THE
STAR CAPTAINS

THE
STAR CAPTAINS

Frigate Command
in the Napoleonic Wars

TOM WAREHAM

CHATHAM PUBLISHING
LONDON

Copyright © Tom Wareham 2001

First published in Great Britain in 2001 by
Chatham Publishing,
99 High Street, Rochester, Kent ME1 1LX

Distributed by
Gerald Duckworth & Co Ltd,
61 Frith Street, London W1D 3JL

British Library Cataloguing in Publication Data
A catalogue record for this book is available from the British
Library

ISBN 1 86176 169 4

Typeset and designed by Roger Daniels

Printed and bound in Great Britain by
Cromwell Press Ltd, Wilts

CONTENTS

(Between pages 96 and 97)

FOREWORD

U P UNTIL ABOUT 1999, on an unremarkable stairway adjacent to the
Nelson Gallery at the National Maritime Museum in Greenwich, hung the
portrait of a naval captain from the time of the Great Wars with France of
1793-1815. The subject was in his late twenties or early thirties and the artist seemed
to have painted his head a little too small for the noticeably corpulent body. The
man's face was fully rounded with pinkish cheeks and on the lips there was a wry
smile. The hair was thin, wispy and seemed to have been tied back in a bow, though
it may also have been cut short behind. His right hand was extended in the classic
pose to rest on the hilt of his sword, whilst the left hand clutched the seam of his
uniform coat. Behind him, in the distance lay a ship, her sails clewed up.

When I first saw this portrait in the 1980s I was struck by the fact that this officer
was unlike the stereotype of the British naval captain that had somehow become
fixed in my mind. The name of the officer painted onto the frame was Captain
James Newman Newman. In an attempt to find out more about him I turned up the
standard library books on naval history but could find no reference to him. As a
result I began to dig deeper – and the work which led to this book (and the PhD
thesis which preceded it) had begun.

It did not take me long to find the comprehensive biographical dictionaries of
John Marshall and William O'Byrne[1] and these were extremely valuable. But what I
quickly discovered was a void in the printed sources available about officers of the
Royal Navy of this period. I could find out more than I was ever likely to need about
Nelson; I could read volumes about Trafalgar, St Vincent, or the other major naval
battles of the period; I could read accounts about selected frigate actions, and I could
read some of the limited number of biographical works about other admirals or one
or two of the more famous frigate captains. But nowhere could I find a general survey
of post captains. What, I wanted to know, was the career of the post captain like?
What exactly did a career in the navy at this time consist of? Was Nelson's career really

so exceptional and if so why? Were the accepted images of Nelson's navy accurate or was there a different truth waiting to emerge? The names of various officers were associated with the career of Nelson, but what course did their careers take outside the theatrical illumination that surrounds our greatest naval hero?

The historian Michael Lewis had produced a comprehensive social history of the Royal Navy of the period – but his study of officers largely stopped at the point they became post captains.[2] On reading this work I immediately wanted to know what happened to them after their promotion, as it seemed to me that this was the most interesting period of their careers. This information was not really available. Without it I began to feel it would not be possible to reach a true understanding of the navy of the period. We knew something about the strategic and tactical achievements; we knew something about how promotion operated – but this was largely dependent on anecdote. We knew a great deal about the ships, but we knew very little about the men who commanded those ships. It was as though they had simply melted away after the wars and no-one had noticed. And in one sense this is exactly what had happened.

What follows is a study, specifically, of the men who commanded His Majesty's frigates between the years 1793 and 1815. I admit unashamedly that the frigate commanders were chosen because the activities in which they were engaged seemed to me to be much more exciting than the much-studied battle-fleet operations of the period. Just as, more recently, the Battle of Britain was partly personified in the (greatly mythologised) image of the Spitfire pilot, so the frigate captain of the Napoleonic Wars has become cloaked in a glamorous mantle. James Henderson, in his study of frigate actions[3] adopted the term 'Star Captains' (from a poem by James Elroy Flecker) and this seems eminently appropriate as a collective name for the elite who commanded the navy's frigates during the Great Wars, and as a title for this book.

That they were the Georgian equivalent of modern media stars is supported by the reception that they often received. On 18 June 1793 the Royal Navy obtained its first and crucial victory at sea when the first French frigate *Cléopâtre* surrendered to the British frigate *Nymphe* commanded by Captain Edward Pellew, in the first conclusive single-ship or frigate action of the war.[4] Almost within a week, to great public enthusiasm, Pellew had been received by the King at a royal levee in St James's Palace and knighted. For, as Pellew's first (and contemporary) biographer noted, 'The capture of the first frigate in a war is always an object of much interest; and the circumstances of the late action, the merit of which was enhanced by the skill and gallantry of the enemy, gave additional importance to Captain Pellew's success.'[5]

However, this enthusiasm was not reserved just for the first frigate capture of the war. Frequently during the course of the war, crowds turned out at Portsmouth or Plymouth or Halifax, Nova Scotia, to watch as prize-frigates and their conquerors returned to port. On shore bands played patriotic airs like Purcell's 'Britons Strike Home', and those watching would join in exhibitions of nationalistic fervour. The arrival of a frigate with a French man of war as a prize seems to have brought the home port to a standstill on more than one occasion; and as the news of a victory spread the excitement often grew. As Captain Philip Broke's wife Louisa reported to her badly injured husband after his success over the American frigate *Chesapeake*:

> This has been a day of great trial to me my belov'd husband … the newspapers we took in the carriage were filled with joy and exultation at your success: and such praise bestowed in the House by Mr Croker and others on your gallant and noble conduct, as was almost too much for your Loo: it was indeed most gratifying to me to hear you so highly spoken and thought of by the whole country.[6]

As the wars dragged on, press claims that the latest action was 'unequalled in the Annals of Naval History' actually became a rather repetitive cliché. Nevertheless, creating or maintaining naval heroes was important to the national morale and the war effort, for the successful frigate captains always seem to have been regarded as dashing and brave, cast in the heroic mould. Among what is sometimes called the 'polite classes' there was 'a highly selective cult of heroism, never focusing on ordinary soldiers or seamen but only on those commanding them [which] was deeply congenial to men intensely proud of their personal status and honour.'[7] Among ordinary people the heroic seaman was as likely to be cast in the form of the incorrigible Jack Tar as Nelson, but in between these two symbols somewhere came those frigate captains who not only acquired sensational riches in the form of prize money, but also fought naval actions which could both stir a populace anxious for an excuse for outbursts of patriotic celebration and reassure an anxious – and powerful – mercantile class. The crucial factor seems to be that the frigate captains not only offered a role model, they also delivered the required deeds in time of war, something which the captain of a ship of the line had less opportunity to do. It is this ability which seems to have dominated the image of the frigate captain in the popular imagination, both during the wars and since the revival of the image in the form of the mature Horatio Hornblower.[8]

In reality the men who commanded His Majesty's frigates were of widely varying characters and qualities. The great majority of them entered the navy as youths of between 12-14 years of age, travelling from all over the British Isles, arriving full of hope with their fathers at Deptford, Chatham, or any of the other major naval dockyards. A small minority had previous experience in the merchant service, though these seem to have been exceptional. For most baptism in the Royal Navy was a shocking and frightening experience – as it was likely to be for any youngster who had not had to tough it out in the more deprived areas of English, Scottish or Irish society. Those who were going to survive this process – and we usually only hear from or about those who did – seem to have accustomed themselves to the lifestyle quickly. From then on there were whole series of hurdles to overcome and only a tiny minority of those who entered as 'young gentlemen' reached the coveted rank of post captain. Even then, not all were given active commands and there was fierce competition for the command of a crack frigate. Between 1793 and 1815 the Royal Navy had the use of approximately 420 different frigates. Although there appears to be some confusion about how many were actually in commission at any one time, it is probably a reasonably safe calculation that the highest figure of 156 frigates was achieved during 1810; whereas at the outbreak of war in 1793 only about 32 frigates were ready for active service or already at sea.

In order to understand the frigate captain it is vital to understand the roles which his ship was expected to perform. Frigates were used in a much more fluid strategy than the ships of the line. Although some were nearly always attached to the battle-fleets, the greater number were usually at sea performing a wide range of patrol or escort duties, often operating in small squadrons or pairs but also on their own for considerable periods of time. Frigates were not expected to engage enemy ships of the line, although there were exceptional circumstances when such actions took place: for example, the French frigate *Serieuse* firing on Captain Sir James Saumarez's *Orion*, 74 at the Battle of the Nile, or Henry Blackwood in the frigate *Penelope* engaging the *Guillaume Tell*, 80.

The whole nature of the workload undertaken by frigates was determined to a much greater degree than in previous wars by the requirement to protect a beleaguered British economy. Sir Charles Middleton was quite clear about this, and stated such in a memorandum drafted at some time in 1793:

> The French being deficient in the great articles of naval stores, their first object will be a general attack upon our trade and supplying themselves by these means of what may be difficult to procure in other ways.
> … In a war of this kind, which I cannot look upon in any other light than a war against trade, and where a large number of trading vessels are to be protected … it will be necessary to have a very large number of frigates, sloops, brigs and cutters … [9]

He was still emphasising the point two years later that the French attack on trade must be successful in the outset, unless our merchant ships are prohibited to sail without convoys, and our cruisers put in order for service and properly arranged before the winter sets in ... for foreign service has been so very great ... that it will become absolutely necessary to husband the use of our remaining ones as much as possible, and particularly in the demands for convoys, passages, messengers &c &c, by the secretaries of state, who have no idea of the numerous services required from our cruisers for the fleet and trade of the kingdom, and the very great difficulties we are put to in complying with their demands, which are generally made on very short notices.[10]

Such complaints about the shortage of cruisers were to reach their apotheosis during the Trafalgar campaign in 1805 when Nelson lamented that lack of frigates would be found engraved upon his heart. Nelson of course was concerned about the need for frigates to operate as scouts for his fleet – at the same time something like 33 per cent of the navy's total frigate force were engaged in some form of trade protection duties. At its peak, in 1801, 47 per cent of the frigates available were engaged in such work.[11] Taken together, the high demand for frigates and the conditions in which they were expected to operate (that is often alone and in extreme weather conditions) put considerable pressure on both their commanders and crews. In such circumstances there was little room for poor performance and the weakest were usually soon weeded out. As a result of this process, frigate command became the training ground for a remarkable fine cadre of seaman-officers – many of whom were ultimately 'creamed-off' by the Admiralty to command the heavier ships of the line, in the process allowing room for the development of more officers of the same calibre.

This book looks at that process and the men who came out at the other end of it as some of the greatest and yet unacknowledged heroes of 'Nelson's Navy'.

> *'West of these out to seas colder than the Hebrides I must go*
> *where the fleet of stars is anchored and the young star-captains glow'*
> (JAMES ELROY FLECKER, *The Gates of Damascus*)

ACKNOWLEDGEMENTS

A book of this nature cannot be completed without the assistance of a range of people and although it is not possible to name everyone who has supported me in some way in the research and production of this book, I would like publicly to offer my thanks to certain individuals.

Firstly, I would like to acknowledge the kindness of the late David Lyon who, rightly or wrongly, seemed instantly to see some merit in this work and provided encouragement at just the right moment.

Dr Michael Duffy of the University of Exeter who, together with Professor N A M Rodger, guided and supported me in producing the PhD thesis which preceded this work. Like many other students of naval history I must also acknowledge the role played by Prof Rodger's *The Wooden World* in launching my research. I am particularly grateful for the friendship, advice and support of Robert Gardiner, whose work on the frigates of this period underpins much of the understanding of their commanding officers. There are many occasions when I have been deeply grateful for the help and support of all three of these people.

On a more formal note I must record my thanks to the Trustees of the National Maritime Museum for permission to quote from the papers in their collections. Also to James Saunders Watson and the Rockingham Castle Estate for permission to read and quote the remnants of the papers of Sir Michael Seymour; Rachel Watson of the Northamptonshire County Record Office was also helpful in obtaining the Seymour Papers for my perusal.

I would like to express my particular gratitude to Alan Giddings of the Manuscripts Department at the National Maritime Museum, and to Clive Powell, previously of that Department. I am sure many researchers will have shared my experience of their unfailing kindness and good humour, often in the most trying of circumstances.

Finally I must thank my parents with whom must lie the guilt for my interest in Nelson's Navy; and last, but by no means least, Chris for giving up many hours of leisure time whilst I diverted to libraries or other sites of maritime interest.

A NOTE ON SOURCES

The raw material for this book is essentially statistical, and the basic data for the research has mainly been drawn from the large official volumes listing, by station, officers and ships in commission between 1793 and 1815, known familiarly as 'The Admiralty List Books'.[12] These, at least for most of the war, keep a month by month track of every ship in commission, its commanding officer, lieutenants and complement, and the station or command to which it was assigned. Using these, it is possible to record the name of every officer commanding every frigate for nearly every month of the wars. Unfortunately, the List Books become inconsistent towards the end of the Napoleonic War and no list remains for the period after 1813. For the final years of the war it is necessary to refer to other sources, including *Steel's Navy Lists* and Government digests which were almost certainly based upon Steel's work (and which ultimately drove Steel out of business).

It must be said at the outset that the List Books need to be used with some caution, for whilst there is no reason for believing that the Admiralty clerks were prone to making many errors, the Lists contain inconsistent spelling of surnames as well as occasional confusion about forenames. Furthermore, it rapidly becomes apparent that the clerks had difficulty in keeping accurate records about appointments. Although the lists were reviewed each month, it is evident that this frequency could only barely keep up with all the changes that were taking place in appointments. Whilst the ships themselves may have moved between stations at an understandably 'leisurely' pace, the men in command could be changed at such speed that, by the time the clerks had entered a man's name against a particular ship, he could be in another ship or someone could have replaced him. Some of this difficulty was undoubtedly caused by the very tardy nature of communications at that time for, although there was a very fast and efficient system of communications between London and the naval ports in the form of the telegraph system, it is very clear that the Admiralty itself had problems keeping up with the appointments made by commanders-in-chief of very distant stations.

In addition to this it was not at all unusual to appoint officers to the command of ships on a temporary basis or as 'Acting Captains'. The status of the appointment in these cases would mean their inclusion in the List Books, although it was not subsequently made clear when the temporary or acting status had become more of a permanent posting. Confusingly, the fact that a captain had been posted to a new ship whilst still in his previous command could lead to his name appearing against both ships for many months. On the other hand, there appear to have been many occasions when, at the moment they had to draw up the month's list, the clerks had no idea who the commanding officer of a frigate was, and no name is recorded.

That this can lead to uncertainty is all too apparent in the Pitcairn Jones 'List of Commissioned Sea Officers'.[13] This consists of twelve A3-sized volumes, being photocopies of notes about all commissioned officers compiled by Commander C G Pitcairn Jones, who used the Admiralty List Books at the Public Record Office to compile a complete list of the ships to which every commissioned officer was appointed throughout his career. To do this he took an annual sample from the List Books, using the month of July in each year, and recorded the officer/ship accordingly. The books constitute a very useful source for finding a quick reference to the ships in which any officer seems to have served. Its drawback is that, as a consequence of the annual sampling method adopted, there can be an eleven-month discrepancy between an officer's real appointment to, or departure from, a ship and the recording of the same in the Pitcairn Jones list. In an attempt to provide a more accurate picture, the data in this book has been collected for every month for the Revolutionary War, and every quarter for the Napoleonic War. This ensures that, as far as is reasonably possible, the dates are accurate to within at least three months.

CHAPTER

I

THE NAVAL OFFICER
AND HIS CAREER

THE SUBJECT OF THIS BOOK is the frigate captain, or rather, the officers who commanded British frigates between 1793 and 1815. Those officers were an integral part of a what might be described as an officer corps and it would be nonsensical to study them without some review of the Royal Navy's officer corps in general. Of course, everybody who has read a biography of Nelson or studied 'Nelson's Navy' has an understanding of the workings of the navy of the period, but the real question is whether we *really* understand how the officer corps was formed and how it functioned. To a certain degree, to see the corps in perspective, it is necessary to look at its reflection: that is, in the form of its nearest contemporary relative, the United States Navy. By looking at the reflection it is much easier to see how it was different – and through that contrast, we can see the Royal Navy much more clearly.

The first rather obvious point to make, however, is that the American navy was a new organisation, since that nation had only existed as such for less than twenty years by 1793. Starting with a clean slate, the US government began by creating the administrative structure of its navy, long before the navy itself existed. In August 1789 Congress had placed the control of the country's naval forces with the War Department, even though the nation had no such recognisable force or vessels. It was really only in 1794, when the US found itself at war with Algiers, that the navy came into being with the construction of six frigates. At the same time Congress legislated for the appointment of a sufficient number of officers to man the ships fully when ready. In fact the conflict with Algiers finished before the ships were completed and work on them was suspended until 1797 when, due to growing tension with France, work resumed. In April 1798 the construction of further vessels was authorised and the Navy Department was established. In 1794 the War Department had appointed just six captains in preparation for commissioning its new ships – that is, one commanding officer for each of the new vessels – but by

April 1798 the corps had grown to fifty-nine officers.[1]

Here then are the first points of comparison. Starting completely afresh, the US Navy Department had attempted to link the size of its officer corps to the size of its fleet by appointing only sufficient officers to man the ships that it had. Secondly, those officers were largely selected from amongst the 350 who had applied in writing to the Secretary of War between 1794 and 1798. Young men wishing to enter the American navy had to submit a letter of application to the Secretary of the Navy, preferably supported by a Congressman, senior naval officer or other man of suitable rank. These letters were read and then filed for future reference, until a suitable vacancy on board a ship existed. In theory, and probably for much of the period up to 1815 in practice, the corps was much more rigorously controlled from the centre than was the Royal Navy, although there were a couple of exceptions to this. The first was in July 1800 when the US had to mobilise quickly in the face of potential hostilities with France. The task of increasing the size of the officer corps from fifty-nine to nearly seven hundred threatened to overwhelm the Navy Department's small administration and it was decided that the officers appointed to command the navy's vessels should be given a delegated authority to select their own officers. In fact this delegation of power lasted for a very short period.

The second exception lay in the commanding officer's ability to make an acting promotion to the rank of lieutenant whilst on active service. In fact, he only had the power to temporarily promote midshipmen, sailing masters or surgeon's mates. Such appointments were supposed to be reported to the Secretary of the Navy for ratification; but apparently it was common for commanding officers to neglect these reports because official confirmation was infuriatingly slow in arriving, if it arrived at all.

The crucial point, however, is that entry to – and employment and promotion within – the US Navy was usually carefully controlled from the centre. Furthermore, the comparatively small size of the US officer corps made it much easier for the central administration to keep a watchful eye on the performance of the members of that corps. All officers received half-pay when not employed and as a consequence the Navy Department was understandably vigilant in dismissing young men of unacceptable quality, discipline or performance.

In the Royal Navy entry, or attempted entry, to the officer corps was considerably less regulated. Aspiring young juveniles entered as Captains' Servants (known as Volunteers after 1794), if the captain of an individual ship could be persuaded to take them on board. There was no means of registering them centrally through the Admiralty. The selection of what became known as 'Young Gentlemen' was by custom and practice the responsibility of the captain. If the lad proved to have the necessary attitude, stamina and ability for a life at sea he might, after three years' active service, be rated as a midshipman. A midshipman could not be promoted to lieutenant until he had acquired a minimum of three years' active sea service and, in theory, had reached the age of 20 (19 years after 1806). It was really only at this point, when a midshipman presented himself for the lieutenant's examination, that he came under the more centralised control of the Admiralty system.

In the American navy attempts were made to regulate the number of commissioned officers and midshipmen to ensure an adequate supply of skilled officers or trainees to man the navy's ships. As even midshipmen received half-pay there was a certain economic pressure on the Navy Department to control its expenditure. In the Royal Navy midshipmen did not get half-pay and there was no attempt to keep the intake of Young Gentlemen in proportion to the size of the fleet. In the United States Navy a midshipman who performed or behaved badly was unlikely to be tolerated for long. He could, literally, be struck off the list of officers. In the Royal Navy there was more chance of one of these less successful officers lurking for many years in the midshipmen's berths of successively less active or attractive vessels, and there are numerous references to older, 'passed' midshipmen. Perhaps the other main difference between the two navies lay in the fact that in the Royal Navy, which was apparently so much more dependent upon the role of 'interest' or influence, the less able young midshipman might just slip through the filter of the lieutenant's examination to reach higher rank. In fact, although we have become accustomed to this idea, the power of 'interest' was not as strong as some naval historians have been led to believe. This will be explained in due course

It is perhaps time to ask why it was that the Royal Navy was, at least on the surface, so different from its American counterpart, and what effect this had on the nature of the officer corps. The obvious, but perhaps not so simple answer to the first part of the question is that the Royal Navy had evolved over more than a hundred years. More importantly, during the eighteenth century it had been involved in a series of conflicts, each of which had inflated the officer corps in order to meet the demand for men to command the fleet. In sharp contrast, the American navy was created from scratch and, like the US constitution, on what were thought to be rational, 'scientific' principles. The Royal Navy had evolved in a much more organic fashion which was inextricably entwined with the customs and nature of British society. Although the Royal Navy was controlled by the machinery of the Admiralty and the administration of the government, it reflected the complications of the British social system. Whilst the American Navy Department was probably no less conscious of social distinctions among its potential officers, it was less likely that these interests would dominate or hamper the efficiency of its operation. By its very essence the American Revolution had attempted to shrug off a social system which depended on innate respect for rank or any historically determined hierarchical position in society. To some degree it had succeeded, and this was reflected in the organisation of its navy.

By 1793 the Royal Navy was just beginning a process of change – a process which was to accelerate in the later stages of the twenty-three years of conflict – but it was still heavily influenced by the mechanisms of patronage and interest. This is because British society generally operated through this process – and the navy was to a large degree that society afloat. It is important to note this because within the American sphere there was much less of a hierarchy to influence promotion and employment. What carried influence in the American service was what Secretary to the Navy Benjamin Stoddert described as 'sprightly young men of good education, good character, and good connections';[2] and by good connections was meant 'respectable' connections. The implications in practice can be seen by the profession of the fathers of young American officers (where known). Some 25 per cent of officers' parents held elective or appointed positions within the Federal Government; a further 10 per cent held state, county or local positions. The remainder seem to have represented medicine, law and the ministry, merchant sea officers or commercial merchants.[3] As will be shown later, many of these professions were represented within the Royal Navy, but there were two crucial differences. Firstly, the officers of the United States Navy were not members of the old landed aristocracy; secondly they *were* to a much greater degree the sons of the commercial and trading classes.

Having drawn these distinctions, it is now necessary to take what may be an unusual step and warn that chasing the issue of 'interest' in the Royal Navy is similar to chasing a mirage. We should not be misled into overstating its importance at the time. 'Interest' was not the sole prerogative of the aristocracy, nor were the sons of the landed families the only ones who benefited from the system. Having now generally introduced the officer corps, it is necessary to focus a little more specifically on the officers of the corps.

It would not be feasible to investigate in detail the career of every officer who held the rank of post captain at any point between the years 1793 and 1815, but a random-sampling method can be used to provide an outline of the officer corps. In this study this has been achieved by taking all of those post captains whose surnames begin with the letters D, E and F, and who were technically available for service between 1793 and 1815: *ie* those reaching post rank before 1815 and who were still alive or had not reached flag rank before 1793.[4] Details of each officer's career after 'posting' (the contemporary term for promotion to post captain) are available from various sources, but two types have been used here. The first is Commander C G Pitcairn Jones's 'List of Commissioned Sea Officers' kept at the National Maritime Museum, Greenwich,[5] which lists the ships in which each officer served; the other type is the biographical dictionaries compiled by Lieutenant John Marshall and William O'Byrne.[6] Although there have been a number of general studies about the career of naval officers, these have tended to avoid events after promotion to post captain, focusing instead on the earlier career.[7] Here, however, we are concerned only with those men who reached the rank of post captain. The 'DEF' sample provides the names of 208 officers.

PROMOTION TO POST CAPTAIN

The first thing to note is that in 1793, the year that war broke out, a considerable proportion of the existing officer corps consisted of rather senior and ageing officers. Approximately 22 per cent of the entire sample had been posted by the end of the American War in 1783. During the years of peace between then and the mobilisation for the Spanish Armament of 1790, the number of commanders being promoted to post captain fell markedly. In fact, only 1.5 per cent of the sample were posted during this period. The Spanish Armament saw a flurry of promotions, with 4 per cent being posted, but then the rate dropped to zero until 1793 when nearly 3.5 per cent of the sample were promoted. It is therefore very clear to what extent naval promotion was tied in with mobilisation and the threat, or actual state, of hostilities. As with the American navy it appears that it was the need to man the fleet which drove the promotion process.

However, even in wartime the promotion process seems to have been uneven: for example, 25 per cent of the sample were posted during the Revolutionary War (between 1793 and 1801, with most occurring during 1795). In 1800 the number of promotions dropped significantly and only one promotion (less than 0.5 per cent) is recorded for that year. Then, in 1801-2, there was an increase, with approximately 4 per cent of captains being promoted during 1801 and a further 8 per cent in 1802. At first sight this is paradoxical because in March 1802 the Treaty of Amiens was signed, bringing about a cessation of hostilities with France. In fact, 16 of the 17 officers promoted in 1802 were promoted on the same day, 29 April, just a month after the Treaty was signed. This will be considered in more detail in due course.

In 1803 war broke out again and between 1803 and 1814, the real years of the Napoleonic War, 39 per cent of the sample were promoted. But once again there is a paradox. Over 8 per cent (17 officers) were promoted right at the end of the war, in 1814. One, George D'Aeth, received his promotion during the flurry of the Hundred Days conflict following Napoleon's brief return from exile. D'Aeth was very lucky: he had been promoted to the rank of lieutenant after serving as a midshipman at Trafalgar but then waited until 1811 to reach the rank of commander. His promotion at the resumption of war with Napoleon in 1815 must have been welcomed as an astonishing piece of good fortune for an officer who expected to live out the rest of his days on a commander's half-pay.

AGE OF THE OFFICER CORPS

If 22 per cent of the corps was actually posted by 1783, it follows that a large proportion of officers were no longer young when war broke out in 1793. Forty-one per cent of the sample were commissioned as lieutenants before the end of the American War. Since the minimum age at which a midshipman was supposed to present himself for his lieutenant's examination was 20 (19 from 1806), it must follow that nearly half of the post captains available to the navy upon the outbreak of war in 1793 were 30 years or more in age. Although there were anecdotes about midshipmen getting round the regulations and obtaining false certificates as to their age, this was probably uncommon, as most of the stories relate to officers with significant interest behind them. The standard ruse, it has been suggested, was to have one's name entered onto a ship's muster book long before actually taking up one's berth – in this way the midshipman could claim the requisite sea time at a much younger age and enter for his lieutenant's examination. Certificates providing proof of age were, so it was rumoured, available at a certain price from the porters at the Admiralty. There are, consequently, many examples of officers who passed for lieutenant and were commissioned at 18 or 19 years of age.[8] However, there seems to be little evidence that the majority of officers entered for and passed the examination prematurely; on the contrary, in many cases officers were commissioned lieutenants at an even later age – a situation which was exacerbated by the slow rate of promotion before 1790 – as examined below.

The group who it would be thought would be the most obvious beneficiaries of this system (apart from the sons of admirals, that is) were the sons of the peerage. However, once again, the evidence does not support the view that the system operated totally to their advantage in any unqualified fashion. For example, of 40 post captains who qualify as the sons of peers[9] only 21 were commissioned as lieutenants before the age of 20. Perhaps equally interesting is the fact that a number of the 'late-qualifiers' had joined the navy either before or during the American War. In other words, the sons of the peerage also suffered from the slow-down in the rate of promotion. There is, of course, another interpretation: this is that the rules governing the lieutenants' examinations were perhaps less rigidly applied after 1793, which would imply that the power of 'interest' grew during the war. Once again, though, it is time to issue a warning. The number of officers entering the navy and being promoted always rose during time of war; statistically therefore we should expect to see a greater number of sons of the peerage being promoted at this time and there were always late starters – Thomas, Lord Cochrane being self-professedly one of these.[10] However, as will be seen shortly, the speed of promotion itself also changed during the last quarter of the eighteenth century.

PROMOTION TO FLAG RANK

At the top of the promotion escalator lay the much sought after position of flag rank. Again, the dearth of promotion between 1783 and 1790 had a knock-on effect, since the escalator actually shortened as the subsequent war progressed. For example, those captains posted in 1783-4, if they lived long enough, could not obtain flag rank until the aftermath of Trafalgar in 1805 (a wait of 21 years), examples being Philip D'Auvergne and Michael de Courcy. Those posted early in 1793, however, might reach flag rank by around 1810, a mere 17 years later. This reduction in waiting time partly arose because of the age factor and the consequent death of many of the older captains on the list. Seven of those posted by 1783 were dead within a few years of the start of the war against Revolutionary France, and approximately one-third (14) of those officers reaching post rank before the end of the American War were dead before Trafalgar. This confirms the fact that many of the officer corps were of senior age and, one suspects, questionable fitness by the outbreak of war. However, the important corollary of this would seem to be that on average, as a body, the officer corps got younger as the war progressed. Ultimately it could also mean that the flag officers would be reaching that rank at a younger age. This may have had a more far reaching effect on the attitude, commitment and professionalism of the corps as the war progressed.

There is also another facet which is highlighted by contrasting the United States Navy. The American navy of this period had no admirals and captain was the most senior rank in the hierarchy. Although the commander of a squadron might be nominated a commodore, this was more of a courtesy title and officially carried none of the perquisites associated with the British flag rank. The difference in the implications for the officer corps was significant. In the Royal Navy, once a man had reached the rank of captain he had to do nothing more than stay alive for long enough to reach the more lucrative senior position. The corps could, therefore, be peppered with the less energetic and less committed. In the American navy, on the other hand, an officer could rise no further than captain and, such was the restriction on numbers, he had to remain reasonably active to retain his position. As previously noted, during the course of the Great Wars with France the average age of the Royal Navy's officer corps fell and admirals may have also been getting to that rank earlier. This could have meant that admirals were surviving longer, thereby reducing the prospect of automatic promotion for senior captains on the list. It is not inconceivable that, without the prospect of guaranteed flag rank, the attention of some captains turned more to the task in hand and their role as commanders of individual ships.

COMMANDS

The real register of the fitness and ability of the officer corps is that found in the officers' employment records and in particular the number of ships commanded by them after posting. Since the Admiralty did not itself keep formal employment records, these have to be compiled from the monthly lists of ships in commission.[11] The data extracted from these and other sources immediately reveals a surprising statistic, for it appears that of the 208 post captains in the sample 61 (nearly 30 per cent) were *never* given command at sea. This high level of unemployment was partly caused by the cessation of war in 1783. About 22 per cent of the sample were posted before 1790 and, of these, twelve were posted at the end of the American War with little prospect of active employment. But there were also officers posted during the course of the American War who were not given employment. Take, for example, the case of Captain William Daniel who was posted in September 1781. Daniel was probably about 43 years old when he was posted. He does not seem to have been given a command before the American War ended and, probably lacking any interest, he was unable to gain employment during the peacetime. When serious conflict broke out again in 1793, Daniel was probably 55 years old and, since he died seven years later, possibly unfit to serve.

Virtually all of the officers posted during the Revolutionary War seem to have been given a command at sea at some stage but, once again, with the end of hostilities around 1801-2, the number of 'never-employed' captains began to rise. Although there would seem to have been little point in promoting an officer and then not employing him, this may have been a deliberate practice by the Admiralty and it is possible that for some officers promotion was being used as a form of superannuation.

One of the key factors that seems to have determined whether or not an officer was given a command following the outbreak of war in 1793 was previous experience of command at sea. Something like 70 per cent of the captains who were posted before 1790 *and* given a command after 1793 had experience of commanding a ship before the outbreak of war with France. By the end of the wars there was even greater competition for command and about 8 per cent of the sample were posted during the last two years of the Napoleonic War, when the competition for command was so great that a post captain often had to consider himself lucky to get even an unrated vessel. Thomas Fellowes, for example, posted in March 1811, was given command of the *Fawn* sloop.

Lack of sea command did not necessarily mean complete lack of employment. Some officers had to be satisfied with the responsibility of commanding districts of Sea Fencibles, a form of nautical 'Home Guard', or with raising levies of seamen in different parts of Britain and Ireland. There were also officers whose inability to take up command was due to factors beyond their control. A few simply died before they could be given command, such as Henry Duncan, who was drowned before taking up his command in 1802 or the 29-year-old James Dalrymple (2) who died after a long illness in 1803, just a year after being posted.[12] It is also possible that many officers simply 'retired' from active service and never again made themselves available. The fact that we cannot be certain about this once again highlights the difference with the American navy where the need to keep a tight rein on expenditure meant that the Navy Department monitored the availability of its officers. There, an officer who 'absented' himself from the active service list was likely to be removed from the list. In the case of the Royal Navy, the disproportion of captains to ships meant that there had to be many unemployed officers and it was almost impossible to tell if an officer was still seeking a command unless he repeatedly wrote to the Admiralty pleading for a ship.

Some captains who were unemployed during the peacetime, entered the merchant marine or some foreign service because they were either more enterprising or financially pressed. A number of captains who were later appointed to frigates did this and it is just possible that by keeping their skills alive they enhanced their prospect for employment when the threat of war loomed once again.[13]

Number of Ships Commanded

The employment statistics reveal that most of the post captains who were given employment could expect to command up to three or four ships during their active career, whilst the more favoured might command five or six. A small number of officers would command seven, eight or even more during the course of their career. Here the researcher of the Admiralty records must exercise a certain amount of caution, for it is not uncommon to find that some officers' names are linked with a questionably high number of ships. This may be a reflection of the communication difficulties faced by the Admiralty clerks in keeping an up-to-date record of which officer was in command of a ship at any given time. It is not uncommon to find both the Admiralty List Books or *Steel's Navy Lists* giving the same captain's name against different ships at the same time. The most likely explanation for this is that post captains may often have been appointed to new ships and the news published, before they had returned their previous ship to port or been succeeded in their previous command.

Frigate Command

There does seem to be an underlying assumption that frigates were 'junior' commands: that is, that they were the type of ship given to the relatively inexperienced commander as a preparation for the more serious task of commanding a ship of the line. To a certain degree, of course, age and seniority on the post captains list went hand in hand; but it certainly appears that neither of these factors bore any consistent relationship to frigate service or lack of it. On the contrary, any such assumption needs to be strongly challenged for, when analysing the *rate* of ships commanded, it becomes evident that many captains were never given frigates even though they did command ships of the line. In fact, disregarding those who had no command at all, 19 per cent of the active captains never appear to have been given frigate command during their career. Furthermore, frigate command was not strictly the preserve of the energetic young officer; nor was the ship of the line the territory of the more experienced or cautious senior captain. At least thirteen of the captains posted during the American War (before July 1783) saw frigate command during the French Revolutionary War, and whilst the majority of these may only have seen frigate command during the French Wars for a brief time, some like the Hon Michael de Courcy[14] and Jonathan Faulknor (2) saw considerable frigate service at 5.5 and 6 years respectively.

RATE OF PROMOTION

The speed at which an officer was promoted from lieutenant to post captain may provide a useful indicator of an officer's ability or interest. As previously explained, there were, at least in theory, formal rules governing the earliest occasion upon which a midshipman could present himself for the lieutenant's examination. Thereafter the system became much more flexible and an officer's progress through the ranks became a matter of interest, ability and – undeniably – luck. Using the commission dates of the sample captains, where these seem to be reliable and are available, it is possible to calculate the average length of time between passing from lieutenant to post captain. (For the sake of ease, the number of years between passing for a lieutenant and being posted will be termed the 'promotion rate'.)

TABLE 1.1 *Average Promotion Rate by Year passed for Lieutenant (DEF Sample)*

N.B. Figures along the top row represent the *maximum* years to reach post captain,
thus 3.75 years would be shown as 4; 16.75 years as 17.

Year passed as lieutenant	>2	4	6	8	10	12	14	16	18	20	20+	Average promotion rate*	Number in sample
1745-59		1			2		1	1	1	2	8	20	16
1760-65							1	3		2	1	17.5	7
1771-1775			4	2	2	1						7	9
1776			1	2			1		1	1		11.29	6
1777		1	2	2			3	3				10	11
1778		5	3				2	1	2		2	10	15
1779							1		1		2	20.75	4
1780							1	1	2	1	1	17	6
1781								3			1	16	4
1782					1	2	1	1		1	1	14.8	7
1783							1					13	1
1784												0	0
1785							1					8.75	1
1786												0	0
1787						1						10.25	1
1788												0	0
1789			1									5.5	1
1790			4	3	1	3	1	2			1	9.7	15
1791			1		1							8.25	2
1792												0	0
1793	1		3	1			1	3				9.45	10
1794			1	5		1	1	2	1			11.2	11
1795			2	2		1	1	1	1			11.43	8
1796			1	1		1	1	1				10.85	5
1797			2	1	1	1	2	1				9.44	8
1798				1	1		3					11.1	5
1799	1	1		1	1	1						6.95	5
1800		2	2		1	1	3	1				9	10
1801		1	1		1		1					7.6	4
1802		1		2	3	1	2					9	9
1803		1			1							5.5	2
1804	1		2	2								6.8	5
1805		1		2	1	1						7.25	6
1806			1		2							7.75	3
1807		1	1	1								5	3
1808			1	2								5.9	3

* Promotion rate given in years

TABLE 1.2 *Promotion Rate from Lieutenant to Captain in Number of Years*

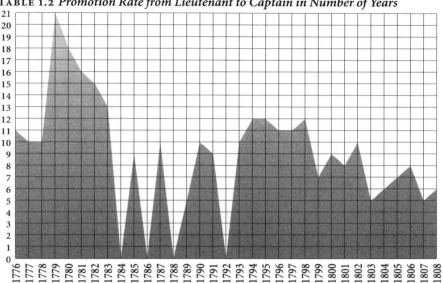

The table clearly shows the almost non-existent promotion rate between 1784 and 1789, the years of peace after the American War. It also shows that very few of those officers commissioned as lieutenant during the American War (*ie* 1776-1783) could expect to be promoted through the ranks in less than 12 years, the highest numbers being promoted at between 12-15 years. It should be acknowledged, however, that an officer promoted during the peace was likely to have a degree of interest or favour to be employed at all – and this might accelerate his individual rate of promotion. The unusually rapid promotion of the lieutenant of 1789 is a good example. This was Percy Fraser, who was promoted from lieutenant to captain in about 5.5 years. A chance remark in a somewhat cynical letter from the young Lt William Lukin to his uncle (Lord Grenville) complaining about the promotion of younger officers reveals that Fraser was promoted young for mentoring the Prince of Brunswick.[15]

After 1790 the percentage of officers passing through the ranks at high speed remained fairly constant, but by this time 46 per cent were reaching post rank after between 4-10 years and 75 per cent of officers reached post rank before 12 years had passed. If we begin by considering those officers passing for lieutenant before 1783, it is probable that those with a promotion rate of between 12 and 15 years are going to be fairly typical whilst those passing at faster or slower rates may be unusual. Those officers passing for lieutenant from 1790 onwards could expect a much quicker transition through the ranks. The average would probably have been around 7-8 years.

Officers with Rapid Promotion Rates

As previously stated, age does not appear to have been the overriding factor in deciding whether a captain was going to get a frigate or ship of the line. The age of the non-frigate officers at the time of their promotion generally ranged between 22 and 40 years,[16] although only a very small number were posted under the age of 28 and one officer, John Dilkes, was probably 48 years old when he was posted. There would therefore be no justification for suggesting either that frigates were strictly the province of younger men or that ships of the line tended to be given to those of more mature age. Nevertheless, as will be seen later, there was most certainly a tendency for frigates to be given to officers as their first post ship.

Whilst it might be stretching the point too far to suggest that those officers who did *not* serve in frigates also happened to be less active in their naval careers, the converse does appear to be true. There is strong evidence that frigate captains tended to have more active careers. Although it is very difficult to explain why some officers never had frigate command, it is abundantly clear that frigate captains positively sought that type of duty. The attractions of the frigate service will be discussed in detail in a later chapter, but for now it is probably sufficient to note that frigate command had its drawbacks and did not suit everyone. Even Collingwood, that most articulate correspondent, stated clearly on one occasion that he would prefer a 74-gun ship above anything else – and that was immediately after Lord Chatham had given him a choice of two comparatively new frigates.[17]

As mentioned earlier, promotion to the rank of post captain brought no guarantee of employment and many officers had to wait a long and anxious time to be given their first ship. Twenty-seven per cent of the captains in the sample experienced a marked delay (*ie* of more than one year) in being appointed to a ship after posting. This is probably no higher than we might expect given that there were always more post captains than there were ships to which they could be appointed. The joy of being posted, which is so clearly expressed in the memoirs of captains of this time[18] was often soon dulled by the growing sense of frustration at not getting a command. Possibly even worse was the tendency to give new post captains temporary commands. This seems to have been less of a problem on distant stations where the commander-in-chief enjoyed almost carte blanche to appoint officers to commands in the knowledge that it would be some time before the Admiralty could send orders countermanding any such move.

On the home station, however, a series of acting commands could be both expensive and unrewarding.[19] The acting captain had no time to build up a rapport with the crew of his temporary command and, unless he was very lucky, little enough time to make his name in action. True, a post captain had merely to sit patiently for long enough and he would automatically be raised to flag rank, but this was not what most naval officers wanted, nor indeed was it the reason that they had joined the navy. It is undoubtedly true that there were some officers who simply avoided serving in any active capacity or who refused the offer of a ship because it did not suit them. However, these latter stood the risk of being 'overlooked' later when they decided that they did desire a command.

A small proportion of officers were posted as flag captains. This meant that instead of being given an independent command, they became the captain of the vessel carrying the admiral – that is, the flagship. This was frequently a sign that the officer enjoyed the patronage of that flag officer, as an admiral could, to a certain degree, select his own flag captain. In actual fact something like 12 per cent[20] of the sample served as flag captains at some stage in their career, and some positively seem to have made a career out of it, as was the case with Sir William Domett. Domett was lucky to enjoy the patronage of the Hood family – and particularly Admiral Alexander Hood (later Lord Bridport) – from an early age. After serving during the American War he was posted as Hood's flag captain. After the war he was given successively a 24-gun ship and then a frigate, but in 1789 he accepted an invitation to become Admiral Millbank's flag captain. In 1790 with the mobilisation for the Spanish Armament Hood, now a vice-admiral, took command of the *London*, and Domett joined him once again. As the crisis faded away, Domett was given the *Pegasus* frigate on the Newfoundland station, but within a year he was back as flag captain, this time to Admiral Goodall in the *Romney*, 50. With the outbreak of war in 1793 he rejoined Hood, this time in the *Royal George*, and remained his flag captain until Hood struck his flag in November 1800. Domett was again given his own command but in February 1801 he became Admiral Hyde Parker's flag captain. He then succesively served in the same capacity under Nelson and Cornwallis until 1804 when he himself reached flag rank.

Domett was clearly a highly skilled and highly regarded fleet administrator. It was also obviously a job that he enjoyed doing, but it would not have been to every officer's taste. The ambition of many officers, as will be explored later, was to be posted directly into their own frigate. Of the DEF sample, only 24 per cent were this fortunate – which rather contradicts any assumption that it was the custom to promote the majority of new post captains into frigates – and 18 per cent of the sample were promoted into ships of other rates without delay. Appointment to a frigate relied on interest or ability (or both) and luck. Henry Digby was one of the lucky ones, but then his father also happened to be the Chaplain in Ordinary to the King. Ross Donnelly[21] was posted directly into the old 28-gun frigate *Pegasus*, possibly because he was well respected for his seamanship, but also because he had the likes of Nelson, Duncan, and the Earl of Tankerville[22] promoting his interests. He was also a favourite of Lord Spencer, who became First Lord of the Admiralty six months before Donnelly's promotion.[23] Philip Durham, on the other hand, was posted directly into the *Hind*, 28 in the Channel, having proved himself as a commander of some ability by capturing a number of privateers; and Charles Dashwood was posted into a frigate from the 18-gun brig *Sylph* after engaging the heavier French frigate *Artémise* in 1801.[24]

The career patterns of something like 34 per cent of captains show a clear and steady progression after posting, from one ship to another. Sometimes this commenced with a frigate or smaller ship, or even a Fourth Rate, and then developed to the command of a 74 or larger ship. It is tempting to suggest that of all the post captains in the navy during the wars with France, this 34 per cent formed the heart of the officer corps; that these were the officers who kept the blockading fleets moving backwards and forwards without ever really obtaining fame or distinction. When it is noted that another 30 per cent of the sample may never have actually served in command of a ship after being posted, this may not seem altogether unreasonable.

Health and Command

There are clear indications that, in the case of at least five officers in the sample, breakdown in health (short of actual death) had a significant effect upon their career. In the case of Sir William Domett, for example, this decline in health came late in his career and after he had reached flag rank. As he may have been in his fifties by this time, we should not read too much into this. Richard Dacres, on the other hand, gives us a prime example of a post captain who was sent to the West Indies, in a frigate, and who subsequently had to resign his command through sickness. Dacres had already spent several years on the Jamaica station when he became ill. Upon return to England he was found a position commanding Sea Fencibles at Dartmouth. The command of Sea Fencibles was frequently given to officers who became incapacitated in some way, but the problem with this duty was that it was sometimes difficult to escape afterwards. Dacres' good fortune was that he was shortly after summoned to be flag captain to Sir William Sidney Smith in the *Pompee*, 80. His luck had not so much to do with Sidney Smith but the fact that Dacres stayed with the ship when the flag was transferred to Vice-Admiral Stanhope for the second battle of Copenhagen, where Dacres earned much praise by organising teams to subdue a serious fire in the dockyard.[25]

Sometimes an officer had to choose just the right moment to prove the reliability of his health. Mauritius De Starck, for example, resigned as lieutenant of the *Salisbury*, 50 because of ill health and his career only seems to have recovered when he offered his services against the mutineers at the Nore in 1797. Illness may actually have saved the career, if not the life, of Edward Dix,[26] who was appointed midshipman of the *Hermione* frigate, which spent a considerable length of time in the West Indies.[27] Dix contracted malaria and then suffered recurrent bouts of fever on two further occasions before being invalided home, fortunate to escape the savage fate of most of the other ship's officers when the crew mutinied.[28] In the case of William Henry Dillon, frequent bouts of sickness in the West Indies hindered his promotion. In his memoirs he recounted how as a lieutenant he was second in line for promotion until it was realised that he was unwell. His patron at the time, Admiral Harvey, ordered him to take sick leave at Tortola in the hope that he might recover, rather than return him to England, for as Harvey reputedly commented, 'That may injure him at the Admiralty'.[29] Furthermore, as even Dillon would probably have recognised, to leave his patron at such a promising juncture would be extremely undesirable. Unfortunately, Dillon's health did not recover sufficiently and, like Dix, he was forced to convalesce in England for several months.

Of course, the officers[30] mentioned here cannot be taken as a representative sample when considering the effect and incidence of poor health. Michael Lewis in *A Social History of the Royal Navy* points out that disease was the greatest cause of death in the Royal Navy[31] and it is obvious that a considerable number of junior officers would have died young. Twenty-four (11.5 per cent) of the sample died during the course of the war, and evidence suggests that the cause was not old age. Of these, two (George Duff and George Downie) were killed in action; whilst John William Taylor Dixon and Henry Duncan (2) were both drowned. The longer term consequences of disease and ill health also had its casualties. James Dalrymple has already been mentioned. Captain Charles Sidney Davers died in 1805, a few months after resigning from the *Active* because of poor health, and John Dolling died whilst captain of the *Suffolk* stationed at the Cape.[32]

Although only two of the sample were killed in action, John Marshall's *Royal Naval Biography* records that a further four were wounded. Here we should take note of the psychology of those submitting their biographical returns to Marshall. Two of those who mention being wounded record that they were 'severely wounded'; the other two mention being wounded in association with important naval episodes (in these cases, Camperdown and Trafalgar). It is an open question how severely an officer had to be wounded before he would make a point of it in his return to Marshall. From a psychological point of view, it is understandable that some officers would mention it to explain gaps in their active service. However, others may simply have taken the view that a wound which did not cause major difficulties or draw attention to a famous event, or result in a pension, was not worth mentioning. Philip Durham, who was shot in the leg and side at Trafalgar suffered long term effects, as his biographer records: 'His wound appeared slight at first, but it was many years before he completely recovered, after narrowly escaping the loss of his leg.'[33]

Francis Douglas, severely wounded at Camperdown, was posted a long thirteen years later. He had been promoted commander in 1800 but by 1805 he was still commanding the guardship at Lymington. Like the command of Sea Fencibles, command of a guardship was another type of post that seems to have been given to those recovering from either illness or the long term effects of wounds, as it usually enabled the captain to live on shore most of the time, often with his family. Douglas never seems to have served after being posted, and was certainly in receipt of a pension after 1815.[34] William Hugh Dobbie,[35] apparently a favourite of Admiral Rainier, was promoted commander by his patron following an attack upon a fort on Baite Island, during which Dobbie was severely wounded. Possibly in order to give him time to recover from his wounds, Rainier made Dobbie the governor of the naval hospital at Madras, although he certainly seems to have recovered well enough by the following year when he served as a volunteer in the search for Linois' squadron in the Indian Ocean. John Draper, probably already suffering from wounds or ill health, died whilst employed as agent for prisoners of war in Huntingdonshire.[36]

At least eighty-six (41 per cent) of the sample were dead by 1822 and were, therefore, unfortunately not included by either John Marshall or William O'Byrne in their autobiographical studies.[37] As a consequence there is little ready information about most of them apart from their commission dates, unless there happens to be an obituary for them in, for example, *The Naval Chronicle*, or unless they submitted a return of their services to the Admiralty.

Promotion and Naval Action

Having raised the issue naval action, it is worth dwelling for a moment on the question of the relationship between promotion and involvement in an engagement. By 1793 it had become customary to encourage and reward officers who fought successful engagements by promoting them or their followers. It is well known that after a major battle, like the Glorious First of June or Trafalgar, there could be a general promotion for most of the officers involved. However, a diverse range of engagements could result in promotion, and statistically it seems that promotion was more likely to arise from a single-ship engagement than from a major fleet action.

Although it has not been possible to check the career details of all of the sample, only ten (*ie* about 5 per cent of the sample) were very clearly promoted at some time because of their involvement in a naval engagement. Of the officers concerned only two of them, Ross Donnelly and John Ferris Devonshire,[38] earned promotion as a result of their presence in a fleet action. In Donnelly's case it was because of his assuming command of the *Montagu*, 74 during the Battle of the First June 1794.[39] Devonshire really received his boost as a result of a single-ship action. However, he was also present at Copenhagen in 1801 as commander of the *Dart* sloop, and became a post captain as a result. It is, then, possible to assert that the majority of those promoted as a result of presence in an engagement were promoted because of single- or small-ship actions. Of the nine officers who fall into this category, approximately half were promoted because of their activities whilst commanding sloops or smaller ships. Others were present in single-ship, mainly frigate, actions. When it came to promotion prospects, therefore, the frigate was the place to be. Having now developed a broader picture of the career of the naval post captain it is appropriate to focus on the frigate captains themselves.

APPENDIX 1. *Post Captains without commands. (DEF Sample only)*

Name	Date Posted	Deceased	Name	Date Posted	Deceased
Joseph Fraine	December 1759	1802	James Donnor	April 1810	1814
Charles Ellys	May 1762	1794	Matthew Flinders	May 1810	1814
Robert Fanshawe(1)	May 1768	1823	William Foote	October 1810	1844
John Ford	June 1763	1796	Robert Evans (2)	October 1810	1828
Thomas Dumaresq	January 1775	1802	Isaac Ferrieres	October 1810	1820
Henry Duncan (1)	February 1776	1814	Francis Douglas	October 1810	1842
William Dudington	September 1777	1817	Sir Bentinck	April 1811	
William Fooks	May 1779	1798	Cavendish Doyle		
William Daniel	September 1781	1800	Robert Merrick	April 1811	1860
Thomas Durell (2)	May 1782	1804	Fowler		
Sir William Henry	May 1782	1809	William B Dolling	August 1811	1834
Douglas			Edward Ellicott	August 1811	1847
Hon Matthew	May 1782	1842	Edward A Down	August 1812	1855
Fortescue (2)			William Westcott	December 1813	1833
James Dundas	September 1790	1811	Daniel		
Charles Dixon	November 1790	1804	Thomas Fife	December 1813	1829
Henry Evans[40]	June 1797	1840	H T Davies	February 1814	1869
Sir Joseph Eyles	December 1799	1806	Peter Fisher	February 1814	1844
Charles Elphinstone	February 1801	1807	Joseph Drury	February 1814	1835
Henry Farnall	May 1801	1806	John Ellis (2)	June 1814	1840
William Day	February 1802	1806	Watkin Evans	June 1814	1817
W H Daniel	April 1802	1838	Thomas Everard	June 1814	Killed in
Henry Duncan (2)	April 1802	1802			Action:
		drowned			N America
James Dalrymple (2)	April 1802	1803	Alexander Fraser (2)	June 1814	1819
T P Durell	April 1802	1836	Edward Flin	June 1814	1820
Daniel Dobree	May 1802	1814	Henry Fanshawe	June 1814	1856
Stephen Folvil[41]	May 1802	1833	Richard Foley	June 1814	1828
Archibald Duff	January 1806	1858	Hon Frederick	June 1814	1867
Philip Dumaresqe	Sept 1806	1819	Fitzhardinge		
Joseph Edmonds	February 1807	1818	Samuel B Deecker	June 1814	1835
Cuthbert F Daly	August 1808	1851	William Dowers	September 1814	1816
William Don	October 1809	1816	George William	June 1815	1873
James Deacon	October 1809	1813	D'Aeth		

THE LURE OF
FRIGATE COMMAND

IN THE PREVIOUS CHAPTER it was suggested not only that frigate command was more than a precursor to what has been seen as the more serious function of commanding a ship of the line, but also that some captains actively sought to command frigates out of preference. There is actually very clear evidence for this. Before moving on to see who the frigate captains were, it is important to look at this evidence and see what it tells us about the navy and the frigate service in particular. There can be no doubt that frigates were seen as glamorous vessels; the correspondents of the *Naval Chronicle,* for example, frequently refer to a frigate as being 'beautiful' – an epithet not usually found when referring to a ship of the line! The more successful frigate captains were also subjected to great adulation. In August 1799, for example, the King received news whilst at the theatre that the frigate *Clyde,* commanded by Captain Charles Cunningham had chased two French frigates and captured one of them, the *Vestale.* 'He immediately stood up in his box, and commanded the news to be communicated to the audience: when "Rule Britannia" was loudly called for from every part of the house, and performed with reiterated applause.'[1] Cunningham was instantly a star captain – until, that is, his own more modest account of the action was received and it was realised that the *Vestale* was less powerful than the British frigate.

The brilliance of some frigate commanders was publicly acclaimed, sometimes even in the face of more outré behaviour. The ever controversial and yet superlative Thomas, Lord Cochrane, for example, was loudly trumpeted by *The Times* when he was sent to lead an attack on a French fleet bottled up in the Basque Roads by Admiral Gambier. *The Times* reported with near glee that Cochrane was being despatched to help. Even when the outcome of the engagement (if it can be so called) was known, *The Times* was anxious to receive Cochrane's personal despatch. When, days later, it arrived the paper produced an inflammatory article with the amazing heading 'Lord Cochrane's Victory'. That Cochrane was enormously popular with all but the Admiralty and some senior captains is made clear by *The Times*'s commentary:

> … the particular fact which most entitles Lord Cochrane to his country's admiration and applause, ought not to have been smothered in the general acknowledgement that his gallantry and judgement 'could not be exceeded by any feat of valour hitherto achieved by the British Navy;' for when the circumstances are better known, we doubt not, an admiring nation will agree with us, that although these are large terms, still they are not extensive enough to include the due praise of this 'judicious' and 'gallant officer', whose daring spirit, and total disregard of all personal consideration in the performance of this service, were not only *never exceeded*, but perhaps *never equalled before*.

Whilst the claim that an action had 'never been equalled before in the annals of naval history' had become a very tired cliché by 1809, there can be no doubt of what the newspaper thought about Cochrane, especially in comparison with the much more senior Admiral Gambier. There was simply no comparison between the dashing, successful and physically striking frigate captain and the cautious, rather too-religious flag officer.

What, though, did naval officers themselves think about frigate service and how did they see it as being distinct from fleet command? To what extent, for example, did they consciously seek appointment to the command of a frigate? It is certainly the officers themselves who tell us that frigate command was greatly sought after. There are two aspects to this: firstly, there are examples from those who were aspiring to frigate service and, secondly, there are the comments of the more experienced post captains.

In one sense the most obvious place to look for evidence of officers' desire for frigate command, or even frigate service, would be among the deluge of letters of appeal which were sent to the First Lord of the Admiralty. However, this source would be unreliable, for a desperate appellant would be only too glad of any form of employment. We get an interesting taste of this from Basil Hall who, as a newly promoted lieutenant, was keen for any appointment. Some adroit political manoeuvring by his father in the House of Commons earned him the support of the Wellesleys – and the current Secretary to the Admiralty just happened to be one William Wellesley Pole. Young Lieutenant Hall very soon found himself holding a commission to join the 74-gun *Invincible*. 'After the first burst of rejoicing was over, at this extraordinary good fortune, I began to disquiet myself, and not in vain, about my appointment, and to wish that, instead of being named to a line-of-battle ship, I had been ordered to join some more active vessel – a frigate for instance.'[2] Hall's response to the situation was to return to the Admiralty three days later and 'beg I might be removed from a line-of-battle ship to a frigate. This change was what my whole heart was set upon.'[3] For his impertinence Hall was soon appointed as lieutenant of the *Endymion*, one of the finest frigates in the navy, commanded by Captain the Hon Thomas Bladen Capel.

In fact Hall had more than just a distant interest in being appointed to a frigate, as he subsequently admits: 'all my thoughts and wishes, asleep or awake, ran so entirely upon frigates, that I badgered the tailors' lives out till my new coat was made, after which I set off to take up my commission, at Chatham ...'[4] Hall's success and boldness are rare. However, as will be shown, the more experienced and renowned the officer, the more confident he would be, not only that his appeal would be heeded at all, but also that he might even specify which frigate he wanted.

It is apparent that there are three main reasons which contributed to the attraction of frigate command.

1. Financial reward. The much considered question of prize money[5] is most often exercised in association with frigate captains. The result is that there is a tendency to see frigate captains as little more than naval privateers. This is a false picture. The occasional capture of a rich prize needs to be offset, for example, against the comparatively lower pay and the costs of frigate command.

2. Independence – the opportunity which frigates usually gave for autonomy of command. Frigates could be sent on independent cruises by the Admiralty or they could be employed in operations which put them outside the orders of the station's commander-in-chief.

3. Glory. Finally there is the matter of the type of kudos referred to in the Foreword – though in the parlance of the time this was usually referred to as honour or glory. One of the best examples of this is to be found in the case of Captain Philip Broke, whose letters reveal him to have been deeply concerned about winning glory in action.[6] The attitudes and practices of captains like Broke indicate that the frigate service was – or was becoming – the elite of the Royal Navy by the time that the conflict ended.

THE REWARD OF FRIGATE COMMAND

In May 1790, at the height of the Spanish Armament and approximately ten years after he was posted, Cuthbert Collingwood, by now fairly high on the list of post captains,[7] wrote to his sister in a tone of almost breathless excitement:

I believe no man can say at present whether this spark will blaze or not …
The Admiral wrote to Lord Chatham[8] to ask for a frigate for me … Captain
Conway came to me a few days after to tell me Lord Ch[atham] had assured
him I should have a 32, which after the great frigates are to [be] preferr'd to
other classes, and for which all are pushing.[9]

Two weeks later he wrote:

Lord Chatham has been particularly civil to me and I think I shall have … one
of the best frigates of 32 guns that we have … You will, may-be, wonder that I
shou'd prefer a frigate to a line of battle ship where my pay wou'd be two
hundred pounds a year more: a 74 I shou'd prefer to anything … And as for the
different emolument; in a frigate the expenses are somewhat less and if I can
get her into the W't Indies I will make the Dons pay me the difference once or
twice a month I hope. The larger frigates are in general more sought after, but I
think I can make mine equal to anything the Spaniards have on one deck.[10]

Collingwood did not serve as a frigate captain during the great wars, but his
comments are a pertinent introduction to the issue of prize money. It should be
noted that according to the second letter, Collingwood wished for a ship of the line
– specifically a 74-gun ship – but he clearly thought that he was being given special
consideration and was obviously far from unhappy at obtaining a frigate. It is not
clear whether, between the two letters, Collingwood had changed his mind about his
real preference, but it is evident from dismissive comments that he made about
64-gun ships[11] that he wanted either to be in the line-of-battle proper or in a frigate
that was capable of both achieving fame through a frigate action or taking prizes.

Both were attractive prospects. Collingwood had previous experience of frigate
command[12] and, as the extract suggests, knew of the advantages to be gained from
serving on the West Indies station.[13] But there was another consideration in
Collingwood's mind. There were certain expenses associated with being a post
captain and Collingwood was well aware that in order to make ends meet as a frigate
captain he would need to be able to make prize money. Therefore, the officer who
pushed for frigate command also had to have something of the nature of a risk-taker
or even a gambler. This applied beyond the monetary sphere: an adventurer was
likely to make a far better frigate captain than an officer who was too cautious.

When it came to the steady income from the officer's salary, frigate captains were
certainly at a relative disadvantage with regard to pay, a situation which only
improved slightly as the wars progressed.

TABLE 2.1. *Daily Pay of Post Captains*[14]

Rate of ship	Guns	Number of men	Daily pay 1796-1806	Daily pay 1807[15]	Number of men	Daily pay[16] 1810-1815
First	100+	850-875	£1	£1-3s	837	£2- 4s
Second	90-98	700-750	16s	19s	738	£1-17s- 6d
Third	64-80	500-650	13s	16s-6d	689	£1-13s- 6d
					640	£1-12s- 6d
					590	£1-11s- 3d
Fourth	50-60	380-420	10s	13s	343	£1- 1s- 6d
Fifth	32-44	220-300	8s	11s	314	19s
					284-294	18s- 4d
					254-274	17s- 9d
					215	16s- 6d
Sixth	20-30	160-200	8s	12s	195	16s-10d
					155-175	16s- 2d

In the early part of the wars a frigate captain's pay equated to 40 per cent of that of the captain of a First Rate ship of the line and 61 per cent of that of the captain of a 74-gun ship. How the rate of pay was arrived at is unclear because at this stage it did not seem to relate to the relative size of the ship's crew. Admittedly, the captain of a Fourth Rate earning 10s per day was commanding, at most, 420 men; *ie* half of the size of the smallest First Rate ship, whose captain was earning 20s (£1) per day. But the ratio does not persist for other rates.

Michael Lewis, in *A Social History of the Navy*, claimed that a captain's pay was somehow linked to the size of crew and the number of guns carried by his ship.[17] This certainly seems possible for the rates of pay between 1793 and 1805 (although the calculation does not work for Fifth and Sixth Rates), but an analysis of the figures for the rest of the war reveals that the link is too tenuous. Even Lewis had to admit that 'The Proportions are not of course exact.' It is possible that rates of pay were calculated upon a complex combination of both number of guns *and* complement. However it was calculated, by 1807 captains of all rates had received a 3/- per day increase (or thereabouts) with the exception of captains of Sixth Rates, who had been given a 4/- increase. In comparative terms frigate captains were now slightly better off, as the captain of a Fifth Rate was earning 48 per cent of the salary of his First Rate colleague and 66 per cent of that in a 74.

By 1810, there had been an enormous increase in the rates of pay for the captains of line of battle ships – in fact, pay had virtually doubled for them. The calculation had obviously become more complicated, because Third Rates and frigates were divided into different rates of pay according to the size of the complement. However, the rate of pay itself was still not calculated according to that differential. The captain of a large Third Rate ship commanded almost exactly twice the complement of a Fourth Rate ship, but his salary was only 64 per cent greater. Furthermore, in comparative terms, the rate of pay for a frigate captain had slumped. The pay of a captain of one of the larger Fifth Rate frigates was now only 38 per cent that of his colleague in a First Rate ship of the line and 58 per cent of that in a 74.

Although officer's pay failed to keep pace with the enormous inflation between 1793 and 1800 (when the value of Sterling had fallen to 56 per cent of its starting value), by the end of the war pay had been increased to bring it back to at least its original worth. Nevertheless, in terms of comparative rates of pay, frigate command was not attractive. On the face of it the differential may appear to relate to the level of responsibility in terms of the number of men and size of the vessel. However, there are two other possible explanations. The first is that the pay was kept lower because it was accepted or understood that frigate captains would supplement their income in a manner not generally available to other captains. This may explain why on occasions the rate of pay for a Sixth Rate ship was slightly higher – that is, that the captain of a Sixth Rate frigate (which being less well armed stood a smaller chance of taking well-armed prizes) needed a little more in the way of regular pay.[18] It might also be suggested that the lower pay acted as an inducement to frigate captains to get to sea and do their job of intercepting enemy trade or taking his warships.

The second possibility may be that the higher pay of the captain of a ship of the line encouraged some captains to opt for the slightly greater financial security of regular income in a battleship: in other words, the salaries of line of battle ship captains included an element of compensation, perhaps as an inducement for the older or less adventurous. This seems to be confirmed by Sir Thomas Byam Martin in an undated memorandum.

> The captain of a ship of the line, though [*ie* even if] much junior in rank[19] to the captain of a frigate, has a higher rate of pay, and for the very sufficient reason following:
> 1st That he commands a much larger body of men, and has much more onerous duties to perform.
> 2nd That the captain of a frigate is almost constantly so employed as to make prize money, which, speaking generally, gives him pecuniary advantages far above the captain of a line-of-battle ship.
> 3rd In war time captains always seek the command of a frigate with small pay, in preference to a ship of the line with larger pay.[20]

One would find it hard to come across a clearer statement. Furthermore, it is worth noting the understated message in Byam Martin's first sentence: frigate captains could be of greater seniority than captains commanding ships of the line!

All naval command implied a certain amount of obligatory expenditure both in war and in peacetime. The captain may, for example, have had to use his personal funds to win the co-operation of dockyard officials in getting his ship ready for sea quickly, or for obtaining just the piece of equipment he needed or wanted. In time of peace captains were expected to host local dignitaries and their families. The officers of a ship calling at a seaside town were usually invited to dine with local dignitaries and were often entertained at balls thrown by the local well-to-do; for the honour of the service, the hospitality had to be returned. On foreign stations such hospitality might carry substantial diplomatic significance. Even at sea it was customary when two ships met for the senior captain to invite the junior to dine – often accompanied by selected members of the wardroom. Naval style being what it was, these could be lavish affairs and those post captains who could afford it provided themselves with very fine tableware and wines.

The importance placed upon 'presentation' is well illustrated by an incident in the career of the young Sir George Elliott, the second son of the Earl of Minto. In July 1803 the unemployed Commander Elliott was attending a ball at Lord Keith's residence in Essex when an urgent message was delivered from the Admiralty instructing him to be at Portsmouth at daybreak to take passage to the Mediterranean to take command of the *Termagant* sloop. In great haste Elliott sped to Portsmouth, leaving virtually all of his clothes and equipment behind and delaying only long enough at Portsmouth to obtain the pieces of cloth necessary to make a new uniform (it was sewn together by the *Victory*'s marine tailors). He arrived in the Mediterranean with none of the paraphernalia usually required by an aspiring commanding officer: livestock, cutlery, plates, glasses, and so on. Fortunately, he was among well-wishers, and Captains Thomas Hardy, John Gore, Ross Donnelly and Richard Moubray all rallied round to provide him with the necessaries (the latter two in particular providing him with chairs, pots and pans). A month after joining the *Termagant*, Nelson promoted Elliott to the 32-gun frigate *Maidstone* following the departure of Moubray, who 'left me numerous things, and the poverty of my establishment was no longer conspicuous'.[21]

Not all officers were as fortunate as Elliott, nor was the timing always so propitious. Philip Beaver, after paying off the *Determinee* frigate in May 1802, was offered another frigate, but declined it, as his biographer recalled, because of his 'absolute inability, in time of peace, to maintain a family at home, and also support the expenses of a table afloat'.[22] Obviously there was a certain amount of social pressure to put on a good show; nevertheless, the advice given to the young Captain Peter Rainier by his uncle, Admiral Rainier, following his posting into the *Caroline* frigate, is interesting: 'keep a very economical table, giving your Officers good white wine, only having a little choice Madeira or Claret for extraordinary visitants. Follow the example of your most economical brother officers in these matters, without becoming sordid, or niggardly.'[23]

The costs of providing entertainment increased according to the status of one's guests. In 1793 Josias Rogers, serving in the Channel in command of the *Quebec* frigate, wrote to a friend: 'I am heartily tired of this rambling channel-service. Besides, I am absolutely spending a little fortune. I am constantly full of great folks, and I need not tell you how very expensive this is to me.'[24] Rogers would have felt this keenly, especially as one of his motivations for returning to sea in a frigate was that his bank had crashed and he had suffered a loss of £2000. The cost of 'great folks' was certainly felt by Captain Samuel Hood of the *Juno*. Being the nephew of both Vice-Admiral Sir Alexander Hood (shortly to become Lord Bridport) and Viscount Hood, he was bound to attract the attention of his family's supporters. In the summer of 1791 he was ordered to take the *Juno* to Weymouth to attend on the royal family. Thomas Byam Martin, who was serving as a lieutenant in the *Juno* tells us:

> The principal preparation however lay in another way, and rested individually with the captain. It became necessary to provide largely and handsomely for the royal table and the numerous train of attendants at lunch, which was in fact providing a daily dinner for them when afloat. This was no small affair for six weeks, and as Captain Hood was at that time a very poor man (nothing but his pay), he had no alternative but to borrow money, so that the honour of being selected for this service ended in his being 700£ in debt, with no other set off against so great an inconvenience but the royal thanks.[25]

In social terms the 'royal thanks' might have had some value, and there can be little doubt that some officers benefited from the sovereign's attention. However, there is little evidence that the King's patronage was guaranteed, and it is hard to find any indication that Samuel Hood benefited as a result. Admirals could also be a problem, as Captain Michael Seymour of the *Amethyst* wrote:

> I sailed on February 8th with Admiral Stopford on board, his furniture, stock, band, secretary, flag and one other lieutenant, captain of marines, chaplain, twelve midshipmen, two mates, his gig's crew, servants &c &c, stores also for the ships here, ... and sixty-three supernumeraries on board from Plymouth

Sound, with forty-eight also of my own crew in the sick list, an entire raw crew of marines, the old having been promoted and cut up, and badly replaced.[26]

This was not an uncommon experience, but the point is that in time of war the cost might be supplemented from prize money. In peacetime there were no prizes to take.[27]

This assumption about the use of a frigate to obtain prize money was common. At about the same time that Collingwood was writing to his sister, Josias Rogers, having learned of his financial loss (mentioned above), apparently consoled his family with the statement that he would simply go to sea and get more.[28] In fact, Rogers had considerable difficulty getting employment and it took the intervention of his patron, Sir Andrew Snape Hamond, and possibly Prince William himself, to move him from his obscurity. By the end of 1793 Rogers was in command of the *Quebec*, a 32-gun frigate, in the West Indies where, according to Gilpin,

> all the frigates and sloops were 'on the wing' as captain Rogers phrases it, to pick up what prizes they could. And it was not without a prudent eye to his own advantage, that he had refused the command of a large ship. He was as active, and judicious in laying out for prizes, as in everything else in which he was concerned.[29]

Rogers had actually been offered a ship of the line but had declined it – probably for the obvious reason. Later in the war, Philip Beaver also commented on the question of prize money:

> My new little vessel is called the *Determinee*, and to a person not conversant with our service, it would appear strange for a man to wish to give up the command of a ship of eighty guns, for one of only twenty-four. But in the former, playing only second or third fiddle, I would have little prospect of distinction; which is not the case in the latter, and before the war concludes, as she sails well, I may perchance fill an old leathern bag. Though my new Quarter-deck is diminutive, it is just as broad a highway to honour, as that of a three-decker.[30]

In all three of these examples there is not only reference to the use of frigates to get prize money, but also a clear indication that the officers concerned have, or would have, declined a larger ship in preference to a frigate. This implies a number of things, but primarily, an ability to pick and choose to a certain degree. This sort of confidence (or might it be arrogance?) was probably determined by the power of one's patron. However, it also implies an ability to move from larger to smaller ship and this was indeed not uncommon.[31]

Prize money, of course, acted as an inducement to captains (and crews for that matter) to be at sea and to be zealous, but it was also thought to be something of a distraction from their essential duties. It is perhaps telling that Josias Rogers's biographer, Gilpin, should comment that Rogers was as active in laying out for prizes as in anything else in which he was concerned – and therein lay the problem with the prize system. There were concerns that the search for prizes might take a frigate captain off station, so much so that in 1804 Sir Charles Middleton, previously a Commissioner of the Admiralty and shortly to become First Lord (as Lord Barham), wrote recommending that Captain's Journals should be frequently inspected to ensure that they were not straying from their stations in search of prizes.[32] The prize system also frequently gave rise to jealousy and bitterness between officers, not least between admirals and frigate commanders who were under direct Admiralty orders. This undoubtedly lies behind St Vincent's enmity towards Sir John Borlase Warren, whom he described as 'a mere partisan, preferring prize money to the public good at all times'.[33] One of the reasons that Bridport apparently resented Sir Edward Pellew's command of an independent frigate squadron was also attributable to this.[34]

PRIZE MONEY

Ascertaining the value of prizes themselves can prove time-consuming and frustrating to the modern historian. Fortunately, under the regulations[35] relating to captures by land or sea, certain shares in all prizes were due to the Greenwich Hospital (for example, the shares belonging to a seaman who had subsequently deserted, or shares not legitimately claimed within three years). As a consequence all prize agents were required to submit an account of the produce of all prizes to the Treasurer of Greenwich Hospital within three months of the first payment to the captors. Agents could be fined £500 for not complying with this regulation.[36] Not all did comply, but the vast majority of agents adhered to the regulation and the Treasurer's accounts are to be found amongst the records of the Greenwich Hospital at the Public Record Office. For the purpose of illustrating this book the contents of the accounts for the period 1793-1798 (particularly where they relate to frigates) are listed below (Appendix 2.1). Although the accounts show the net sum received from sale of hulls, cargo, head money and salvage, this was not actually the sum that was paid over or due to the captors, as there were various deductions that had to be made, like the Prize Agent's fee.

Richard Hill, in his recent work on the naval prize system, has estimated that some £30 million was received in prize money during the course of the wars.[37]

According to the Greenwich Hospital accounts the total net figure for prize payments during the first two years alone was somewhere in the region of £691,800. Because of the delay in condemning and selling prizes or dealing with legal disputes, it could take several years for money to be distributed; hence many sums won during the first few years of the wars would not be declared in the Hospital accounts until some time later, if at all. For example, to the above sum should be added a proportion of the prize money for the French corvette *Jean Bart*, which was taken by Sir John Borlase Warren's squadron in April 1795; unfortunately Hemmons, the agent appointed to act for this prize, never submitted his accounts to the Greenwich Hospital. Of the total given above, £489,613 was made up from individual prizes, stores and head money. The balance was almost completely provided by the prizes taken at the Battle of the First of June 1794. The Channel Fleet under the command of Admiral Lord Howe gained £201,096 from that battle alone, that is just over 29 per cent of the prize money for the whole period.

A study of the accounts immediately shows how prominent the frigates were in taking prizes. In fact, frigates were involved in captures to the value of approximately £463,635 (that is, just over 67 per cent of the total). Other rated ships gained prize money totalling approximately £227,365 (33 per cent). This gives us an indication of the comparative success of frigate captains in taking prizes – the figures suggest that the officers and crew of a frigate were twice as likely to gain than their comrades in larger ships. But in general the difference may have been even greater because the 'other rates' figure is inflated by one particular prize: the capture of the French East Indiaman *La Constitution* by the *Leopard*, 50 commanded by Captain John Maude. William Henry Dillon serving on board the frigate *Thetis*, commanded by Captain John Hartwell, recalled arriving at St Helena in June 1793:

> We found lying here our consort the *Leopard* and several East India ships. The battery saluted the Commodore with 15 guns, the compliment being returned by us. The first person that made his appearance on board was Captain Maude. He had, it seems, taken a large French East Indiaman, and also, when in the Channel, a French Privateer. The Indiaman was named the *Constitution*. It had originally belonged to our East India Company and was a very fine ship with a valuable cargo.[38]

Hartwell and his crew had themselves just taken two valuable prizes, a French merchantman *La Trojan* and the *Mongoff George*, both of which fell victim through ignorance of the outbreak of war. As *Thetis* was sailing under Admiralty orders her captain could expect to retain his full three-eighths share of any prize money.[39] Maude suggested that the *Thetis* and the *Leopard* might share the value of their prizes. This was a common practice, particularly among frigate squadrons, as it enabled all to share from the good luck of one of the group whilst reducing the level of loss if the prize were subsequently lost. Hartwell, conscious of the prospective value of his two captures, refused, a decision which he must have bitterly regretted, for *La Trojan*, which had already been sent back to England with a prize crew, was retaken by the French. The *Mongoff George* was successfully delivered to England and sold for £35,057-18s-6d; of which the officers and crew received £21,378. John Hartwell's share would have been just over £8000. It was a poor recompense, for Dillon anticipated that the value of *La Trojan* would have been in the region of £120,000.[40]

Maude's prizes, on the other hand, all returned to England successfully. *La Constitution* alone realised £145,287-9s-8d, although the crew only appear to have received £66,889 of this. John Maude himself received over £25,083, the equivalent of £1,203,984 at 1996 rates.[41] This, together with the £8031 which was paid out in prize money for the *La Victoire* captured by Maude and the *Leopard* earlier in the year, equated to over 227 times his annual salary and made him a very rich man indeed. Maude and his crews' prize money for this one capture amounted to 16 per cent of the total prize money awarded (in the period under review). If the *Leopard*'s prize money is disregarded, captains of line of battle ships gained only about £109,000 plus the prize money from the First of June (£210,096) which was shared with seven frigates.[42]

The main issue here, however, is that of the prize money gained by frigate commanders. It must first of all be noted that, as far as all naval captains were concerned, the prize system contained a number of hazards. One of the greatest dangers lay in the problem of identifying which vessels were eligible for seizure. At the beginning of the wars there were no guidance notes available for sea officers and although the 1793 Prize Act was available, it was not the sort of document which could easily be used by the majority of sea officers. There was even some confusion over what legally constituted 'blockade' and it took a ruling in 1798 by Sir William Scott, Judge of the High Court of Admiralty, to clarify matters somewhat. The situation became much more difficult from 1803 onwards when Channel ports under French control were placed under two different levels of blockade, with those ports from which invasion forces might be launched being under strictest blockade.

Behind the strategic interest of blockade lay the underlying need of both sides of the conflict to undermine each other's economy by effectively breaking trade embargoes and continuing an export trade. Napoleon attempted to seal off the continent with the issuing of the 'Berlin Decree' in November 1806, to which Britain responded through Orders in Council forbidding neutral vessels to trade between

French controlled ports. This should have made the frigate captain's job easier, but in fact the government capitalised on the situation by selling licences to some neutral vessels to continue trading. Frigate captains on the Channel Station, therefore, found that increasing amounts of their time was spent chasing and boarding vessels legally licensed by His Majesty's government.[43] This could lead to further difficulties. The owners or merchants with cargo in a vessel wrongly detained could seek redress and reparation from the captain of the naval vessel involved, and the cost of this could be high. In May 1813, for example, Thomas Bladen Capel – an extremely able commander (with over eight and a half years' experience as a frigate captain) – now commanding the 74-gun *Hogue*, captured and burnt an American merchant vessel which the owners subsequently claimed was sailing under licence. Two years later, when the appeal was heard before the High Court of Admiralty, the decision went to the owners and Capel found himself liable for £4000 compensation. To cover this eventuality the Government retained a fund to bail out officers who got into such difficulties, provided those officers were deemed to have acted reasonably and in good faith.

In spite of these pitfalls, substantial sums could be, and were, made by captains during this period. Not surprisingly, the names of the most successful prize-taking frigate captains during the first two years of the war will be familiar. Perhaps the most successful of these in 1793-4 was Sir Andrew Snape Douglas of the *Phaeton*. Douglas was already a senior captain by the outbreak of war, having commanded a squadron of frigates during the American War. He was knighted by the King during one of the monarch's peacetime summer excursions at Weymouth, and was given the *Phaeton* in 1793. In April 1793 in company with three other ships Douglas captured a copper-bottomed French privateer, the *General Dumourier*, 22 guns, which was found to be carrying 680 cases of silver. By remarkable coincidence, later on the same day, he captured a Spanish galleon, the *St Jago* or *St Iago*.[44] He wrote to his uncle, Sir Andrew Snape Hamond:

> The two prizes are of immense value, exceeding Commodore Anson's ... You may easily imagine, as success has a very sensible effect upon the human mind, how much we are elated at this stroke of fortune, and I feel much gratified at having been the principal feature in the picture ... *Phaeton* sails remarkably well ...[45]

Phaeton's share in the capture was approximately £52,000, which gave Douglas a personal share of £13,000 (the equivalent of nearly £624,000 at mid 1990s rates).[46] Douglas's successes might have accrued still further. Lord Howe, who clearly and understandably was rather pleased at Douglas's success, rewarded him:

> Lord Howe gave me a distinguishing pendant, and the command of all the
> frigates of the fleet[47] formed into a separate squadron. This was the first
> appointment of the kind that had ever taken place; and, as such, I considered
> it a very honourable one, although it was very fatigueing.[48]

Nearly a year later Howe appointed him his flag captain, just in time for the battle
of the First of June 1794, during which Douglas received a serious head wound from
which he never really recovered. He eventually died as a result of the wound in 1797.
Nevertheless, in approximately eighteen months whilst in command of the *Phaeton*,
Douglas managed to take prizes which brought he and his crew a total of
approximately £75,000.

Other successful prize-takers included Sir Richard Strachan, who was posted at
the end of the American War in 1783 and served in the West Indies as a frigate
captain during the intervening peace. In 1793 he was appointed to the *Concorde*
frigate in the Channel, where he operated in a frigate squadron with Sir Edward
Pellew in the *Arethusa* and Sir John Borlase Warren in the *Flora*. The amount of
prize money received by Strachan between 1793 and 1798 amounted to £6477 (or
£9715 if sailing independently) over 54 per cent of which came from his capture of
La Pauline, which alone sold for £22,426-18s-11d gross. Likewise, both Pellew and
Warren showed considerable success in the first six years of the war, Pellew taking
approximately £10,300[49] and Warren £8932, though the latter also stood to gain
further prize money from the proceeds of the *Jean Bart* corvette, *Robuste* and *Etoile*,
captured in company with the rest of Warren's frigate squadron (*Galatea*, Richard
Keats, *Anson*, Philip Durham and *Artois*, Edward Nagle), which brought the four
frigates a share of £8190 cash payment.

Strachan, Warren and Pellew, of course, commanded frigate squadrons; the two
latter most famously as independent squadrons operating from Falmouth a few
years later. All three served longer than average as frigate captains,[50] and it is easy to
see exactly why Pellew was so reluctant when the time came not only to surrender
his frigate, but also to return to the control of the fleet admiral who had previously
been unable to claim his customary one-eighth share of the frigate's prize money.

Whilst the vast majority of prizes were taken on the Channel and Cork Stations
during 1793-8, there is clear evidence that valuable prizes could be captured
elsewhere. John Woodley in the *Leda*, in company with the 50-gun ship *Romney*,
Captain the Hon W Paget, took four French vessels in the Mediterannean in June
1794, which brought the *Leda*'s crew a total of £4087-18s-6d in cash. Captain

Edward Foote and the crew of the crack frigate *Niger* received £11,096-17s-7d for the capture of the Spanish brig *Natalia* and the *Caradad* in January 1797; clearly there were major advantages to be had from sailing in one of the navy's finest frigates. Thomas Fremantle and the crew of the *Tartar* received £3142-11s-8d as their share of prize money from the capture of the French frigate *La Sybille* and several other vessels.

The example of Fremantle highlights another facet of prize money: that is, the reward for taking an enemy frigate. The capture of a frigate brought a number of bonuses. First of all, there was considerably more kudos in taking an enemy frigate, and some officers were honoured as a consequence. A successful frigate action brought both public notice and the very strong possibility of a better command, with promotion for the junior officers. Financially, a captured frigate made a better prize because, provided she was not too badly damaged during the battle, the ship, complete with guns, stores and rigging, could be purchased for the service. For the Admiralty it was a relatively cheap way to acquire another frigate, but the navy would still pay more than prospective merchant purchasers could or would afford. To the value of hull, stores and weapons would have been added the bounty known as head money – that is, the £5 bonus for every member of the enemy's crew at the start of the action. The sums received for captured frigates *usually* greatly exceeded that of both merchant vessels and privateers. Richard Hill has estimated that the average proceeds for a privateer were in the region of £1063 net; and on average about £2500 for a merchant vessel.[51] During the first few years of the wars Edward Pellew and the crew of the *Nymphe* received £7798 for the capture of the French frigate *Cléopâtre*. Saumarez and the crew of the *Crescent* shared £5239 in cash with Joseph Sidney Yorke in the *Circe* for the capture of the French frigate *La Réunion*.

The advantages of agreeing to share prize money with other ships in the squadron applied equally when it came to captured enemy frigates. In April 1796 Pellew's squadron chased and captured the *Unité*, although it was Frank Cole in the *Revolutionnaire* whose ship actually engaged the French frigate. Just days later the squadron ran into another French frigate, the *Virginie*, and captured her, although on this occasion it was Pellew himself in the *Indefatigable* who took the prize. However, all of the frigates took a share in the joint proceeds of the two prizes, as follows:

Frigate	Commander	Share of Prize Money
Argo	Richard Burgess	£2810
Indefatigable	Sir Edward Pellew	£4205
Amazon	Richard Carthew Reynolds	£3929
Concorde	Anthony Hunt (2)	£3401
Revolutionnaire	Frank Cole	£3862

AUTONOMY

Given the sort of financial reward discussed above, it is easy to see why it has often been implied that prize money was the main attraction of frigate command. But there were other types of reward. Frigate captains benefited from a degree of independence which was not, even could not be, applicable to the captain of a line of battle ship attached to a fleet or squadron. For the officers and crew of a crack frigate, under a good captain, the experience could be very agreeable, as Basil Hall recalled:

> I should be happy indeed, could I describe, in suitable terms, the delightful sort of life we led in the *Endymion*, during the two or three years which followed our abortive attempts to drive the French out of the Peninsula, by means of two or three thousand unarmed Galician peasants. During the remaining months of 1809, all 1810, and for the greater part of 1811, we had almost as free a roving commission as any corsair could have drawn up for himself.[52]

And to underline the fact that prize money was not everything, Hall finished on a dry note:

> It so chanced, however, that in all this busy period of the most active possible cruising, flirting, and feasting, there did not occur a single adventure deserving of that name, or such as would figure in a novel. We often got scent of French frigates, but never ran one of them home … Neither, with all our opportunities, and apparently with the choice of our own cruising ground, did we ever pounce on a prize worth the trouble of catching; or, to speak more correctly, did we ever catch one, in which the chase was not by far the most interesting part of the adventure.[53]

The research for this book unearthed few overt comments from captains about autonomy, but the value placed upon it is best judged from the reaction of those officers who suddenly found that they had lost their independence. As mentioned above, there is the example of Edward Pellew's fury at discovering that he and his squadron were to be put under the command of Lord Bridport, after several years of successfully cruising in the Channel. On finding out that he was not only to lose his frigate but also his officers and crew, he dispatched a furious and bitter letter to Spencer, First Lord of the Admiralty, written in the unconventionally challenging third person: 'he [Pellew] dares to say … that language does not furnish words sufficiently strong to express his feelings upon such merited hard treatment; nor can time, however soothing on most other occasions, blot from his remembrance,

47

circumstances so debasing to the reputation of an Officer … .' And Pellew's parting comment was as sharp as one of the *Indefatigable*'s broadsides: 'to your Lordship he leaves the regret of having occasioned them.'[54]

There is also the case of Lord Cochrane, who claimed (rather dubiously) that his independent cruising orders from the Admiralty had been embargoed by the port admiral at Plymouth and re-copied under his own authority. The effect of this was to place Cochrane under the port admiral's orders and entitle him to a share of any prizes that the *Pallas* took.[55]

However, the idea that frigate captains simply roved the high seas looking for prizes should be carefully avoided, for it was not the case. Frigates were usually attached to a particular squadron or division of one of the fleets, and even though their commanders were often left alone to deal with situations as they arose, they were usually under orders of varying rigidity. This, probably fairly typical, example was sent by Nelson to Captain William Parker of the *Amazon* frigate in December 1804:

> I am going off Toulon to see that all is safe, and it is my present intention to return to 97; but should a heavy gale of NW wind come on I shall not allow myself to be driven to the southward of the straits of Bonifacio … but shall go to Madalena, at which place I shall certainly be before the 7th January; therefore, if you have no chance of getting hold of the squadron from the sketch I have given you of my intentions, and you have many bullocks for us, I would recommend your going to Madalena, and landing Mr Ford and the cattle, that they may be taken care of.
>
> … Should you have much spare time … between the time of your arrival and the 7th January, I would recommend your cruizing off the Coast of Corsica, and try and get the *Naurice*, a store-ship, which loads timber in the Gulf of Saone … If she is there, you may either take or destroy her, and the French have, they say, 4000 troops ready for embarking at Ajaccio.[56]

Sometimes a frigate captain's orders could be deviously ambiguous. In 1793 Lord Hood, commanding the Mediterranean fleet, dispatched Captain George Lumsdaine in the *Iris*, 32 with both the *Mermaid* frigate, Captain John Trigge, and Commander Thomas Byam Martin in the *Tisiphone* sloop, under his command to deliver presents to the Bey of Tripoli. Both Martin and Lumsdaine were summoned to Hood's cabin in the *Victory* prior to their departure and were informed that they were also charged to deliver a dispatch for the consul at Tunis. Such great emphasis was laid on this latter point that both officers were left puzzled as to its importance and the rather curious way in which their orders had been expressed. In due course, Martin in the *Tisiphone* was sent ahead of the small squadron to sail into Tunis and return. On approaching Tunis he realised that a French frigate lay in wait for him, preceding him into the port. Anxious not to break the rules of neutrality, Martin entered the port, delivered the dispatch and sailed back to join his squadron. On their successful return to the fleet Lumsdaine and Martin found themselves under threat of court martial for failing to obey orders. It then became apparent that Hood had intended Lumsdaine to use the *Tisiphone* as bait, hoping that if the French succumbed to the temptation to seize her, Lumsdaine and the rest of the fleet would have a general excuse to attack all French shipping in the neutral ports along the African shore. In the end, Lumsdaine was court-martialled but fully acquitted.[57]

The loss of autonomy could be felt even more acutely by the frigate captain if the admiral decided that, for whatever reason, he was going to travel in that frigate itself. In February 1809 Sir Michael Seymour left Plymouth in the *Amethyst* to take up his station blockading Lorient. As passenger he carried Admiral Sir Robert Stopford, the commander of the blockading squadron. The *Amethyst* struggled through very foul weather, constantly changing course as the wind shifted to threaten her with a lee shore, but at least Seymour knew his destination: that is until 'wearing, and pushing hard to get round the Saints for my passage to this station, I first heard from my amiable, excellent Admiral that he meant to call at Glenans to give the L'Orient squadron ... some orders.' The frustration of this situation can only really be appreciated by reading the full letter from Seymour to his brother captain, Edward Hawker.[58]

Where frigate commanders would appear to have had the most freedom was, as Cochrane was aware, under direct Admiralty orders. But this was granted to a minority. In the month of July in the years 1793 to 1795, for example, between 15 and 20 per cent of the frigate force was sailing under Admiralty orders, but this included those on convoy duty as well as those cruising or sailing under secret orders. In the same month for 1796-7 only 6 per cent and 3 per cent respectively of the frigate force was engaged on these duties (although during these two years there *also* existed the independent frigate squadrons under Pellew and Warren, who were also engaged on cruising duties in the Channel). During the second war the number of frigates sailing under independent orders seems to have been generally less than 9 per cent of the available force.[59] These statistics all reinforce the view that only a minority of frigate commanders were really given the opportunity to cruise independently by the Admiralty. Having said this, it must be noted that many flag officers rewarded the frigates under their command by giving them limited periods in which to cruise in pursuit of enemy vessels or contraband.

PRESTIGE

The writings of officers serving in frigates make it instantly obvious that they themselves saw their time in frigates as being distinctly different from service in ships of the line. Exactly how they expressed this varied according to their age and rank. For example, frigate service was very popular with young midshipmen because it was more adventurous, although often the reason that some of them gave for this popularity had more to do with money. The narrative of William Henry Dillon records his feelings as a midshipman at anchor in Plymouth Sound in 1793:

> A French frigate, *la Blonde*, came in here as a prize one day. The official account of her capture as well as that of several others afterwards, always created a great deal of excitement amongst the Mids of the *Defence*, as we were, comparatively speaking, doing nothing, whilst our frigates were making prizes daily.[60]

and

> Several of the Mids became dissatisfied with the duty of a line of battle ship. They were not only anxious for more active service, but also to touch some Prize money. Their applications to the Captain [Gambier] to remove them into frigates annoyed him, and he used frequently to declare, 'You are all frigate mad'.[61]

Dillon was perhaps particularly attracted to the money; others were not. The young Abraham Crawford, serving as midshipman on board the frigate *Revolutionnaire*, commanded by Captain Twysden, recalled :

> Everybody, even to the least boy in the ship, felt an interest in her fame; and the histories of the chase and capture of the *Bordelais* and *Determinee*, two large French privateers, were so familiar to me, that I almost fancied I had been a sharer in the frigate's wonderful exploits upon those memorable occasions. [62]

What both Dillon and Crawford were expressing was a sense of identification with the frigates involved. The ships were exciting and glamorous and the boys wanted to be associated with that.

This sense of identification had another dimension in that, in the dockyard towns in particular, the famous frigates would be well known to other seamen and the public. Being part of the crew of one of those frigates would, therefore, bring its own prestige and peripheral benefits.

Another young midshipman commenting in similar vein was Frederick Chamier, who was moved from the *Salsette* frigate to a 74-gun ship: 'I confess I did not much like the change, for in those days a certain stigma was attached to midshipmen who belonged to line-of-battle ships, while the midshipmen of frigates were the aristocracy of their grade in the profession.'[63] The midshipmen of frigates were considered – or at least they considered themselves – the cream of their rank because they were usually deeply involved in their frigate's operations. If one of the major activities of a frigate was the 'cutting-out expedition' – that is, sending in boats of seamen to board and capture an enemy vessel in a hostile port – one of the major duties of a frigate's midshipmen was to lead those boats, usually under the direction of the first lieutenant. A frigate's midshipman was therefore not only likely to be wealthier[64] than his ship of the line counterpart because of his share of prize money, but he was also likely to be more experienced in terms of seeing action.

Captain Frederick Marryatt, who served as a midshipman in the *Imperieuse* under Captain Lord Cochrane, referred to this in his unashamedly autobiographical first novel *Frank Mildmay*. Transferred from the frigate to the admiral's flagship – 'I should have much preferred remaining in the frigate, whose captain also wished it, but that was not allowed' – Marryatt found himself just one of between sixty and seventy midshipmen.

> They were mostly youngsters, followers of the rear-admiral, and had seen
> very little, if any, service and I had seen a great deal for the time I had been
> afloat. Listening eagerly to my 'yarns', the youthful ardour of these striplings
> kindled, and they longed to emulate my deeds. The consequence was
> numerous applications from the midshipmen to be allowed to join the
> frigates on the station; not one was contented in the flagship.[65]

And it was not just the midshipmen of frigates who were conscious of a difference between themselves and the crews of other ships. In 1794 Lieutenant John Surman Carden was in his twenties and apparently languishing on board a ship of the line, the *Queen Charlotte*. Although he was under the command of his patron, he realised that as the junior of nine lieutenants his chances of promotion in a First Rate ship of the line were remote: 'I could not do myself the injustice to remain the junior of nine lieutenants in any ship during a hot war, While any other situation afloat would offer me brighter prospects of furtherance in the Service, and as such … I felt myself entitled to become first Lieutenant of a Frigate.'[66]

Frigates, therefore, offered the chance of pecuniary reward to those who served in them, whilst at the same time the nature of frigate service enabled the officers and crews to experience a much more direct role in the activities in which they were engaged. This can be explained quite simply. For the officers of a frigate sent out on patrol or cruising, their detachment from the close watch of the admiral gave them a sense of autonomy and an encouragement to use their initiative which would have been stifled when attached to a fleet. This autonomy and initiative could pay huge dividends both in terms of fame and prize money. Even for the ordinary seaman, being one man in a crew of 300 (as opposed to one man in a crew of between 700 and 900), could only make everyone's personal contribution the more important and less anonymous. It is this simple fact which enabled some frigate captains to develop extraordinary relationships with their crews. It also enabled the crews to develop a very keen sense of self-identity, especially when they came together as a team in one of the frigate squadrons. In 1795, for example, when Sir Graham Moore, captain of the *Syren* frigate, joined Sir Richard Strachan's frigate squadron in the Channel, he noted in his journal:

> There is the strongest attachment to each other among the crews of these three frigates [*Melampus*, *Diamond* and *Syren*]. I have always encouraged and promoted it as much as I could, as I think it of very great importance to the service, that ships acting together should be on the most cordial terms with each other.[67]

It is certain that the crews of frigates, serving together for considerable periods, developed a close affinity and under a good captain could be welded into a very efficient team. This close relationship was probably reinforced by the arrangement to share prize money. Both Pellew's and Warren's frigate squadrons agreed to share their prize money; and it was common for two frigates on a cruise to make the same agreement. This could only have fostered the sense of mutual interest and support between the crews of the associated ships. It may be for this reason that although the Admiralty adopted a policy of dispersing crews of line of battle ships when they were paid off (apparently to prevent the development of potentially radical associations), frigate crews were often turned-over complete to another frigate – usually under the same captain. Edward Owen, for example, was allowed to transfer his entire crew and officers on three different occasions.[68] Michael Seymour was allowed to transfer his entire crew from the *Amethyst* to the *Niemen*. Sir Edward Pellew was allowed to transfer the crew of the *Nymphe* across to the *Arethusa* and subsequently to the *Indefatigable*.[69] The difficulties caused when this did not happen are well illustrated by the story of the very promising Captain Thomas Twysden, who had commanded frigates for nearly five years by 1801 when he was commanding the crack frigate *Revolutionnaire*.

> Having been ordered into Plymouth to refit one winter, under Lord St
> Vincent's administration, the whole of his ship's Company was taken from
> him. Consequently he had to re-man the frigate. When he had accomplished
> that task, and going to sea with a new crew, he was so dissatisfied with their
> lubberly proceedings that it brought on a fit of passion, during which he fell
> down in his cabin a dead man.[70]

When seamen from frigates were dispersed to different ships of the line they were sometimes recognisably different from the seamen from other ships. Crawford, who had himself been serving under Captain Edward Owen in a frigate, joined the First Rate *Royal George* and noted of her crew:

> Those who had served chiefly in ships of the line, or passed much of their
> lives in guard ships, ... were well skilled in slang, and even their ordinary
> conversation was garnished and interlarded with a superabundance of oaths
> and obscenity. The collection from sloops of war and gun-brigs might be
> known by an absence of good breeding, and a certain slouching vulgarity
> and slovenliness of appearance; while those of the frigate-school differed
> widely from both. Of this they seemed themselves aware, avoiding as much
> as they could an intimacy with the others, and forming as much as possible,
> a society apart.[71]

This is a fascinating comment by the observant Crawford. Unfortunately, of course, he does not state exactly how the frigate seamen differed, but it can be inferred that Crawford thought them less vulgar in their language and possessing more pride in their appearance. The implication was that they were in some way of a higher quality. This may be wishful thinking on Crawford's part but it is worth pointing out his choice of the words 'frigate-school' to describe some form of collective identity. Furthermore, Crawford's observations were not limited to the hands:

> In the *Clyde* I felt myself to be an officer of some little consequence. I
> frequently was placed in charge of the deck, and never was ordered to
> perform any duty but such as comported with my years and standing in the
> service. In my new ship, on the contrary, I was but one, and I believe the

youngest one of a host of passed midshipmen, who were no more regarded, nor their feelings consulted, as to the duty they were required to perform, than if they had entered the service the day before.

... What, for instance, can be more wounding to the feelings of a young man, who has passed his examination and is qualified in all respects – by birth, by years, and by experience – to fill the situation, and do the duty, of a lieutenant, than to be ordered, as I have been, to attend with a boat upon the captain's pleasure, laqueying him like the menial who stands behind your chair, or opens your carriage at the opera?[72]

This is another deeply interesting comment from Crawford, principally because it gives clear evidence of the class consciousness that was increasingly manifest in the officer corps at the beginning of the nineteenth century. It should be said that in his *Reminiscences* Crawford rarely speaks in such a tone, but here there is an element of bitterness arising from his changed circumstances. It must be remembered that the cause of this emotion is the fact that Crawford feels his self-esteem reduced: in other words, on board the *Clyde* he enjoyed a higher status than in the line of battle ship.

There may have been a number of factors at play here. First was the culture of command created in the frigate by his former captain, Edward Owen, which may have given Crawford a higher shipboard status than his rank or seniority would attract on board a ship of the line. This would certainly seem to be at the root of Crawford's discontent. On the other hand, given the comments that have been presented from other sources, it is equally likely that it was the nature of service in a frigate that gave the greater feeling of worth. This is quite easily explained. Crawford himself points out that in a line of battle ship he was just one of a larger number of 'passed midshipmen'. But it was not so much a matter of rank as of number. In a frigate there were simply fewer men to carry out the same number of duties, and therefore every officer, even a midshipman, had to carry a heavier responsibility. Furthermore, the nature of frigate duties meant that the crew would be under greater strain for longer periods, and under a good commander this could lead to a high level of (largely unacknowledged) teamwork among both hands and officers. In the *Clyde* it is unlikely that Midshipman Crawford was expected to carry out the menial duties he experienced in the *Royal George*, not because of his social status, although this would undoubtedly have had a bearing on the matter, but because he could not be spared for it.[73] Likewise, if he was not kept 'laqueying' around by Captain Owen, it was probably because Owen's duties kept him away from the type of activity or social requirements in which many captains indulged.[74]

There is another point, of course, which is that Crawford's commanding officer in the *Royal George* was the captain of a line of battle ship rather than a frigate, and it may have been more important for him to give a visible display of his status in having junior officers waiting around for him. Just as on land the number of one's servants provided a visible gauge of social importance, so at sea might the number of junior officers. This raises a tantalising question. If command of a ship of the line was seen as being socially more prestigious, why were so many officers keen to command frigates? Was it perhaps that professional interest was beginning to assert itself over the considerations of social class?

HONOURS

For the post captain the most tangible symbol of prestige, apart from being given employment or command of a squadron, was probably the acquisition of either a knighthood or elevation to the peerage. The obvious question to ask at this point is whether a post captain stood a better chance of obtaining this sort of recognition in a frigate or a ship of the line? The captain of a ship of the line actually stood little chance of gaining a knighthood, even after a major fleet action. Scrutiny of the rewards after two such engagements will serve as an illustration.

The Battle of Cape St Vincent
Commander-in-Chief: Admiral Jervis was raised to the peerage as Baron Jervis and Earl St Vincent. He was also given a pension of £3000 pa
Vice-Admirals: Thompson became a baronet. Waldegrave already had a title[75] as the son of a peer and declined a knighthood. So he was given an Irish Peerage
Rear-Admirals: Parker became a baronet
Captains: Captain Robert Calder (Jervis's flag captain) received a knighthood because he was sent home with dispatches. Other captains received a gold medal. Commodore Nelson, technically a rear-admiral, although this was only known at home at the time of the battle, was also knighted

The Battle of Camperdown
Commander-in-Chief: Admiral Duncan was created Baron Duncan and Viscount Duncan of Camperdown
Vice-Admirals: Onslow became a baronet
Captains: Trollope and Fairfax were sent home with despatches and made knights-banneret (Fairfax was Duncan's flag captain). All other captains received a gold medal (with the exception of Williamson who was court-martialled for cowardice and found guilty)

From this it can be seen that it was really only the flag captain and the bearer of dispatches who could expect to be knighted following a fleet engagement.[76] At Camperdown there were sixteen British ships of the line involved; at St Vincent there were fifteen. Numerically speaking, therefore, the ordinary post captain involved in a major engagement had little chance of being honoured.

During the wars there were approximately forty-seven single-ship frigate actions. In twenty-seven of these engagements the enemy ship was either captured or destroyed. In only five cases (possibly six) was the captain honoured. The reason for this would seem to lie partly in the nature of the ships involved in the engagement.

The first knighthood awarded to a frigate captain was that given to Edward Pellew in June 1793, following the capture of the French frigate *Cléopâtre* by the *Nymphe*.[77] This being the first contest between the two navies, it is hardly surprising that a British victory should be celebrated. What was ignored at the time was the fact that the French frigate could fire a broadside of only 286 pounds compared with the *Nymphe*'s 322 pounds, though as in virtually all similar engagements the crew of the British ship was significantly smaller. Four months later the *Crescent* captured the French frigate *Réunion* in what was the second successful frigate action of the war.[78] The *Crescent*'s captain, James Saumarez was also knighted, though the honour on this occasion was somewhat soured by the fact that an attempt was made to make him pay a fee for his knighthood. In November 1793, he wrote to his brother:

> I am not quite so pleased with a letter from Mr Cooke, who has the distribution of the fees[79] which he says are due from those who receive the honour of a knighthood, and which amount to £103 6s 8d. In reply to this I have referred him to whoever paid the above fees for Sir E Pellew, on whom that honour was conferred on a similar occasion … I think it hard to pay so much for an honour which my services have been thought to deserve.[80]

The *Crescent* was a much closer match to her opponent. In May 1794, however, the tiny 28-gun *Carysfort* captured the *Castor* which had been taken from the Royal Navy three weeks previously. The broadside weight of the British frigate was only 73 per cent that of her opponent and therefore this could be regarded as a significant victory. However, her captain, Francis Laforey did not receive a knighthood. The reason for this would seem to have been a dispute which immediately broke out as to whether the *Castor* could justly be regarded as a prize or as salvage. The Admiralty seem to have considered that she was salvage as she had not been taken into an enemy port. Laforey and his officers disputed the ruling and won their case.[81]

In April 1795 the 12-pounder 32-gun frigate *Astraea*, under the command of Lord Henry Paulet, captured the 40-gun *Gloire*, a French frigate whose formidable broadside weighed 112 pounds more than the *Astraea*. Paulet received no knighthood, but then he was already titled. The disparity between the two frigates was significant, but the crucial difference may have been that the *Astraea* was not totally alone during the action. Although she alone engaged the *Gloire*, other ships under the command of Rear-Admiral Sir John Colpoys were also in chase.[82] This was not the case in June 1796, however, when the British frigates *Santa Margarita*, Captain Thomas Byam Martin and *Unicorn*, Captain Thomas Williams, engaged two French frigates north-west of Scilly. As a result of the engagement Martin, in the 12-pounder *Santa Margarita*, captured the slightly heavier *Tamise*, whilst Williams, who was also the senior captain, in the 18-pounder frigate *Unicorn* captured the smaller French frigate *Tribune*. Perhaps because it was convention, it was the senior captain, Thomas Williams, who received a knighthood, although it was probably the captain of the *Santa Margarita* who had overcome the greater odds.[83] Edward Brenton apparently thought that Williams had been knighted because he had overcome a ship of superior force;[84] this was certainly not the case, although he might equally have been knighted for capturing two French frigates.

Later in 1796 Lord Amelius Beauclerk in the *Dryad* captured the smaller French frigate *Proserpine*. Apart from the fact that Beauclerk was already titled, the capture of a smaller ship no longer seemed to have attracted public attention to any noteworthy degree. In October of that same year Richard Bowen in the 32-gun 12-pounder *Terpsichore* captured the 34-gun 12-pounder Spanish frigate *Mahonesa* after an action described by William James as 'as fair a match as an English officer would wish to fight, or an English writer to record'.[85] By late 1796 even a fair match was no guarantee of obtaining honours and Bowen received virtually no reward. It was sad treatment for an officer who had led his crew so well, and even William James later thought Bowen's treatment was unjust. Even more tragically, Bowen was killed less than two years later during the ill-fated attack on Santa Cruz. In Bowen's death the navy lost a brilliant captain and, in a repetition of the earlier event, even Nelson's attempts to get a monument erected as a memorial to Bowen in St Paul's Cathedral were rejected as the attack on Santa Cruz had been a failure.[86]

In October 1798 Thomas Byam Martin, now commanding the 18-pounder *Fisgard*, engaged and captured the slightly more heavily armed French frigate *Immortalité*. This was his second important and successful frigate engagement, but Martin again received no public honour. In fact the first real honour conferred on Martin was that of the Order of the Sword, by the King of Sweden in 1808 following an engagement with a Russian 74. He did eventually receive a knighthood in the summer of 1814, but neither of these accolades was the result of his command of a frigate.[87] Between 1798 and 1806 there were small numbers of single frigate actions – but many of these involved smaller opponents or demonstrated other clear reasons why a knighthood was not conferred on the commanding officer – as for example in the case of the capture of the French *La Forte* by the British frigate *Sibylle* in the Indian Ocean in 1799, where the English Captain Edward Cooke was mortally wounded.

After the resumption of war against Napoleonic France in 1803 there was no early reason for celebrating a frigate action. In fact, the first three possible frigate engagements of the war (all in 1805) gave just cause for concern. In February 1805 the *Cleopatra*, commanded by Sir Robert Laurie, was forced to surrender to a larger French frigate; five months later the *Blanche*, Captain Zachary Mudge, was captured by the *Topaze*. Finally, days after the loss of the *Blanche*, the *Aeolus*, commanded by Lord William Fitzroy, rather conspicuously and suspiciously avoided an engagement with the French frigate *Didon* – although, to be fair to Fitzroy he claimed that his orders were to deliver vital dispatches and that these were more important.[88]

In July 1806, however, the tide changed when another British frigate, also called the *Blanche* and commanded by Captain Thomas Lavie captured the similarly armed French frigate *Guerriere* off the Faro Islands. Shortly after bringing his prize into Yarmouth, Lavie was given a knighthood. The reason for this distinction seems to have no direct bearing on the nature of the action itself, for it was not so different from earlier unmarked engagements. It is possible that Lavie's action was noted as being the first successful action of the 'new' conflict; or, that somebody felt that it was time to offer some tangible encouragement to the frigate commanders. It is also possible that Lavie was honoured because of his success in completing a specific mission. The *Guerriere* was one of three French frigates sent into the waters between Iceland, Greenland and Spitzbergen to prey on British and Russian whalers. In spite of the *Blanche*'s success and the fact that two other British frigates continued to hunt for the remaining French raiders, the French squadron continued its activities until September, when they returned to Lorient having destroyed a total of twenty-nine English or Russian merchant vessels.[89]

In October 1806 the 22-year-old Captain Peter Rainier, of the 18-pounder frigate *Caroline,* braved the overwhelming force of a Dutch light squadron off Batavia Road to capture the 12-pounder frigate *Maria Riggersbergen.* Rainier was the nephew of Admiral Peter Rainier, who had been Commander-in-Chief of the East Indies station until the previous year. As a prize the *Maria Riggersbergen* was probably not so remarkable, but Rainier's action in taking her was. There was no official recognition of this action – perhaps because Rainier was so young, and perhaps because he had been eased through the ranks so blatantly by his uncle. He had been commissioned as a lieutenant in January 1802 and, according to his own papers, he was posted into the *Dedaigneuse* in February 1805.[90] But there may have been another reason why he received no honours, as will be explained after the next case.

In 1809 Captain Michael Seymour was granted a baronetcy following his second capture within twelve months of a French frigate in the Bay of Biscay. Seymour was one of only two frigate captains to have been so honoured for a single-ship action during the whole course of the wars. In fact, Seymour was the last frigate captain to be honoured at all until 1813, when Philip Broke took the *Chesapeake*, for which he also received a baronetcy. Broke's case is somewhat exceptional in that Britain was absolutely desperate for a naval victory against the big American frigates, and Broke provided the result so desperately craved. This is not to detract from the achievement of the *Shannon*, which was the result of a brilliant action, but merely to put the reaction to the event into context.

What will not be apparent from the information given, but will nevertheless be found to be true, is that with the exception of Broke and the *Shannon*, no honours were awarded to frigate captains for actions on foreign stations. All were granted for engagements around the coast of Britain or off the west coast of France. This might explain why Rainier and Bowen were not honoured for actions in the East Indies and Mediterranean respectively, although it does not explain why certain deserving frigate actions in 'Home Waters' were not rewarded: for example, Laforey received nothing when the *Castor* was captured some 200 miles north-west of Ferrol on the Spanish coast. Nor does it explain why Byam Martin was never honoured.

In a curious way it might explain why William Hoste, the captain of the *Amphion* and commodore of the victorious frigate squadron at the Battle of Lissa (in the Adriatic) in 1811 received no knighthood as a result of an action which was widely regarded as brilliant at the time. Certainly Hoste was made a baronet in July 1814, and then a knight commander of the new Order of the Bath at the beginning of 1815. But then a number of victorious frigate captains were honoured in June 1815, including Peter Rainier, John Phillimore and Edmund Palmer. For Hoste the recognition came too late to be either effective or appreciated.

Just as with the acquisition of substantial prize money, the award of honours and title was a rare event. There can be no doubt that these provided the inspiration or goal for many commanders, but when one considers the small number who achieved such rewards, they cannot stand alone as the reason why frigate command was so popular. For this it may be necessary to look elsewhere.

APPENDIX 2.1.

Prize Agents' Accounts, Greenwich Hospital Treasurer' Accounts (1793 – mid-1798)

Captor	Prizes	Net Proceeds (£-s-d)	Actual pay (£)
Orpheus, 32 (Henry Newcombe)	Helene, Jeune, Iphigenie, La Surprise, La Desir	2132-3-2	2123
Leopard, 50 (J Maude)	La Victoire	8243-6-6	8031
Boyne, 98	La Guidelou	1437-19-8	1367
Flora, 36 (J B Warren)	Republique Francais	156-19-0	
Assistance, 50 (A K Legge) Lapwing, 28 (Henry Curzon) Fury, 16 (J Hanwell) Scout, 16 (Frank Sotheron)	Salvage of the brig Saltom	1012-0-0	
Edgar, 74 (A Bertie) Bedford, 74 (R Mann)	La Reine de Goleande, Providence, and Thomas and Sally salvage	5406-17-0	
Juno, 32 (Sam Hood)	L'Entreprenant	116-9-2 (includes HM)	
Phaeton, 38 (Sir A Douglas) Weazle, 12	Prompte privateer Plus HM to Phaeton only	6437-0-0	
(W Taylor)	601-1-0		
Nymph, 36 (Sir E Pellew) Venus, 32 (J Faulknor)	La Sans Cullottes French privateer + HM	297-9-17 265-4-10	275
Nymph, 36 (Sir E Pellew)	La Cleopatre + HM	8250-0-0	7798-17-1
Crescent, 36 (Saumarez) Circe, 28 (J S Yorke)	La Reunion + HM	5318-9-11	5239
Spitfire, 16 (P C Durham)	King George – a recapture	802-15-0	
Spitfire, 16 (P C Durham)	Afrique + HM; St Jean, St Marguerite	257-5-3	
Phaeton, 38 (Sir A Douglas) Weazle, 12	Poisson Volant	514-0-0	266 138

Captor	Prizes	Net Proceeds (£-s-d)	Actual pay (£)
(W Taylor)			
Cleopatra, 32 (A J Ball)	Brig Peggy – salvage	473-8-8	462-7-8
Tisiphone, 20 (A Hunt)	L'Outarde	1400-0-0 1327-11-9	920
Juno, 32 (S Hood)	Penthievre	2000-0-0 (part)	1306
Leopard, 50 (J Maude)	La Constitution	40,000-0-0	38,467
Childers, 14 (R Barlow)	Le Patriote, Le Triton	178-0-10	
Boston, 32 (G W A Courtenay)	L'Hirondelle privateer	710-10-2	611
Lizard, 28 (T Williams)	Sans Cullotte, Valiant Custine Allen and Dorothea, 2 cargoes of wheat, Endraught	293-16-0 471-3-0	273 435
Nymphe, 36 (Sir E Pellew) Circe, 28 (J S Yorke)	L'Espiegle	1267-11-5	1212
Circe, 28 (J S Yorke)	Le Didon, L'Auguste Diane, Le Vaudreuil Le Jeune Felix	1313-3-10 3360-7-2 3401-18-6	1542
Hannibal, 74 (J Colpoys)	L'Etoile du Matin	1077-12-8	967
Melampus, 36 (T Wells)	La Pomone, La Babette, L'Engageante + HM	2752-8-8	2561
Concorde, 36 (Sir R Strachan)	Meriam – salvage	72-0-0	53-13
Thetis, 38 (J Hartwell)	Mongoff George	22,850-14-0	21,378
Arethusa, 38 (Sir E Pellew) Flora, 36 (Sir J B Warren) Concorde, 36 (Sir R Strachan)	La Pomone, La Babette (Nymphe and Melampus in company)	2769-2-8 (part) 2672-1-1 (part) 2478-1-8 (part)	2582 2598 2384
Juno, 32 (S Hood) Powerful, 74 (W A Otway)	Le Palme Le Penthieuse Ship George – salvage	530-18-8 1867-19-2 641-17-4	342 1239 530
Hebe, 38 (A Hood) Southampton, 32	Experiment – recapture	243-4-9 236-17-10	224

Captor	Prizes	Net Proceeds (£-s-d)	Actual pay (£)
(Hon R Forbes)			
Leopard, 50 (J Maude)	La Constitution (see above)	70,140-18-8	28,422
Venus, 32 (W Brown)	Mary of Bristol – recapture	202-13-2	
Blonde, 32 (J Markham)	Lady Washington & cargo	1383-0-1	
Vanguard, 74 (J Stanhope)	Le Blonde	484-9-8	
Bellerophon, 74 (T Pasley) Phoenix, 36 (Sir R Strachan)	Le Blonde (Phaeton and Latona in company)	486-12-7 306-12-1	419 213
Nymphe, 36 (G Murray)	La Pomone, La Babette, L'Engageante	2585-3-0 (proportion)	2417
Flora, 36 (Sir J B Warren) Arethusa, 38 (Sir E Pellew) Concorde, 36 (Sir R Strachan)	La Pomone, La Babette, L'Engageante	2071-13-2 2150-6-5 1913-18-4	1947 2039 1806
Flora, 36 (Sir J B Warren) Sheerness, 44 (W G Fairfax)	La Vipere (Druid, Fury and Echo in company)	975-17-8 621-6-0	943
Nymphe, 36 (G Murray)	La Gute Hoffming (a note* as with above)	201-8-0	180
Bellona, 74 (G Wilson)			
America, 64 (Hon J Rodney) Severn, 44 (G Tripp) Carysfort, 28 (F Laforey) Hornet sloop, 16 (C Pul)	Lust en Vleyt – Dutch recapture (Alfred in company)	1079-8-0	
Ceres, 32 (R Incledon)	Catherine – recapture; Petite Victoire + HM	446-10-10	362
Phoenix, 36 (Sir R Strachan)	La Pauline	14,447-15-3	14,198
Scourge, 16 (G Brisac)	Sans Cullotte + HM La Bonne Mere	781-12-8 2619-2-9	703 2373
Ganges, 74 (A Molloy Adml) St George, 98 (Gell: Capt)	St Jago and Gen'l Dumourier	47,779-7-1	42,006

Captor	Prizes	Net Proceeds (£-s-d)	Actual pay (£)
(A Dickson)			
Edgar, 74 (A Bertie)	St Jago and Gen'l Dumourier	46,219-18-4	43,110
Phaeton, 38 (A Douglas)		20,906-2-2	16,291
Flora, 36 (Sir J B Warren)	Queen, Donna Maria brig – recaptured on company with		519-1-6
Arethusa, 38 (Sir E Pellew)	Diamond and Diana		542-17-3
St Margarita, 36 (E Harvey)			524-5-9
Artois, 38 (E Nagle)			484-11-9
Diamond, 38 (Sir Sidney Smith)			541-19-2
Nymphe, 36 (Sir E Pellew)	For return of duties only for La Cleopatre and L'Espiegle		287-9-2
Arethusa, 38 (Sir E Pellew)	La Revolutionnaire (Diamond in company)		2534-2-6
Artois, 38 (E Nagle)			2391-16-10
Galatea, 32 (R G Keats)			2301-16-1
Diamond, 38 (Sir Sidney Smith)			2559-18-1
Alcide, 64	L'Eclair, Vrai Patriote		72-18-9
Lowestoft, 32 (W Wolseley)			49-19-9
Illustrious, 74			82-17-4
Leda, 36 (G Campbell)			49-13-3
Colossus, 74			110-3-5
Vulcan fireship			40-14-8
Conflagration fireship			43-9-5
Camel storeship			36-0-5
Victory, 100			122-12-1
Agamemnon, 64			101-18-0
Leviathan, 74			101-8-2
Aimable, 36 (Sir H Burrard Neale)			52-18-9
Robust, 74			71-19-5
Niger, 32 (R G Keats)	Krone Van Bremen, Catherine – recapture	1000-0-0 47-3-6	
Nimble cutter (Lt J Smith)			
Nimble cutter (Lt J Smith)	Pettite Victore	33-16-0	
Ardent, 64	Sacra Famiglia		115-17-8
St Albans, 64			204-14-8
Castor, 32 (T Troubridge)			110-14-3
Mermaid, 32			129-12-3

Captor	Prizes	Net Proceeds (£-s-d)	Actual pay (£)
(J Trigge)			
Flora, 36 (Sir J B Warren)	Drooning Gaard, brig Triumph		1161-11-2
Arethusa, 38 (Sir E Pellew)			1186-8-11
St Margarita, 36 (E Harvey)			1119-17-7
Concorde, 32 (Sir R Strachan)			1077-10-5
Melampus, 36 (T Wells)			1140-15-3
Orion, 74 (V-A Sir A Gardner)	Sans Cullottes	152-1-1	
Fleet under the command of Lord Howe in the Channel	Sans Pareil, Juste, Northumberland, Achille, Impetueux, America, with others	201,096-13-0	
Pomone, 44 (Sir J B Warren) Galatea, 32 (R G Keats) Anson, 44 (P C Durham) Artois, 38 (E Nagle)	Jean Bart corvette		2011-4-2
La Pomone, 44 (Sir J B Warren)	Prizes taken between 13 Feb and 2 Mar 1795 Phoenix, Le David, L'Oimontaise	4151-16-8 1919-12-8	
Alligator, 28 (W Affleck)	Sans Pareil and Fiend Tout		252-2-6
Nymphe, 36 (G Murray)	Pomone and Babet (22 Jan 1795) Engageante	953-0-9 970-18-2	
Venus, 32 (J Faulknor)	Sans Cullotte		232-11-9
Aimable, 36 (H Burrard)	La Moselle Apr-Jul 1795		973-14-6
Phaeton, 38 (A Douglas) Circe, 28 (J Yorke)	Venus and Ant Jan 1794		190-0-3 232-2-11
Phaeton, 38 (A Douglas)	Experiment, March 1794		231-16-10
Phaeton, 38 (A Douglas) Weazle, 12	Prompte, Poussaint Vollante, May-Jun 1795		212-1-5 88-7-11
Phaeton, 38 (A Douglas)	General Washington		128-10-6

Captor	Prizes	Net Proceeds (£-s-d)	Actual pay (£)
Weazle, 12			61-12-4
Phaeton, 38 (A Douglas)	General Dumourier and St Jago (1st) Blonde		31,601-17-5 301-18-10
Galatea, 32 (R Keats) Artois, 38 (E Nagle)	Revolutionnaire (2nd) 14 Jun- 4 Sep		1121-6-8 1197-1-3
Diana, 38 (J Faulknor)	Queen and Donna Maria 9 Mar 1795		477-10-2
Crescent, 36 (Saumarez) Hind, 28 (A Cochrane)	Espoir 29 Jun 1795	443-14-8	
Crescent, 36 (Saumarez) Lively privateer	Club de Cherbourg	113-14-9	
Latona, 38 (E Thornborough)	Ambiteux (2nd)		140-9-2
Lively, 32 (G Burlton)	Joseph Favorius (1st) Tourterelle		924-10-11 571-12-10 6588-3-5
Phaeton, 38 (A Douglas)	St Jago (2nd)	14,725-17-9	
Aimable, 36 (H Burrard) Dido, 28 (C Hamilton) Lowestoft, 22 (B Hallowell)	La Mozelle		215-4-4
Leda, 36 (J Woodley)	Sybille, Cerasine, Adele, Beste		4087-18-6
Melampus, 36 (R Strachan) Seaflower, 16 Sprightly, 10 Daphne, 20	Sundry captures 3 Jul 1795 with Hebe in company		1485-7-6 238-13-4 189-19-10 132-1-9
Pomone, 44 (J B Warren)	Prizes 12 Feb-12 Mar 1795 Phoenix, Le David, L'Omontaine Expedition, Maria Francois, Fidelle		4151-16-8 1919-12-8 592-5-3
Artois, 38 (E Nagle)	Expedition Maria Francois, Fidelle		525-10-7
Artois, 38 (E Nagle)	Quartide, Hassinglande Revolutionnaire (3rd) Head money of [?above]		78-3-5 534-9-8 351-8-1
Concorde, 36	Prizes 9 Mar 1795		1734-3-6

Captor	Prizes	Net Proceeds (£-s-d)	Actual pay (£)
(A Hunt)	*Phoenix, David, L'Omontaine*		1732-8-7
Aigle, 38 (S Hood)?	*L'Elaine* Jun-Jul 1793		52-2-7
Nemesis, 28 (S H Linzee)	*L'Elaine* and *Vrai Patriot*		50-9-3
Tisiphone, 20	*Vanneaux*, Jun-Jul 1793		15-10-3
Meleager, 32 (C Tyler)?	*Vanneaux*,*L'Elaine* and *Vrai Patriot* Jun-Jul 1793		75-5-5
Lowestoffe, 32 (W Wolseley)	*Jacobin* May 1794		138-4-0
Dido, 28 (C Hamilton)			110-5-7
Swallow, 16			12-6-9
Imperieuse, 38 (C Cunningham)			97-19-7
Scout, 14			105-11-6
Tartar, 28	*General Washington* privateer		135-14-2
Lowestoffe, 32 (W Wolseley)	*Mozelle* May 1794		1021-6-5
Dido, 28 (C Hamilton)			896-15-2
Diana, 38 (J Faulknor)	*Quartide, Haesingland* Sep 1794		62-13-9
Cleopatra, 32	Cargo of the *Bacchus* (taken West Indies)		1048-18-3
Thetis, 38			1192-8-8
V-Adm Murray			362-10-2
Thetis, 38	Cargo of the *Hamilton* and retaken snow *Charlotte*		188-2-10
Hussar, 28 (Lord Garlies)?			159-8-3
Esperance, 16			119-10-4
V-Adm Murray			71-18-6
Crescent, 36 (Saumarez)	*Club de Cherbourg*		443-10-10
Hind, 28 (A Cochrane)			
Phaeton, 38 (A Douglas)	*Dumourier* and *St Jago* (3rd)		3874-1-0
Hebe, 38 (P Minchin)	7 prizes (*Vasure, Maria Louisa, Pencheur* etc)		1528-9-10

Captor	Prizes	Net Proceeds (£-s-d)	Actual pay (£)
	Jul 1795		
Pomone, 44 (J B Warren) Galatea, 32 (R Keats) Anson, 44 (P Durham) Artois, 38 (E Nagle)	Jean Bart (2nd)		851-9-5
Romney, 50 (F Sotheron) Phaeton, 38 (R Stopford) Latona, 38 (A K Legge)	Bonne Citoyenne corvette and Betsey brig Mar 1796		2037-14-1 1761-4-10 1789-19-7
Pomone, 44 (J B warren) Anson, 44 (P Durham) Galatea, 32 (R Keats) Swinger, 14 Teaser, 14 Penelope cutter	Kent recapture Oct 1795		703-14-9 708-12-6 593-19-7 80-12-3 100-18-7 73-19-2
St Margarita, 36 (E Harvey)	Alert, Espion, Volontaire Aug 1794		79-2-3
Galatea, 32 (R Keats)	Revolution HM		421-12-11
Flora, 36 (J B Warren)	St Joseph Jun 1793		3436-1-0
Aimable, 36 (H Burrard) Juno, 32 (S Hood)	Boneaux, Harnoll, Hamilton, La Maria Agathe Apr 1793		184-3-6 207-6-3
Aimable, 36 (H Burrard)	La Courier May 1793		105-19-6
Beaulieu, 40 (J Sailisbury)	America recapture Dec 1793		472-15-7
Argo, 44 (R Burgess)	Unite and Virginie Apr 1796		2103-11-5 707-17-7
Stag, 32 (Yorke)	Betsey and Bonne Citoyenne		1748-8-11
Concorde, 36 (A Hunt)	Kent recapture		580-3-2
Arethusa, 38 (E Pellew)	Phoenix, David and L'Ormentaire Revolutionnaire (2nd) Revolutionnaire (3rd)		1836-8-7 1220-15-1 530-7-7

Captor	Prizes	Net Proceeds (£-s-d)	Actual pay (£)
	Quartide and Haesingland		81-17-9
Indefatigable, 44 (E Pellew)	Gentille, Temeraire, Minerve, Unite and Regeneration (1st) (2nd)		1011-5-11 916-19-6
Indefatigable, 44 (E Pellew) Amazon, 36 (R C Reynolds) Concorde, 36 (A Hunt) Revolutionnaire, 38 (F Cole)	Unité and Virginie		4205-19-6 3929-2-10 3401-4-2 3862-16-9
Phaeton, 38 (A Douglas)	Dumourier and St Jago (4th)		1204-6-0
Iphigenia, 32 (P Sinclair)	Elizabeth French privateer		109-7-3
Tartar, 28 (T Fremantle)	Sybille, Alebe, Betsie		3142-11-8
Warren's Sq	Robuste 1 Dec 1796 Etoile		2861-11-0 2467-2-6
Dryad, 36 (Beauclerk)	Voteur		1039-10-0
Cleopatra, 32	'Sundry prizes'		331-19-0
Melampus, 36	Etna		4917-11-4
Sybil, 28 (C Jones)	Diana aka Vesta		134-18-10
Phaeton, 38 (R Stopford)	L'Anne Nov 1796		109-5-9
Southampton, 32 (Forbes)	Experiment		232-17-9
Venus, 32 (W. Brown)	Mary		171-10-3
Jason, 38 (C Stirling)	Gentille Marie, Union, Bonette Jean Marie (share) Robuste Tartar		1777-11-7 816-7-3 188-6-2 684-13-10 1279-11-3
Stag, 32 (Yorke)	Approcate, Sarah		1346-7-0
Niger, 32 (Foote)	Natalia Caradad		8014-10-0 3082-7-7
Latona, 38 (A K Legge)	Jean		107-6-8
Diamond, 38 (R Strachan)	Amarante Esperance		4266-19-3 92-12-2

Captor	Prizes	Net Proceeds (£-s-d)	Actual pay (£)
	Pere Maria		272-11-4
Diana, 38 (J Faulknor)	Alert, Volontaire, Espion Comet Cromhout (1st) Cromhout (2nd) Abielle	482-19-2 1319-4-2 5946-4-4 2051-4-10 286-16-0	
Quebec, 32 (J. Cooke)	Aspie	933-12-1	
Unicorn, 32 (T Williams)	Cromhout (2nd) Rover Eclair		2042-13-5 104-2-1 362-12-7
Phoebe, 36 (R Barlow)	Atlanta		3413-14-3/4
Syren, 32 (Gosling)	SansPeur Robinson		133-4-3 178-4-2
Arethusa, 38 (T Wolley)	Gaite Aug 1796		4514-1-2
Cambrian, 40 (A Legge)	Betsey Oct 1797		348-11-0
Phaeton, 38 (R Stopford)	L'Actif Mar 1797		940-19-0
Flora, 36 (R Middleton)	Incroyable Apr 1797		1293-19-4
Latona, 38 (A K Legge)	Tartare Feb 1797		61-1-5
Stag, 32 (Yorke)	Alliance		1243-5-1
Minerve, 38 (Cockburn)	Mutine de Regla Felice Belerno Marseilleise	19,649-0-0 6921-8-0 3693-4-0 68,483-7-0	
Pique, 38 (D Milne) Charon, 44	Lacedaemonian Mar 1796		269-19-1 145-15-9
Stag, 32 (Yorke)	L'Yppocrate and Hirondelle, Franklyn Swallow		443-10-8 29-18-9 81-8-11
Proserpine, 28 (W Lake)	Unity and Concorde		2174-7-4
Stag, 32 (Yorke)	Prizes 17 Sept-20 Oct 97		993-17-4
Melpomene, 38 (C Hamilton)	Espiegle		114-13-5
Jason, 38	Revanche and Queen of Naples		47-5-10

Captor	Prizes	Net Proceeds(£-s-d)	Actual pay (£)
(C Stirling)			
Aimable, 36 (Lobb)	Triumphant	3794-5-3	
	Le Chasseur	517-14-9	
Scourge (Warren)		1657-16-7	
Phoenix, 36 (Halstead)	3 prizes (inc La Dificile)		694-0-6
Spitfire, 16 (Seymour)	Jacoba		13,473-4-10
Stag, 32 (Yorke)	Recovery		62-14-3
	Brunette, Indien, Decoverte, Adamante, Arcade, Recovery		986-2-0
Anson, 44 (Durham)	Jason		1,475-7-6
	Belleisle		75-11-4
Magnanime, 44 (De Courcy)	Echo		513-2-8
Shannon, 32 (A Fraser)	Dugay Trouin		2445-13-1
Magnanime, 44 (de Courcy)	Tierelete		304-1-2
Niger, 32 (E Griffith)	Danerhafte May 1798		198-18-3
Arethusa, 38 (T Wolley)			227-10-8
Melpomene, 38 (C Hamilton)	Triton		892-19-7
Phaeton, 38 (R Stopford)	Chesseur, Brunette and Converte		867-18-0
	Adamant and Arcade		1168-14-9
Melpomene, 38 (C Hamilton)	Friendship Dec 1797		1471-6-0
Jason, 38 (C Stirling)	Courier, Golden Grove Benton La Mare Several 12-28 Aug 1797		3146-2-4 1745-18-2 441-1-8
Phoebe, 36 (R Barlow)	Nereide Jul 1798		13,018-6-2
Stag, 32 (Yorke)	Alliance		178-2-4
Pique, 38 (D Milne)	Recovery Oct 1797		103-9-3

HM = head money.
* A note here explains that 'Mr Toulmin being a Bankrupt' £57-10-4d must be paid to the Hospital from his Commission.
Source: PRO Adm 68/314.

APPENDIX 2.2. *List of Frigate Engagements*

27 May 1793	*Venus*, Captain J Faulknor, engages the French frigate *Semillante*
18 June 1793	*Nymphe*, Captain Edward Pellew, captures the French frigate *Cléopâtre*
31 July 1793	*Boston*, Captain George William Augustus Courtenay, engages the French frigate *Embuscade*. Courtenay is killed
20 October 1793	*Crescent*, Captain James Saumarez, captures *La Réunion*
24 October 1793	*Thames*, Captain James Cotes, engages and drives off the *Uranie*, but is then captured by a French squadron
29 May 1794	*Carysfort*, Captain Francis Laforey, captures the *Castor*
8 June 1794	A British squadron close to Guernsey is saved from a superior French squadron by the *Druid*, Captain Sir James Saumarez
30 December 1794	*Blanche*, Captain Robert Faulknor, captures *La Pique*. Faulknor is killed but Lieutenants Frederick Watkins and David Milne assume command
10 April 1795	*Astraea*, Captain Lord Henry Paulet, captures *La Gloire*
24 June 1795	*Dido*, Captain George Towry, and *Lowestoffe*, Captain Robert Middleton, capture the French frigate *Minerve*
28 September 1795	*Southampton*, Captain James Macnamara, engages the *Vestale*
20 April 1796	*Indefatigable*, Captain Sir Edward Pellew, and *Amazon*, Captain Robert Reynolds, and *Concorde*, Captain Anthony Hunt, capture the *Virginie*
8 June 1796	*Santa Margarita*, Captain Thomas Byam Martin, captures the French frigate *Tamise*
8 June 1796	*Unicorn*, Captain Thomas Williams, captures the *Tribune*
9 June 1796	*Southampton*, Captain James Macnamara, cuts out a corvette in the Mediterranean
13 June 1796	*Dryad*, Captain Lord Amelius Beauclerk, captures *La Proserpine*
13 October 1796	*Terpsichore*, Captain Richard Bowen, captures the Spanish frigate *Mahonesa*.
13 December 1796	*Terpsichore*, Captain Richard Bowen, engages the French frigate *Vestale*, which escapes after striking
7 January 1797	*Indefatigable*, Captain Edward Pellew, and *Amazon*, Captain Robert Reynolds, attack the *Droits de L'Homme*. *Amazon* and *Droits de L'Homme* are wrecked.
30 May 1798	*Hydra*, Captain Sir Francis Laforey, destroys the French frigate *Confiante*
23rd June 1798	*Seahorse*, Captain Edward Foote, captures the *Sensible*
29 June 1798	*Pique*, Captain David Milne, captures the *Seine*
20 October 1798	*Fisgard*, Captain Thomas Byam Martin, captures the *Immortalité*
14 December 1798	*Ambuscade*, Captain Henry Jenkins, captured by the French corvette *Baionnaise*

9 February 1799	*Daedalus*, Capt Henry Lidgbird Ball, takes the *Prudente*
1 March 1799	*Sibylle*, Captain Edward Cooke, captures *La Forte*
20 August 1799	*Clyde*, Captain Charles Cunningham, captures *Vestale*
20 October 1799	*Cerberus*, Captain James Macnamara, attacks a squadron of 5 Spanish frigates
1 March 1800	*Nereide*, Captain Frederick Watkins, captures the *Vengeance* privateer
20 August 1800	*Seine*, Captain David Milne, takes the *Vengeance* frigate
16 February 1805	*Cleopatra*, Captain Sir Robert Laurie, taken by the *Ville-de-Milan*
19 July 1805	*Blanche*, Captain Zachary Mudge, captured by *Topaze* and two other French ships
29 July 1805	*Aeolus*, Captain Lord William Fitzroy, avoids an engagement with French frigate *Didon*
10 August 1805	*Phoenix*, Captain Thomas Baker, captures *Didon*
18 June 1806	*Blanche*, Captain Thomas Lavie, takes *Guerriere*
18 October 1806	*Caroline*, Captain Peter Rainier, attacks Dutch squadron and captures the frigate *Maria Riggersbergen*
10 November 1808	*Amethyst*, Captain Michael Seymour, captures the *Thétis* just before the arrival of the *Shannon*, Captain Philip Broke
10 January 1809	*Horatio*, Captain George Scott, with others takes the *Junon*
5 April 1809	*Amethyst*, Captain Michael Seymour, takes *Niemen*
13 December 1809	*Junon*, Captain John Shortland, taken by four French frigates. Shortland is killed.
12 September 1810	*Africaine*, Sir Robert Corbet, surrenders to two French frigates. Corbet killed.
19 August, 1812	*Guerriere*, Captain James Dacres, taken by USS *Constitution*
25 October 1812	*Macedonian*, Captain John Carden, taken by USS *United States*
29 December 1812	*Java*, Captain Henry Lambert, taken by USS *Constitution*
6 February 1813	*Amelia*, Captain Hon. Frederick Paul Irby, engages the French frigate *Aréthuse*
1 June 1813	*Shannon*, Captain Philip Broke captures USS *Chesapeake*
5 January 1814	*Niger*, Captain Peter Rainier, and *Tagus*, Captain Philip Pipon, capture the French frigate *Cérès*
8 February 1814	*Phoebe*, Captain James Hillyar, captures USS *Essex*
25 February 1814	*Eurotas*, Captain John Phillimore, engages the French frigate *Clorinde* which later surrenders to *Dryad*
26 March 1814	*Hebrus*, Captain Edmund Palmer, captures the *Etoile*
15 January 1815	*Endymion,* Captain Henry Hope encounters the US frigate *President* and nearly forces her to surrender. *President* escapes, only to surrender to other ships hours later

THE FRIGATE CAPTAINS

S O FAR WE HAVE SURVEYED a sample of the officer corps to find out what was generally happening to the navy's post captains. It is now time to consider the data relating specifically to the navy's frigate captains because this enables us to clarify a range of aspects about the operation of the navy of this period. For example, it is not unusual to find naval historians referring to a quick promotion for a particularly favoured or well connected officer – but what exactly was a quick promotion? There are also some specific issues relating to frigate command that need to be clarified. It often seems to be assumed that frigate command was given to younger, junior captains. Was this really the case? Either way, how long could an officer expect to be in command of frigates and what would happen to him thereafter? How many frigates would he command and for how long? Was there a limit placed on the amount of time an officer commanded frigates? Who got the best frigates? Did frigate command, with its very distinctive demands and rewards, attract officers from any particular social background – and did this change as the wars progressed? Finally, if frigate command was more arduous, it must have been more hazardous. What effect did this have on occupational mortality?

SPEED OF PROMOTION

As stated in the first chapter, one of the most valuable statistical tools for analysing the career of large numbers of officers, is that of the rate or speed of promotion. This can tell us what the general trend was in terms of its effect on the officer corps in general, and it gives us a measure of the individual officer. What is very clear is that the speed of promotion in general increases towards the latter part of the century. For example, an officer passing for lieutenant before 1771 was likely to wait an average of 20.62 years to reach post captain. Thereafter the waiting period was considerably reduced to about 8.5 years, though in fact we have to notice the effect of the years of peace after the American War. Those officers who reached the rank

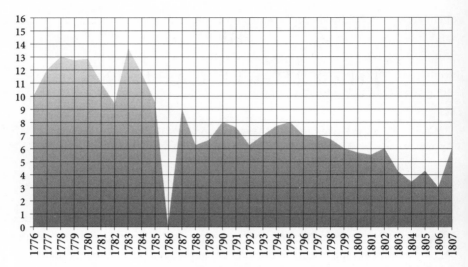

FIGURE 3.1. *Average Promotion Rate in Years (from Lieutenant to Captain) of Frigate Captains, by date of promotion to Lieutenant*

(NB: In 1786 there were no recorded promotions of lieutenants).

of post captain before 1790 did so on average in about 10.5 years; those posted from the time of the Spanish Armament onwards, within just under 6 years.

The chart shows graphically the fall in waiting period from a peak at the end of the American War until 1806, when the excessive number of captains on the list begins to cause another decline in promotion.

What is curious is that, on the whole, officers who became frigate commanders were promoted approximately 3 years quicker than captains who did not. In the DEF sample used earlier, lieutenants commissioned before 1790 took an average 14 years to reach post rank – as opposed to 10.4 years in the frigate captain sample: those commissioned after 1790 took 8 years (DEF sample) but only 5.9 years within the frigate captain sample. The number of officers included in the comparative samples would necessarily mean that of the two, the frigate captain sample would be the more reliable. But it could also suggest that many of the men who went on to become specialist frigate commanders were displaying qualities as young officers which enhanced their promotion prospects.

What is more significant is that the speed of promotion for frigate captains actually gets faster as the war progresses. Whilst it might have been expected that there would have been a temporary acceleration to reflect the mobilisation at the start of the war, it might also have been expected that the rate would slow down as the corps of post captains grew larger and there was increasing difficulty in giving them active commands. In fact, this does not begin to happen until 1807. Since it could not have been predicted that the wars would conclude in 1815, something else was working to ensure that many of the frigate captains were reaching post rank with as little delay as possible and, on average, much faster than officers who were not given frigate commands after posting.

NUMBERS OF FRIGATE CAPTAINS

Approximately 670 captains were given command of frigates between the years 1793 and 1815. It is not possible to be precise about the number because the records are not complete – and even where they are, there is some ambiguity about some of the names given. It is possible that a further 100 names could be added, but the brevity of their commands would render their inclusion almost pointless. We will return to this question a little later.

The number of officers being 'created' by promotion to the rank of lieutenant was

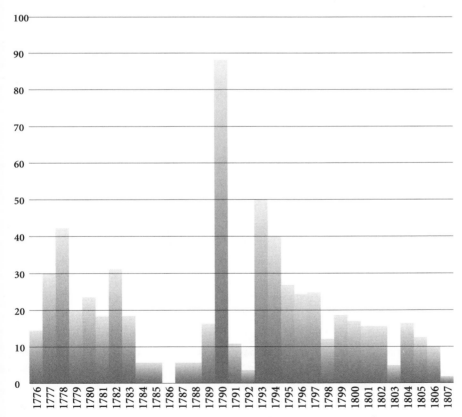

FIGURE 3.2. *Number of Midshipmen Promoted to Lieutenants Each Year*

closely related to the threat or potential threat of hostilities. Looking at those officers who later were to become frigate commanders this relationship is dramatically demonstrated by the years in which they were commissioned as lieutenant.

Up until 1776 a small number of midshipman in the sample were being promoted each year.[1] The number increases dramatically in 1776, appears to peak in 1778 (and again in 1782) and then falls away during the following years of peacetime. It will be recalled that in the previous chapter, where the DEF sample was considered, only three lieutenants were found to have passed between 1784 and 1789.

In 1787, the year of the Dutch Armament, the number passing returned to its normal level for the inter-war years. In 1790 Britain found itself close to war with Spain over the Nootka Sound crisis, often referred to as 'The Spanish Armament', and the number of promotions suddenly exploded as ships were brought out of ordinary and crews hurriedly scrambled together. Of course, the mobilisation came to nothing, and the Admiralty suddenly found itself with a greatly enlarged and largely unemployed officer corps. Not surprisingly, promotions again declined until war really broke out in 1793. Then after about 1795 the number of promotions began to fall. At this point again there must be an artificial cut-off point, because none of the frigate captains identified passed for lieutenant after 1808. Even those four frigate captains who did manage to pass for lieutenant in 1806-1808 may have squeezed in because of special favour, and because of who they were: Lord James Townshend (youngest son of the Marquis of Townshend), Edward Troubridge (son of Admiral Sir Thomas Troubridge) in 1806; the Hon Henry Peachey (son of Baron Selsey) in 1807 and Sir David Dunn in 1808.[2]

We can see in Table 3.1 the pattern of promotion to post captain. In 1782 and 1783, right at the end of the American Revolutionary War, there was a significant increase in the number of officers being posted. To a certain degree this seems curious, for we would expect to see the flood of postings at the beginning of the war, followed by a steady trickle. It seems unlikely that the demand for more officers would increase at the end of the war and, in any case, it could be argued that the Admiralty could hardly predict the date of the end of the war. The increase in 1782 and 1783 may reflect the need to reward the lieutenants and commanders who had served through most of the conflict, prior to placing them on what may have been permanent half-pay.[3] The historian Michael Lewis argued that the increased promotions at the end of a war might have reflected a conscious act of charity by the Admiralty:

TABLE 3.1. *Number of Frigate Captains (1793-1815) by Year Posted*

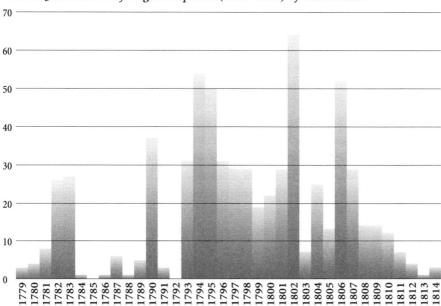

Year Posted	Number	Year Posted	Number	Year Posted	Number
1779	3	1791	3	1803	7
1780	4	1792	0	1804	25
1781	8	1793	31	1805	13
1782	26	1794	54	1806	52
1783	27	1795	50	1807	29
1784	1	1796	31	1808	14
1785	0	1797	29	1809	14
1786	1	1798	29	1810	12
1787	6	1799	19	1811	7
1788	1	1800	22	1812	4
1789	5	1801	29	1813	1
1790	37	1802	64	1814	3

The Government ... did realise by now that it could never again hope to give many thousands of its servants work on full pay, and it knew that all these thousands faced the certainty of a drab, penurious existence on half pay ... For such people promotion would not give employment (and therefore full pay), but it would give them the better half pay of their new rank.[4]

This seems to imply an unlikely degree of philanthropy in an eighteenth-century institution: it is not inconceivable, but on the other hand one must never overlook the likelihood of 'political appointments'. In 1782 The Duke of Portland became Prime Minister and in the following year Howe became First Lord of the Admiralty and, in succession, both Hugh Pigot and the Hon John Leveson Gower, became First Naval Lords of the Admiralty. The growth in postings in 1782 and 1783 may, therefore, also reflect the return of political favours. This seems even more likely because at least six of those officers posted in 1782-3 went on the become Members of Parliament.[5]

The year 1790, once again, witnessed a large increase in the number of postings in response to the Spanish Armament; and then the number of postings peaks at the beginning of the French Revolutionary War. More interestingly, perhaps, this table reveals two further peaks. The first of these is in 1802 when fifty-four officers were posted in April, the month following the signing of the Treaty of Amiens.[6] Although it is not immediately apparent why this should have happened, it is possible that, as in 1782-3, the Admiralty recognised the need to reward officers for services rendered. A second peak occurs in 1806. This may well arise from a general promotion after the Battle of Trafalgar and is a factor which is echoed in the promotion of lieutenants. Equally, it may reflect the appointment of Grenville as Prime Minister, following the death of Pitt in January 1806. Once again this is supported by the fact that at least four of those officers posted during 1806 became Members of Parliament and also that one of the officers posted later in the year (on 25 September) was the Hon Sir Anthony Maitland, son of the Earl of Lauderdale who became First Lord of the Admiralty in September. Curiously, the data for the frigate captains also reveals the fact that there appear to have been particular dates on which an extraordinary number of officers were posted. For example, twenty-one officers in the frigate captain sample were posted on 22 November 1790, presumably an indication of the mobilisation during the Spanish Armament; and fifty-four were posted on 29 April 1802 – that is, 8 per cent of the entire sample on a single day.

AGE OF POST CAPTAINS

When considering age it is important to bear in mind that there was no set age at which an officer became a post captain – only when he was supposed to be eligible to sit the lieutenant's examination. Contrary to popular imagination, frigate command was not just the domain of the young, freshly promoted post captain, although there was always a desire to have men of ability in command of frigates – indeed the nature of the job absolutely demanded it. The problem for the Admiralty was that by 1793 few of the men available had sufficient experience. With little fresh blood brought in during the peacetime years, a significant number of those promoted in the first two years of the war were older men – but these were also men

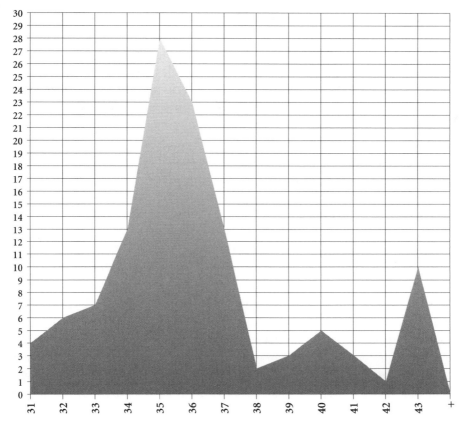

FIGURE 3.4. *Numbers of Post Captains and their Ages in 1793*

of outstanding ability. Once these had been put into position the Admiralty began to 'cherry pick' from what were likely to be the most promising younger men.

At the outbreak of war, the majority of captains were in the age-range of 34-37 years, whereas by the end of the wars the common age for a frigate captain at the time of posting was somewhere between 23 and 26 years. However, in 1793 there were active frigate captains who were noticeably older than 37 years, some of whom were quite senior captains, while others were just posted late. Possibly the oldest of these latter was William George Fairfax; born in 1739, he entered the navy in 1750 and passed for lieutenant in 1757. He was therefore 53 years old when the war with Revolutionary France war broke out.

Some of these older officers may have been of questionable health or fitness for service, but assumptions cannot be made. Fairfax stands as a good example: he was commander of the 44-gun *Sheerness* until March 1795, when he was transferred to the *Repulse*, 64. In 1796 he was appointed as Duncan's flag captain on board the *Venerable*, 74 and fought in that ship at the Battle of Camperdown in the following year. Duncan sent Fairfax home with dispatches reporting the victory and the elderly captain received a knighthood for his pains. He was still in command of the *Venerable* in 1799, but in 1801 he reached flag rank and saw out most of the next war in peaceful retirement, dying in 1813. Old he may have been, but by no means unfit or inactive.

Among the youngest captains in 1793 were Edward Buller, son of the Bishop of Exeter; the Hon Robert Forbes (1), younger son of Lord Forbes; and William Bentinck. Both Buller and Forbes passed for lieutenant in 1782 and were posted in 1790 (both slightly faster than average). Bentinck was even more fortunate, for he passed for lieutenant in 1782 and was posted in the following year, which also happened to be the year that his father, Lord Portland, became First Lord of the Treasury. Buller was actually born in 1764 and was therefore 29 when posted. He entered the navy at the age of 12 and became a commander in April 1783 at the age of 19 – perhaps explaining why Marshall should choose to describe him as 'a mere boy' at that juncture of his career.[7]

It should not need pointing out that those who seem to have been posted at a young age were generally, at the same time, those posted the quickest. These will be looked at in some detail shortly. Of the older captains, it is worth noting that the most significant clusters of promotion of older commanders occurred at times of crisis. In 1790, at the time of the Spanish Armament, twenty-four captains were posted who were over the age of 31: that is, the majority of the captains in the sample posted during that year (68 per cent). In fact, when the crisis arose the Admiralty seems to have turned to those officers who had been passed-over for posting in 1783. If, for example, we take the twenty older officers posted in 1790 and who were between the age of 31 and 35, we can track backwards over the years to 1782 and 1783 when eight and seven officers respectively of the same 'generation' were posted. The twenty men posted in 1790 were, in a sense, the forgotten generation of post captains of the post-war period. With the outbreak of war against Revolutionary France a similar situation is evident, for as the navy swung into operation to commission its ships once again during 1794 and 1795 in particular, there was a heavy concentration of posting of older commanders: twenty-seven over the age of 30 in 1794 (77 per cent of those posted), and twenty-three in 1795 (44 per cent). The posting of older commanders then gradually declined until 1802 when, with the Peace of Amiens collapsing, twenty-two of that age group were posted (40 per cent).

The age of some of the older captains is largely confirmed by checking the dates at which they passed their lieutenant's examinations. Of those posted in 1794, Robert Barton, for example, passed in June 1776, Charles Paterson in February

1777, and Charles V Penrose in August 1779. Of those posted in 1795, George Burlton passed in August 1777, W G Lobb in December 1777, and Henry Lidgburd Ball in August 1778. Given that most of these officers should have been about 20 years of age at that time, it can be seen that they were significantly older than average when they were finally posted.

It is also worth reflecting for a moment on those older officers who were posted in 1802. Philip Somerville, for example, who was one of the longest serving frigate captains of the period, died at the age of 54 in December 1817.[8] He was therefore born in 1763 and aged 39 when posted. James C Crawford was born in 1760 and was therefore 42 years of age when posted. Crawford actually did not enter the Royal Navy until he was 17 years of age, having served for several years in the merchant service.[9]

THE YOUNGER CAPTAIN

The fact that the speed of promotion was increasing does not mean that only the younger officers were being promoted. It was not unheard of for an officer to enter the navy at a slightly later age and then reach post rank in a comparatively short time. A good example of this is found in the case of David Milne (see below). However, it must also be acknowledged that having 'good connections' – or 'interest' as it is more usually known – played an important role in rapidity of promotion to the rank of post captain. Three of the officers promoted to post rank in 1794, for example, were about 22 years of age and at the same time were well connected. These were George Cockburn, Robert Gambier Middleton and the Hon Charles Elphinstone Fleeming. Cockburn, like so many officers, was fortunate in that he had become the favourite of the commander-in-chief of a foreign station. In this case the station was the Mediterranean and the Admiral was Lord Hood. As soon as Hood was able to identify a vacant frigate command, he ordered Cockburn into it with a temporary commission[10] and then wrote to the Admiralty telling them what he had done, requesting their formal confirmation of Cockburn's new rank. This confirmation was forthcoming, although it was not always,[11] and Cockburn became a post captain at the age of 21.

Robert Gambier Middleton was the nephew of Sir Charles Middleton, who in 1794 also happened to be a Lord of the Admiralty. Like Cockburn, Middleton was serving in the Mediterranean at the time and, given his family connections, there can have been little doubt that confirmation would be forthcoming in this case. The Hon Charles Elphinstone Fleeming was the son of Baron Elphinstone, a Scottish peer;[12] his mother was a granddaughter of the Earl of Bute and Charles also seems to have been a nephew of Viscount Keith.[13] With Dundas as Secretary of War it was hardly likely that such a well connected young Scot was going to have too much difficulty when it came to promotion.

We can find another example in the following year. The Hon Henry Hotham appears to have been just 18 years of age when posted.[14] Both Henry Hotham and William Hotham, his cousin, were posted in the Mediterranean while Admiral Hotham, Henry's father, was commander-in-chief of that station. Both of the youngest captains posted in 1797 were well connected with the peerage. The Hon Sir Charles Paget was the younger brother of the Earl of Uxbridge and Sir William Hall Gage was almost certainly related to Baron Gage of Castlebar. There is more certainty surrounding the rapid promotions of 1798. Sir Henry Heathcote was 21 years of age when posted and was the son of Sir William Heathcote, Bart, MP for Hampshire.[15] The Hon Charles Herbert Pierrepoint was the son of Earl Manvers and was possibly 20 years of age when posted. The Hon Thomas Bladen Capel was the youngest son of the Earl of Essex, and was 22 years old when posted.[16] The remaining officer posted at some rapidity in 1798 was Josiah Nisbet.[17] The fact that he was Nelson's step-son was, of course, material in his quick promotion; however, that relationship was also partly responsible for the subsequent destruction of his career.[18]

It is also worth noting, for example, that some of the fast movers during the Napoleonic War also happened to share the surname of flag officers: examples include Augustus Leveson Gower in 1802, James Richard Dacres (2), the Hon Archibald Cochrane, Sir Thomas John Cochrane, Sir George Francis Seymour in 1806, and Edward T Troubridge in 1807. So there is clearly some connection between promotion and 'interest'. However, it is easy to overstate this association. Even allowing for the names quoted above, the correlation only applied to a minority. Many other officers were promoted who were not so well connected, and many of these were men of particular ability. It is very clear that competence attracted the attention of senior officers and so an able lieutenant or commander lacking political or aristocratic connections could also acquire significant service interest.

However, the chances were that it would take them longer to get to the rank of post captain. David Milne, for example, was 32 years of age when he was posted. Born in 1763, he did not actually enter the navy until he was 16 years old, somewhat later than usual. Although he saw much active service as a midshipman during the American War, he lacked any real interest and opted for service with the East India Company until 1793. After the outbreak of war his abilities were quickly recognised by Sir John Jervis and he was promoted from lieutenant in January 1794, to post captain in October 1795.

Another example is that of James Bowen (1), who clearly made rapid progress because of ability, being promoted from lieutenant in June 1794, to post captain in September 1795.[19] Bowen came from a Devon family closely connected with the sea;

his father was captain of a merchantman, and at a young age James and his younger brother Richard (also to become a frigate captain) went to sea in the Canada and Jamaica trade. The seamanship that James learned in the merchant service enabled him to gain the rank of master under Lord Howe, and it was with Howe's support that he was promoted quickly. The cases of Bowen and Milne are important because they stand as good evidence that rapid promotion was not necessarily dependent on an aristocratic background, but could be won through the acquisition and display of professional qualities. Furthermore, it is worth noting that these displays of skills were noticed by very senior naval officers (*ie* Jervis and Howe), suggesting that they were particularly observant of the aptitude and activity of junior officers.

LENGTH OF FRIGATE COMMAND

The fact that an officer was promoted to the rank of post captain was in itself no guarantee that an individual possessed the necessary talent for command. Whilst it seems unlikely that the Admiralty would have bothered to promote an officer and then not employ him, we have already seen that this was not an unusual occurrence. The proposition can be reversed, because we can also say that just because a post captain was given a frigate there was no certainty that he would be suited to that type of service. The crucial tell-tale is whether an officer remained in command of a frigate or frigates, and for how long. Many officers were tried out, but a significant number were found to be wanting when it came to the essential qualities.

Before turning to review the longevity of officers' frigate command there is a special factor which has to be acknowledged. There is strong evidence that the Admiralty imposed a rule whereby captains of a particular seniority on the list were obliged to relinquish frigate command. The rule seems to have been imposed on officers when they had reached about ten to twelve years' seniority, which means that there would also be a co-incidental age-ceiling for frigate captains – but there were also reasons why the rule was not applied consistently, and this will be considered shortly.

Although the Admiralty did not keep service records at this period, it did record on a monthly basis who was in command of which ship, and where they were stationed.[20] Collating the information from these enables the historian to build up a record of each officer's service. For example: Captain Robert Barton,[21] who was posted in April 1794, was appointed to the 9-pounder frigate *Lapwing* in August of the same year and continued in command until April 1798 (a period of 3 years and 9 months). He was then immediately given the 12-pounder frigate *Concorde*, which he commanded from May 1798 until April 1800 (a further period of 2 years). His total frigate command period therefore was 5 years and 9 months, or 5.75 years. For the sake of convenience this period will be referred to as a captain's 'frigate service'.

At the shortest, there are command periods recorded of a single month where, in almost every case, the command was an acting/temporary appointment or was probably immediately altered by the Admiralty or commander-in-chief. (The possibility of an error by the Admiralty Clerk making the entry also cannot be ruled out.) At the highest end of the scale, the maximum length of frigate service would seem to have been that of 11 years and 9 months, being the period served by Philip Somerville, although his total was only a few months more than that of Edward W C R Owen.

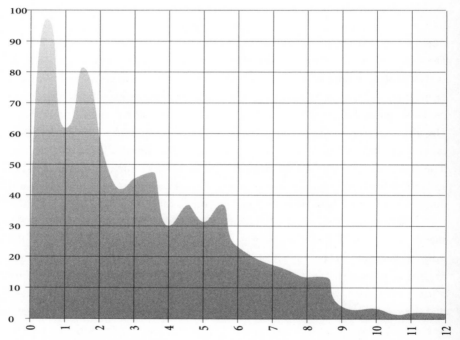

FIGURE 3.5. *Frigate Captains – Total Length of Service 1793-1815 in Years*

Overall, the median length of a captain's frigate service was approximately 3 years and 6 months, but, as can be seen from this chart, only a small minority actually served for this period. The variation in total service is enormous and at a later point closer examination of the longer-serving frigate commanders will be considered, but at this stage it is the relationship between an officer's age and length of frigate service which needs to be examined. This can be done in the first instance by using the same formula as previously; that is, by assuming that the majority of officers were approximately twenty years old at the time they passed for lieutenant.

TABLE 3.2. *Total Frigate Service (between 1793-1815) of Post Captains (in full years) by Year Commissioned as Lieutenant*

Numbers of Captains and their Length of Frigate Service in Years between 1793-1815

Year Passed for Lt.	> 1.	1	2	3	4	5	6	7	8	9	10	11
1776	3	5	4	1		2						
1777	5	9	2	3	5	2	3	1				
1778	11	12	8	2	4	2	1	2		1		
1779	1	3	7	3	3	1	2		1			
1780	3	4	6	1	5		3					
1781	3	2	2	3	4	1		1	1		1	
1782	5	3	5	4	4	4	3		2		1	1
1783	2	3	3	4	1	3	2					
1784		2	2						1			
1785		2	1				1		1			
1786												
1787					1	1	1	2				
1788		1	1			1	1		1			
1789		1		2	6	1	3	1	2	1		
1790	13	13	14	14	13	11	7	1	2		1	
1791	4	1		2		2		2				
1792						1	1					
1793	8	8	10	8	4	6	2	1	3			1
1794	8	7	5	6	2	9	1	2	1			
1795	5	4	3	3	6	1	2	1	2			
1796	6	6	3	3		2	3		2			
1797	4	8		2	2	2	2	2	3			
1798	1	4	2	1	2			1			1	
1799	7	3	3	2		1		3				
1800	5	4	4	1	2					1		
1801	4	3	4	2	1	1	1		1			
1802	4	2	5		2	1						
1803	2	1				2						
1804	2	7	2	2	1	2						
1805	5	1	1	2	1			1				
1806		1		1								
1807	1											

The first thing to note about this table is that it shows fairly quickly that long frigate service was not necessarily restricted to younger men. Some of the longer serving frigate captains were already between the ages of 31 and 35 years when war broke out in 1793. Four older individuals stand out as long-serving frigate captains. They are John Erskine Douglas, who was commissioned a lieutenant in 1778. He was promoted to commander in May 1795 and then quickly to post captain in June of the following year. Within two months he was in command of the 9-pounder frigate *Garland,* which he commanded until January 1798, when he was given the larger 12-pounder *Boston.* He was still in command of the *Boston* in November 1804 – a command period of something like 9 years and 3 months. Ross Donnelly was commissioned a lieutenant in 1782, but not posted until June 1795. He then accumulated a very respectable 10 years in command of frigates, his final command being a very brief period in the 12-pounder *Franchise* in 1807, before going on the command the *Ardent,* 64. Another older captain with long frigate service was Graham Moore. He was commissioned lieutenant in 1782, promoted to commander after the Spanish Armament, and then posted in April 1794 when he was probably at least 32. He was given successively the 12-pounder *Syren* and 18-pounder *Melampus,* until the end of 1801 when the Peace of Amiens interrupted service generally. Then, from August 1803 for approximately a year, he commanded the 24-pounder *Indefatigable.* His total frigate service amounted to something like 8.25 years. Perhaps one of the most extraordinary records is that of Philip Somerville, who was commissioned a lieutenant in 1782, promoted to commander in 1796, and then posted in 1802. From August 1802 until the early part of 1814 he commanded frigates without interruption, going on to command line of battleships and eventually dying in 1817.

All four of these officers were important frigate commanders and they will be discussed again in due course. The point to emphasise here is that although they were long serving and *older* officers, they started in frigate command as relatively 'junior' officers on the list. However, considerable service was also given to some fairly senior captains, like Sir Edward Pellew, who was posted in 1782 and commanded frigates for over six years after the outbreak of war in 1793. Jonathan Faulknor, posted in the same year as Pellew, served in frigates for six years. Other senior officers with significant spells in frigate command included Sir Alexander Cochrane, Richard Strachan and the Hon Michael de Courcy. Of course, with the dearth of promotions between 1783 and 1790, these officers may not have featured high up on the captains list by 1793 (although their advance from 1790 onwards would have been considerably faster). But in the first five or six years of the Revolutionary War there was no shortage of junior captains. So why were these comparatively senior captains being given frigates for such long periods? The reason will become clearer shortly, but for now it must be emphasised that the presence of these and other officers in frigates for considerable periods contradicts any suggestion that frigate command was any form of 'probationary command'. Frigate service was not just a precursor to the command of a ship of the line, yet at the same time there is evidence that a time limit was placed on frigate service.

It is not possible to find an exact correlation between age/seniority and length of frigate service, because the simple fact is that, between officers posted in the same year and post captains of similar age, there was wide variation in the length of frigate command which they experienced. Neither age nor seniority, therefore, were the dominant factors in determining the length of frigate command. Yet it is also apparent that for the older officer, provided he was fit and able to carry out the arduous duties associated with frigate command, there was no reason why he might not accumulate many years in command of frigates.

Variations in the Length of Frigate Command

Approximately 18 per cent of the captains who qualify as frigate commanders during the wars commanded a frigate for a period of less than twelve months. In many cases information regarding their careers as frigate captains is almost irretrievable. Temporary command was not popular among post captains, especially when it was for really short periods and those who lived long enough to be included by John Marshall in his *Royal Naval Biography* may well have considered such a brief command too insignificant or uneventful to have been worth noting. Something like 6 per cent of frigate captains spent only two or three months commanding a frigate, whilst a further 9 per cent commanded for between three and six months only. Despite the brevity of these commands it would be erroneous to assume that the officers concerned were particularly deficient as post captains. Their abilities or inclination may have lain in a different activity. This is certainly suggested by the fact that approximately 60 per cent of those who commanded a frigate for less than twelve months often had substantial commands in other rated ships during their career.

TABLE 3.3. *Length of Frigate Service According to the Year Posted, and Showing the Number of Officers in Each Case*

Year posted	>1yr	1	2	3	4	5	6	7	8	9	10	11
1779	2	1										
1780	1	3										
1781	2	3	2		1							
1782	7	8	5		2	2	2					
1783	3	7	10	3	2	1	1					
1784		1										
1785												
1786		1										
1787	3	2	1									
1788					1							
1789		3	1						1			
1790	8	10	5	4	3	3	2		2			
1791			1		1				1			
1792												
1793	2		4	3	1	6	10	2	3			
1794	5	9	6	7	7	7	4	4	3	2		
1795	5	7	3	3	12	9	4	1	3	1	1	
1796	6	7	6	2	5	2	2	1				
1797	5	1	6	6	3	5	2				1	
1798	2	4	9	6	1	3	1		2			1
1799	1	5	2	4	5				1		1	
1800	0	4	2	3	6	2	2		3			
1801	2	3	2	5	4	4	3	2	4			
1802	10	14	9	10	4	7	2	6	1			1
1803		1		2	1	1	2					
1804	4	6	4	3	1	3		2	1	1		
1805	4	3		1	4			1				
1806	14	13	10	6	3	6						
1807	9	9	5	3	2	1						
1808	3	3	2	3	1	1		1				
1809	5	5	2	2								
1810	10	2										
1811	4	1	2									
1812	3	1										
1813	1											
1814	3											
TOTAL	124	138	99	76	70	62	37	22	23	4	3	2
%	19	21	15	11.5	10.5	9.4	5.6	3.3	3.5	0.6	0.5	0.3

There were, however, probably numbers of officers who for one reason or another either did not shine when given the command of a frigate or who were extremely unlucky. For example, approximately 16 per cent of short-term frigate commanders would appear to have had no other command after their brief spell in a frigate, and another 12.5 per cent may have commanded other rated ships before being given a frigate – only to have this also taken away from them. It may be that these officers totally lacked the 'interest' to get themselves further employment. However, this seems unlikely: the fact that they managed to get promoted to post rank and given a frigate at all suggests that they had some weight behind them. It is possible that they were raised to post captain and given a few months in a frigate before being effectively superannuated – a generous gesture which, as we have previously noted, may have been a possibility. However, it is also a possibility that when it came to command of a rated ship their abilities fell noticeably short of requirements.

We can be more assured about the 7 per cent who were promoted to frigate command close to the end of the war, because the end of the conflict simply closed down the chance of command (and the qualifying period for this survey). We can also be sure about at least two officers who were drowned, three who were killed in action, and one who was court-martialled and dismissed from the service. Since few of the officers with brief frigate service will feature again in this work it is worth reviewing the careers of a few of them to sample the reasons why their frigate career was so brief.

Officers with Brief Frigate Service

Edward Codrington[22] who was posted in April 1795, at the age of 25 years appears to have commanded the 12-pounder frigate *Druid* for between two and six months in the middle of 1796. The grandson of a baronet after whom he was named,[23] he attracted the patronage of Lord Howe shortly after entering the navy, and it was probably for this reason that he passed his lieutenant's examination and was promoted to post captain in less than two years. His first post command was the *Babet*, 22, which he was given quickly after posting. In 1796 he commanded the 12-pounder frigate *Druid* off the coast of Portugal for approximately six months[24] until she was paid off.[25] He then seems to have been unemployed for a number of years, which might be explained by the fact that his patron, Lord Howe, died on 5 August 1799. In the summer of 1804 he was offered the command of the *Argo*, 44, but turning this down he was given instead the *Orion*, 74, which he appears to have accepted with some reluctance and which was under his command at Trafalgar.[26] In 1809 he commanded the *Blake*, another 74, spending several years serving on the coast of Spain before reaching flag rank in 1814. Since Codrington did not marry until some time after the paying-off of the *Druid*, it is possible that his period of leisure was made more attractive by a reasonable inheritance and these may have been key factors influencing the length of his frigate service.

Sir Isaac Coffin commanded the 18-pounder *Melampus* from May 1793 to March 1794. He was posted in June 1782, and was 34 years of age when war broke out in 1793. His command of frigates, indeed of any ship, during the Great Wars was brief mainly because the focus of his sea-going career dates before the period in question. The son of a Boston (Massachusetts) customs officer, Coffin entered under the patronage of Rear-Admiral Montagu and then won the support of Sir Samuel Hood (later Lord Hood), under whom he served as a volunteer[27] in the West Indies. Posted to the *Shrewsbury*, 74, he immediately fell foul of Admiral Rodney and was court-martialled. As a result of this he was sent home in the *Hydra*, 20 and paid off. In 1786 he was given the *Thisbe* frigate and commanded her for two years before again being court-martialled, this time for signing a false muster. He was dismissed and then struck off the list before being reinstated after a sensational court case. In 1790, largely at the instigation of Lord Hood, Coffin was once again given a frigate, this time the *Alligator*, 28. Confirmation of this continuing patronage comes unequivocally from a revealing extract from the memoirs of Sir William Hotham, who recorded:

> At the close of the year 1790 I was appointed Second lieutenant of the *Alligator*, a 28-gun frigate commanded by Captain Coffin, then under orders for the Halifax station. The tide of prejudice, however, ran so much against this commander that, young as I was, and he not bearing the character that promised much allowance for age or inexperience, I was very much alarmed at the prospect and got a month's leave of absence, principally for the purpose of having, if it were possible, this commission cancelled. My friend on this (as on all other occasions) was *Lord Hood*,[28] who was then on the board, and to whom I communicated my apprehensions, begging his furtherance of the object I solicited. His reply to me was decisive 'I am much inclined to serve you,' he told me, 'but if you take my advice you will, after your leave has expired, join the *Alligator*…'.[29]

Sadly for Coffin, once again his command was to be relatively short-lived. The frigate being anchored at the Nore during stormy conditions, Coffin leapt bravely over the side to save a drowning seaman. Although the rescue was successful, Coffin was injured in the process. Following the paying-off of the *Alligator*, Coffin travelled extensively in Europe until May 1793, when he was appointed to the 18-pounder frigate *Melampus*. In March of the following year, however, he was injured yet again and was forced to invalid himself out of active sea service. He was given a position as regulating captain, and as commissioner on several stations until he became both rear-admiral and a baronet in 1804.

It would seem that his early career was financially lucrative for his biographer recorded that 'The judicious investment of his pay and prize money by one of his cousins made him rich',[30] and in his will he left endowments to found several nautical schools in America. Ultimately, it would appear that it was injury which forced Coffin out of both frigate command and active sea service. Two other points are also worth noting in Coffin's case. Firstly, in March 1794 when he received the critical second injury, he was still active in frigate command in spite of the fact that he had been on the list of post captains for nearly twelve years. He was therefore, a comparatively senior captain. Secondly, he appears to have been good at the job, having commanded three different frigates during peace-time and making substantial prize money.

Sir Francis Hartwell, Bart, commanded the 18-pounder frigate *Thetis* for approximately eight months after the outbreak of war in 1793. Born the third son of the Lieutenant Governor of Greenwich Hospital in 1757, he commanded a cutter during the American War and captured what Marshall described as a 'very valuable French West Indiaman'.[31] Possibly as a result he was made commander in January 1779 and post captain before the year was out. According to Pitcairn Jones' list, Hartwell seems to have commanded Third Rates during the intervening peace and was given the *Thetis* in 1792. He was therefore a very senior post captain by the outbreak of war and, chronologically, would have become a flag officer by 1797. Instead, however, he became firstly Commissioner of the Victualling Board until 1796, then Superintendent at Sheerness. By 1814 when he decided to retire, he was Deputy Comptroller of the Navy Board. As has been previously noted, 35 years of age was not too old to command a frigate, but Hartwell's position in the upper echelons of the Navy List (in fact his frigate service ended after he had been on the captains' list for about fourteen years) seems to have made it more unlikely that he would continue with active sea service. The fact that he was given successive administrative positions suggests that his strengths lay in other quarters.

James Carpenter, whose frigate command totalled approximately twelve months, was 33 years of age when war broke out. He had entered the navy under Captain John Jervis (later, of course, Earl St Vincent) and had also served for a time in Rodney's flagship during the American War. He was clearly a protégé of Jervis's, for as a lieutenant he was appointed to Jervis's flagship in 1793, where, in the West Indies, Jervis promoted him to commander of the *Nautilus*. When Martinique fell in March 1794, the French 28-gun frigate *Bien Venue*[32] was captured and given to Carpenter, who was posted for this purpose. He was moved rapidly to the *Veteran*, 64 and then in around December of the same year, was given the 12-pounder 32-gun frigate *Alarm*. Some eight months later he commanded the *Quebec*, a frigate of similar armament to the *Alarm*, and which he probably brought back to decommission following the death of her former commander, Josias Rogers. It is apparent that much of Carpenter's service was in the West Indies, for in 1800 he was invalided home from there, having had command of the *Leviathan*, 74 in which he had been Sir John Duckworth's flag captain and had captured some valuable prizes. Unfortunately on his voyage home, Carpenter was captured by the French and sent to Spain as a prisoner of war. He was later released after the direct intervention of St Vincent. Between 1803 and 1810 he was placed in command of a section of Sea Fencibles, a role which was not unusually given to officers who were suffering from some lapse in health. In 1811, having recovered, he became Duckworth's flag captain once again, this time in the *Antelope*, 50 a year before he reached flag rank. According to Marshall,[33] Carpenter saw no further service. Obviously there are gaps in Carpenter's career that it is difficult to explain. He was on active service in the West Indies almost continually until the end of 1795, and this may have affected his health, which could account for the apparent gap between the end of 1795 and 1799.[34]

From the examples considered thus far the suggestion must be that seniority on the list played a part in the rate of ship which might be made available to a post captain. Whilst no captains were both in command of a frigate and near the top of the captains list, seniority did not rule out significant periods in command of a frigate. The other factor which seems to have played upon the length of frigate command relates to personal skills and ability. As we have seen above, it is clear that officers with marked administrative and organisational skills were frequently given jobs which took full advantage of those qualities; examples might be Hartwell among the above and Sir William Domett in the last chapter.

Number of Frigates Commanded

Obviously there was a wide variation in both the number of frigates that an officer might command during his career and the length of time that he spent in them. An 'average' frigate captain would probably spend something like three years in command of frigates – and would probably command two frigates during that time. However, around 49 per cent of frigate captains commanded just one frigate. Nevertheless, when we cross-reference the number of commands with the length of time spent in the ships, we quickly see that a number of frigate commanders served in just one or two frigates, but for much longer than the average period: captains like Samuel Ballard, who commanded the *Pearl* for 6 years; Philip Beaver who commanded the *Acasta* and the *Nisus* for a period of 5.25 years; Sir Philip Broke, who commanded the *Druid* and then the *Shannon* for 8.5 years; or Richard Hawkins who commanded the *Minerva* alone for 7 years.

This prompts the question: why were certain captains kept in frigate service for much longer than others? Similarly, why were they retained often in the same frigate for long periods? Frigate command was highly desirable and there were many officers clamouring for commands, so there can be no suggestion that there were significant numbers of incompetent frigate commanders being quietly 'overlooked'. On the contrary, it seems much more likely that there was a positive reason for keeping these men in frigates, and sometimes in *particular* frigates, for long periods.

One further aspect should be highlighted before moving on: 20 per cent of frigate captains were given a frigate either immediately or within a few months of posting and whilst their aggregate frigate service varies widely, in general their frigate service is longer than the average of the whole frigate captain list. Captains posted quickly into frigates had a frigate service of on average 3.9 years as against 3.1 years; and whilst they, in common with all of the other frigate captains, commanded an average of two frigates, their wider careers tended to include the command of more ships. In other words, those officers posted directly into a frigate, served in frigates longer and commanded more ships generally, and factors seemed to be operating which gave them a more than usually active career in frigates.

SOCIAL BACKGROUND

One cannot move on from a general discussion about the frigate captains without some consideration being given to their social background. There is a problem here in that it is, and was, much easier to identify an aristocratic background than someone of more humble origin. However, the following comparison uses the same source material as Lewis in *A Social History of the Navy, 1793-1815*,[35] so the comparison is significant. Lewis calculated that the social background or class of the parents of all the naval officers in his study broke down as follows:[36]

	percentage		*percentage*		*percentage*
Titled (Peers/Baronets)	12.0	MP	1.0	Church	8.7
Gentry	27.4	Navy	24.1	Medicine	2.8
Public Office	5.7	Army	7.3	Others	11.0[37]

It has been possible to identify the parental-social background of 148 frigate captains. These are as follows:

	percentage		*percentage*		*percentage*
Titled Family	43.1	MP	3.9	Church	4.6
Gentry	9.8	Navy	17	Medicine	2.6
Public Office	10.5	Army	5.2	Other	3.3

To a large degree the comparison is misleading, because Lewis was considering a much bigger group over a much longer period than that for the frigate captains. What can be observed, however, is that Lewis's three most significant groups were the gentry, naval families and then the titled families. Within the frigate sample the most significant groups are the titled families, naval families and those holding public office. It should also be noted that the percentage of sons of government officials and Members of Parliament is larger in the frigate sample. This would seem to suggest that within the frigate captain sample there was a higher number of fathers in prominent positions. Furthermore, it is possible to mark a change during the course of the war by separating parental background according to the period in which an officer was posted.

TABLE 3.4. *Social Background of Frigate Captain Sample (in percentages) by Year of Posting*

Background	pre-1793	1793-1800	1801-1814
Titled	33	34	61
Gentry	10	11	8
Public Office	6	17	4
MP	6	4	2
Navy	30	11	17
Army	3	7	4
Church	6	6	2
Medicine	0	6	0
Other	3	4	2

There are perhaps three important trends suggested by these figures. The most obvious relates to the enormous rise in the number of young aristocrats commanding frigates from 1801 onwards. In fact, after 1801, there was growing criticism of the numbers and professional qualities of some young titled officers, but at the same time there was a sense that only 'gentlemen' possessed the requisite qualities to make a good commander. This potential contradiction is well illustrated by Frederick Marryat, who described serving with a frigate captain who was not a gentleman, and concluded:

> Impressment and the want of officers at the early part of the war, gave him an opportunity of becoming a lieutenant ... The service had received serious injury by admitting men on the quarter-deck from before the mast; it occasioned there being two classes of officers in the navy – namely, those who had rank and connections, and those who had entered by the 'hawseholes', as they were described. The first were favoured when young, and did not

acquire a competent knowledge of their duty; the second, with few exceptions, as they advanced in their grades, proved, from want of education, more and more unfit for their stations.[38]

There was a middle line as we shall see in due course.

The second trend is that relating to the apparent decline in the sons of naval officers commanding frigates from 1793 onwards (some naval officers were also titled, of course, but here we are concerned with those whose fathers were 'ordinary' officers). Although there appears to be a reduction from 1793 onwards, what the figures probably reveal is the much greater advantage that the sons of naval officers had in the pre-war navy. In a period when there was a seriously reduced opportunity for employment and even less chance of promotion, the men who probably stood the best chance of getting to sea were the ones who had the closest contact with active sea officers. As the navy expanded from 1793 onwards, this relative advantage declined. As a result we see the third trend: that is, the growing influence of men in public office, be it Members of Parliament, government or Admiralty official, colonial service or customs officers, and a consequent growth in 'political appointments'. However, it is worth remembering what was going on in the officer selection process for the American navy over this period. The findings here suggest that in Britain, whilst the landed families continued to predominate to an astounding degree, the situation in America (ie the state of hostilities from 1775 onwards) created the opportunity for the newer social groupings based on trade, new money and public office, to rise in prominence.

Given the hardship of the life at sea, one might wonder what it was that drove the sons of titled families to take up such a career in preference to others. The popularity of the Royal Navy can be gauged by looking at the male siblings of a sample group of forty-eight families with at least one son in frigate command. Obviously, we would expect eldest sons to remain at home for, unless the family was impoverished as in the case of the Dundonalds, the first-born would normally expect to inherit the family estate. However, of the forty-eight titled families checked here, ten had eldest surviving sons in the navy. Seven of these were the sons (or in one case nephew) of naval officers, and six of them also had a younger brother in the navy. Where a career was found to be necessary or chosen for elder sons, the Royal Navy was much more popular than either the army (four elder sons) or public office (one elder son). The remaining 69 per cent of elder sons do not seem to have needed to enter any profession.

The preference for a naval career continues with second sons where, out of forty-eight, twenty-one entered the navy, nine the army and two the church. In fact for virtually all families the navy seems to have been the single most popular profession.

TABLE 3.5. *Profession of Sons of Sample Group of Titled Families*

Name	eldest	2nd	3rd	4th	5th	6th	7th	Date Lt	Father RN?
De Courcy	Army		RN					20/11/1776	No
Finch			RN	Army	Church	RN		30/08/1777	No
Northesk		RN	Army					07/12/1777	Yes
Saumarez	RN		RN	Army	Surgeon	PO		25/01/1778	No
Ranelagh	RN	Army		Army	Army	RN		21/01/1782	No
Forbes		RN		RN				28/06/1782	No
Curzon		Army	RN	Church	RN			01/02/1783	No
Gardner	RN	RN	Army					12/01/1784	Yes
Paulet		RN						12/03/1789	No
Legge		RN		RN	Church	Church		03/08/1789	No
Garlies		RN	Army	Church		PO		08/08/1789	No
Fitzroy		Army	RN	RN	Church			17/03/1790	No
Byng	RN							01/11/1790	Yes
Murray		Army	RN	EICo				03/11/1790	No
O'Bryen		RN	RN	Army	Army			19/11/1790	No
Boyle		Army	RN					22/11/1790	No
Herbert		RN	Church	Church	Law			05/04/1793	No
Elphinstone	Army	RN	PO	PO				22/04/1793	No
Colville	RN	Army						29/07/1793	Yes
Wodehouse		RN	Church	Church				06/01/1794	No
Hotham	Army	Church	RN					06/06/1794	Yes
Kerr			RN	Army				01/11/1794	No
Maitland		RN	Army					04/03/1795	No
Cochrane, T	RN							27/05/1796	Yes
King			RN	Army	Church	PO	RN	16/06/1796	No
Aylmer	Army		RN					17/12/1796	No
Irby		RN	Church	Army	Church	Army	RN	06/01/1797	No
Dundas	RN	Army		Church	RN	Army		23/03/1797	Yes
Falkland		RN						30/03/1797	No
Mackay			Army	RN				27/03/1798	No
Cochrane, A		Army	PO	Church	EICo	RN		19/05/1798	No
Pleydell-Bouverie		RN						16/02/1799	No
Bennett			RN					02/08/1799	No
Rodney		RN	PO	RN				29/08/1799	Yes
Elliott	PO	RN						12/08/1800	No
Stuart			Army	RN	RN	PO		21/03/1801	No
Cathcart	RN	Army						02/09/1801	No
Cadogan		Church	RN	EICo	Army	Army	RN	12/04/1802	No
Duncan		RN						21/04/1803	Yes
Pakenham		Army	Army	RN	Church			29/06/1803	No
Powlett		RN	Army					03/04/1804	No
Percy		PO	Church	RN	Army	RN	Army	30/04/1804	No
Gordon		RN	Army	Army	PO	RN		02/07/1804	No
Waldegrave	RN	RN						20/07/1804	Yes
Proby	RN							24/10/1804	Yes
Maude			Church	RN	Church	RN		29/03/1805	No
Townshend			Church		RN			31/01/1806	No
Peachey		RN	Church					05/01/1807	No

(Key: RN – Royal Navy; PO – Public Office; EICo – East India Company. Source: *Debrett's Peerage*, 1834.)

Previous page Sir Edward Pellew: a little used portrait by Opie, probably painted when Pellew was in his prime as a frigate captain. The portrait gives a good representation of the powerful impression he made as one of the navy's superlative frigate commanders.

Left Aquatint by Robert Dodd of the first successful frigate action of the war, the capture of the *Cléopâtre* by Edward Pellew's *Nymphe*, herself a French prize from the previous war. Pellew was rewarded with a knighthood for this engagement.

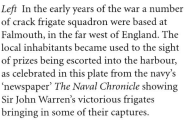

Left In the early years of the war a number of crack frigate squadron were based at Falmouth, in the far west of England. The local inhabitants became used to the sight of prizes being escorted into the harbour, as celebrated in this plate from the navy's 'newspaper' *The Naval Chronicle* showing Sir John Warren's victorious frigates bringing in some of their captures.

Right Sir John Borlase Warren: a portrait dating from shortly after his days as commander of a frigate squadron. A keen seaman and sensitive frigate commander, Warren is much under-rated because of his less successful period as Commander-in-Chief on the American Station during the War of 1812.

Above Sir James Newman: a good example of the unacknowledged and forgotten frigate heroes of the war. Newman perished tragically along with virtually all of his crew when his ship was overwhelmed by a storm on Christmas Day 1811.

Right Sir Harry Neale: deeply respected by the crew of his frigate which broke away from the mutiny at the Nore. Neale inherited a Baronetcy before getting frigate command and later became MP for Lymington in Hampshire.

Left Edward Owen: possibly one of the finest and most professional frigate commanders of the Napoleonic period.

Below John Phillimore: a controversial character. Is his wit and capacity for irreverence reflected in this portrait?

Left Sir Michael Seymour. The attractive personality of the man is clearly conveyed here.

Below Robert Faulknor: a volatile and ultimately troubled personality. After killing a seaman in the West Indies, Faulknor was unable to rest and took to pacing the quarterdeck during the night.

Opposite page The Death of Faulknor: one of very few naval officers of the period apart from Nelson whose death was portrayed in print.

Left Blockade duty was the lot of many a frigate captain. As suggested by this illustration of the entrance to Brest (from *The Naval Chronicle*), close reconnaissance required great seamanship and cast-iron nerves, but it made British officers as familiar with enemy waters as their French counterparts.

Left William Hoste. The victor of the Battle of Lissa, and beloved by Nelson, Hoste died embittered by the lack of recognition awarded him by an ungrateful government and nation. For most of his career, Hoste was impoverished by the obligation to support a spendthrift father.

Right Samuel Hood. Unlike some of his more famous relatives, Hood had a joy of sailing which was remarked upon.

Above Peter Rainier: one of the young 'Star Captains' par excellence. This superb portrait provides a stunning impression of the youthfulness of some of the navy's most brilliant frigate commanders.

Opposite page David Milne. With years of experience as a Mate in the East India Company service, Milne provides a fine example of the thorough seaman who was recognised and promoted by an observant Admiralty.

Left Sir Peter Parker: one of the few frigate captains killed during combined operations. This portrait is also interesting in recording the changing fashion among naval officers in the first decades of the nineteenth century.

Below Joseph Sidney Yorke: achieved an outstanding record patrolling with his frigate in the English Channel.

Above Sir James Saumarez: a brilliant squadron commander from an aristocratic Guernsey family. It was fitting that one of his finest achievements was in engaging a French Squadron within sight of his own home. Ironically, Saumarez was one of the few officers who never really enjoyed frigate command.

Right The Hon Courtenay Boyle. Third son of the Earl of Cork, and distantly related to the Earl of Sandwich, Courtenay Boyle was an early protégé of Nelson but never achieved the spectacular success of the more humble William Hoste.

Above Rewards for successful frigate actions could be more than merely honorific. Patriotic organisations might make valuable awards, like presentation swords or commemorative silver. This elaborately decorated salver was given to Captain Broke by his home county of Suffolk to celebrate his victory over the *Chesapeake*.

Right Frigate captains rarely led their own boarding parties, the fate of Philip Broke struck down on the deck of the *Chesapeake* underlining the reason why. Luckily, *Shannon*'s crew was too well drilled to feel the loss of leadership, and the American frigate was already beaten at than point in any case.

Left George Nicholas Hardinge. He was killed in action on 8 March 1808 when his 36-gun 18-pounder frigate *San Fiorenzo* engaged the heavier French frigate *Piémontaise* in the Indian Ocean in a running fight lasting three days.

Below John Shortland: mortally wounded in December 1809 when his frigate, the *Junon*, was surprised by two French frigates. Although surviving the capture of his ship, Shortland had one leg amputated above the knee and grape removed from his hand. Possible moved before he had sufficiently recovered, he died weeks later.

In the case of the more impoverished families, the chance of prize money might have been an obvious motive for a naval career. Similarly, younger sons, might make a substantial income from the same source, if they were very lucky, and might thus increase their opportunities for a lucrative marriage and social elevation. However, there may have been another more ideological reason why the navy was popular with this social group, as will become clear later.

MORTALITY AMONG FRIGATE CAPTAINS

Accidental death was an accepted hazard of the seaman's life during the age of sail. Indeed, as Michael Lewis demonstrates, the dangers of the sea resulted in greater loss of life than engagement with the enemy.[39] Disease was the main cause of loss of life, accounting for as many as 50 per cent of the deaths of seamen during the period, but accidents, either to the individual or to ships, accounted for a further 41 per cent.[40] The frigate, at sea in all conditions and in all areas of the world, was more likely than a ship of the line to suffer from natural weather hazards. It is therefore not surprising that the reason why some frigate captains served only briefly was simply that they did not long survive their appointment. For example, the list of short-term captains would include the name of John Morrison, who was appointed to the 12-pounder frigate *Circe* in October or November 1806. The *Circe* had been under the command of Captain Jonas Rose since early in 1805, and had been on the Leeward Island station for approximately one year. Morrison's career had been relatively uneventful, although as a commander he had been involved in Abercromby's expedition to Egypt in 1801 when he had commanded the *Thisbe* frigate, probably reduced to a troopship.[41] On that occasion he failed to attract the attention of a senior officer and he continued as a commander until he was finally posted in May 1806 (he had passed for lieutenant over fifteen years earlier!). His first post command was as acting captain of the 74-gun *Northumberland*. He was then given the *Heureux*, 22, an ex-French privateer mounting 12-pounder guns, and it was whilst commanding this ship that he was appointed to the *Circe*. If the news reached him of his appointment to the larger *Circe*, Morrison must have been delighted, for it had taken a long time for him to become a captain of a frigate. Now he had been given the two-year old *Circe* which, whilst she had a reputation for being rather crank, was thought to be good and fast in manoeuvres.[42] Sometime in the later part of 1806 Morrison set sail in the *Heureux* to join his new command, but, sadly, somewhere between Halifax and the Leeward Islands, the *Heureux* disappeared without trace. His career as a frigate captain had quite literally sunk before it had even started.

Both George William Augustus Courteney and John Eveleigh commanded a frigate for less than a year before being killed in action. Just as the role of the frigate frequently exposed it to hazardous weather conditions, so too its role rendered it much more likely than, say, a 74-gun ship, to come into contact with the enemy.

In the case of the vast majority of officers who served as captains of frigates it has been possible to verify the year in which they died. Out of 624 such officers 155 (25 per cent) died or were killed during the course of the conflict. For some of these death came after their period in command of a frigate, but for 74 officers (48 per cent of those in the frigate sample who died during the years 1793-1815), death coincided with their command. Twelve officers were killed during some form of action whilst in command of a frigate, starting with G W A Courtenay of HMS *Boston*, killed in action against the French frigate *Embuscade* in 1793;[43] but only eight of these were during frigate engagements as such.[44] Edward Riou, for example, was commanding the frigate squadron at the Battle of Copenhagen in 1801 when he was killed by a shot from the Danish batteries. Conway Shipley of the *Nymphe* was killed in the act of leading his boarders on to a French brig-corvette during a disastrous cutting out expedition in the Tagus in 1808;[45] the fact that he was the only officer in the sample found who had died in the course of this type of activity illustrates how rare it was for captains to actually lead such expeditions themselves. Nonetheless, Richard Bowen, of the *Terpsichore* was killed whilst leading a landing against Tenerife in 1797 and, in a less well known example, Peter Parker of the *Menelaus* was killed whilst leading a combined force of seamen and soldiers during an attack up the Chesapeake in 1814.[46]

Twenty-six captains died whilst in command of their frigates in either the East Indies or the West Indies, including Lord William Stuart, who had just relinquished command of his frigate and died on the passage back to England from the West Indies. To this should be added Philip Beaver of the *Nisus* frigate, who died as a result of a longer term debility he is thought to have contracted in Batavia. It cannot be ascertained whether all of these died from some form of fever, but given the reputation of the stations involved, this would seem to have been the most likely cause of death. If so, then fever accounted for at least 36 per cent of the deaths of active frigate commanders. Other illnesses are also occasionally encountered. W H Dillon tells us, for example, that Captain Thomas Twysden of the *Revolutionnaire* suffered some form of seizure and was found dead in his cabin shortly after leaving port.[47]

The other common cause of death was that of drowning. Ten captains died either through shipwreck or foundering, or as in the case of Bridges Taylor when his boat overturned attempting to land in heavy surf at Brindisi in the Adriatic.[48] A less common cause of death was that occasioned by duelling. In fact, only Hassard

Stackpoole of the *Statira* was so killed whilst in command; though in 1809 the infamous Lord Falkland was also eventually killed in a duel eighteen months after being removed from the *Quebec* for his unreliable and, some claimed, insane behaviour.[49] Only one captain was definitely killed during the course of a mutiny, and that was the infamous Henry Pigot of the *Hermione* in 1797. Finally, Edward Pakenham was killed when the *Resistance* blew up in the East Indies in 1798. Fire and explosion were not uncommon, but Pakenham was the only frigate captain to have been killed in this way during the wars.

Approximately 50 per cent of those officers who died between 1793 and 1815 may have died from a more non-specific disease or old age. This almost certainly explains why 80 per cent of those who died whilst inactive passed away after 1807, for many of these fifty-one officers were significantly older officers, as in the case of William Fairfax, who had entered the navy in 1750; or there were those who had entered during the American War like George Henry Towry, who the *Naval Chronicle* described as 'an old post captain' who died of a 'Quinzy' in 1809. From the point of view of frigate captains, however, the greatest danger lay in contracting one of the diseases endemic to both the East and West Indies stations.

CHAPTER IV

THE TYPICAL
FRIGATE CAPTAIN

O NE OF THE PROBLEMS historians have in trying to understand the naval captain of this period, is that there is no conception of the ordinary officer. In popular imagination the naval captain is perceived as being either one of two extremes – the heroic Nelson or the brutal Bligh. One was extraordinary, the other probably misrepresented. Neither of these figures represents the typical captain of the period. Part of the problem also lies in the fact that no two officers or their careers are entirely alike. However, it is possible to say something about the characteristics of the average frigate captain's career – although this will still be highly dependent on when it started. For example, an officer passing his lieutenant's examination during or at the end of the American War was likely to have to wait 10-11 years to reach post rank. But if he passed that examination after the mid-1780s, the chances are that the threat or actual outbreak of war would accelerate his promotion to within 6 years.

In this latter case he might well be slightly younger. He would probably command two or three frigates over a total period of 3-4 years, but after 8½ years on the list he would either find himself on the beach on half-pay or, if he was fortunate, in command of a ship of the line. In fact, these circumstances describe sixty-eight frigate captains, although it must be admitted that not all of these officers were 'typical'. The list of 'typical' captains would include, for example, Lord Cochrane, whom no-one could describe as an ordinary naval officer. Furthermore, Cochrane's career was terminated in unusual circumstances after 1809 when his endeavour to publicise what many people saw as Admiral Gambier's disgraceful inaction at the Basque Roads led him into controversial political activity. As a criteria, therefore, the length of frigate command needs to be used with a little caution. Of course, the frigate career of other officers was terminated because of factors beyond either theirs or the Admiralty's control, such as through death or illness. Captain John Turnor, for example, had not long relinquished command of the 32-gun frigate *Orpheus* for the old 64-gun *Trident* when he died in 1801.

Some of the 'typical' frigate captains would certainly have stronger interest than others, though of course, the value of this should not be assumed. On first sight it might be tempting to think that Lord Cochrane or Lord James Townshend, son of Viscount Townshend, would have had sufficient interest to guarantee their careers. However, Cochrane's interest was almost always more trouble to him than it was worth; and Townshend, in spite of his connections, was not promoted to lieutenant until he was 21 (although his promotion through the ranks thereafter was fast, from lieutenant in January 1806 to post captain in June 1809).

Other officers struggled with slightly less obvious interest. Christopher Cole, for example, had the advantage of three brothers in influential positions. One was the Chaplain of Greenwich Hospital; another was vice-chancellor of the University of Oxford and domestic Chaplain to the Duke of Clarence; and the third, his older brother Frank, was a navy captain and a close friend of Sir Edward Pellew. His rate of promotion was actually rather slower than expected, partly because of an unfortunate twist of fate. Early in his career he obtained the patronage of Rear-Admiral Sir Francis Samuel Drake. Drake secured for him a position as lieutenant on board the *Crown*, 64 commanded by Commodore Sir William Cornwallis, in the East Indies. Unfortunately, when Cole eventually arrived in India to join his new ship, he learned that Drake was dead, and 'all hopes of speedy promotion were consequently abandoned by him; nor did he obtain the rank he had so long sought after until 1793.'[1] Ironically, another gamble actually paid off. In 1799 he was given the choice of being promoted to commander on half-pay, or remaining as a lieutenant and sailing with Admiral Lord Hugh Seymour, who was due to take up his position as commander-in-chief of the Leeward Islands station where, as has already been noted, the mortality rate almost guaranteed promotion. He opted for the latter and shortly after was promoted commander and given a captured 20-gun ship, the *Surinam*. In 1801 Seymour, now commander-in-chief, died and was succeeded by Sir John Duckworth, who also became a patron of Cole. Early in 1802, Duckworth posted Cole into the *Southampton* frigate and Cole's career was assured.

One of the key career elements revealed by the employment records relates to *where* these officers served. Here it must be said that the Admiralty List Books are a little imprecise when it comes to providing information about an officer's or frigate's whereabouts. To a degree this is disappointing, especially as one of the reasons for the List Books was to provide the Admiralty with a regularly updated reference to the disposition of its ships in commission. However, since there had to be some vagueness about a ship's activities (because of the shortfalls of communication), it was obviously thought sufficient to record the whereabouts of each ship according to its general or command disposition. Thus virtually all frigates allocated to the

Channel Fleet command were listed in the Books under 'Channel Fleet', or 'Grand Fleet' as it became known during the Napoleonic War. Under this heading they could be anywhere between Spithead and the coast of Portugal, and they might be at anchor or cruising (even though there was a separate listing for ships formally 'Cruising' under what seems to have been Admiralty Orders – see below). However, frigates attached to particular squadrons within the Channel command area might be listed under the name of the squadron commander, as with 'Duncan's Squadron', 'Warren's Squadron' or 'Pellew's Squadron'.[2]

For the purpose of this book the stations on which these 'typical' frigate captains served has had to be simplified to eight stations, as follows:

The Channel Fleet: This includes ships at Spithead, although these were usually listed separately. However, although the List Books do not specify as such, it would also include ships not actually in company with the Channel Fleet, but on patrol and blockade work off the French Channel ports and eastern Atlantic seaboard as far south as Portugal.

The North Sea: This includes Duncan's Squadron between August 1796 and May 1800; and the Nore, Baltic, and frigates recorded as being at the Texel.

East Indies: This includes ships at the Cape of Good Hope, a crucial position, commanding as it did the route to India. For most of the wars the East Indies station stretched from the Cape to China and although after 1805 the station was divided and the Cape became a station in its own right,[3] it has been treated here as the one station.

West Indies: This includes Jamaica and the Leeward Islands and, perhaps questionably, those frigates sent to South America.

North America: Including ships on the eastern seaboard of the North American continent, Nova Scotia and Newfoundland.

Mediterranean: This is apparently straightforward as the Mediterranean is the only station so easily defined by geography. However, it should be noted that the Adriatic command came under this station and that in the west it extended to Cape St Vincent and Cape Spartel. Furthermore, even when the Mediterranean Fleet under Jervis was forced to leave the station in 1797, the ships were still nominated as being on the 'Mediterranean Station'. Sir John Orde's command based at Cadiz was treated in the same way.

Port: Where possible all references to ships being in Portsmouth, Plymouth, or the Thames yards are included in this category, particularly where it is stated that they are fitting and stowing for Channel or 'foreign' service. It is perhaps the one category which should be treated with extra caution as it is not always possible to differentiate the status of a ship at Plymouth/Hamoaze or Portsmouth/Spithead. Spithead and Hamoaze being moorings, it is not unusual to find frigates fitting or stowing at these positions. Ships moored at St Helen's, east of the Isle of Wight and Cawsand Bay, off Plymouth, are also included in this category; both were the normal assembly place for convoys and in the case of St Helens, also for ships awaiting a favourable wind to take them down the Channel.

'Cruising & Convoy': This category is in many ways the most interesting. The protection of trade was fundamental to the duties of any commander-in-chief of all stations, although the degree of demand obviously varied. Frigates recorded as being on almost any station in the List Books could also be undertaking convoy escort duties or patrols on the orders of the station commander. This category, however, appears to apply to a varying number of frigates kept in reserve for particular duties. By keeping a pool of frigates under direct Admiralty orders, it was possible for their Lordships to issue instructions promptly without having to observe the normal protocol of writing either first, or simultaneously, to the commander-in-chief.

The frigates recorded under 'Cruising & Convoy' were, in fact, a form of reserve who could be ordered into action at short notice to meet particular contingencies. For example, in August 1798, with the rebellion in Ireland barely suppressed, the Admiralty became concerned about French transports assembling in La Rochelle and Brest. These forces were preparing to depart for an uncertain destination, but the most likely target was guessed to be Ireland. Some of the Admiralty's pool of frigates were quickly ordered to join single ships or squadrons on station between the coast of France and Ireland. The *Boston*, under John Erskine Douglas, for example, was ordered to join Robert Barlow in the *Phoebe* (another frigate in the pool) off the Channel Islands. Barlow in fact arrived at Plymouth on 18 July for a refit and, two weeks later, was instructed to return to station off Guernsey as soon as possible. Both frigates were then attached to a large frigate formation under Francis Fayerman in the *Beaulieu*, who was actually part of Sir Richard Strachan's squadron. In this way the regular cruising squadrons could be reinforced without detaching other frigates from their normal station.

Another ship in the pool at this time was the *Melampus* under Captain Graham Moore. During August 1798 she was sent to join the frigate *Doris* (attached to the

Cork station) and help her escort a convoy to Belfast Lough. In this instance one of the pool of frigates was ordered on convoy duty as a precautionary measure to reinforce an existing escort who might have been in jeopardy.

However, this form of exigency was not the only reason a frigate might be sent on convoy duties at the direct order of the Admiralty. It is also appears that captains who attracted their Lordships' displeasure could find themselves detained on a less than rewarding task. An example of this could be found in the case of Captain Woodley Losack who, it will be seen from the following tables, spent approximately 46 per cent of his frigate career on Cruising & Convoy duties. Losack was not promoted with any great speed – in fact, his promotion rate was very slow (approximately 12 years). In 1810 he was given the new 36-gun 18-pounder frigate *Galatea*, and sent to join Schomberg's squadron based at the Cape. In May 1811, when Schomberg's squadron became involved in a heavy action with some French frigates, the *Galatea* suffered heavy damage[4] and Losack himself was badly wounded. In his public letter reporting on the action, Schomberg was critical of Losack and implied misconduct on his behalf. On his return to England Losack demanded a court martial to clear his name, but the Admiralty refused, stating that they were perfectly satisfied with his conduct. However, Losack was then promptly dispatched off on Cruising & Convoy work and the suspicion must remain that he had fallen out of favour.[5]

In another example, Captain Lord Augustus Fitzroy seems to have found himself in disgrace whilst serving under direct orders. In May 1796 his frigate the *Imperieuse* was sent into dock. A rather tart note in the Admiralty Board Journals records that Captain Fitzroy was to be 'acquainted that their L'dships cannot help feeling much surprise that a far greater number of men (63 No.) have been suffer'd to desert from [the *Imperieuse*] than have deserted from any other ship in similar situation.'[6] When he did get his ship to sea he was attached to Duncan's fleet with orders to cruise off the Naze for a week – hardly a rich hunting ground. A month later Fitzroy was put under the orders of Captain Robert Watson in the *Isis* and sent to St Helena with orders to wait there three months and return with the East Indies convoy.

There was another operational reason why it was useful to have a pool of frigates available for direct order from the Admiralty. A frigate sent on a specific mission or escort duty might have to cross several stations in the process. Without direct Admiralty Orders the commander of such a frigate would fall under the direction of whichever senior officer he happened to encounter and could be detained. Direct orders from the Admiralty usually over-rode those of the local commander – unless, of course, the strategic situation had changed dramatically enough to justify his intervention.

To find out on which stations these 'typical' officers served in command of frigates, their frigate service has been divided according to the percentage of time spent on each station. For a comparison, the results are shown in two tables, one for the first war and one for the period from mid-1801 until 1814. Obviously the career of some officers spans both periods, across the Peace of Amiens. Those officers have been placed according to the majority of their frigate service.

TABLE 4.1. *The Station Disposition of 'Typical' Frigate Captains (1793-1801) given as a Percentage of Frigate Service*[7]

Captain	Channel	Cruising/Convoy	North Sea	East Indies	West Indies	North America	Med	Port
Alms, J		10	32		22			36
Bagot, R	25		16		61			
Bayntun, H			7		86			7
Berkeley, V C	31	13			13		18	27
Bowen, W							95	5
Buller, E	31	28		23				18
Cole, F	81	11						8
Downman, H							100	
Drew, J	64	21						15
Fayerman, F	62	5	17				4	12
Fremantle, T							97	3
Griffith, E	86	12						2
Harvey, J					92			8
Harvey, T	24				76			
Lane, R	28	10	8		45			10
Lee, Sir R	29	29			40			2
Linzee, S	11	3		27			49	10
Ogilvie, W	56		4		33			7
Raper, H	14				71		3	12
Robinson, M	73	9						18
Rowley, C	49		32			15		5
Seater, J	24		8		47	21		
Stephens, G				90				10
Turner, J				100				
Waller, T							93	7
White, C			100					
Woodley, J	24	11			8		51	5
Per cent of time	26	6	8	9	22	1	19	8

TABLE 4.2. *Station Disposition of 'Typical' Frigate Captains (1801-1814)*

Captain	Channel	Cruising/Convoy	North Sea	East Indies	West Indies	North America	Med	Port
Ballard, V					86			14
Bullen, C							88	12
Byron, R		7				93		
Cochrane, Lord	23		10			13	41	13
Cole, C				90	10			
Crawford, J	27	36		27				3
Cumberland, W	21	7			57			14
Curtis, L		38		56				6
Dick, J	14					86		
Deans, J W D	100							
Dunn, R D	60			8			28	4
Grant, C	65		8		28			
Hamond, G E	43	26					26	5
Hancock, J	6	28	60				6	
Heywood, E			89		11			
Harris, G	43			57				
Hawker, E					17	83		
Hill, H	86					14		
Hope, H							100	
Kerr, A	50					50		
Livingstone, T			10				80	10
Lloyd, R	14				33	53		
Losack, W		46		54				
Lumley, R						33	67	
Mason, F	73		27					
Mends, R	73				27			
Miller, G	46	15			31			8
Montagu, W	29			71				
Oswald, J	50		17				33	
Pelly, C			6	56		25		12
Quilliam, J			47			53		
Raggett, R	26	47	16					10
Richardson, C	56			35	9			
Rose, J	45				55			
Serrell, J	57		*8		43			
Skene, A		7	38			45		10
Stackpoole, H			14		86	*9		
Stuart, J	92					8		
Townshend, Lord						100		
Wainwright, J				91			9	
Walker, J		34	3	23	29			11
Per cent of time	27	7	8	12	15	16	12	3

The table for the first war contains twenty-seven names. What is immediately striking is that over half of the officers concerned spent over 70 per cent of their frigate service on *one* station. Most of them were in the East or West Indies, or the Mediterranean: that is, on a distant station. Only four captains commanded frigates mainly in the Channel or North Sea. It is also quickly apparent from the percentage of time spent on each station which were the most active for the frigate captains – the Channel Station, followed by the West Indies and the Mediterranean.

The second table contains forty-one names, a larger number as we would expect, because the period is longer and the navy larger. Of these, seventeen captains (41 per cent) spent more than 70 per cent of their frigate service on one station, eleven of them (27 per cent) on a distant station. The percentage of frigate time spent in the Channel and North Sea was virtually the same as during the first war. The main change seems to have been in the longevity of commissions on distant foreign stations.

Taking both periods together, nearly 40 per cent of typical captains served at some time in the West Indies. It is therefore, easy to see why that station featured so largely in the concerns or ambitions of officers of the period. Service in the West Indies could give that important break, as we have seen in the case of Christopher Cole. The opposite side of the coin is well illustrated by the case of Captain Josias Rogers. Rogers made a substantial sum from prize money as a sloop commander during the American War, sufficient to be able to purchase a small estate near Lymington and to build a new house,[10] only to face ruin when his bank suddenly crashed around 1790. According to his biographer, Gilpin, Rogers responded very jauntily to this calamity by claiming that he would simply go to sea and get more. When war broke out in 1793, Rogers appears to have lobbied Sir John Jervis[11] (even turning down the offer of a ship of the line) until he was given a frigate, the *Quebec,* and joined the Jervis-Grey expedition to the West Indies, where, 'In a little time he took nine ships, which was a greater number, than all the other cruisers together had taken.'[12] There was the chance of profit, but there was also a risk. Josias Rogers took the risk hoping not only to remake his fortune from prize money but also to gain from the mortality rate on that station by taking his younger brother with him as a junior officer. His gamble did not pay off, for both men were dead within weeks of each other. Ironically a number of other frigate captains ran this risk and survived the immediate peril only to succumb to the longer term breakdown of health that followed malaria.[13]

Less frigate time was dedicated to the West Indies during the second war than during the first. Furthermore, long individual commissions in the West Indies tended to concentrate in the earlier period.[14] This reflects the fact that the major expeditions to secure the West Indies, and the British colonies there, really all took place during the first war.[15] In spite of the efforts of the Grey-Jervis expedition of

1793-4, the French recovered their bases at Guadeloupe and St Lucia and were able to spread their influence over other islands, increasing the threat of native revolt. From Guadeloupe the French were able to send both privateers and frigates out to attack British trade[16] so the continued presence of a strong force of British frigates on this station was essential through both wars.

Frigate presence on the East Indies station increased slightly during the second war. In many ways the East Indies station with its long trade routes and valuable cargoes made it an ideal cruising ground for the frigates. The second war did, of course, see the Mauritius and Java campaigns, and action against piracy. However, when the number of captains involved is considered (as opposed to the proportion of time), a greater number were sent to the East Indies, including the Cape, after 1801 – 24 per cent of the captains as opposed to 15 per cent for the first war. In other words, after 1801 more captains were sent out there, but for shorter commissions.

As with the West Indies, the major battle for the Mediterranean as a whole was concentrated in the years preceding 1805. This is not to say that there was not much activity thereafter, nor is it to devalue the enormously important role played by Collingwood. With both of these stations, however, it is clear that other theatres of war became a higher priority after 1801. Although the danger from across the North Sea was reduced (though not in any way mitigated) by the Royal Navy's victories at Camperdown, the two battles of Copenhagen and several landings of troops on the Baltic coast,[17] there continued to be much activity in the North Sea and virtually a continual presence in the Baltic after 1807. During both wars there were major, and usually disastrous, amphibious campaigns within the North Sea station,[18] which were demanding on both frigates and frigate captains. These deployments were not popular. Sir Michael Seymour in the frigate *Amethyst* was diverted from his favourite station – cruising in the Channel and Biscay – to assist with the Scheldt expedition in 1809. He wrote to his brother-in-law, Captain Edward Hawker, describing himself as 'hurried and worried to death with the strange accumulation of this expedition intended against the 'Scheldt', shipping etc. etc. at Antwerp, all suddenly and confusedly brought together ... *Amethyst* was sent from Plymouth, where I was sadly hurried, ... I have no wish this way but to get Westward.'[19] Nevertheless, with so much activity on that station, it is hardly surprising that frigate presence in the North Sea seems to have remained constant.

In the second war there was a greater frigate presence in the Channel and Channel ports (34 per cent as opposed to 30 per cent). Again, there are clear reasons for this. With the collapse of the Peace of Amiens and very obvious signs of a planned French invasion, British naval strategy was for a while dominated by the need to guard against an invasion flotilla crossing the Channel. This statistical comparison, of course, relies on the inclusion of the number of captains in 'Port' which fell from 8 per cent of total time to 3 per cent during the second war. It is well known that from the spring of 1800, when St Vincent was appointed Commander-in-Chief of the Channel Fleet and during his subsequent tenure at the Admiralty, captains and their frigates were kept out of dock and away from port as much as possible. This was a policy which was deliberately introduced to counteract what was seen by St Vincent as a growing threat of mutiny and a lack of discipline amongst the officers in the Channel Fleet.[20] The policy caused considerable complaint and grievance. In November 1800, for example, Lady Martin (mother of Sir Thomas Byam Martin, captain of the 18-pounder frigate *Fisgard*) wrote to Sir Henry Martin of her son:

he is very much hurried preparing for sea, though it seems impossible for him to go next Friday as ordered, as he has defects in his ship that must be made good, particularly in a mast. He and all the fleet are (with reason) outrageous with Lord St Vincent; he hurries them so much, that the seamen, after their long cruises, are working night and day, and no time for them to get on shore. [21]

In fact it might have been expected that the second war would show an even higher level of Channel activity than the first, given the threat of invasion (and in a sense it does, because numerically there are more frigates operating in the Channel than during the first war). However, the statistic for the Channel activity for the first war may be distorted because of the activity of the frigate squadrons like those under Edward Pellew, John Borlase Warren and Richard Strachan. Francis Cole, whose name appears listed as a typical frigate captain during the first war, was one of those officers who served with Pellew's squadron, and he spent approximately 81 per cent of his time on that station. Ironically, his name appears in the table almost by accident, his career having been cut short by his sudden death in 1798. Many of the captains who served with the Western Squadrons went on to have much longer frigate careers: Philip Durham, Robert Barlow, Richard Keats, Robert Carthew Reynolds, Israel Pellew, James Young and Graham Moore.

The most obvious statistical difference between the two tables relates to time spent on the American seaboard. This reflects the greater presence demanded on that station following the outbreak of war with America in 1812. In actual fact, the proportion of time spent by frigate captains on that station was probably even greater than indicated here, because the records in the Admiralty List Books become fragmented towards the end of the period, just at the time that greater concentration was being focused there. Richard Byron, it can be seen, spent approximately 93 per cent of his frigate service there commanding the *Belvidera*. He commissioned the *Belvidera* in February 1810, and she was not paid off until 1814.[22] John Dick in the *Penelope* was part of Admiral Sir John Borlase Warren's squadron[23] from the middle of 1807 until early 1811, during which time he seems to have spent much time between Halifax and Martinique. He was part of Philip Beaver's squadron escorting troops to the latter island and was closely involved in the attack there in 1809, securing Fort Trinité with a party of his crew.[24] Lord James Townshend, like Byron, was also part of Broke's squadron on that station.

BACKGROUND AND INTEREST

Few of those listed above and who were included in Marshall's *Naval Biography* seem to have made any mention of their background, and only a small number appear to have been well connected in any sense at the time of their entry into the navy. There is, as might be expected, a scattering of men who were either following in family tradition or were influenced by their father's career in entering the navy. Edward Buller's father, for example, was both a Member of Parliament and a member of the Admiralty for many years. John Harvey's father was a post captain and his uncle was Admiral Sir Henry Harvey. Other officers were connected with the peerage (*eg* Lord Townshend), diplomats (*eg* H W Bayntun) or other well placed relatives. Here one feels obliged to mention Christopher Cole again, who was a younger brother of Frank Cole, a close friend of Edward Pellew, and who had another brother serving as domestic chaplain to HRH the Duke of Clarence.

Patronage

It is well recognised that the patronage of a senior officer in a powerful position was crucial to obtaining a desirable appointment. For example, Henry Hill and H W Bayntun were protégés of Sir John Jervis, and Sir Roger Curtis acted as patron to J C Crawford. Edward Griffith was not only a protégé of Jervis, but he also appears to have been related to Admiral Sir John Colpoys. These officers were able to take full advantage of any special opportunity which was given to them by their patrons and used this to advance their careers. Sometimes the patron was able to assist on more than one occasion. Charles Richardson, for example, was a protégé of Viscount Duncan, who specifically requested his services in his flagship. Richardson also served on a number of occasions with Sir Richard Strachan, both as a midshipman and then, years later, as a lieutenant when Strachan was not only a rear-admiral of the blue but had also been awarded his KCB.

Some officers struggled in spite of strong backing. John Hancock was supported in his early career by both Captain Robert Kingsmill (a Member of Parliament 1779-80 and 1784-90, and a rear-admiral in 1793) and Sir John Colpoys (rear-admiral in

1794). Having passed his lieutenant's examinations in 1785, he continued serving with Colpoys until 1787 when he decided that the continuing peace gave him little prospect of promotion or better employment. Disillusioned, he decided to quit the service.[25] In 1790 during the excitement of the Nootka Sound crisis he once again joined Colpoys, who was now commanding a 74-gun ship. Despite Colpoy's patronage Hancock failed to secure advancement in the general promotion which followed, and once again resigned. After a short period friends persuaded him to change his mind and in 1798 he found himself serving under the commander-in-chief of the Jamaica station, Admiral Sir Hyde Parker, 'whose lasting friendship he had now the good fortune to obtain'.[26] Sadly for Hancock, Hyde Parker was then recalled before his friendship could result in promotion. Hancock continued with what, it must be emphasised, was a far from mediocre career until 1804 when his services under Sir William Sidney Smith earned him a letter of approbation from Lord Melville, then First Lord of the Admiralty. In the following year Melville was impeached and Sir Charles Middleton (Lord Barham) became First Lord. Hancock simply struggled on until 1815 when, like so many others, he was faced with definitive redundancy. Ironically, Hancock's service was remarkable and there is no doubt that he was not only an excellent seaman, a brave and skilled military commander, but also a humane captain. It is certainly no wonder at all that he should have come to the attention of senior and powerful officers. Unluckily, those officers were never in a position to help him when it was necessary. Furthermore, it must be seriously doubted that Hancock's example was unparalleled.

What Hancock's career illustrates is the fact that, although 'interest' could be of enormous value to a captain, it was not enough on its own. As noted above, only a minority of the sample (whose entries in Marshall's *Royal Naval Biography* have been checked) seem to have had any significant 'interest' other than that attracted by a display of talent. A talented officer could still get appointments, particularly as it would have been in the interest of any admiral or commander-in-chief to have men commanding frigates who were good seamen, enthusiastic, energetic and popular with their crews. All other things being equal, good seamen were less likely to lose their ships and stood a better chance of outsailing enemy vessels, whether merchantmen or men-of-war, and they were more likely to have the confidence of their officers and crew. An enthusiastic and energetic captain would not have to be repeatedly 'encouraged' to take his ship to sea.[27]

Sometimes even the best seamen captains could fail to please. Among the papers of Samuel Hood at the National Maritime Museum is his letterbook compiled whilst commanding the *Juno* and a small frigate squadron off the coast of Smyrna in 1793-4 and containing letters to his commander-in-chief, Admiral Lord William

Hotham. One, a letter dated 24 November 1794, positively howls with protest that he is not delaying putting to sea, and complaining of the poor local craftsmanship and lack of timber to replace two of his frigates' bowsprits. A captain who was popular with his crew, provided that he was not unlucky, would be more likely to achieve success by any criteria, and it is no coincidence that some of the most successful frigate captains also appear to have been popular with their crews (most of the time!). This recognition of a captain's talent would of course be rewarded even more if the captain concerned was thought to be lucky with prizes, of which the admiral got a share. Ability and talent reflected glory as well as attracting it.

FRIGATE PROGRESSION

About 48 per cent of those captains selected on the basis of average frigate service, commanded two frigates; 23 per cent commanded three frigates; and 29 per cent just one. It should not be assumed that because an officer commanded just one frigate, he was in any way less valued. His one frigate might have been a particularly crack ship; a desirable command which he might wish to hold onto for as long as possible and which served his purposes. Samuel Ballard, for example, though not a typical frigate captain was, after a short period as acting captain of the *Tremendous*, 74, given command of the 12-pounder frigate *Pearl* in March 1796. His command of her was continuous until February 1802, when she was paid off; a period of six years. The *Pearl* was an old frigate, but being one of the highly regarded *Niger* class frigates, her performance was still up to par. She was fast, highly manoeuvrable, with plenty of room for the accommodation of the crew below decks and she was dry.[28] Marshall tells us that in his six-year commission in the *Pearl* Ballard destroyed or captured eighty enemy vessels; and the *Pearl* served on many different stations. It is, therefore, not surprising that Ballard does not seem to have been pressing for a different frigate. Within the sample of typical frigate captains can be cited the example of Francis Cole, who commanded the captured French frigate *Revolutionnaire* for three years, almost until his death. *Revolutionnaire* [29] was a very large, fast frigate – on the Cork station she was nick-named 'the Irish racehorse' – and at the time of her capture she was thought to be the largest frigate in the possession of the Royal Navy.[30] It is doubtful that Cole wanted a better ship for, had this been the case, his commodore and great friend, Edward Pellew, would certainly have seen to it.

Frigate captains were certainly not hesitant in complaining if they felt their ship to be poor or inadequate. Robert Barrie, a great favourite of William Windham Grenville, Baron Grenville, used an argument along these lines to great effect. In 1806, when Grenville became Prime Minister (and his brother Thomas became

First Lord of the Admiralty), Barrie wrote to him complaining about the frigate which he had commissioned but a few monthly previously, the old and rather small 28-gun 9-pounder frigate *Brilliant*. (It is worth mentioning at this point that Barrie, who was posted in April 1802, had not been given an appointment at all until Grenville was returned to office. His commissioning of the *Brilliant* was obviously a result of some heavy lobbying of his friend.) On 17 April 1806, Barrie wrote apologising to Grenville for calling upon his favour once again,

> but I am urged to do so by my disappointment and chagrin – I can gain neither honor or profit in the *Brilliant*. Very lately I chased for two days a Privateer and her Prize without being able to come up even with the Merchant ship, and two days ago the *Boadicea* (n.b. no flyer) fairly ran us out of sight in eight hours.[31]

By August 1806, Barrie was commanding the 18-pounder frigate *Pomone*.

It must be acknowledged that the *Brilliant* was an old and comparatively poorly armed frigate by this time. However, what is revealing about this particular case is the fact that the *Brilliant* had served several of her earlier commanders very well. Henry Blackwood, in particular, made great use of her when he outmanoeuvred and fought off two superior French frigates off Santa Cruz in July 1798.[32] Therefore, one has to be circumspect about the reasons Barrie's behind complaint – especially in the light of subsequent events.[33]

In the vast majority of cases where an officer commanded more than one frigate, he progressed from smaller to heavier frigates. Naturally all captains wanted to have a ship which stood the best possible chance of success against the enemy. In terms of design characteristics this meant speed and manoeuvrability, and also best possible armament. The tendency, then, was to hope for better (at this time usually synonymous with larger) ships as a career progressed. The following tables show that this was clearly the rule, though there are exceptions. Richard Dalling Dunn, for example, commanded the 38-gun 18-pounder frigate *Armide* after the 40-gun 18-pounder *Acasta*. However, the *Acasta* was one of only a handful of frigates of that rate, and they were in any case only marginally more powerful than the 38-gun ships. It is unlikely that Dunn would have regarded the move as a regression. What is equally significant is that in the several years between commanding the *Acasta* and *Armide*, Dunn commanded a couple of ships of the line. On the other hand, there would appear to be no obvious explanation why Henry Hope should have moved from the relatively new 18-pounder frigate *Leonidas* to the older 12-pounder *Topaze* (although since he was in the former for only 6-8 months it might have been a temporary appointment).

Table 4.3. *Armament of Frigates Commanded by Typical Frigate Captains (First War)*

	First Frigate	Second frigate	Third Frigate
Alms, J	28-gun, 9pdr	36-gun, 12pdr	
Bagot, R	32-gun, 18pdr	32-gun, 12pdr	36-gun, 18pdr
Bayntun, H W[34]	28-gun, 9pdr	36-gun, 12pdr	32-gun, 12pdr
Berkeley, V C	44 gun	36-gun, 18pdr	
Bowen, W	36-gun, 18pdr		
Buller, E	44 gun	36-gun, 18pdr	
Cole, F	36-gun, 18pdr		
Downman, H	34-gun, 12pdr		
Drew, J	32-gun, 18pdr		
Fayerman, F	40-gun, 18pdr		
Freemantle, T	28-gun, 9pdr	38-gun, 18pdr	
Griffith, E	32-gun, 12pdr	38-gun, 18pdr	
Harvey, J	32-gun, 12pdr		
Harvey, T	28-gun, 9pdr	32-gun, 12pdr	
Lane, R	32-gun, 12pdr	40-gun, 18pdr	
Lee, Sir R	28-gun, 9pdr	32-gun, 12pdr	
Linzee, S	28-gun, 9pdr	36-gun, 12pdr	
Ogilvie, W	36-gun, 12pdr		
Raper, H	36-gun, 12pdr		
Robinson, M	28-gun, 9pdr	38 guns [35]	38-gun, 18pdr
Rowley, C	28-gun, 9pdr	32-gun, 12pdr	38-gun, 18pdr
Seater, J	36-gun, 12pdr	36-gun, 12pdr	44 guns [36]
Stephens, G	36-gun, 12pdr		
Turner, J	28-gun, 9pdr	32-gun, 12pdr	
Waller, T	36-gun, 18pdr		
White, C	28-gun, 9pdr		
Woodley, J	28-gun, 9pdr	36-gun, 18pdr	

During the first war there was still a heavy reliance on 28-gun 9-pounder ships as first frigate commands. Only about 25 per cent of typical frigate commanders were given the heavier 18-pounder frigates as their first command. By 1800 half of the 28-gun frigates had been paid off, and then the remainder were gradually withdrawn from service until 1813 when the class disappeared with the sale of the old *Carysfort*. None of the captains in this group was given a 9-pounder frigate as his second frigate command and, indeed, the table clearly shows the transition towards larger and heavier frigates.

TABLE 4.4. *Armament of Frigates Commanded by Typical Frigate Captains (Second War)*

	First Frigate	Second Frigate	Third Frigate
Ballard, V	28-gun, 9pdr	38-gun, 18pdr	
Bullen, C	38-gun, 18pdr		
Byron, R	36-gun, 18pdr		
Cochrane, Lord	32-gun, 12pdr	38-gun, 18pdr	
Cole, C	32-gun, 12pdr	36-gun, 18pdr	36-gun, 18pdr
Crawford, J	36-gun, 18pdr	38-gun, 18pdr	38-gun, 18pdr
Cumberland, W	36-gun, 18pdr	36-gun, 18pdr	
Curtis, L	36-gun, 12pdr	36-gun, 18pdr	38-gun, 18pdr
Dick, J	36-gun, 18pdr		
Deans, J W D	36-gun, 18pdr		
Dunn, R D	32-gun, 12pdr	40-gun, 18pdr	38-gun, 18pdr
Grant, C	32-gun, 12pdr	38-gun, 18pdr	
Hamond, G E	36-gun, 18pdr	38-gun, 18pdr	
Hancock, J	48-gun, 18pdr[37]	36-gun, 18pdr	
Harris, G	38 gun[38]	38-gun, 18pdr	
Hawker, E	36-gun, 18pdr		
Heywood, E	32-gun, 12pdr	36-gun, 18pdr	
Hill, H	32-gun, 12pdr	38-gun, 18pdr	
Hope, H	36-gun, 18pdr	38-gun, 12pdr	44-gun, 24pdr[39]
Kerr, A	32-gun, 18pdr	40-gun, 18pdr	
Livingstone, T	44-gun[40]	38-gun, 12pdr	
Losack, W	36-gun, 18pdr		
Lloyd, R	38-gun, 18pdr	38-gun, 18pdr	
Lumley, J	28-gun, 9pdr	32-gun, 18pdr	
Mason, F	38-gun, 18pdr	38-gun, 18pdr	
Mends, R	32-gun, 12pdr	36-gun, 12pdr	38-gun, 18pdr
Miller, G	32-gun, 12pdr	38-gun, 18pdr	
Montagu, W[41]	32-gun, 12pdr	38-gun, 18pdr	
Oswald, J	38-gun, 18pdr	40-gun, 18pdr	36-gun, 18pdr
Pelly, C	28-gun, 9pdr	32-gun, 18pdr	
Quilliam, J	32-gun, 12pdr	38-gun, 18pdr	
Raggett, R	38-gun, 18pdr		
Richardson, C	28-gun, 9pdr	36-gun, 18pdr	
Rose, J	32-gun, 12pdr	32-gun, 12pdr	36-gun, 18pdr
Serrell, J	36-gun, 18pdr		
Skene, A	28-gun, 9pdr	38-gun, 18pdr	38-gun, 18pdr
Stackpoole, H	36-gun, 18pdr	38-gun, 18pdr	
Stuart, J	36-gun, 12pdr	36-gun, 18pdr	
Townshend, Lord	32-gun, 12pdr		
Wainwright, J	36-gun, 12pdr		
Walker, J	28-gun, 9pdr	32-gun, 18pdr	36-gun, 18pdr

During the second war, only 15 per cent of first frigate commands were 9-pounder frigates (as opposed to 44 per cent in the first war). The 18-pounder frigate was beginning to predominate; furthermore, we can see an increase in the number of 38-gun frigates, some being allocated to captains as their first commands.

Continuous Service

The progression of frigate captains from smaller to heavier frigate is only really significant if that progress forms a more or less continuous period of activity within each individual officer's career. In other words, if the three years of frigate service is actually scattered through a career of, say, ten to fifteen years, it would become less significant. During the first war 70 per cent of the typical frigate captains served in either one frigate for the whole period or moved from one frigate to another with very little intervening unemployment (*ie* nothing longer than six months).[42] In addition, three captains actually commanded larger ships of the line between periods of frigate command. Charles Rowley, for example, commanded the *Prince George*, 90, whilst both John Seater and Samuel Hood Linzee commanded ships of 64 guns. Importantly, all three officers subsequently returned to command frigates thereafter, reinforcing the assertion that frigate command was not regarded as having lesser status than fleet service in a ship of the line.

Even where captains appear to have experienced longer periods of unemployment, the picture may not be as straightforward as it appears at first sight. Richard Lane, for example, seems to have been without a ship for six months, according to the Admiralty Lists, but it is possible that he may have had temporary command of the *Nymphe* during this time. Thomas Fremantle, likewise, may have commanded the *Inconstant* during a gap in his service. Edward Griffith, commanded the *Niger* frigate for several months at the end of 1797. According to the Admiralty records he was then unemployed until he was given the *Diamond* frigate in 1799. According to Marshall,[43] however, the gap in his employment record seems to coincide with nearly a year as temporary commander of the new fir-built frigate *Triton*, after its commander John Gore was badly injured by a block falling from the rigging. Griffith was the nephew of Admiral Sir John Colpoys and received his break into frigate command following the mutiny at the Nore in which he played a critical part.[44] Fortunately these anomalies are rare.

Of those captains in the first war sample only Bayntun, Berkeley and Lee seem to have had significant periods of unemployment during their frigate service. In summary therefore it can be asserted that over 70 per cent of typical frigate captains underwent virtually continuous frigate service during the first war.

Of those forty-one captains in the sample for the second war, 56 per cent experienced continuous service during that period. Eleven captains would appear to have commanded line of battle ships during gaps in frigate service: that is, 27 per cent as against 11 per cent in the first war. Christopher Cole, for example, commanded the *Culloden*, 74 in the five year period between his frigate commands. Graham Eden Hamond also commanded a 74, whilst John Hancock (1), Charles Richardson (2) and Hassard Stackpoole all commanded 80-gun ships between frigate service. Seven captains would appear to have experienced significant unemployment in between frigate service.[45]

The conclusion must be that during the first war the typical frigate captain might expect a greater chance of three years' continuous employment within the frigate service. During the second war there was less chance of continuous frigate service, but there was a much greater opportunity of serving in a ship of the line in between frigates. This may reflect the overcrowding of the officer corps and the increasing demand for employment. The experienced frigate commander could often expect some form of active service employment, even though the competition for a frigate became harder after 1801. The rate of unemployment remained more or less the same in both wars and officers may have been obliged to accept other types of command as a way of keeping in favour and demonstrating their commitment to the service.

Towards the end of the wars it appears to have become accepted that commanding a troopship, for example, was a necessary preliminary to frigate command. Even a frigate in active service might be ordered to strike its guns into the hold and, armed *en flute*, prepare to take on the temporary role of a troopship. This was particularly the case from the outbreak of the Peninsular War. However, the officer commanding a frigate armed *en flute* at least had the reassurance that his ship would be fully restored as a cruising frigate before too long. The post captain in command of an old, and reduced, ship of the line was in a much more trying position, since it was unlikely that the ship would revert to its more warlike role. An example of this is found in the career of John Phillimore, who in 1810 was given the troopship *Diadem* (an old 64-gun ship armed *en flute*, with most of her guns removed). Captain Andrew Drew, who wrote an obituary of Phillimore commented that the *Diadem* was 'not a very agreeable service for a dashing young officer' but as aspiring officers tended to refuse the lesser commands the Admiralty made troopship command a stepping stone to promotion 'and with post captains the high road to the command of a frigate'. [46]

Earlier Career

At some point a question must arise as to the relationship of pre-war command and seniority to length of frigate service. This was touched upon previously, but here the focus is on the average or typical frigate captain. About 9 per cent of typical frigate captains serving between 1793 and 1815 were actually posted before 1793, but of these six officers only three actually had commands before the outbreak of war. These happened to be James Alms, John Drew, and Sir Edward Buller, who are also the most senior officers in the sample. These three were promoted through the ranks much quicker than Berkeley, Robinson or Cole who were promoted before 1790 but not given commands. This implies a link between speed of promotion and employment both before and during the war. Certainly at the beginning of the war seniority played a role in employment. Of the 122 captains posted before 1793, thereby being senior captains on the list, some 17 per cent served in frigates after 1793 for longer than the average term (as opposed to 5 per cent serving for the average term).

Later Career

An indication of how highly an officer's capabilities were regarded may have been given by his service after frigate command. A favoured officer might expect to have been given further employment after his frigate time and, of course, the reverse may also be true. A poor frigate commander may not have been an attractive prospect as captain of a ship of the line. Without closely assessing each officer's biographical details it would be impossible to be sure about the application of the latter point; but it is relatively easy to identify which officers, upon completion of between three and four years service in frigates, were re-employed in ships of the line. The confusing factor here, of course, is the end of the war. Typical frigate captains completing their frigate time in the later years of the war, when there were an increased number of captains clamouring for employment, were less likely to be successful in their applications than those completing frigate time in the first war. This is confirmed by the fact that 52 per cent of typical frigate captains serving during the first war went on to command ships of the line before 1815. Of those frigate captains serving during the second war, only 37 per cent succeeded in this way. Ultimately, as might be expected, a higher proportion of officers in the first war sample went on to reach flag rank than those in the second: that is, 71 per cent as opposed to 49 per cent. Of those first war officers reaching flag rank, all but two[47] achieved this before 1815. Those who did not reach flag rank were either dead or superannuated.

CHAPTER
V

THE STAR CAPTAINS

I N CHAPTER III it was shown that a small number of captains were given
extraordinarily long periods in command of frigates (Table 3.3). It was also
shown that some captains were still commanding frigates after they had been
on the list of post captains for at least twelve years (Table 3.2), thereby reaching a
position of some seniority. In this chapter those officers will be identified and their
careers assessed. If the average length of frigate service was approximately 3.5 years
and approximately 91 per cent of frigate captains served for not more than 6 years,
it follows that the fifty-three remaining officers were extraordinary, even if judged
only by their frigate time.

Having identified the longest-serving frigate captains using the statistical data
from the employment records, we will also have identified the officers who, for
whatever reason, may have been best suited for frigate command. Naturally, for
various reasons this list will not be exclusive, as there were excellent frigate captains
whose careers were shorter than those listed in Table 5.1. The next task is to review
the factors within these officers' careers that made them especially suited to this type
of service. Some of the names on this list will already be familiar to the student of
naval history, particularly where those names are associated with frigate actions.
However, the point to stress here is that successful frigate actions were the product
of a good captain, crew and frigate – the culmination of skill, seamanship and
leadership/command. A successful action could not make a good captain out of a
poor one.

RATE OF PROMOTION, SOCIAL BACKGROUND AND INTEREST
Whether social background was a significant factor in the make-up of good frigate
captains is an obvious first question. It is important because if all of the names on the
above list came from well connected families, it could reasonably be argued that the
length of their careers was simply the result of interest. Speed of promotion is usually

TABLE 5.1. *Frigate Captains with more than Six Years Frigate Service*[1]

Name	Date Posted	Frigate Service (Years)	Years between Posting and End of Frigate Service*
Richard Goodwin Keats **	June 1789	7.00	12
Charles Hamilton **	Nov 1790	8.75	12
Thomas Williams **	Nov 1790	8.00	
Lawrence W Halstead	May 1791	7.25	
Harry Burrard Neale **	Feb 1793	7.25	
Joseph Sidney Yorke **	Feb 1793	8.00	
The Hon Arthur Kay Legge	Feb 1793	8.00	
Robert Barlow **	May 1793	7.75	
Philip Charles Durham **	June 1793	8.25	
George Cockburn **	Feb 1794	8.75	
Thomas Graves (4)[2]	March 1794	9.25	
Graham Moore **	April 1794	8.25	
Richard King (2) **	May 1794	7.50	
Edward James Foote **	June 1794	8.00	
James Newman	Aug 1794	7.25	
Philip Wilkinson	Sept 1794	7.25	
Charles John Mansfield	Oct 1794	7.00	
John Gore (2) **	Nov 1794	9.25	
The Hon Charles Herbert	April 1795	8.50	
Henry Blackwood **	June 1795	8.25	
John Erskine Douglas	June 1795	9.25	
Ross Donnelly **	June 1795	10.00	12
Thomas Le Marchant Gossellin **	July 1795	7.25	
James Macnamara (2) **	Oct 1795	8.00	
Stephen Poyntz	Oct 1796	7.00	
Robert Laurie	July 1797	10.00	13
Edward W C R Owen **	April 1798	11.50	15
David Atkins	May 1798	8.50	
The Hon Thomas Bladen Capel **	Dec 1798	8.50	12
Charles Adam **	June 1799	7.50	
Adam Mackenzie	Sept 1799	8.75	14
Thomas James Maling	Sept 1800	8.50	
George Wolfe	Dec 1800	8.50	
William Selby	Dec 1800	8.00	
George Mundy	Feb 1801	8.00	
Henry Vansittart **	Feb 1801	8.25	
Philip Bowes Vere Broke **	Feb 1801	8.50	13
George Sayer (2)	Feb 1801	7.25	13
Frederick L Maitland **	March 1801	8.00	
William Parker (2) **	Oct 1801	7.50	
William Hoste **	Jan 1802	7.75	12
Stephen Thomas Digby	April 1802	8.25	12
The Hon Duncan P Bouverie	April 1802	7.50	
Richard Hawkins	April 1802	7.00	12
Philip Somerville	April 1802	11.75	12
Clotworthy Upton	April 1802	7.50	
Bridges Watkinson Taylor	Aug 1802	7.75	
Charles Malcolm **	Dec 1802	7.50	12
The Hon George Elliott (2) **	Jan 1804	9.25	
James Hillyar **	Feb 1804	7.75	
Lord George Stuart (2)	March 1804	8.75	
John Tower	May 1804	7.25	
Fleetwood B R Pellew **	Oct 1808[3]	7.00	

* where 12 years or more. ** after the name indicates the officer had an entry in the old *Dictionary of National Biography*. Twenty-eight of the officers on this list are recognised in this fashion.

a good indicator of interest, but it is also a sign of ability: 67 per cent of the officers listed above were promoted in seven or less years and 34 per cent in four years or less. Therefore, only about a third benefited from noticeably rapid promotion. Several officers, however, should be noted for a spectacular race through the ranks: George Cockburn (one year), the Hon Charles Herbert (two years), the Hon Thomas Bladen Capel (one year), Charles Adam (one year), William Parker (two years). These officers were extremely well connected, with powerful interest.

George Cockburn was a favourite of Nelson and had won the approval of Jervis, who was commander-in-chief in the Mediterranean where Cockburn's promotions took place. Cockburn's rapid promotion was unquestionably based upon his abilities, particularly as a seaman,[4] and although he certainly had the patronage of Lord Hood when he entered the navy, much of his powerful interest was won by merit. Cockburn's father was an MP and some of his brothers had success in their own careers: his eldest brother became a general and later Governor of Bermuda; another brother, also a general, became Governor of Curacoa and Honduras; others achieved high rank in the church and consular service.

The Hon Charles Herbert was the second son of the Earl of Carnarvon and had a number of powerful connections, including the Byng family; while the Hon Thomas Bladen Capel was the youngest son of the Earl of Essex, and served as a lieutenant under Nelson at the Battle of the Nile. It was Capel whom Nelson selected to deliver his dispatches overland after the battle, thereby marking him for extraordinary favour for, not only had Nelson promoted him commander immediately after the battle, but by sending him home with dispatches, he ensured his protégé yet further promotion. The fact is that Capel had only been promoted lieutenant in April 1797. Nelson made him a commander on 2 October 1798, and less than three months later he was a post captain.[5] This favour demonstrates an adroit move by Nelson, for when Capel as commander of the *Mutine* brig was sent to Naples to begin his journey overland to Britain, his second-in-command was lieutenant William Hoste (another Nelson protégé) who, upon the departure of Capel, was promoted to become a commander and captain of the brig.[6]

Charles Adam and William Parker both benefited from powerful naval interest. Charles Adam was the son of the Rt Hon William Adam, Lord Chief Commissioner of the Scottish Jury Court.[7] He also just happened to be the nephew of Admiral George Keith Elphinstone (later Lord Keith) under whom he served and was promoted on several occasions. Adam's promotion might have been considerably faster. His uncle, Elphinstone, promoted him to acting captain of the *Carysfort* frigate in the East Indies. Upon his return to England, he was rather bluntly informed by the First Lord that owing to an irregularity in his certificates his lieutenant's commission had been disallowed and he was actually only a midshipman! He re-sat his lieutenant's examination the next day and in a short time became a post captain for the second time before the age of 20.[8] William Parker was the nephew of John Jervis (later Earl St Vincent), and although this may be sufficient to explain his rapid promotion, it is worth noting that his early service, as a midshipman, was in the West Indies where the mortality rate, together with the necessity of placing midshipmen in charge of prizes, meant that an energetic young officer would soon be noticed and promoted. This would certainly have been the case with Parker who had a good friend in his own captain, Sir John Duckworth, who was also a friend of the family.[9] Parker does not seem to have been related to the contemporary flag officer of the same name, but there is evidence that he benefited from the interest of his grandfather, the Earl of Macclesfield.[10]

The value of social or political connections should not be over-stressed, although these may have played some part in the speed of promotion. Social background would obviously continue to have an effect throughout the captain's career, notwithstanding the fact that he was on the automatic ladder of promotion. Interest founded on social or political connections, in theory, could have helped to secure employment – but to what extent did this happen? If interest was the crucial factor which it is often made out to be, there would be a concentration of well-connected officers among the list of long serving frigate captains. In fact, among the fifty-three names identified above, there were certainly a number with strong interest behind them. Approximately eleven captains were closely connected with the peerage or other ranks of the landed gentry. Sir Harry Neale (*aka* Burrard), for example, was the nephew of a baronet (and actually inherited during the course of his career as a frigate captain). The Hon Arthur Kay Legge was the son of the Earl of Dartmouth; Sir Charles Hamilton was related to the Duke of Brandon; the Hon Charles Herbert was the second son of the Earl of Carnarvon; Sir Henry Blackwood was the son of an Irish baronet; the Hon Thomas Bladen Capel was the son of the Earl of Essex; Frederick L Maitland was a cousin of the Earl of Lauderdale; the Hon Duncan Pleydell Bouverie was a son of the Earl of Radnor; the Hon George Elliot, son of the Earl of Minto; Lord George Stuart (2) was grandson of the Marquess of Bute.

However, there were also post captains of aristocratic stock who did not flourish in their naval career,[11] and as a consequence their names do not appear on this list: for, whilst powerful social or political interest could be enormously helpful, it was not enough on its own to guarantee employment. There usually had to be a degree of professional interest also, and this tended to accumulate where there was evidence of professional ability. Frederick Lewis Maitland, for example, was well connected, being a cousin of the Earl of Lauderdale. St Vincent had been a friend of his late father, and as a consequence promised to promote him whenever the opportunity should occur.[12] But in addition to this, Maitland was an exemplary seaman and excelled as a cruiser, both when a commander and later as a frigate captain. It was not without reason that Captain Michael Seymour of the *Amethyst* wrote admiringly to his brother-in-law, Captain Edward Hawker of the *Melampus*: 'In Company with Maitland, who is the best cruiser I ever met with, we have taken *La Patrie* [letter of marque of 22 guns], ... *Le Serpent* [letter of marque], ... *La Caroline* brig, ... *La Vanturier*, schooner, letter of Marque...'[13]

The difference between family connection and professional interest is well illustrated in the example of a cousin of F L Maitland, Captain John Maitland (2). John Maitland not only benefited from the family connection but he was also the second lieutenant of the *Lively* under the acting command of Captain George Burlton when she encountered the French frigate *Tourterelle*. The following quotation from a letter dated 17 March 1795, just a few days after the action, from the King to Spencer, First Lord of the Admiralty, illustrates the matter rather nicely:

I am much pleased with the gallant action of the *Lively* with the *Tourterelle* French frigate transmitted to me by Earl Spencer, and with Captain Burlton having been in consequence promoted to the rank of post captain, and the first Lieutenant to that of Master and Commander. As the second Lieutenant Mr Maitland conducted himself very well I trust he will soon meet with the same favour; being a man of good family will I hope also be of advantage in the consideration, as it is certainly wise as much as possible to give encouragement, if they personally deserve it, to gentlemen.[14]

Maitland's promotion to commander did not actually occur until December 1796. A good word from even the King himself could not guarantee that an officer could bypass the usual practice of the service *unless* he was particularly able and there were senior officers who wanted him promoted. The use of the provision 'if they personally deserve it' should not be overlooked. There is probably no reason for believing that Spencer was any less discriminating about promotion than, say, St Vincent, who came from the other side of the party-political divide and succeeded him at the Admiralty; but there is no doubt that he was critical of Spencer's record on this subject.[15] John Maitland later served as a frigate captain for a total of just over five years.

The question of social background and frigate command is further illuminated in the correspondence of St Vincent, in a letter dated April 1802 to Admiral Markham:

> Captain Capel will look to a higher rate than the *Aurora*: she will do for
> Captain Wolfe, Lord Spencer's friend, who I wish very much to employ ...
> Captain Fane has been very strenuously recommended for employment; he
> being an honourable, his fitness for a storeship is doubtful, therefore you had
> best put him in one of the vacant sloops.[16]

It was therefore not thought appropriate to keep well-connected officers in the less glamorous ships of the service. Note also that George Wolfe (who also features in the list of the longest serving frigate captains) had nevertheless attracted St Vincent's attention in spite of the fact that he was 'Lord Spencer's friend'.

One other factor which should be mentioned about John Maitland is that his father was also a naval captain. At least six of the names on the above list were the sons of naval officers.[17] Seven more had very strong naval connections: William Parker (nephew of St Vincent); Charles Malcolm (nephew of Admiral Thomas Pasley); James Newman (related to the Hood family); Philip Wilkinson (nephew of Sir Philip Stephens, Secretary to the Admiralty and related to Viscount Ranelagh); Stephen Poyntz (distantly related to the Spencers); Charles Adam (grandson of Lord Keith); and the previously mentioned George Wolfe (who had the strong patronage of Lady Spencer in particular).

A number of the other officers on the list provided details of their family background to John Marshall for his *Royal Naval Biography*. The church, army, public office (including Parliament) and medicine are represented among the occupations of the fathers concerned. Others are less clear. What, for example, does one make of the fact that Captain Thomas Maling's father was 'Mr Maling of West Donnington, County Durham'.[18] Others like Richard Hawkins or James Hillyar[19] simply do not seem to have wanted to provide information about their family background. Only eight of the captains on the list were sufficiently involved in politics to become Members of Parliament and half of these were elected to Parliament some time after the end of the Napoleonic War.[20]

POSTING AND APPOINTMENT

As noted earlier, a display of ability on a foreign station brought a strong chance of advancement by the local commander-in-chief. However, comparatively few of the officers on this list were posted on foreign stations by the direct patronage of the station commander. In the case of at least 60 per cent, promotion to post captain came by order of the Admiralty. In only about seven cases did promotion arise because of the patronage of the local station commander, the majority of these occurring on the Mediterranean station. George Cockburn and James Macnamara, for example, were promoted by Lord Hood in the Mediterranean in 1794 and 1795 respectively; George Elliott was promoted by Nelson in 1804. In addition to these, Capel, Hoste and Hillyar were posted by Admiralty Order whilst serving under Nelson's command on the same station and at Nelson's very direct intervention. F L Maitland was promoted by Lord Keith during his tenure as commander-in-chief of the Mediterranean station. Lord George Stuart and Fleetwood Pellew were both posted in the East Indies, the latter during his father's period as commander-in-chief. Other officers may have had strong family connections or patronage, but their elevation to post captain was not achieved on an overseas station.

Approximately 22 per cent of the longest serving officers were posted direct into a frigate, most of these promotions occurring in the early years of the war (before 1796). Parker and Hoste were posted into frigates after four to six months delay later in the war; and during the second war Charles Malcolm, the Hon George Elliot, James Hillyar, Lord George Stuart and Fleetwood Pellew were all posted directly into a frigate. Such a posting depended on both a powerful friend and a recognition of ability. This is why many of the names on this list are familiar; some, because of their connection with Nelson, others because their activities earned them a degree of fame. On the other hand, it must be borne in mind that officers with little ability are unlikely to have remained in frigate command for long periods. Of the names on the list given above twenty-seven, or 51 per cent, were in continuous command of frigates, without a break, which strongly suggests that they had considerable interest or ability, or both. A further six captains experienced short breaks in between frigates, of six to ten months. At least nine others experienced longer breaks coinciding with the Peace of Amiens and, as already noted, their inactivity was more likely the result of wider de-commissioning of frigates than a conscious decision not to employ them. This leaves only eleven frigate captains (21 per cent) who actually served for significant periods in ships of other rates or were unemployed for long periods within the span of their frigate service.

Furthermore, virtually every captain on the list progressed from lighter to heavier frigates. Even where superficially it appears that a captain was given command of a smaller or less powerfully armed frigate, there were mitigating factors. For example, Sir Robert Barlow transferred from the 18-pounder frigate *Phoebe* to the 12-pounder frigate *Concorde* in 1801. Although this meant a reduction in firepower, the *Concorde* was a fast frigate captured from the French, and thus thought to be a desirable command. Similarly the Hon Duncan Pleydell Bouverie was given the captured 12-pounder Dutch frigate *Braave* for about three months in 1803. Upon leaving her he was unemployed for about eighteen months until he was given the 9-pounder frigate *Mercury*, which he kept for ten months. Dutch-built ships were not well regarded, whereas the *Mercury* was one of the *Enterprize* class frigates which performed well in a head-sea and were highly manoeuvrable.[21]

Thomas Gossellin, likewise, was given an 18-pounder frigate[22] for three months, but was then immediately given the 12-pounder frigate *Syren*, which he retained for five years. Although small, *Syren* was one of the highly manoeuvrable *Amazon* class frigates. Ross Donnelly ended a very successful five-year commission in the 18-pounder frigate *Narcissus* with a few months cruising in the captured French 12-pounder frigate *Franchise*, a less powerful ship but faster and actually larger. Nevertheless, it must be re-emphasised that these apparent exceptions were of minimal duration.

These captains were, therefore, by the criteria that has been analysed and defined earlier, exceptional officers. This raises the obvious question of what it was that made them exceptional. What factors might offer a clue to their special abilities?

STATION

An analysis of the stations on which the specialist frigate captains served during their frigate service (Table 5.2) reveals a number of interesting points. Firstly, the majority of these officers served repeatedly on one station. This is particularly true of officers operating in what can be described as 'home waters' (North Sea, Channel, and coast of Ireland).[23] Richard Keats, Thomas Williams, Philip Durham, Richard King (2), Edward Owen, George Wolfe, Joseph Sidney Yorke, the Hon A K Legge and Frederick Maitland all appear to have served more or less exclusively in home waters (which admittedly covered a huge area) and on convoy or patrol work. Robert Barlow could also be added to this list for, of his 7.75 years frigate service, all but about a year were spent either in home waters, or on cruising/convoy duties. This included, incidentally, a 2.5- year spell serving in the Western Squadron under both Pellew and Warren. Service off the Texel also seems to have retained several frigate captains. Philip Somerville commanded both the *Nemesis* and the *Rota* frigates there between November 1808 and the end of 1809. Lord George Stuart similarly commanded the *Aimable* and the *Horatio* frigates off the Texel between 1809 and 1813.

Alternatively to the concentration on service in home waters, many of the longer serving officers were repeatedly sent to one particular station – or at least served there in several successive ships. George Cockburn, for example, commanded both the *Meleager* and the *Minerve* in the Mediterranean between late 1794 and November 1801. Edward Foote commanded the *Niger* and the *Seahorse* on that station between December 1796 and September 1800. Henry Blackwood commanded the *Penelope* in the Mediterranean between October 1799 and February 1802; and was back there again in the *Euryalus* towards the end of 1805.

TABLE 5.2. *Service Details of Longest Serving Frigate Captains*[24]

Captain	Frigate	Approximate Dates	Station
Keats, R G	Niger	Jan 1793 – Mar 1793	Convoys & Cruising
	Galatea	Jun 1794 – Dec 1795	Convoys & Cruising
		Jan 1796 – May 1797	Warren's Squadron
	Boadicea	Jul 1797 – Feb 1801	Channel
Hamilton, C	Dido	May 1793 – Dec 1793	Channel
		Jan 1794 – Nov 1794	Mediterranean
	Melpomene	May 1795 – Nov 1801	Convoys & Cruising/ Channel
		Feb 1802 – Aug 1802	Leeward Islands
Williams, T	Lizard	Jan 1793 – May 1794	Convoys & Cruising
	Daedalus	Aug 1794 – Jul 1795	Convoys & Cruising
	Unicorn	Jul 1795 – Feb 1797	Cork
	Endymion	May 1797 – Dec 1797	Home waters
		Jan 1798 – May 1799	Cork
		Jul 1799 – Feb 1801	Convoys & Cruising/ Channel
Halstead, L	Venus	Jan 1795 – Oct 1795	Home Waters
	Phoenix	Nov 1795 – Aug 1797	Home Waters
		Sep 1797 – Aug 1798	Coast of Wales
		Sep 1798 – May 1799	Cork
		Jun 1799 – May 1802	Mediterranean
Neale, H	Aimable	Mar 1793 – Mar 1795	Mediterranean
	San Fiorenzo	Jul 1795 – Oct 1800	Home Waters
Yorke, J S	Circe	Feb 1793 – July 1794	Home/ various
	Stag	Aug 1794 – Feb 1800	Home/ various
	Jason	Apr 1800 – Apr 1801	Convoys & Cruising
Legge, A K	Niger/Latona	Jul 1793 – Apr 1797	Home/ various
	Cambrian	May 1797 – Aug 1801	Home waters
Barlow, R	Pegasus	Jul 1793 – Jul 1794	Home waters
	Aquilon	Aug 1794 – Oct 1795	Home waters
	Phoebe	Nov 1795 – Apr 1798	Western Squadron
		May 1798 – Mar 1799	Channel/ Convoys & Cruising
		Apr 1799 – May 1801	Cork
	Concorde	Aug 1801 – Nov 1801	Newfoundland
		Feb 1802 – May 1802	Home Waters
Durham, P	Hind	Nov 1793 – Oct 1794	Channel/ Convoys & Cruising
	Anson	Nov 1794 – Feb 1796	Channel
		Feb 1796 – Feb 1798	Western Squadron
		Mar 1798 – Nov 1799	Channel
		Dec 1799 – Apr 1801	Channel/ Convoys & Cruising
	Endymion	May 1801 – Nov 1801	Secret service/ Convoys & Cruising
		Feb 1802 – May 1802	Home Waters
Cockburn, G	Meleager	Sep 1794 – Feb 1797	Mediterranean
	Minerve	Mar 1797 – Feb 1802	Mediterranean
	Phaeton	Aug 1803 – Nov 1803	Convoys & Cruising
		Feb 1804 – Nov 1805	East Indies

Robert Laurie commanded three different frigates off Nova Scotia and North America between 1801 and 1810. His only other station was the Channel for several years at the start of his frigate service. Clotworthy Upton served on the Cork station on three different occasions: in the *Lapwing* in 1805; the *Sybille* both from February 1808 to February 1809, and again between 1810 and 1813.

CAREER ACTIVITIES

A survey of the careers of these frigate captains begins to reveal a range of distinct features: that is, activities which are almost peculiar to frigate service, and which they all experienced to some degree. These can be summarised as follows:

1. Significant engagement with an enemy frigate usually, but not necessarily, resulting in its capture (possibly in company with other ships).

2. A record of capturing a significant number of enemy armed vessels and privateers.

3. Being a consistently successful cruiser.

4. Direct assistance in military operations with land forces.

5. Rigorous blockade and patrol duty in the Channel.

6. Command of a frigate squadron.

To this list could perhaps be added the acquisition of prize money, but as that is really a direct consequence of activities already identified, it would simply confuse matters. Furthermore, prize money was not an accurate yardstick against which to measure the calibre of a frigate captain. Luck and skill were of equal importance in obtaining prize money and a lucky captain might potentially get prizes with the minimal application of skill; an unlucky captain could not make up in skill for not being in the right place at the right time!

Unfortunately, information on the careers of certain officers is rather scant. The case of Captain Richard Hawkins provides a good example. Hawkins had a fairly distinguished career as a midshipman and, as lieutenant of the *Theseus*, 74, was wounded at the Battle of the Nile. He was posted in 1802 but given no command until 1807 when he was appointed to the frigate *Minerve*. Although he commanded her for seven years, it has been possible to find only one incident

Captain	Frigate	Approximate Dates	Station
Graves,T	Venus	Nov 1795 – Apr 1796	North Sea
		May 1796 – Feb 1800	Newfoundland
		Mar 1800 – Nov 1803	Leeward Islands.
		Feb 1804 – Aug 1805	Cork
Moore, G	Syren	Aug 1794 – Jul 1796	Channel
	Melampus	Aug 1796 – Apr 1798	Channel
		May 1798 – Aug 1798	Convoys & Cruising
		Sep 1798 – Mar 1800	Cork
		Apr 1800 – Nov 1801	Jamaica
	Indefatigable	Aug 1803 – Aug 1804	Channel
King, R (2)	Aurora	Nov 1794 – Jul 1795	Channel
	Druid	Sep 1795 – Feb 1797	Channel
	Sirius	Jun 1797 – Aug 1802	Home Waters
Foote, E	Niger	Aug 1794 – Nov 1796	Channel/ Convoys & Cruising
		Dec 1796 – Sep 1797	Mediterranean
	Seahorse	Apr 1798 – Sep 1800	Mediterranean (mainly)
		Jan 1801 – May 1801	Convoys & Cruising
		Feb 1802 – Aug 1802	East Indies
Newman, J	Vestal	Sep 1794 – Jul 1795	Home Waters/ Convoys & Cruising
	Ceres	Sep 1795 – Aug 1797	Mediterranean (mainly)
	Mermaid	Sep 1797 – Aug 1798	Jamaica
		Sep 1798 – Mar 1799	Channel
	Loire	Apr 1799 – Feb 1802	Channel/ Convoys & Cruising
Wilkinson, P	Hermione	Dec 1794 – Jul 1797	Jamaica
	Success	Jul 1797 – Nov 1797	Nova Scotia (and Jamaica?)
		Dec 1797 – Mar 1799	Channel/ Convoys & Cruising
	Unicorn	Apr 1799 – May 1801	Channel
	Naiad	Aug 1801 – Nov 1801	Channel
	Hussar	Aug 1802 – Feb 1804	Channel
Mansfield, C	Andromache	Apr 1795 – Aug 1796	Leeward Islands
		Nov 1796 – Nov 1798	Mediterranean
	Dryad	Dec 1798 – May 1802	Cork
Gore, J	Triton	Oct 1796 – Apr 1801	Mediterranean
	Medusa	May 1801 – Nov 1804	Mediterranean
		May 1805 – Feb 1806	East Indies
Herbert, C	Amphitrite	Sep 1795 – Aug 1797	Channel (mainly)
	Amelia	Sep 1797 – Feb 1802	Channel
	Uranie	Nov 1803 – Aug 1804	Jamaica
		Jan 1805 – Nov 1805	Convoys & Cruising
Blackwood, H	Brilliant	May 1796 – Feb 1798	North Sea
		Apr 1798 – Oct 1798	Newfoundland
	Penelope	Nov 1798 – Sep 1799	Channel
		Oct 1799 – May 1802	Mediterranean
	Euryalus	Aug 1803 – Aug 1805	Cork & Channel
		Aug 1805 – Nov 1805	Mediterranean

recorded about his activities, this being the chase of a French brig in September 1808. Even John Marshall had to finish his biographical entry with the rather despairing comment that Hawkins 'does not appear to have had any opportunity of distinguishing himself whilst in her [*Minerve*].' He was subsequently placed on half-pay.[25]

The six categories given above would begin to suggest a set of criteria for defining the successful frigate captain; indeed, one of the categories actually uses the word 'successful', although no attempt has been made at this stage to define success. That will follow. The term is used in reference to cruisers because that is how they are sometimes referred to by John Marshall. Unfortunately, Marshall himself did not try and explain how this was measured, and all that can be said is that some officers had a reputation for being successful cruisers, which sometimes earned them the envy or admiration of their brother officers.

The first factor on the list is that of the successful frigate action. This was in many ways the most spectacular display of ability, but it is also problematic in determining speciality. This is because there was a significant number of officers who fought successful frigate actions but did not have an extraordinarily long career in frigates. To understand fully the nature and importance of frigate actions requires consideration of both categories of frigate captains, so an analysis of frigate actions will be postponed until the next chapter.

Capture of Significant Number of Enemy Armed Vessels and Privateers

A successful single-ship engagement would of course attract attention but the number of what can be defined as true single-ship actions constitutes only a very small minority of the incidents in which frigates became engaged. The basic bread-and-butter duties of the frigates were to undertake patrols, safeguarding British trade and harrying that of the enemy. Much of this could be carried out in the form of 'close blockade' of the French channel ports, where they could not only watch enemy naval movements, but also intercept coastal traffic. A natural corollary of this was the engagement and capture of the smaller enemy armed naval vessels and privateers. In fact, this particular function became increasingly important for, as the line of battle ships of the French navy successively failed to escape the blockade or were defeated in major fleet actions, and the coastal blockade denied an adequate supply of imports, the French resorted to raiding tactics, utilising their smaller armed ships and those financed by French privateering interests. In fact, right at the start of the war in 1793, the French Convention took steps to encourage such activities by abandoning the state's right to a share of prize money, offering a premium for the fitting out of corsairs,

Captain	Frigate	Approximate Dates	Station
Douglas, J E	Jason	Jun 1794 – Dec 1794	Convoys & Cruising/ fitting
	Garland	Aug 1795 – Dec 1797	North Sea
	Boston	Jan 1798 – Apr 1799	Channel
		May 1799 – Nov 1804	Nova Scotia
Donnelly, R	Pegasus	Jul 1795 – Mar 1796	Convoys & Cruising
		May 1796 – Feb 1797	North Sea
	Maidstone	May 1798 – Jan 1800	Jamaica
		Feb 1800 – Dec 1801	Channel/ Convoys & Cruising
	Narcissus	Dec 1801 – Feb 1805	Mediterranean
		Feb 1805 – May 1805	Home waters
		Aug 1805 – Nov 1805	Leeward Islands
		Feb 1806 – Aug 1806	Convoys & Cruising/ Cape
Gossellin, T	Diamond	May 1796 – Jul 1796	Channel
	Syren	Aug 1796 – Jan 1800	Leeward Islands
		Feb 1800 – Nov 1800	Channel
		Jan 1801 – Aug 1801	Jamaica
		Aug 1801	Jamaica
	Melampus	Feb 1802 – May 1802	Jamaica
	Latona	Nov 1804 – Aug 1806	Channel
Macnamara, J	Southampton	Jul 1794 – Jul 1797	Mediterranean
	Cerberus	Feb 1798 – Mar 1801	Cork
		Aug 1801 – Feb 1803	Jamaica
Poyntz, S	Solebay	Sep 1797 – Apr 1799	Leeward Islands
		May 1799 – Sep 1800	Jamaica
	Beaulieu	Jan 1801 – Feb 1802	Channel
	Melampus	Nov 1804 – Aug 1807	Channel/Convoys/ Cruising
Laurie, R	Andromache	Dec 1798 – Aug 1801	Channel
		Aug 1801 – Feb 1804	Nova Scotia
	Cleopatra	Aug 1804 – May 1805	Nova Scotia
	Milan	Aug 1805 – May 1808	Nova Scotia
		Aug 1808 – Jul 1810	North America
Owen, E C W R	Nemesis	Jan 1801 – May 1802	Channel/Nelson's Sqd
	Immortalite	Aug 1802 – Feb 1806	Convoys & Cruising/North Sea
	Clyde	May 1806 – Jan 1811	Channel/ Texel
	Inconstant	Jan 1811 – Jan 1813	Texel
Atkins, D	Iris	May 1802 – Aug 1802	Channel
	Ambuscade	Nov 1802 – Nov 1803	Channel
	Seine	Feb 1804 – Jan 1811	Channel
		(Feb 1805 – Nov 1806)	West Indies
Capel, T B	Meleager	Nov 1800 – Nov 1801	Jamaica
	Revolutionnaire	Aug 1802 – Oct 1802	Convoys & Cruising
	Phoebe	Nov 1802 – Nov 1805	Mediterranean
	Endymion	Feb 1806 – May 1808	Mediterranean
		Aug 1808 – Jul 1810	Convoys & Cruising
Adam, C	Sybille	Feb 1802 – May 1803	East Indies
	Chiffonne	Aug 1803 – May 1805	North Sea
	Resistance	Nov 1805 – Jan 1810	Channel/ Convoys & Cruising

compensating for losses, and shortly thereafter, exempting prize goods from any form of duties.[26] The opening years of both wars saw an eruption of privateering activity, and although this usually died back again, there were significant peaks in 1797 and 1810.[27]

To some extent, therefore, the mark of a good frigate captain could be gauged by his success in taking enemy vessels. Whilst virtually all captures could be condemned as prizes, thereby earning the captors monetary reward, the capture of an armed vessel had to carry greater weight because of the risk involved in taking her. Furthermore, it is clear that the captains of many French privateers were highly experienced seamen, who even after being captured, could after exchange return again and again to their activities in the employment of different merchants. The bravery and skill of the privateer commanders and crews should not be underestimated. Privateers were known to resist capture ferociously and their captains often had superior knowledge of the waters in which they were sailing. It has to be admitted that in contemporary sources there is little discussion on this point. Frigate captains do seem to have been primarily interested in the glory associated with a single-ship action or the possibility of a quick fortune that a lucky prize might bring. Whilst an individual captain may have taken a certain amount of pride in capturing smaller armed vessels, it was not likely to attract a great deal of public attention. Nevertheless, it has to be suggested that someone in seniority *did* take notice of this sort of success, because nearly 30 per cent of the officers in the list of specialist frigate captains appear to have excelled in this activity.

There might have been a pecuniary motive behind this: an officer who had a record for capturing enemy vessels was also more likely to bring in the prize money, and it would be in the interest of a station commander to have that captain under his command. Richard Keats, Marshall tells us, as captain of the *Boadicea*, 'distinguished himself as an indefatigable cruizer, and captured several very formidable French privateers.'[28] These included *l'Invincible Buonaparte*, *L'Utile*, *Le Requin*, and the *Milan* which were captured by *Boadicea* alone; but there were others which were captured in consort with other frigates. Charles Hamilton, who commanded the *Melpomene* for approximately seven years, most of which was spent in the Channel on patrol and convoy duties, captured nearly fifty enemy vessels.[29] These included the privateers *Triton* and the *Auguste* which was captured after a dogged chase of sixty hours.[30] Thomas Williams was fortunate in that he was appointed to command the *Lizard*, 28 just before the outbreak of war. Dispatched to patrol in the Channel to provide protection to unsuspecting merchant vessels, he was also on station to capture several privateers before May 1793, and then patrolling off Rotterdam in the same year he captured the *Trois Amis*. In April 1798,

Captain	Frigate	Approximate Dates	Station
Mackenzie, A	Brilliant	Nov 1801 – Feb 1802	Nelson's Sqd
	Magicienne	Aug 1803 – Nov 1804	Channel
		Feb 1806 – Nov 1806	Jamaica
	President	Feb 1808 – Jul 1810	South America
	Undaunted	Nov 1810 – Jan 1811	Convoys & Cruising
	?Venus	Jan 1811 – Jul 1813	Leeward Islands/ Leith
Maling, T	Diana	Nov 1801 – Aug 1803	Mediterranean
		Aug 1803 – May 1804	Channel/Convoys & Cruising
		Aug 1804 – Feb 1806	Jamaica
		May 1806 – May 1807	Cork
	Undaunted	Feb 1808 – Jul 1810	Convoys & Cruising/ Portugal
Wolfe, G	Galatea	May 1802 – Nov 1802	Cork
	Aigle	Feb 1803 – Jan 1811	Channel
Mundy, G	Carysfort	May 1802 – Nov 1802	Convoys & Cruising
	Hydra	Nov 1802 – Aug 1804	Channel/Convoys & Cruising
		Nov 1804 – Jul 1810	Mediterranean
Vansittart, H	Magicienne	Aug 1802 – Nov 1802	Channel
	Fortunee	Feb 1803 – May 1804	Channel
		Aug 1804 – Aug 1806	West Indies
		Nov 1806 – Nov 1807	Channel
		Oct 1807 – Nov 1811	Cork
Broke, P B V	Druid	May 1805 – May 1806	Channel/Cork
	Shannon	Aug 1806 – Jan 1811	Channel/North Sea
		Mar 1811 – 1814	North America
Sayer, G	Galatea	Nov 1805 – Feb 1809	Leeward Islands
	Leda	Jan 1810 – Jan 1814	East Indies
Maitland, F L	Loire	Nov 1802 – Aug 1806	Cork
	Emerald	Feb 1807 – Feb 1809	Channel
		Feb 1809 – Jan 1811	Cork
Parker, W	Alarm	May 1802 – Nov 1802	Channel
	Amazon	Feb 1803 – Nov 1805	Mediterranean
		Nov 1805 – Jan 1810	Channel
Hoste, W	Greyhound	May 1802 – Feb 1803	Mediterranean
	Amphion	Feb 1806 – Jan 1811	Mediterranean
	Bacchante	Jul 1812 – Jan 1814	Mediterranean
Digby, S T	Vestal	May 1805 – May 1806	North Sea
	Argo	Aug 1806 – Feb 1808	Convoys & Cruising
		May 1808 – Aug 1809	Jamaica
		Nov 1809 – Jul 1810	Convoys & Cruising
	Theban	Nov 1810 – Jul 1814	Channel/Convoys & Cruising
Bouverie, D P	Braave	Feb 1803 – Apr 1803	Cape
	Mercury	Nov 1804 – Aug 1805	Channel
	Aimable	Nov 1805 – Feb 1806	Channel
	Medusa	May 1806 – Nov 1806	Channel/Convoys & Cruising
		Feb 1807 – Nov 1807	Cape/ South America
		Feb 1808 – Jan 1813	Channel/Convoys & Cruising

patrolling off Madeira in the large 24-pounder frigate *Endymion*, he captured the 100-ton *Revanche*;[31] and in May 1800 he captured the Bordeaux raider *Scipion Français*. Joseph Sidney Yorke likewise was given a frigate at the beginning of the conflict and was able to take a number of privateers in the Channel (see below). The Hon Arthur Kaye Legge, stationed on the coast of France in the *Cambrian* captured several large privateers, including the *Caesar* and *Pont de Lodi*, both of which were taken in March 1797.[32] Robert Barlow in the *Phoebe* also captured several commerce-raiders in 1798; John Marshall tells us that this included three French privateers mounting 58 guns in all; and in March 1800, *L'Heureux* of 22 brass 12-pounder guns.[33]

The operation against privateers continued throughout the wars. George Wolfe in the *Aigle* captured, among others, an 18-gun French privateer off the Western Isles in September 1810, after a 134-mile chase lasting thirteen hours.[34] The privateer in this instance was the *Phénix*, commanded by the highly experienced Jacques Perraud, who had only recently been released from prison in Britain after being captured by the *Powerful*, 74, off the coast of Ceylon. Further afield, Stephen Poyntz in the *Solebay* captured a number of privateers in the West Indies and later in his career, in 1805 whilst captain of the *Melampus*, he captured a 28-gun Spanish private ship of war, the *Hydra*.[35] Possibly one of the most successful frigate captains in this field was Charles Malcolm in the *Rhin*. Of his prizes the *San Joseph* had been a highly successful privateer, making a profit of 94,599 francs from one of its captives alone; and there was also a valuable by-product of this capture in September 1810, when Malcolm found on board a complete set of signal books issued for use by French telegraph stations along the coast.[36] Other names associated with the capture of privateers include Philip Durham, John Erskine Douglas, Duncan Pleydell Bouverie, Frederick Maitland, Graham Moore, George Cockburn, Edward Foote, David Atkins, John Gore and John Tower.

Before moving to the next feature of the frigate captains' activities, it is worth noting that many of those captains who were successful against privateers spent long periods commanding frigates in the waters around the British Isles. This is crucial, because if one of the advantages possessed by privateer commanders was their knowledge of the Channel and North Sea waters, gleaned because of their (often pre-war) merchant marine careers, the same experience seems to have been acquired, albeit more slowly, by frigate captains who were retained in the same waters during the wars. They were thus able to develop their own knowledge and familiarity with the areas in which they were to patrol.

Captain	Frigate	Approximate Dates	Station
Hawkins, R	Minerva	May 1807 – Jul 1812	Channel
		Jan 1813 – Jan 1814	North America
Somerville, P	Nemesis	Aug 1802 – Aug 1805	Channel/Convoys & Cruising
		Nov 1805	Nova Scotia
		Feb 1806 – Nov 1807	Newfoundland
		May 1808 – Aug 1808	Convoys & Cruising
		Nov 1808 – Feb 1809	Texel
	Rota	May 1809 – Jan 1810	Texel/fitting
		Jul 1810 – Jan 1811	Ireland
		Jul 1812 – Jan 1814	Channel/Convoys & Cruising
Upton, C	Lapwing	Feb 1805 – Aug 1805	Cork/ North Sea
	Aimable	May 1806 – May 1807	North Sea
	Sybille	Aug 1807 – Nov 1807	Convoys & Cruising/ Gambier's Sqd
		Feb 1808 – Feb 1809	Cork
		May 1809 – Aug 1809	Newfoundland
		Jan 1810 – Jan 1813	Cork/Ireland
		Jul 1813	Newfoundland
Taylor, B W	Thames	Feb 1806 – Feb 1807	North Sea
		May 1807 – Nov 1807	Convoys & Cruising
		Feb 1808	Mediterranean
	Apollo	May 1808 – Jan 1814	Mediterranean
Malcolm, C	Chiffonne	Feb 1803	East Indies
	Narcissus	Nov 1806 – Aug 1809	Channel
	Rhin	Aug 1809 – Jan 1813	Channel
		Jul 1813 – Jan 1814	Leeward Islands
Elliott, G	Maidstone	Aug 1803 – Nov 1804	Mediterranean
	Aurora	Aug 1805 – Feb 1806	Newfoundland
		May 1806	Mediterranean
	Modeste	Nov 1806 – Jul 1812	East Indies
	Hussar	Jan 1813 – Jan 1814	East Indies
Hillyar, J	Niger	May 1804 – Nov 1807	Mediterranean
	Phoebe	Nov 1809 – Jan 1810	Baltic
		Jul 1810 – 1811	Cape
		Jul 1812 – Jan 1814	Convoys & Cruising
Stuart, G	Sheerness	May 1804 – Feb 1806	East Indies
	Duncan	May 1806 – Feb 1807	East Indies
	Aimable	Aug 1807 – May 1808	North Sea/ Convoys & Cruising
		Feb 1809 – Jul 1810	Texel
	Horatio	Nov 1810 – Jan 1813	Texel
		Jan 1813 – Jan 1814	Channel
Tower, J	Iris	Aug 1806 – Nov 1809	Channel
	Curacoa	Jan 1810 – Jan 1811	Channel
		Jul 1812 – Jan 1814	Mediterranean
Pellew, F B	Psyche	Feb 1808 – Nov 1808	East Indies
	Phaeton	(?) Feb 1808 – Jul 1812	East Indies
	Resistance	Jan 1813 – Jan 1814	Mediterranean

The Consistently Successful Cruiser

A frigate captain who was successful in capturing privateers was also likely to be more broadly successful as a cruiser. But the definition of this success is not necessarily as straightforward as it might seem. A cruiser might have been considered effective because he prevented enemy coastal shipping from sailing, which would be a success in terms of longer term strategy. However, it is doubtful if this is the meaning of the term when used during the wars. Almost certainly, to their contemporaries, the frigate captain who was a successful cruiser was the one who consistently captured enemy vessels and had them condemned as prizes – at least ten of the names on the list of frigate specialists appear to have scored highly in this category. In September 1804 a squadron of four frigates, under the command of Captain Graham Moore in the *Melampus*, captured a squadron of Spanish treasure ships carrying at least three million dollars in specie. Both Moore, and another of his captains, John Gore, feature on the list of longest serving captains (another, Samuel Sutton, may well have retired on the proceeds, as there was a gap in his naval service until he reached flag rank many years later!).[37]

There was clearly an element of luck in taking prizes. Thomas Byam Martin writing in his journal of Charles Rowley, the captain of the *Boadicea* in 1801, observed that although Rowley had been at sea consistently since 1793, 'cruizing with a zeal and activity that deserved better luck, for according to his own words "he had never seen a shot fired in anger, or even the flag of an enemy". And I do not recollect any instance of his being more fortunate after he left my squadron.'[38] Revealingly, Rowley had commanded two frigates for a total two and a half years by the time he was given the *Boadicea*. His total frigate service was only about three years and three months!

How, then, should 'a consistently successful cruiser' be defined? One of the captains to whom John Marshall applied this term was Joseph Sidney Yorke. Yorke was born in 1768, the youngest son of the Lord Chancellor. He entered the navy at the age of 12 and served as Admiral Rodney's aide-de-camp at the Battle of the Saintes in 1782. Following the war he served with Sir Charles Douglas on the coast of America for a number of years. In 1789 he was promoted to lieutenant and in the following year he was elected Member of Parliament for Reigate in Surrey where his family had considerable property. In February 1793, at the age of 25, he was posted as captain of the 28-gun frigate *Circe* in the Channel Fleet.

The extent of Yorke's success as a cruiser is undeniable. Steel's *Prize Pay List* records Yorke's prizes as follows:

TABLE 5.3. *Prizes taken by Captain Joseph Sidney Yorke in the frigates* Circe, Stag *and* Jason *during the Revolutionary War*

Date of Capture	Prizes or Salvage	Net Value[39] (to nearest £) where known
Mar 1793	Salvage for the *Pelican*, Danish brig	
Mar 1793	*Diane*, *Vaudreuil* and *Jeune Felix* merchantmen	£12,470
May 1793	*Didon* and *L'Auguste* privateers	£1838
May 1793	*Le Courier* privateer (taken with HMS *L'Aimable*, Capt H B Neale)	
Oct 1793	*Réunion* French frigate	£5318 (part)
Nov 1793	*L'Espiegle* French sloop of war (taken with HMS *Nymphe*)	£1267
Jan 1794	Salvage of *Venus* brig, and *Ant* sloop	£190
Aug 1795	Ordnance stores of the *Alliance*, Dutch frigate (taken with HM Ships *Reunion*, *Vestal* and *Isis*)	£1424
Feb 1796	Salvage of the *Betsey* (shared with rest of squadron)	}
March 1796	*La Bonne Citoyenne*, French corvette (shared with rest of squadron)	} £1748
Nov 1796	*Le Franklin*, French privateer (shared with Vice-Admiral Colpoy's fleet)	£30
Feb 1797	*L'Appocrate*, French privateer, and salvage of the ship *Sarah*	£1346
Feb 1797	Salvage of the *Swallow* (taken with HMS *Unite*) and French privateers *L'Appocrate* and *Hirondelle*	£524
Feb 1797	*Atlantic* (American ship for which compensation was paid to *Stag* and her crew)	£81
Feb 1797	Salvage of the *Recovery*	£62
July 1797	*Bothcraft/Bothchaff? Maria*	£368
Sept 1797	*Chasseur*, *Brunette*, *Indien* and *Decouvert*, French privateers	
Sept 1797	Salvage of the *Adamant*	
Sept 1797	Salvage of the *Nordstern* and proceeds of the *Cocyte* (both taken with HMS *Phaeton*, Capt the Hon R Stopford)	
Oct 1797	Salvage for *Le Venus y Cupido*	
Oct 1797	Salvage of the *Arcade* (and possibly another ship called *Recovery*)	
May/June 1798	*Maria Perotte/Rustia* and an unnamed sloop; salvage of the *Sea Nymphe* and the *Mary*, sloop.	£1007
June 1798	*Jonge Marcus*	
Aug 1798	*La Francine*, chasse maree (taken with HMS *Ambuscade*, Capt Henry Jenkins, and *Nimrod* hired cutter).	£76
Nov 1798	*L'Hirondelle*	
Nov 1798	*Resolu*	
Nov 1798	Salvage of the *Fame*	
Dec 1798	*Resource*, *Faucon* and *Sans Soucie*	
April 1799	*Nymphe* (American ship taken with HMS *Phaeton*)	£708
Oct 1799	Salvage for the *Sarah* and the *James*	
Oct 1799	*Amiable Maria*, *La Paz* and *L'Heureux Premier*	
Jan 1800	*Ursula* (taken with several others)	£105
Jan 1801	*Venus*	
April 1801	Salvage for the *Trafficker*	
May 1801	*Dorade*	
? 1801	*Le Poisson Volant*, French privateer	

In addition, the Greenwich Hospital Accounts record the following payments which it is not possible to allocate to the above table:

17 Sep – 20 Oct 1797	'Various prizes'	£993
- - -	'For five ships'	£986
- - -	The *Elizabeth*	£1073
- - -	The *Two Brothers*	£347

To understand this table it is essential to remember that salvage money was paid for any vessel retaken after capture by an enemy privateer or man of war. In all, whilst in command of frigates Yorke was centrally involved with the capture of at least fifty-six vessels in an eight-year period. Prize money for just thirty-four of these vessels totalled nearly £30,000[40] – a colossal sum when it is remembered that a frigate captain's pay at this time amounted to £146 per year.

Although it was not a pre-requisite for cruising success, Yorke spent virtually all of his frigate career in home waters or on convoy escort duties. James Macnamara apparently cruised with great success off Jamaica which, as has already been noted above, could be a very rich area for prizes. On the other hand, there were factors which made stations poor cruising grounds. It was sometimes claimed that the Channel could be a poor area for cruising, particularly after the initial year of a war when most of the unsuspecting, richer prizes had already been taken or were blockaded in port. In fact, this view more likely reflects a strain of naval officers' despondency at being kept on the more wearing Channel duties. On some other stations frigate captains like William Hoste, patrolling for unenviable periods in the Adriatic, were obliged to burn most of their prizes because they lacked sufficient crew to man them, and because of the very practical difficulties of getting them to an Admiralty Court.

Whilst the value of all of Yorke's prizes has not been ascertained, it must be assumed that Yorke was able to amass a substantial income from them. Certainly, for most officers, what mattered was the value of the prizes that they took. It has already been shown that prize money was generally accepted as a legitimate method of supplementing a captain's income. Indeed, it was rigorously defended. A common complaint of sea officers was that their reward was over-emphasised and that others questioned their right to profit from it. In 1808, Captain William Hoste, ruminating from his cabin in the *Amphion* in the Adriatic, commented on news of the Admiralty's decision to cut the captain's share of prize money:

> A parcel of old fograms who are very quietly seated over their Christmas fire,
> do not allow for many a sleepless night of watching and anxiety that we have.
> They forget that in our service, when others take it by turns to watch, the
> Captain must always be on the alert, and that if the chances are in his favour
> in the prize way, it is more than over-balanced by constant anxiety and care.[41]

Three years later, in 1811 an anonymous post captain wrote:

> What must an indifferent person think … when he is told, that a common

clerk in the Admiralty or Navy Office, or even the porter at any of the dock-yards, who has no responsibility attached to his situation, who has no laborious duty to perform, no sleepless nights to disturb his quiet, no anxiety from storms or tempests, no danger to apprehend ... has more of the public money than a captain commanding the largest frigate in His Majesty's navy... and, if such be the state of a captain's pay in general, what must it be in the West Indies; more particularly now, when the little chance of success, by prizes, is totally at an end?[42]

Direct Assistance in Military Operations with Land Forces

The incidence of naval land deployments, either in terms of direct co-operation with the army or independent action using only seamen and marines, is realistically a subject which demands attention in its own right. It must be observed, however, that this aspect of naval activity has been largely unacknowledged and probably continues to be underestimated. Indeed, one naval historian has recently noted that 'Some writers on the army in the Napoleonic Wars suggest that landings and amphibious operations were rare.'[43]

In actual fact amphibious operations were undertaken almost continuously throughout the wars (see Table 5.5 at end of chapter). These could be strategic operations on the scale of major troop landings, such as the army of approximately 40,000 troops landed at the Helder in 1799 in an attempt to drive the French from Holland; the 16,000 men landed in Egypt in 1801 to defeat the remnant of Napoleon's Army of the Nile; and the 40,000 troops landed in the Scheldt during the disastrous Walcheren expedition in 1809. However, there were many smaller expeditions. Often these were initiated by frigate captains seizing an opportunity which arose because they were on the spot. A very good example of this is the capture of Palinuro in the Gulf of Salerno in November 1811 by the Hon Henry Duncan in the *Imperieuse* and Charles Napier in the *Thames*, with troops of the 62nd Regiment from Sicily. On this occasion the *Imperieuse* had been operating independently against Neapolitan forces until she was joined by the *Thames*. On 21 October the two frigates approached the port of Palinuro and saw a large quantity of merchant vessels and naval stores assembled in the harbour. Duncan realised he did not have adequate forces to make a purely naval attack so he sent Napier to Sicily to request a detachment of troops from Lt-General Maitland. The reinforcements arrived on 28 October, and on 1 November a combined force of troops, marines and seamen, under the command of Napier, landed to attack the town. A fort overlooking the town was successfully stormed and French troops driven off, but the harbour was protected by a battery and fortified tower which prevented the troops approaching. Duncan summoned Napier back on board the *Thames* and the two frigates then closed upon the fort, silencing its batteries after a fifteen-minute cannonade, and enabling the troops to take it.[44]

Frigates were certainly deeply involved in smaller operations against Mauritius and Reunion in 1810, and Java in 1811,[45] and there were many expeditions against hostile islands in the West Indies.[46] Frigates were also employed in operations co-operating with foreign troops, like Sir John Borlase Warren's frigate squadron attempting to land arms and supplies to French Royalists in the Quiberon Peninsular in 1795. Later, frigates were regularly used to provide assistance to Spanish guerrillas or to Italian regulars, and this sort of naval support for land forces peppers the careers of many of the frigate captains who were mainly active during the Napoleonic War. In fact, nearly 30 per cent of the specialist frigate captains played an active part in amphibious operations. These activities were particularly common along the coast of Spain and southern Italy where difficult interior terrain meant that roads tended to concentrate along the coastline. Frigates could anchor close to the shore and open fire with their broadsides onto the coast roads – thus providing a firepower which, in calm weather, was heavier and more effective than many army batteries could provide. In 1806, for example, Captain William Hoste in the frigate *Amphion* intercepted a French column advancing along the coast road between Catanzaro and Crotone in Calabria, southern Italy. Anchoring close to the shore, the *Amphion* soon broke the French column, who were forced to flee inland up the mountainside to avoid the effect of *Amphion*'s broadsides.[47]

The officer most famous for this sort of activity was Lord Cochrane, captain of the *Imperieuse* frigate, who during 1808 carried out a series of raids upon the Catalan coast. In July of that year, following an appeal from Spanish guerrillas who were investing the coastal fort of Mongat, Cochrane destroyed the roads leading to the fort, so that the besieged French troops could neither escape nor receive reinforcements. Having left the French to ponder their possible fate at the hands of the Catalan guerrillas, Cochrane returned the following day and succeeded in obtaining the surrender of the fort after 'a couple of well-directed broadsides'.[48] Cochrane was little short of a specialist at this sort of operation, for he appreciated the possibilities which his frigate gave him. In his autobiography he commented:

> It is wonderful what an amount of terrorism a small frigate is able to inspire on an enemy's coast. Actions between line-of-battle ships are, no doubt, very imposing; but for real effect I would prefer a score or two of small vessels, well handled, to any fleet of line-of-battle ships.[49]

Cochrane's role was enthusiastically endorsed by the *Naval Chronicle,* which commented, following the attack on the French Fleet in Basque Roads:

Seeing what Lord Cochrane *has* done with his single ship upon the French shores, we may easily conceive what he would have achieved if he had been entrusted with a sufficient squadron of ships, and a few thousand military, hovering along the whole extent of the French coast, which it would take a considerable portion of the army of France to defend. Thus, and thus alone, may Spain be saved.[50]

Cochrane in the *Imperieuse* was often able to act alone, that is without the assistance of allied forces, against enemy land forces. He was not unique in this. Captain Frederick Watkins of the frigate *Nereide* scored a spectacular success, almost by accident, in September 1800. Ordered to cruise in search of a French frigate south of Jamaica, the *Nereide* with a schooner in company, arrived off of the Dutch-held island of Curacoa. Shortly after his arrival Watkins received a deputation from the inhabitants who were alarmed at the depredations of republican forces in the west on the island. It transpired that the Dutch colonists had decided that capitulation to the British was to be preferred to falling into the hands of the French. Watkins was somewhat taken aback, as he had no troops with which to hold or defend the colony, but he agreed upon terms with the Government of the Island, and accepted its capitulation formally on behalf of His Britannic Majesty.[51]

Cochrane and Hoste are both well known to naval historians for amphibious operations, but other less well known frigate captains, whose names feature on the list of specialists, were also deeply involved in this at different times. Right at the beginning of the Revolutionary War, Captain Charles Hamilton in the 28-gun frigate *Dido* in company with the *Aimable,* Captain Harry Burrard (Neale), acted in consort with 300 Corsican irregulars to attack a French held fort, and the latter was also involved at the siege of Bastia. Later, in the *Melpomene,* he was given command of a number of ships with responsibility for landing troops in the Helder.[52] Thomas Williams in the *Endymion* provided active assistance to the army in suppressing the Irish rising of 1798.[53] Captain Philip Durham in the razeed frigate *Anson* was part of Warren's frigate squadron in the attempt to assist Chouan rebels at Quiberon in Brittany, in which exercise he was accompanied by the slightly better known Richard Goodwin Keats. Following the destruction of the Royalist forces, after a confused and half-hearted attempt by the emigré officers to raise a revolt, Warren became so depressed that he sent Durham back to England to explain to the Admiralty the cause of the failure of the expedition.[54] Thomas Le Marchant Gosselin, captain of the *Syren* frigate, was part of the small squadron under the command of Lord Hugh Seymour sent to take Surinam in 1799.[55] James Macnamara, the captain of the *Southampton* frigate and a close friend of Nelson, served in Nelson's squadron and gave active assistance under Nelson's orders to the Austrian and Sardinian armies in 1794-5. Macnamara was also among the officers under Nelson's command involved in landing troops on Elba in 1796 to take possession of Porto Ferrajo.

Less well known than Macnamara was George Mundy, son of an MP for Derbyshire. Mundy served under Samuel Hood in both the *Juno* and *Aigle* frigates and was present as a midshipman at the sieges of Calvi and Bastia. Posted in 1801, he was sent once again to the Mediterannean, where Collingwood described him in glowing terms: 'His vigilance and activity are exemplary; he is a clever young man.'[56] By 1808 Mundy in the *Hydra* frigate was deeply involved in assisting Spanish forces on the coast of Catalonia. Operating with guerrillas at Badalona, Mundy seems to have become deeply sympathetic to their struggle, so much so as to become politically involved with their cause.[57] Captain Thomas Bladen Capel – a protégé of Nelson – was also highly active in the frigate *Endymion* with Spanish irregular forces. Other specialist frigate captains who were actively involved along the Spanish coast were William Parker in the *Amazon* (especially around Galicia and Ferrol, where on one occasion he landed at the head of a party of his own seamen – a task which was usually delegated to the first lieutenant of a frigate); Duncan Pleydell Bouverie (MP for Downton in Wiltshire), in the *Medusa* frigate, serving under the orders of Home Popham;[58] and John Tower in the *Curacoa* on the coast of Catalonia.[59]

Four of the specialist frigate captains were actively involved in the attack on Java in 1811: James Hillyar in the *Phoebe*, George Sayer in the *Leda*, and Fleetwood Pellew in the *Phaeton* and, perhaps most significantly, the Hon George Elliot in the *Modeste*. Sayer actually had command of the squadron blockading Batavia in advance of the arrival of the main expeditionary force.[60] Elliot's role is remarkable because the whole expedition was only really successfully launched by the enthusiasm of Elliot's father, Lord Minto, Governor General of India. Minto not only pressed forward with the expedition against the reluctance of the commander-in-chief (Admiral Edward O'Bryen Drury, who fortuitously died a few months before the departure of the expedition), he decided to accompany the expedition in person, travelling in his son's frigate. It was fortunate that he did so, for the acting commander-in-chief, Commodore William Broughton, seems to have been just as reluctant as his predecessor. Broughton claimed that he was being careful not to endanger the expeditionary force in what were unreliably charted waters. He sent the *Minto* schooner ahead to explore the waters to the west of Borneo but then refused to accept the reports that he received from her commander.[61] According to George Elliot's own account of the expedition, it seems that Broughton, who was known to be a difficult senior officer, resented Minto's intervention in the affair and decided to vent his anger on Elliot himself. In a turn of events that could almost be seen as farcical, on the return of the *Minto* schooner Broughton dispatched Eliot in the *Modeste*, with the Governor General on board, into the uncharted waters regardless of the 'perceived' dangers. The farcical element was compounded by the fact that Broughton also ordered Elliot to approach Batavia to ascertain whether a superior force of French frigates had arrived there as suspected.[62] The relationship between Elliot and Broughton actually worsened as the attack on Batavia developed. Elliot personally took command of the right wing of the British forces during the attack, but when Broughton heard of Elliot's whereabouts, he immediately ordered him back on board the *Modeste*. To Elliot's clear jubilation, Broughton was superseded next day by Admiral Robert Stopford, who promptly returned Elliot to his duties on shore.

Finally, before leaving this section on combined operations, it should be noted that Philip Somerville commanded the *Rota* in the expedition against the Scheldt in 1809; and Lord George Stuart (2) who commanded the *Horatio* frigate, led a party of seamen and marines against French troops near Cuxhaven in 1809, thus enabling the Duke of Brunswick's forces to embark safely.[63] There were even officers who might be considered specialists in combined operations. One who excelled in this duty was Philip Beaver of the *Acasta* and then *Nisus* frigates. Unfortunately, Beaver died as a result of an illness whilst in command of the *Nisus*, after an aggregate of five year's service, and so does not feature in the list of long-serving captains.[64]

Zealous Blockade and Patrol Duty in the Channel

Earlier in this chapter it was noted that a number of the specialist frigate captains served almost exclusively in the waters around the British Isles and the Bay of Biscay. In addition to these a further twenty-one (40 per cent) of the captains on the list served for noticeably long periods in these waters. Being stationed in home waters inevitable involved blockade duty of some form, a role which was considered by many officers as one of the most unrewarding and punishing of duties. John Surman Carden, captain of the *Macedonian*, was ordered to join Sir Philip Durham's squadron blockading Rochefort in 1811. He wrote of this:

> I was to keep just outside the range of shot and shell of the Isle of Aix;
> sometimes I had a small cruiser under my orders, but generally alone. – And
> though I can aver that at no time did I ever feel a hardship in the execution of

my Orders received … Yet I must say this was the most harassing Duty I had at any time to perform. – All night we had to row guard to meet the probability of Fire Vessels, or Rafts, & and all day Boats & Ship under weigh to intercept the Coasting Trade.[65]

Sir Andrew Snape Douglas, who was given command of a frigate squadron in the western approaches in 1793, described his duties as 'very fatiguing',[66] and indeed this appears to have been the common experience of those engaged on blockade work. Then there was the ever-present danger of accident at sea, a factor heightened in the close inshore work required on blockade and a worry never far from the minds of frigate captains. Some of the anxiety this could cause is evident in the following letter from Captain William Prowse of the *Sirius*, which was blockading Brest, written to his commander-in-chief, Admiral Cornwallis, in July 1803:

It is with great concern I have to acquaint you that yesterday, in Company with his Majesty's ship *Boadicea*, … with a moderate breeze, the ships about three cable's length distance, when the *Sirius*' situation required her to be tacked, and having stern way … the *Boadicea* standing under her stern, with a strong weather tide, which set her on board the *Sirius* … I am exceedingly sorry to state that, from this unfortunate accident, his Majesty's ship under my command had her rudder broken off about five feet from its head and entirely torn from the stern-post, part of the quarter galleries and the upper part of the stern frame materially damaged … I shall proceed without a moments loss of time to Plymouth.[67]

Prowse had only been in command of the *Sirius* for nine months when this accident occurred and, it being his first frigate command, one can understand that he might have been somewhat anxious about Cornwallis's response.

Ship-handling in these conditions was undoubtedly fatiguing as Douglas put it, but it also could lead to nervous conditions and what would probably be recognised today as extreme levels of stress. Added to the worries of station-keeping was that wider responsibility that blockade duty signified. This concern was undoubtedly in Edward Pellew's mind when on the stormy night of 16 December 1796, Vice-Admiral de Galles fleet escaped from Brest carrying French troops bound for Bantry Bay. Pellew in the *Indefatigable*, accompanied by his old friend Frank Cole in the *Revolutionnaire*, and the *Duke of York* lugger watched as twenty-nine warships and several other storeships set sail under cover of darkness. Pellew first sent the lugger to warn Sir John Colpoys, commanding the offshore squadron, and then sent the

Revolutionnaire with fresh intelligence of the enemy's activity. The lugger found Colpoys and passed on the message from Pellew, but later Cole was completely unable to locate the offshore squadron – which unbeknown to the frigate commanders seems to have fallen back up the Channel. Pellew with his small force was left alone to attempt to frustrate the French fleet. To make matters worse, Pellew then lost contact with the enemy and could only surmise that they had headed south for Lisbon or the Mediterranean. He dispatched the lugger again to warn the Admiralty and himself headed south.

> God knows … if I shall be doing right, but left in a wilderness of conjecture I can only say that the sacrifice of my life would be easy if it served my gracious King and my country … I trust myself to you, my Lord [Spencer], upon this perhaps the most important crisis of my life.[68]

During the later part of the wars the serious threat of an invasion being launched from the French Channel ports led to a greater intensity of blockade work in the Channel. Graham Moore, Philip Wilkinson, Henry Blackwood, Ross Donnelly, Thomas Gossellin, Stephen Poyntz, David Atkins, Adam Mackenzie, George Wolfe, George Mundy, Henry Vansittart, Philip Broke, Duncan Pleydell Bouverie, Philip Somerville and, of course, Edward Owen, all commanded frigates in the Channel between the outbreak of the Napoleonic War and the end of 1805, when the destruction of the French fleet at Trafalgar effectively ended the invasion threat. Some of these officers went on to continue with blockade work in the Channel or North Sea. Of this list it could justifiably be claimed that Edward C W R Owen was the blockading frigate captain *par excellence*.

Owen was the son of a naval captain and the godson of Rear-Admiral Sir Thomas Rich. His name was apparently entered on the books of the *Enterprize* when he was only four years old – though, in spite of this his rate of promotion was formally no faster than average. Although he was not posted until April 1798, he was actually appointed acting-captain of the *Impregnable*, 98, carrying his godfather's flag, in 1796.[69] He appears to have become unpopular with seamen during the Spithead Mutiny in 1797, and this almost certainly delayed his appointment to further command for a time.[70] Although he seems to have enjoyed the strong support of Sir John Colpoys, who chose him as his flag captain immediately after the Spithead Mutiny, the fact that Colpoys' flagship was the *London*, which had been at the centre of the mutiny, led to Owen's appointment being countermanded. He was given command of a division of gun-brigs at the Nore later in 1797, but his really noteworthy service began from 1801 when he was given command of the *Nemesis* frigate. From that point onwards he was employed almost continuously in the Channel, where he was attached to the Dungeness squadron which had the responsibility for watching Boulogne and the other ports in the Narrow Seas. At the end of 1805 he was made commodore of the squadron in which he had served for so long. Owen had certainly attracted the attention of his senior officers: Lord Melville, First Lord of the Admiralty, wrote of him to Lord Keith in October 1804, 'I have taken a very strong prepossession in his favour and would always conceive any business to be in safe hands that is entrusted to him.'[71]

From his appointment to the *Nemesis* in 1801, Owen served continually in command of frigates until the middle of 1813 – a period of approximately 12½ years. This factor makes him not only one of the longest serving frigate captains, but also one of the most senior, for by the time he left the 18-pounder frigate *Inconstant*, he had been a post captain for some 15 years. There is other evidence for his popularity and success. Abraham Crawford, who served with him, records that Owen was permitted to take his entire crew from one frigate to another on three separate occasions.[72] As commander of the *Immortalité* he was engaged on the coast of France for nearly two years without real respite, regularly carrying out attacks on the French invasion flotillas which Crawford described as 'a very tedious piece of work'.[73] An attempt was made to reward them with a 9-10 week cruise to the west of Havre, as Crawford recalled, much to the delight of the crew:

> War had been declared for some months with Spain, and the newspapers teemed with accounts of the Spanish prizes and their riches, which were almost daily arriving in England. It was with joyful hearts and fond anticipations of success that we started upon this cruise. Besides, we began to be weary of a service where nothing was to be got but deuced hard knocks and a very profitless share of honour, which we all, at least the greater part of us, would very willingly exchange for a few of the doubloons that were showering so plentifully upon the more fortunate cruisers[74] to the westward.[75]

Sadly for the crew of the *Immortalité*, they succeeded in taking a small Spanish privateer only.

Owen's competency and undoubted knowledge of the French coast led to his being chosen both to test Fulton's experimental 'torpedoes' and to lead attacks against the French invasion flotillas using Congreve's rockets. It is perhaps not surprising that Crawford should have held Owen in great esteem. After all, it was the captain's responsibility to inspire and enthuse the young gentlemen and junior officers serving under him. Crawford elaborates on this relationship saying that Owen,

> possessed himself of a vast fund of professional knowledge, both practical and theoretical, he was ever ready and happy to impart instruction to those who sought it. To the youngsters of the ship he was of incalculable benefit; and I have never met an officer who took the same pains or possessed the same happy method of instilling knowledge of their duty into the minds of his young *élèves* as Captain Owen.[76]

There were of course other officers who had a reputation for making an effort with the training of their midshipmen. Edward Pellew himself employed a teacher on board of his frigate. These commanders made a powerful impression on the young officers-in-training, and there are many well-known examples: the relationship between Nelson and William Hoste (amongst many protégés); Cochrane and Frederick Marryat; Captain Philemon Pownoll with the young Edward Pellew; Samuel Hood and Thomas Byam Martin. Other captains, like Robert Barlow and Ross Donnelly, were renowned for being good captains, with the result that there was some competition to have a son or near relation placed aboard their frigates.

It is perhaps also a sign of Owen's ability and reputation as a frigate commander that Admiral Sir William Hotham, who was at one time Owen's senior officer as commodore of the frigate squadron blockading Boulogne, should in referring to the latter's keenness to engage the enemy, follow an acknowledgement that he was an 'able and skilful officer' with the critical observation, 'It is melancholy to perceive what men will do for the sake of a little popularity, and how many valuable officers there are who upon this point are weak enough to forget what they owe to their own characters and the real benefit of the service.'[77] Success clearly also had its price.

Command of a Frigate Squadron

At least nine of the officers on the list of frigate specialists were given command of their own frigate squadrons at some time during the wars (at least two others commanded 'light' squadrons). Captain Edward Owen was made commodore of a frigate squadron just eight years after posting. Sir Charles Hamilton, who was posted in 1793, was given command of a small frigate squadron off the coast of Corsica in 1794. Sir Thomas Williams, posted in 1790, was given command of a frigate squadron stationed at the entrance to St George's Channel at the beginning of 1798. Lawrence Halstead, posted in 1791, was commanding a squadron of frigates blockading Elba by the latter part of 1800. Sir Graham Moore was in command of a frigate squadron in 1804 when he captured three Spanish treasure ships; he had been posted in 1794. Ross Donnelly, posted in 1795, had command of a squadron in the Mediterranean around 1802. Thomas Gossellin, posted in 1795, had charge of an inshore squadron in 1805. Philip Broke, posted in 1801, commanded a frigate squadron off the American coast by 1812. Sir William Hoste, posted in 1802, commanded a frigate squadron before the Battle of Lissa in 1811. From these dates it would appear that elevation to commodore usually took place about eight years after posting, though in some cases it was after eleven years, when the captains concerned were really quite senior officers.

One of the reasons for this degree of seniority was the Admiralty's recognition that captains could not be asked to serve under an officer below them in the post captains' list, as the commodore of a squadron. Even special appointments made over the heads of more senior officers could be problematical, as for example in 1809 when Captain Lord Cochrane was chosen to lead the attack against the French fleet in the Basque Roads. Although on this occasion Cochrane was not appointed as commodore, he was brought into the fleet specially to lead the attack. There was much discontent at this partiality, and the poor relationships engendered in Basque Roads led almost directly to the court martial of Admiral Eliab Harvey. An incident of perhaps more direct relevance occurred in 1798 when an officer was required to lead an attack on the Saas Lock at Ostend. The idea for the attack came from Captain Home Popham, who had succeeded in getting political and military support for the operation before really approaching the Admiralty. Almost before the Admiralty had a chance to influence events, there was a strong lobby for Popham to command the squadron. The First Lord, Spencer, wrote with clear irritation to Henry Dundas:

> Captain Popham should remember that he is a very young captain, that he never commanded a ship-of-war of any description (as far as I know) in his life; and I am not without apprehensions that his being placed in command of a squadron on this occasion may give great disgust and offence to the profession who are suitably irritable on these matters[78]

Popham in fact had only reached three years' seniority at this point, and the Admiralty's solution was to provide him with vessels which were not really 'post ships', commanded by very junior officers. One might be forgiven for speculating whether the ensuing debacle at Ostend might have been avoided if more experienced officers had been involved.

LIMITING THE LENGTH OF FRIGATE SERVICE

It must now appear quite clear that many officers were aware of the attraction of frigate command and those who were ambitious and successful pressed the Admiralty or their patron for command of one of the better Fifth or even Sixth Rate ships. It has been observed that the rate of pay of the captain of a frigate was considerably lower than that of the battleship captain, and it is likely that this differential was maintained to encourage good captains into the, frankly, less attractive side of sea command. It is, however, quite possible that this financial inducement was insufficient to draw the good commanders into the battle fleets of their own volition, and that, as a consequence, the Admiralty had to impose some form of semi-official and arbitrary limit on the length of time a captain could command a frigate. Although it has not been possible to find any official record of an Admiralty decision restricting the length of frigate service, the fact is that towards the end of the second war, captains began referring either directly or obliquely to a time limit. For example, in July 1813 Sir John Borlase Warren wrote to Captain Philip Broke of the frigate *Shannon*, 'I suppose you do not wish to change the *Shannon* for the *Chesapeake*, as your time of service in a frigate is so near over.'[79] In November of the same year Broke himself received a letter from Captain D P Bouverie:

> You may have heard that I continued in my old ship [the 18-pounder frigate *Medusa*] on our old station, and without having any reason to complain of my luck till the spring, when it was voted that I had been long enough in a frigate, and I was offered a seventy-four; but I thought it a favourable time to get a little respite, and I have since been a gentleman at large, and wandering about the country. Now, however, we are likely soon to be fixed, I having bought a small place near Lymington.[80]

It certainly seems possible that the Admiralty fostered the *belief* in some form of official limit, because it could then be conveniently and selectively invoked to remove captains from frigates where desirable. In March 1810, for example, trouble erupted on board the *Naiad* frigate, leading to a petition from petty officers and crew stating their refusal to put to sea under the command of the frigate's new captain, Henry Hill. This was not a very unusual occurrence but was often a symptom of a poor commanding officer, and at the subsequent court martial eight of the crew were tried for inciting mutiny and most were reprieved. Marshall tells us, 'In the following year, Captain Hill left the *Naiad*, having arrived at that standing on the list which precluded his continuing any longer in the command of a frigate. He has not since been afloat.'[81] By this time Hill had been a post captain for ten years, and whilst many frigate captains had their frigate service terminated by this juncture, quite a few served longer (see following Table 5.4). In fact, Hill's removal sounds suspiciously like a 'rule' being invoked as a convenient method of replacing him without either causing major embarrassment or setting a dangerous precedent by visibly giving in to the crew's demand. This is especially likely as, according to O'Byrne, Hill was frequently winning the approbation of the Admiralty and was, much later (in 1845), granted the Good Service Pension.

One method of testing whether some sort of ruling was being operated is to list all of those captains with average or above average frigate service[82] according to their year of posting, and then see how many years passed between their posting date (when they would have been first placed on the Captains List) and the date on which their frigate service finished.

TABLE 5.4. *Seniority of Captains at the end of their Frigate Command*

| Year Posted | Number of Years on the List by the end of Frigate Service | | | | | | | | | | | |
	> 6	6	7	8	9	10	11	12	13	14	15	16/17
1782									3	2	2	3
1783								4	4	2	2	2
1790	1	3	2	3	2	1	3	2				
1791	1						1					
1792												
1793	3	1	5	5	13		1					
1794	6	3	8	7	2	4	4	1				
1795	3	5	14	2	4	3	3	1	1			
1796		2			3	6	2	1				
1797	7		1	1	1	3	6		1			
1798	4			4	2	3	2	3	1		1	
1799	1	2				4	4			1		
1800	1		2	1		5	7					
1801	1			1	3	6	5	1	3			
1802	2	2	1	6	6	3	6	10				
1803			1			3	1					
1804	2		4		1	6						
1805					3	1						
	32	18	38	30	40	48	45	23	13	5	5	5
Per cent	11	6	13	10	13	16	15	8	4	2	2	2

NB. The statistics for this table do not include captains with less than two years frigate service, or those captains who died in service.

If the Admiralty were operating some comprehensive form of time limit for frigate service based on seniority, it would show here, because there would be a consistently high number of officers whose frigate service ended at the same time. Of those officers posted in 1793 thirteen (46 per cent) ended their frigate service in the same year, but that year was 1802, right in the middle of the Peace of Amiens. As already noted, a number of captains were placed on half-pay at this time, either temporarily or permanently. This is underlined by the figures for the posting year 1795, when fourteen captains (39 per cent) are shown to have ended their frigate service seven years later – that is, once again in 1802.

Disregarding the effect of the Peace of Amiens, it is clear that approximately 84 per cent of captains ended their frigate service by the time they had eleven years seniority on the list. Philip Broke received his letter from Sir John Borlase Warren twelve years after being posted; Bouverie was withdrawn after eleven years and Hill had the 'rule' applied to him after ten years. It is possible that, ordinarily, a flexible time limit of ten to twelve years was operating. This conclusion is reinforced by a comment made in the *Memoir of Robert Dudley Oliver*, written by his nephew, Viscount Lifford.[83] Lifford explains that following Trafalgar, Collingwood offered Oliver the command of the *Mars*, 74: 'He accepted this offer, as he was within a few months of having been ten years post captain, when it was usual to oblige a captain to take a line-of-battle ship' – or at least, to leave his frigate! By the end of 1805 Oliver had completed six and a half years of frigate service, and had command the *Melpomene* frigate since at least May 1803. There may have been a further incentive – Oliver's health had recently declined. This was certainly not serious enough to threaten his career, because he lived on until 1850, but it may have been an encouragement to give up the more rigorous existence of the frigate commander.

TABLE 5.5. *Combined Operations 1793-1815*

	Object	Commanded by	Frigates involved
1793	West Indies	R-A Gardner	*Heroine* (A H Gardner)
			Iphigenia (P Sinclair)
	Forrelli	Commodore Linzee	*Lowestoffe* (W Wolseley)
			Nemesis (Lord A Beauclerk)
1794	Martinique and Guadeloupe	V-A Jervis	*Beaulieu* (J Salisbury)
			Assurance (V C Berkeley)
			St Margarita (E Harvey)
			Solebay (W H Kelly)
			Blonde (J Markham)
			Winchelsea (Lord Garlies)
			Quebec (J Rogers)
			Ceres (R Incledon)
			Rose (E Riou/M H Scott)
			Blanche (R Faulknor)
			Terpsichore (S Edwards)
	Port au Prince	Commodore Ford	*Penelope* (B S Rowley)
			Hermione (J Hills)
			Iphigenia (P Sinclair)
1795	Quiberon Bay	Commodore J B Warren	*Pomone* (Warren)
			Anson (Durham)
			Artois (Nagle)
			Arethusa (M Robinson)
			Concorde (A Hunt)
			Galatea (Keats)
			Jason (C Stirling)
1796	St Lucia	R-A Christian	*Charon* (J Stevenson)
			Beaulieu (L Skinner)
			Arethusa (T Wolley)
			Hebe (M H Scott)
			Undaunted (H Roberts)
			Astraea (R Lane)
			Laurel ? (R Rolles)
	Colombo	Capt A H Gardner	*Heroine* (A H Gardner)
1797	Santa Cruz, Teneriffe	R-A Nelson	*Seahorse* (T Fremantle)
			Terpsichore (R Bowen)
			Emerald (J Waller)
	Trinidad	R-A Harvey	*Arethusa* (T Wolley)
			Alarm (E Fellowes)
	Porto Rico	R-A Harvey	*Tamar* (T B Martin)
			Arethusa (T Wolley)
1798	Ostend	Capt H Popham	*Circe* (R Winthorpe)
			Vestal (C White)
	Minorca	Commodore Duckworth	*Argo* (J Bowen)
			Aurora (J Caulfield)

	Object	Commanded by	Frigates involved
1799	Transport of Russian troops to Revel, Holland		*Hebe* (W Birchall) *Romulus* (J Culverhouse) *Ulysses* (T Pressland) *Blonde* (D Dobree) *Niger* (J Larmour) *Espion* (J Rose)
	Helder, Texel	V-A Mitchell	*Melpomene* (Sir C Hamilton) *Latona* (F Sotheron) *Shannon* (C D Pater) *Juno* (G Dundas) *Lutine* (G Monkton)
April 1800	'Secret Expedition' [Ferrol]		10 frigates armed *en flute*
1800	Quiberon Bay and BelleIsle	Sir Edward Pellew	*Amethyst* (J Cooke) *Fisgard* (T B Martin) *Amelia* (Hon C Herbert) *Diamond* (E Griffiths) *Doris* (Lord Ranelagh) *Thames* (W Lukin)
	Ferrol	R-A J B Warren	*Indefatigable* (Hon H Curzon) *Amelia* (Hon C Herbert) *Amethyst* (J Cooke) *Stag* (R Winthorpe) *Brilliant* (Hon C Paget)
1801	Baltic	Adm Hyde Parker	*Desiree* (H Inman) *Amazon* (E Riou) *Blanche* (G E Hammond) *Alcmene* (S Sutton)
	Neutral islands in the West Indies	R-A Duckworth	*Diana* (J P Beresford) *Unité* (T Harvey) *Southampton* (J Harvey) *Andromeda* (J Bradby) *Amphitrite* (C Ekins) *Proselyte* (G Fowke)
1803	Leeward Isles	Commodore Sir S Hood	*Emerald* (O'Bryen)
1804	Goree, then coast of America	Capt E Stirling Dickson	*Inconstant*
1806	Cape	Capt Home Popham	*Leda* (R Honeyman) *Narcissus* (R Donnelly)
	Buenos Ayres	Capt Home Popham and Maj-Gen Beresford	*Narcissus*
1807	Copenhagen	Adm Gambier and Lt-Gen Lord Cathcart	*Sybille* (C Upton) *Franchise* (C Dashwood) *Nymphe* (C Shipley) *Africaine* (R Raggett)

	Object	Commanded by	Frigates involved
	Madeira	Sir S Hood and Maj-Gen Beresford	*Africaine*, (R Raggett) *Shannon* (P Broke) *Alceste* (M Maxwell) *Success* (J Ayscough)
	Monte Video	R-A G Murray and Lt-Gen Whitelocke	*Leda* (R Honeyman) *Unicorn* (L Hardyman) *Medusa* (D Pleydell Bouverie)
	Alexandria	Capt B Hallowell and Maj-Gen Fraser	*Apollo* (E Fellowes)
1809	Rio	Capt Yeo	? *President* (Mackenzie) ? *Surveillante* (Collier)
	Withdrawal from Corunna	R-A Sir S Hood	*Endymion* (Hon T B Capel)
	Calabria	R-A G Martin and Gen Sir John Stuart	? *Spartan* (J Brenton)
	Ras al Khyma, Persian Gulf	Capt Wainwright and Lt- Col Smith	*La Chiffonne* (J Wainwright) *Caroline* (Gordon)
	Martinique	R-A Sir A Cochrane and Lt-Gen Beckwith	*Acasta* (Beaver) *Penelope* (J Dick) *Aeolus* (Lord W Fitzroy) *Cleopatra* (S J Pechell)
	Vigo	Capt Crawford	*Venus* (Crawford) *Lively* (M'Kinley)
	Walcheren	R-A Sir Richard Strachan	*Amethyst* (M Seymour) *Fisgard* (W Bolton) *Salsette* (R Keats) *Clyde* (E Owen) *Lavinia* (Lord W Stuart) *Perlen* (N Thompson) *Rota* (P Somerville) *Statira* (C Boys) *Aigle* (G Wolfe) *Euryalus* (Hon G Dundas) *Dryad* (E Galwey) *Nymphen* (K Maxwell) *Heroine* (H Christian)
1810	Amboyna and Banda Neira, East Indies	Adm Drury	*Dover* (Tucker) *Cornwallis* (Montagu) *Caroline* (C Cole) *Piedmontaise* (Foote?)
	Mauritius	Capt J Rowley	*Psyche* (J Edgecumbe) *Cornelia* (H Edgell) *Doris* (C Cole) *Cornwallis* (W Montagu) *Phoebe* (J Hillyar) *Iphigenia* (H Lambert)

Object	Commanded by	Frigates involved
		Magicienne (L Curtis)
		Boadicea (J Rowley)
		Sirius (S Pym)
		Nereide (N Willoughby)
		Africaine (R Corbet)
		Nisus (P Beaver)
		Clorinde (J Briggs)
		Menelaus (P Parker)
St Maura, Mediterranean	Capt G Eyre	*Belle Poule*
		Leonidas (Griffiths)
Guadeloupe	Sir A Cochrane and Lt-Gen Beckwith	

	Object	Commanded by	Frigates involved
1811	Batavia, East Indies	R-A Stopford and Lt-Gen Auchmuty	*Leda* (Sayer)
			Nisus
			Caroline
			Phoebe
			Cornelia
			Modeste
	Cadiz	Sir R G Keats and Lt-Gen Graham	*Druid*
	Palinro	Capt H Duncan	*Imperieuse* (Duncan)
			Thames (C Napier)
	Ponza	Capt Napier and Lt-Col Coffin	*Thames* (Mounsey?)
	St George	Capt Hoste and Capt Lowen (army)	*Bacchante* (Hoste)
1814	Baltimore	Sir A Cochrane and Maj-Gen Ross	*Loire* (T Browne)
			Narcissus (J Lumley)
			Severn (J Nourse)
			Menelaus (P Parker)
	Genoa	Sir J Rowley and Lt-Gen Lord W Bentinck	*Iphigenia*
	Oswego, Lake Ontario	Sir J Yeo	*Prince Regent*
			Princess Charlotte
	Ragusa	Capt W Hoste	*Bacchante* (Hoste)
	Washington	Sir A Cochrane	*Hebrus* (E Palmer)
			Severn (J Nourse)
			Menelaus (P Parker)
			Seahorse (Gordon)
			Euryalus (C Napier)
1815	Guadeloupe	Admiral Sir P C Durham and Sir James Leith	??
	New Orleans	Sir A Cochrane and Maj-Gen Hon Sir E Pakenham	*Seahorse* (Gordon)

CHAPTER
VI

ACTIONS AND AFTERMATH

A BOOK ON FRIGATE CAPTAINS would be incomplete without touching on the subject of frigate actions in at least some depth. There are already many books dealing with the sea fights that took place between 1793 and 1815 and there is nothing to be gained from repeating their outlines; nevertheless, combat lay at the heart of the activities of the men who served in or commanded frigates and the subject must be considered. This chapter examines a select number of engagements, but concentrating on the experience of combat, and its significance in the careers of the officers involved – not just during the battle but also after the guns fell silent, an aspect rarely addressed in conventional naval histories. Not all of the specialist or longest serving frigate captains identified in the previous chapter fought single-ship engagements, and the following analysis will focus on a small number of officers who distinguished themselves in action more than once or whose actions merit consideration for a combination of reasons. This is largely determined by the nature of the source material available.

Over the last century or so numerous works have been written on the subject of frigate actions during the Great Wars with France.[1] Virtually all of them have one thing in common: they are concerned primarily with the manoeuvres of the ships and the circumstances in which they came together. They are also notable for generally ignoring the men who managed and fought those actions. The reasons for this may be rooted in the fact that the crews, and even the officers, have become obscured over the passage of time. To society in general the ordinary seaman, even at the time, was usually perceived as just a name in a ship's muster book or, occasionally, a name printed in the casualty list of a newspaper. As the nineteenth century wore on the officers also faded into obscurity. Perhaps this is an inevitable process of history, but in this case it is also a product of the sparse source material available to the historian.

There is a popular image, perpetuated by the writers of naval fiction, of naval captains sitting round endlessly re-tracing the courses of famous actions, or those in which they were personally engaged. If these discussions did take place, and there is some evidence to suggest that they did, those participants rarely seem to have committed their experiences to paper. Of the many hundreds of naval officers who served during the Great Wars with France, only a tiny minority produced any form of autobiographical work, and a minuscule proportion of these were involved in a frigate action. This is not to say that such works are entirely lacking. At a stretch, the category might include Cochrane's *Autobiography of a Seaman*, but, strictly speaking, Cochrane was never involved in a ship-to-ship frigate engagement. William Henry Dillon provides a very vivid description of a battle between two brigs and this may serve well to illustrate a single-ship action,[2] but there would have been a great deal of difference between commanding a brig and a frigate in action. Possibly the only frigate captain to write an autobiographical memoir which included an account of a single-ship action was John Surman Carden, who commanded the frigate *Macedonian* when she was captured by the American frigate *United States* in October 1812. The problem with this account is partially revealed 260 pages into the work when Carden explains why he has written his memoir:

It was near the conclusion of my Visit at Swindon Hall, at Dinner with some of Mr Surman's Friends, when the subject of the Frigate's Battle [*Macedonian*], with the *United States* ... became the Topic of Conversation, & I found by the Sentiment of one of the Company, that He or they little understood the true state of the subject in question.[3]

Reading between the lines, one may infer that Carden was stung by remarks made at dinner and decided to write a corrective account. His description of the engagement is actually very short and not terribly informative – perhaps because it is so defensive. In truth, genuine firsthand accounts of such actions, by officers in particular, are hard to find. Most of the information that survives from the participants either take the form of ships' logs, the official dispatch written in the immediate aftermath of the event, or the rare personal accounts which (like Carden's) were written some years later. In both former cases the accounts tend to be impersonal and it is difficult to learn anything of the nature of the participant himself.

For the great majority of frigate actions, the standard reference source is William James's *A Naval History of Great Britain*. It is worth dwelling on this work for a moment to understand its significance to this subject, especially as James is still generally regarded as veracious and reliable. James had been employed for several years as a proctor in the Admiralty Court at Jamaica and he was resident in America at the time of the outbreak of the War of 1812. Being a member of a hostile nation, he was placed under arrest, and during this time he was able to observe the effects of the American naval successes during the war, particularly in relation to the defeat of the British frigates *Java*, *Macedonian* and *Guerriere*. This inspired him to write a narrative which developed into the much larger history of the wars, first published in 1822-4. In his Introduction to *The Naval History* James states that, in his search for a true account, he studied ships' logs, Gazette letters, other primary sources, and also wrote to a number of participants. On the question of official correspondence written immediately after an engagement, James noted that the letters were 'very imperfect'; captains were mentally and physically exhausted after the action, and as he puts it, many were simply 'far more expert at the sword than at the pen'.[4] He also placed an advertisement inviting officers to contribute information and wrote to a number of individuals. Not all of the officers to whom he wrote were willing to respond. Although he received three hundred replies, several officers were reluctant to talk about actions in which they were engaged, and some certainly wanted to play-down their activities. Many simply do not seem to have responded to his enquiries and in some cases there was outright hostility towards him. James suggests that this may have been the result of a prejudice against him within the service because he was not himself a naval officer and because he was prepared to be critical. The response to James might be contrasted with the much greater degree of co-operation that Lieutenant John Marshall received when compiling his *Royal Naval Biography* in 1823.

Notwithstanding the success that John Marshall had in *his* appeals for autobiographical information, it is possible that, as in all wars, the participants felt a reluctance to communicate their experiences once the war was over. Marshall's work (like that of James) is of course written as a third person narrative. This effectively creates an editorial barrier between the contributor and the reader, who cannot tell if the entry is the officer's statement or Marshall's. Among the Rainier Papers at the National Maritime Museum is a curious undated document written by Captain Peter Rainier,[5] detailing the course of his career and the list of prizes that he took as captain of the frigate *Caroline*. It is quite possible that this is a copy of a document prepared for Marshall, but whatever its purpose, it is written in a dispassionate prose that gives no description of the actions in which Rainier was involved nor insight into his character. This is a great pity because Rainer was one of the more interesting young captains of the Napoleonic War. It is also possible that this was typical of the sort of response to his enquiries that James received. If this was the case then it is hardly surprising that his *Naval History* reveals little about the men who commanded His Majesty's ships of war. There is another factor which may help explain the attitude of some officers towards James. His biggest fault was his determined patriotism which, at best, was unforgiving of perceived failure, and at worst led him to make unfair and ill-judged pronouncements. This is very much illustrated by his treatment of Captain John Phillimore of HMS *Eurotas*. But of this, more later.

If he had less co-operation than he might have liked, at least he had recourse to the ships' logs, but a reliance on the log of a frigate was even less likely to provide information about the men involved in an engagement. The information in ships' logs followed age-old conventions, and were usually entered in a brusque, almost notational language. Here, for example, is the complete log entry for what is now perhaps the most studied frigate action of the entire period, the engagement between the British *Shannon* and the American *Chesapeake*, on Tuesday 1 June 1813:

PM. Light breezes and fine. Observed the Enemey's Frigate Chesapeake under weigh. Kept away to gain an offing. 1. The enemy rounded the light house. Up foresail & down jib (steering offshore). 3.20. Cape Ann North 6 or 7 Leagues, the Enemy still coming down under all sail, with several small craft & a large schr apparently armed round him. 3.40. In topsails & staysails. Chesapeake closing fast with 3 Ensigns & a white flag at the fore having on it 'Free Trade & Seamans Rights'. 5.10. Beat to Quarters. Hoisted the Jib and filled the topsail. 5.30. Filled the Maintops'l and kept a close luff, the Enemy coming down under his topsails and jib. 5.40. He luff'd up on our W.Q. within Pistol Shot & gave three cheers. 5.50. Commenced action within hail. After three broadsides the Enemy appeared unmanageable, & having shot away our Jib Stay fell on board of us. Grappled the Enemy & boarded him & after an action of ten minutes succeeded in hauling down his flags.

Cleared the Enemy & sent the Jolly Boat to exchange prisoners. In boarding, lost the life of Mr. Watt, 1st Lieut – & sev'l men. Capt very seriously wounded by one of the Enemy, whilst endeavouring to rescue him from his own men. Could not ascertain our own loss or that of the Enemy from the lateness of the Evening and … parts of our people having boarded the Chesapeake. Out Yawl, having repaired her & sent her to exchange prisoners. Found our masts considerably wounded & the rigging & hull of the ship considerably cut up.[6]

From this example, it should be clear why James's history became the work that it is, and why subsequent books on frigate actions have tended to be de-personalised. From James it is possible to learn something of the movement of frigates in action, but nothing of the men who manoeuvred them.[7] To learn more about the personal experience of a frigate action it is necessary to trawl a number of disparate sources, and even so, there is no detailed account of one single action. What follows, therefore, is a form of montage.

THE EXPERIENCE OF BATTLE

The first point to make is that, of the 670 or so captains of frigates during the twenty-two years of conflict, probably only 4-5 per cent actually commanded a frigate during a single-ship action (specifically, an action between two frigates). The vast majority of engagements in which frigates and their crews were involved were associated with the taking of privateers and smaller armed vessels, cutting-out expeditions or combined operations against land-based forces. A single-ship frigate action was uncommon – hence the impact a victory or defeat made when it occurred. Nevertheless, it is clear that such an action was something that many captains longed for. The possibility of meeting and taking an enemy frigate in a single-ship action was without doubt one of the great motivators of the young officers aspiring to frigate command. Indeed, it could sometimes become almost an obsession, which perhaps explains the extraordinary state of readiness of the *Shannon* under Captain Philip Broke.[8] Broke's attitude is best revealed in the letters he wrote home to his wife. On one occasion, in the depth of depression, he wrote:

> I would give any of the French frigate Captains all the prize money I should obtain by taking him if he would only come out voluntarily to give me an opportunity of going home with honor ... but I must stay by old *Shannon* so long as she will bear with me and perhaps she may be gracious enough to make me some return for my constancy – either in laurels or in lucre.[9]

The capture of an enemy frigate might mean not only glory, but could also result in substantial prize money, and (less frequently) honours. Combat was the ultimate trial of the captain of a frigate, for during an engagement the team of men which constituted his officers and crew were tested to the utmost. The importance of the regime a commander had established is, perhaps, best illustrated by the fact that many frigate actions were won by the speed and skill with which a crew repaired their rigging during a lull in the action. It was not uncommon for opposing ships to fight themselves to a temporary standstill: that is, when the damage sustained rendered it impossible for them to continue manoeuvring or controlling the ship. In these circumstances the outcome could be determined by the ability of a crew to get their ship back into a state of combat readiness before the enemy. If the commander had adequately trained his crew in seamanship and gun-handling and had sufficiently nurtured their morale and health, and ensured that the ship and its stores, armament and fittings were in the best possible state of preparedness, he had taken all the steps he could to ensure that the ship might fight on an equal basis with an opponent – having mastered all possible elements under his control. Under such circumstances the ultimate outcome could depend heavily on the quality of the enemy, wind and weather – factors *beyond* his control.

However, there was another vital factor – leadership. Anyone who has studied the activities of Nelson at the Battle of Cape St Vincent, for example, will be aware how vital and decisive the decisions and example of one man can be, when in a leadership position. The ability of a frigate captain and his officers to provide leadership in action was crucial – probably more so than in a fleet action, because the opponents focussed solely on each other without the distraction of other participants. Once a frigate cleared for action, there was a clearly understood hierarchy of control. Midshipmen and lieutenants were usually responsible for divisions of guns and gun crews. The first lieutenant was usually on the quarterdeck with the captain. The captain gave immediate direction to the men at the helm or the ship's master, who would issue the necessary commands to reef sails, brace the yards, or any orders necessary to manoeuvre the ship. If the captain was incapacitated, even temporarily, control passed to the lieutenants in order of seniority. If all of the commissioned officers were incapacitated it was probable that the crew would be unable to continue the action, as there would be no co-ordination of manpower to either manoeuvre or fight the ship. However, before the situation had become this critical, it was more likely that the remaining officers would either break off the action, or surrender to prevent unnecessary slaughter (there were in reality few officers willing to fight 'to the last man').

From this it can be seen that the culture of command a captain created on board his ship was a vital element when it came to combat. Ultimately, much depended on the man himself. Although a new commander or post captain would probably have spent, at the very least, eight years as a midshipman and lieutenant, there was no guarantee that he would experience combat during this period. However, if he did, the chances are that it would be in some form of leadership position, either commanding a division of guns, or perhaps leading a cutting-out expedition or boarding party. These would introduce or even harden him to the horrors and difficulties of combat, but unless his existing captain was killed during an action, there was little that could prepare him in advance for the pressure of command in a single-ship action. The responsibility would be so much greater and it would only be natural for officers to wonder how they would respond when their time came.

Whether it was an issue which was widely discussed has yet to be proven, but there is at least one case where two frigate captains are known to have considered how they would cope with taking a frigate into action.

The evidence for this is to be found in the correspondence (originals now lost) between Captain Michael Seymour of the *Amethyst* and Captain Edward Hawker of the *Melampus*. The two men were perhaps unusually close, Seymour having married one of Hawker's sisters, and Hawker having served as lieutenant in the *Spitfire* sloop when Seymour was her commander. Writing to each other as both friends and brothers-in-law, their correspondence was particularly candid. A week following his successful action against the French frigate *Thétis* in November 1808, Seymour wrote to Captain Edward Hawker about the action, commenting: 'Thanks to heaven, my mind was clear, and I felt during the greater part of the action delighted, at ease, under occasional anxiety, and on <u>one</u> or <u>two</u> critical occasions, under apprehensions.' Occasional apprehension he may have had, but this was not apparent to the frigate's master, Robert Fair, who noted afterwards: 'I was much struck when on the moon's rising at a most critical period of the fight and revealing the *Thétis* returning gallantly to the contest, he turned to me, and said, "Look, Fair, what a subject for a painter!"'[10]

Seymour's courage and cool confidence enabled him to gain sufficient detachment from what was going on around him and gave him the psychological time and space in which to plan, anticipate and react during the course of the action. Seymour's confidence might be contrasted with the example of John Surman Carden. Although Carden tells us nothing about his state of mind during the action between the *Macedonian* and *United States*, there was another eye-witness to the event who does. This was the seaman Samuel Leech. Leech appears to have had a dislike for all of the captains under whom he served and he certainly had no love for Carden. He noted that Carden was more than usually fretful before the encounter with the *United States*. Carden was aware that a state of hostilities existed between Britain and the United States and it seems that he received intelligence at Madeira that an American frigate was operating on the eastern side of the Atlantic. Leech noted:

> our captain appeared more anxious than usual; he was on deck almost all of the time; the 'look-out' aloft was more rigidly observed; and every little while the cry of 'Mast-head there!' arrested our attention ... Thus we passed several days; the captain running up and down, and constantly hailing the man at the mast-head ... Indeed he seemed almost crazy with some pressing anxiety.[11]

When, eventually, the American frigate was sighted, Carden made a critical tactical error. In the Royal Navy it had become standard practice to try and maintain the weather gage: that is, to keep to windward of an opponent, as the windward ship has more control over when and how to come to close action. The leeward ship, in this case the *United States*, has to close against the wind, a much more difficult task. Furthermore, the leeward ship stands more chance of her broadside going over the enemy, whereas the broadside of the windward ship, if fired low when the ship is heeling towards the enemy, may just ricochet off the sea into the opponent's hull. These were standard tactics, but completely wrong in this situation. With her much more powerful armament, the *United States* did not need to close with the *Macedonian* and her longer range guns could hit the smaller British frigate before fire could be returned. This danger was anticipated by David Hope, Carden's first lieutenant. He urged Carden to bring the *Macedonian* down on the *United States* as soon as possible, for the British frigate would also be able to rake the bows of the American in the process. Carden though, stuck adamantly to his original plan and then, when he did decide to close, Captain Stephen Decatur in the *United States* maintained *his* advantage by slipping downwind and keeping his distance.

Although gallantly fought, the *Macedonian* had little chance against the more powerfully armed and better commanded American frigate. Carden's anxiety had made it difficult for him to think creatively and he was unable to analyse what was going on. As a result he was unable to appreciate the tactics suggested by Lieutenant Hope.

Pre-engagement anxiety would be a factor affecting both officers and crew, and it was probably something which would only intensify whilst waiting for the action to start. It is important to remember that it often took a long time for opposing frigates to come to close quarters. The norm would appear to have been between three and five fours – that is, three to five hours between first sighting the enemy and coming into close engagement. In the case of the *Chesapeake* and *Shannon*, for example, the action itself lasted barely fifteen minutes. However, the two ships were in visual contact from at least 1pm on the afternoon of the action, nearly five hours before finally engaging at 5.50pm. Even then Broke did not beat to quarters until 5.10pm. Engagements often took place after a much longer delay than this. In April 1804, for example, the *Wilhelmina*, a 12-pounder 32-gun frigate armed *en flûte*, commanded by Captain Henry Lambert, first sighted the French privateer frigate *Psyché* at daybreak on 9 April. The two ships did not actually engage until 5.30am on the 11th. This delay was partly the result of a deliberate tactic by Lambert to lure the *Psyché* away from a valuable merchantman which he had been escorting and the delay was then extended slightly by the intervention of a squall which prevented the ships closing. After a furious engagement, the badly damaged *Psyché* escaped.[12] In one of those strange twists of fate, in February 1805 Lambert, now commanding the 36-gun 18-pounder frigate *San Fiorenzo*, captured the same French frigate (now a national frigate rather than a privateer) after a chase lasting 39 hours.[13]

The atmosphere on board a frigate waiting to engage was vividly captured by Midshipman Abraham Crawford, recalling an occasion when the *Immortalité*, Captain Edward Owen, chased a French frigate off the French coast:

> We immediately gave chase ... the drum beat to quarters, and a very few minutes sufficed to have the ship ready for action. Although the chase, when first seen, was not far from us ... we did not get within hail of her for nearly an hour, affording leisure for serious thought and reflection at such a time. And certainly, after the bustle and excitement attendant upon a sudden call to quarters at night is over – when the guns are all cleared and laid, and everything at quarters is now in its proper place – when expectation and anxiety, by the protracted chase, are raised to a painful degree – and a silence, a stillness almost breathless, only broken at times by a whispered order from a Lieutenant giving some necessary directions – succeeds to hurried preparation, I own I have felt, at such a time, a thrilling solemnity, approaching to awe, which I never knew when the broad clear day gave light to such scenes. Then the dusky figures of the sailors, with arms bared, and heads and loins girded for the strife, or their hats ornamented with bits of oakum twisted hard for vents, appear of larger proportions, seen by the doubtful light, as with folded arms, and bent, determined brows, they pass, from time to time, with silent step, between you and the fighting lanterns, whose feeble rays scarcely serve to penetrate the gloom – the whole offering a picture not unworthy of the painter's art.
>
> ... anon the Commodore's voice, bidding the men 'stand to their guns' disturbs the transient calm. In an instant the crew start into activity and animation...[14]

If the chase was likely to be a long one, the chances are that the captain might not clear the ship for action immediately, or perhaps he would let the crew stand down to eat. It was actually rare for a frigate to come into close action in less than a couple of hours. One of the very few examples where this did occur was in the engagement between the 12-pounder 32-gun *Thames*, commanded by Captain James Cotes, and the considerably heavier French frigate *Uranie* in October 1793. In this case the two frigates sighted each other at 9.30am, only to lose each other for forty-five minutes in 'thick weather'. At 10.15am when the French frigate was again sighted she was already bearing down on the *Thames*. There was limited opportunity to manoeuvre and there was a clear determination by the French to attack the smaller vessel. The ensuing close action continued for four hours until the *Uranie* broke it off, having failed to board the British frigate.

The circumstances in which opposing frigates first sighted each other could be a major factor in determining how quickly the ships engaged. It is no co-incidence that in the majority of cases opposing ships sighted each other around daybreak. There *were* a small number of night-time actions – usually encouraged by the certainty over the nature of the stranger, probably because she had been sighted during daylight hours or was betrayed by her behaviour – but a night action involved certain risks. Whilst there was always the difficulty of identifying a genuine enemy in the dark, there was the additional problem, if engaging near a coastline, of maintaining an adequate lookout for rocks and shallows. It was precisely this latter point which led to the loss of the *Amazon*, Captain Robert Carthew Reynolds, and nearly also caused the loss of the *Indefatigable*, commanded by Sir Edward Pellew, in January 1797. For eleven hours during the hours of darkness, in terrible weather, the two frigates had been so intent on engaging the French 74 *Droits de l'Homme* that all three combatants ran into the Bay of Audierne without realising it. The shore was not seen until the frigates were two miles from the land. The engagement was then hurriedly broken off as the two frigates desperately braced round their yards in an attempt to escape from the shore. The French 74 was by this time too badly damaged to make the attempt, and rolled on her side in the surf. The *Amazon* also ran aground and six of her crew, stealing a boat, were drowned in an attempt to reach the shore. It says much for Reynolds and the men under his command that within a few hours they had been able to build rafts for all of the remaining crew, so that even the wounded were ferried ashore in safety. Pellew, in a display of consummate seamanship, was able to claw the *Indefatigable* out of danger and back to Falmouth. Against this sort of risk the frigate captain had to decide whether it was better to shadow the other ship until morning and hope that she did not escape during the hours of darkness. At first light on a clear day the top-hamper of a square-rigged ship might be visible from as much as twenty miles away, and it is probably this early morning disclosure, together with the tactic of shadowing during the hours of darkness, that accounts for many of the first sightings being recorded at daybreak, or shortly thereafter.

As has been previously noted, the men who served in His Majesty's frigates have left very little information about what it was like to experience a frigate action. There is, however, one account of an action by what might be described as a third-party witness. This was Captain R W Eastwick, commander of a merchantman in the East Indies country trade.[15] In February 1799 his vessel, the *Endeavour*, fell prey to the French frigate *La Forte*, which was wreaking havoc amongst English shipping in the Bay of Bengal. *La Forte* was a very large and heavily armed frigate mounting 24-pounder guns. In an attempt to put a stop to her depredations, the British frigate *Sybille*, mounting smaller 18-pounder guns, was sent to try and intercept her. The two frigates met on the night of 1 March, and Eastwick, a prisoner on board the *Forte*, was a firsthand witness to the engagement. Although confined below decks for part of the engagement, was able to view the action from what he described as a small port-hole.

The *Sybille*, commanded by Captain Edward Cooke, approached the French frigate from the windward side and, showing no light, fooled the French officers into thinking that she was an unsuspecting merchant vessel:

Suddenly, having got into a proper position ... all the tarpaulins which had covered the lanterns and hidden the lights on board of the *La Sybille* were removed as if by magic, and an illuminated large English ship exposed to view. She was now within two cables' lengths, and luffed to the wind on the starboard tack, and the next instant the whole broadside of a well-directed fire was poured into *La Forte*. Then edging down, after the discharge, before the wind, the *La Sybille* came fairly alongside ...[On board the *Forte*, the] decks had been raked with the small grapeshot that came like hail from the 24-pounders[16] of her opponent, and in a moment all was shouting and noise and confusion. Whistles were piped, orders were cried out, and the crew were hurried up to serve the guns, urged on by their officers. The Admiral was killed early in the action, and the captain fell next ... He was cut in half by a chain-shot whilst trying to rally his crew, who, having been fairly caught a napping, were all in alarm and confusion. The execution wrought amongst their ranks by the sudden broadside was dreadful, and the whole ship resounded with the shrieks and groans of the wounded, making a noise that was sickening to hear ... The musketry rattled, and between the thunder of the guns, as broadside after broadside was returned, there came the lesser but constant discharges of the brass swivels mounted on the quarter-deck...

At this point the remaining officers of the *Forte* attempted to break off the action. However, the gunners on *Sybille* were now ordered to direct their fire at the rigging of the French frigate.

La Forte's shrouds were presently shot away, and soon afterwards her masts went by the board one after another with an awful crash, carrying all the top hamper with them, until the deck became an inextricable mass of tangled rigging, and the frigate lay a helpless cripple upon the water …

… The din and noise were awful; the great ship shook and quivered under every discharge of her guns; a suffocating smell of gunpowder smoke pervaded the whole vessel, we being to leeward; and every second or third minute there came a great crash, most startling in the dark, and we heard a shot go rioting through the prison we were confined in, and did not know whether the next might not carry us all off. From overhead came the trampling of feet, the cries of the wounded, the crashing sounds of falling spars and top hamper, heard between the thundering of the cannon and the lesser roar of the small arms…

… At last the action began to draw to a close. The discharges of cannon were less frequent, and *La Forte*'s men being all engaged in trying to set sail, the rattle of musketry on the quarter-deck above our heads almost ceased.

At this point, Eastwick and his fellow prisoners were released and made their way on deck as the French frigate surrendered.

The value of Eastwick's account lies in the fact that he was a helpless witness to the engagement. Unable to take an active part, he had no distractions and experienced it fully through the senses of sight, sound and smell. Eastwick himself observed of his own experience:

The excitement of action was wanting, which assists men to face fire, and at times hardly to heed it. And added to all was the terrible sense of uncertainty as to what was happening, with whom we were contending, and whether the *La Forte* was winning the day or losing it.

Eastwick's point is highly pertinent in suggesting how the officers and crews of frigates coped with the horrors of naval warfare. To the men at the guns in particular, a frigate action consisted of a frantic race to load, aim, fire, and reload their gun as quickly as possible, probably in the hope that the more and sooner they could inflict damage on the ship opposite them, the less chance there was that they would receive injurious or deadly fire in return. A well disciplined and trained crew would focus all of their concentration and energy on this activity unless they were called away to manoeuvre the ship, repair rigging, or join a boarding party. Whilst a certain number of gun crews were able to maintain this essential activity efficiently, the ship would still fight – but if the level of activity dropped below a critical point, if the individual guns became undermanned, or the number of guns firing declined too far, the balance of the action would swing against them. As this happened, the rate of fire would drop and members of gun crews would have more time to become aware of what was happening around them. It would be at this point that morale would break down and an undisciplined or demoralised crew would flee from their guns. There were occasions where this happened aboard British frigates, but it was unusual. That it did not was largely due to the officers and the culture of command that the captain had instilled on board. This will be looked at in more detail in the next chapter.

It should be noted, however, that in some ways Eastwick's account is much more akin to the experience of a seaman than an officer. For much of the action Eastwick was confined below deck and his view of what was happening was probably similar to that of the seaman glimpsing the enemy through the gunport. The captain and officers on the quarterdeck were all too well aware of what was happening during the course of the action. To a very large degree their ability to deal with and react to changes in the course of the action ultimately defined whether they would be victor or vanquished. Crucial to this was the degree to which a captain had developed the skills, abilities and confidence of his officers, for if the captain himself was incapacitated during the action, the officers had to step into the breach of command. In the encounter described above,[17] Captain Cooke of the *Sybille* was mortally wounded part way through the action, and the subsequent victory was achieved under the direction of Lieutenant Lucius Hardyman. The victory over the *Forte* was therefore a testimony not only to Cooke's regime on board the ship but also to a system of officer training and promotion which, although it may have seemed haphazard, also usually worked.

Before proceeding to look in more detail at specific single-ship frigate engagements it is important to reiterate that, just as there is some evidence that captains discussed how they would cope in an engagement, there is also evidence that tactics were considered in detail. Furthermore, it is clear that there was a highly committed professional element within the corps of frigate captains who were keen to see the development of fighting tactics and gunnery. Nevertheless, it is very difficult to find officers committing their ideas or discussions to paper – apart from the occasional comment in the *Naval Chronicle*. However, in 1820 Sir Howard Douglas produced *A Treatise on Naval Gunnery*.[18] Towards the end of this work the author states that his chapter on frigate tactics is primarily the result of his discussions with two officers in particular, and that he has quoted them substantially (without denoting where!) in the chapter itself. The two officers concerned were Philip Broke and Samuel Pechell. Broke is, of course, famous for the action between the *Shannon* and the *Chesapeake* in 1813, when the gunnery of the British frigate devastated the crew of the *Chesapeake* in minutes. Pechell, however, is less well known, probably because he never had the opportunity to fight a single-ship action. Nevertheless, Pechell was one of the great advocates of regular and 'scientific' gunnery drill. Like Broke, he had elevation and ranging marks fitted to the guns of his frigate, and had his gun crews practising with the same method. Both officers served in frigates on the American station under Sir John Borlase Warren, who also happened to be Pechell's uncle, and both followed with great concern the activities of the American frigates during the War of 1812. It is clear from Douglas's comments that Pechell and Broke analysed the course of these actions (and probably of others also) and drew up tactics for fighting the bigger, more heavily armed Americans. In his youth Sir John Warren himself had been a frigate commander of considerable merit, and with Pellew, commanded the independent frigate squadrons operating out of Falmouth between 1795 and 1797. Pechell actually entered the navy on board the *Pomone*, commanded by Warren, in 1796, so he would have had firsthand experience of the activities of the frigate squadron and Warren's method of command.

ROBERT BARLOW

Robert Barlow, one of the longest serving frigate commanders, was also one of the most successful. Barlow commanded the 36-gun 18-pounder frigate *Phoebe*, to which Pechell was transferred when the frigate squadrons were disbanded. The *Phoebe* was based at Falmouth with the rest of the ships of the squadrons and it is hard to believe that there was no interchange of ideas about tactics, training and techniques of command. It was from Barlow that Pechell learned about gunnery, and it is strongly implied in a paper produced by Pechell some years later,[19] that Broke also picked up similar ideas from captains under whom he served as a lieutenant, possible the Hon Charles Herbert in the *Amelia*, or Captain James Macnamara in the *Southampton*.

Barlow scored two major successes in single-ship actions. On 21 December 1797, whilst cruising approximately 200 miles due west of Brest, the *Phoebe* captured the 12-pounder 36-gun French frigate *Néréide* during a night action in which the French ship had the advantage of the weather gage. *Phoebe* was, however, a heavier frigate, being armed with 18-pounder guns, and after several hours the damage and casualties on board the *Néréide* forced her captain to strike. William James, in unusually complimentary fashion, noted of this action: 'The relative proportion of loss proves, however, that, had more been required of, more could have been performed by, Captain Barlow, his officers and ship's company.'[20] At the time of this engagement Barlow had commanded the *Phoebe* for approximately two years.

Barlow's success was not just the result of having the superior frigate. On a dark night in February 1801 (during her one year outside home waters), the *Phoebe* encountered the 40-gun French frigate *Africaine* just east of Gibraltar. After a two-hour close engagement the French frigate struck, and a fortnight later Barlow brought his prize into Port Mahon. It has to be said that this was probably one of the bloodiest frigate actions of the war. The *Africaine* was carrying troops bound for Egypt, and the gunnery of the *Phoebe* caused devastation on her opponent's decks. Even William James had to remark that the French casualties were 'truly dreadful', suffering, as she did, 200 killed and 143 wounded.[21] Marshall tells us that 'For his courage and excellent conduct on this occasion Captain Barlow was deservedly rewarded with the honor of a knighthood, [on] June 16, 1801.'[22]

By the time of this second action Barlow and his ship had been together just over five years, time enough to weld his crew into an effective team. Both frigates suffered severe damage as a result of the action and while the Royal Navy's tactic of aiming shot at the hull rather than the rigging of an enemy vessel may well account for the disparity in casualties, the discipline and morale of the crew of the *Phoebe* remained intact after two hours of close action, whereas the crew of the *Africaine*, despite their superior armament, were unable to sustain the action in the face of the superior British gunnery. Pechell served in the *Phoebe* during both of these engagements and undoubtedly learned much from the experience. What the example of Barlow and the *Phoebe* also appears to demonstrate is that keeping good officers and crew together, particularly on a familiar station, was an important ingredient for an effective frigate. Of course, Barlow and his crew demonstrated their abilities on other occasions also, capturing for example three French privateers, mounting in all 58 guns; also *L'Hazard*, 10 guns, laden with spices, ivory and gum from Senegal, valued at £10,000; and *L'Heureux* of 22 brass 12-pounder guns.

FRANCIS LAFOREY

The promotion of Francis Laforey to post captain in 1793 was directly due to his father (Vice-Admiral Laforey) sending him home with dispatches following the capture of Tobago. For the next six and a half years he commanded the *Carysfort*, 28, *Aimable*, 32 and then the *Hydra*, 38 on the Leeward Islands station (which he knew very well) and on the Channel station. Laforey appears to have been a very well respected and popular officer, certainly earning rare approval from William James.[23] On 29 May 1794, nine months after being given command of his first frigate, the British 28-gun frigate *Carysfort*, Laforey fell in with the French (previously British) 32-gun frigate *Castor* towing a Dutch merchant brig. The *Castor* cast off her prize and an action commenced which lasted an hour and fifteen minutes, at the end of which *Castor* hauled down her colours. *Carysfort* got off very lightly and lost only one man killed. The harm to the *Castor* was somewhat greater, having had her masts and hull damaged, and sixteen men killed.[24] James, in his assessment of the action, praised Laforey and 'a very new ship's company' for having captured the *Castor*. However, he also mentioned the fact that the French seamen were themselves unfamiliar with the frigate as she had only recently been taken from the British.

On getting back to port, Laforey and his crew had to fight to get the *Castor* condemned as a prize, as the Navy Board tried to claim that *Castor* was not a prize but a case of customary salvage, as she had not actually been taken into an enemy port by her French captors. Captain Laforey and his officers resisted and eventually the judge of the High Court of Admiralty ruled that she was a lawful prize.

Laforey's second single-ship action took place on 30 May 1798, a year after he had taken over command of the heavy 38-gun frigate *Hydra*. Accompanied by a bomb vessel and a cutter, Laforey was patrolling in the Channel off of Le Havre. As day broke, lookouts on the *Hydra*, which was far to windward of her consorts, sighted a small French squadron consisting of the 36-gun frigate *Confiante*, a 20-gun corvette and a cutter attempting to break out of Le Havre and escape to Cherbourg. Laforey ordered the squadron to close with the enemy, but the *Hydra*, being the fastest vessel, rapidly left her consorts behind. The French squadron had, by now, spotted the British ships and hurriedly wore in an attempt to regain the safety of Le Havre. At 6am, *Hydra* came under fire from both the *Confiante* and the corvette, and returned fire. At 6.30am the French ships separated and Laforey now concentrated on attacking the *Confiante*. The two ships exchanged broadsides in a running fight until 7.15am when the French frigate, under full sail, ran herself on shore. Manoeuvring his frigate, Laforey continued to cannonade the *Confiante* until a falling tide forced him to haul off to deeper water. The action had by this time attracted attention from Le Havre, and troops began to assemble on the shore to prevent the *Hydra* approaching closer. On the following morning Laforey realised that the French crew had abandoned ship, and he dispatched boats to set fire to the grounded frigate. This was successfully accomplished, despite what James describes as a constant though ineffectual fire from the troops along the shore.[25]

Although one wonders exactly why Laforey did not send his boats in under cover of darkness, the question is academic, for as James triumphantly concluded, 'This dashing service was performed without injury to a single man on board, or belonging to, any one of the three British vessels ... From the number of slain left on board and the state of her decks, the *Confiante* appeared to have sustained a severe loss.'[26] In February 1801, nearly eight years after he had been promoted to the rank of post captain, Lafory was transferred to the command of the 74-gun *Powerful*, and then, in 1803, to the *Spartiate*, 74. In 1805 the *Spartiate* was part of Rear-Admiral Cochrane's squadron in the West Indies, and joined Nelson in the search for Villeneuve's fleet which culminated at Trafalgar.

RICHARD BOWEN

Laforey had the advantage that his father was a flag officer who was close at hand when the opportunity came to give his son's career the essential boost it needed. Promoted to post rank, Laforey quickly proved himself a successful frigate commander. Other officers, of course, had to do more to prove their potential before reaching post rank. One of these, of more humble origin but equally respected as a frigate commander, was Richard Bowen. Born into a Devon family, Bowen and his brothers began their seagoing careers in the merchant service. In 1778 Richard joined the *Emerald* frigate, and after passing his lieutenant's examination, served continuously throughout the American War. It is a clear sign of both his competence and the favour in which he was regarded that he seems to have been employed for most of the ensuing peace, commanding a brig in operations to suppress smuggling. By the end of 1790, Bowen had earned a reputation as a highly skilful navigator, and was appointed to command a division of ships sent to take convicts and supplies to the new colonies in what is now Australia.

Returning to England in May 1793, he was appointed lieutenant on board Jervis's flagship, the *Boyne*, for the expedition against the West Indies. There can be little doubt that Jervis had previously recognised his abilities, for Bowen had also served temporarily with him during the Spanish Armament. By April 1794, within the space of twelve months, Jervis had promoted him captain of the frigate *Terpsichore*. Later that year, in what might now be seen as a portentous incident, he was badly wounded in the face by a musket shot whilst leading the embarkation of troops from Fort Mathilda on the island of Guadeloupe. In the middle of the following year the *Terpsichore* was sent back to Portsmouth to refit. A few months cruising in the Channel was followed by instructions to sail to Gibraltar, which he did with a strong recommendation from Jervis: 'Captain Bowen, who is a child of my own, is selected to command the small naval force at Gibraltar; and you will find in him the most inexhaustible spirit of enterprise and skilful seamanship, that can be comprised in any human character.'[27]

For the next few months *Terpsichore* was employed patrolling east of Gibraltar, but her crew were becoming increasingly affected by debilitation and disease. In early October 1796 Bowen was forced to put to sea, leaving some thirty of his crew behind in hospital, and within a short time the situation deteriorated when an equal number of those remaining on board also became ill. As day broke on 13 October, a strange sail was sighted off Carthagena. This proved to be the slightly heavier Spanish frigate *Mahonesa*, and it was quite clear from her movements that she was intent on engaging the British frigate. With his frigate seriously short-handed, Bowen may well have considered the wisdom of engaging for, as James points out, if his ship was seriously disabled he might have insufficient skilled seamen to repair any damage or jury-rig the ship; on the other hand, if he was successful, he might not have enough crew left to take the Spaniard as a prize. Nevertheless, Bowen continued on his course and, when the two ships were in close range, defiantly fired a shot at the enemy frigate. The Spanish vessel instantly replied with a full broadside and the two ships engaged closely for an hour and twenty minutes. By the end of this period, both ships had sustained heavy damage and the *Mahonesa* tried to break off the action. During the lull that followed there began a frantic race between the two crews to try and repair the extensive damage to both running and standing rigging. The contest was won by the crew of the *Terpsichore* and twenty minutes later, the ship was jury-rigged, re-armed and in a position to re-engage her opponent. Wisely, the *Mahonesa*'s commander decided to strike his colours rather than fight on.

After eighty minutes of working their guns it was the men under Bowen's command who were able to respond quickly to orders to carry out repairs and then prepare the guns for action once again. The disparity between the performance of the two crews is partly explained by the fact that the *Mahonesa* suffered between 50 and 60 casualties during the action, whilst the Terpsichores had suffered none. Morale of the latter remained high whilst that of the Spanish crew fell progressively as the action developed and casualties were taken. Ultimately the root cause of this must have been the comparatively superior gunnery of the *Terpsichore*, for which Bowen – who had been the frigate's commander for over two years – and his officers could claim full credit.[28]

Within just two months the *Terpsichore*'s damage had been repaired at Gibraltar and she was back at sea. As the daylight grew at dawn on 12 December, 20 leagues off Cadiz, the *Terpsichore* sighted the 36-gun French frigate *Vestale* lying-to about 4 miles to windward. Bowen immediately gave the orders to tack and give chase. The *Vestale* also tacked and stood away to windward in an attempt to avoid contact. During the afternoon, with the wind increasing, the *Terpsichore* sprang both her fore and main topmasts, but Bowen pressed on under courses until the early hours of the following morning when, being close inshore, he gave orders for the frigate to wear away to avoid running aground in the darkness. Although he had now lost contact with the French frigate, either through luck or an acute ability to predict the likely behaviour of his opponent, she was sighted again at 8am. Now, however, it was *Terpsichore* which had the weather gage and gave chase to the French frigate as she headed for Cadiz. An hour and a half later, however, the *Vestale* suddenly hove-to, awaiting the approach of the British frigate. What happened next seems a little curious. According to William James, the French frigate neither raised her colours nor fired a shot. Bowen brought the *Terpsichore* to within thirty feet of the *Vestale* and hailed them several times. Receiving no response, he gave the orders for his gun crews to open fire and the French ship immediately returned the broadside, only then running up her colours. An hour and forty minutes later the *Vestale* surrendered, having suffered heavy casualties and damage. Immediately after the flag was struck one of the French guns was discharged, killing one of *Terpsichore*'s boys, seriously wounding Bowen's brother George, who happened to be the only lieutenant on board, and wounding four seamen.

By the time that Bowen managed to get a prize crew on board the French frigate, she had lost all of her masts and bowsprit and was drifting into shoal water. As Bowen himself was short of men, he could spare only the *Terpsichore*'s master, a midshipman and seven seamen to take possession of the prize. The *Vestale* herself was in a pitiful condition, especially as she had suffered over 20 per cent casualties, and few of the crew were in any condition to assist as the frigate's liquor store had apparently been broached. Nevertheless, despite having no anchor, the small prize crew managed to bring-to the drifting frigate in less than three fathoms of water and hold her until Bowen brought the *Terpsichore* in to attempt to tow her to safety. Unfortunately, the attempt failed and Bowen apparently stood out to sea to avoid running aground during the night.

Bowen then appears to have made an astounding error of judgement. At some point around dawn, lookouts on the *Terpsichore* sighted another ship and Bowen, either fearing interference from another hostile vessel or being tempted by the prospect of another prize, allowed himself to be drawn away in chase. The stranger eventually hove-to and proved to be a Swedish vessel and not eligible as a prize. The distraction was to prove very costly. At some time during the night, the crew of the French frigate recovered sufficiently to overwhelm the small British prize crew, carry out repairs, work the ship out of the shallows and set sail for nearby Cadiz. Bowen arrived back just in time to see his hard fought prize being towed into the safety of Cadiz harbour.[29] It was not surprising that Bowen received little official acknowledgement for this action – and six months later he was dead, having been killed leading a landing party in the ill-fated attempt to capture Tenerife.

THOMAS BYAM MARTIN

Richard Bowen's name is probably fairly familiar because of his association with Nelson. An officer who is somewhat less well-known, but was scoring some spectacular results as a frigate captain, was Thomas Byam Martin. Martin was the son of a naval captain who became Resident Commissioner at Portsmouth in 1780. In 1786 Martin joined the frigate *Pegasus*, which was commanded by Prince William Henry (later William IV).[30] He was employed almost constantly between 1786 and 1790 and, immediately after the Spanish Armament, he was appointed as lieutenant to the *Juno* commanded by Captain Samuel Hood. Hood was a consummate seaman and it was almost certainly under his command that Martin honed his ship-handling skills. In his journal Martin commented of the *Juno* under Hood's command:

> if the salvation of the kingdom had rested on this single ship she could not have been kept more constantly at sea. Summer or winter, blow high, blow low, she was always cruising, and often went out for no better purpose than that of fighting with the winds in the Channel.[31]

In 1794 Vice-Admiral Lord Hood, probably at the recommendation of Captain Samuel Hood, appointed Martin to the *Modeste*, a recently captured French frigate. Martin was 21 years of age but had made a highly favourable impression by his displays of 'judgement and skill'.[32] Then, in the following year, he was given temporary command of the *Artois* frigate in the absence of her real captain, Edmund Nagle. The *Artois* was a highly desirable command, being a new 38-gun frigate mounting 18-pounder guns, and regarded by her normal captain as the best sailing ship in Sir John Borlase Warren's frigate squadron. Martin quickly won the approbation of Warren himself, and in turn quickly came to appreciate his senior officer. After his term in the *Artois* came to an end Martin asked to be attached to Warren's Squadron once again, but instead he was given the smaller *Santa Margarita* frigate and sent to the Cork station.

At 2am on the morning of 8 June 1796, whilst north-west of Scilly, Martin in the *Santa Margarita* and Captain Thomas Williams in the 18-pounder frigate *Unicorn* sighted to leeward the French frigates *Tribune* and *Tamise* and a corvette. The French ships attempted to escape but at 1pm, failing to outrun the British frigates, they opened fire with their stern-chasers, the corvette having previously separated to shadow the other ships at a distance. At 4pm the *Tamise* suddenly bore up in an attempt to rake the bow of Martin's frigate, but Martin responded quickly by following the manoeuvre of the French frigate. As the two ships ran alongside, a furious cannonade was exchanged and after only about twenty minutes the *Tamise* struck her colours. The casualties aboard the British frigate were comparatively light, whereas the crew of the *Tamise* suffered 51 killed or wounded out of a crew of 306.[33]

The other French frigate attempted to avoid engagement with the *Unicorn*, but after a chase of 210 miles she was taken following a close engagement of little more than thirty-five minutes. Williams, as senior captain, received a knighthood. In his Gazette letter he noted that during the early moments of the course of the action 'I had the pleasure to see Captain Martin manoeuvre his ship with the greatest judgement' to avoid being raked.[34] Martin was honoured with the Freedoms of both Dublin and Cork for this action and received the usual gift of plate from the City of London.[35] Before the year was over Martin had come to further attention, firstly by capturing a Dutch frigate which had mutinied and had anchored in the Clyde; and then by capturing a well manned 16-gun privateer in the Channel.

In December 1796 Earl Spencer, First Lord of the Admiralty, wrote appointing Martin to the *Tamar*, commenting: 'I hope your having the command of her will be the means of enabling you to pursue with success the course you have so fortunately begun, and entitle you to further distinction and credit,'[36] and adding his view that the *Tamar* was 'one of the finest frigates in the navy'. Indeed, although she was built of fir, the *Tamar* was one of the crack *Artois* class frigates.[37] Martin however was not happy with the change nor does he appear to have been overjoyed to find that the *Tamar* was bound for the West Indies as part of Rear-Admiral Harvey's squadron. He complained about this, the ship and its crew in a letter to Spencer and received an almost acid response which clearly closed down any possibility of a change in either ship or assignment. In spite of his reservations, in the West Indies Martin distinguished himself both in combined operations with Abercromby's forces in the attack on Porto Rico, where the effectiveness of the frigate's gunnery was commented on by Rear-Admiral Harvey himself[38] – and in capturing enemy privateers, for which the interested parties of Antigua, Martinique and Barbados awarded him plate, two presentation swords and 300 guineas.

In November 1797 Martin's health broke down and he exchanged into the 64-gun *Dictator* in order to return to England for recuperation. By September of the following year his health had recovered and he was appointed to the 38-gun frigate *Fisgard*. This ship had been captured from the French in 1797 and was found to be an experimental design, with a very sharp hull form and screwjacks so that the rake of the fore and main mast could be more easily adjusted. In some conditions she was probably fast but, typical of many French frigates, she pitched and rolled heavily in bad weather. She was also prone to leaks.[39] On the positive side, in spite of the break in his command of the *Tamar*, he was able to turn over many of his best seamen from her. This was a clear indication that he was well favoured as some had also been able to follow him from his previous frigate the *St Margarita*.[40] Even the *Fisgard*'s new first lieutenant, John Surman Carden, was impressed at the readiness of the ship when she sailed to search for a large privateer operating somewhere off of Brest in the mid-October 1798. According to Carden:

> We met with strong gales, when we made Ushant on the French Coast, and then stretched out into the Atlantic Ocean – We every day made much progress in the organization of our crew at the Great Guns &c., at which our Gallant Captain shewed much tact and experience, which gave to all confidence ... [41]

At dawn on 20 October the *Fisgard* sighted the larger French frigate *Immortalité* (armed with 24-pounder guns) and gave chase. By midday the two frigates were engaged in close action, but after twenty-five minutes the gunnery from the French frigate had cut *Fisgard*'s stays, braces and running rigging to such an extent that she became uncontrollable. The commander of the *Immortalité* decided at this point to make off rather than take advantage of the British frigate's desperate situation. This turned out to be a serious mistake, for within half an hour the seamen on the *Fisgard* had repaired the damage sufficiently for her to resume the action. As the chase continued, Martin himself supervised the firing of the bow-chasers, and it was through his skill or luck that at least one of his shots damaged the top hamper of the *Immortalité* sufficiently to enable the British frigate to catch up.

The action recommenced and the gunnery on both sides was so determined that by 3pm both ships had sustained heavy damage, the *Fisgard* receiving many shot below the waterline and having six feet of water in the hold. Throughout the action Martin closely directed the manoeuvres of his frigate until Carden was able to lead a boarding party to take their opponent. Both ships limped back to port, and Martin received further acclaim, a whole service of plate from the City of London, and the Freedoms of both Exeter and Plymouth. In accordance with the usual practice, Carden was made a commander, though (considering his later performance as captain of *Macedonian*) one cannot help wondering whether Martin thought that he really deserved it. Carden had served in the *Fisgard* for but a few weeks, and following his promotion was kept on half-pay for some time, not being posted until over seven years later. In his Gazette letter Martin almost damned him with faint praise: 'I should wish to recommend the steady good conduct of Mr Carden, ... on this occasion, but not to the prejudice of any other person.'[42]

A successful frigate commander had to possess and make full use of a wide range of skills and abilities. These could be crucial to the fighting of a successful frigate action – but different activities required different expertise, and a commander needed to be able to call on all of the appropriate skills to meet each particular circumstance. The fact that a commander could fight several successful ship-to-ship engagements did not mean that he would automatically excel in other activities. Martin's career as a frigate commander provides a very good example of this. During the year 1800 Martin and the *Fisgard* were attached to Sir John Borlase Warren's squadron blockading Brest and harrying French trade in the Bay of Biscay. During June and July the squadron launched a series of spectacular cutting-out expeditions and boat attacks on vessels moored inshore.[43] This spell of good luck eventually ran out during a cutting-out expedition on the Isle of Noirmoutier which was apparently planned by Martin himself.[44] The combined boats of the squadron had, on this occasion, been sent in to take three armed vessels together with fifteen French merchantmen. Unable to remove the vessels, they were destroyed and the party began its return journey, only to find that the tide had dropped unexpectedly fast and they were high and dry. Stranded, the party came under heavy fire from both troops and shore batteries, and were forced to drag one of the smaller French vessels some two miles across the mudflats. Half of the party were able to escape but they left 92 seamen, marines and officers behind, some wounded, to be taken prisoner.[45] Although contemporary response was to treat the expedition as a success, it must now be evident that to lose half of one's force because of a miscalculation of wind and tide or a failure to observe their effect, was a serious failure – especially for Martin, an able and experienced seaman. Despite the debacle at Noirmoutier, Martin continued on very active service in the *Fisgard* until the Peace of Amiens. In February 1802, having been a post captain for eight years and four months, he relinquished his command at Plymouth and so ended his career as a frigate commander, although his naval career continued for many years with great distinction and he gained the curious distinction of gaining a Swedish knighthood before being rewarded with English honours in 1814.

DAVID MILNE

What constituted a successful frigate engagement is not always clear cut. Victory could be accompanied by heavy cost and the outcome could be a messy affair, as illustrated by the engagement between the *Droits de l'Homme* and the *Indefatigable* and *Amazon*. Another example of this is to be found in the career of Captain David Milne. Born the son of an Edinburgh merchant in 1763, Milne entered the navy at the age of 16 during the war with America. For the next four years he saw considerable active service at the second siege of Gibraltar, the operation at St Kitts in January 1782, and the action off Dominica in the following April. His return to England coincided with the declaration of peace and having no prospect of employment, Milne entered the East India Company service. Between 1782 and 1785 he served as fourth mate in the East Indiaman *General Eliott*, and then completed three further voyages in the same ship as second mate between 1786 and 1791. Few young naval officers can have gained such valuable experience outside the Royal Navy during the years of peace as Milne. The experience was to reveal itself in his subsequent career.

At the outbreak of war in 1793 he re-entered the navy and was appointed to the *Boyne*, Jervis's flagship for the West Indies campaign. Less than a year later Jervis promoted him to lieutenant of the *Blanche* frigate, which had recently been given to the somewhat fiery Captain Robert Faulknor. In January 1795 the *Blanche* encountered and engaged the French frigate *Pique*. During the course of the action the French frigate ran on board the *Blanche*, and the English frigate's two lieutenants, David Watkins and David Milne, hurriedly attempted to lash the *Pique*'s bowsprit to their own main mast in order that they could board her. With French marksmen firing down onto the English frigate's deck, this was a dangerous and difficult operation, and with his habitual recklessness Faulknor rushed to assist his officers personally, only to be shot and killed. Command devolved upon Watkins who successfully completed the action, forcing the *Pique* to strike. As the *Blanche*'s boats had been destroyed during the action, the only way to take possession of the crippled French frigate was to swim to her, and it was Milne who performed this task, rather endearingly accompanied by his Newfoundland dog!

In recognition of his gallantry Milne was promoted to commander in April 1795 and six months later he was posted as captain and given command of the frigate *Matilda*, with special responsibility for supervising transports. This may not have been the most glamorous task, but Milne's rise had been spectacular – from second mate in the East India Company to post captain in the Royal Navy in less than three years. His star continued to rise, for less than three months later he asked to be transferred to the *Pique*, which had now been entered into naval service, and his request was granted. Initially, the *Pique* was stationed at Demerara with orders to ensure the protection of the West Indies trade, and it was in this role that Milne gave a bold demonstration of the sort of decision-making that was often forced on a detached frigate commander. In July 1796 a group of merchant vessels failed to make the designated rendezvous for an escorted convoy back to England and a delegation of anxious West Indies merchants visited Milne to plead for his assistance. Milne decided that there was no other recourse but to leave his station and escort the ships back to England himself. On arrival at Spithead on 10 October the first thing he did was dispatch a letter to the Admiralty explaining his decision and enclosing the letters of appeal from the Governor of Demerara and local merchants.[46] Although, strictly speaking, Milne had deserted his station, his actions were seen as fulfilling his instructions to protect the West Indies trade, and his judgement was commended by the Admiralty. Subsequently Milne and the *Pique* were attached to the Channel squadron.

At daybreak on 29 June 1798 the *Pique* was cruising off Brest in company with the frigates *Jason* and *Mermaid* when an enemy frigate, which proved to be the French *La Seine*, was sighted off the Penmarcks. A general chase ensued southwards towards the coast of France, and by 9am the *Piques*, being closest, was the first to engage, opening fire with her bow-chasers. At 11am the two ships drew alongside each other and exchanged broadsides, continuing for over two and a half hours until a shot from the French frigate shot way the *Pique*'s main topmast and she fell astern. At this point the *Jason* arrived, commanded by Captain Charles Stirling, who was the senior captain; Stirling immediately shouted to Milne to drop anchor. It is unclear whether this was an order or a warning, but either way, the shout was misunderstood or ignored. Milne ordered more sail to be set, and then both the *Pique* and the *Jason* ran aground. Amidst the general consternation it was seen that the *Seine* had also not only run aground herself but had lost all of her masts as a consequence. With all three crews frantically trying to extricate themselves, the tide began to rise, bringing greater problems. The *Jason* was now lying closer to the French frigate, with her bows aground. As the tide rose, her stern swung towards the enemy, who wasted no time in reloading their guns and pouring several raking broadsides through the *Jason*'s stern. As *Jason* began to sustain heavy damage, especially to her sails and rigging, Milne, desperate to come to *Jason*'s assistance quickly, ordered all of his men to lift several round shot and run with them towards the bows. The shift in weight lifted the stern sufficiently for the ship to spin slightly once her yards were braced round to get four of his guns to bear on the *Seine*. However, he could fire no more for fear of hitting the *Jason*. At this point the *Mermaid* arrived, and the *Seine*, recognising the hopelessness of her position despite the condition of the British frigates, promptly struck her colours.

The immediate aftermath of this action is worth noting in some detail. To Milne's great chagrin, it was found that the *Pique* had bilged and she had to be destroyed to avoid her being salvaged by the enemy. *Jason* on the other hand was saved, largely due to the extremely capable seamanship of the commander of the *Mermaid*, Captain James Newman. Newman is one of those fascinating characters whom one rarely reads about despite his being very active as a frigate commander for many years of the war. His adroit ship-handling was demonstrated on numerous occasions but never remarked by the chroniclers of the time. In fact, even *The Times* commented obliquely that *Pique, Jason* and *Seine* would all have been lost 'but for the assistance afterwards afforded them by others that fortunately happened to be in the fight'.[47] This was scant recognition.

Whilst the crew of the *Jason* set about re-rigging and repairing their ship, Milne and his crew attempted to take possession of the *Seine*. This was not straightforward. The action had terminated so close inshore that it had attracted an enormous crowd of onlookers and some of the French crew managed to swim ashore. On board there was both carnage and confusion the *Seine* having suffered 170 dead and 100 wounded, some of whom, it was being claimed, had been shot by their own captain as they abandoned their guns. This actually seems rather unlikely, given the punishment the French gun crews were inflicting on the *Jason* until the end of the engagement. Also on board was a lady who had taken passage from Mauritius, and who had survived the horrific punishment the ship received. The French gunner and three of the crew were permitted to escort her safely ashore and, surprisingly, returned afterwards to imprisonment. Milne also permitted the French captain to go on shore, and with equal honour, though perhaps less surprisingly, he too returned on board at the allotted time. Furthermore, whenever the tide fell, the frigate was visited by groups of curious French visitors who, possibly in company with the prize crew, managed to break into the *Seine*'s stores and consume quantities of arrack. Drunkenness added to the confusion.

Although it is tempting to wonder exactly how or why it was that Milne allowed this situation to develop, it has to be remembered that his first priorities would have been to deal with his own dead and wounded and then to supervise the stripping of the wrecked *Pique* before it was destroyed. Eventually, order was restored, the *Seine* refloated, jury-rigged and sailed to Portsmouth where a correspondent for *The Times* noted her arrival:

La Seine, French frigate, brought in here is one of the finest vessels of her class, although much shattered by the action. All her masts were shot away, and also her rudder. To the stumps of the former, jury masts are fastened; and the English flag is suspended over the Republican colours from a temporary ensign staff.

And then with a macabre touch, 'The face of the figure head of *La Pique* is nailed over the figure head (a woman) of the prize which makes a strange appearance.'[48] Earlier, the paper had dismissed the loss of the British frigate by describing her as a 'very old and crazy ship' whose 'loss is to be estimated as little more than the value of her old iron'. Her crew, in typical sailor fashion, clearly felt very differently about her.

If the crew were pleased about their potential prize money, Milne's prize agent, James Halford, was understandably overjoyed. Probably on the same day that the frigate was brought successfully into Portsmouth he wrote to Milne:

> I most sincerely congratulate you on your gallant action and success ... The Public hold your conduct in proper estimation but will never be able to reward you according to your merits. Your claim to command *La Seine* is so good that no one doubts it. Your application to Lord Spencer and Mr Dundas therefore will I flatter myself produce a favourable answer by this post. I know the latter expressed himself in such a way at dinner yesterday ... [49]

Sure enough, shortly afterwards Milne and his entire crew were formally transferred to the *Seine*, though this is perhaps hardly surprising since, in a literal sense, they were already in occupation.

An illustration of what Milne and his crew might have achieved had they not run out of water, followed in August 1800 whilst the *Seine* was cruising in the Mona Passage. At 8.30am on the 20th she sighted and gave chase to a stranger which proved to be the French frigate *Vengeance*. Although the two ships were close enough to exchange shots from their respective bow- and stern-chasers by 4pm, *Seine* did not get close alongside her opponent until 11.30pm. For half an hour the two ships exchanged broadsides in the darkness and the French gunnery inflicted sufficient damage on the *Seine*'s rigging to force her to drop astern. During the following hours, both crews carried out repairs, but when day broke the French frigate had failed to escape her pursuer. At 7.30am Milne gave the orders to close with the *Vengeance* once again, and from 8am until 10.30am the two ships engaged furiously at close range until the *Vengeance*, having lost most of her masts and with considerable hull damage, struck her colours. In his letter to the Admiralty, Milne reported that the *Vengeance*'s losses had been 'very great', probably about 110-120 dead and wounded; but the *Seine* too had her casualties, 13 dead (including her second lieutenant, George Milne) and 29 wounded.

MICHAEL SEYMOUR

In the example of the *Seine* and the *Pique* something of the nature of the aftermath of an action was evident in the sequence of events described. What is clear is that because of its nature – a destructively bloody and damaging occasion – an action was always going to be a messy affair, either in terms of its destructive nature or because of the disorganisation that it engendered. In reality it could never be as romantic and clear cut as the engravers or subsequent storytellers would have it believed. This negative side could to some degree be balanced by the more positive promise of prize money, honours or promotion for the victors. It is this aspect that makes the example of Captain Michael Seymour so interesting. Seymour's story is one of a hard-working, skilful officer who achieves honour and fortune by dint of perseverance. In many ways he was probably typical of the core of long serving frigate captains – although in other ways he was also exceptional.

Seymour was born the son of a clergyman in County Limerick in 1768. By the age of 13 he was serving on board the 50-gun *Portland* commanded by the Hon James Luttrell. In 1783 Luttrell retired because of ill health, but recommended Seymour to another Irish captain, the Hon Michael de Courcy, commanding the *Europa*, 50. Sent to the West Indies, Seymour contracted yellow fever and was invalided home in September 1785. Upon his recovery, Seymour appealed to Luttrell for help. Luttrell was too ill to assist his protégé, but recommended him instead to Captain George Cranfield Berkeley, who was also the MP for Gloucester. Berkeley met Seymour, took a liking to him, and became his very active patron. With Berkeley's backing, Seymour found employment firstly in the *Pegase*, 74, guardship at Portsmouth, and then in the *Magnificent*, 74, the guardship at Weymouth, in which he was made master's mate. In this Seymour was fortunate, for only a minority of officers or young gentlemen managed to find employment during the years of peace. In 1790, at the time of the Spanish Armament and at the age of 22, he passed his lieutenant's examination and continued in the *Magnificent* for a further year when he appears to have been placed on half-pay. With the outbreak of war in 1793, Seymour was appointed as fifth lieutenant of the 74-gun *Marlborough*, commanded by his patron Berkeley.

The *Marlborough* took a severe pounding at the Glorious First of June (1794), and during the course of the action Seymour's left forearm was broken by grapeshot. The ship's surgeon advised that the forearm be amputated, but Seymour refused to allow this. This is hardly surprising; the loss of the limb may have seemed to threaten his future naval career and it is possible that he did not think the wound warranted such drastic action. Unfortunately, the delay allowed the onset of gangrene, and Seymour ended up losing more of his arm than might have been initially necessary. Following the ship's return to England, Seymour returned to his parents' home in poor health and probably suffering from severe depression, exacerbated by the fact that he had been refused promotion following the battle.

In August 1795 Seymour was promoted to the rank of master and commander, almost certainly as the result of some heavy lobbying by both Berkeley and James Luttrell's sister, who happened to be the Duchess of Cumberland. This seems to be confirmed by the fact that Seymour was not actually given a command until the following June, when he was appointed to the acting command of the *Fly* sloop. Shortly afterwards he was given the *Spitfire* sloop, operating under the orders of the commander-in-chief at Plymouth, initially Admiral Sir Richard King and subsequently Vice-Admiral Sir Thomas Pasley. Under Seymour's command the *Spitfire* took a number of highly valuable prizes, including several French privateers. Part of this success was undoubtedly due to Seymour himself, who was rarely off the deck and when close to the French coast often conned the ship himself with his charts on the ship's capstan.[50] Furthermore, the *Spitfire* was worked hard and her decks leaked almost constantly so that in strong winds neither officers nor crew slept in the dry.

With the enthusiastic backing of both Berkeley, who was now a vice-admiral, and his commander-in-chief, Seymour was promoted to post captain in November 1800, at the age of 32, somewhat later than the average. However, he obtained no permanent command until February 1806 when he was given the 36-gun 18-pounder frigate *Amethyst*. The *Amethyst* was initially employed on the Cork station, but at the end of 1807 she was sent to join the blockade of Brest and the coast of Biscay. In August 1808 the *Amethyst* was joined by the frigate *Emerald*, commanded by the Hon Frederick Lewis Maitland, a nephew of the Earl of Lauderdale. It was not unusual for frigates working together to develop close affinities. In the case of the *Amethyst* and the *Emerald* it would seem that the commanding officers got on well; in fact, Seymour described Maitland as the best cruiser he had ever met.[51] The two ships certainly seemed to have hunted as a pair, as subsequent events will show, and also seem to have agreed to share prize money. Entries in the *Amethyst*'s log assiduously record the presence, arrival and departure of the *Emerald*, even when she is glimpsed on the horizon, with a frequency which suggests a degree of affection.

On 9 November, whilst the *Emerald* was absent, the *Amethyst*, patrolling approximately a mile from the Isle Groix, heard the report of two guns being fired in the south-east. An hour later a sail was seen running to the westward. Seymour ordered all sails set in chase and the frigate cleared for action, although the exact nature of the chase was probably not really known until an hour later when the two ships began to exchange fire with stern-chasers and bow-chasers respectively.[52] Warning rockets were set off to attract the attention of other English ships, and the crew of the *Amethyst* saw three flashes in response from somewhere in the north-east. The chase was the French 40-gun frigate *Thétis*, carrying troops and provisions for Martinique. In terms of combatants, the *Thétis* was greatly superior, having 436 men on board, as opposed to the *Amethyst*'s 261, and having a greater broadside weight. By 9.30pm the two ships were in close action, with the French captain repeatedly trying to take advantage of his larger manpower by boarding the *Amethyst*. These attempts at boarding were repelled but by midnight the two ships had become locked together in heavy action. Shortly after 12.20am Seymour ordered his men to board the French frigate, which was now on fire in several places, and the *Thétis* surrendered. The *Amethyst* herself had suffered considerable damage during the action, and now had 3 feet 6 inches of water in her hold. The human cost had also been severe: *Amethyst* had sustained 70 killed and wounded, whilst the crowded decks of the *Thétis* had suffered a terrible carnage, there being 236 killed and wounded.

Seymour's first task after the surrender of the *Thétis* was to make both ships secure. A number of prisoners were transferred to the *Amethyst*, which was a comparatively simple task as both ships were locked together. Next, the anchor of the prize was lowered, first to stop her drifting, and then to bring her to whilst the *Amethyst* was disentangled. She also then anchored close by. This was accomplished at about 1am, some twenty-five minutes after the action ceased. At this point a ship of the line was observed approaching from the north-east – the general direction of Lorient – and alarm set in when the stranger failed to reply to the recognition signal. However, the vessel proved to be the 74-gun *Triumph* commanded by Captain Thomas Hardy, which hove to and provided surgical assistance with the wounded. By 2am the prize had lost all of her masts and a second British ship, the *Shannon*, commanded by Philip Broke, also arrived to give assistance. By the evening of 11 November the efforts of seamen from all three ships working on the *Thétis* had completed temporary repairs and rigged jury masts and she was taken in tow by the *Shannon*, which parted company on the afternoon of the 12th to begin the journey back to Plymouth.

That morning, having completed their first priority of securing the prize, the crew of the *Amethyst* concentrated on getting their own frigate back into order – especially as *Amethyst* was still making water at the rate of five inches an hour. Later that afternoon the *Amethyst*'s dead were buried, and all possible sail was made in the wake of *Shannon* and the prize. Two days later on the afternoon of the 14th *Amethyst* approached Plymouth Sound with signals flying for assistance, and by 5.40pm she was securely lashed alongside the hulk *Tholen*. *Amethyst* was to be out of action for 71 days, nearly half of these being in dock. Three tasks were undertaken with greatest priority. The wounded had to be cared for; promotions and rewards secured; and the ship readied for repair.

The wounded seamen and marines were removed to hospital. Two midshipmen had also been severely wounded in the action, and one of them, Richard Gibbings, one of the leading boarders and a relative of Seymour's, had received a head wound that proved mortal, a musket ball fired from the rigging of the *Thétis* having entered his skull and exited from his right eye. Both men were taken to Seymour's own home to be nursed by his wife Jane, but Gibbings survived just ten days.

Immediately after Gibbings' funeral Seymour went to London, residing for several days at a house in Princes Street, off Hanover Square. It had been intimated to him that he might receive a knighthood if he appeared at Court, but he simply refused to go. Instead of the knighthood he was awarded a celebratory medal, thus becoming possibly the first officer to receive a medal for a frigate action. Most of the *Amethyst*'s officers were promoted. Blennerhasset, the first lieutenant, was promoted to commander, though he never reached post rank.[53] The second lieutenant, William Hill, was promoted to first. The purser was promoted to a ship of higher class (where the remuneration of his profession would be that much greater). Seymour was invited to select one of his midshipmen to be promoted lieutenant, and the master, Robert Fair, was to be removed to a vessel of a higher class if acceptable to him. However, Fair was an old and loyal follower of Seymour, and the offer was declined. There were cash gifts also. Lloyd's presented the officers and crew who had been wounded with £625, and Seymour received £100. As was fitting for an Irishman, he was also presented with the Freedoms of Cork and Limerick. Perhaps less gratifying was a rather pompous letter from Lord Gambier, congratulating him and also reminding him:

> we must not forget, <u>Who</u> it is that gives us the ability to contend with our enemies, and gives the victory; I therefore hope, if you have not already done so, that you will take the earliest opportunity when all your people return on board, to assemble them, and read the Thanksgiving After a Victory, and other suitable thanksgivings and Psalms.[54]

Sadly, Seymour's response to this letter is not recorded.

Just over ten weeks later, on 25 January 1809, *Amethyst* slipped from her moorings in Hamoaze and joined six other frigates anchored in the Sound, including her consort *Emerald*. Once again, *Amethyst* and *Emerald* were sent to cruise in the Bay of Biscay where they were given specific instructions to look out for a newly built French frigate, the *Niemen*. The *Niemen* had been launched at the end of October 1808, and Captain Rodd, cruising in the frigate *Indefatigable*, had picked up intelligence that she was due to sail from Bordeaux in an attempt to break the British blockade. Rodd had dutifully passed on the intelligence to the Admiralty,[55] who appear to have passed the intelligence to other commanders. There is certainly a suggestion that Seymour and Maitland believed that they had personally been sent on a cruise to search for the *Niemen* as a form of reward for the capture of the *Thétis* because Seymour was outraged to encounter the frigate *Naiad*, also searching for the *Niemen* on what he considered to be his own cruising ground.

On 31 March the unwelcome *Naiad* disappeared over the horizon and on 5 April, in the middle of the morning, when both *Emerald* and *Amethyst* were approximately 100 miles due west of the Ile d'Oleron, a frigate was seen standing to the east-south-east. *Emerald* was at this time to the north-east, and with a fresh breeze whipped up by squalls, *Amethyst* made all sail in chase. Seymour pressed his frigate hard for the remainder of the day, at one point carrying away the jibboom, but pushed on, rigging another and making even more sail. By evening it was clear that the *Amethyst* was closing on an enemy frigate and Seymour ordered the ship cleared for action. By 7.25pm *Emerald* had been left far behind and with darkness closing in there was a danger that Seymour would lose his quarry. Indeed, for some anxious time the chase was lost to view entirely but, the sky clearing for a moment, the frigate was again seen beam-on running to the west. Both ships seem to have observed each other at the same moment, for the French frigate hauled her wind onto the larboard tack again and made all sail from the *Amethyst*. As if still doubting the evidence of his eyes, Seymour ordered the private signal to be made, but this was not answered, and at 10.30pm Seymour ordered the bow-chasers to commence firing.

For three hours the chase continued with the two frigates firing bow-chasers and stern-chasers respectively. By 1.15am Seymour had brought the *Amethyst* to within a mile of his opponent and he luffed and fired the starboard broadside. The ships now commenced a close action. By 3.15am both frigates had lost main and mizzen masts, and the French frigate was on fire in several places. There was at this point some extraordinary confusion, for the officers on the *Amethyst* observed a light being lowered on the French ship and assumed that this was an indication that she had struck. Ten minutes later the English frigate *Arethusa* arrived. The French frigate suddenly hoisted her light again and fired two guns at her. The *Arethusa* replied, firing a full broadside into the stricken French frigate, which promptly surrendered to her. The French frigate was indeed the *Niemen* and Captain Robert Mends of the *Arethusa* immediately sent a boarding party to take possession whilst at the same time sending his surgeon to assist on board the *Amethyst*. Mends described his arrival in a letter to another frigate captain (Charles Adams of the *Resistance*), on the morning after:

> Last night about One O'clock we observed a considerable firing to leeward evidently of ships engaging, which continued till past four, when we arrived

up and found them to be two frigates, each with only her foremast standing, the action having nearly ceased left nothing for the *Arethusa* to do, but to fire a few shot, when the Enemy hoisted a light as a signal of having struck. On the return of the boat, I found the English frigate to be the *Amethyst*, Captain Seymour, who with his usual good fortune, zeal and ability had followed his chace tho' a dark night, beaten him, and needed not the aid of a Friend to complete his conquest.[56]

The *Amethyst*'s chase of the *Niemen* had taken both ships approximately 140 miles south-east across Biscay, and the final part of the engagement had taken place only about 12 miles off of the north coast of Spain.[57]

It is at this point that we encounter another facet of the aftermath of a frigate action, and one which was not that uncommon. The intervention of the *Arethusa* was in some ways unfortunate. It is clear from Mends' letter to Charles Adam that the action had really been fought and won by the *Amethyst*. However, the *Niemen* had actually surrendered to the *Arethusa* who, not having been part of the engagement, was undamaged and therefore able to send a boat with a prize crew to take possession of her. Furthermore, the arrival of the second frigate encouraged the French captain to claim that in fact the *Amethyst* had surrendered to *him*, but that he had then been forced to surrender ultimately to a fresh opponent. Notwithstanding the admission made by Mends to Charles Adam, he immediately lodged his own claim to a portion of the prize money, stating that the *Niemen* had only surrendered after he had fired several broadsides at her.

What Mends either did not know, or chose to ignore, was that by arrangement the crew of the *Emerald* were due a share of the prize money and that *Emerald*, although left far astern, was also engaged in the chase of the *Niemen*. For years afterwards a bitter legal wrangle was fought between Seymour and Maitland on one side, and Mends on the other, resulting in strong personal animosity between Seymour and Mends.[58] This animosity almost certainly had its roots in the hours immediately following the action, for even as the three frigates lay close together, Mends attempted to take some advantage of the prize. As Seymour supervised the care of his wounded and the repair of his ship, he received a letter from Mends informing him that he had

this morning sent a Lieut. and fifteen more seamen on board to fish her [*ie Niemen*'s] foremast which is badly wounded and get up a jury fore topmast, which I perceive they are about; yesterday they reemed her guns and cleaned her decks. I apprehend that she had a great many men killed as a number of bodies were thrown overboard by our people … As I suppose you were furnished with a complete set of Maps out of the *Thetis*, I should (not having any) very much like to have these [*ie* from the *Niemen*]. The private stores of the Captain and officers we had better divide between the two ships, then each party might do as they wished with their own share. Oil, paint and nails, of neither of which have we any, I should propose doing the same thing with; nor have we one broom or scrubbing brush in the ship. I should like to send for three or four pipes of the ship's wine to serve out to the prisoners, which the Purser shall account for at what the rest might sell. We have no candles on board and will fairly account for what we could be supplied with, but I believe all I have as yet mentioned would only go to waste. The cushions on the lockers in the Cabin would suit me very well if you do not want them yourself or if any value be set on them I will become a purchaser. If you want them take them: I have not yet put my cabin to rights as Indeed I have not had workmen to spare from the ship's duty.…

I caught a cold in my eyes yesterday which has made me very blind today, and afraid to show my head on deck. I wish to have my surgeon on board as soon as he can be spared in case of accident and should a ship of force come in sight having the appearance of an enemy, shall be under the necessity of withdrawing (for the time being) my people.[59]

There is much in this letter that might have infuriated Seymour. Firstly, the tone of Mends letter is presumptuous, considering that it was addressed to the captain who had actually fought and defeated the captured French frigate. Then there is the reference to the French charts (see below) and the disposal of the French officers' private stores, and finally the rather self-centred last paragraph. Seymour would not have been happy at the last-minute intervention of another British ship at his moment of triumph; the fact that the officer commanding that ship was now assuming rights to some of the prize would have been like salt to the wound. The effect which Mends' rather pathetic excuse for not making a personal appearance would have had on an officer who had spent many hours chasing and fighting an enemy frigate, and then putting his ship and crew to rights, speaks for itself. Furthermore, Seymour would have known all too well that what Mends was suggesting was tantamount to breaking-cargo and therefore not only illegal, but potentially threatened to cheat Maitland and the crew of the *Emerald* from any share that they might have.

His response seems to have been blunt and icy, for Mends responded hastily:

My dear Seymour, I agree with you respecting the private stores, let them
remain where they are and be brought to account that way. Tis to me exactly
the same thing. I mentioned receiving from *Le Niemen* what might have been
accommodating to my officers, more on their account than my own. I also
agree with you on the almost mispropriety of removing any thing from a
prize for our own use. As it generally leads to a belief on the part of the
people that they are not dealt justly by, but then my regulation in such cases
is that whatever might be so taken, even poultry, is to be paid for at a market
price.

However, even his attempts to placate Seymour, he caused greater irritation by
referring again to the French charts which, evidently, Seymour wished to retain for
his own first lieutenant (who would expect to be made commander as a result of the
action):

As you do not want the charts for yourself, Hill's claim in this instance will I
hope not be done injustice to if it yields to mine, as had the condition of our
two ships been reversed I should unquestionably have held yours next in
priority to my own. If you prefer those on board her to what you have, send
for them, take your choice ... I am glad to hear you say that few French wines
fetch such a good price at Plymouth and think *our* [author's emphasis] prize
will turn out a very good one ... Believe me Seymour I am much more
pleas'd at your not acceding to my proposal in the manner you have, than to
have done so with reluctance.[60]

Even whilst the repairs were going ahead off of the Spanish coast, and he was dealing
with the interference from Captain Mends, Seymour found time to write a jubilant
letter to his brother-in-law, Edward Hawker, captain of the frigate *Melampus*:

You will be rejoiced to hear that *Amethyst* is in the habit of seeing and
thrashing French frigates, though not of getting them to herself ... the flying
Niemen, which is the fastest sailor I ever met with, and only the old luck, and
keeping large after dark, after losing sight of her, and being beaten to pieces
by the wind of her, and an admirable look out by Fair (the present Captain
Fair[61]), who is a great treasure to me, gave us a view of him.[62]

The afternoon and evening of 6 April were spent clearing the wreckage of the fallen
masts and rigging, repairing damage, and rigging jury masts. On the afternoon of

7th the *Amethyst* was in a suitable condition to receive prisoners of war, and 66 men were transferred from the *Niemen*.[63] Repairs continued, as did the squally weather, until 9 April, when all possible sails were set to take the frigate back to Plymouth. The journey took four days and *Amethyst* anchored in Plymouth Sound at 10am on 13 April.

On arrival there were some personnel matters to be dealt with. The first lieutenant, William Hill, would undoubtedly be promoted; the second and third lieutenants had not actually been on board the *Amethyst* during her recent engagement – one having not yet joined and the other being in charge of a prize – so Seymour was keen to ensure that his second lieutenant, Edward Crouch, was duly promoted. James Gledstanes Jacob was appointed second and, by mutual request, Richard Incledon, who was acting lieutenant, was promoted and appointed as third to the *Amethyst*. There were other crew matters to be dealt with: William Ruler, an 'infirm old seaman', requested and was given leave to go to his home in Scotland in an attempt to recover his health, having a form of consumption and diseased liver.[64]

Seymour wrote again to Hawker: 'All my friends in town are anxious for me to go up [to London]; but I decline, as the Admiralty have been very civil, and have done all that I have asked, except making Fair from November 10 last as I wished him 2nd,[65] but will make him … on his time being up, and passing.'[66] Seymour's reference, once again, to the pressures placed upon him to show himself at Court reveal what might be an unexpected degree of modesty in a frigate captain. On the following day Seymour learned that he was to be made a baronet. He wrote to Hawker:

So I am, you see, right in not going to town to beg – pressed as I have been by many to do so. To one in particular, I was compelled to reply, and truly said, that I went the last time 'to do justice to an excellent set of officers and men, and now by letter, and promotion the Admiralty have done everything I could expect, I then did not ask anything, and have no idea of going to beg, and perhaps be disappointed.

I have written my best thanks, and shall be off on leave to give personal thanks to my gracious Sovereign, and pay my fees (400£) I hear, by return of post on my leave coming down.[67]

Seymour's attitude could, of course, be attributed to personal pride, but what belies this is both his reference to his officers and men and the irony in his inclusion of the reference to the fees. Some months later, Seymour wrote again to Hawker on the subject:

... my expenses are enormous, and I shall be a poor miserable rascal of a Baronet, nor be able to afford the woman I love most on earth a carriage which she ought to have, for she deserves every comfort I can afford her ... and I do not want the cash to hoard it, for my boys must work their way ... I have no interest, and am treated respectfully and politely by all the folks ... I am sure the middle line of life is the happiest, and moderate circumstances as to rank and state, though I love decency and comfort.[68]

Seymour was being modest about his financial gains. His earlier career in the *Spitfire* had been pretty lucrative, and the prize money for the *Niemen* alone totalled £29,979-2-10d (net).[69]

In the following October, he was appointed to command the *Niemen* and, happily, was able to take all of his officers and crew with him. The frigate served on the coast of Ireland until May 1812, when Seymour was appointed to the 74-gun *Hannibal*. He retired from the Navy in September 1814 but was recalled to command the guardship at Sheerness in 1818. In 1829 he was appointed Commissioner of Portsmouth Dockyard and then, in 1832 he was raised to the rank of rear-admiral of the blue and appointed commander-in-chief of the South American Station. Unfortunately the climate at Rio did not suit his health and he died there on 9 July 1834.

JOHN PHILLIMORE

The final action to be considered is more likely to be known because of its aftermath than the battle itself. This is the encounter on 25 February 1814 between the French 40-gun frigate *Clorinde* and the British 24-pounder 38-gun frigate *Eurotas*, commanded by Captain John Phillimore. The *Eurotas* was one of a number of frigates hurriedly built out of pine and armed with lightweight 24-pounders in an attempt to meet the threat of the heavy American frigates during the War of 1812.

Phillimore, who was 33 at the time of the action, was like Seymour the son of a clergyman, though this time from Leicestershire. Phillimore had entered the navy in the *Colossus* in 1795, under Captain George Murray, who remained his active patron in a number of ships for much of his early career. He was present in the *Colossus* during the battle of Cape St Vincent. In 1798 he was still serving in the *Colossus* when she was wrecked on the Scilly Isles. A few years later he was present at the Battle of Copenhagen though, serving in the *London*, he was not involved in the centre of the action. In May 1804 he was promoted to the rank of commander, but was not given a command until October 1805 when he was appointed to the *Cormorant* armed vessel on the North Sea station. In September 1806 he was given the *Belette*, an 18-gun brig-sloop. Even though he was promoted to post captain in October 1807, he remained in the *Belette* until 1809 when he was temporarily appointed to command the *Marlborough* during the Walcheren expedition, with responsibility for the direction of the hired transports.

In June 1810 he was appointed to the 64-gun *Diadem*. The *Diadem* was by this time fitted out as troopship and rated on the establishment of a 32-gun frigate, a situation which resulted in difficulties in obtaining adequate stores and equipment. In complaining to the Admiralty about this, Phillimore found himself subject to a reprimand. In fact, Phillimore's subsequent career appears to have been subject to a number of controversies which centred on erratic relations with senior officers. His career actually started under a shadow since he suffered from some form of speech impediment. At his examination for lieutenant, the examiners were in some doubt as to whether he would be able to communicate his orders sufficiently – nevertheless, he was promoted to lieutenant, which suggests that he was seen as a strong enough candidate in all other respects.[70]

As a midshipman, his patron, Captain George Murray, described him during the Battle of Cape St Vincent, as being 'like a young lion in action'.[71] In 1807, during Gambier's operation against Copenhagen, Phillimore landed with troops under the command of Wellesley and participated in the attack on Kioge. Phillimore obviously gained Wellesley's approbation as the latter subsequently presented him with several field pieces which were used as 'boat-guns' on ships that he commanded during the rest of his career. The campaign was also witness to another of those contradictory incidents which dogged his career. For some reason Phillimore fell foul of Gambier during the campaign and a row ensued, following which Gambier sent the *Belette* to reconnoitre the enemy positions. Phillimore dropped anchor close to the Crown Battery and simultaneously engaged both it and a flotilla of fifteen gunboats. Vastly outclassed, the 18-gun *Belette* nevertheless drove off the gunboats before Gambier, alarmed for the brig's safety, ordered her withdrawal. It is in fact possible that Phillimore became trapped by a shift in the wind and could not withdraw, because the fleet's boats had to be sent in to tow her to safety. Whatever lay behind the incident, the show of bravado was much appreciated by the crews of the other ships of the fleet, who cheered the *Belette* as she passed by. Gambier then selected Phillimore to convey the dispatches back to London after the fall of Copenhagen, a favour which guaranteed his promotion to post captain. Still in the *Belette*, Phillimore returned to the Baltic where he further demonstrated his abilities by escaping from a Dutch ship of the line and a frigate by boldly sailing through shoal water where they could not follow.

By 1810 the demand for commands had become so great that Phillimore's appointment to command the troopship *Diadem* was reluctantly accepted as a necessary step to more agreeable service. The *Diadem* may not have been the most dashing command, but Phillimore apparently made use of the experience to develop a very advanced style of command. For example, he believed strongly in the necessity of giving his crew leave on shore. He reduced the chance of desertion by making two messmates bondsmen for a third, neither of the other two getting their leave until the third had returned. It was a policy which paid dividends, as the *Diadem* suffered few desertions, and as a policy it appears to have made Phillimore a popular captain with his seamen. However, his policies were not universally approved, even by some liberally minded officers. Lord Cochrane, for one, apparently remarked that he wondered how Phillimore was able to maintain discipline when the 'government of his ship was marked by such a degree of mildness'.[72]

Phillimore's desire to treat his crew fairly inevitably led him into further difficulties with his senior officers. In a very revealing incident, Phillimore fell foul of Admiral Sir George Berkeley upon his arrival in the Tagus in 1811. Shortly after dropping anchor, Phillimore gave some of his crew leave to go on shore, unaware that Berkeley had issued a general order that no seamen were to be on shore after sunset. The order was not discovered until too late because, we are told, the Admiral's Order Book was so vast that the lieutenant sent to copy the orders did not see the order until after the prohibited hour. The offending seamen were arrested and taken on board Berkeley's flagship where they were fined 30 shillings each. Phillimore remonstrated with the admiral, explaining that the fault was his, but this simply led to a long and furious argument. In the end the men were fined and Phillimore reimbursed them from his own pocket. In retaliation, Berkeley sent the *Diadem* off on a series of frustrating errands, ending in a further row where the admiral publicly humiliated Phillimore at a ball organised by a personal friend. Days later Berkeley demanded a court martial and was asked to prepare charges against the troublesome captain; but on arrival in England, Phillimore and the *Diadem* were appointed to Home Popham's squadron operating on the Spanish coast, and by 1813 the charges had been quietly dropped. In May 1813 Phillimore was appointed to the brand new 24-pounder frigate *Eurotas*, building at Blackwall on the Thames.

From being something of a 'black sheep', Phillimore's fortunes had turned around so that he was now in command of a highly desirable and powerful frigate. This may be due to the support of Lord Keith, who was both his patron and commander-in chief of the Channel Fleet. This interest may also have helped to ensure that he had a crew, and the *Eurotas* was able to put to sea with virtually a full complement of 330 men. Even so, many of these seemed to have been unfit, and the great majority appear to have had little experience of seamanship. As a result, one observer commented, the frigate was lucky to return safely from her maiden voyage.[73] On return to port, Phillimore requested a survey of his crew, and was quickly given 60 extra seamen. With this additional intake, Phillimore was soon able to turn the motley complement of the *Eurotas* into an efficient ship's company. However, by October the frigate herself was in need of some degree of refit and at the same time Phillimore was being pressed to get to sea to join Commodore Malcolm's squadron blockading Brest. He dutifully set sail though the frigate's topsails had not been finished, reporting to his commander-in-chief, Lord Keith, that 'a greater part of the running rigging has been condemned by the Surveying Officers, and therefore I hope your Lordship will do me the favour to allow such running rigging to be sent out … which will enable the *Eurotas* to continue at sea for a considerable time.'[74]

In January 1814 the *Eurotas* sighted three French frigates and shadowed them for three days in the hope that they would encounter another British ship and thus be able to engage them. After a chase of 500 miles no friendly ship had been encountered and Phillimore decided to sail between two of the French frigates during the hours of darkness, engage them on both sides and then, using the *Eurotas's* superior speed, sail off, hoping that the two frigates would engage each other in the confusion. However, he lost contact with the French frigates during the night and by dawn they were far astern and soon disappeared. Then a few weeks later, at 2pm on 25 February, the crew of the *Eurotas* sighted the French frigate *Clorinde* heading for Brest. Phillimore immediately gave orders to chase and at 5pm, following a shift in the wind, *Eurotas* passed under the stern of the French frigate, discharging a raking broadside from her starboard guns. She then closed on the *Clorinde's* quarter and the two ships exchanged close-range broadsides. The fire from the French frigate was, as James describes it, 'well directed' with the result that in the space of about twenty minutes the British frigate lost her mizzen mast; within minutes the *Clorinde's* fore topmast also fell. An attempt by the latter to cross the bows of the *Eurotas* was adroitly avoided by Phillimore and his crew, who managed to pour another raking broadside into the stern of the *Clorinde*. The two frigates again closed to exchange broadsides at close range. By 7.10pm the *Eurotas* had lost all of her masts and was rolling unmanageably. The French frigate, who had lost her main and mizzen masts, set sails on what remained of her fore mast, and escaped out of gunshot.

The damage to the British frigate was certainly greater than that inflicted on the *Clorinde*, but the French frigate had lost 70 killed or wounded as opposed to the 60 casualties in *Eurotas*. Among the latter, however, was Phillimore himself, badly wounded in the shoulder by grapeshot in the early stages of the action. Despite repeatedly fainting from loss of blood, Phillimore remained on deck and in command until the *Clorinde* broke off the action. The British crew were now hastily put to work repairing the damage to their frigate, which seems primarily to have been to the masts and rigging. By 11.30pm, with jury masts rigged, the *Eurotas* was underway again in pursuit of the *Clorinde* who, having declined the opportunity of re-engaging her crippled foe, was now six miles away. Unfortunately, before the *Eurotas* could catch up with the French frigate, two more British warships hove into view. These were the 36-gun frigate *Dryad*, commanded by Captain Edward Galwey, and a brig-sloop. The captain of the French frigate, realising the hopelessness of his position – his crew had still not repaired the damage to their masts and rigging – quickly negotiated terms of surrender to the *Dryad*. The officers and crew of the *Eurotas* could only watch as the ship which they had fought became the prize of another.

The chagrin of the *Eurotas*'s officers and crew must have been exacerbated by another factor. The *Eurotas* carried a main deck battery of 24-pounder guns, whilst the *Clorinde* had only 18-pounders. Superficially, the British frigate should have inflicted severe damage on her opponent. Instead, with the exception of the damage to her masts, her hull was found only to be 'in want of between a small and middling repair' to make her fit for service in the Royal Navy; repairs which the Dockyard at Portsmouth estimated could be completed within two months.[75] This discrepancy in armament and outcome led the historian William James to publish an acid account of the action in his *Naval History of Great Britain* in 1826. James pointed out that there could be little deficiency in a crew who, having fought a close-range action for several hours, could so speedily repair their frigate and seek a resumption of the engagement. The problem lay in the ship's gunnery, and for this, James implied, Phillimore himself was to blame. Specifically, James pointed out that the log of the *Eurotas* demonstrated that the crew of the frigate had only been put to gunnery practice on average of once a week:

> … here was a frigate, fitted out purposely to be a match for one of [the large American frigates]; and we have not a doubt that, before he fell in with the *Clorinde*, Captain Phillimore expressed a very strong desire to encounter the [American frigate] *Constitution*. Under these circumstances, no pains should have been spared to make the crew of the *Eurotas* expert cannoneers. We have seen the means that Captain Broke took to teach his men how to point their guns with great effect, and we have seen in what a short space of time these guns, thus skilfully directed, tore to pieces an equal antagonist …

When James's work was published Phillimore responded to this criticism by travelling to London and thrashing James with a cane, an assault which cost him a fine of £100.

Phillimore's response to the criticism was probably prompted by a number of factors and may, incidentally, illustrate why many other naval officers felt the way they did about James – hence the reluctance of many to co-operate with him when researching his work.

In the first place, much of James's criticism relies on the detailed accuracy of the captain's log. As noted earlier, there were (and are) limitations to the value of ships' logs as evidence; and this will be demonstrated further in the next chapter. To rely on the evidence of a log alone to publicly criticise an officer and crew who have fought a hard and bloody action is unwise, particularly so soon after the event.

The second factor is that Phillimore himself was severely wounded during the action. In a letter to the Admiralty he reported:

> I suffered and must continue to suffer for the remainder of my life from the wounds in the arm and breast which have so long endangered my life and confined me to my bed for 24 weeks besides which I received five subsequent wounds of a more trifling nature which for some time subjected me to considerable pain.[76]

The wounds continued to trouble him ever afterwards. Although awarded a CB in 1815, he remained unfit for further service for several years. In 1823 he was appointed to the frigate *Thetis*, serving on both sides of the Atlantic for three years until the ship was paid off. The long lasting effects of his wounds, however, continued to trouble him, and he eventually died as a result of these in March 1840.

The third point involved James's assessment of the efficiency of the armament on board the *Eurotas*. As previously noted, the *Eurotas*, like some of the other ships of her class, was built out of pine. Pine was not only a cheaper material for shipbuilding, but its use also speeded up the production of new ships at a time when the Admiralty urgently required more frigates to blockade the long American coastline. However, the issue was complicated by the perceived threat from the heavier, 24-pounder-armed American frigates, which had already overpowered three of the standard British 18-pounder ships. Frigates of *Eurotas*'s class could not bear the weight of the usual 'long' 24-pounders, and attempts were made to solve this problem by the production of lighter, shorter barrelled main-deck guns. The *Eurotas* and her sister ship the *Cydnus* were fitted out with two different designs of experimental 24-pounder guns, the former carrying those developed by William

Congreve, and the latter a 24-pounder gun designed by Henry Blomefield. The Congreve pattern looked like an elongated carronade, while Blomefield's resembled a truncated conventional gun, but both were shorter in the barrel and lighter in construction than the standard 24-pounder. The aim of these changes in design was to make it possible for what was basically a *Leda* class frigate – a ship designed to carry twenty-eight 18-pounder guns as its main armament – to carry twenty-eight 24-pounder guns. By making the weight of the guns themselves lighter, it was thought that the firepower of a frigate could be improved without increasing the number of men required in the gun crews.

The Admiralty were keen to prove that the Congreve design gun was both suitable and practical for use at sea, but their wish to utilise these guns on a more general basis was opposed by the Board of Ordnance, which was headed by Blomefield himself. Whatever lay behind the conflict of opinion – and it is probable that some political interests may have been involved as Congreve had the ear of the Prince Regent – Phillimore found his new frigate armed with experimental guns which the Admiralty was keen to prove in action. On joining Commodore Malcolm's squadron off Brest in September 1813, a trial of the new guns had been witnessed by a number of the squadron's commanders. The guns were fired double-shotted eight times in quick succession. They performed well and were handled easily with smaller crews. However, the performance of the guns was found to be different in action. As one of the *Eurotas*'s officers later recalled:

> we found Congreve's experimental 24-pounders very light guns to work; but they were so lively that the allowance of powder was very soon obliged to be reduced one third, and subsequently one-half; about an hour and a half from the commencement of the action, one of them made a jump and actually touched the beams of the fore-castle-deck; in fact, it was so hot that we were obliged to discontinue using it.[77]

In other words, the more the guns were fired the hotter they became; as they became hotter they responded to the detonation of powder within the barrel with greater force, increasing the recoil. To some extent this was true of all guns, but acutely so of the lightweight Congreves. Such a violent recoil, of over two tons of cannon, amidst a deck crowded with frantically active gun crews would have been dreadful; and this was overlooked by William James. In an attempt to ease the recoil of the guns, the weight of powder in each charge was reduced – but the effect of this was to lower the velocity with which the shot hit the enemy ship. It was this factor which, Phillimore claimed, explained the comparatively slight damage inflicted upon the

Clorinde. That the Admiralty were concerned enough about the guns' behaviour is confirmed by the fact that the Navy Board and the Board of Ordnance both sought reports on the effectiveness of the guns during the action. The Navy Board ordered a survey from Portsmouth Dockyard on 'the effect of the Fire of the *Eurotas* upon the Hull, Masts and Yards of the *Clorinde*'.[78] As previously mentioned, the Dockyard inspectors concluded that the damage was not severe. However, their report makes very little of the fact that the mizzen and main mast had been brought down by the *Eurotas*'s guns, the bowsprit had been shot through and that, although the actual fore mast remained (but not the fore top or fore topgallant masts), this had also been damaged by shot. Hours after the engagement, when the *Clorinde* surrendered to the *Dryad*, she was realistically in no condition to re-engage. The *Eurotas*, on the other hand, had been sufficiently repaired – and no doubt her guns would have cooled sufficiently to enable them to be double-shotted once again.

Only a few weeks before this inspection, the artillery expert Henry Shrapnel was sent by the Board of Ordnance to undertake an inspection of the guns of the *Eurotas* at Plymouth, and, reading between the lines, to prove the inferiority of Congreve's guns. The inspection was carried out in the presence of Lord Keith, Vice-Admiral Domett and Rear-Admiral Martin, and it was, therefore, hardly surprising that Shrapnel was cautiously discreet. His observations backed up both the Board of Ordnance's concerns and Phillimore's report of the action: '… with regard to the merits of the *Eurotas* Guns in the late action *whether the French ship Clorinde has been more disabled by the Fire from the Eurotas than might have been the case had she been armed with Guns already in the service* [Author's emphasis] I beg leave to refer this opinion to Naval Officers.'[79] Looking at the guns themselves he noted:

if the Metal is not of a sufficient substance or is thin in any one part whatever, I consider such kind of ordnance very unfit for service – from the extreme heat which it must speedily acquire from the inflammation of gunpowder, and is besides very liable to be fractured even by common grape shot … The *Eurotas* frigate has two of her Carronades [*ie* the Congreve guns, which were of carronade form] No 10 and No 14 disabled. No 10 has every appearance of being struck by a grape shot only which has fractured the extended part of the Muzzle and which I do not believe would have been the case had they been made with the usual swell of the muzzle common to all other guns … In the action with the *Clorinde* it was found necessary to reduce the charge of the guns on board the *Eurotas* to four pounds of powder which charge can never be considered sufficient for the projecting of two 24 pounder shot or forty eight pounds weight with a sufficient velocity, and

from the examination of the coins I found the Base rings of the Guns had
from the violent action penetrated their coins to a considerable depth.[80]

Shrapnel's findings seemed to confirm the account given by Phillimore and his
officers; and even the Portsmouth Dockyard inspectors found two of the *Eurotas's*
shot still embedded in the mast and spirketting of the *Clorinde*, a testament to their
low velocity. Nevertheless, political interest seems to have prevailed and the
Admiralty ordered more Congreve guns for general use within the navy.

The aftermath of the action between the *Eurotas* and the *Clorinde* is therefore a
complex one, but at the end of the day it was Phillimore who was left in an extremely
uncomfortable position. Not only had he been seriously wounded, but he had also
failed to take a less powerful French frigate as quickly as might have been expected,
had lost out on prize money because of the untimely intervention of the frigate
Dryad, and was also at the centre of a political row in which he had, to all intents
and purposes, demonstrably undermined the position of his senior officers and the
Admiralty. For an officer with a previous record and reputation like Phillimore's,
this might have meant a very depressing and serious outcome. Yet within a few years
he was again in active service and would probably have continued longer had not
his health finally broken down. One of the factors that may have salvaged Phillimore
from his situation was his style of command. In many ways Phillimore's approach
to the men serving under him was more in tune with changing attitudes and values
evolving at the beginning of the nineteenth century. As one of his officers noted in
an obituary: 'his mind was constantly employed in endeavouring to ameliorate the
condition of his fellow creatures, but particularly British seamen ... a kind protector
to those over whom he was placed in authority.'[81]

VICTORY
The question of styles of command will be dealt with in the next chapter, but before
leaving the subject of actions and their aftermath, there are two factors that should
be emphasised. Firstly, provided casualties suffered in the process were not too
heavy, a victorious frigate engagement usually brought fame, rewards and
professional kudos. In the case of officers like Sir Edward Pellew and Sir Michael
Seymour, for example, the rewards of victory were evident in the honours they
received. Such officers were also likely to receive gifts of silver plate from Lloyds and
the award of the Freedom of various cities. For those who were in a state to
appreciate it, the arrival at port with their prize was a moment to be savoured. There
are several brief descriptions of these events, but the spirit of that moment in
perhaps best sampled in a letter written by Thomas Haliburton, a resident of

Halifax, Nova Scotia, recalling many years later, the moment that the *Shannon* arrived back in port.

> I was attending divine service in St Paul's Church at that time, when a person was seen to enter hurriedly, whisper something to a friend in the garrison pew, and then as hastily withdraw. The effect was electrical, for whatever the news was, it flew from pew to pew, and one by one the congregation left the church. My own impression was that there was a fire in the immediate vicinity of St Paul's; one movement soon became so general that I, too, left the building to enquire into the cause of the commotion. I was informed by a person in the crowd that an English man-of-war was coming up the harbour with an American frigate as her prize! By that time, the ships were in full view, near St George's Island, and slowly moving through the water. Every housetop and every wharf was crowded with groups of excited people, and, as the ships successively passed, they were greeted with vociferous cheers.[82]

The irony of course is that Broke himself was too seriously injured to enjoy the moment. The reality of naval warfare was (and still is) horrific for those who have to experience it. There are very few writings that convey what it was really like but, by coincidence, Thomas Haliburton himself reveals something of its nature. In their excitement to see the prize, Haliburton and a friend borrowed a boat and rowed out to the two frigates as soon as they anchored. They were refused permission to board the *Shannon* but somehow they got on board the *Chesapeake*.

> The deck was not cleaned … and the coils and folds of rope were steeped in gore as if in a slaughter house … Pieces of skin, with pendant hair, were adhering to the sides of the ship, and in one place I noticed portions of finger protruding, as if thrust through the outer wall of the frigate … it was a scene of devastation as difficult to forget as to describe. It is one of the most painful reminiscences of my youth … and it made upon me a mournful impression that, even now, remains as vivid as ever.[83]

CHAPTER

VII

IN COMMAND

I N THE FINAL ANALYSIS the success of a frigate captain was dependent on his possession of the skills and abilities necessary to enable him to 'command'. Two hundred years later these attributes would be recognised as 'leadership' skills; but this word is certainly not one commonly found in the naval writings of the period. By the time an officer was promoted to post captain during the Great Wars with France, he would probably have spent some twelve years in an environment from which he was expected to learn how to command both officers and men. Although there were attempts to provide formal training for officers in the guise of the Naval College at Portsmouth, the focus there was heavily on seamanship, navigation, mathematics, physics, and so forth – all aspects relating to the practical side of fighting and ship-handling.[1] There was nothing to assist the young officer in understanding how to command people. Such understanding was therefore supposed to be assimilated through experience during the six years as a 'young gentleman', midshipman or master's mate, followed by the four to five years as a lieutenant. At the end of this period of time the fortunate ones were appointed commander of their own vessel – but a small vessel with a small crew. Usually only by having proven their abilities at this level did they gain post rank and the command of a rated ship with a crew of two hundred or more.

It is possible to see in this structured system a training process at work, in which the trainee learned by imitation. Moreover, the process was heavily dependent upon good role models. The examples of Lord Cochrane, Ross Donnelly and Edward Owen have already been noted in this capacity, though one would also have to acknowledge Nelson's huge contribution in this area. If there was little formal training in 'command', there were certainly tools to assist. The oldest of these were the *Regulations and Instructions relating to His Majesty's Service at Sea*.[2] These actually contained little guidance about handling either men or officers, although they did insist, for example, that a captain was never 'by his own authority, to discharge a commission or warrant officer, nor to punish or strike him'.[3] However, a post captain could suspend or confine one of those officers pending court martial, which suggests that the *Regulations* existed to literally 'regulate' the powers of the commanding officer rather than to encourage good relations with his officers. The real value of these regulations is demonstrated by the fact that Regulation IV, restricting the ability of any commander to inflict more than twelve lashes, was regularly ignored. The *Regulations* were amended by Sir Charles Middleton (Lord Barham) in 1806, possibly in an attempt to instil a degree of acceptable practice and uniformity to ship management, but, once again, there was little to give direct guidance to the commanding officer.

The reason for this absence of advice probably lay in the reluctance of the Admiralty to trespass onto the quarterdeck of individual captains. That senior officers in the navy were conscious of the difficulty that existed here is evident, for example, from a chance remark in a letter from Lord Keith to Admiral Markham in 1803: 'Captain Mitford is a gentleman, but, I have heard, a little harsh in his command. It is a difficult subject to mention or I would [talk] to him on the subject; it is of high importance to keep men in temper at this time.'[4] Mitford was not a frigate captain, but the reference indicates the difficulty that senior officers experienced in tackling severity among their officers, especially when there was no official framework or detailed rules and regulations to guide officers in the practice and method of command. In spite of this apparent reluctance – and one might understand why many admirals would have been reluctant to trespass on the captain's territory – it is clear that the issue was one of which a number of commanding officers were themselves aware.

It may have been this which prompted David Steel in 1804 to publish a volume by an anonymous 'Captain in the Royal Navy' entitled *Observations and Instructions for the use of the commissioned, the junior and other officers of the Royal navy on all the material points of professional duty ...*[5] The anonymous captain was in reality Commander John Davie, who was to be posted in 1809, and had served for a number of years as first lieutenant under Captain Jonathan Faulknor in the frigate *Diana*. It is more than possible, therefore, that Davie was writing with the benefit of firsthand experience, some of which was gained from observing Faulknor. What is particularly important about Davie's work is that almost from the beginning it gave voice to some of the issues relating to command: 'The first object of every captain in His Majesty's navy on his appointment to a ship must be to have those officers with him whose dispositions he is acquainted with, and upon whose abilities and attention *his*[6] character, comfort and happiness are, in a great measure, dependant.'[7]

Davie went on to explain that if the captain was not able to choose his own officers he would be 'tenacious of his authority' and afraid to delegate. Furthermore, only a captain fully satisfied with his first lieutenant, 'upon whose abilities the whole movement of the ship depends', would be able to leave the 'whole internal management to his direction'. The point of this was to enable the captain to retain a certain amount of distance, enabling him to concentrate without the encumbrance of the 'day-to-day'; again, in modern management terms this would be recognised as a valid technique, sometimes referred to as 'helicopter vision'. The author went on to explain further: 'Every captain of a ship of war should recollect ... that the exertions of [the first lieutenant] ... will be in proportion to the confidence reposed in him, and that interference in his department, and unnecessary orders, are the most certain means of damping his zeal and ardour.'[8] Furthermore, it was the duty of the first lieutenant to manage the other officers and, through the divisional system, the crew. Under this system the crew were literally divided into Divisions, each being the responsibility of a junior lieutenant, assisted by midshipmen and warrant officers. It was the duty of these to ensure the care of the seamen, inspecting their clothing, bedding, food and ultimately their health. The divisional system, therefore, represented a management hierarchy. Although a number of enlightened officers had already tried and adopted the system, it was not formally recommended until the amended *Regulations* of 1806.

Davie, however, was certainly advocating it in 1804, noting that 'an officer who commands seamen should make himself acquainted with their dispositions and character, in preference to any other consideration. By this he will be enabled to improve every favourable opportunity of rendering the discipline subservient to his command.'[9] Vitally, Davie was not concerned simply with maintaining discipline; he was also concerned about motivation. He advocated, for example, officers taking every opportunity to encourage young seamen to improve their skills, thus raising their status within the ship – and therefore within the wider seafaring community. In what would appear to be almost revolutionary thinking he noted that the largest part of the crew – the afterguard and waisters – were the ones upon whom 'the whole drudgery of the ship devolves. These men have not only the burden, but every dirty and inferior duty to execute; to them I conceive an officer's principal attention should be directed, and every encouragement and inducement made use of to reconcile them to the service, and to acquire a knowledge of seamanship.'[10] In this there is more than a whiff of that philosophy of self-improvement which became so prevalent later in the nineteenth century. Here, seamanship is seen as the means of self-improvement, but what is really important is the recognition of the relationship between low-status/low self-esteem, and the need for an officer to play an active role in encouraging men to rise above this situation.

The divisional system, therefore, was included in the amended *Regulations* of 1806 because it was already being operated by a number of post captains. The *Regulations* also attempted to encourage a degree of uniformity between the regimes on different ships. One of the major causes of grievance and disruption occurred when a new commanding officer assumed his position and introduced his own particular rules for the internal discipline and management of the ship. It often took some time to become familiar with changes to routines which may have been in operation for many years, and the result was often an increase in punishments.[11] In his study of discipline on the Leeward Islands Station, John D Byrn noted that '74% of the men flogged within the first six months of the arrival of a fresh captain had no previous history of disciplinary problems on their ships'.[12]

The influence of a new captain upon those under his command cannot be over-emphasised. The case of Captain Henry Jenkins of the *Ambuscade* serves as a good example here. Jenkins was posted in 1795 and, within a year was given command of the *Carnatic*, 74. In April 1798 he was transferred to the 12-pounder frigate *Ambuscade*. On 14 December, he encountered the French corvette *Baionnaise* and during the course of the ensuing engagement, the crew of the British frigate suddenly lost both morale and discipline and abandoned their guns, enabling French boarders to take the ship. According to William James[13] the crew of the *Ambuscade* were in a very bad state of discipline which had not been improved by Jenkins's behaviour since taking command. The latter had brought with him, from his previous ship, a party of favourite seamen whom he nominated the 'Gentlemen Carnatics', whilst the frigate's crew he publicly termed the 'Blackguard Ambuscades'. This thoughtless and provocative treatment obviously created serious divisions among a crew who should have been working closely as a team. The result was disaster. Jenkins probably survived the consequent court martial only because his judges were unable to decide which half of the crew to blame, and the fact that he looked so ill, still suffering the effects from the wound he had received during the action.

Captains' Order Books

The particular requirements of a new captain were generally presented in the form of the Captain's Order Book containing what were often referred to as his 'standing orders'. A number of these have survived, and in many cases they prefigure both the work of John Davie and the amended *Regulations*. The contents of the captains' order books tend to be similar, concentrating on the role and duties of the first lieutenant, officer of the watch, and so on. There is usually a surprising degree of concern with seamen's clothing, bedding and the need to keep the 'tween decks dry and aired for health reasons. Individual captains brought their own style to the orders. Captain Edward Riou's order book for the frigate *Amazon* in 1799, for example, was very detailed, containing 64 different orders.[14] Those of William Parker, who followed Riou in command of the *Amazon*, were much shorter.[15]

There is also no noticeable difference between the orders of a frigate captain and those of the captain of a ship of the line. The concerns are largely the same. However, to a certain degree this may depend on the type of duty on which the ship was engaged. Edward Griffith of the 90-gun *London* included an order that, when at sea he was to be informed 'should we at any time lose sight of the Commr in Chief or his lights'.[16] This was less likely to be of concern to a frigate on a cruise! Similarly, J C Purvis of the *Princess Royal*, another 90, included orders to ensure that at the change of watch the relieving lieutenant signed the log to confirm that he had had the exact position and distance of the ship ahead made clear to him.[17]

Some of the order books drawn up for frigates do contain elements suggesting an awareness of crew management, particularly when it came to the relationship between the captain and his first lieutenant. The management of officers was probably much more important than management of the crew, since the latter were commanded through the former and getting this relationship wrong could lead to serious problems. Charles Dashwood, who was later to command frigates for a period of five years, experienced just such a problem when commanding the sloop *Sylph* in 1800. Dashwood was concerned about the behaviour of his first lieutenant, a Lieutenant Pyne. Following an ugly incident involving dockyard artificers who had boarded the sloop to carry out repairs, Pyne was found guilty of maltreatment and Dashwood reported to his commander-in-chief: 'I have had many opportunities of observing the great warmth of temper of that officer, and I am as apprehensive of unpleasant consequences from his violent and unconciliatory mind, the harmony and discipline of the *Sylph* having suffered much since his appointment to the situation of Senior Lieutenant ... .'[18]

Frederick Hoffman, first lieutenant of the *Diamond*, provides an example of a poor relationship between captain and first lieutenant. In August 1806 the apparently easy-going Captain Thomas Elphinstone of the frigate was replaced by Captain George Argles:

unfortunately for himself and in some measure for the service, [he] courted a kind of left-handed popularity among the seamen, and neglected the officers. The consequence was, that in less than two months the discipline of the ship became so relaxed that the crew, from being one of the smartest in the fleet, was now the slackest.[19]

In this quotation it is clear that the vital relationship and confidence between the commissioned officers on the ship had disintegrated and Hoffman, for one, felt that his authority had been undermined.

In his order book Edward Riou, commanding the frigate *Amazon*, placed great emphasis on the importance of the first lieutenant in the command structure: 'The duties of the First Lieutenant depend so much upon the zeal, activity and strength of constitution of the officer that it is impossible to point out how much, and what is or what is not expected of him.' To this end the relationship between the captain and his first lieutenant were to be made clear: the latter 'ought to be made acquainted with every direction the captain may give', but in return 'by no means should he adopt an erroneous system too prevalent amongst officers of that rank, of carrying on the duty and ordering the different services in the ship to be performed according to their own ideas of propriety without previously acquainting, and with a proper deference obtaining the consent or orders of the captain.'[20] Here then it can be seen that Riou recognised the importance of keeping his first lieutenant fully informed, but at the same time, emphasised where authority lay; and, to emphasise this point, Riou repeated it in the next paragraph of his orders. The first lieutenant would, in commanding the junior officers, have the benefit of the captain's confidence, thus reinforcing his own authority over the rest of the crew. But, on the other hand, it was clear who was the captain.

Obviously not all captains kept such close control, and the response of lieutenants to the relationship varied. When Lieutenant Frederick Hoffman had joined the frigate *Diamond* in March 1806, he found the situation on board rather strange. His new colleagues informed him that the captain, T E Elphinstone, 'was highly nervous, and that he left everything to the first Lieutenant, except the discipline of his cook'. Furthermore, 'he was not fond of punishment with the cat.'[21] The culture of command in the frigate was therefore clearly different from Hoffman's previous experience. Whether this was genuinely because Elphinstone lacked confidence, as Hoffman implies, or because he adopted a more delegated command style, is now difficult to say. However, Elphinstone was an older, experienced, captain who had commanded the *Diamond* for over three and a half years by the time that Hoffman joined.[22] After three and a half years he may well have felt pretty secure in his command and therefore may have had no difficulty in delegating some of his authority, particularly as (according to Hoffman) he said he would leave sailing to the first lieutenant, whilst he would be the fighting captain.

When William Parker assumed command of the *Amazon* after the death of Riou in 1801, he issued his own orders, and these included a section specifically written for the seamen themselves. In other words, whereas the common practice seems to have been to provide one set of orders for the use of both officers and men, Parker provided a specific section of nine simply-written orders which addressed the people directly and was headed 'Regulations to be observed by the Ship's Company of HMS Amazon'. The first of these, for example, stated: 'When any Duty is ordered, every man is to go as fast as possible to the station appointed to him, and there wait in <u>silence</u> for the orders of his officers, which he is to obey as briskly and as well as he can without speaking, for the men are to be properly silent whenever Duty is performing.'[23]

Another order allows a glimpse of Parker's philosophy and also his attitude to punishment:

> The ship's Company are always to keep their Hammocks very clean and well lashed up (A sure sign of a good seaman). The men of every mess are to keep their Berths clean; they are never to throw the Bones or any part of their provisions about the Deck and they are never to Piss on the Decks or to throw dirt of any kind over the gunwale nor out of the Ports, the Head is the place for such purposes – If any man is found making a dirt below, he will be made to sweep all the decks, until he finds another equally neglectful of this order.[24]

There is evidence here of a very enlightened culture of command, made even more remarkable by the fact that Parker was just 21 years of age and had been promoted with great speed. It is hardly surprising, therefore, that he met with the enthusiastic approval of both Nelson and Sir John Borlase Warren, under both of whom he served.[25] Parker was to have a long and distinguished period of frigate command (nearly eight years) and was clearly influenced to some degree by Captain Edward Foote of the *Niger* frigate under whom he also served for some time.[26]

ATTITUDES TO DISCIPLINE

In the case of Parker it is perhaps possible to see a new attitude towards the maintenance of discipline. The example of Thomas Elphinstone in 1806 has already been noted above. In the same year the seaman Robert Wilson recorded in his journal the arrival of Captain Patrick Campbell on board the *Unité* frigate in 1806 and commented:

> We soon found the good effects of his joining us, for he ordered no sticks, etc, to be used by the Boatswain and his Mates, and no person to be punished without his knowledge, and did away with the formality of touching our hats

at quarters, except when particularly spoken to. At the same time the ship's company were kept in their good state of discipline with less severity, for the crew did their duty more cheerful.[27]

To some degree this change in attitude may have been a consequence of the presence of growing numbers of young aristocrats in the navy as the war progressed.[28] Consider, for example, Sir William Hotham's recollection of his time as a lieutenant on board the *Inconstant* frigate commanded by Captain Augustus Montgomery, the 'natural' son of Lord Pembroke.

> I always have, and always shall, look back upon my being under the command of this officer as the happiest period of my professional life … and it was a very curious thing, and I think unique in the service, that the four commissioned officers of the *Inconstant* frigate were all public school-men … The ship was in a state of discipline highly creditable to the service, nothing like severity appeared; and the quarter-deck was the parade of gentlemen, without, to those under them, any worrying tricks of brief authority.[29]

According to Linda Colley[30] the British ruling elite underwent a major transformation at the end of the eighteenth century as it became increasingly aware that political, industrial and economic development in Europe and North America threatened to undermine its continued existence. As one of the main roles of the aristocracy had always been to provide leadership in time of war, the Great Wars against France provided a stage on which the young men of the ruling class could attempt to fulfil this role and reassert their collective position. In so doing new role models were created in the officer corps of the navy and changes became apparent in attitudes towards command.

Probably one of the most famous role models was that provided by Lord Cochrane whose very noticeable style of command involved 'leading from the front' and not asking those under his command to undertake any task he would not do himself. This meant, in effect, that he had to be (and be seen to be) as skilled as those he commanded in order to win their trust and respect.[31] The impact of this style of leadership is well illustrated by one of his protégés, Frederick Marryat. In *Frank Mildmay*, Marryat described Cochrane (whom he names 'Lord Edward'), as follows:

> Lord Edward was a sailor every inch of him, he knew a ship from stem to stern, understood the characters of seaman, and gained their confidence. He was, besides, a good mechanic – a carpenter, rope-maker, sail-maker, and

cooper. He could hand, reef, steer, knot and splice; but he was no orator – he read little, and spoke less. He was a man of no show. He was good tempered, honest, and unsophisticated, with a large proportion of common sense. He was good humoured and free with his officers; though if offended he was violent, but soon calm again; nor could you ever perceive any assumption of consequence from his title of nobility.[32]

The understanding that lay behind this approach to leadership was clearly expressed by Basil Hall:

it is very well known that much instruction in the difficult art of command may be taught through the medium of obedience alone. For the mere knowledge of what is required to be done, will not always be accompanied by an acquaintance with the best way of accomplishing a given piece of service. We must understand the nature of the instruments by which the work is to be executed, otherwise our force is wasted, our tools blunted, and the whole task bungled. Unless, indeed, a commanding officer have learnt, from actual experience, what it is to feel as a subordinate, not once or twice, but on a great variety of occasions, he will hardly be able to turn the capacities of those under his command to their full account. Instead of cementing his crew into one compact mass, and so bringing their united forces to bear upon the objects required by the public service, he will waste and dissipate their strength by misdirected applications of their divided and often conflicting energies, while his own temper may too frequently be lost in punishments, which might have been spared, had he only learned, by personal experience, what were likely to be the feelings and wishes of his inferiors.

But an officer who, in his own person, has gone through a full course of rigid obedience ... will be able, under like circumstances, to produce very different results from those just described. He will find little or no difficulty in divining the feelings of those under his orders; and though, if the number of his crew be great, there must ever be a considerable diversity of sentiment amongst them, yet, in most cases, he will be enabled to strike a pretty fair average as to the general wish, and thus secure the hearty co-operation of the majority of those he desires to put in motion.[33]

The weakness of Hall's point of view is that although experiencing discipline 'as a subordinate' was a part of the every day training of all 'young gentlemen' in the navy, it did not prevent the development of a number of brutally severe officers. To

210

'experience' had to be added a different attitude towards the people below deck. Changing attitudes may perhaps be ascribed to two factors: firstly an application of the concept of *noblesse oblige* and, secondly, an ability or willingness among some officers to begin seeing the seamen under their command as fellow, if not quite equal, human beings. It is impossible to ignore signs of a changing attitude to what was described as the 'lower orders', from at least the last decade of the eighteenth century. To some degree this change had been forced upon the upper levels of society as a reaction to the upheavals of the French Revolution, and the mutinies of 1797 had brought further alarm. The fact that the seamen of the Channel and North Sea fleets had demonstrated their potential power without showing any real wish to overthrow the established order had troubled some of the more socially sensitive members of the upper classes. Certainly, some naval officers were in sympathy with the grievances of the seamen if not their methods or organisation. But the message that seems to have been gleaned from the great mutinies was about the need for a more paternalistic approach by those in power: in other words the post captain as father-figure rather than deity. This paternalism dove-tails with the concept of *noblesse oblige*. A year after the mutinies, for example, in June 1799 George Fitzroy, Earl of Euston (and later Duke of Grafton) observed in a letter written from Ireland, where the propertied classes had even more reason to be alarmed:

Acts of outrage from the lower orders will follow imperiousness and oppression from those above them, therefore disorder must prevail here till the interest of the two countries become the same, and through the intimacy of the connection, a spirit of charity to the poor, and justice and civility to inferiors, shall diffuse itself among the people of property, and most especially the middle orders.'[34]

The recognition of a need for a change in relationships is clear in this letter.

The significance is increased when it is noted that the recipient was Morton Pitt, who was associated with the Clapham Sect of the Evangelical Movement. There can be no doubt that the Evangelical Movement played an important part in changing attitudes, though the extent of this is hard to establish without considerable research. Neither the Clapham Sect, nor the wider Evangelical Movement, can be described as a liberalising movement. In many ways their philanthropy towards the poor was aimed at defusing any possibility of threat to the established order. Yet at the same time, the activities of the sect's members brought them into contact with a poorer class in whom they could find certain redeeming qualities. Some of the leading members of this sect were closely connected to members of both

Government and the Admiralty, and there is no doubt that there were also naval officers who shared or were influenced by their views. The best known example is Lord Gambier, who was – and to some degree still is – castigated for introducing his religion into his professional activities. It is also clear from Lady Chatterton's *Memorials* of Gambier that there was a lively correspondence between leading Evangelical activists like Hannah More, Henry Thornton and William Wilberforce, and Sir Charles Middleton, the Pitts and other families with naval connections like the Legges and Bouveries, and of course Lord Gambier himself.

When it comes to identifying the religious leanings of frigate captains, the issue becomes more difficult. Philip Broke, for example, appears to have closely followed the regulations regarding religious observance at sea. He even annotated a book of sermons to make them suitable for him to use during services on board his ships. His personal letters to his wife Louisa also contain the occasional revealing comment, as for example in his letter of 18 June 1809, from off Bordeaux: 'We have had a fine day and been to church, I got one volume of Haggitt's sermons, amongst the books by *Seine*, and am confirmed in the idea I had of their being the fittest discourses of any I know for a general congregation, and particularly for the middling and lower classes.'[35] This and other chance remarks do lead to the suspicion that Broke was at least in sympathy with some of the Evangelicals' tenets. Philip Beaver, who had reached the rank of lieutenant before the war, spent several years assisting in an unsuccessful attempt to establish a colony of English settlers and freed slaves on the island of Bulama, off the coast of Sierra Leone. This may well have been the same colony with which the Clapham Sect was involved through two of their leaders, Henry Thornton and Granville Sharp. This is obviously not sufficient evidence to prove that Beaver himself was an Evangelical, but the link is tantalising.

Most probably, the more sensitive captains adopted a more pragmatic paternalism, taking ideas from people like the Evangelicals without the 'baggage' that accompanied their philosophising. This seems to have been the case with captains' attitude to religion generally. As Captain Anselm Griffiths of the *Leonidas* noted, there was a role for religion at sea in providing comfort in time of fear – and a role for chaplains in setting a moral example on board and acting as an advocate for transgressors. Ultimately, however, the attitude towards the people was determined by the captain himself.

The paradox is that the growing number of aristocrats in the officer corps led it inexorably towards greater social awareness whilst at the same time, for a while at least, the concept of paternalism embodied in *noblesse oblige* also spread. Thus we find officers like Captain Philip Beaver of the *Acasta* frigate writing to another officer:

Recollect ... that numbers of your people have been impressed, and are the unwilling victims of our temporal, though urgent interests. Such considerations, added to the tantalising breaches of the ties of home, which the very nature of the services renders necessary, should make every good officer desirous of establishing the comfort of his crew ... Endeavour to grant some respite in port, if the tenour [*sic*] of your instructions will admit it. The refitting, stowing stores, squaring yards, working boats, and drying sails, with all the minor minutiae, leave but little leisure ... Jack knows well enough what is necessary, and therefore does not relish a too frequent mustering of hammocks and bags, polishing of iron work, and other artificial modes of teasing the time ...[36]

Anselm Griffiths went much further, producing a manual for all aspiring officers and advised:

If in the management of a ship's company after the attainment of all the essentials of discipline, activity, sobriety and obedience, &c. they were left more to themselves, there would not be any thing which bore even the semblance of ... [mutiny]. Much dissatisfaction does arise from a too constant interference with them, from the attempt to keep them fidgeting about trifles and works of supererogation, all with a view to employ their minds. This seems a want of knowledge of human nature. Such perpetual fiddle faddle and interference only disgusts. The experience of many years has taught me, that if dealt with kindly, they may safely be left in their leisure hours from their duty, to their own resources and amusements. [37]

Griffiths commanded frigates for over five years and wrote his manual immediately after the war. His attitude towards command was clearly not unique.

Whilst there may have been a growing tendency in some quarters to try and make the quarterdeck the preserve of gentlemen, there was also a view that it was the characteristics of the gentleman that was required. This was rationalised, again by Basil Hall:

The opinion will hardly be controverted, that persons who are the most gentlemanlike in their habits of thought, in sentiment, and in manners – supposing their talents and opportunities alike – generally speaking, make the best officers ... what is indispensably required in the naval profession, above all others ... [is] the essential spirit, if I may so term it, of a gentleman.

This quality in the character of an officer must, by some means or other, be made to predominate, and, as it were, to exalt all the others...

... the power placed in an officer's hands ... is of such a nature, that, unless it be regulated by the principles which form the distinguishing features in the character of a gentleman, it is apt to degenerate into tyranny and oppression.[38]

In other words, the best commanders were those who were impelled by a character that was determined by their social and cultural background. This would seem to be where *noblesse oblige* is activated to the benefit of the crew and it is interesting that Hall juxtaposes the 'character of a gentleman' with 'tyranny and oppression'.

Of course there were examples of titled commanders who were the antithesis of the character that Hall advocates – Lord William Fitzroy, for example – but the point is that Hall is talking about the principle and good future practice of command, rather than an exposition of past bad practice.[39] Hall was also able to add a justification for the need for the gentleman officer, and this was quite possibly grounded in real experience.

The sailors, who are very quick-sighted to the merits and faults of their officers, and form critics of great correctness, understand the distinction perfectly between a well-bred or high-caste officer, and one who, not having been born in a class where good manners are an essential characteristic, has not contrived to adopt them from others. Above all things, a ship's company like to be commanded by gentlemen; and there is nothing they hate or despise in an officer so much as that coarseness of thought and behaviour which belong to their own class.[40]

It is important to note that Hall advocates officers who are 'gentleman-*like*' or who had *acquired* the essential characteristics of the 'gentleman'. He could not rule out the development of such qualities by officers who had learned the skills of command during the war years. This was part of a new professionalism which he was keen to encourage.

Changing attitudes to command were certainly evident earlier, particularly when it came to the application of discipline, and flogging in particular. Some officers, even before 1797, had learned to handle their crews in a manner which brought them both loyalty and respect. One of the best examples is that of Captain Philip Cunningham, whose name has already been cited several times. During the mutiny at the Nore in 1797, the crew of Cunningham's frigate *Clyde* were torn between their loyalty to their captain and the cause of the mutineers. In the end, forced to make a choice between the Delegates and Cunningham, the crew chose the latter. Writing some time later, Cunningham commented:

> In those ships too, where good discipline was maintained, the general behaviour of the Crews, during these turbulent scenes, was marked with the least violence … In a ship so managed, where strict discipline is enforced, the good men have confidence in their commander, and even feel a positive obligation to him for the protection he affords them against those who would be guilty of theft, drunkenness, idleness or want of cleanliness, were they allowed to commit such offences with impunity, and to pass unnoticed.[41]

Throughout the mutiny the crew of the *Clyde* had carefully retained the disciplinary structure on board ship, even handing a miscreant over to Cunningham for punishment. This respect and desire for order would appear to have been common on the lower deck and is well explained by Cunningham. However, it is crucial to understand what is meant by 'strict discipline', for it is easy to confuse this with harsh discipline.

Like the attitude to crew management, attitudes towards discipline gradually changed as the wars continued. Captains like Charles Cunningham and James Newman were practising more enlightened disciplinary regimes well before the mutinies of 1797, but the greatest change seems to come about during the second war. As we have seen, the Admiralty took steps to try and revise the *Regulations*, such as they were, to meet both changing attitudes and new ideas about what we would call 'best practice'. Not all officers were able to cope with the changes and it is possible that some found their confidence undermined by more liberal attitudes and coped only by imposing greater severity on their ships.

This may well have been the case with Captain Robert Corbett, who gained a place in naval history in September 1810, when, as commander of the frigate *Africaine*, he was killed whilst engaging two French frigates simultaneously in the Indian Ocean. By this time, however, he had already gained a less welcome notoriety for severity. Corbett was promoted to lieutenant in 1796 and appears to have been constantly in employment during the first war. Indeed he distinguished himself as commander of the *Fulminette* cutter during Abercromby's expedition to Egypt in 1801. He was promoted to the rank of commander in April 1802 and then, on the resumption of war, was sent to the Mediterranean in command of the sloop *Bittern*.

Up to this point Corbett's promotion had been slow. However, it is clear that his performance as a commander was respected, most particularly by his commander-in-chief, Nelson. In June 1804, for example, the crew of the *Bittern* stood to the sweeps for 36 hours without break to chase and capture the French privateer *L'Hirondelle* and her two English prizes. No doubt the chance of good prize money was a major factor in motivating the crew, but it is also to Corbett's credit that the ship was swept a distance of over 60 miles when there was no wind. It was hardly surprising that Nelson should praise the zeal of both commander and commanded. Nelson's approbation of Corbett continued into 1805 when he made him acting captain of the *Amphitrite* and then the *Seahorse* frigates. However, Corbett was not confirmed in post rank until over a year later, by which time, of course, his benefactor was dead. In mid-1806 he was given the frigate *Nereide* and took part in operations in the Rio de La Plata. The *Nereide* was then sent to the East Indies, where the commander-in-chief was Sir Edward Pellew.

Corbett's reputation for severity seems to have first appeared soon after he was appointed acting captain of the *Seahorse*. According to Captain Thomas Bennett, previously a lieutenant in the *Seahorse*, 'his punishments were sometimes severe, and occasionally irregular...', but, Bennett also believed, 'during that time, I never saw a man punished who did not richly deserve it; I have more than once heard the good seamen congratulate each other upon being commanded by an officer who made every one, *from the highest to the lowest*, do their duty; for under Corbett there was no skulking or leaving the ship's duty to be done by the *willing* hands.'[42]

Bennett also confirms that at the same time an anonymous letter appeared accusing Corbett of tyranny and oppression. In August 1808 Corbett, now in command of the *Nereide*, was sent to Bombay to refit. Whilst there he fell seriously foul of Pellew and at the same time his crew again complained of cruelty and oppression on board the frigate. Corbett protested his innocence of the charges and demanded a court martial. This could only be convened at the Cape and Corbett was ordered to take the frigate there – unfortunately nobody thought to explain this to the crew who, thinking their protest had been ignored, promptly mutinied. The mutiny was quickly quelled and upon arrival at the Cape, ten men were tried for mutiny, nine being subsequently pardoned, leaving one to die by way of example. Corbett's trial followed that of the alleged ringleaders of his mutinous crew. There can be no doubt from the evidence presented at the court martial that the regime on board the *Nereide* was harsh and that the men were subjected to arbitrary discipline and unnecessary beatings. In fact the punishment record on board the *Nereide* is certainly the harshest this writer has come across. Between 16 August 1806 and 30 September 1808 (a period of 224 days) 134 floggings were inflicted on the crew – an average of one every day-and-a-half. Furthermore, approximately a third of all of these were for 18 or more lashes.

In his statement of defence at the Court Martial, Corbett made some acutely interesting comments. For example, he claimed that 'No man feels or more dislikes the unpleasant part of a Captain's duty, but as a duty I trust I shall never be found to neglect it.'[43] This was an appeal to his peers, to the officers judging him, the insinuation being that command was a task entrusted to post captains, and inherent in that task was the need to carry out duties which were naturally unpleasant. Corbett's appeal implied that these were necessary for 'the good of the service', a concept with which all officers were familiar. His defence continued by stating that authority had been vested in post captains by the legislature and that it was the responsibility of individual captains to regulate the severity or leniency of the punishment. This much was certainly true, although as we have seen, by 1809 attempts were being made to encourage the latter. However, Corbett then went on to explain how he interpreted the situation: 'I find my instructions upon that head are to follow the customs of the service. I have done so.'[44] A sentence later, the real weakness of Corbett's defence was revealed. 'The consequences in two instances have been unpleasant, but who can always answer for consequences? I have used no new method of punishment; no instruments unheard of or forbidden by law.' To the latter part of Corbett's statement, the officers of the court martial could have no answer, and it was probably for this reason that he was acquitted on virtually all counts. However, the more intelligent captains would probably have been disturbed at Corbett's shrugging off of 'consequences'. For the captain of a ship *was* responsible for the consequences, because he was bound by a duty of care for the ship and all on board. It was for this reason that captains usually referred to 'His Majesty's Ship ... under my command': neither ship nor crew were theirs, but they were responsible for them both.

During the later part of his defence, Corbett went on to expound the circumstances attaching to the complaint from the crew of the *Nereide*. It was in this that we really learn about Corbett's weaknesses as a commander. For example, he explains that during the cruise 'a sulky indifference to punishment superseded all endeavours to avoid it by exertion or activity'.[45] In other words, punishment was his only means of motivating his crew to exert themselves and 'if fear has any influence in preventing crimes, the more severe in appearance the better'. From the range of misdemeanours which attracted a flogging aboard the *Nereide*, it is clear that Corbett's use of the word 'crime' carries a very broad definition. Several men were flogged for selling their clothes, and the marine Joshua Orchard received 17 lashes for 'tearing his clothes'. Others were heavily punished for straggling whilst collecting water or, as in the case of the marine Richard Mason who received 17 lashes, for 'stealing water'.

It is certainly true that there were some difficult cases on board the *Nereide*, but many of the misdemeanours were a reaction to Corbett's total inability to find any method of motivating his crew other than by fear of punishment. In fact, towards the summing up of his defence he actually referred to the need to keep such men 'under terror'. The response of many of the crew was not so much to see Corbett enforcing discipline well, as to see a man overstepping natural justice and imposing tyranny. It was a far cry from the styles of command being adopted by other officers and it led to Corbett's posthumous castigation by William James and others. Yet there were some who saw a different side of him. Jenkin Jones, second lieutenant of the *Africaine*, claimed that even though the crew of that ship initially mutinied when they learned that Corbett was to command them, he subsequently won their respect. There is some slight evidence that this might have been the case. The Africaines appear to have been a proud and efficient crew, and Corbett may have latched onto this as a means of motivating them. For example, some two weeks after taking over command, an anonymous letter was thrown through the quarter-gallery window, threatening his life. He summoned the crew on deck to ask if they were dissatisfied with the way they had been treated. Naturally nobody in their right mind would be prepared to admit to this under these circumstances and, on the contrary, the crew of the *Africaine* expressed their satisfaction. Corbett's response was to promptly stand down the marines who had been standing guard over his cabin and the quarterdeck. Similarly, a short while later, when it became evident that the ship might be going into action, the crew apparently voluntarily and cheerfully gave up their evening grog at Corbett's suggestion that 'It shall not be said we wanted Dutch courage to thrash these Frenchmen.'[46]

Shortly after the *Africaine* was captured by the French frigates *Astrea* and *Iphigenie*, in 1810, rumours began to circulate that the *Africaine* was captured because her crew refused to stand to their guns. It was also suggested that they had preferred to be shot down than suffer any longer under Corbett's command. The assertion is, frankly, ridiculous. The Africaines fought long (for two-and-a-half hours) and suffered 47 dead and 113 wounded before surrendering. The casualties included Corbett, mortally wounded, the master, first and second lieutenants, first lieutenant of marines, both master's mates and three midshipmen. Corbett may have been at fault in allowing his ship to be becalmed and isolated between two French frigates, but it cannot on this occasion be said that his crew refused to serve.

In many ways, Corbett epitomises the dilemma that may have faced may officers at this time. Brought up in a navy where life was tough and unforgiving, they were unable to understand changes that were taking place around them and, in their isolated positions, they were unable to adapt. From our perspective some two centuries later, it is particularly hard to understand these officers. Corbett stands condemned by the complaints of his own men, his inadequate defence statement at a court martial and the contents of his log whilst commanding the *Nereide* (the log for the *Africaine* having unfortunately disappeared, probably when the ship was captured). When it comes to an assessment of a captain's disciplinary regime, however, the ship's log proves to be a very unreliable tool.

The evidence of the ship's logs

Any analysis of a command must inevitably consider the issue of discipline at sea and, in the process, will have to consider the evidence contained in any particular captain's or frigate's logs. No researcher can avoid looking at these for they are, in many ways, vital sources of information about the activities of a captain and his frigate. The problem is that they are dangerous tools to use when studying the culture of command of any individual officer and the researcher needs to be aware of the pitfalls.

The captain, lieutenant and master of a frigate were expected to maintain a log of each voyage or commission and to present these to the Admiralty at regular intervals or when the commission ended. Certain information was recorded in the logs: weather conditions, ship's position on a daily basis, number of miles run in each 24-hour period, any adjustments made to sails, masts or yards, any ships encountered, details of any action, records of accidents and/or men lost at sea, stores taken on board or discharged, amount of drinking-water on board, how the crew were employed, any damage sustained by the ship – and any formal punishments ordered by the captain. Invariably it is the latter that has attracted the attention of many researchers and, ironically, it is probably the most unreliable and misleading of all the information contained in the logs.

The punishment record was supposed to – and usually did – record the name of the offender, the nature of the offence committed and the number of lashes inflicted. Part of the problem is illustrated by the following example from the log of the *Penelope*, commanded by Henry Blackwood, for 16 May 1800.[47] The captain's log records that one George Towzey received 36 lashes for contempt, drunkenness and neglect of duty; and that a Charles Tapper received a similar punishment for disobedience of orders. On consulting the lieutenant's log[48] for the same day, the following punishments are recorded: Patrick Bagley, 48 lashes; George Towzey, 36 lashes; Samuel Tupper [*sic*], 36 lashes; Samuel Patterson, 18 lashes – all for drunkenness.

It is clear, therefore, that discrepancies can exist between officers' records of the same event. There are a number of possible reasons for this. The first is that logs may not have been written up on a daily basis. In a frigate beset by a heavy gale the writing up of the log was unlikely to be the officer's first concern. Details of position, wind strength and direction, and navigational data were initially recorded on the log-board and, as these were vital to the safety of the ship itself, there can be no doubt that they were noted with care. However, this is not the case with the details of a punishment inflicted perhaps before a storm developed. So the formal entry in the log may have had to wait several days before completion. Secondly, it is most likely that the captain's log was not actually written up by the captain himself, but was delegated to the captain's clerk or another trusted member of the crew. It is possible that a busy captain did not always check the details before signifying his approval of the contents. Thirdly, and perhaps rather cynically, some captains may have been inclined to suppress some details regarding punishments – after all, the tide was turning against the practice of severe and arbitrary punishment. So the actual record of punishments in the log may be unreliable.

The second factor contained in the logs that can be misleading is the name of the offender. It is not unusual to find that a log appears to give an erroneous name in connection with a punishment. Anyone who has read ships' logs will be all too well aware of the frequency with which suspiciously similar but not identical names recur in relation to floggings. It would not have been difficult to confuse a 'John' with a 'James' and, using the standard abbreviations of the time, mark 'J^{no}' in the log instead of 'J^{as}'. Likewise, a surprising number of seamen appear to have adopted pseudonyms at sea, only to let these lapse after a period of time, so that it is possible to find two names for the same man.

The third factor relates to the severity of the punishment. There was no regulation governing the number of lashes which should be inflicted for each type of misdemeanour; hence there was wide variation recorded in the logs. But it is not always clear whether a log records the number of lashes ordered or the number actually inflicted. For example, some of the more meticulous commanders noted in their log when a victim collapsed part way through a flogging, before the ordered number of punishments had been inflicted. This can account for uneven numbers of lashes – since the usual practice was to order small numbers of lashes in units of six (6,12,18,24), and thereafter in dozens (36, 48, and so on). In many cases, a recorded seven or eight lashes is actually the limit reached before the ship's surgeon intervened. However, it is impossible to say whether these incidents were always noted – so we cannot be sure whether the log records the sentence or the punishment itself. Furthermore, there were some officers who did deliberately avoid an adherence to set levels of punishment. Anselm Griffiths of the *Leonidas* was certainly one of these. In his *Hints on Seamanship* he had commented:

Severity of punishment defeats its own object, and only tends to harden and disgust. To award a given number of lashes to any particular crime, is like administering the same medicine to all constitutions. Character should have its full effect, and on different men the punishment in severity is very unequal. Eight or nine lashes to one man, being as much as twenty to another. I am quite of opinion with Mr Colquhoun, that it is not severity of punishment, but the certainty that *some* punishment will attach to certain crimes, which has the desired effect.[49]

Finally, there is the issue of the nature of the offence. When studying ships' logs it very quickly becomes clear that commanders followed a particular formula for categorising offences. The most common terms for these were 'Uncleanness' (or 'Dirtiness'), Theft, Drunkenness, Neglect of Duty, Disobedience of Orders, Quarrelling (or Fighting), Desertion, Insolence (or Contempt), Striking a Superior Officer and Mutiny (or Mutinous Expressions). The frequency with which these terms recur confirms that they were widely recognised among the officer corps and accepted by the Admiralty. However, we cannot be certain in all cases how the terms were applied, nor that they were applied consistently. Some of the terms would seem to be relatively easy to explain. For example, 'Theft' almost invariably refers to robbery of other seamen's property or possibly of ship's stores, though there were variations. Robert Corbett punished three of the *Nereide*'s crew for 'stealing water' – presumably when supplies were low and water rationed more than usual. This seems to be harsh, but in a sense they were stealing from their shipmates, an action which was always dealt with severely, sometimes by being made to run the gauntlet. The seriousness of the offence was outlined by Frederick Marryat:

> There is, perhaps, no crime that is attended with such serious consequences on board a ship as theft. A succession of thefts undiscovered will disintegrate a ship's company, break up the messes, destroy all confidence and harmony, … for whom can a person suspect, when he has lost his property, in so confined a space, but those who were acquainted with its being in his possession, and with the place in which it was deposited? – and who are these but his own messmates …[50]

In a smaller warship like a frigate the consequences of theft were clearly considerable.

'Drunkenness' seems an easy category to define, though it must be remembered that the consumption of large amounts of alcohol was integral to the life at sea, especially when water was often unpalatable. In this case, the offence seems to have occurred when the individual was deemed incapable of carrying out his duty. 'Uncleanness' or 'Dirtiness' seems mainly to have applied to urinating or defecating anywhere but at the heads. There was a tendency for seamen to urinate over the side or through open gun-ports – and occasionally an individual defecated below decks and then disposed (or attempted to dispose) of the faeces through the gun-ports. This was obviously an unhealthy, not to say antisocial practice, and was understandably punished. 'Desertion' too is a category which we ought to be able to define, though some captains did punish men for *attempting* to desert, and Corbett gave three seamen 24 lashes each for 'straggling' when collecting water. They were, therefore, punished on suspicion of being about to commit an offence; an action which would have fitted in completely with Corbett's method of command.

With most of the other categories of offence, we have some difficulty. It is unclear, for example, what exactly constituted 'Neglect of Duty'. John Byrne suggests that this offence was one of negligence or carelessness, such as a marine not keeping his musket clean or a seaman losing an item of his clothing overboard.[51] They were not, as such, wilful acts of disobedience. 'Disobedience of Orders' may have been regarded as slightly more serious, in that it probably applied when a member of the crew either failed to observe or deliberately flouted the captain's orders. Here it should be emphasised that the term most probably applied to the Captain's Standing Orders, rather than his direct orders – as disobedience to a direct order would probably have attracted a charge of mutiny.

'Insolence', 'Contempt', 'Striking a Superior Officer', 'Mutinous Expressions' and

Captain	Ship	Days in Period Sampled	Number of Punishments for outright offences against Authority	Punishment per Day Ratio
Newman	Ceres	225	4	1:56
Blackwood	Penelope	457	0	0
Digby	Aurora	365	7	1:52
Baker	Phoenix	173	3	1:57
Broke	Shannon	163	6	1:27
Griffith	Topaze	365	6	1:61
Seymour	Amethyst	781	9	1:86
Corbett	Nereide	224	10	1:22

(Source: Log Books *Amethyst* ADM/L/A/118, Adm 51/1807, Adm 51/1859; *Penelope* ADM/L/P/85, Adm 51/1377; *Topaze* ADM/L/T/154, Adm 51/1673; *Aurora* ADM/L/T/240, Adm 51/1231; *Phoenix* Adm 51/1532, ADM/L/P135;. *Shannon* Adm 51/2861; *Ceres* Adm 51/1256; *Nereide* Adm 51/1941. PRO Adm 51 series are captains' logs; NMM ADM/L series are lieutenants' logs.)

outright mutiny, are all clearly recognisable as acts challenging the commander's authority. Yet even the most popular commanders appear to have suffered in some way with this behaviour from members of the crew.

The comparisons given above from a sample eight log books show quite clearly that Corbett's command suffered from the greatest number of challenges – as might be expected given the other source information available about him – but it is surprising to find that Broke also appeared to suffer from a similar problem. Although events were to prove that Broke had created a most deadly and efficient fighting team, it is possible that this could only be maintained through what was often described as a 'taut' regime. It is interesting to note, for example, that virtually all of the challenges to authority faced by Michael Seymour occurred *before* the *Amethyst* captured her second French frigate, the *Niemen*. Thereafter he appears to have suffered no disciplinary problems which required the lash. If the figures from his log are to be relied upon, it would prove a quite remarkable instance of a crew turning into a committed team as a result of success in battle.

Blackwood, despite his reputation for being hard on his crew, likewise appears to have suffered from no challenges to his authority (in one of the largest sampling periods). Blackwood, like Newman and Seymour, was an excellent seaman and a superlative frigate commander. As such, he is more likely to have had a crew who respected him; possibly made up of a high proportion of volunteers. If so, challenge to his authority was unlikely. But this leaves the paradox of Broke's log. Closer inspection reveals that all but one of the offences were committed by marines rather than seamen – a common occurrence in other logs. Challenge to authority on the *Shannon* came not from the seamen but from the marines, who were always considered to be of a different character to the rest of the crew.

The problem of drunkenness has already been referred to, but an interesting result arises from a comparison of this offence on the sample group of frigates.

Captain	Ship	Days in Period Sampled	Percentage of Punishments arising from drunkenness
Newman	Ceres	225	12
Blackwood	Penelope	457	50
Digby	Aurora	365	20
Baker	Phoenix	173	42
Broke	Shannon	163	38½
Griffith	Topaze	365	17
Seymour	Amethyst	781	40
Corbett	Nereide	224	15

The commanders who punished on the most occasions for offences involving drunkenness were Blackwood, Baker, Seymour and Broke. In the case of the first three, drunkenness was the most frequent misdemeanour committed on their ship. On the *Shannon*, the two highest offences were equally 'Drunkenness' and 'Insolence/Contempt' – a relationship which may not be co-incidental. The crucial point is that these four all appear to have been much more rigorous in punishing drunkenness than the others in the sample. Again it is probably no co-incidence that of the group, these four are the ones most associated with spectacular and successful engagements whilst commanding their frigate. Their opposition to drunkenness has to be closely associated with their endeavour to keep their crew in a high state of efficiency and preparedness for action. The demands of such a condition were not compatible with incapacity through alcohol and as a consequence it was not tolerated. This is symptomatic of a high level of professionalism, a quality that should certainly be associated with the commanders concerned.

From this it should not be inferred that an officer who did not have reason to order punishments for drunkenness was in any way lax in his attitude to the discipline and efficiency of his crew. James Newman, for example, was a comparatively lenient commander and suffered little from either drunkenness or challenges to authority on board the *Ceres*. He too fought a highly creditable action against a much heavier French frigate in October 1798, when his subsequent frigate, the 32-gun 12-pounder frigate *Mermaid*, encountered the 44-gun 18-pounder French frigate *La Loire*.[52] Although neither side was able to claim a victory in that conflict, the failure on the *Mermaid*'s part had more to do with the intervention of a heavy storm than anything else.

Although incapacity through alcohol consumption may generally have been deemed the real offence, it is quite probable that some commanders perceived drunkenness to be more of a problem than it really was, or that they took an unrealistically puritanical position with regard to it. This is well demonstrated in a comparison between Captain James Newman and the commander who succeeded him in the *Ceres*. In April 1797 Newman exchanged command of the *Ceres* with Captain Robert Otway of the *Mermaid* in order that Newman, who was suffering from malaria, could return home. Otway was far from happy with the state of affairs on board his new frigate. A month later, at the end of May 1797, the *Ceres* ran aground in the West Indies. Otway wrote to Hyde Parker:

> on taking command of the *Ceres* I found a great want of regularity in her, the Ship's Company were accustomed in a great measure, to do as they pleased, and Drunkenness, seldom considered as a crime, having from my infancy

trained up in the Service with different ideas; – I of course was endeavouring to put a stop to such pernicious example; not having been but a Month on board, when she struck, I was able to effect but little, I then seriously felt the want of a disciplined ship's company, little or no attention paid to my Orders, not the smallest exertion: The Spirits broached, and the greatest part of them Drunk, and at a time, when the water was gaining on the pumps, seven men cut the Barge adrift and made their escape to the shore ...

I much dispare with such a crew, it will be some considerable time before the *Ceres* will be fit for service ... As you may be led to imagine ... that I am a well man'd ship I have selected a List of Old Men, Boys, and Foreigners that form a great part of this Ship's Company.[53]

It is curious that Otway should make such an issue about drunkenness on board the *Ceres*, for as we have seen it was not a significant problem for Newman and he appears to have had no particular need to apply severe discipline over the matter. This could be taken to confirm Otway's allegation that Newman was too lenient on this issue, more so than, for example, the officers with whom he is compared above. On the other hand, there can be no doubt that Otway was attempting to lay the blame for grounding the ship on his crew.

His allegation that they 'wanted' discipline at a time of crisis simply does not ring true. The men he is describing do not sound like the same crew which had performed so well just six months previously. On 2 November 1796 Newman, whilst still in command of the *Ceres* had given chase to a strange sail about 500 miles north of Bermuda. As the chase continued the winds increased and the *Ceres* lost her fore topmast and stunsail, and consequently the chase. Within a short time the frigate was caught in a severe storm, Newman ordered the remaining topgallant masts and yards struck and reduced sail. At 3.30am, in a heavy sea, the frigate lost her main mast. Forty-five minutes later the fore mast collapsed across the bows, carrying away the bowsprit, followed fifteen minutes later by the mizzen, which fell over the quarter. For the next few hours the crew struggled furiously to clear the wreckage and attempt to bring the frigate under control, an attempt which was not helped when a heavy sea pooped the ship, smashing the cabin windows and the jolly boat. Nevertheless, by the end of the morning the crew had rigged a jury mizzen and brought the ship to. The gale continued throughout the next day with hard squalls and a heavy sea. During the afternoon the ship was hit by another tremendous sea which stove the launch, washed the spare spars off the booms, and swept away from the starboard side of the deck the topgallant and topsail yards and sails, gangway stanchions, hammocks, flag chest, scuttle butts and hen coops. The weather conditions only really improved on 6 November, by which time the crew had erected sheers to create jury masts and yards and were able to bring the frigate back under control and get her back to Antigua.[54] The crew described by Otway do not sound like the same men who came through this experience so creditably. It was not the crew who had changed, but their commander.

What, then, can be concluded about Newman's style of command? The *Mermaid*'s log for the period 25 April 1797 to 11 July 1798[55] (252 days) records no punishments at all. It is hard to believe that no punishments were inflicted during this period but then the frigate was very active on the Channel station, taking a number of prizes and later engaging the *Loire* in October 1798. Although there may be some justification for questioning Newman's regime in the *Ceres* on the assumption that he might not have been firm enough, there is definitely a sense in which he appears to have been fair (the small and consistent number of lashes inflicted, for example). There are also indications that he was caring of the men under his command. For example, in January 1798 he wrote to the Admiralty on behalf of Sam Wilkinson, an able seaman who had been sentenced at a court martial in the previous November to 300 lashes for desertion. Half of the punishment had been inflicted, and presumably Wilkinson was in the process of recovering from this when the *Mermaid* was ordered to sea. Newman wrote that Wilkinson was still on board and

> he has been released several times when the ship was cleared for action, and always went cheerfully to his duty.
>
> I am therefore induced to request that their Lordships will be pleased to remit the remainder of the punishment and also that they will be further pleased to give direction for him to be entered on the ship's books from the time he was punished at Spithead, as the Inclemency of the weather rendered it absolutely necessary to supply him with a considerable quantity of slop cloathing since that time and he has no wages due to pay for them.[56]

It is quite possible that Newman had problems maintaining an adequate level of discipline with the harder members of his crew. His usual punishment was 12 lashes and even an unrepentant marine, Daniel Murphy, received only 18 lashes for his third offence (during this period). This may have given some of the crew the opinion that Newman was a 'soft' captain – by many accounts something despised by seamen in general – and would perhaps explain Otway's complaint. What contradicts this is the extraordinarily high level of seamanship and team-work displayed by Newman and his crews on many occasions.[57]

What the case of Newman demonstrates is that 'discipline' was not the same thing as 'command'. Officers like Newman and Seymour led highly effective frigate crews, achieving high levels of success in their activities without the imposition of severe or brutal disciplinary regimes. One is tempted to believe that these ships were 'happy ships' where the crews felt they were valued and had a personal investment in their performance. Confident and contented seamen were led by confident and contented officers – and so the command structure was well balanced.

At the opposite end of the scale were officers like Corbett, whose case has been looked at in some detail. Corbett was never fully confident about either his own ability to lead or of the willingness of his crew to follow. This is hardly surprising since he seems to have had great difficulty in building a positive relationship with his crew. Corbett, probably like many others, was wont to assume that his crew were all bad, before he had had the opportunity to discover their qualities – or lack of them – for himself. Indeed, on first joining the *Africaine* he announced to the assembled crew that he believed them all to be a set of cowards, afraid to be led by a brave man: hardly a statement on which to base a positive relationship.

From this it can be seen that one of the keys to 'command' was the ability to develop a highly positive relationship with the other officers and the 'people'. On the more confined decks of a frigate on constant and active duty, the opportunity to establish and cement this relationship was much greater than in a ship of the line. As a result many of the best examples of 'command' and 'leadership' are to be observed in the frigate commanders of this period. The corollary of this were the achievements of the Royal Navy's frigates, and their contribution to the defeat of Britain's enemies by military activity or economic blockade.

POSTSCRIPT

T HE OBJECT OF THIS WORK, and the research that lay behind it, was to throw some light into a dark area in our knowledge of the naval history of the Great Wars. The focus has always been on the men in command rather than the seamen – although I would be the first to acknowledge that good seamen were as important to the success of a frigate as her officers or commander. The simple fact is that, until recently, many of these commanders were as obscure as the men they commanded. Admittedly there was some biographical information available, but no-one had attempted to survey this, to collate the data into any form of comparative study of officers of the period. In many ways this book is a social history of the Royal Navy, because it is more concerned with the men and their relationship with the service than with their military activity. However, there are numerous books already on frigate actions, and I can see no need to repeat the contents of those. Those wishing to study the tactics of frigate engagements will find much of their requirement satisfied by William James's *Naval History of Great Britain*, though they will need to look elsewhere for the contextual background for such actions.

In the process of producing this book a number of issues have been clarified and I hope that these are now apparent to the reader, in whatever degree. First of all, it is now evident that the officer promotion process was organised and controlled to a greater extent than previously appreciated. In order to produce an officer corps which could hope to win the naval wars against Britain's enemies, it was recognised that a progressive ethos of professionalism had to evolve in a subtle conjunction with the conservative practices of the eighteenth-century navy and society. Social privilege and status were still enormously powerful factors in society in general and these forces had to be acknowledged, respected and yet controlled within the navy. One has to admire the tough stance taken by St Vincent during his tenure as First Lord of the Admiralty, and remember that some of the voices of criticism raised against him came from those privileged levels of society who were suddenly frustrated in their attempts to wield influence at the Admiralty.

Inevitably a filtering system had to be at work in the navy, because there were always more officers than ships. It becomes clear that by the later years of the war the unfit and unsuitable were being sifted out, to the benefit of both the service and the war effort. Admittedly, some unsuitable aristocrats slipped through the mesh, but this was inevitable: change to a profession based truly on merit could not be achieved overnight, especially when some of the personnel in control were committed to the older system of patronage. Even then it has to be recognised that many of those who controlled promotions and appointments in the navy were more concerned with obtaining the best possible tools to defeat the enemy than re-building a professional organisation for the future

The second result of this work has been the emergence from the shadows of a number of admirable and inspiring frigate commanders. Some, like Broke, Hoste and Cochrane were already well known – and were likewise well known to me before I started work. As the research for this book developed and I found letters, personal papers, logbooks and so forth, some of these officers began to take on a three-dimensional shape and something of their personalities began to emerge. When I started I had no idea who these characters would be, and even now I am well aware that there are many officers waiting to be 'discovered' by whoever has the time to undertake the necessary research. My regret is that there is not room in this work to do more justice to the men concerned. They cannot all be named here but a recapitulation of some of the names should serve to illustrate the point. For example, there is Philip Cunningham, already an older officer when war broke out in 1793. Cunningham's logs and correspondence reveal a man who was dedicated to his profession and deeply humanitarian in his approach to his men. There is James Newman, who was mentioned in the introduction to this book, and who was lost so tragically with virtually all of his crew in HMS *Hero* on Christmas Day 1811. There is a long obituary of Newman in the *Naval Chronicle*,[1] and of course there are the logs of the ships that he commanded. But, as far as I have been able to ascertain, no personal papers have survived. Then there is Sir Michael Seymour, the captain of the *Amethyst* during two stunning frigate actions. Seymour emerges from the darkness as a character of great humour and intelligence, dedicated to his duties and a superb seaman. Sadly, virtually all of his personal papers seem to have been destroyed and, in the main, we are left with a few fragments of correspondence and a highly edited biographical volume produced by one of his descendants. Originally I intended to include an entire chapter on Seymour and the activities of the *Amethyst* in this book. However, in the final analysis such an intense focus on one officer in this book seemed inappropriate and somehow unfair to some of the other officers concerned.

Whilst on the issue of what has been excluded, I should say that much personal information about the officers has been left out. The past may be a foreign country, but its people are definitely not strangers. The correspondence and personal papers of frigate commanders reveal in sharp detail how much the emotions and concerns felt by them are shared by us today. There is Broke's homesickness and worry about his distant wife's pregnancy; Graham Moore's melancholy and loneliness, confiding in his personal diary of his longing for a marriage he cannot afford; there is Seymour's anticipation of an evening by the fireside sharing naval yarns with his brother-in-law and fellow frigate captain. And generally we can learn of the officers' worries about promotion and their anxiety about the future.

A chapter on the personal side of the frigate commanders was considered but it too has been excluded – partly because there is still much material waiting to be discovered. Curiosity has, it must be said, taken me to the homes of some of these officers. Broke Hall still stands, externally little changed from the time that Broke lived there. The home that Seymour occupied at the end of the war is also still extant near Andover in Hampshire. Tragically, during the writing of this book the house built by Captain Josias Rogers shortly before he went back to sea and died in the West Indies was demolished because it was considered too draughty and uneconomical to maintain. Two functionally modern detached houses now stand on the site.

The research behind this book contains a substantial amount of statistical evidence; much of this has been included so that it can be used by anyone needing a 'yardstick' against which to assess any particular officer's career. As stated in the Foreword, one of the aims of this work was to provide an objective scale for measuring an officer's career – other, that is, than the careers of either Nelson or Hornblower. I trust that the tables will assist in this purpose.

Finally I hope that in a modest way this book may lighten the obscurity of the many excellent frigate commanders whose names have been largely forgotten. I would be gratified if something in this work encouraged researchers, museums and/or enthusiasts to do more justice to the names and achievements of the lesser known officers of 'Nelson's Navy' and perhaps introduce them to a wider public.

NOTES

FOREWORD

References are given in shortened form; full
details can be found in the Bibliography.

Abbreviations used in the Notes:
DNB – *Dictionary of National Biography*
NMM – National Maritime Museum
PRO – Public Record Office

1   Marshall, *Royal Naval Biography*, and
    William O'Byrne, *Naval Biographical
    Dictionary*.
2   Lewis, *A Social History of the Navy*.
3   Henderson, *The Frigates*.
4   For an account of this action see James,
    Naval History, I, 106.
5   Osler, *Life of Admiral Viscount Exmouth*, 91.
6   NMM LBK 58/2: Louisa Broke, 11 July
    1813.
7   Colley, *Britons: Forging the Nation, 1707-
    1837*, 180.
8   Hornblower, Ramage, Aubrey, Bolitho – all
    the fictional heroes of hugely successful
    modern novels are based (at least at first) on
    this image.
9   Laughton, *Barham Papers*, II, 365-7.
10 *Ibid*, II, 412-3.
11 Statistics drawn from Admiralty List Books:
    PRO Adm 8 series.
12 PRO Adm 8/69-/100: Admiralty List Books.
13 NMM Ref GRE 359(42) (083.81):
    Commander C G Pitcairn Jones, 'List of
    Commissioned Sea Officers'.

CHAPTER I

1   McKee, *A Gentlemanly and Honorable
    Profession*, 3.
2   *Ibid*, 46.
3   *Ibid*, 73ff.
4   The commission dates for these officers has
    been drawn from Syrett & DiNardo,
    Commissioned Sea Officers.
5   NMM Ref GRE 359(42) (083.81):
    Commander C G Pitcairn Jones, 'List of
    Commissioned Sea Officers'.
6   Marshall, *Royal Naval Biography*; O'Byrne,
    A Naval Biographical Dictionary.
7   For a general background see Lewis,
    England's Sea Officers; and his *A Social
    History of the Navy*.
8   For example, the Hon George Elliott who, in
    July 1800, went for his lieutenant's
    examination in London, with a certificate
    stating he was 21 years of age: 'I was sixteen
    and four days …' – Elliott, *Memoir of
    Admiral the Hon Sir George Elliott*, 25.
9   To check this captains outside of the test
    sample have been included to increase the
    size of the sample.
10 Ultimately there can be no doubt that being
    the son of a peer could give a distinct
    advantage when it came to early promotion
    to lieutenant. For example, the Hon Henry
    Duncan passed aged 17; the Hon G
    Cadogan at a very questionable 14 years.
11 The Adm 8 series volumes at the PRO.
12 *Naval Chronicle*, IX (1803), 423.
13 Although this could, in certain
    circumstances, be deleterious – as in the
    career of Sir William Sidney Smith. In 1790,

Sidney Smith, having no employment in the Royal Navy, decided to offer himself as a 'mercenary' officer in the Swedish Navy. In June of that year he played an important role in the defeat of Russian naval forces in the Bay of Viborg. For these services, King Gustavus knighted him, and on return to Britain Smith both applied for, and was granted, permission to use the title which the knighthood conferred upon him. The title was regarded with some ridicule by his brother officers and may have gone some way to explaining the subsequent attitude that many took towards 'the Swedish knight'. However, there was another reason. Six British naval officers had been killed whilst fighting for the Russians. Smith had, in a real sense, been fighting his own comrades.

14 Marshall, *Royal Naval Biography*, I, 332.
15 British Museum, Add 37,912 (f182): Grenville Papers, Letter from Lukin to Windham, dated 3 November 1795.
16 Ignoring for the moment the rather exceptional William Don, who was 70 years of age.
17 See Hughes, *The Private Correspondence of Admiral Lord Collingwood*, 26.
18 Dillon (ed Lewis), *A Narrative of my Professional Adventures (1790-1839)*, II, 99-100; Anon, *Service Afloat or The Naval Career of Sir William Hoste*, 72-3.
19 Take, for example, the case of Captain Michael Seymour. Posted in August 1800, Seymour commanded two ships briefly during 1801. The Peace of Amiens then intervened and he received no employment during 1802. In 1803 he was appointed to the *Ville de Paris* briefly. In 1804 he was given the *Colossus* for a couple of months, and then nothing until February 1805, when he commanded the *Illustrious*, briefly. In January 1806 he was sent to the *Warrior* for several months. In June 1806, after a period of nearly six years he was given his first permanent post command, the frigate *Amethyst*.
20 This *estimate* is based on the career information collected by John Marshall for those officers whose surnames begin with the letter D only.
21 See Marshall, *Royal Naval Biography*, I, 663.
22 The earl's son John Astley Bennett may have

been taken as a midshipman on Donnelly's ship.
23 Spencer may have considered it unseemly to promote one of his favourites before the usual one-year term as commander had expired.
24 James, *Naval History*, III, 145.
25 See Marshall, *Royal Naval Biography*, II, 29.
26 *Ibid*, X, 55.
27 The Admiralty List Books show that *Hermione* was in the West Indies continuously from July 1793 until the mutiny in later 1797. She had served on that station prior to that date also.
28 See Pope, *The Black Ship*.
29 Dillon (ed Lewis), *A Narrative of my Professional Adventures (1790-1839)*, I, 307-8.
30 Other officers suffered in various ways: Ross Donnelly, for example had to resign command of the *Invincible*, 74 because of the onset of a cataract.
31 Lewis, *Social History of the Royal Navy*, 402ff.
32 See Vice-Admiral Elphinstone's return of officers promoted etc: PRO Adm 6/65.
33 Murray, *Memoir of the Life and Services of Admiral Durham*, 62.
34 See Marshall, *Royal Naval Biography*, X, 217.
35 *Ibid*, IX, 136.
36 *Naval Chronicle*, XXXIX (1814), 264.
37 Marshall, *Royal Naval Biography*; O'Byrne, *A Naval Biographical Dictionary*.
38 Marshall, *Royal Naval Biography*, III 3, 411.
39 Even then Donnelly's promotion was not automatic. In spite of a number of representations on his behalf, including one by the Earl of Tankerville, he did not receive promotion to commander until a month after the event, whereas promotion was usually instantaneous.
40 Possibly given command of Sea Fencibles.
41 Possible post for Levy of Seaman in 1803.

CHAPTER II

1 Marshall, *Royal Naval Biography*, II, 80, and James, *Naval History*, II, 385.
2 Hall, *Fragments of Voyages and Travels*, 1,II, 194 –6.
3 *Ibid*, 1,II, 194 -6.
4 *Ibid*, 1, II, 207.

5   See for example: Hill, *Prizes of War*; Lewis, *Social History of the Royal Navy*, 316-30; Marcus, *Heart of Oak*, 124-6; Pope, *Life in Nelson's Navy*, 231-41; Lavery, *Nelson's Navy*, 109-110.

6   NMM LBK 58/1-1: For example, Letter 280, 9 April 1811; Letter 359, 28 May 1813.

7   He reached flag rank in 1799: Syrett & DiNardo, *Commissioned Sea Officers*.

8   First Lord of the Admiralty 1788-95.

9   Hughes (ed), *Correspondence of Lord Collingwood*, 23.

10   *Ibid*, 26.

11   'Their most common employment is the convoy, which is a constant worry: in the line they are the weakest ships, for which reason when any detachment is made they are the ships ...'. *Ibid*, 26.

12   Collingwood's first frigate was the *Pelican*, a 24-gun post ship which foundered in August 1781. In 1782-3 he also commanded the new 44-gun *Mediator* for a brief time. Both commands were in the West Indies.

13   It should be remembered that Collingwood was writing at the time of the Spanish Armament and, therefore, it was anticipated that hostilities would break out with Spain, leaving the rich South American trade routes open to attack. Elsewhere in the letter Collingwood expresses a fear that he might be sent to the East Indies where no prizes would be available since the Spanish had *comparatively* few interests there, their main colony being the Philippines. Although many captains may have dreamed of capturing one of the Spanish 'Manila' treasure ships, their voyages were infrequent.

14   Sources for this are as follows: *Steel's Navy Lists* (August 1797; May 1798; June 1799 etc, to 1805; January 1807 to March 1808; August 1810 etc, to 1815).

15   This increase in pay seems to have been effective from September 1806.

16   Daily pay for this period is based on a division of the given annual figure before deduction of income tax but *after* deductions of 3d per Pound for the Widows' Fund, 1s per month to the Chest and 6d per month for the Royal Hospital. See *Steel's Navy List*, August 1810.

17   Lewis, *A Social History of the Navy*, 296.

18   Although this would not have prevented

19   him taking merchantmen.

     That is, junior on the list of captains. Martin is not implying that all captains of line of battle ships are junior to frigate captains.

20   Hamilton (ed), *Journals and Letters of Sir Thomas Byam Martin*, III, 342.

21   Elliott, *Memoir of Admiral the Hon Sir George Elliot*, 36-7.

22   Smyth, *The Life and Services of Captain Philip Beaver*, 156-7.

23   NMM RAI/201: Rainier papers. Also transcribed in Parkinson's *War in the Eastern Seas*, 432-6.

24   Gilpin, *Memoirs of Josias Rogers*, 88.

25   Hamilton (ed), *Journals and Letters of Sir Thomas Byam Martin*, I, 157.

26   Seymour, *Memoir of Rear-Admiral Sir Michael Seymour*, 58-9.

27   Captains could submit a claim for the reimbursement of costs when carrying important passengers, but these claims were not always accepted.

28   See Gilpin, *Memoirs of Josias Rogers*, 69.

29   *Ibid*, 96.

30   Smyth, *The Life and Services of Captain Philip Beaver*, 152.

31   Some other cases of this may be found, for example, in the careers of Charles Elphinstone Fleeming (Marshall, *Royal Naval Biography*, I, 577); James Hillyar (*ibid*, II, 849); George Hope (*Naval Chronicle*, XXIX [1818], 424); Richard Goodwin Keats (*Royal Naval Biography*, I, 342); Francis Laforey, (*ibid*, I, 446); Henry Matson (*ibid*, II, 743); Ben Hallowell (*ibid*, I, 465); and arguably Josias Rowley (*ibid*, I, 622). In the last case, however, there were very specific reasons for his move to a frigate, this being to lead a frigate squadron in the Indian Ocean (see James, *Naval History*, V, 166-187; also Parkinson, *War in the Eastern Seas*, Chapters XXI and XXII).

32   See Laughton (ed), *Letters and Papers of Charles, Lord Barham*, 39.

33   Letter to Admiral John Markham in Markham (ed), *Selections from the Correspondence of Admiral Sir John Markham*, 60.

34   Parkinson, *Edward Pellew, Viscount Exmouth*, 196.

35   These are concisely included by Steel in the *Prize Pay Lists*.

36   Steel's *Prize Pay Lists* (London 1802), xii.

[37] Hill, *The Prizes of War*, 246.

[38] Dillon (ed Lewis), *A Narrative of my Professional Adventures (1790-1839)*, I, 79.

[39] A frigate sailing under the orders of a fleet or port Admiral lost one-eighth of its prize money to that flag officer. See previous discussion.

[40] Dillon (ed Lewis), *A Narrative of my Professional Adventures (1790-1839)*, I, 77.

[41] For the reader's information the comparative value of Sterling with 1996 was as follows:
1793 – £48.06.
1800 – £26.98.
1810 – £25.63.
Figures supplied by the Bank of England Information Office, December 1996.

[42] *Niger*, 32, A K Legge; *Latona*, 38, Edward Thornborough; *Pegasus*, 28, Robert Barlow; *Phaeton*, 38, William Bentinck; *Aquilon*, 32, Hon Robert Stopford; *Southampton*, 32, Hon Robert Forbes; *Venus*, 32, William Brown. Listed in Brenton, *The Naval History of Great Britain*, I, 143-4.

[43] Hill suggests that approximately 20,000 Licences were issued annually up to, and including 1811: *Prizes of War*, 53.

[44] James, *Naval History*, I, 100.

[45] *The Naval Chronicle*, XXV (1811), 357,

[46] Douglas was sailing under the command of Rear-Admiral John Gell, bound for the Mediterranean, but the prizes were taken on the Channel Station. Lord Howe, commander-in-chief of that station would therefore have received £6500.

[47] The Channel Fleet.

[48] *The Naval Chronicle*, XXV (1811), 358.

[49] Hill estimates that Pellew made a total of £300,000 in prize money during the war: *Prizes of War*, 70.

[50] Warren served 4.75 years; Strachan 6 years and Pellew 7 years.

[51] Hill, *Prizes of War*, 194 and 179.

[52] Hall 1, III, 284.

[53] *Ibid*, 286.

[54] Parkinson. *Edward Pellew, Viscount Exmouth*, 214.

[55] Cochrane, *The Autobiography of a Seaman*, 87.

[56] Phillimore, *The Last of Nelson's Captains*, 123-4.

[57] Hamilton (ed), *Journals and Letters of Sir Thomas Byam Martin*, I, 177-91,

[58] Seymour, *Memoir of Rear-Admiral Sir Michael Seymour*, 61.

[59] Sample figures are as follows:
August 1806 = 5%; August 1807 = 20%; July 1810 = 7%; July 1812 = 8%; July 1813 = 9%. All statistics drawn from the Admiralty List Books, PRO Adm 8 series.

[60] Dillon (ed Lewis), *A Narrative of my Professional Adventures (1790-1839)*, I, 101.

[61] *Ibid*, I, 110.

[62] Crawford, *Reminiscences of a Naval Officer*, I, 30.

[63] Chamier, *Life of a Sailor*, 170.

[64] This is of course theoretically speaking. A midshipman was usually only as wealthy as his allowance made him, so a midshipman from a well-off family was likely to be well provided for. On the other hand, of course, the autobiographical reminiscences of all officers of this period associate the midshipmen's berth with long periods of poverty.

[65] Marryat, *Frank Mildmay*, 66.

[66] Carden, *Memoir of Admiral Carden*, 153.

[67] Gardiner, *Memoir of Sir Graham Moore*, 14.

[68] Crawford, *Reminiscences of a Naval Officer*, I, 65.

[69] Parkinson, *Edward Pellew, Viscount Exmouth*, 213.

[70] Dillon (ed Lewis), *A Narrative of my Professional Adventures (1790-1839)*, I, 147.

[71] Crawford, *Reminiscences of a Naval Officer*, I, 240.

[72] *Ibid*, I, 242.

[73] Although it is noticeable how many frigate officers lay stress on their own ability to go aloft and carry out other manual tasks associated with seamanship. It may be that where there was a tendency for all officers to 'lend a hand' there was a blurring of social differences at sea among the younger and junior officers – and that this might have contrasted strongly with life on board a ship of the line. One might compare the greater *camaraderie* in modern elite branches like the Submarine Service.

[74] It might also be noted that on those occasions when the midshipmen from the *Immortalité* went on a late night social spree, they do not appear to have been concerned about the seamen having to wait in boats for them at the seashore. Crawford, *Reminiscences of a Naval Officer*, I, 78.

75 Lord Radstock.

76 Nelson was knighted presumably because he carried the rank of commodore and/or because technically he was a rear-admiral. The knighthood was, therefore, a compromise.

77 See James, *Naval History*, I, 106.

78 *Ibid*, I, 114-16.

79 An interesting reminder of the eighteenth-century practice of sinecures.

80 Ross, *Memoirs and Correspondence of Admiral Lord de Saumarez*, I, 116.

81 Laforey inherited a baronetcy a few years later on the death of his father.

82 James, *Naval History*, I, 316.

83 James notes that the cannonade between the *Santa Margarita* and the *Tamise* lasted 20 minutes, whilst that between the *Unicorn* and the *Tribune* lasted 35 minutes; an odd disparity given the relative broadside weights. But see also reference in the next chapter. See *Naval History*, I, 365ff.

84 *Ibid*, I, 368.

85 *Ibid*, I, 399.

86 *Ibid*, II, 67

87 Marshall, *Royal Naval Biography*, I, 491.

88 James clearly felt that Fitzroy, son of the Duke of Grafton, had acted with less than the usual zeal. Two months later the *Aeolus* was part of a squadron under the command of Sir Richard Strachan which attacked a similar sized French squadron. James virtually accused Fitzroy of cowardice as a result of both incidents and, in 1823, Fitzroy was forced to publish a pamphlet refuting James's insinuations: James, *Naval History*, IV, 56-64; and 3-11.Fitzroy was dismissed by court martial in April 1811, for oppressive and tryannical behaviour, but was quietly reinstated five months later: Marshall, *Royal Naval Biography*, VIII, 448.

89 James, *Naval History*, IV, 162.

90 See NMM RAI/201/1-11. John Marshall states that his official posting was on 17 January 1806: *Royal Naval Biography*, II, 977.

CHAPTER III

1 1771 (1); 1772 (3); 1773 (5); 1774 (3); 1775 (2).

2 Troubridge was promoted from midshipman to post captain in approximately 1 year and 9 months; Townshend in 3½ years. Peachey and Dunn took between 5½ and 6 years – however, their frigate command would seem to have been of very brief duration.

3 Lewis, *The Navy In Transition 1814-1864*, 67-8.

4 *Ibid*.

5 Sir Edward Pellew, Sir Isaac Coffin, Sir Thomas Troubridge, John Markham, Sir Eliab Harvey and Sir William Sidney Smith.

6 The treaty was signed on 27 March 1802.

7 Marshall, *Royal Naval Biography*, I, 350.

8 Obituary in the *Naval Chronicle*, XXVII (1812), 176.

9 Marshall, *Royal Naval Biography*, I, 83.

10 Pack, *The Man who burned the White House*, 30.

11 See for example the cases of James Macnamara, John Cooke (2) and Charles Napier.

12 Marshall, *Royal Naval Biography*, I, 577.

13 See also *Debrett's Complete Peerage*, 394.

14 *Ibid*, 552.

15 Marshall, *Royal Naval Biography*, II, 123; William O'Byrne, *Naval Biographical Dictionary*, I, 490.

16 Marshall, *Royal Naval Biography*, II, 195; O'Byrne, *Naval Biographical Dictionary*, I, 167.

17 Marshall, *Royal Naval Biography*, II, 184.

18 The reader is directed to almost any biography of Nelson for a fuller account of this sorry tale.

19 For the story of James Bowen's promotion see Lewis, *Social History of the Navy*, 54-5.

20 Admiralty List Books, PRO Adm 8 series.

21 Marshall, *Royal Naval Biography*, I, 530ff.

22 Marshall, *Royal Naval Biography*, I, 635; O'Byrne, *Naval Biographical Dictionary*, I, 207.

23 That is, Sir Edward Codrington, Bart.

24 Here the *Dictionary of National Biography* and the Adm 8 records disagree. According to the Admiralty Lists, Codrington was replaced in command of the *Druid* by Sir Richard King.

25 She became a troopship in 1798.

26 'I think my Master Codrington will be very glad to get rid of his *Orion*, for he hates the thing, and took the ship *a la maniere d'aquit*, as many others have done.' Admiral

Markham to St Vincent, 26 November 1806, in Markham (ed), *Selections from the Correspondence of Admiral Sir John Markham*, 63. Another reason for Codrington's reluctance may have been his marriage and the birth of a son whom he had not had to leave before (see Howarth, *Nelson the Immortal Memory*, 312).

27 Coffin had already been made commander, but had no ship. See entry in *Dictionary of National Biography*.

28 Author's emphasis.

29 Stirling, *Pages and Portraits From the Past*, 31-2. In fact, Hotham's opinion of Coffin did not improve with experience. It is clear that he despised Coffin for lacking the tact and manners of a gentleman, yet he had to admit that not only was Coffin 'one of the best practical seamen in the Navy' but he 'steered, reefed and hove the lead, better than any man on board his ship. He was thoroughly master of any business he undertook', *ibid*, 34.

30 Amory, *The Life of Admiral Sir Isaac Coffin*, 54. Amory also records that Coffin was given command of the *Venus* frigate after 1796, but this is not recorded in the Admiralty List Books.

31 Marshall, *Royal Naval Biography*, II, 60.

32 The *Bien Venue* was renamed the *Undaunted*.

33 Marshall, *Royal Naval Biography*, I, 528; O'Byrne, *Naval Biographical Dictionary*, I, 170.

34 See entry in *Dictionary of National Biography*.

35 Lewis, *A Social History of the Navy*, Chapter 1.

36 Note the following statistics are taken from Lewis's Tables I and II (pages 31 and 36 of *A Social History of the Navy*). The statistics have been re-grouped for the purposes of this book.

37 This includes 6.7 per cent of 'working class' origin.

38 Marryat, *Frank Mildmay*, 167-8.

39 Lewis, *A Social History of the Navy*, Chapters 12-13.

40 *Ibid*, 420.

41 James, *Naval History of Britain*, III, 83.

42 See Gardiner, *The First Frigates*, 101.

43 James, *Naval History*, I, 110-14.

44 Edward Cooke has been included here even though he died as a result of his wounds several days after the engagement.

45 James, *Naval History*, IV, 328-9.

46 *Ibid*, VI, 186.

47 Dillon (ed Lewis), *A Narrative of my Professional Adventures (1790-1839)*, I, 147.

48 *Naval Chronicle*, XXXI (1814), 352.

49 Tolstoy, *The Half-Mad Lord*.

CHAPTER IV

1 Marshall, *Royal Naval Biography*, IV, 502.

2 The western frigate squadrons, for the duration of their existence, were listed separately from the Channel Fleet, even though geographically they acted within the same station. Duncan's Squadron was listed separately from the North Sea command. See PRO Adm 8/75-76. The size of Warren's Squadron varied between one and six frigates, being at its strongest from March 1796 to November of that year. Pellew's Squadron was never as large, averaging three frigates, but consisting of five on three different occasions.

3 Parkinson, *War in the Eastern Sea*, Chapter 14.

4 James, *Naval History*, V, 293-4.

5 Marshall, *Royal Naval Biography*, IX, 32.

6 PRO Adm 7/229: Admiralty Board Journal Minutes, 1796 (I am grateful to Robert Gardiner for drawing my attention to this case).

7 Some statistics may not total exactly 100 per cent.

8 Serrell certainly served in the Baltic towards the end of the second war, for some time. Unfortunately his service there is not recorded in the List Books.

9 Stackpoole was certainly serving in American waters in 1814.

10 Gilpin, *Memoir of Josias Rogers*, 54.

11 Duffy, *Soldiers, Sugar and Seapower*, 106-14.

12 Gilpin, *Memoir of Josias Rogers*, 98.

13 For example, the Hon Henry Curzon, Charles Ekins, and Alexander Fraser.

14 See Table 5.2. Even among the longest serving frigate captains there was a tendency for service in the West Indies to concentrate before the period 1793-1803.

15 1793-4 Expedition under Sir John Jervis; 1795-6 Expedition under Rear-Admiral

Christian; and the Expedition of 1796-7 under Admiral Harvey (then station commander-in-chief).

16 Duffy, *Soldiers, Sugar and Seapower*, 155.

17 Including a landing against the port of Stralsund in 1807, which had been the base for a number of privateers.

18 The Helder in 1799 and the Scheldt/Walcheren in 1809.

19 Seymour, *Memoir of Rear-Admiral Sir Michael Seymour*, 79.

20 See for example, Sherrard, *A Life of Lord St Vincent*, Chapter XI.

21 Hamilton (ed), *Journals and Letters of Sir Thomas Byam Martin*, I, 291.

22 Marshall, *Royal Naval Biography*, IV, 619.

23 Warren was commander-in-chief of what became the combined Halifax, Jamaica and Leeward Island station, from 1812 to 1814 when he was succeeded by Vice-Admiral Sir Alexander Cochrane.

24 Marshall, *Royal Naval Biography*, II, 558. Also James, *Naval History*, V, 69.

25 Marshall, *Royal Naval Biography*, IX, 4.

26 *Ibid*.

27 NMM MKH/246.

28 See Gardiner, *The First Frigates*, 98.

29 Gardiner, *The Heavy Frigate*, 93.

30 James, *Naval History*, I, 236.

31 British Library Add 59004: Grenville Papers, Letter f184.

32 James, *Naval History*, II, p250.

33 Whilst the *Brilliant* may have been small and comparatively lightly armed, and was neither fast nor able to bear a press of sail, she was highly manoeuvrable. All of her class were considered to be comfortable ships in heavy weather and it may be that it took a particularly good seaman to get the best out of her. This is ironic because Barrie was wrecked in the *Pomone* in October 1811, although the formal verdict blamed the poor navigation of the master.

34 Bayntun commanded five frigates in all during the war with Revolutionary France. The last two were, however, for very short periods. They were the *Lowestoft*, a 32-gun 12-pounder ship and the same sized *Quebec*, which had also been the third frigate he commanded.

35 This was the *Indefatigable* which was being razeed from a 64-gun ship at the time. Robinson's commission was one of

'caretaker' as it only lasted two months, the ship's designated commander, Sir Edward Pellew, being at sea during the fitting out.

36 The *Mediator* (she was an ex-Indiaman and although rated as a frigate was barely worth the description).

37 The *Lavinia* launched in 1806 and one of the heaviest frigates built for the Royal Navy.

38 The *Sir Francis Drake*; purchased from the East India Company.

39 In 1812 briefly commanded the *Salsette/Doris* for some months before being given the *Endymion*.

40 The *Mediator* purchased in 1804 (see note 36 above).

41 Montagu's second frigate was actually the purchased East India Co frigate *Marquis Cornwallis*. By 1806 it had been down rated to a troopship and renamed *Akbar*, although according to the Admiralty List Books it was rated as a Fifth Rate. The ship was not restored to frigate status, with a 24-pounder main battery, until 1813. Because of this ambiguity it has not been included in this table.

42 It has been assumed that a gap of up to six months might be the result of delays in communication. Any gap longer than this has been taken as a definite indication of unemployment (unless contradicted by Pitcairn Jones).

43 Marshall, *Royal Naval Biography*, I, 548.

44 Manwaring and Dobree, *The Floating Republic*, 81ff.

45 Although Pitcairn Jones thought that Jonas Rose may have commanded a 26-gun ship during this time.

46 Drew, 'Memoir of John Phillimore', 276.

47 Those two being Thomas Harvey (2) who reached flag rank in 1821, and Hugh Downman who did the same in 1825. See Syrett & DiNardo, *Commissioned Sea Officers*.

CHAPTER V

1 A bracketed number following the name indicates that there were several naval officers with the same name. It has become the convention to identify the different officers in this fashion and the author has

followed the numbering allocated in Syrett & DiNardo, *Commissioned Sea Officers*. It should be noted that this system of numbering pre-dates the list and will be found in some contemporary sources.

2 There may be some doubt about Thomas Graves' record. According to Pitcairn Jones, he commanded the *Blenheim*, 74 in 1804. But the Admiralty List Books record his command of the *Venus* frigate for a further year. It has been difficult finding verification of his career record.

3 One of the difficulties with Fleetwood Pellew's records is that he was promoted early by his father on the East Indies station, and the Admiralty List Books become confused about both his service and his promotion – as no doubt their Lordships themselves were!

4 See for example Pack, *The Man Who Burned the White House*, 29-30. Also see comments in Morris, *Cockburn and the British Navy in Transition*, 28.

5 Syrett & DiNardo, *Commissioned Sea Officers*, 72.

6 Pocock, *Remember Nelson: The Life of Captain Sir William Hoste*, 79-80.

7 O'Byrne, *A Naval Biographical Dictionary*, I, 3.

8 Phillimore, *The Last of Nelson's Captains*, 74.

9 *Ibid*, 60.

10 See a letter from St Vincent quoted in *Ibid*, 80-1.

11 For example: the Hon F Aylmer, the Hon J A Bennett (died 1812); the Hon William Cathcart; the Hon Archibald Cochrane; the Hon Lord Viscount Falkland (possibly insane; killed in a duel in 1809); the Hon Robert Forbes (1); the Hon George Poullett.

12 Marshall, *Royal Naval Biography*, I, 381.

13 Seymour, *Memoir of Sir Michael Seymour*, 73.

14 Althorp MSS quoted in Aspinal, *The Later Correspondence of George III*, II, 2, 328 note 1.

15 The following extract from a letter of St Vincent to Sir John Carter, is fairly blunt. 'The circumstances of the war, and numerous connexions of the Spencer Family, have contributed to swell the list of post-captains and commanders to an enormous size, insomuch I have determined not to promote to those ranks, except in cases of extraordinary merit and service, until the worthy on half-pay are provided for ...', Smith (ed), *Letters of Lord St Vincent*, I, 331.

16 Markham (ed), *Selections from the Correspondence of Admiral Sir John Markham*, 2.

17 The others were Hamilton, Halsted, Durham, King, Owen and, of course, Fleetwood Pellew.

18 Marshall, *Royal Naval Biography*, II, 302.

19 For a wider discussion on this issue see Lewis, *Social History of the Navy*, 27ff.

20 Members of Parliament and year of first election are as follows:
Charles Hamilton (1790-1801) – it should be noted that there is a dispute here between Syrett & DiNardo's dates and those given in Marshall; Sir Harry Neale (1790); Joseph Sidney Yorke (1790); Philip Durham (1830); George Cockburn (1818); the Hon Charles Herbert (1806); George Mundy (1818); the Hon George Elliott (1832). See Syrett & DiNardo, *Commissioned Sea Officers*.

21 See Gardiner, *The First Frigates*, 99.

22 The *Diamond*.

23 However, please note the earlier remark that the Channel Station extended down to the coast of Portugal.

24 PRO Adm 8 series.

25 John Marshall, *Royal Naval Biography*, III, 329.

26 For a detailed discussion on this subject, see Crowhurst, *The French War on Trade*.

27 *Ibid*. A clear indication of the level of activity can be seen in the statistics for the number of French seamen captured in privateers for each year of the war given in Appendix 1.

28 Marshall, *Royal Naval Biography*, I, 342.

29 *Ibid*, I, 411.

30 Crowhurst, *French War on Trade*, 116.

31 *Ibid*, 66.

32 See *Steel's Prize Pay List 1793-1802*, 45.

33 Marshall, *Royal Naval Biography*, II, 44.

34 *Ibid*, II, 310.

35 *Ibid*, I, 753; O'Byrne, *Naval Biographical Dictionary*, II, 921.

36 Crowhurst, *French War on Trade*, 102.

37 Marshall, *Royal Naval Biography*, II 104.

38 Hamilton (ed), *Journals and Letters of Sir Thomas Byam Martin*, I, 77.

39 PRO Adm 68/314-/315: Greenwich Hospital Treasurer's Accounts.

40 PRO Adm 68/314-/316.

41 Anon, *Service Afloat*, 132.

42 Anon, *A Letter to the Rt Hon Lord Viscount Melville on the Present Condition of Officers in the Royal Navy...... By a post captain.*

43 Lavery, *Nelson's Navy*, 310.

44 James, *Naval History*, V, 259.

45 Parkinson, *War in the Eastern Seas*, Chapters 11 and 12.

46 For these see Duffy, *Soldiers, Sugar and Seapower*; and Parkinson *War in the Eastern Seas.*

47 Anon, *Service Afloat*, 122.

48 Cochrane, *The Autobiography of a Seaman*, 144.

49 *Ibid*, 148.

50 *Naval Chronicle*, XXI (1809), 372.

51 James, *Naval History*, III, 38-9; also, Duffy, *Soldiers, Sugar and Seapower*, 317-8.

52 Marshall, *Royal Naval Biography*, I, 411.

53 *Ibid*, I, 387.

54 Murray, *Memoir of the Naval Life and Services of Admiral Sir Philip Durham*, 36.

55 O'Byrne, *A Naval Biographical Dictionary*, I, 415; Duffy, *Soldiers, Sugar and Seapower*, 314-5.

56 Collingwood to Nelson: quoted in Marshall, *Royal Naval Biography*, II, 333.

57 According to Marshall, Mundy became the advocate of the Simotines of Badalona, adopting the role of their advocate and having to deal with what he considered to be the imbecilic leadership of the Spanish Junta.

58 For an example of Pleydell Bouverie's activity during this period see Popham, *A Damned Cunning Fellow*, 205.

59 Marshall, *Royal Naval Biography*, IV, 897.

60 James, *Naval History*, V, 295ff.

61 Parkinson, *War In the Eastern Seas*, 415.

62 Elliot, *Memoir of Admiral the Hon Sir George Elliot*, 75.

63 Marshall, *Royal Naval Biography*, I, 864.

64 Following his successful co-ordination of landings in the West Indies, General Maitland wrote of him: 'His arrangement, and presence of mind, render him peculiarly qualified for joint operations', and Sir Alexander Cochrane wrote, 'the direction of all the naval operations connected with the army was left entirely with Captain Beaver, of the *Acasta*, who conducted the service with all the correctness and celerity which I expected of him.': Smyth, *Life and Services of Captain Philip Beaver*, 189. Beaver was also centrally responsible for the success of Abercromby's landing at Aboukir Bay, and his journal description of this event is vivid: *Ibid*, 143-146.

65 Carden, *Memoir of Admiral Carden*, 252.

66 *Naval Chronicle*, XXV (1811), 353.

67 Leyland (ed), *Blockade of Brest*, I, 104, letter 81.

68 Quoted in Parkinson, *Edward Pellew*, 169.

69 See *Dictionary of National Biography.*

70 Crawford, *Reminiscences*, I, 57.

71 Lloyd (ed), *The Keith Papers*, III, 97.

72 Crawford, *Reminiscences*, I, 65.

73 *Ibid*, 119.

74 This may well be a reference to the capture of a squadron of Spanish treasure ships by Sir Graham Moore's frigate squadron in 1804. See James, *Naval History*, III, 278.

75 Crawford, *Reminiscences*, I, 159.

76 *Ibid*, I, 72.

77 Stirling, *Pages and Portraits from the Past*, I, 204. This type of comment is reminiscent of similar attitudes struck by other officers towards that other most active frigate captain, Thomas Cochrane.

78 Quoted in Popham, *A Damned Cunning Fellow*, 59.

79 Quoted in Brighton, *Admiral Sir P B V Broke, Bart; A Memoir*, 301.

80 *Ibid*, 311.

81 Marshall, *Royal Naval Biography*, I, 319; O'Byrne, *Naval Biographical Dictionary*, I, 512.

82 In this instance service of more than two years has been taken as the minimum guideline.

83 Lifford, *Memoir of Robert Dudley Oliver*, 37.

CHAPTER VI

1 For example: Henderson, *The Frigates*; C R Low, *Famous Frigate Actions.*

2 Dillon (ed Lewis), *A Narrative of my Professional Adventures (1790-1839)*, II, 91ff.

3 Carden, *Memoir of Admiral Carden*, 259-60.

4 James, *Naval History*, I, xxvi.

5 NMM RAI/201/1-11.

6   PRO Adm 51/2861: Captain's Logs, HMS *Shannon*, 1 Sept-29 Nov 1813.

7   For a contemporary criticism along similar grounds see Glascock, *Naval Sketch Book*, 97ff.

8   Broke was not the only frigate captain to go to unusual lengths to try and seek an action. Captain Henry Hope issued a challenge to the American frigate *United States* to meet him in a frigate duel. The action was forbidden by Hope's commodore (Sir Thomas Hardy), because the *United States* was a much heavier frigate than Hope's *Endymion*.

9   Quoted in Padfield, *Broke and the Shannon*, 67.

10 Seymour, *Memoir of Sir Michael Seymour*, 52.

11 Leech, *Thirty Years from Home*, 70.

12 James, *Naval History*, III, 267.

13 James, *Naval History*, IV, 18.

14 Crawford, *Reminiscences*, I, 186-7.

15 Eastwick, *A Master Mariner*, 130-51.

16 Eastwick was mistaken as to calibre: the fire was probably from the *Sybille*'s 32-pounder carronades.

17 James, *Naval History*, II, 365ff.

18 Sir Howard Douglas, *A Treatise on Naval Gunnery*.

19 Pechell, *Observations upon the Defective Equipment of Ship Guns*, 4.

20 James, *Naval History*, II, 105.

21 James, *Naval History*, III, 127.

22 Marshall, *Royal Naval Biography*, II, 44. See also Brenton, *The Naval Hisory of Great Britain*, I, 545, which also records that the *Phoebe*'s first lieutenant, John Wentworth Holland, was promoted commander and then, shortly after, post captain.

23 James, *Naval History*, I, 229; and Stirling, *Pages and Portraits from the Past*, I, 148.

24 James, *Naval History*, I, 229.

25 James, *Naval History*, II, 133.

26 James, *Naval History*, II, 135.

27 *Naval Chronicle* IV (1800), 365.

28 James, *Naval History*, I, 398.

29 James, *Naval History*, I, 402.

30 Martin's name had actually been entered on the books of various ships from 1780, when his father became Resident Commissioner.

31 Hamilton (ed), *Journals and Letters of Sir Thomas Byam Martin*, I, 153.

32 *Ibid*, 247.

33 *Ibid*, 262. Also See James, *Naval History*, I, 366.

34 Hamilton (ed), *Journals and letters of Thomas Byam Martin*, I, 262.

35 In this instance from the Committee of Shipping.

36 Hamilton (ed), *Journals and Letters of Sir Thomas Byam Martin*, I, 270.

37 See Gardiner, *The Heavy Frigate*, 86.

38 Hamilton (ed), *Journals and Letters of Sir Thomas Byam Martin*, I, 272.

39 See letter from Robert Stopford to Byam Martin in Hamilton (ed), *Journals and Letters of Sir Thomas Byam Martin*, I, 318.

40 Carden, *Memoir of Admiral Carden*, 102.

41 *Ibid*, 102.

42 Hamilton (ed), *Journals and Letters of Sir Thomas Byam Martin*, I, 277.

43 See for example James, *Naval History*, III, 15.

44 Marshall, *Royal Naval Biography*, I, 494.

45 *Ibid*, III, 16-17.

46 PRO Adm 1/2136: Captains Letters M, 1796.

47 *The Times*, Monday 16 July 1798.

48 *Ibid*.

49 NMM MLN/35/4: Milne Papers, Halford to Milne, 14 July 1798.

50 Seymour, *Memoir of Rear Admiral Sir Michael Seymour*, 25.

51 *Ibid*, 73,

52 For a detailed account of this action see James, *Naval History*, IV, 376-80.

53 See Syrett & DiNardo, *Commissioned Sea Officers*. Blennerhasset became a retired commander in 1844.

54 Carden, *Memoir of Admiral Carden*, 57.

55 PRO Adm 1/139: Letters of Commander-in-Chief Channel Fleet, Letter J812.

56 Rockingham Castle WR(S)8: Seymour Papers ['Watson of Rockingham (Culme-Seymour)'], Mends to Adam, 6 April 1809.

57 The captain's log records that the land was visible by dawn.

58 The final accounts for the sale of the *Niemen* were not settled until July 1811. Mends and the *Arethusa* appear to have shared, but *Emerald* was cut out of the reward. Interestingly, a note in the High Court of Admiralty Papers (PRO HCA/2/366), John Hawker's Account for the sale, states that no deduction was made for the cost of resisting the claim of the *Emerald*.

59 Rockingham Castle WR(S)9: Seymour Papers, copy letter from Mends to Seymour, from *Arethusa*, 7 April 1809.

60 Seymour Papers, Rockingham Castle, WRS(S)9, Mends to Seymour, *Arethusa*, 7 April 1809.

61 Fair, the master, was promoted to lieutenant as a result of this action on July 1809.

62 Seymour, *Memoir of Sir Michael Seymour*, 72.

63 At the start of the action the *Niemen* had a complement of 339 men and boys; 47 were killed and 73 wounded in the action: James, *Naval History*, V, 16.

64 Subsequent correspondence reveals that Ruler became too ill to return at the allotted time and was marked down in the muster books as having 'Run'. Seymour later received a letter from a Doctor reporting on Ruler's condition and Seymour petitioned the Admiralty for permission to discharge him as unfit. PRO Adm 1/2520: Captains' Letters, S 1809, Letter S47.

65 This suggests Seymour wanted Fair as his own second lieutenant.

66 Seymour, *Memoir of Sir Michael Seymour*, 74.

67 *Ibid*, 76.

68 *Ibid*, 79.

69 PRO HCA/2/366: John Hawker's Account for the sale of *La Niemen*, 18 July 1811.

70 Drew, 'Memoir of John Phillimore', 276.

71 *Ibid*.

72 *Naval Chronicle*, XXXI (1814), 243

73 *Ibid*.

74 NMM KEI/38/4: Keith Papers, Phillimore to Keith, 18 October 1813.

75 NMM POR/D/30: Portsmouth Dockyard Report to the Navy Board, 21 April 1814.

76 PRO Adm 1/2347: Captains' Letters, P 1814, Letter P355.

77 Marshall, *Royal Naval Biography*, Supplement Part 1, 248.

78 NMM POR/D/30: Portsmouth Dockyard Report to the Navy Board, 21 April 1814.

79 NMM KEI/38/6: Keith Papers, Shrapnel to Keith, 25 March 1814.

80 *Ibid*.

81 Captain Andrew Drew: quoted in old *DNB* entry.

82 [Thomas Haliburton], 'The Arrival of the *Chesapeake* in Halifax in 1813', 161.

83 *Ibid*, 165.

CHAPTER VII

1 Lavery, *Nelson's Navy*, 89-90; Lewis, *A Social History of the Navy*, 143-9.

2 Lavery (ed), *Shipboard Life and Organisation*, 9-51.

3 *Ibid*, 16, Regulation V.

4 Markham (ed), *Selections from the Correspondence of Admiral Sir John Markham*, 117. Interestingly, Mitford was never a frigate captain and in December 1803 he was presumed drowned when the *York*, 64 which he was commanding disappeared in the North Sea.

5 Extracts of this have now been published in Lavery (ed), *Shipboard Life and Organisation*, 263-75.

6 Author's emphasis.

7 Lavery (ed), *Shipboard Life and Organisation*, 263.

8 *Ibid*, 263-4.

9 *Ibid*, 267.

10 *Ibid*, 265.

11 See the comments in Robert Wilson's Journal, in Thursfield (ed), *Five Naval Journals*, 243. Wilson served as a seaman on board the frigate *Unité*, commanded by Patrick Campbell, an officer with a fine reputation. See also Robinson, *Jack Nastyface*, 149-150.

12 Byrn, *Crime and Punishment in the Royal Navy*, 94.

13 James, *Naval History*, II, 273-280.

14 Lavery (ed), *Shipboard Life and Organisation*, 119-82.

15 NMM JOD/45: Captain's Standing Orders, December 1802, HMS *Amazon*, Captain William Parker (John Skynner's copy).

16 NMM OBK/10: Additional Rules and Orders for the Better Government of HMS *London*, Order 34.

17 NMM PRV/20: General Orders and Regulations for the Government and Interior Discipline of HMS *Princess Royal*, Capt J C Purvis, April 1793.

18 PRO Adm 1/815: Sir Thomas Pasley's Despatches as C-in-C Plymouth, March 1800.

19 Hoffman, *A Sailor of King George*, 239.

20 Lavery (ed), *Shipboard Life and Organisation*, 127.

21 Hoffman, *A Sailor of King George*, 227-8.

22 Elphinstone passed for lieutenant in 1780

23 NMM JOD/45: Captain's Standing Orders, December 1802, HMS *Amazon*, Captain William Parker, (John Skynner's copy).

24 *Ibid.*

25 See in particular, Warren's letter to St Vincent (Parker's uncle) in Phillimore, *The Last of Nelson's Captains*, 154.

26 In May 1795 *Niger* was sent out on a cruise. Parker wrote home to his Mother: 'The *Niger* is a very nice little frigate of 32 guns, and Captain Foote is one of the best men that ever was ... Captain Foote has a vast number of books, so I had a fine choice. In general I read Shakespeare's plays. Captain Foote desired me to read those which were taken from the History of England, and I compared them to the History, which was very amusing ...': *ibid*, 40-41.

27 Thursfield (ed), *Five Naval Journals*, 145.

28 Lewis, *A Social History of the Navy*, 31.

29 Stirling, *Pages and Portraits from the Past*, I, 42.

30 Colley, *Britons: Forging the Nation*, 164ff.

31 For an example of this, see the incident in board HMS *Genereux* in Cochrane's *Autobiography of a Seaman*, 36 – though one must always treat Cochrane's accounts with a certain degree of circumspection.

32 Marryat, *Frank Mildmay*, 118.

33 Hall, *Fragments of Voyages and Travels*, II, 106.

34 Quoted in *Memorials of Admiral Lord Gambier*, I, 367-8

35 NMM LBK 58/1 & 58/2: Transcripts, Letter 215

36 Smyth, *The Life and Services of Captain Philip Beaver*, 171.

37 Griffiths, *Observations on Some Points of Seamanship*, 114.

38 Hall, *Fragments of Voyages and Travels*, II, 151.

39 It must be acknowledged that some officers were highly critical of young aristocrats being promoted prematurely because of their 'interest'; furthermore, they were often condemned for being too harsh. Such views were expressed by the likes of Nelson, St Vincent and Collingwood.

40 Hall, *Fragments of Voyages and Travels*, II, 164. This also throws interesting light onto John Wetherell's antagonism towards Captain Philip Wilkinson, who he believed was the son of a Harwich barber. See Forester (ed), *The Adventures of John Wetherell*.

41 NMM CUN/3: Cunningham Papers, 'A narrative of occurrences that took place during the mutiny at the Nore in the months of May and June, 1797; with a few observations upon the Impressment of seamen and the advantages of those who are employed in his majesty's navy; also on the necessity and useful operations of the articles of war', 120

42 Letter from Captain Thomas Bennett, *United Services Journal* (3, 1832), 399.

43 Lavery (ed), *Shipboard Life and Organisation*, 403.

44 *Ibid*, 403

45 *Ibid*, 405.

46 Jones, 'Character and Conduct of the Late Captain Corbett Vindicated', in *United Services Journal* (3,1832), 162-71.

47 PRO Adm 51/1377: Captain's Log, HMS *Penelope*.

48 NMM ADM/L/85: Lieutenant's Log, HMS *Penelope*.

49 Griffiths, *Observations on Some Points of Seamanship*, 115.

50 Marryat, *The King's Own*, 7.

51 Byrn, *Crime and Punishment in the Royal Navy*, 177.

52 James, *Naval History*, II, p154.

53 PRO Adm 1/248: Hyde Parker's Dispatches, Robert Waller Otway to Hyde Parker, 30 May 1797.

54 See PRO Adm 51/1256: Captain's Log, HMS *Ceres*, 2-8 November 1796.

55 PRO Adm 51/1257: Captain's Log, HMS *Mermaid*.

56 PRO Adm 1/2226: Captains' Letters, N 1797-8.

57 See, for example, *The Naval Chronicle*, III (1800), 78, Plymouth Reports, 7 January 1800.

POSTSCRIPT

1 *Naval Chronicle*, XXX (1813), 361.

BIBLIOGRAPHY

1. PRIMARY SOURCES

1.a. Manuscript Material

Public Record Office, Kew (PRO)

Adm 1/106: Admiral's Despatches, Channel (Colpoys).
Adm 1/136: Letters of C-in-C Channel Fleet (Lord Gardner).
Adm 1/137: Letters C-in-C Channel Fleet.
Adm 1/139: Letters of C-in-C Channel Fleet (Lord Gambier).
Adm 1/248: Admiral's Despatches (Hyde Parker).
Adm 1/814: Admiral's Despatches, C-in-C Plymouth, 1799 (King).
Adm 1/815: Admiral's Despatches, C-in-C Plymouth, March 1800 (Sir Thomas Pasley).
Adm 1/1528: Captains' Letters, B 1803.
Adm 1/1531: Captains' Letters, B 1804.
Adm 1/1534: Captains' Letters, B 1805.
Adm 1/1537: Captains' Letters, B 1806.
Adm 1/2225: Captains' Letters, N 1795-96.
Adm 1/2226: Captains' Letters, N 1797-98.
Adm 1/2517: Captains' Letters, S 1807.
Adm 1/2519: Captains' Letters, S 1808.
Adm 1/2520: Captains' Letters, S 1809.
Adm 1/2521: Captains' Letters, S 1809.
Adm 1/2339: Captains' Letters, P 1813.
Adm 1/2341: Captains' Latters, P 1812.
Adm 1/2347: Captains' Letters, P 1814.

Adm 6/65: Admiral's Despatches, Vice-Admiral Elphinstone (Lord Keith).
Adm 8/69-/100: Admiralty List Books.
Adm 12/M367: Admiralty Digests, 1806.
Adm 12/M470.35: Admiralty Digests, 1806.
Adm 37/2615: Muster Book, HMS *Niemen*, October 1809.
Adm 37/709: Muster Book, HMS *Amethyst*, April 1808 – February 1809.
Adm 51/1231: Captain's Logs, *Aurora*, January 1797, and January 1798.
Adm 51/1256 Captain's Logs, HMS *Ceres*.
Adm 51/1257: Captain's Logs, HMS *Mermaid*.
Adm 51/1377: Captain's Logs, HMS *Penelope*.
Adm 51/1532: Captain's Logs, HMS *Phoenix*.
Adm 51/1532: Captain's Logs, HMS *Narcissus*.
Adm 51/1673: Captain's Logs, HMS *Topaze*.
Adm 51/1807: Captains' Logs, HMS *Amethyst*, 14 April – 30 June 1808.
Adm 51/1859: Captains' Logs, HMS *Amethyst*, 1 July 1808 – June 1809.
Adm 51/2861: Captain's Logs, HMS *Shannon*.
Adm 68/314-/316: Greenwich Hospital Treasurer's Accounts.
HCA/2/366: High Court of Admiralty Papers (Account for *Le Niemen*).

National Maritime Museum, Greenwich (NMM)

NMM ADM/L/P/85: Lieutenant's Logs, HMS *Penelope*.
NMM ADM/L/P/135: Lieutenant's Logs, HMS *Phoenix*.
NMM ADM/L/T/240: Lieutenant's Logs, HMS *Aurora*.
NMM COO/2/B1- /B3: Captain Edward Owen's narrative of the Walcheren expedition.
NMM CUN/1-4: Charles Cunningham Papers.
NMM CUN/6-7: Captain's Log, HMS *Clyde*.
NMM ER: Captain Edward Riou's Papers.
NMM JOD/45: Captain's Standing Orders, December 1802, HMS *Amazon*, Captain William Parker (John Skynner's copy).
NMM KEA: Captain Richard Keat's Papers.
NMM KEI: Lord Keith's Papers.
NMM LBK 58/1 & 58/2: Typed transcription of Captain Philip Broke's letters to his wife.
NMM MKH: Samuel Hood and Lord Bridport's Papers.
NMM MLN4: Milne Papers.
NMM MS78/146: Captain Ross Donnelly's Letter Book, 1798-1803.

NMM OBK/10: Additional Rules and Orders for the Better Government of
  HMS *London*.
NMM PRV/20: General Orders and Regulations for the Government and Interior
  Discipline of HMS *Princess Royal*, Captain J C Purvis, April 1793.
NMM RAI: Captain Peter Rainier's Papers.
Pitcairn Jones, Commander C G, 'List of Commissioned Sea Officers'
  (not published).

British Library, London
Add 59,004: Grenville Papers (Letters of Captain Robert Barry).
Add 34,918: Nelson Papers.
Add 35,195-35,196: Spencer Papers.

Rockingham Castle, Northamptonshire
WR (S): Seymour Papers ('Watson of Rockingham [Culme-Seymour]').

1.b. PRINTED SOURCES

The Naval Chronicle, 40 vols (London 1799-1818).
Steel's Prize Pay List 1793-1802 (London 1803).
Steel's Navy Lists (particularly August 1797; May 1798; June 1799 etc to 1805;
  January 1807 to March 1808; August 1810 etc to 1815).
The Times.
Debrett's Complete Peerage (London 1834).

Amory, T C, *The Life of Admiral Sir Isaac Coffin, Bart* (Boston 1886).
Anon, *Service Afloat or The Naval Career of Sir William Hoste* (London 1887).
Anon, *Letter to the Right Honourable Lord Viscount Melville on the Present
  Condition of Officers in the Royal Navy, By 'A Post Captain'* (London 1811).
Brenton, E P, *The Naval History of Great Britain*, 2 vols (2nd ed, London 1837).
Brighton, Rev J G, *Admiral Sir P B V Broke, Bart: A Memoir* (London 1866).
_____, *Admiral Of The Fleet Sir Provo W P Wallis: A Memoir* (London 1892).
Burrows, H (ed), *The Perilous Adventures and Vicissitudes of a Naval Officer
  1801-1812* (London 1927)
Carden, J S, *Memoir of Admiral Carden* (Oxford 1912).
Chamier, Captain F, *Life of a Sailor* (London 1833).
Chatterton, Lady Georgiana (ed), *Memorials Personal and Historical of Admiral
  Lord Gambier* (London 1861).

Childers, Colonel Spencer (ed), *A Mariner of England* (reprint London 1970).

Cochrane, Lord T, *Autobiography of a Seaman* (London 1890).

Crawford, Captain, A *Reminiscences of a Naval Officer*, 2 vols (London 1851, new edition 1998).

Dann, J C (ed), *The Nagle Journal: A Diary of the Life of Jacob Nagle, Sailor, From the Year 1775 to 1841* (New York 1988).

Douglas, Sir Howard, *A Treatise on Naval Gunnery* (London 1820).

Elliott, the Hon Sir George, *Memoirs of Admiral The Hon Sir George Elliott* (London 1863).

Foote, Captain Edward, *Captain Foote's Vindication of His Conduct When Captain of His Majesty's Ship Sea-Horse* (London 1807).

Forester, C S (ed), *The Adventures of John Wetherell* (London 1954).

Gardiner, Sir Robert, *Memoir of Sir Graham Moore* (London 1844).

Gilpin, W, *Memoir of Josias Rogers Esq* (London 1808).

Glascock, W N, *Naval Sketch-book*, 2 vols (London 1826).

Griffiths, Captain Anselm, *Observations on Some Points of Seamanship with Practical Hints on Naval Economy* (Portsmouth 1828).

Hall, Captain Basil, *Fragments of Voyages and Travels*, 3 vols (Edinburgh & London 1831).

Hamilton, Sir Richard Vesey (ed), *Letters and Papers of Admiral of the Fleet Sir Thos Byam Martin, GCB*, 3 vols (Navy Records Society, London 1898, 1901 & 1903).

Hoffman, F, *A Sailor of King George* (London 1901, new edition 1999).

Hughes, Edward (ed), *The Private Correspondence of Admiral Lord Collingwood* (Navy Records Society, London 1957).

James, William *The Naval History of Great Britain*, 6 vols (8th ed, London 1902).

Laughton, Sir John Knox (ed), *Letters and Papers of Charles, Lord Barham*, 3 vols (Navy Records Society, London 1907-1911).

Leech, Samuel, *Thirty Years from Home, or A Voice from the Main Deck* (Boston 1843, new edition London 1999).

Lewis, M.A (ed), *Sir William Henry Dillon: A Narrative of my Professional Adventures (1790-1839)*, 2 vols (Navy Records Society, London 1953 & 1956).

Lifford, Viscount, *Memoir of Robert Dudley Oliver Esq, Admiral of the Red, by his nephew* (London 1851).

Lloyd, C (ed), *The Keith Papers* (Navy Records Society, London 1955).

_____, *Above and Under Hatches: Being Naval Recollections in Shreds and Patches with Strange Reflections by James Anthony Gardner* (London 1955).

_____, *The Naval Miscellany Vol IV* (Navy Records Society, London 1952).

Lovell, Vice-Admiral W S, *Personal Narrative of Events from 1799 to 1815, with Anecdotes* (London 1879, reprinted 1971).

Low, C R, *Famous Frigate Actions* (London 1898, reprinted 1970).

Mark, William, *At Sea With Nelson* (London 1929).

Markham, Sir Clements (ed), *Selections from the Correspondence of Admiral John Markham during the Years 1801-4 and 1806-7* (Navy Records Society, London 1905).

Marshall, Lieutenant John, *Royal Naval Biography*, 12 vols (London 1823-1830).

Marryat, Frederick, *Frank Mildmay, or The Naval Officer* (London 1864).

_____, *The King's Own* (London 1896).

Murray, Captain A, *Memoir of the Life and Services of Admiral Durham* (London 1846).

Napier, Major General E, *Life and Correspondence of Admiral Sir Charles Napier, KCB* (London 1862).

Nicholas, Sir N H (ed), *Dispatches and Letters of Vice Admiral Lord Viscount Nelson*, 7 vols (London 1844-1847).

O'Byrne, William, *A Naval Biographical Dictionary* (London 1849).

Osler, Edward, *Life of Admiral Viscount Exmouth* (London 1835).

Parkinson, C Northcote (ed), *Samuel Walters: Lieutenant, RN* (Liverpool 1949).

Parsons, G S, *Nelsonian Reminiscences: Leaves From Memory's Log* (London 1843, new edition 1998).

Pechell, S, *Observations upon the Defective Equipment of Ship Guns in a letter addressed to Vice Admiral Sir Harry Neale* (Corfu 1824).

Plunkett, Captain the Hon E, *The Past and Future of the British Navy* (London 1847).

Ralfe, J, *Naval Biography of Great Britain*, 4 vols (London 1828).

____, *Historical Memoir of Sir Robert Waller Otway, Bart* (London nd).

Robinson, Rear-Admiral H R, *Sea Drift* (London 1858).

Robinson, W, *Jack Nastyface: The Memoirs of an English Seaman* (London 1836, new edition 1973).

Ross, Sir John, *Memoirs and Correspondence of Admiral Lord de Saumarez*, 2 vols (London 1838).

Seymour, R, *Memoir of Rear-Admiral Sir Michael Seymour, Bart KCB* (London 1878).

Smith, David Bonner (ed), *Letters of Lord St Vincent 1801-1804*, 2 vols (Navy Records Society, London 1922 & 1927).

Smyth, Captain W H, *The Life & Services of Captain Philip Beaver* (London 1829).

Stirling, A M, *Pages and Portraits from the Past: Being the Private Papers of Sir*

William Hotham,GCB, Admiral of the Red, 2 vols (London 1919).

Thursfield, Rear-Admiral H G (ed), *Five Naval Journals* (Navy Records Society, London 1951).

Warren, Sir J B, *A View of the Naval Force of Great Britain by An Officer of Rank* (London 1791).

2. SECONDARY SOURCES

2.1. General Works of Reference

Dictionary of National Biography, 66 vols (London 1885-1901).

Colledge, J J, *Ships of the Royal Navy*, Vol 1 (London 1987).

Hepper, David J, *Warship Losses in the Age of Sail, 1650-1859* (Rotherfield 1994).

Lyon, D, *The Sailing Navy List* (London 1993).

Syrett, D & DiNardo, R L, *Commissioned Sea Officers of the Royal Navy, 1660-1815* (Navy Records Society, Aldershot 1994).

2.2. Monographs and Biographies

Anson, Captain W V, *The Life of Admiral Sir John Borlase Warren* (London 1914).

Balleine, G R, *The Tragedy of Philippe d'Auvergne* (London 1973).

Barnes, J, *Naval Actions of the War of 1812* (New York 1896, reprinted 1969).

Boudriot, Jean, *History of the French Frigate 1650-1850* (Rotherfield 1993).

Byrn, Jr, J D, *Crime and Punishment in the Royal Navy: Discipline on the Leeward Islands Station 1784-1812* (Aldershot 1989).

Colley, L, *Britons: Forging the Nation 1707-1837* (New Haven & London 1992).

Crowhurst, Patrick, *The French War on Trade: Privateering 1793-1815* (Aldershot 1989).

Duffy, M, *Soldiers, Sugar and Seapower* (Oxford 1987).

Dugan, J, *The Great Mutiny* (London 1966).

Duncan, N, *Duncan of Camperdown* (Diss 1995).

Forester, C.S, *The Naval War of 1812* (London 1957).

Gardiner, Robert (ed), *The Line of Battle: The Sailing Warship 1650-1840* (London 1992).

Gardiner, Robert, *The First Frigates: Nine-Pounder and Twelve-Pounder Frigates, 1748-1815* (London, 1992).

_____, *The Heavy Frigate: Eighteen-Pounder Frigates, Vol 1, 1778-1800* (London 1994).

_____, *Frigates of the Napoleonic Wars* (London 2000).

Gore, J, *Nelson's Hardy and His Wife* (London 1935).

Henderson, J, *The Frigates: An account of the Lesser Warships of the Great French Wars 1793-1815* (New York 1970).

Hill, Admiral R, *The Prizes of War: The Naval Prize System in the Napoleonic Wars* (Stroud 1998).

Hood, Dorothy, *The Admirals Hood* (London nd).

Howarth, David & Stephen, *Nelson: The Immortal Memory* (London 1988).

Hubback, J H & E, *Jane Austen's Sailor Brothers* (London 1905).

Kay, J T de, *Chronicles of the Frigate Macedonian, 1809-1922* (New York 1995).

Lavery, B, *Nelson's Navy: The Ships, Men and Organisation, 1793-1815* (London 1989).

Lavery, B (ed), *Shipboard Life and Organisation 1731-1815* (Navy Records Society, London 1998).

Lewis, M A, *England's Sea Officers* (London 1948).

_____, *A Social History of the Navy, 1793-1815* (London 1960).

_____, *The Navy In Transition 1814-1864: A Social History* (London 1965).

_____, *The Navy of Britain: A Historical Portrait* (London 1948).

Leyland, J (ed), *Blockade of Brest,* Vol 1 (Navy Records Society, London 1898).

Lloyd, C, *The British Seaman* (London 1968).

_____, *Captain Marryat and the Old Navy* (London 1939).

_____, *St Vincent & Camperdown* (London 1963).

_____, *Lord Cochrane* (London 1947).

Mackesy, Piers, *War in the Mediterranean* (London 1957).

Mahan, Captain A T, *The influence of Sea Power upon the French Revolution and Empire*, 1793-1812 (London 1893).

Manwaring, G E, & Dobree, B, *The Floating Republic,* (London 1966).

Marcus, G J, *A Naval History of England: The Age of Nelson* (London 1971).

_____, *Heart of Oak* (Oxford 1975).

Masefield, J, *Sea Life in Nelson's Time* (2nd ed, London 1971).

Mason, M, *Willoughby the Immortal* (Oxford 1969).

McKee, C, *A Gentlemanly and Honorable Profession* (Annapolis 1991).

Morris, R, *The Royal Dockyards during the Revolutionary and Napoleonic Wars* (Leicester 1983).

_____, *Cockburn and the British Navy in Transition* (Exeter 1997).

Nash, M D, *The Last Voyage of the Guardian, Lieutenant Riou, Commander, 1789-1791* (Capetown 1990).

Pack, James, *The Man Who Burned the White House* (Emsworth 1987).

Padfield, P, *Broke and the Shannon* (London 1968).

Parkinson, C Northcote (ed), *The Trade Winds: A Study of British Overseas Trade during the French Wars, 1793-1815* (London 1948).

Parkinson, C Northcote, *War in the Eastern Seas, 1793-1815* (London 1954).

_____, *Britannia Rules: The Classic Age of Naval History, 1793-1815* (Gloucester 1987).

_____, *Edward Pellew, Viscount Exmouth* (London 1934).

Perrett, B, *The Real Hornblower: The Life and Times of Admiral Sir James Gordon* (London 1998).

Phillimore, Admiral Sir Augustus, *The Last of Nelson's Captains* (London 1891).

Pocock, Tom, *Remember Nelson: The Life of Captain Sir William Hoste* (London 1977).

_____, *A Thirst for Glory: The Life of Admiral Sir Sidney Smith* (London 1996).

Poolman, K, *Guns Off Cape Ann* (London 1961).

Pope, D, *The Black Ship* (London 1963).

_____, *The Devil Himself: The Mutiny of 1800* (London 1987).

_____, *Life in Nelson's Navy* (London 1981, reprinted 1997).

Popham, Hugh, *A Damned Cunning Fellow: The Eventful Life of Rear-Admiral Sir Home Popham* (Tywardreath 1991).

Price, Anthony, *The Eyes of the Fleet: A Popular History of Frigates and Frigate Captains, 1793-1815.* (London 1990).

Rodger, N A M, *The Admiralty* (Lavenham 1979).

_____, *The Wooden World* (Glasgow 1986).

Russell, Lord, *The Knight of the Sword* (London 1964).

Sherrard, O A, *A Life of Lord St Vincent* (London 1933).

Talbot, J E, *The Pen And Ink Sailor: Charles Middleton and the King's Navy, 1778-1813* (London 1998).

Thomas, D, *Cochrane: Britannia's Last Sea-King* (New York 1978).

Tolstoy, Nikolai, *The Half-Mad Lord: Thomas Pitt, 2nd Baron Camelford* (London 1978).

Tucker, S C & Reuter, F T, *Injured Honor: The Chesapeake-Leopard Affair, June 22, 1807* (Annapolis 1996).

White, D, *The Frigate Diana* (London 1987).

2.3. Articles

Beeler, John, 'Fit for Service Abroad: Promotion, Retirement and Royal Navy Officers, 1830-1890', *The Mariner's Mirror* 81/3 (August 1995).

Brown, D K, 'Speed of Sailing Warships 1793 – 1840', in *Les Empires En Guerre et Paix: 1793-1860*, Les Journées franco-anglaises d'histoire de la marine 1990.

Drew, A, ' Memoir of John Phillimore', in *United Services Journal* (June 1850).

[Thomas Haliburton], 'The arrival of the Chesapeake in Halifax in 1813, as described by Thomas Haliburton', *American Neptune* 57/2 (1998).

Owen, H, '"I shall make five sons of mine fight for their King and Country": The Naval sons of William IV and Mrs Jordan', *The Mariner's Mirror* 83/1 (February 1997).

2.4. Theses

Slope, N, 'HMS Trent, A Social Survey: 5 April 1796 – 25 July 1797'. Unpublished MA Thesis, Thames Valley University.

INDEX

Page references in **bold** indicate tables

GREENGATES

Persephone Book Nº 113
Published by Persephone Books Ltd 2015
Reprinted 2017 and 2022

First published by Victor Gollancz and by
Frederick A Stokes, New York in 1936

Endpapers taken from the design for a 1935
floor linoleum © MODA/Mary Evans Picture Library

Typeset in ITC Baskerville by
Keystroke, Wolverhampton

Printed and bound in Germany by
GGP Media GmbH, Poessneck

9781910263037

Persephone Books Ltd
8 Edgar Buildings
Bath BA1 2EE
01225 425050

www.persephonebooks.co.uk

GREENGATES

by

R C SHERRIFF

✳✳✳✳✳✳✳

with a new preface by

JULIET GARDINER

PERSEPHONE BOOKS
BATH

PREFACE

✳✳✳✳✳✳✳✳

R[obert] C[edric] Sherriff is best known for the harrowing play *Journey's End* set over four days in an infantry officers' dug-out in March 1918, towards the end of the First World War. The drama is based on the letters that Sherriff, who was severely wounded at Ypres, sent home from the trenches. The play was first performed in 1928 with Laurence Olivier, then twenty-one years old, in the lead role, and it ran for over two years at the Savoy Theatre and is still revived in the West End today. Yet after the success of his masterpiece, Sherriff seemed unable to produce another play that caught the public's imagination in the same way. His career as a writer was in the doldrums when, sitting in a deck chair on the promenade at Bognor Regis, he had an idea for a novel that indeed was to revive his popularity. *The Fortnight in September* (Persephone book no.67) is set in a world that Sherriff knew intimately, 1930s suburban life among the middle and lower-middle classes: he had been born in Hampton Wick in 1896 and lived there with his mother, until they moved to nearby Esher.

The Thirties is a much maligned period in Britain's history – characterised by WH Auden as 'a low, dishonest decade', a judgement he pronounced while sitting on a bar stool in New York's Lower East Side, having fled the approach of war in Europe. And the titles of several subsequent books add to this condemnatory view: *The Devil's Decade, The Dark Valley, Borrowed Time* and, most recently, Richard Overy's *The Morbid Age*.

Indeed, it was a bleak time for many. Britain was a deeply divided society with high levels of unemployment and under-employment in the north, the lowlands of Scotland and the mining villages of South Wales. In these areas of traditional industries such as shipbuilding, textiles and iron and steel manufacture in decline, there was chronic – sometimes acute – poverty, malnutrition, sickness, the constant spectre of the hated means test, and a general feeling of hopelessness with no solutions forthcoming from the National Government.

However, life was somewhat different in large areas of the Midlands and the South East. By the mid-1930s the British economy was slowly picking up with the growth of light industries to serve the domestic market – engineering, the manufacture of synthetic textiles, electronic components, pharmaceuticals, more and more cars rolling off the pro-duction lines, plus an increasing demand for 'white goods' for the home. Perhaps most important of all – and part of the reason for the boom in consumer demand – was an increasingly robust construction industry that was slowly building new dwellings to re-house the thousands who were displaced as the result of the demolition of acres of insanitary, overcrowded slum dwellings in London and other large cities. Labour was cheap, materials plentiful, and mortgages and credit easy to obtain at low rates of interest; so it was not only government subsidies to local authorities to build huge new estates of council houses to rent, such as Wythenshawe near Manchester and Becontree in Essex, that enabled the 1930s explosion of home construction.

The decade was also synonymous with the rapid growth of suburbia. This was initially ribbon developments, usually of semi-detached, owner-occupier houses strung out along arterial roads radiating from cities; later such houses were more often grouped into estates for the middle and more prosperous lower-middle classes. Such houses were usually built by 'spec' developers, rather than to commission. Some of the builders, such as Wates or John Laing, were large, others were small firms which had to sell the first few houses in a new road or close to be able to finance the rest of its development.

'Architecture in the 1930s in Britain played a larger role in cultural debate than at any time since the height of the Gothic Revival eighty years before,' says the architectural historian Alan Powers. There was the work of émigré architects from Nazi Germany such as Walter Gropius, Ernö Goldfinger, Erich Mendelsohn and Berthold Lubetkin; the Russian Serge Chermayeff; the Canadian Wells Coates; and then there were natives like Maxwell Fry and Oliver Hill. They designed such iconic buildings as the De La Warr Pavilion in Bexhill-on-Sea, Marine Court in Hastings, the Midland Hotel in Morecambe, and (in North London) the Lawn Road flats in Hampstead and various other avant-garde buildings. Almost all these were in the south, where the wealthy clients of Bauhaus-influenced architects managed to persuade often reluctant local author- ities to grant permission for stark, concrete habitats. These

✳✳✳✳✳✳✳✳✳✳

are the buildings that typify the Thirties today – houses looking like an ocean liner in dry dock, smooth, sinuous white
curving walls, punctuated by Crittall metal windows with often
porthole windows on stairs and landings, and above all a flat
sun roof, signifier of all that was modern (or *moderne* in the
architecture-speak of the time). As WH Auden put it in 1937
in his poem 'Letter to Lord Byron':

> We're entering now the Eotechnic Phase
> Thanks to the [National Electric] Grid and all those
>   new alloys. . .
> Huge plate-glass windows, walls absorbing noise. . .
> And all the furniture is chromium-plated.

Functional, not ornamented, regular 'machines for living', in
Le Corbusier's words.

The interiors offered a model of what we now revere as
minimalism. Light streamed in through large plate-glass
windows, bouncing off white walls, polished parquet floors
were laid in a herringbone pattern, and the spacious rooms
were lined with fitted wardrobes and cupboards in pale
plywood or light oak. There was a sparse scattering of simple
boxy furniture that looked less substantial than the heavy
reproduction Jacobean designs with carvings and 'barley
sugar stick' legs that tended to be the default design of most
British furniture between the wars. The curtains were maybe
a Christopher Heal or Duncan Grant print, or there was a
plain, rough-textured fabric at the windows, a cubist or 'jazz'
rug, designed by Marion Dorn perhaps, on the floor, a few

select books housed in a 'Penguin Donkey', a portable wooden bookcase by the Isokon design company; the odd well-chosen vase and perhaps a streamlined art deco ornament, possibly incorporating a clock: modernist, sleek, elegant – if not exactly oozing cosy comfort.

However, these 'flat roofer' architects and the houses and flats they built constituted a small minority of the 1930s house-building boom. Even though the vision appears in a dilute form in such settlements as Silver End in Essex, which provided houses and facilities for the workforce of the Crittall metal window factory on the paternalistic Bourneville or Port Sunlight model of earlier decades, these were not the sort of houses that Sherriff lived in or wrote about in *Greengates*. In his quietly wry, true to life and frequently rather moving novel (published by Victor Gollancz, who would publish George Orwell's *The Road to Wigan Pier* the following year), Sherriff again excelled as the acute miniaturist and profound observer of human foibles and frailties that readers will recall from *The Fortnight in September*. When this was published in 1931 its author was described as a worthy successor to Charles Dickens, and it established Sherriff's reputation as a sharp and perceptive chronicler of lives that, despite their undramatic domestic banalities, often reveal greater truths than might initially appear.

Greengates is ostensibly about a house built in the 1930s, about how and why a retired couple, the Baldwins, came to buy it, and how it changed their lives. Its subject matter holds up a mirror to the social and cultural preoccupations of the decade: the desire for a home of one's own, the slow seepage of an attenuated form of modernism into a profoundly traditional society, the nuances of class, status and taste. It also addresses the urgent question of the changing nature of the countryside, with the fall in land values and the concomitant encroachment of the town, and the urbanisation of England (an issue pursued by the architect of Portmeirion, Clough William-Ellis, in his book *England and the Octopus* and by others).

Tom Baldwin had been 'in insurance' in the City, a man of regular dress and habits who, at 58, had been looking forward to retirement. There was so much that needed doing in the gaunt late Victorian terraced house in Brondesbury Crescent off the Edgware Road in north-west London where he and his wife Edith (or Edie in moments of affection) had lived all their married life, for which, as a regular commuter on the 8.15 a.m. train, he had never had time. The house needed redecorating and 'brightening up' – a fact highlighted by the fact that the simply designed modern-looking clock that Tom had been presented with on his retirement just didn't look right on the old-fashioned mantelpiece in the fusty, gloomy dining room. The garden needed a lot of hard work too – to bring the tired shrubs, the patchy lawn and the wilting flowers back to glory. And, of course, Tom and Edith would have time to do the crossword puzzle together, read companionably on either side of the fire in the evening, go for walks, take outings on the Green Line bus or even go to the occasional matinée.

Only it didn't work out like that.

Tom found that the little jobs in the house remained dispiritingly unfinished and, despite strenuous hours of double digging and the application of bags of chemical fertiliser, the garden failed to revivify and he concluded that the soil was simply worn out. Nor did his study of history that he had hoped would yield some new discoveries, a long-lost language perhaps, prove fruitful. Publishers rejected the manuscript he submitted, declining to publish his retelling of Britain's island story, which, in his view made it more accessible than the dusty tomes he had been obliged to plough through for *his* research.

Moreover, with Tom's retirement, the Baldwins' marriage was under strain. Previously the couple had enjoyed talking through their days over dinner served by their elderly, somewhat curmudgeonly maid, Ada. Tom would relay office gossip that amused Edith, while she would recount the people she had met out shopping, the bargains she had managed to pick up, the gossip of Brondesbury Terrace. But now, since the couple were together all day, their separate spheres merged and there was nothing to talk about in the evenings. Edith, who had been looking forward to the companionship of retirement, instead found the comfortable routines she had established over nearly forty years disrupted. Her habit of taking a little nap after lunch in an armchair by the fire was no longer possible since 'her' armchair had been thoughtlessly requisitioned by Tom (who had expected a three-course lunch rather than the bread and cheese Edith had been used to eating) to read the 'picture paper' as he smoked his pipe. If she wanted a rest, Edith had to retire to their cold bedroom.

It was as if, like the tired soil in the garden, the previously contented energetic life of the couple was leaching away; there was nothing to enjoy in the house in the same way any more, nothing to look forward to.

Unexpectedly, all that changed. One autumn Saturday, Edith managed to persuade a reluctant Tom to go for a country walk that they had enjoyed during the many weekends when Tom was working, but they hadn't taken for a long time.

The couple toiled breathlessly through the familiar woods and fields until they breasted the hill that looked down on a small village in a valley, where stood the teashop where they had always ended their hike with tea and scones by a crackling fire.

But what now greeted the Baldwins' gaze was no longer the familiar tranquil rural scene but a sea of churned-up mud, bulldozers, half-built walls, piles of planks and bricks, all evidence of intensive building activity. Descending the steep slope with trepidation, they discovered that a new housing estate was being built and, to Edith's amazement, the Baldwins found themselves accepting the invitation of a personable young estate agent to take a look round the show house. They were enchanted with it.

Strictly speaking, 'Welden' did not qualify as the suburbs: indeed Tom Baldwin rejoices in leaving suburbia (the Edgware Road!) for the countryside. But it soon would. The gap between the urban and the rural, the green belt, that was supposed to confine the urban sprawl, was more like a number of pocket-handkerchief sized green spaces strung out like bunting rather than a chastity belt of refusal. Yet everything was done by the developers of such estates to emphasise the rural rather than the urban. No roads or streets, just closes and crescents and avenues and drives: the houses given names such as 'The Brambles' 'The Limes', 'The Hollies' and 'Woodland Grove'.

As the poet John Betjeman, 'a child of the past', says in *Metroland,* his 'ode to creeping surburbia' televised in 1963, as he takes the Metropolitan line from Baker Street through the green and leafy country of Hertfordshire, pausing awhile to admire Neasden and Wembley, 'lured by the lush country-side', it is home to the city clerk, turned countryman again and yet connected to the city by train. Soon, the 'mild country acres of Bucks, and Herts and Middlesex' will yield to 'Metroland'; and houses (like the one that Tom and Edith found so attractive) will stand on fields that once were bright with buttercups, and oaks and elms rose above the rooftops. 'The country had come to the city, north down Hertfordshire way' and city workers and dwellers wanted to claim a patch of that bosky rurality.

Soon the Baldwins had made their decision to purchase a house they would call 'Greengates'. The next few weeks were a whirlwind of activity: putting 'Grasmere' on the market, and, since it was to be the start of a new life, a root and branch transformation, arranging for their heavy old furniture to be sold at auction. They spent days trailing round the shops choosing furniture, curtains and kitchen equipment to be as like those they had seen in the show house as possible.

Like *The Fortnight in September, Greengates* was enthusiastically received when it was published in 1936. Writing in *The Listener,* the farmer and novelist of the countryside, Adrian Bell (*Corduroy,* published in 1930, had been a bestseller) called it 'that rarity, a complete novel . . . one that is completely experienced, whose success is both local and cumulative . . . in which every detail tends towards the whole'. And he instanced as evidence of Sherriff's exquisite mastery, his description of the evening before the sale of the Baldwins' furniture and effects at 'Grasmere' when Tom Baldwin, arriving home 'dropped his umbrella in Lot 1 and hung up his hat on Lot 2'.

I was brought up in a Thirties house designed by my father in 1934. It was named 'The Laurels' in honour of a rather scrubby hedge that separated our house from next door. But the attraction of concrete and plate glass seems to have by-passed my father's aesthetic horizons – or more likely, he had dismissed them, as he drew plans for council houses, branch libraries and a cricket pavilion. 'The Laurels' (built in the Hertfordshire countryside, as was Sherriff's 'Greengates') was exactly as children draw houses, square, with a chimney at each corner, its symmetry emphasised by wooden framed windows on either side of the front door, which was reached by a curving crazy-paving path flanked by standard roses, a castellated wall hung with swags of heavy chains surrounding the front garden. And, almost inevitably, there was a low front gate set in the wall, painted a green that was midway between British racing green and leaf green, a colour as ubiquitous in the Thirties as Farrow & Ball's 'Downpipe' or 'Elephant's Breath' is today. And this gate had another characteristic Thirties idiom carved into it, a rising sun, its rays stretching out to signal the new day.

In this, our house was similar to 'Greengates', but not *nearly* as grand: we did not have a maid's bedroom since we did not have a maid – just a 'char' who came in to 'do' for my mother two or three times a week. Our furniture was still in the reproduction Jacobean style – probably bought from Drages in Oxford Street, Maples or Waring and Gillow rather than Heal's or Dunn's of Bromley. We had an uncut moquette three-piece suite, a rust-coloured chenille cloth to protect the highly polished oak dining table, lazy-daisy embroidered linen head-rests on the arm-chairs, and ash trays on a leather strap over the arms of the easy-chairs. We didn't have a print of 'The Laughing Cavalier' (which could be obtained by saving up coupons from cigarette packets) hanging over the beige and brown tiled fireplace, but I do recall a picture of rollicking abbots above the oak sideboard upon which were lined a crystal decanter and a row of matching sherry and port glasses, which were only activated at Christmas or on special occasions. The walls were papered with porridge coloured – and textured – paper with a deep border of leaves in autumnal tints. In our house, culture got a nod from an upright piano on which my mother played familiar arias from Handel's *Messiah* every Sunday evening, a Bakelite wireless on a small mahogany veneer table standing below my father's complete set of Charles Dickens' novels, housed in a purpose-built alcove.

'Greengates' owed rather more to the influence of the 'flat roofers' than my childhood home. Its expanses of glass and airy interiors pushed it considerably further along the 'moderne' spectrum than our house, and the rising sun on its eponymous gate really was to prove a new dawn for Tom and Edith Baldwin.

****

In March 1938, a doctor, writing in the medical journal *The Lancet* identified what he described as 'suburban neurosis', which seemed particularly to affect women since they now had more leisure what with the shopping being delivered, modern houses that were easy to clean, and electrical appliances to help do this with less elbow grease. The rupture of the extended family that a move to the suburbs often entailed did not appear to have entered the equation yet, as it would a couple of decades later (this is described in Michael Young and Peter Wilmott's sociological survey *Family and Kinship in the East End of London*).

Much thought was given to how to alleviate this isolation in the 1930s by trying to foster a community, rather than just a collection of proximate houses. But these attempts rarely met with success. Newcomers, particularly those relocated from the slums, were doubtless delighted to get away from the hugger-mugger life of urban overcrowding, valuing their new privacy as paramount, the neat privet hedges around their front gardens metaphorical fortress walls, 'minding your own business' and 'keeping yourself to yourself' their mottoes.

The gentle charms and the reassuring details of domestic life which Sherriff so brilliantly captures were to figure in a number of books and films in the decades after *Greengates* was published. The disruption of war, the separation of families, the loss of houses and possessions, had made the home a sanctuary to be treasured, the comfort of loved objects an anchor to a normal, calmer peacetime life as captured by Jan Struther's Mrs Miniver articles in *The Times* and, most poignantly, in David Lean's proseletysing film, *Brief Encounter* based on a play by Noel Coward and starring Celia Johnson. This showed how the pull of the home, hearth and the familiar (including a dull, pipe-smoking husband) would keep a housewife steady in rejecting the temptation of a charming and virtuous stranger (Trevor Howard), who promised a new life and fresh horizons.

RC Sherriff had a rather more adventurous life than his fictional creations: the era of the silent film was all but over by the 1930s and movie moguls, desperate for writers who could pen convincing dialogue, alighted on Sherriff. He was shipped out to Hollywood (accompanied by his mother), as were Aldous Huxley and P G Wodehouse, but, unlike them, Sherriff was rather successful, writing the script for the film of H G Wells' novel *The Invisible Man,* and later the feel-good film version of James Hilton's sentimental novel of school life, *Goodbye Mr Chips.*

But the lure of his natural habitat proved too strong: Sherriff (and his mother) returned to suburban Surrey, the environment he understood so well, with its rigid nuances and indicators of class. He died in 1975 aged seventy-nine in Kingston-upon-Thames, where he had been educated at the grammar school, and only a few miles from where he had been born. A life lived full circle.

Juliet Gardiner London 2014

GREENGATES

CHAPTER I

In FROSTY DAYS GONE BY, the chief lunch-hour entertainment for the City of London was the watching of men raise horses that had fallen in Cornhill. To-day there is a better supply of sand to keep up the few horses that remain, and the loiterer has turned to less exciting things. A workman with an electric drill can command a five-deep audience, a man clicking spoons between his fingers to the music of an organ can do almost as well. Police have to be called to regulate the crowd when a water main bursts, and any old building can draw a mass of sky-gazers during the first dangerous days of its demolition. On fine days the whole City enjoys a few minutes in the fresh air between the end of lunch and the beginning of the afternoon: but for so short a time the entertainment must be free and the Londoner's principle is that anything is worth watching for nothing, particularly other people in trouble and other people working.

Mr. Baldwin enjoyed his own quiet form of entertainment, and frequently, for a few minutes after two o'clock, you would see a slight, well-dressed man, with grey hair and a thoughtful, clean-shaven face, leaning against the parapet of London Bridge, watching the barges unload.

Sometimes, on a fine day, a few boys would perch up on the parapet beside him, eat sandwiches and throw the crusts to the gulls.

But usually he was almost alone, with the river beneath him and the clattering steps of passers-by. He was alone one autumn afternoon, for a raw east wind was blowing up the Thames, a hint of frost lay in the air, and people hurried across the Bridge for the shelter of the narrow streets.

It was not an exciting entertainment at the best of times, but the blue-jerseyed, toiling backs on the wharf were a change from those that only moved to toss a few papers into a wire letter basket, and the smell of mud and tar was healthier, to Mr. Baldwin's way of thinking, than floor polish and centrally heated mahogany. The river had not changed as the streets had changed: they would never change this distant view of Tower Bridge, or the red, muddy swirl, or block out these last remaining stretches of London sky. The Bridge gave command of the open air, in the City you crept like an insect in a rut.

The giant cranes on the far side of the river were the only arrivals in recent years. Sometimes Mr. Baldwin crossed the Bridge to watch them slowly raise themselves like stiff, lumbago-stricken monsters, curtsey and drop fat bales of merchandise into open hatches as neatly as one would drop a seed into a hole. But generally his conservative eye preferred the blue-jerseyed, toiling backs, the skilful twist that took a rolling barrel through a narrow door.

Despite the cold wind he stayed beyond his usual time this afternoon. His lunch hour closed at a quarter past two, but even when he turned and walked away, he hesitated, and wandered down the side streets. He pictured the whole staff busy at the afternoon's work and the one empty desk behind the glass screen. He felt like a small boy playing truant, for he rarely failed to be back on the stroke of time. But when Wilson, the Manager, had passed him as he had left for lunch, he had said, "Don't hurry back to-day."

So Mr. Baldwin loitered against his will. The City still fascinated him: he could still probe into forgotten corners and find unexpected things. It fascinated him but had never made him feel at ease. Every inch of it was too fantastically valuable: the ownership of a few square yards would keep a man in luxury for life and you could not love a piece of land that could bury itself in its own gold. Every inch of it had been so many times disturbed, so honeycombed with wires and pipes, tunnelled and vaulted, chewed and spat out by mechanical excavators, turned over and built over, fought over and schemed over. Even when they had hollowed out the space for the new office lavatories they had found a Roman Milestone and a wooden water pipe from Cromwell's day. The best Museums of London still lay underground.

No one appeared to look with unusual interest at Mr. Baldwin as he walked into the office at three o'clock. The Cashiers were busy as they always were on the days following Michaelmas: the telephone was ringing, several clients stood at the rail with papers spread before them— everything was so exactly the same, so normal that he could not avoid a slight sense of disappointment. A day of such consequence to him might at least have sent a ripple across those bowed, working heads.

As Chief Cashier, he occupied a screened-in corner to himself, but glass played so large a part in the screens that the official behind them was always known as the goldfish. His desk was clear of official papers, but it still remained for him to clear out the personal relics that had accumulated there; a strange assortment that had travelled with him from desk to desk in his gradual rise to the screened-in corner; odd things that for some reason or another had not been destroyed or taken home.

For once and for all he had got to decide what to do with his Menu of the Staff Jubilee Dinner, held at Gatti's in 1889. It had been too valuable to destroy but too dangerous to take home, for Denny had been on the staff in those days, and Denny had become a famous black-and-white artist a few years later. Amongst the high-spirited after-dinner scribblings on the Menu card was an authentic, early Denny—unfortunately a somewhat indecent Denny. To rub it out would have been vandalism, to take it home and risk Edith seeing it would have been unthinkable, and so it had lain amongst this jetsam, dusty and fading, for thirty-six years.

It occurred to Mr. Baldwin that one of the Juniors might like to have it, but there would be no purpose in giving it away unless he pointed out the reason for its value, and to do that would scarcely be in keeping with his position as Chief Cashier. The card was still creased where he had folded it for his pocket on that distant night: it had been his first Dinner: he had been in the office five years and he was to marry Edith in the summer. Huîtres—Potage Russe —Whitebait—Duckling—somebody had scrawled here, " Where are you going when this is over ? " He tried to decipher the names, and the misty pencil scrawls took misty form—ghosts in high collars—in frock coats that dangled to boot heels hitched to the crossbars of absurdly high stools: flickering gas jets over each office desk, a baking heat from fifty jets when a pea-soup fog demanded lights all day. A curious crowd round the first telephone, touching it as if it were a bomb—a whiskered Messenger screwing down a copying book in a machine that looked like Caxton's printing press—pulling out clammy, sodden letters, folding them and stamping them. The Queen was nearly seventy and they used to wonder how much longer the head of a girl would appear on her lilac postage stamps. The office itself had scarcely changed, except for the central heating and electric light. The Management prided itself upon its old foundation and tried to retain the atmosphere of the past. The door was the same that the merry party had used on their way up West for the Gatti's Dinner, but they had climbed on to a growling iron rimmed omnibus, young Mr. Baldwin beside the driver, with a lamp-lit view of a swaying tail and sweating haunches. Everybody above the rank of office boy had worn a top hat in those times, and a woman in the City was as rare as a horse to-day. And the streets themselves: swirls of dust on an August evening; a mire on a winter night; unbelievably quiet when the staff worked late at overtime. Now and then the clip-clop of a hansom, taking a City Magnate to the station . . . so near to yesterday that the closing of the eyes brought back the very sounds. . . .

He lay the Menu card aside, for despite years of indecision he still had a few more minutes to decide its fate. These casually collected relics linked themselves together and formed a panorama. He propped up the lid of his desk, for he did not want anyone to see what he was doing. There were a few picture postcards from men on their holidays: Bexhill, Lowestoft—one from an adventurer who had gone to Guernsey: a report of an Inter-Office Chess Match, kept for its record of " T. H. Baldwin, 1. F. Cass, o "—report of an Office Cricket Match: " Baldwin, run out, 3." There was a cigarette picture of Mornington Cannon, the jockey, a few fossilised pieces of india-rubber and a sweepstake ticket. Amongst the fluff and cake crumbs in a corner there lay a small splinter of anti-aircraft shell that he had picked up in the doorway of the office. He destroyed the papers but he dropped the splinter into his pocket. There was a musty sentiment about old papers that was best forgotten, but the sentiment of this jagged, glittering piece of steel was of another kind. It conjured up cold starlight nights of loneliness, with whistle and truncheon, when for a few dark hours he had been a different kind of man from the Baldwin who had defeated F. Cass at chess and the Baldwin run out for three in the office cricket match.

He scraped a few nibs and paper clips together, dropped them into an envelope and put them in his pocket. The desk was empty, he lowered the lid and was surprised to see Henslip the Messenger just closing the main doors. He had been dreaming in his desk for over half an hour, but he was glad the time had passed so quickly.

He knew exactly what was going to happen now. Strictly speaking it was a secret shared by the staff and withheld from him alone, but he had shared the secret with the others so many times in the past that it could not hold any surprise for him now.

First of all, Henslip the Messenger disappeared into the Manager's room. Then he emerged, went downstairs and returned with a small brown-paper parcel. After another

short disappearance he re-emerged and passed with a
furtive importance from one member of the staff to
another whispering something to each. Each member of
the staff, upon receiving the whisper, glanced curiously
towards Mr. Baldwin's desk, slid off his stool and disappeared into the Manager's room.

He saw the girls file downstairs from the typewriting
rooms and follow the men: gradually the office emptied
until Mr. Baldwin sat alone behind his glass screen. Then
there was a hitch. The telephone rang, Henslip hurried
with an impatient grunt to answer it, and called out,
" Mr. Robins !—Somebody wants to report a Fire
Claim ! " A harassed Junior came out of the Manager's
room, and for a few moments Mr. Baldwin sat listening to
words that seemed now to eddy back from the past—
" Yes—I see—curtain blew into candle flame—have you
got your policy number ?—Never mind, I'll turn it up.
I'll send you a Claim Form. Good-bye."

Henslip was fidgeting outside the telephone box. He
hustled the Junior back to the Manager's room and crossed
the silent office to Mr. Baldwin's desk.

" Will you come into Mr. Wilson's room, sir ? "

Mr. Baldwin looked up from an almanack with an
attempt at surprise.

" Yes. All right. I'll come now."

He was glad to feel so calm and controlled, for he had
been dreading this moment for days. He waited until
Henslip had gone, then tore the Gatti's Menu into little
squares and threw them into the fire as he passed on his
way to the Manager's room. It seemed to be the right and
only moment to destroy it.

Mr. Wilson had a spacious, cheerful room, flooded with

sunlight on fine mornings, for its windows were upon a side street with low buildings opposite. Now the lights were on and above the buildings lay a green strip of smoky sky. On the mantelpiece stood a photograph of Mr. Wilson's wife, for it was a custom of successive Managers to have some personal decoration in this room. At one time Mr. Baldwin had had visions of a photograph of Edith standing there, but things had not worked out that way.

The whole staff, men and girls, were grouped round the walls, and Mr. Wilson stood behind his desk, his tea tray pushed aside to make way for the brown-paper parcel.

" Are we all here ? "

" Yes, sir," said Henslip, closing the door.

It is embarrassing for people who know each other to stand together in a crowd. Young ones, unused to the ceremony, shuffled, looked down at their feet or at their fingernails, older ones gazed with bland smiles at Mr. Baldwin, the sort of smiles used at weddings, turned on very carefully to half pressure to prevent them wearing out too soon. Mr. Baldwin took up his position a little in front of the rest, like a prisoner about to hear sentence at Court Martial. He smiled feebly at Mr. Wilson, then lowered his eyes to the edge of the Manager's desk. Henslip stood nearest him and he caught the slight odour of long-used flannel that always rose from the Messenger's red, polished face. A coal popped in the fire, and there was silence. Then Mr. Wilson cleared his throat and began.

" Mr. Baldwin. The staff has asked me to hand you this little souvenir on the occasion of your retirement. I need hardly say what a sad occasion it is for us although I'm sure it's a very happy one for you. We shall miss you, for although we may be able to fill your official position we cannot replace your personality."

There were some appreciative murmurs, and Mr. Wilson turned to the staff.

" Mr. Baldwin joined the staff of this office in 1884: he has given honourable service for forty-one years. He could tell us some interesting stories of the naughty nineties if he wanted to—even of the eighties, too ! There's no need for me to enlarge upon Mr. Baldwin's virtues, for they are known to you all. The office will remember him as a loyal and devoted servant: we personally shall remember him as an upright gentleman. We all wish you, Mr. Baldwin, many years of the happiness and leisure that you so justly deserve, and we hope you will often come in to see us. We ask you to accept this little present as a token of our esteem."

Mr. Wilson waited for the polite applause to die away, then drew aside the brown paper and revealed a neat square clock in varnished oak. He picked it up with a smile and put it down again on the corner of the desk nearest Mr. Baldwin.

It was Mr. Baldwin's turn. He took a step forward, his fingers fumbled the clock as he turned to face the staff. He did not feel like Mr. Baldwin at all, he was a strange, light-headed person who had had some vague connection with a Mr. Baldwin in the past, who began to recite words that this Mr. Baldwin had taught him.

" Mr. Wilson, Ladies and Gentlemen. I really can't tell you how much I—I value this lovely present. I shall always keep it to remind me of the days in the old office, because they've been good days. I'm sorry they're over, and I'm going to miss you all. It's very kind of you to think of giving me such a beautiful present. Thank you very much . . . very much indeed."

The short speech, with its abrupt close took everybody by surprise and there was an awkward little silence before Mr. Wilson nodded to Henslip to open the door. The telephone began calling out like a spoilt child annoyed at being left alone: someone hurried off to soothe it, the girls and the Juniors edged along the walls and disappeared. Some of the senior men shook hands with Mr. Baldwin, others, less senior, nearly did. Gradually the room emptied and Mr. Baldwin was alone with the Manager.

He had never felt at ease with Wilson. Five years Mr. Wilson's senior, it had been difficult for him when this tall, puckered man arrived from the Head Office to take command.

" Well, Baldwin—you're a gentleman of leisure now ! "

" Yes," said Mr. Baldwin with a faint smile.

" What are you going to do with yourself ? "

" Oh, there's a good many things been waiting for this to happen. Garden, you know—and books to read—and—and hobbies——"

" That's right. Hobbies are the thing."

Henslip the Messenger tapped at the door and peeped in.

" Shall I do the clock up for you, Mr. Baldwin ? "

" Yes, do please—Henslip."

The Manager himself took the clock across to Henslip and Mr. Baldwin followed with the paper and string.

" I'll find a stronger bit of string than that," said Henslip.

The Manager turned back into the room and offered Mr. Baldwin a cigarette.

" Don't forget to look us up sometimes."

" Certainly," replied Mr. Baldwin, knowing quite well that retired members of the staff were a curse when they came wandering round, wasting people's time.

" Is your wife keeping well ? "

" Quite."

" That's good."

The Manager's eyes were upon a pile of letters waiting for his signature, and Mr. Baldwin held out his hand.

" Well, good-bye, Mr. Wilson. Thanks for the nice things you said in that speech."

Mr. Wilson smiled. " I meant it. Well, good-bye."

He met one of the Juniors as he went downstairs for his overcoat and hat: a pleasant lad who lived somewhere out in the country and had an hour's train journey to get home. He stopped, flashed a smile at Mr. Baldwin and said: " We're going to miss you a lot, sir—the way you always help us "—the boy played football on Saturday afternoons and Mr. Baldwin had sometimes helped him to get away sharp at one o'clock by taking a bundle of letters from him and doing them up himself—" we've just been saying so downstairs . . . how decent you've been to us . . . thanks. . . ." The boy's library book slid from under his arm and clattered on the stairs, there was a dive for it . . . a laugh . . . a flustered handshake . . . a cold hand, still damp from washing. " Don't be silly," said Mr. Baldwin. " I've never done anything."

" You've done lots and we're going to miss you. Don't forget to come in and see us sometimes, sir." Another smile and the boy was gone. Something flew up and stung

Mr. Baldwin at the back of his nose and he hastened downstairs to the lavatories.

A little later, with a neat brown parcel under his arm, he rumbled the main door to and joined the broad stream of home-goers. The last moments in the office had seemed unreal to him, but everything was cool and normal here: the same brown, shining street—the same swinging of umbrellas and bobbing of white folded newspapers—the same giant buildings filled with light—the same deep murmur—the same narrow strips of remote, unnoticed sky.

CHAPTER II

WHEN A MAN RETIRES, and time is no longer a matter of urgent importance, his colleagues generally present him with a clock. But the unmeant irony is balanced by an equally unmeant appropriateness, for while a man in retirement is no longer governed by hours and minutes, he very frequently wants to know the time.

Mr. Baldwin felt unreasonably self-conscious standing on Broad Street platform with the clock under his arm. Although it was done up in brown paper and nobody could possibly guess what it was, he could not help feeling that a placard reading " RETIRED ! " hung round his neck.

The crowd around him, companions of a thousand journeys, seemed detached and remote from him now. The bond that had held him to them had snapped at four o'clock when the door of the office closed. His spirit was no longer with them, but his body would have to stand amongst them on the platform and sit amongst them in the train until a porter called out " Brondesbury Park ! " He was glad when the train came in, and the clock, with his hat on top of it, lay on the luggage rack above his head.

An elderly man in the far corner had also placed a parcel on the luggage rack, and Mr. Baldwin wondered whether he, too, had received a clock that afternoon. Then the man leant forward and began a vigorous

Bσ

conversation with a friend. Mr. Baldwin caught the words
" stocktaking next week . . . late evenings . . . more business in the spring," and he knew that the old man's parcel
contained no clock: he could not make him a spiritual
companion for the journey home. All these other passengers, the old man included, would go to the City to-
morrow morning and be on this train to-morrow night.
With a deepening loneliness he opened his evening paper.

The train drew out and side-stepped clumsily across
the points. The chilly night had been observed by the
railway authorities, and they had caused a stuffy, metallic
smell to ooze in warm clouds from beneath the seat and
up Mr. Baldwin's trouser legs. He watched the familiar
electric signs pass by for his last inspection and began to
realise how little he had prepared himself for what had
happened this afternoon. Freedom—leisure: they were
words for inspiration, and he was like an old canary with
its cage door open, crouching on the furthest end of its
perch. He had made no plans. If he had thought of it at all
he had rarely planned anything beyond an extra half
hour in bed and a morning in the garden, but mostly he
had put the matter uneasily from his mind. Retirement,
he had told himself, could take care of itself when it came.
It meant decay: the beginning of the end and he had no
desire to premeditate it.

But now he began to think as a marooned man might
think as he calculates the time his food will last. There
was his scrap-book with a good many cuttings waiting to
be stuck in: a picture frame to repair and some drawers
to clear out: there was the garden: an afternoon walk
and books he had been waiting to read. He had been
given his reward for forty years of work. He had yearned

a thousand times for freedom, and now that it had come he was afraid of it. It was the fear of a man who, having habitually enjoyed two apples a day, is suddenly called upon to eat six in the same period.

He was a man of method; he had planned his leisure in such a way that its whole span was comfortably filled —no part being overcrowded and no part empty. Home usually at six, there was a half-hour's rest and talk with Edith, a walk until dinner-time, his diary, business and books from then until bed, with a visit to the pictures once a week and an occasional theatre in the West End. For Saturday afternoons there was always a football match to watch in the Park and for Sundays there was the garden, tea with friends and some pleasant, aimless pottering. In the past, without a moment's boredom, he had comfortably enjoyed four hours of leisure each day: his problem was how to dispose of twelve. If he were an old man he could doze away the extra hours before the fire, but he was not an old man: he was only fifty-eight.

He decided to postpone the problem until after dinner and turned again to his paper. There was nothing of special interest on the first page and he was just about to fold it over to the centre when his eye caught a small headline and paragraph in the lower right-hand corner—

" TRAGEDY OF RETIREMENT "

It hit him in the stomach and dried his mouth. His eyes jerked away and strove to make a panic-stricken escape through the maze of print above: but they came to blind alleys: a morbid curiosity clutched at them and tried to draw them back. A devilish spirit broods over newspapers at certain times: a spirit that records " Death from Gnat Bite " on the morning a man wakes up with a small red lump on his wrist—that tells of diphtheria epidemic in the village he is on his way to for his holiday. Mr. Baldwin fumbled the paper—tried to turn it over and lose himself in other news—but in his heart he knew that defeat was ahead: even if he kept his eyes from the paragraph he would never have the strength to throw the paper away: he might put it in a drawer at home and return to it like a murderer to his crime: he might torture himself for weeks but read it in the end. He accepted the inevitable, and lowered his eyes:

" An inquest was held this morning on the body of John Herbert Stoner, 63, a retired Civil Servant, of 97 Lincoln Road, Ruislip, who was found hanging to a beam in his garage last Friday. It was stated that the deceased was a strong, healthy man, but since his retirement two years ago had become very depressed, lost interest in things and worried over imaginary troubles. His wife stated that he had no hobbies. The coroner, in returning a verdict of suicide while temporarily insane, said that tragedies due to retirement were increasing. . . ."

Mr. Baldwin lowered the paper. He felt better for having faced it. In an unexpected way he felt happier. There was no madness in his family: in any case, he had no garage and no beam, and he would never dare abuse the gas-oven while Ada ruled the kitchen. He had read the ultimate, most pitiful thing that could happen from retirement, and gained strength from it. He pitied Mr. Stoner —and despised him. He had killed himself through not knowing how to live: he had been picked out of eternity, given a tiny pinpoint of precious light and blotted it out with a rope over a garage beam: a sordid, pitiful crime.

Near by, another paragraph that recalled memories:

" President Hindenburg to-day celebrated his 78th birthday by unveiling a Memorial to his famous victories at Tannenberg. A huge crowd stood bareheaded and silent as the aged President, erect and soldier-like, performed the simple dedication. It is interesting to recall that President Hindenburg took part in the War of 1870 as Adjutant to a battalion and retired from active service in 1911 at the age of 64. . . ."

Mr. Baldwin turned his face from the yellow atmosphere of the carriage to the cold, dark, fleeting things outside. Inspiration gripped him and overwhelmed him. Fate had shown him the first paragraph to test his courage; and now it had pointed to this other, and left him in silence to think. It pointed a way, threw open doors, and shafts of exultant light rushed in.

A splendid thing had happened: he was still a young man—well under sixty—fit and healthy—keen on things: keener than ever in his life—and he was gloriously free, with a pension and at least fifteen years of full activity before him.

An hour ago he was thinking of retirement as the first step into the grave: the leisure promised for forty years had turned to a mockery—had come too late—he had dreaded it, faced it and accepted it, and now he was filled with a fierce, defiant happiness.

The golden age for a man who had lived wisely lay between sixty and seventy-five. Men had climbed from the valleys to the mountain tops in that time. There was Hindenburg, a retired soldier in 1914: world-famous at seventy—President of Germany at nearly eighty: Gladstone returned to power at seventy-six and was still a great Prime Minister at eighty-three—dozens of others—Shaw, at seventy, writing masterpieces, and here was he, coming home to retirement, thinking about one foot in the grave at fifty-eight!

It was the fashion to think of retired City clerks as finished and done with at sixty—fit for nothing but doddering into the Park and dozing over the fire. No more was expected of them: their pens were taken away: they were sent home and forgotten. He would show people that there was more to it than armchairs, slippers and memories.

In his rising excitement he crossed his legs, kicked the man opposite and apologised more heartily than he had ever apologised before. The train took wings and plunged through the night: his retirement was not going to be a hopeless chloroforming of time: instead of a " Tragedy of Retirement " he would supply the Press with a novel headline when his time came: " Man who achieved Fame after retirement from City."

He would take stock of himself: then make his plans. " I've a sound, clear brain: a tough, steady health, and no delusions. I know quite well that I am not a genius, but that is all to the good. If genius were to flame out at fifty-eight I would probably be certified.

" My course is quite clear: instead of dabbling in anæmic hobbies with the cheerless object of killing time I will select one aim: one intense purpose, concentrate my whole mind and every ounce of enthusiasm upon it and work my way to recognition.

" Anything against it?—Any reason why I shouldn't ? "

Why did not other retired City men of fifty-eight, with the bonds of an irksome job broken and a pension at their backs, adventure down the roads of burning inclination ? Because they never thought about it. Because they were too tired or lazy. Because they accepted the feeble tradition that retirement meant the end.

Nobody seemed to realise that the idea of sending men to retirement at fifty-eight or sixty was an antiquated tradition going back to the days when life ended ten years earlier than it did to-day. Retiring age had not been advanced to meet the times but men still accepted it in its old, worn out meaning, and merely used their additional span to fade away more slowly.

" I was the pioneer. I blazed the trail: I was the first man to show that in these great days of golfing grandmothers, men too can take advantage of the new meadows of fertile life that science has reclaimed from the marshes of disease ! "

That would be a good thing to say at one of his lectures, for one day he might be hailed as the man who invented a new grafting operation. One day it would become the normal thing for every man to graft a new and fascinating career upon the broken stump of his dull City life.

As the train left Camden Town he settled himself to the exciting business of selecting his new vocation. One or two people had got out, and he could stretch his legs and think better.

He ruled out at once the professions that demand a life's apprenticeship. Even if he wanted to be a lawyer, or a doctor or an architect it was too late, and he had no regrets. Men had gone into the Church at sixty, but the

Church demanded qualities he could not claim. Astronomy?—a short cut to fame was to discover a new star with
a home-made telescope. It was an idea worth thinking
about: he had read books of popular astronomy and been
fascinated, but the practice demanded mathematics which
he detested. He would not be an astronomer. Science?
No. Literature? No. You had got to grow up with literature and have something you specially wanted to write
about. Geology?—Browsing upon hillsides?—He was
getting warm.

He had known all along what he was coming to but
he wanted to test his choice by deliberately throwing other
possibilities in the way. He wanted to whittle things down
to the one fascinating thing that had always lurked in the
backgrounds of his mind. He would become an Historian.
Not merely a fireside one, but one who went out and
explored and discovered. It offered a glorious fullness to
winter evenings and sunlit days. There were a thousand
fascinating books to study—a thousand earthworks on the
downs of England, Roman fortresses and Norman castles.
Very few of them had been properly explored. The whole
pageant lay ready for him: he had but to give the signal
for the trumpets to sound and the doors to fly open. In
dark evenings by the fire he could study, make notes and
draw conclusions: in the summer he would plan excursions with Edith to historical sites. He could begin with
short articles that would throw new light upon obscure
questions, bringing him into touch with men of his own
enthusiasms—thence to more important work, full-sized
books—lectures. It demanded no more than the qualities
at his disposal: common sense, imagination, and a great
desire.

He began to plan his time, no longer how to fill it, but how to fit everything in.

First came health. He could afford the extra half hour in bed that made all the difference between a sleep-clogged morning and a clear brain. He could allow an extra five minutes in dressing that enhanced the self-respect: the extra five minutes essential to the full enjoyment of a herring. Half an hour with the paper to keep abreast with the times, and then the garden.

He had clung to the garden until now as the one straw that would keep him floating above dark pools of terrifying leisure. Now the garden would take its place as a subsidiary thing: a hobby for health's sake, with great interest thrown in.

He would rejuvenate that bald, worn out patch behind the house: reorganise it, build a rockery, refertilise it with clean chemical manures—coax that sickly laurel hedge into a billowing green gift to privacy: dig, and plant and perspire in the open air, wash and lunch.

Edith would enjoy his retirement. Lunch together would be far pleasanter than her frugal little lunch alone. He had forgotten what a difference his retirement would make to Edith, for the brief companionship of week-ends and evenings had never been enough.

But it would be in the afternoons, and in the quietness of the nights when, free from the weariness of a day in the City, he would settle down to work on his new career. It would be for those long quiet hours to prove that a man is not finished and done with when he retires from a City office. The long quiet hours that would lay the foundations for fascinating summer days. . . . " Ladies and Gentlemen, I have much pleasure in introducing Mr. Thomas

Baldwin, who is going to tell us of his fascinating discoveries at Pevensey Castle. As you all know, Mr. Baldwin has "——" Brondesbury Park ! "

Brondesbury Park ? He started up, dazed and blinking. Only four passengers remained : poor devils who would have to get up in the dark to-morrow morning, drag themselves to the station and go to the City to another day of dreary work. In the evening they would travel back once more : sit wedged together in this stuffy metallic air, in this dull, yellow light, with musty advertisements twitching overhead. Backwards and forwards, backwards and forwards for years—poor fellow prisoners.

One or two glanced up at Mr. Baldwin as he rose. They did not realise that he was saying good-bye : that his sentence was over. An hour ago his release had seemed but the opening of a door that led to another, even drearier cell. Now he had discovered a different, secret way that led to sunlit horizons—to quivering fields of new, exciting life.

He reached for his hat—a parcel under it ?—of course, they had given him a clock !

Stars of frost glittered on the platform and crunched under foot. He trotted up the steps, said " Good night ! " to the ticket collector and turned down the dark, tree-lined road that led to his home.

CHAPTER III

THE WIND HAD FALLEN, and a gathering fog was rusting the lights in the avenue that led from the main road. The stream of passengers trickled away in different directions, and Mr. Baldwin and a solitary boy with a small bag were the only ones to turn off into Brondesbury Terrace. The boy disappeared into the second gate: Mr. Baldwin's house lay a hundred yards further on, with a lamp-post in front of it that gave a glow to its placid brown face.

" Grasmere " was his own freehold property, built in 1871 and purchased by him as the result of a legacy from his uncle in 1912. The price was £700 and Mr. Baldwin was in the habit of telling intimate friends that it was the best investment he had ever made—(his other being in the Bank of Paraceta, upon the advice of a cousin).

He estimated that the rise in the value of house property since the war had increased the value of " Grasmere " to something like £1,000. He had lived there as a tenant for fifteen years before he became its owner, so it had been his home for the greater part of his career. It was a nice, semi-detached house of brown brick, relieved in front by a few quiet lozenge patterns in red and blue: a tall, thin house with a slate roof and gothic chimneys. Ada, their servant for the past seventeen years, inhabited its two perpendicular extremities—the basement kitchen and the attic bedroom. The dining-room, with bow windows upon the road, communicated by sliding doors with the drawing-room, and French windows opened from there on to the garden by way of an ironwork balcony and a few steps. An old-fashioned, uncomplaining house that had never been spurred to discontent by better things in its neighbourhood.

Mr. Baldwin hitched the clock firmly under his arm to open the gate. For some months past the front gate had been opening with increasing difficulty, with a resentful squeak that robbed the door-bell of all importance. He made a mental note of the gate as one of the things he would now have time to attend to. He could save a good deal by setting aside half an hour a day for minor repairs.

He heard his wife's familiar " All right, Ada ! " as he rang the bell. The basement stairs had begun to trouble Ada of recent years and they were in the habit of saving her the climb when they knew for certain who was at the door.

Edith stood under the hall light, and Mr. Baldwin gave her the traditional kiss. She gave no sign to suggest that this was not just another ordinary homecoming on a late autumn night.

" Was there much fog in the City ? It's been coming up here since tea-time." She looked out for a moment before she closed the door.

" Nothing to speak of," said Mr. Baldwin. " It began to look bad at lunch-time, but it cleared up. The late trains are going to catch it."

He hung up his hat, dropped his umbrella into the stand, and with the parcel under his arm went into the dining-room without removing his overcoat. There was a faint perfume: a big fire was blazing, and a smell of warm leather came from the front of the armchair. The room was at its best in the winter warmth, for the sun had a way of pointing out things that the standard lamp forgave. The sun made the purple velvet mantelpiece cover look like a cloak at an open-air pageant: the lamp gave back its dignity.

Mr. Baldwin put the parcel on the table beside Edith's work-basket. He stood casually beside it and Edith came and peered at it over her glasses.

" Got your scissors handy ? "

" What is it, Tom ? "

" Just a little thing the staff gave me. You open it."

He went into the passage and took longer than usual to remove his overcoat. He wanted her to enjoy the surprise by herself. He heard the rustling of paper, judged his time, and returned.

" Isn't that awfully nice !—it's so neat and simple."

She put it on the table and stepped back to admire it. The old walnut-wood pendulum clock on the mantelpiece, with its round, keyhole eyes, stared in mild curiosity at the little quick-ticking newcomer—reassured itself and continued its placid beat without further interest. It was a doleful clock at the best of times, but it looked at its worst at twenty-five past six, when its hands gave it a dreary, drooping moustache.

" What an awfully nice thing to have done. Wasn't it a surprise ? Weren't you pleased ? "

"They all gave something towards it," said Mr. Baldwin. There was no point in telling her that everybody got a clock when they retired.

" We'll have to find a nice place for it. Where do you think ? "

" That's what I've been wondering," said Mr. Baldwin. " We can't move that old chap up there."

" And the one in the drawing-room matches the other things."

It was a problem. The normal clock-space of the house was filled.

" What about the bedroom ? " he suggested.

" Yes. We could easily have it there. It's got a nice, quiet tick. I expect it's Swiss."

" It's the latest thing," returned Mr. Baldwin. He wondered what Edith was really thinking, for in his own heart he was disappointed. The price mattered nothing, but for a man in his position it might have been a little better: it was such a " local " affair, so obviously subscribed to by the people at his Branch alone. There were dozens of men now working at the Head Office and at other Branches who had at one time or another worked with him. It would not have cost much time or trouble to invite them to subscribe their small expression of regard. What was the clock worth ?—£3 ? He must have given fifty half-crowns in his time towards other men's retiring and wedding presents. He shook off the sordid thought and turned to the fire.

The room was warm, the curtains drawn—Edith's chair was drawn up as usual to the table so that she could do her work beneath the light. His armchair stood ready for him with his slippers beside it. Everything was the same: Edith was the same, for beyond speaking of the clock she had asked no questions. He was determined to tell her nothing for the time being of the plans he had made in the train, for although she always encouraged him in the things he did, he knew that she did not share his fascination for the past. If, on a holiday, he pointed to a ruined castle she was only fascinated by its frame of nature: the noble trees and the sky beyond it. The ruins meant little to her in themselves: she did not share his gift of breathing life into the dead relics of endeavour, of conjuring clattering hoofs from the space where a drawbridge once spanned a grass-grown moat. He would begin his work alone, and draw her gently into it as time went by. If success and recognition came to him, then her pride would be his chief reward.

He spread his knees to the warmth of the fire: the first fog signal of the evening crunched in the distance. It was very still and quiet outside. Through a chink in the curtain he could see the grizzled crown of the laurel hedge that he was going to rejuvenate. Edith, by the table, had put her work-basket on a chair beside her and was counting stitches in a low whisper, just loud enough to let him know that he need not talk unless he wished to. The old clock on the mantelpiece tocked sonorously with its pendulum: the new clock on the table ticked with the hurry and lightness of a sparrow's heart.

As a rule they talked freely during the half hour between Mr. Baldwin's arrival home and his walk before dinner. Edith would detail the domestic events of the day: he would tell her of incidents in the office and adventures in the train. He understood why Edith was silent now, for just as he had always avoided thinking about his retirement so it had become their habit never to allude to it. They had carried on during the past week as if his retirement had been thirty years away: the matter had not even been mentioned at breakfast that morning, and Edith could have no idea what he was feeling now that it had happened. She might be expecting him to burst into song : she might equally expect a flood of tears. It was clearly up to him to say something, but the more he thought, the less there was to say—he had cleared up his desk : at four o'clock he had retired : they had given him a clock and he had come home. She knew that, and as far as he could see there was no point in telling her.

He gave an artificial yawn and drummed his fingers on the arm of his chair.

" Well. It's all over."

Edith did not look up from her work. " It must have been a funny day."

He gave a short laugh and poked the fire. " It was rather. Quite ordinary, really. That was the funny part."

She lowered her work and drew the clock towards her. " It's nice to have this—to know they wanted to give you something."

He turned his head, and caught the soft, dark profile of her face beneath the lamp. Edith meant home, the City meant work, and he had thought of them as rigidly apart. But suddenly they wove themselves together : he knew that the office had been almost as much her life as his and that she would feel its loss. She had shared his thoughts, and hopes, and disappointments. The gossip he had brought home each night must have built a little Branch office in her mind, staffed by the men he talked about, buzzing with the incidents he told her of, furnished with a queer jumble of brass rails and mahogany pulpits and patches of mosaic floor : things distorted by memory, and by the shy, bewildered eyes that saw them.

For once or twice in the early days, Edith had called for him at the office before going on to a theatre. Of late years he had preferred her not to face the turmoil of the City alone, but he remembered her face as she used to sit waiting on the leather window seat, the awed, wondering eyes that roved round the brass fittings and polished partitions: the quick jerk of her head as one man called across to another: the furtive peepings at men whom she knew were his friends but whose names she did not know—he had tried to identify them afterwards—" that fat man with the big moustache—he's Burtenshaw "—" Who was the tall man sitting near the fire ? "—" Oh, that was Watson—you know—the man I told you about who plays tennis well."—" Oh, *that's* Mr. Watson !—I pictured him quite different, somehow." He had never questioned her upon what she thought of the office itself. As they used to go out together her tapping heels would seem to press patterns of their dining-room carpet on the cold mosaic floor. He shifted his chair a little, and with his eyes on her needlework, began to talk.

" Funny how it was just like any other day. You know—the going up in the train—the getting there—hanging up my hat and coat and going to my desk. Couldn't somehow believe I was doing it for the last time—one or two agents who knew I was going dropped in to shake hands. Then there was lunch just the same—— "

" What did you have ? "

Such an ordinary, everyday Edith asked the question that Mr. Baldwin had to stop to collect himself. It was such a regular, nightly question of hers that it was necessary to reassure himself that he had not dozed and dreamt his retirement; that he was not sitting back in his

Cᴳ

armchair at the end of an ordinary day—with an ordinary day ahead. It even made him forget what he had had for lunch.

"Let's see—what was it? Oh—stewed steak, sprouts and baked potatoes."

"You're always having stewed steak lately."

"They do it very well at the Unicorn. Then cheese, and coffee."

Once started, there was plenty enough to say. He told her everything that had happened after lunch: from his stroll to London Bridge until the end. When he came to the clearing out of his desk he was reminded of something: he dived into his pocket and produced the fragment of anti-aircraft shell.

"That brings back memories!" Edith looked at it in curiosity. It took her a little while to realise what it was.

He told her about the presentation so lightly and casually that he might have been an onlooker instead of the principal figure. The time flew by: Edith had turned her chair to the fire and so absorbed were they that neither noticed Ada come in to lay the dinner until a wheezy cough disturbed them.

"Where shall I put this?" She was holding the new clock in her hands as though it were a box of spiders.

"Oh—on the sideboard, Ada. We're going to put it in our bedroom."

Anything new that came into the house was an irritant to Ada's ordered mind, and it remained an irritant until it had found a settled place. She indicated quite clearly by the way she carried it that she did not consider it had a decent shape for a clock. Ada herself looked rather like a plump but sombre Christmas cracker in her stiff,

billowy uniform and even stiffer starched apron: the bow
that secured the apron behind looked the stiffest thing of
all. She put the clock on the sideboard and eyed it de-
fensively before she turned to lay the cloth, as though she
half expected it to say something cheeky.

Her arrival to set dinner was the signal for Mr. Baldwin
to go for his walk. As Edith went upstairs to tidy herself she
paused at the landing window to watch her husband, with
his hat at a jaunty angle, swing out of the gate, whistling
a tune. He looked up and down, deciding upon his
route: she saw him swish his walking stick and stride off
into the fog-streaked night. She felt inexpressibly happy
and relieved. He had behaved wonderfully and far
beyond her wildest hopes: she had even been prepared
that night to open the door to an old and broken man:
instead had come a buoyant, youthful figure, ten years
younger than the man who had gone for his morning
train.

It delighted her, but puzzled her a little. He had told
her everything as though he were describing something
that had happened to some other man: he had not mentioned his plans for the future as though they, too, were no
concern of his and belonged to someone else. But if she
were certain of one thing it was that his mood was not
artificial and forced: she knew that he was not just
throwing a brave face upon an inward fear: she knew him
well enough to know that he was genuinely happy and she
wished now that she had bought the chicken that Sainsbury's had recommended, and made a celebration dinner
of it. As it was she had played for safety with cutlets and
stewed pears. But it was not too late to change into her
velvet dress. She turned on the light, drew the blinds and

began her preparations for dinner with a thankful, jubilant heart.

When dinner was over, and Edith had gone up to bed, Mr. Baldwin settled himself by the fire and took a final wander round the past before he locked the door and threw away the key. It hardly seemed decent to allow the future to bubble so gaily and noisily before the past had received a proper, reverent burial, so he draped his mind in respectful sentiment and sent it quietly away to pay its homage.

Best were the early football days, lost almost in a mist as the ball was lost towards the end of a winter game: the hurry to be off on a Saturday morning: the sandwiches munched behind the lid of a desk: the journey out to fields—the mud, the dusk: the glow from washing off the mud and the drowsy, limb-stretched journey home. Winter billiards tournaments: the Lord Mayor's Show from the office window: cricket matches and sweepstakes. The office had returned his services in things besides money, for it had given him friends, and life with them outside the office doors. Even if there were no great moments to look back upon there were none to make him ashamed: he had never been in trouble through betting or other silly things that some men did. It would have been pleasant to have retired as a Manager, for besides the dignity it would have added an annual £50 to his pension. But it mattered less now than it might have done. The worry of Managership took a physical and mental toll: he was fresher and stronger than Wilson would be when he retired, and the compensation was coming to him now. He had not missed a Managership through lack of brains: he had missed it because he had not been cut out for it—because he had really been cut out for something else. . . .

Something else. He rose from his chair and went to the bookcase. Behind the glass doors stood the great twelve-volume *History of England* that his fat Uncle Henry had given him, in the spirit of a balloon unloading ballast. He had never had time to do more than glance at them. He saw them now as the stout companions that would accompany him upon the first part of his journey. He would study them: every volume, every page, carefully and thoughtfully: to build the solid background he would need. With a tingle in his fingers he opened the doors and drew out Volume I. It was half-past ten, and out of the stillness came the plaintive hooting of a fogbound train. The sound no longer filled him with oppressive thoughts of a chilled platform wait in the morning: he peered out at the hazy, bitten road and drew the curtains tighter. The room was warm and the fire would last an hour. He drew a small table up to the armchair and got a pencil and some paper to jot down notes of his reading. It occurred to him with a slight pang that, having left the office, he would in future have to buy his own pencils, but that would be a trivial thing beside the compensating blessings.

CHAPTER I

Prehistoric Britain

(The South Downs—wiry turf—wind blowing through his hair—vague humps of an earthen fortress—buried flint arrowheads waiting for the spade. The very title of the Chapter stirred the blood.)

" There were still no Straits of Dover when the earliest

aborigines drifted in a westerly direction across Europe,
into the tangle of marsh and forest that was to form the
British Isles. . . . His rude weapons, of flint and stone, have
been found in river drift and in the caves that were his
dwelling-places . . . the greater part of the North Sea was
a marshy plain . . . the worst of the ice age had passed
away. . . . ''

He sat up with a start: the big book, falling to the
ground, awakened him. Twenty past eleven !—he had
dozed for half an hour. It was silly to try and begin work
like this: the stress of the day had tired him more than he
had realised. To-morrow night would be different—he
would be fresh and alert and could work for hours.

He picked up the book, retrieved the pencil that had
disappeared down the cleft of the armchair, turned out
the light and went up to bed.

Tired though he was, it took him some little while to
settle down, for cheap clocks, like crickets, chirp stronger
as the night wears on. First he had to get up to cover his
new present with a towel. A little later he had to get up
again to put the clock, towel and all, into the wardrobe
cupboard.

CHAPTER IV

WHEN MR. BALDWIN AWOKE to his first morning of retirement he discovered that he did not really need the extra half hour in bed that he had planned. All that he needed was to hear the clock strike eight and to tell himself there was no necessity to get up. Having done that he had no further desire to stay in bed. But breakfast for the future was to be at nine o'clock: to rise at the old time would have meant a half-hour wait for breakfast in the dining-room, and Ada, who had accepted the alteration with very bad grace, would have taken a gloating delight in keeping them waiting. So they remained in bed and told each other how nice it was.

Edith could not hold out till the scheduled time, and got up at twenty-five minutes past eight, but Mr. Baldwin stuck it until the dining-room clock chimed the half hour. He ignored the strangled ticking in the wardrobe cupboard and, going to the bathroom, began his toilet in as leisurely a way as possible in order to take advantage of the extra ten minutes he had allowed himself.

But here again was a difficulty. An extra minute spent with his shaving brush in working up an extra special lather resulted in the quickest shave he had ever had. Deliberation with studs and cuff-links brought further undesired expedition and he was well ahead of time when a problem arose to delay him. He was automatically pulling on his City trousers when he realised that he had given no consideration to the dress required for his rough mornings in the garden. City trousers were obviously wrong, and he began to search the wardrobe for something appropriate: he examined a pair of grey flannel trousers that he watched football matches in, but decided they were too good at present: his plus-fours were out of the question, and after turning everything out he decided upon a shiny pair of blue serge. He completed his gardening costume with an old woollen cardigan and when he came whistling downstairs, care-free and comfortable, at ten past nine, he found that an unpleasant incident had happened.

On the stroke of nine Ada had brought in the fried herrings. Edith could hear her husband rummaging about upstairs, but not wishing to hurry him on the first morning of his retirement, had told Ada to keep his herring hot for him until he came down. This simple request had startling consequences. Ada, already sizzling, blew up——

" How am I going to get cleared away and washed up and finished with the bedrooms before the tradesmen come ! How can I answer the kitchen door when I'm still making the beds upstairs ? "

Edith knew quite well that Ada was not a contortionist and had simply replied that now Mr. Baldwin had retired they would need to adjust one or two things.

" Adjust things ! " cried Ada—" turning 'em upside-down, that's what it is !—everything upside-down ! How am I going to make up the time I lose in cooking breakfast half an hour late—and then having it lying in the oven ? I suppose there'll be a big lunch to cook now as well."

Ada had gone out and slammed the door, and Mrs. Baldwin knew that this quivering bang was the first shot in what might prove a long and difficult guerilla war. She knew that Ada was a good servant, but like many good servants of mature years, she regarded the disturbance of settled habits as she would the desecration of an altar. She was apparently lying in wait for Mr. Baldwin and almost trod on his heels as she followed him into the dining-room with his herring.

" It's dried up," snapped Ada, and banged the door again. Mr. Baldwin looked round in surprise.

" Hullo !—what's up with Ada ? "

He laughed when Edith told him.

" She's right, you know ! If we hadn't got Ada we'd be coming down to breakfast at ten o'clock ! Nine o'clock sharp in future, and no messing about ! "

But Edith knew that this simple resolution would only smooth out one small detail.

" And it's not dried up at all," he added. " It's fine."

A herring on a hurried working day meant the consumption of the roe and the obvious portions only. This morning Mr. Baldwin explored the intricate, bone-ridden sections below : he took the fish to pieces as a craftsman would a delicate watch. He was in buoyant spirits : there was enormous satisfaction in seeing harassed, half-breakfasted men hurry by towards the station.

" Look !—there goes old Anderson !—he's only got five minutes : he's always late—comes dashing into the station as the gates close. He'll have a heart attack one of these days."

He reached for the marmalade and spread his toes in his slippers : he had half expected the call of a dying habit when he saw his old travelling companions go by, but he was thinking too eagerly of the garden, and the settling down to Chapter I of the History in the afternoon. The fog had disappeared: it looked dull and rather cold outside, but a good morning for hard work.

" What do you think I ought to do first ? The lawn— or the hedge out there ? "

Edith suggested that he should begin by sweeping up the leaves, and he heartily agreed. Sweeping, he said, was an excellent exercise for the stomach muscles and would give him a ravenous appetite for lunch.

" I shan't be able to give the whole morning to the garden: it'll just have to be a quick look round to-day. There's a whole crowd of things to do."

He began ticking them off on his fingers—" I'll have to try and get up to Boots' to open that library subscription : I've got to write in to the Railway Company for the rebate on my season ticket—then I must get some gardening gloves—there's a whole lot of things——"

Edith said he might like to come up with her at half-past eleven, when she went shopping, but he waved this aside.

" It would mean we should both be hanging about wasting time, and after all, there's not a lot of daylight for the garden. I tell you what ! Let's go up together after tea ! "

That suited Edith better, too.

" What sort of lunch would you like ? " she asked. " I suppose you'd like the same sort that you have in the City ? "

" Good heavens, no !—I shall have exactly what you always have when you're alone."

Edith laughed. " I never have anything ! "

" What !—you don't have *anything* ? "

" Only a snack—sometimes a little salad, or bread and cheese. When I'm busy I just have a cake and some coffee at Lyons."

Mr. Baldwin was surprised and concerned.

" You ought to have more than that, Edie : you're looking thin, you know. Let's split the difference—just a chop or something, and cheese. It'll do you more good than salad."

" You always have coffee after lunch in town—I expect you'd like a cup . . ."

" Certainly not ! It's easy in a restaurant. It's too much of a bother at home and I really don't want it. Order in a crate of beer."

He rose from the table and clapped his hands together : from the distance came the rattle of a train.

" I don't want you to alter anything, Edie." He stood behind her chair and squeezed her shoulders. " It's going to be fine, lunching together every day. I hated those stuffy dining-rooms in the City—that awful smell of food : other people sitting right on top of you, making noises with their mouths."

Edith laughed. She got up and gathered together the breakfast things to save Ada's time.

" Do I ever make a noise with mine ? "

" Never ! "

She rang the bell, and Ada came ostentatiously down-stairs with a duster in her hand to show that she had been disturbed from doing the bedrooms.

Edith took the breakfast things into the passage and piled them on the table beside the kitchen stairs. She took the cloth on to the garden steps and shook the crumbs out for the birds. When she returned to the dining-room, Mr. Baldwin was in the armchair by the fire, reading the picture paper.

They took two papers; one for the news, the other for the pictures. Mr. Baldwin took the newspaper with him to the train, and it was Edith's habit, after breakfast, to sit for a little while in the window seat and glance through the picture paper before beginning her morning's work.

It was a very little thing; just a habit—but it was the first gentle step in the ladder of her day's work. Now suddenly this step had given way, and she was not lissom enough, on the spur of the moment, to leap this unexpected space. She stood aimlessly by the table; she looked across at the window seat, and then at the picture paper in her husband's hands. His silver head just showed over the back of the chair, and the other paper, *his* paper, lay beside him. She felt as bad as Ada to allow such a small thing to disturb her. Quietly closing the door, she went down to the kitchen and filled a jug of water for the ferns in the drawing-room. It was funny how Tom seemed to think that because he had retired, she had retired, too.

Mr. Baldwin looked up at the clock and threw down the paper. This would never do: ten o'clock and nothing done. By this time the whole staff had arrived in the office, the post was opened and everybody had begun work. He put on the old shoes he had selected for gardening, went through the drawing-room and opened the French windows.

It was an occasion, this first entrance to the garden: it was the entrance of a new Manager—a live wire—come to pull together and inject new life into a neglected old concern.

It occurred to him how dismally the old Mr. Baldwin had neglected it. From October to March he had scarcely seen it in daylight except at week-ends, and week-ends gave no time to do anything important. In the spring and summer a man used to come in once a week, and the man had just done enough to prevent Mr. Baldwin from taking an interest himself. Edith had some rose trees and a pair of gloves for gathering occasional blossoms, and that was the sum total of the garden activities of the past. From now on things would change. He reviewed his property from the balcony before descending the steps.

Everything was dark, and threadbare, and asleep. A sparrow hurriedly gathered up the last breadcrumb from the shaken tablecloth and disappeared.

Despite his neglect of it, the possession of this land gave Mr. Baldwin more solid satisfaction than the house itself. His ownership extended far beyond the surface and the things that grew upon it: it extended down and down, for thousands of miles, a vast wedge that tapered slowly away, until as a minute pin-point it met everybody else's land at the centre of the earth. He owned grass and gravel, clay and rock, possibly a section of a subterranean river and any amount of volcanic fire. He could dig it, blast it, tunnel it if he chose: do anything with it except keep pigs, forbidden by the Council: he could have a dense wood or a sunken garden with statues, a pond, or a sugar-loafed hill. As it was he had a prematurely bald lawn surrounded by a gravel path: flower borders, some shrubs and a few fruit

trees in the broad strip at the bottom, the whole surrounded by a stout wall of brown brick.

His thoughts flew to this land whenever his morning
paper foretold the collapse of civilisation. He reckoned, at
a pinch, that he could grow enough to keep Edith and
himself alive. He had tested this during the war when he
had set two rows of potatoes and produced a number of
pallid little globules that tasted of soap. Malnutrition had
been the cause of this, for his pride in a great annual
cluster of nasturtiums had been somewhat dampened
when he read in his gardening book that nasturtiums
flourished at their best in " any poor soil."

For some time past he had been studying a gardening
book, and practically knew by heart " What To Do in
October." But the doing of most of these things was
dependent upon certain preparatory things that should
have been done in the spring. Edith had struck the right
note when she had suggested sweeping up the leaves.
" Leaves," said his book, " should be swept from lawns
and paths, being heaped up in an odd corner of the
garden and left to decay."

The leaves that came from their own trees were
negligible in quantity, but a walnut tree in a neighbour's
garden overhung the Baldwins' land and presented them
annually with a sodden, brandy-coloured carpet. Sometimes it threw them a few mildewed nuts in return for the
nourishment that its roots sapped up from Mr. Baldwin's
garden, but usually it only gave leaves. Mr. Baldwin went
to the tool-shed to find a broom.

Piles of discarded newspapers, broken deck-chairs,
empty paint tins and cardboard boxes creep into tool-
sheds like rats into a granary. Mr. Baldwin could scarcely

get in: the shed presented a morning's work in itself, but he set this aside for the first wet day. The tools were very rusty and needed a great deal of greasing to bring them back to efficiency. This also could wait.

He pulled out the besom broom, shook the cobwebs off it, and examined it. It was hopelessly worn out—nothing more than a toothpick—its few remaining strands had rested so long on the ground that they were turned stiffly up like an old-fashioned barber's quiff.

He decided to burn the broom later on and use its ashes to nourish the lawn. He threw it aside and began work with the rake. But most of the leaves got through the rake, and after a fruitless ten minutes he decided to go and see if there was an old broom he could borrow from the house.

He would gladly have used his fingers—even his shaving-brush—to sweep up the leaves had he foreseen the unhappy results of his endeavour to bring about a friendly alliance between the garden and the kitchen. He leant the rake against the tool-shed and went light-heartedly towards the house without the slightest conception of the packet of trouble he was putting his head into.

The whole enterprise seemed blighted from its beginning, for in the first place Mr. Baldwin, once in the garden, had the greatest difficulty in regaining an entrance to the house. He discovered that during his short absence the French windows had been closed and these windows, once closed, could only be reopened from the inside.

It seemed a little absurd to go round and knock at his own front door, so he took the easier and more reasonable course of going down the basement steps to the kitchen entrance.

The baker's boy was blocking the kitchen door with his basket, and Mr. Baldwin had to stand by and wait while the boy signed the book and searched for some change. This took an irritatingly long time, and Ada increased Mr. Baldwin's embarrassment by looking at him steadily over the boy's shoulder with a suspicious, hostile stare that made him feel like a pedlar waiting to be sent off with a flea in his ear.

But worse things were to follow. The boy having departed, Mr. Baldwin went into the doorway and said in a friendly, jocular voice: " I say, Ada—I wonder if you can let me have an old broom to get up some leaves? Any old thing'll do."

There was nothing demanding in his manner, and a polite refusal from Ada would have ended the matter without the slightest difficulty. But the reception of his harmless, polite request was astounding: never before had Mr. Baldwin seen such an evil light gather in a woman's eyes.

" A broom—to sweep up leaves ! " she shouted— " *leaves !*—when there ain't a decent broom in the house for the carpets ! Here am I trying to get the bedrooms finished half an hour late—and tradesmen at the door every half-minute ! No !—there *ain't* a broom—not for leaves there ain't ! "

She stooped down, picked up a small cake of mud that Mr. Baldwin had brought in on his heel and flung it out of the door with a hiss of disgust.

Mr. Baldwin was speechless: he had seen Ada sulky: he had heard her grumble occasionally when her rigid routine was upset—but he had never seen her like this. Her nose was white with anger: two vivid little patches of colour had risen to her cheek-bones: demented little strands of hair fluttered over her forehead. She stood back from the table like a wounded animal at bay.

Then suddenly his own anger came: he was angry at Ada for her senseless behaviour and angry at himself for blundering into a humiliating situation. He saw clearly now that he should have gone to the dining-room, spoken first to Edith and ordered the broom to be sent up to him. By coming into the kitchen he had placed himself on the level of a tradesman's boy: Ada was playing on her own ground: even his costume was too shabby and ridiculous for a show of dignity.

But he knew that he could not draw back now. A stiff, long-handled broom was leaning in a corner by the kitchen range, beside a dust-pan. He crossed to it, picked it up and said in a light, easy voice—" This'll do. We'll get a new one for the house."

He felt better with the broom in his hand: he had spoken as if Ada had never given vent to her outburst at all: he began to feel that he might still come out of it with dignity, but when he turned, Ada was facing him again: she was blocking his retreat: for a horrible moment he pictured himself struggling with his servant for a broom—dreadful newspaper headlines flashed before him—" Brondesbury man charged with assaulting elderly servant. . . ."

Then Ada blazed up more fiercely than before:

" That's my broom !—put it down ! " she shouted.

" It happens to be *my* broom," he said—and shame rushed over him. It was not his broom—every inch of it was Ada's—two dark patches on the handle worn by Ada's hands—the bristles worn diagonally across from the

Dg

patient motion of her arms: it was steeped in her personality as his old, favourite razor was steeped in his.
What would he feel if Ada came to his bedroom and took
his favourite razor to peel potatoes?

He would still have laid it down if Ada had given him
a chance, but suddenly she stood away, flung the loaf of
bread on the table and burst into a high-pitched, cackling
laugh.

" All right !—go on !—take it ! I don't care if the house
turns into a pig-sty !—It's nothing to do with me !—I'm
only a servant ! " And she gave the dust-pan a kick that
sent it, by a fluke, straight into the cupboard and back
into its place.

He paused in the doorway with the broom under his
arm.

" I ought to give you notice for this, Ada."

" I take my notice from the mistress."

There was a queer, husky dignity in her voice that made
him glance back in surprise. As he had turned to the steps
leading up to the garden a pale shaft of sunlight had
flashed in his eyes and when he looked back the kitchen
was filled with brooding shadows. He could see little else
beyond the bright yellow square of fire in the kitchen
range and a row of moon-like plates that took the reflection and shone like faded amber lanterns. Ada was almost
lost in the shadows by the cupboard door: she was standing quite still: it might have been a solitary, discarded
waxwork of Mrs. Noah, set aside and forgotten in a twilit
store-room.

As Mr. Baldwin went up the steps towards the garden
he noticed another tradesman's boy, standing with his
mouth wide open, beside the coal-cellar door. He had

probably witnessed the whole sordid affair and would pass it round Brondesbury.

He no longer wanted the broom: it humiliated him to hold it, but he had got to use it now. He ostentatiously flicked some leaves from the crevices of the flower border: its handle was smooth and warm from the heat of the kitchen and it seemed almost cruel to let the frail old thing grow cold. After a little while he leant it against the wall and used the rake again. Ada's shrill voice was upstairs now, in one of the bedrooms, and through the open window he could hear Edith quietly and patiently making reply. The altercation was a long one, then finally a door slammed and there was silence.

It was pitiful to have this happen upon the first morning of his new life. He wanted peace, and dignity, and happiness, and Ada had destroyed them all. She had made him feel like a naughty little boy—then a senseless bully who had forced a broom from a defenceless old woman and threatened her with dismissal because she was in his power and too old to find another place.

The sun took Ada's part, and disappeared behind a misty cloud to show its contempt for him: the morning grew suddenly cold and dank: the leaves, too, stood up for Ada and clung to the path, to show that, even if they also were small and defenceless, they were not going to give in to a bully.

He plodded on, but his heart was no longer in his work: he took up a little pile of defeated leaves and stacked them in a corner behind the apple trees. He was stooping over them, flattening them down, as a quiet step came behind him and he turned to find Edith standing by.

She was dressed to go out shopping, in a neat brown

costume and white gloves, and he felt ashamed when he saw her troubled, unhappy face. She had borne the whole brunt of this silly incident and he knew that, whatever she had felt, she had stoutly taken his part. He brushed his hair aside with a grimy hand and smiled.

" Hullo, dear—off to the shops ? "

" Yes. I'll have to be getting along." She nodded towards the little pile of leaves. " That's going to be fine for the garden next spring. You'll have to let me have some for my rose trees."

" I think it'll buck things up," he said, and he saw Edith glance towards the broom. " Did I hear Ada shouting about upstairs ? "

Edith began buttoning her gloves.

" Tom, dear—I know Ada's silly—but it *is* hard on her. You see, she's only got that one broom, and she keeps wanting it all the morning."

Mr. Baldwin gave a careless laugh.

" Such a fuss about nothing !—I haven't hurt the thing —look at it ! Anybody'd think I was going to smash it to bits ! "

" It's not that, Tom. Ada wants it, you see."

She looked at him with her shy, level grey eyes. It was like her to take his part with Ada, and Ada's part with him.

" Surely we can afford another ! "

" Of course we can—if I'd known you wanted one, dear."

He leant on his rake and took one of Edith's gloved hands. " I'm sorry, Edie. I don't *want* the broom ! If only Ada had explained like a reasonable human being. She was *abominably* rude. We can't allow it : if it happens again she must go."

Edith gave a little laugh.

" We'd never get another like her. You know that, Tom. They simply won't come nowadays, where there's a basement. We must try and be patient with her, and leave her alone. She *is* a good worker."

He knew that perfectly well. No servant had stayed with them as long as Ada. Even her crotchetiness was a disguised quality, for it rarely occurred except when her routine was threatened. But no power on earth would persuade him to creep back to the kitchen with the broom. He nodded carelessly towards it and began raking the path.

" I've finished with it now, if she wants it." He paused, and went on with a return of his old enthusiasm. " You know, Edie, that gardener fellow used to burn all the leaves and grass cuttings. Just shows what gardeners are : don't care a rap when it's not their own garden. We'll stack everything here and dig it all in along the borders next spring."

" You've made a wonderful difference already," said Edith. " Don't overdo it to start with or you'll be stiff to-morrow. I'll be back just before one."

" You might leave those French windows open when you go in, Edie."

As she went down the basement steps with the broom, she saw him leaning on his rake, gazing over the lower wall, towards the houses in Alma Road.

CHAPTER V

Soon after twelve o'clock Mr. Baldwin decided to act upon his wife's suggestion and shorten his first morning's gardening to avoid excessive stiffness next day. He pulled a few obstinate leaves out of the prongs of his rake, added them to the neat pile he had made against the wall and looked at the cleared space under the walnut tree with satisfaction. The leaves, when stacked, had yielded so obediently to the pressure of his foot that he was confident they would begin decaying without delay.

He carefully scraped his shoes and went up the iron steps into the drawing-room. He could hear Ada moving about in the kitchen, so he went upstairs with confidence, washed his hands and came down to rest by the dining-room fire.

To sit by the fire at twelve o'clock on a week-day morning was so definitely associated with a bilious attack or a cold that he had to assure himself more than once that he was in normal health. It was very pleasant to feel the soft breath of leisure round his elbows, but he was not entirely at his ease. On the previous night he had closed the door on the past and set his face to the future, but this morning he was beginning to discover that the door was warping badly, and things he had meant to shut away were drifting through the cracks. When he had gone to the tool-shed for the rake the sudden twilight had twisted the shed into the shape of the dim-lit office safe from which, at that hour of the morning, it was his custom to collect the money deposited on the previous night. For a moment his hands had passed the rake and groped automatically for more familiar things—a canvas bag of coin—a bundle of notes in an elastic band—a wad of postal orders and a pile of multi-coloured cheques. And now, as the clock chimed half-past twelve he glanced over his shoulder, half expecting to see Mason and Palmer pass him on their way to lunch. He was disturbed, and rose abruptly from his chair: it was no part of his plan to let this happen. He had intended to work in the garden until the moment lunch was ready: his programme was upset, and he was unprepared for a sudden, empty space of time. The quietness of the room and the emptiness of the road made him feel that everyone in the world was at work but him: that he had slept, and been forgotten when an army had moved on.

He picked up the morning paper and crossed to the window seat: he had a sudden aversion from settling himself slackly by the fire. Having read most of the news after breakfast he turned to the gardening notes: " Dahlia tubers must now be lifted and stored. . . . " He flicked the paper impatiently to the financial columns—advice of that kind irritated a man who had no dahlia tubers. The ordinary papers never quoted his shares in the Bank of Paraceta, but he occasionally bought the *Financial Times* to find that the stock he had bought as a bargain at 75 was steady at 2½. News that Gilt-edged were soaring left him cold. He laid the paper down and glanced round the room. He had no desire to begin his reading until he could settle down, according to plan, in the afternoon.

He decided to begin turning out one of the drawers in his bureau. It was a job he had set aside for a wet day and he began with an uncomfortable feeling that he was breaking into his emergency ration.

The drawer was chock full of papers: old envelopes, unfamiliar looking with Edwardian stamps—an ancient Book of Rules of the Acacia Tennis Club, long defunct—a complete set of receipted Gas bills, 1905–1924. . . .

Ada came in to lay lunch. His back was towards her and he did not look round, but he could tell by her quietness that her evil mood had passed: he could feel that her eyes were upon the swollen waste-paper basket, but she closed the door so quietly that he scarcely heard it.

From his seat at the bureau he had a clear view down the road and he found himself growing amused and interested in things that he had never had opportunity of observing before. Towards one o'clock the road had come to life: and he could watch the eddying of life in a back-water unseen by the City man who passed each day by the main stream. One or two tradesmen's boys cycled up to houses and took parcels in with a hurry suggesting belated orders for lunch. Then came a thin, erratic stream of school children: quick, tapping heels: two small girls bouncing a ball. A woman came to a gate, bundled one of them in and shooed the other off to a nearby house—two boys in green caps came by and lingered at another gate while they looked at some foreign stamps. Then one went in and the other went on.

Hard on the heels of the returning school children came the mothers with parcels and shopping baskets, and Mr.

Baldwin suddenly realised that he was watching something to which his own wife belonged: he began to look
out for her, and grew impatient to see so many other
women return ahead of her. At last she came—he waved
to her from the window: she looked surprised, as though,
lost in thought, she had momentarily forgotten that he
was at home: then she smiled, waved back, and hurried
in, frowning and shaking her head in comic despair at the
squeaking gate.

To sit lunching in his own home, with Edith opposite
him and the fire gently fluttering behind, was a great
improvement upon the noisy Coffee Room at the Unicorn
with its smoky ceiling and perpetual smell of soup and
beer. A drizzling rain had come on: it darkened the room,
threw up the glow of the fire and set the stage invitingly for
his first afternoon's work upon his history books.

He was in no great hurry to begin: he was content for
the moment to anticipate the pleasure of settling down to
his new studies. He wanted to sit back in his chair, smoke
a cigarette and enjoy a placid, rambling talk with Edith
for half an hour. But Edith was not good at conversation
after lunch, it was her habit to rise directly her meal was
over so that Ada could clear the table and leave her undisturbed for her afternoon's nap by the fire.

Mr. Baldwin began discussing improvements to the
garden, but Edith was restless. She tried to respond but her
remarks were dull and pointless, and after a little while
she rose and began collecting the plates and glasses
together. He looked up in surprise and disappointment,
then rose himself and went to the windows.

" Lucky I got those leaves stacked before the rain set
in," he said. " It'll soak into them and help them rot."

Edith heartily agreed, and helped Ada to clear the lunch away. When she returned to the dining-room she found that Tom had settled down in her favourite arm-chair by the fire with a thick, musty-looking volume from the bookcase resting on his chest.

There were two armchairs in the dining-room. One faced the light from the windows and was narrow, hard and shiny: the other had its back to the windows and was broad, well worn and comfortable. For many years, on week-days when Tom was at the office, it had been Mrs. Baldwin's habit to draw the curtains, settle down in the broad, comfortable chair with her eyes from the windows and doze for half an hour in the twilight by the fire. She looked forward to it, not only for the relaxation, but because it completely refreshed her for the rest of the day: it had become both a luxury and a vital need: the pleasantest of all combinations.

Now Tom was in her chair, and for the second time within a few hours she found herself the slave to a habit that showed its teeth when it was disturbed. It demanded to know what her husband would have done if he had returned one day from lunch in the City to find her calmly sitting at his desk: it angrily pointed to a selfish, sprawling man depriving her of her one hard-earned indulgence.

He had worked for forty years to earn the pleasure of sitting by his fire on a week-day afternoon: he had gone to work in the dawn of winter days: through snow, and blinding rain—he had sat for hours in bitter, fogbound trains—for six months at a stretch he had scarcely seen his home by the light of day. He had earned his retirement a hundred times and now she was resenting his first day's rest because it upset her forty winks in her favourite chair. She got her needlework and tried to settle down in the narrow, slippery chair opposite him.

" That's a nice fat book you've got there," she said.

" M'm," murmured Mr. Baldwin—and she accepted the signal for silence.

She knew quite well that if she explained things to him he would immediately jump up and give her the chair— but what could he do ? The chair she was sitting in was too far from the window to give sufficient light to read on a dull day, and unless she drew the curtains the pleasure of her siesta was destroyed. He might take his book into the drawing-room, but she could not think of him sitting in that cheerless place without a fire in order that she could sleep comfortably in the warmth.

Normally she sat up to the table with her needlework when Tom came home in the evenings : this hard, slippery chair was good enough for sitting in after dinner : but for relaxing in—dozing in, it was impossible. The seat was so high that she could see straight out into the wet, dreary road.

A laundry van drew up at the house opposite : two children in mackintoshes trotted past on their way to afternoon school—a nondescript man was going in and out of the gates along the opposite side distributing pamphlets—afternoon things that Mrs. Baldwin would not have seen in the ordinary way, with the curtains drawn and her face away from the windows. She hitched herself up on the slippery leather seat and tried to concentrate upon her needlework. Despite her discomfort habit brought on a drowsiness, but the light from the tall, gaunt windows dug through her eyelids, and when her

head nodded she slipped down the seat. The chair was like
a bathing chute.

Tom was breathing heavily through his nose. She began
to think he had fallen asleep, until he turned a page so
unexpectedly that it made her jump. His deep breathing
came from concentration. She began to wonder why he
was reading an old thing that had stood neglected in the
bookcase for years and years.

From her unaccustomed seat the light from the window
revealed the room in a disconcerting way. It showed her
how faded the covering to the mantelpiece had become:
it disclosed a thin, meandering crack in the wallpaper.
The room had never pleased her: it had always been too
crowded with furniture, and the windows were too big
to take the kind of curtains she would like to hang. She
had often made plans to improve things but even with
her husband's full salary there had never been quite
sufficient: from now on there would be less.

Tom was really dozing now: the big book lay on his
chest: his lips were parted but his new teeth had failed
to respond and were set in an uncanny grin. She liked
him better in his smart City clothes than in the shiny blue
trousers and old brown cardigan he had put on for
gardening: he had taken pride in his clothes and she
hoped that his retirement would not lead him into slovenly
habits. It was hard to believe that his working days were
over: he would pass for fifty anywhere, with his slight
figure and thick silver hair. He looked more like a lawyer,
or a clergyman, with his thin, clean-shaven face and
deep-set eyes.

She rose from the hopeless chair, tiptoed out of the room
and went up to the spare bedroom to try the curtains she

was working on. They were not ready to try yet but she felt that she must move about—do something, do anything to ward off the panic that began to grip her.

She held the curtains to the windows but scarcely noticed how they were progressing. She lowered them, and stood looking down the deserted road. The cool air of the bedroom seemed to clear her mind: it gave her the chance she needed, to collect her thoughts and put them in some kind of order.

For months she had known that her husband's retirement was coming and yet her preparations had only been for him: how would he respond to it?—What would he do? She had thought of him individually all the time, and for some unconceivable reason had never considered it as a dual problem that would profoundly affect them both. She had thought her own life would go on exactly the same: that all her long-set plans and habits would remain serenely undisturbed; she had looked forward to devoting herself to the happiness of her husband in his retirement, and now, before a single day had passed, some trivial incidents had come to throw a cruel, revealing light upon the fragile ground that had supported their past happiness.

Happily as they had always lived together, she knew to-day more clearly than ever before that this happiness depended upon a regular, daily period of absence from each other. Given this, their companionship was perfect, and it was the realisation that this vital bulwark was destroyed that brought Edith to the verge of panic. She knew that they had no deep well from which to draw their mutual interests. Their evenings were made pleasant by an exchange of anecdotes: of incidents that had occurred in the other's absence. His were of things that had happened in the City—rumours he had heard—ideas he had got from talking with men in the train. Hers were of conversations with people she had met during shopping—of new shops discovered—a dozen things that had happened during his absence from the house.

Their supply of conversation, like a battery that quickly exhausts itself, needed a long period of daily rest for recharging. There would be a desperate squeezing of the battery in the long, winter nights ahead.

She saw now how futile had been her vision of a cheerful, resourceful woman, encouraging a husband to face the demoralising fears of retirement. She had foreseen Tom's battle, but she had not foreseen her own; and while his battles were clear to understand and easier to grapple with, hers were obscure—the more difficult because she must fight on lonely fields in secret. If he chose to discuss his difficulties she might still be able to help him, but she could never discuss hers: the very mention of them would come as a blow in his face. How could she say that his constant presence in the house was making her life unhappy? That his only way of helping her would be to go out, and stay out, for eight hours a day?

The happiness of their married life; their contentment in each other's company, had been the breeding-ground of the difficulties they were now to face, for the result had been that they had never sought for mutual friends. She had her own friends at the Bridge Club and another circle at the Welfare Centre where she spent one afternoon a week: his friends had mostly been colleagues of his office and companions of the train—as remote from her as her friends were from him. Now his were cut away from him, and he had apparently made no plans to seek others: already—for nearly twenty-four hours, he had spoken to no one but Ada and herself. The Ada conversation had not been inspiring and she herself had run dry after lunch and had come up to a cold spare bedroom to seek things to talk about at tea.

Week-ends came to mind, when the weather had kept them indoors, inactive and together for hours at a stretch: she remembered how perilously close they had come to a dead end: moments when both felt themselves groping for something else within each other's minds—never finding it—and wondering whether anything else was there to find.

She knew that he was interested in other things and she had tried to respond, but there was an impatience in his nature that prevented him from lingering behind with her to explain elementary points. Sometimes, on holiday, he would surprise her by stopping dead before some old building or ruined castle: he would stand in rapt silence for minutes on end, then say, " Isn't that magnificent ! " She had always agreed, but had never discovered magnificence in decay. Mustiness, beetles and long-dead bones never stimulated her as would a field of corn or a roadside of spring flowers, but these he would pass with his eyes fixed on a crumbling, decayed tooth of stone ahead.

When he said, " Can't you picture knights in armour riding over that moat ? " she had to detach her mind from a heap of rusty cans in a weed-grown ditch. She admired him for his visions but was faithful to her own.

Sometimes he tried to interest her in finance, but money was bewildering unless you had it: money was only real in a purse, or divided into neat piles upon tradesmen's books on the kitchen table.

She resolved to try harder to join him in his interests: she determined to work tactfully at finding friends who would mutually satisfy them. For the time being she could think of nothing else. Gone for ever were those refreshing comings together in the evenings—that cheerful " What have *you* been doing to-day ? " She tried to stifle the dread of a man eternally sprawling in the dining-room armchair —pottering in the garden—coming in, going out—looking out of the windows with his hands in his pockets—knowing minute by minute what she was doing—with nothing new to talk about—nothing to say—from now on—right on—until the end.

He had worked for his retirement and had given her a home and leisure while he worked. Now he must have the leisure, and she in her turn must work for his retirement—work desperately to give him the happiness he deserved.

The clock downstairs struck three : another hour before tea would be ready. It was extraordinary how the afternoons had always slipped by in the past without thought of time. She held up the curtains again and saw that in their present state they were at least an inch too long.

Mr. Baldwin did not hear the clock strike three : the mist and drizzle were things of the past : a blue, unruffled sea stretched before him and the cliffs of Dover trembled in an August haze. He was at Cæsar's elbow in the prow of a galley and behind them lay eighty squat transports with eight thousand silent, armoured men. They had left Boulogne with the midnight tide and now, against the

skyline, they could see a horde of painted Britons following them along the cliffs. They could hear their distant
shouting as they clambered up and down the gulleys—
their chiefs in chariots—some ardent warriors stumbling
along the bouldered shore. Cæsar had decided to wait
until the tide had turned, and then run eastwards to where
his scouts had told him there were no cliffs to scale. The
wind and tide, remarked Cæsar, would bear them faster
than their enemies could follow over the rough downs.
They would probably land in the evening, unopposed.

Mr. Baldwin laid the book down and sat gazing into the
fire : on a day like this he had seen those unaltered downs
—and sea—and sky. He could picture every detail of that
great adventure of two thousand years ago : the Gallic
cavalry gripping their frightened horses in the flat-
bottomed transports—the Britons sweating across the
stiff, chalky turf—the blue sky and the blue sea—England's history beginning at two o'clock on an August
afternoon.

His ability to visualise these things so clearly was proof
beyond doubt that his instinct had guided him to his true
vocation. He was glad that he had not been an Historian
all his life, for that would have robbed him of the pleasures before him now. Page 35 : he slipped a pipe-cleaner
in to mark the place. Before he went to bed he would
have left Cæsar and the Druids behind; to-morrow he
would probably lend the first William a hand in compiling
his Domesday Book.

No one, the book remarked, had ever discovered what
language those ancient Britons spoke, or whether they
had any form of writing. What a chance for somebody !
Supposing, in his explorations, he were to discover a stone,
E G

covered in hieroglyphics—a key to the first tongue spoken in Britain? His name would then join history itself. He decided that he would make his first Field Excursion very soon: Edith and he would make a day's pilgrimage to the site of one of the earliest monuments . . . Stonehenge, or Avebury, or if it rained, the British Museum. . . .

"Tea ready, Ada?—Why, goodness!—it's four o'clock!"

"I expect you've been having a nap, sir." Ada was her old self again: the broom incident was apparently forgotten and forgiven, and he was very thankful.

"Nap!—I should think not!—I've had a quiet couple of hours with a fine book. All about Ancient Britain, Ada."

"Ah—those were the days, sir." She put a plate of toast in the fireplace and went out as Edith came in.

"What have *you* been up to, Edie?"

"Just fitting curtains to that spare room."

"You're always busy on something. You never seem to rest."

He got up briskly and came to the table.

"Now that we'll always be having tea together we ought to get a little table and have it by the fire."

She was glad to find him in such buoyant spirits. They decided to make an evening journey to the shops. There was his subscription to open at Boots' Library—a letter to post to the Railway Company, applying for a rebate on his season ticket, and a pair of gardening gloves to buy.

"There's more to do now than when I was at the office," he said.

CHAPTER VI

THE DOMESTIC DISTURBANCES arising from Mr. Baldwin's retirement began to settle down in the course of a week or two, and things seemed to adjust themselves to a new routine.

Ada discovered that the later rising and later breakfast of Mr. and Mrs. Baldwin gave her, too, an extra half hour in bed, and at sixty-seven that was no small comfort on a frosty morning. There was now a more elaborate meal to prepare for lunch: a very muddy pair of gardening shoes to clean each morning and a certain amount of additional clearing up to do after Mr. Baldwin. Beyond that, things were very much the same as they used to be.

For the master was a considerate man on the whole, and never intentionally gave additional work. He occasionally asked her for a jam jar, or some other small thing for the garden, but he always applied through the proper channel: asking Mrs. Baldwin in the dining-room and allowing the request to be conveyed through her. He never came into the kitchen again, and by means of a slight adjustment to the latch of the drawing-room window he was able to go out and come in from the garden without leaving the window open and allowing the house to get cold.

He was always out in the garden soon after breakfast: he dug all the borders and raked the lawn until it looked as if somebody had played football on it: he bought a pair of clippers and pruned the shrubs until they looked almost indecently naked: he did this, she suspected, to provide material for bonfires of which he never tired: he said the ashes contained potash salts invaluable to all shrubs and trees, but the scheme appeared to lose its purpose when you had to burn the trees and shrubs to secure the ash to fertilise them. When he had burnt everything he could find in the garden, he cleared out the tool-shed and burnt most of its contents, including the handle of his rake that fell into the fire one day while he was having lunch. He asked her, through Mrs. Baldwin, to let him have all inflammable rubbish from the house—such as cardboard boxes, straw packing and newspapers. When those supplies failed he went up and routed about in the boxroom and burnt some discarded curtain poles and an old Venetian blind. He told her that hard-wood ashes were particularly rich in potash salts and Ada had to keep a wary eye on her washhand-stand.

When rain prevented bonfires he would bring old furniture down from the boxroom and paint it in the toolshed. He suspected mice in the shed, and bought a trap and a quarter of cheese. One day he caught one, and the house was upset for a whole morning while it was decided how they should do away with it. They had no cat, so Mr. Baldwin had a bucket of water brought out to drown it in. He stood for a long time over the bucket and pointed out to Mrs. Baldwin what pretty little things mice were, when you really looked at them—what bright eyes they had and what beautiful little coats they possessed. When Mrs. Baldwin remembered that mice could swim he seemed relieved: he began to suggest tying a stone to the trap and submerging it, trap and all—but as he elaborated on the scheme he suddenly felt like Borgia and stopped. It was a problem. One could not hang a mouse, or cut its throat: to bury it alive would merely assist its natural instinct. Eventually he put the mouse, trap and all, into a fruit bag and, smuggling it up to the Park, waited until no keepers were in sight and let it out into a shrubbery. He came home looking very pleased.

But after a week or two Ada began to feel that things were not going quite as they should. Mr. Baldwin took to coming in from the garden for a rest at eleven o'clock and would often finish up at twelve. This she could understand, for the garden was not a catch on a cold damp morning for a man past middle age. But his doings in the afternoons puzzled her. For the first few days he settled down by the fire directly after lunch and read a book till tea-time: but after the first week or so he no longer remained concentrated for the whole afternoon, and she would often hear him roaming about, poking the fire, opening the window a little, or closing it. She would hear the sharp snick of the curtain rings as he jerked the curtains back: she would hear him in the hall—drawing his stick out of the metal stand: he would go for a walk and return so soon that he could scarcely have gone beyond the end of the road. She would hear his stick plunk back into the stand and his chair draw up to the fire again.

Sometimes she found slips of paper that he had left lying about—scribbled all over with stuff he had copied out of his books. One day she accidentally tore some of these up with an old sale catalogue: she prepared for trouble but it never came: he didn't seem to miss the notes, and never enquired about them.

Sometimes, when she came in to lay tea, she would

catch him standing at the window, chinking some coins in his pockets, staring down the road. When he saw her he would turn round almost guiltily, pick up his book and start to read again.

One day he talked about turning the spare bedroom into a study and they tried to get an old table from the boxroom through the door. But it would not go, and after a half-hearted struggle he gave it up. He said it didn't really matter, and in any case it would mean an extra fire, coals to bring upstairs and more clearing up. So they took the table back and forgot about it. He knocked his pipe out into the dining-room fender a good deal nowadays and Ada was relieved that the spare room was not going to be his study.

He would often clear out drawers after tea and put a pile of old stuff aside to throw away. Then he would change his mind and put it all back, which was all to the good because he could clear it out again later on. One day he bought a scrap book and began sticking in old photographs, bits cut from newspapers and all manner of things that were never made to be stuck anywhere. This made the dining-room table sticky and she had to mention it to Mrs. Baldwin.

It was worse one day when he went out and bought some sticks of glue. He melted them in an old enamel cup over the dining-room fire and mended the leg of a chair. But the glue boiled over and stank the house out, and they had to open all the windows and let a cold east wind blow through the house.

Ada was puzzled, and worried. She understood that retired men played golf, but Mr. Baldwin did nothing but potter in the garden and read his book—and these things grew patchier and more erratic as the days passed by. He neither had friends nor sought them, and this too seemed queer to Ada.

But if Mr. Baldwin puzzled her, she understood and pitied her mistress with all her heart. Few things passed Ada's notice and it had been a genuine shock to her, on the first afternoon of the master's retirement, to see him sitting in Mrs. Baldwin's chair, and Mrs. Baldwin perched unhappily in the hard one opposite him. She respected her mistress's hour of rest in the darkened dining-room and moved and worked quietly in the kitchen below: her work had been disturbed that afternoon as she thought of her mistress sitting up there, wide-eyed in a room full of cheerless light.

She pitied the patient quietness with which her mistress faced the breaking up of her old habits and ways of life: Mrs. Baldwin treated her husband with the tender indulgence of an invalid, and it was a new shock to Ada when, on the night of the glue incident, she heard voices raised in anger, speaking one over each other—almost shouting—she heard him say: " How *can* I melt a tin of glue in the tool-shed without a fire !—don't you *want* the furniture mended ? " And Mrs. Baldwin had cried out: " Oh, don't *nag* ! Leave me alone ! "

It was a new thing for them to quarrel violently like this, but it happened again in the same week. Mrs. Baldwin had given up trying to have her rest in the dining-room, and had taken to going up to her bedroom, cold though it was, and resting in the chair with a quilt over her knees. One very cold afternoon she had asked Ada to light the fire up there, and she had sat by it between tea and dinner, alone.

After dinner, from the top of the basement stairs, Ada heard raised, angered voices again—and the closed doors muffled them into sounds that were almost like cries of pain.

" You seem to think," shouted Mr. Baldwin, " that we've got as much money as we had before I retired ! What's the matter with the dining-room ? Isn't there room for the two of us in here ! "

Mrs. Baldwin did not have a fire in the bedroom next day, but although it was very cold, she went up a long time before dinner and sorted out the things in her wardrobe.

Then came the morning when Mrs. Baldwin came into the kitchen and asked Ada if they could have a little talk.

Ada, disturbed but flattered, pulled up a chair for her mistress and the two sat opposite one another at the kitchen table—a thing that had never happened before.

It may have been the peculiar light in the basement, but Ada suddenly thought how much older her mistress looked. There were deep shadows under her eyes and she looked pale and tired.

" I'm a bit worried over expenses, Ada, and I'm wondering if there's any way we can cut things down." She looked frankly into Ada's face and spoke as if she were reciting something she had long rehearsed.

" You see, Mr. Baldwin's income has been reduced by nearly three pounds a week, and now that he has lunch at home it naturally adds about ten shillings to the housekeeping."

" But surely," exclaimed Ada, " the master saves a lot more than ten shillings by not going to London every day ! "

Mrs. Baldwin glanced away, and did not meet Ada's eyes when she replied.

" I know—but Mr. Baldwin wants to put a little aside. He thinks I ought to be able to carry on the same—and we must try, Ada."

" You never had scarcely any lunch at all, m'am—and the master wants meat, and pudding, and cheese."

" I know. But we must try and give him a good lunch after his gardening."

Ada's father had been a proper gardener: he had worked from eight o'clock till one—and lunched on bread and cheese, but she did not mention this. They had a long talk and decided there were no definite things they could do without. They would be a bit more careful all round: Ada said she would wash everything except the sheets and table-cloths and they would save a good part of the laundry bill.

Mrs. Baldwin rose with a grateful smile.

" I don't know what I'd do without you, Ada."

And as the door closed, Ada's bosom swelled with pride. A few weeks ago she had felt sorry for herself. She had believed herself to be the solitary, unappreciated victim of Mr. Baldwin's retirement, left to suffer alone. Now she realised that she was the mainstay of the house: that she was sorry for *them* : mostly for the mistress—but a little more than previously for the master since she had had this talk.

She had never realised how much money went in rates and taxes, in insurance and other things until her mistress had so frankly told her: to drop three pounds a week was a lot when these big expenses went on the same, and she understood now why Mr. Baldwin did not play golf or have parties in to dinner.

But she still thought they ought to find some people and ask them to tea. They used to have lots of friends, but these had gradually left the neighbourhood and they had never troubled to replace them. They had been sufficient to each other while they only had a few hours together each day—but now ? . . . it was a great pity.

They had taken to going to the pictures in the afternoons instead of the evenings, as they used to, but that meant every evening of the week was spent at home. The mistress had her Tuesday afternoons at the Bridge Club and Fridays at the Welfare Centre, but the master seemed to resent her doing even that and always said, " You're late," when she came in. As for him, he never seemed to meet anybody at all. They ought to take retired men in hand and teach them to do things, like they did blind people.

The trouble was that it was not just an awkward period that would come to an end—as if he were temporarily out of a job—it was something that must go on, for always. It *was* the end.

But Ada was going to play her part. She would do all she could. She found an error of sixpence in the baker's book—sixpence, naturally, on the wrong side. She put the book grimly aside to await the baker's arrival. She would give him something to think about for quite a long time.

CHAPTER VII

Octo ber darkened into winter; a winter that broke no records for excessive mildness or excessive cold: leaden mornings—shrouded afternoons that stole away into the darkness with fog signals as their minute guns— a high wind one night that unravelled Mr. Baldwin's leaf heap and restacked it against the kitchen door.

Mr. Baldwin never missed his morning in the garden, but as the novelty wore off and his concentration lessened, he would often fall to brooding over things that were continually happening to irritate and worry him nowadays. When he had gone out one morning to prune the laurel hedge in the front garden a man had come along and tried to sell him a roll of linoleum. The man had stood at Mr. Baldwin's elbow as he had worked outside his gate, and begged and pestered until Mr. Baldwin had been forced to return to his back garden.

For days afterwards, as he dug the shrubbery, he found himself repeating under his breath the cutting things he should have said to the shameless beggar: he would work himself up into a sullen anger that would smoulder on until it was time for lunch. He would forget about it then, but it would come back next morning and he would work himself up all over again.

And frequently, as he worked, or read by the fire, or went for his walk in the Park, he would worry about

Edith. She was so different these days. Whenever he settled down opposite her for a good long talk she would begin to fidget and look round the room like a caged animal: she would make pointless, absent-minded replies and finally make a feeble excuse to get away and sit alone in her bedroom. On the other hand, when he wanted to settle down to read quietly, she would suddenly try and start a conversation, and would look unreasonably upset when he gently reminded her that he wanted quiet.

She had discovered that he was reading history, and would frequently disturb him with some absurd remark about castles or something—or ask an idiotic question.

At first he had been patient, and replied as clearly and as briefly as possible: later on it angered him because her interruptions sounded like attempts to humour an invalid or encourage a dilatory child. She had changed in an extraordinary way.

But more serious was her hopeless inability to adjust herself to their lower income. While he economised in the smallest detail she persisted in going to an absurdly expensive hairdresser in Maida Vale to have her hair waved. He liked her to look smart, but to have her hair done once a fortnight, at her age, was not playing the game in their present circumstances. He had reduced his own hairdressing expenses to the extent of ninepence a visit by confining himself to a hair-cut, and shampooing his hair himself when he got home.

But while he saved, she squandered. She bought new things for the house that they could no longer afford. When he protested against the expensive stuff she had bought for the dining-room mantelpiece she had asked whether he wanted the house to fall into rack and ruin !

It infuriated him to see her posing as the heroic protector of the house, making him feel a fool who was attempting to destroy it. They had got to face a few faded things around them now that his income had shrunk from ten pounds a week to seven pounds. It needed courage and she had not revealed it.

Sometimes when he was pondering on these unpleasant things during his walk, he would suddenly pull himself up and try to remember if he had actually been round the Park ten minutes previously: he had been thinking so deeply that everything surrounding him had sunk away. He began to fear that his memory was failing, and never left home without a card in his pocket containing his name and address.

But there were times when he was sorry for Edith, and ashamed at himself for losing his temper with her: it was not her fault that she failed to grasp the big things of life: that she could not discuss politics, or finance, or history. When she tried, her attempts were so futile that his annoyance often turned to pity. But he admired her hatred of cheap and tawdry things. When he had persuaded her that they could no longer afford luxury seats at the Cinema, she had replied that she would rather go once a fortnight in the best seats than every week downstairs.

But what annoyed him most of all was her constant suggestion that he was lonely, and ought to find more friends.

It was such an easy suggestion to make: anyone would have thought he could walk out into the street and pick up friends like cigarette ends. Once upon a time there had been plenty of nice people in the neighbourhood, but they had gradually drifted away, and those who had come to take their places were not up to the standard he desired. To tolerate commonplace bores for the sake of talking was a nauseating business and he was happy enough in solitude if Edith would only stop worrying him about it.

This came to a climax one afternoon when Edith took the matter into her own hands and brought two women from the Welfare Club back to tea. He was amazed and humiliated when she brought them into the dining-room without a word of warning. He was reading by the fire in his gardening clothes—in an old woollen jersey. He had kicked his shoes off and there was a hole in the toe of one sock. Despite this : despite the ruination of his afternoon's work, he had done his best for Edith's sake to join in the inane tea-table chatter. But he had swallowed his cup of tea as quickly as possible and asked to be excused. He had taken his book and gone to sit in the cold drawing-room. When he had heard the front door close on the two women and had returned to the dining-room he was astonished to find Edith in tears.

" How could you be so rude, Tom ? It made me feel terrible."

" Rude ? What on earth are you talking about ? "

" Walking out of the room like that. I didn't know how to face them. Mrs. Wheeler's the wife of a Bank Manager."

" What's that got to do with it ? "

" It isn't as though they were common."

" Who said they were ? "

" The way you treated them—and I only brought them back because I thought you'd like to . . ."

He lost his temper.

" What about *me* ! . . . What d'you think *I* felt . . . when you come crashing in with a couple of inane women without even . . ."

He had never finished. She had risen, escaped from the room and hastened upstairs. As she went out she had turned her face from him as though she were ashamed.

He sat by the fire, dejected and miserable. He understood why she had invited the women back: he pictured her planning it—selecting the women whom she thought he would most like to meet. He groped for his book and tried to read. What right had Edith to think him lonely ? His mind was stored beyond the famines of loneliness.

But the incident had its effect. A few evenings later, while they were at dinner, Mr. Baldwin suddenly said:

" D'you remember the Tarrants, who lived next door ? "

" Yes, of course," said Edith.

" They weren't bad people at all. They're living in Wembley now. I think we might ask them to dinner one evening and have a game of bridge."

In due course the Tarrants came. It was a big occasion to have people to dinner. Edith began planning the dinner days ahead: if a couple of soles in the North Sea felt their ears burning a night before they were caught it was because of a long discussion between Ada and Edith as to the manner of their cooking. Mr. Baldwin went down to Kensington to buy some new cards and scoring tablets: Edith bought flowers, some paper serviettes and a bottle of claret.

Their guests arrived in a small but noisy car and the quietness of " Grasmere " was soon broken by Mr. Tarrant's boisterous voice. He had got on well of recent years: a bit better, in fact, than Mr. Baldwin had bargained for. He was rather inclined to talk of the " old

days " and poke fun at Brondesbury Terrace as though
the Baldwins, too, were no longer living there.

But it was a cheerful evening: Ada rose to the occasion
with a delicious dinner and Mr. Tarrant had two helpings
of everything. The Baldwins, however, lost five shillings
and sixpence between them at bridge and Mr. Tarrant
drank nearly half a bottle of whisky. When the buzz of the
little car died away and the door slammed and quietness
reigned again, the Baldwins returned to the dining-room
and opened the windows to let out the smoke. There were
a few crumbs on the carpet: on the table were scattered
cards and scoring tablets, an ashtray heaped with cigarette
ends, an empty syphon and a shallow whisky bottle. Mr.
Baldwin's throat ached with so much unusual talking,
and after Edith had gone to bed he reckoned the evening
had cost nearly two pounds: over half of their week's
housekeeping money gone up in smoke in three hours.
They could not entertain sufficiently often to make it
worth while.

He was too tired to read: he followed Edith to bed
before his usual time but something was disturbing him
and he could not sleep. It was something unconnected
with the Tarrants' visit, something that kept whispering
about a veil of make-belief that grew thinner every day—
and that he was powerless to do anything to repair its
worn-out fabric.

It was on a morning in mid-December that the veil
gave way and fell aside. It happened suddenly: he had
been digging for half an hour with scarcely a glance
above the shoulder of his spade: telling himself that every
spadeful turned would bring its reward in the spring.
Then he had straightened himself: the sudden change of

position dazed him for a moment—his head cleared, and for the first time he saw the garden for what it really was. He faced the reality that for weeks he had struggled to drive away.

It was no good. This sour, worn-out soil was beyond human aid and chemical manure: he might as well give massage and tonic to a starving man. He had tried to believe that it was merely neglect that prevented flowers from blossoming in past years—that gave a scraggy dismalness to the shrubbery and a barrenness to his fruit trees.

But it was more than that. It was the suffocation of these gaunt, brown brick walls. He looked with revulsion at the discoloured patches of brickwork where years ago some kind of sheds must have stood behind the shrubbery. Every ounce of nourishment had been sucked out of this dark, crusty soil. It was not a garden—it was a life prison for a few pallid things that had been taken from fertile homes to linger in a seasonless, walled-in obscurity. The aged apple tree with its branches trained against the brickwork looked like some gnarled old man with outstretched arms manacled to a dungeon wall. The garden was old and tired, and wanted to be left alone: he might as well try to coax sap to flow up the dead limb of a tree. He would toil through the winter, and the spring would pass this garden without a smile.

He put his spade in the tool-shed, and went into the house to rest by the fire. The corner stone had fallen and he knew that it was only a matter of time for the rest of his splendid plans to crumble away. He had expected everything around him to remain fresh and young out of respect for his pretence at remaining young himself. The

F G

dining-room was old and dull because the young man and girl who had furnished it were old themselves. If he resented the worn leather of the armchairs and the heavy, faded curtains they could equally resent the puckered hands that pulled them about.

After a while he was surprised to feel an urge to return: he wanted to go on working in the garden and he went out of the French windows of the drawing-room and down the iron steps with a new desire: no longer the lusty champion who had come to rescue it, but a fellow prisoner to keep it company in its patient bondage.

It was Edith's habit to retire early and leave her husband to read alone for an hour before following her to bed. It happened one night that she had left her library book in the dining-room, but desiring not to disturb him, had tried to make do with a magazine. But towards eleven, still feeling wide awake, she slipped on her dressing-gown and went softly downstairs to get her book.

He did not hear her come into the dining-room, and the sight of him made her cry out in dismay. He was not reading: he was sitting huddled in his chair, his book sprawled on the floor beside him, his face buried in his hands. Her first thought was of sudden illness, but when he turned towards her she could see far more than physical pain—there was a misery that she had never seen in his face before—a despairing appeal that broke all the barriers that weeks of petty squabbling had built between them.

Her library book was forgotten: she went over to him and put her hand on his bent shoulder.

" What is it, dear ?—has anything happened ? "

He poked the fire and coaxed up a little tongue of flame. He made her sit down, and he told her everything. Of the garden she knew, for she had watched, day after day, his work grow more listless and mechanical, but of the hope locked in his dusty history books she did not know until this moment: she had never guessed the fantastic heights to which they had beckoned him and how terribly they had failed him when he had held out his hands to them for help.

" But I can help you, dear ! You know I'm interested in everything you do."

He shook his head.

" You know you can't, Edie. No more than I could help you make a curtain or bake a cake. To do any good I want to talk about it with people who know *more* than me !—Don't you see ?—it's— it's a sort of loneliness, just to go on reading and reading—passing over things I don't understand because there's no one to explain. It doesn't lead anywhere—and—oh—it's not only that, Edie—it's everything. When you're always in a house with lots of time you see so many things that want doing—it gets on your nerves—and worries you. Everything's so old and shabby, dear. . . . No !—it's not your fault: you do wonders with it—it's—it's beautifully clean: it's just old— and you know it makes me feel old . . . and—and finished."

It was on the tip of her tongue to say that the old castles he liked so much were much older and shabbier, and hadn't even got roofs, but something told her not to say it. She remained silent and he went on: he was calmer now.

" I meant to start all over again when I left the office—
a sort of new life—with new interests—but it's just like the
garden, Edie—you can't set wonderful new things in worn
out soil and expect them to grow. We've been set here so
long, Edie, we've taken root, and I might as well try and
change the colour and shape of the leaves on an old tree—
if you see what I mean."

Edith did not altogether understand, but she was over-
whelmingly grateful that such a small thing as a forgotten
library book should have given them the chance of
drawing together again.

The little tongue of flame had disappeared: she pulled
her dressing-gown round her knees.

" I'm so glad you told me, Tom. We can see everything
together now, and it'll be so different. We've lots to be
thankful for—we're both well—and we're not really poor.
We can think out lots of ways of passing the time."

He quivered at that. " It's terrible to think of it like
that, Edie—it's terrible to think of just ' passing the
time ' when there's not much left and it's so terribly
precious."

" But there *are* things to do, Tom !—we can do all sorts
of useful things !—things to make the house better, too.
We'll both start making mats to-morrow—you know,
those big woollen ones—they're easy and it's quite fascinating work—yours can go down here by the fire in place
of this thin thing—and mine'll go in the hall."

Mats ! He smiled for the first time and Edith was delighted to see that he was pleased. Mats !—he thought—
the man who was to emerge as an inspired historian—
sitting by the fire making mats.

" We could do up some of the rooms ourselves—lots of

people do nowadays—all the inside painting and everything—and I can help in your reading ! I'll read, too—
the same books after you and then we can talk about
them. Perhaps we could both join some society and go to
meetings and things."

They rose and went up to bed. They were silent, but
neither slept. Both heard the whirr and strike of the
dining-room clock long into the small hours of the
morning.

To confess to failure, thought Mr. Baldwin, might in
itself be claimed as a minor success: but to admit that
one is facing a blind alley does not flatten walls and
produce a distant horizon.

CHAPTER VIII

Mr. Baldwin had wondered why pensioned business men never did anything really important with their retirement. He had argued, with every appearance of reason, that a man's brain is fully matured and at its best between sixty and seventy: that the highest positions in politics, the law and the Church are rarely given to men before they reach this age, and that a man retiring at sixty from a City office, with an alert mind and a sound body, ought to be fit for something more than a slow vegetation into obscurity.

He had wondered why so few of them used their freedom to do anything big, and a grim three months' struggle had shown him the reason. A brain that has been hungrily aware of life for sixty years is stored to its capacity: a man may draw from it lavishly and refill it with the kind of goods that he has fashioned it to hold, but he cannot clear it out and fill it with new stock of a different shape and size. The old fittings are simply not made to take them: they either reject them or collapse under the strain.

But like the vast majority of people Mr. Baldwin thought he was different from the rest, and while fate, in its normal, plodding way tried its utmost to make him realise that he was the same, he stubbornly refused to believe it. Ambition had stirred him to rebellion, but now a consuming dread was fighting desperately in alliance. A man can face his declining years with equanimity if satisfying achievements lie behind him, but Mr. Baldwin was not prepared to lie back and admire a cashier's box as the monument upon the peak of his career.

And there was a deeper and more frightening spectre in the background. The past three months had given him a sample of what lay ahead if he lost courage and gave in. Sometimes, in unguarded moments, his mind had sunk into a dark vision of hopeless, endless, terrible days, suffocated by a drooping pair of faded velvet curtains— a nauseating brown carpet patterned with clusters of bloated grapes and pergolas—a tool-shed—grinning walls—scraps of paper blowing down a desolate road— the eternal tock of a pendulum—the rustle of settling coal and the click of a neighbour's gate. When these thoughts gripped him he would struggle back, grope for his history book and hold it tight—or hurry into the garden and grip the handle of his spade until strength and calmness returned. He would emerge with a dogged resolution that even if ambition failed he must go on because he dared not face the alternative, for deep in these chasms of despondency lay the memory of an evening paper—with something about a beam in a garage and a piece of rope.

The night of his confession to Edith had come as a heaven-sent relief. Even if it had humiliated him, the broad gates of sympathy that Edith had thrown open had given outlet to his pent-up, brooding disillusionment. He felt a happiness that he had not known since the night of his retirement: he was able to call a truce with himself: gather his demoralised forces: reorganise them and prepare for a new campaign in a short season of rest. He realised how ridiculous it had been to imagine himself the

only man who had ever visualised inspiring things to be
done after retirement from an office. Every ambitious
man had plans like his: he was one of thousands and not
a solitary adventurer after all. But the knowledge that the
vast majority of these thousands were defeated by circumstances did not discourage him: it hardened his resolution
to succeed.

His original plans had been based upon a wrong
foundation. Sensational achievement needed more than
he was prepared to risk. It would mean a gamble—the
selling of everything he possessed, the making of a
hazardous journey into the wilds and a return with
unique discoveries. Only then could he write books and
gain the authority to lecture. For Edith's sake these wild
dreams would have to go. Too many men, all more
experienced than he, were engaged upon the research
work he had planned to do in England, and to persist in
this would be a vain and futile waste of time. For a little
while he was content to rest, confident that with calm
and reasoned reflection a new horizon of endeavour would
reveal itself.

Edith wasted no time in playing her own part. On the
day after her husband's confession she returned from her
morning's shopping with an unwieldy parcel containing
the necessary ingredients for two large mats of tasteful
design. There were two threading hooks, a box of gaily-
coloured wool and two broad pieces of canvas upon which
the designs of the mats were traced.

The whole thing was a great success. Although Mr.
Baldwin scoffed at it and said it was an old woman's job
and a waste of time, he soon got fascinated by it. To sit
opposite each other for hours in the evening and try to

draw conversation from dry reservoirs was courting disaster, but for each to sit with the beginnings of a useful mat upon their knees, to dip into a common basket for stubby lengths of wool and to thread them deftly into their allotted spaces was to spend a pleasant hour with long periods of unnoticed, sympathetic silence, and dinner was frequently upon them before it was expected.

And then one day came the inspiration that Mr. Baldwin had been waiting for. It came, in fact, from Edith. She had been trying to read his history books in order to discuss them with him but she soon realised its futility. She understood little of the hopelessly dull tomes he was trying to digest and she frankly confessed that the ecclesiastical troubles of the fourteenth century were Greek to her. He did not tell her that they were Greek to him as well, but it pleased him to know of her failure. There had been too much suggestion of late that Edith, still with her normal occupations around her, and capable of doing them successfully, was the strong protecting partner—but by chance her confession of failure contained the inspiration.

"Why don't they write the stuff in an interesting, human way that ordinary people can understand? There's nothing between children's books and these great, dull things that aren't written for ordinary people at all."

He did not say much in reply, but he went for a long walk that night, impelled by a new, restless excitement. He knew exactly what Edith meant and there must be thousands like her. Thousands would enjoy a new interest in history if it were given to them in an interesting, intelligent way. The books he had been trying to read had defeated him because they were written by a man without a glimmer of humour or humanity: his failure had demoralised him and suddenly he began to thank his stars that he had failed. Gradually the mists cleared, and he saw the colossal mistake that had nearly broken his heart. He had been trying to become a dry-as-dust historian like the author of his books: he had tried to follow him when he was totally unsuited for that kind of thing. He was a normal intelligent man in close sympathy with worldly people: he delighted in history for its romance and humanity—not for its intricate technicalities of religion and politics. The murder of Becket was exciting but the reasons for it were dull: what they had to eat on the Field of the Cloth of Gold was infinitely more interesting than what they talked about. Action: sweating, swearing, marching men—grand processions—banquets and tattered banners were the things that stirred him: and those were the things that he would rescue from these musty books, bring to life, sharpen and light up for the thousands who had no patience for ten-volume slabs of dullness.

After dinner that night he began an essay upon the Roman Invasion. He called it " Enter Cæsar " and when it was finished he gave it to Edith to read. She was entranced.

" It's wonderful, Tom !—It's twice as good as all those stodgy old books put together !—I never knew you could write like that ! "

" Did you feel it—held you ? " he asked; " did you feel you wanted to go on ? "

" Wanted to go on !—I was disappointed when it was over ! It was a lovely bit where the Ancient Britons picked up big stones off the beach and threw them at the Romans when they'd used all their arrows ! "

He laughed self-consciously.

" That's only imagination, of course—but I expect they did."

" It's imagination that the man who wrote those books never had. That's why you've made it worth reading about and he didn't."

She pressed him to send it to a publisher. They selected one from their Sunday paper who was advertising a book about the Emancipation of Crete, and first thing Monday morning Mr. Baldwin went out to get an envelope big enough to take his manuscript flat. He enclosed a letter suggesting he should write, say, a dozen such episodes in the same style and have them published in one volume.

Christmas came with a shy flutter of snow, and Mrs. Baldwin's sister from Beaconsfield brought her husband to spend the day. The year turned with a week of black frost and all the while Mr. Baldwin's ears were developing an acute sense for the snick of the gate-latch and the heavy boots of the postman. Every night now, after Edith had gone to bed, he sat at the dining-room table surrounded by paper and pencils and open books: he wrote *The Landing of the Conqueror* and *Runnymeade: England Asserts her Freedom*. He even toyed with a flight of fancy—of King John losing the Crown Jewels in the Wash—but he finally decided to stick to fact. Edith read each as it was written and declared them perfect.

The arrival of the Christmas Sales catalogues brought many cruel false alarms. Mr. Baldwin had discovered in the past that when you deliberately wait for a letter and watch every post for its arrival, the letter never comes.

So he would lie in bed towards the postman's time and say to himself again and again, " I don't expect a letter to-day: of course there won't be a letter to-day." But that did not work either—because sure enough there wasn't a letter.

But it came at last: by the unusual post at eleven o'clock. Edith was on the point of going shopping and Mr. Baldwin had just come in for his break in the morning's gardening.

Edith collected the letter from the mat: she knew it immediately by the name on the back of it. She took it to her husband and left him to open it alone, but she could not bear the suspense of waiting until she had returned from shopping: she stood in the hall, slowly putting on her gloves. The silence in the dining-room seemed interminable: then she heard him moving about, and the rattle of the brass curtain rings as he flicked back the curtains in his old habit. Her heart fell, for the sound was ominous.

He came out of the dining-room and said, " D'you want to see it ? "

The envelope, carefully slit, lay on the table, and beside it lay the essay. He held the letter out to her. The publisher regretted that there was no demand.

Mr. Baldwin was surprised by the vehemence of his wife's outburst. What did publishers know about what people wanted ? Look at the stuff they published !—and why couldn't they have written sooner instead of keeping them in suspense ?

" I suppose they get lots of things to read," said Mr. Baldwin. He was quite calm: he seemed scarcely to mind. He was putting on his gardening gloves as he spoke, and went almost at once through the drawing-room and back to the garden.

Edith read the letter again, and looked at the essay, beautifully written in Tom's clear round hand. It seemed strange and unfamiliar after its long absence. She glanced through the drawing-room windows before she left, and saw him kneeling on an old cushion, weeding the path.

To observant people in Brondesbury Terrace Mr. Baldwin became a " character "—to some rather a tragic one, to others a figure of fun, according to the way they thought about such things. They would see him potter out in his overcoat and new brown-kid gloves, potter down the road and potter back. Sometimes he would disappear in the direction of the Park and not be seen for an hour: at other times he would merely go the length of the road. As the days drew out, the darkness no longer shrouded his departure with his wife for their evening's shopping— in March they went by twilight, by April in broad daylight, and often the Harrington family, who lived opposite, got some free amusement out of the way the old man and lady returned, the old man walking a few paces in front: impatiently swinging round and waiting at the gate for the old lady. " They've had another row ! " said the Harrington family. " Poor old thing—the way he nags her." They often noticed the old lady sitting at her bedroom window the whole afternoon: sometimes for a part of the evening: they would see her open the dining-room window, and laugh when the old man slammed it again a few minutes later.

" There he goes again ! Isn't he getting old ! "

" They must be on good terms to-day, he's been to get a bag of cakes."

" Sort of old boy who'll drown himself one day," said Mr. Potter from the large corner house. " There was a case in the paper yesterday. Fellows like that with nothing to do ought to be put into a Home."

But even the most observant neighbours failed to attach any significance to the departure of Mr. and Mrs. Baldwin on Saturday the 28th October at two o'clock in the afternoon. " Off to the Pictures," thought Miss Freeland next door.

But they were not off to the Pictures. Neither Miss Freeland nor anyone else in Brondesbury Terrace who saw them go out so normally had the faintest notion of the star that was guiding the footsteps of Mr. and Mrs. Baldwin that afternoon.

CHAPTER IX

Saturday, the 28th October: a date that Tom and Edith Baldwin were to remember with feelings close to reverence: a date of deliverance.

Towards the end of the first winter of her husband's retirement Mrs. Baldwin began to lose all confidence in her power to help him. It became impossible when every word was taken as a rebuke or an accusation of laziness to be angrily denied: she began to feel towards him as one would to an old, sick animal—to be fed, occasionally soothed, but for the most part to be left alone. She persuaded him to send his essays to several other publishers, but his faith in them had gone, and it was difficult to endure his gloating " I told you so," when they were returned.

It was hard to understand why the failure of these essays should have so broken his spirit. He had undertaken them so light-heartedly that failure seemed scarcely a matter for tragic concern.

But beyond doubt their failure had marked the beginning of a terrible change in him. One by one his interests faded, and all that came to replace them was a morbid concern for his health. He would put on two woollen jerseys before venturing into the garden, then button his overcoat to his neck and return in half an hour with fear in his face and the news that he was dripping with perspiration and would catch a chill. On her return from shopping Mrs. Baldwin would often find the thermometer lying out of its case on their bedroom dressing-table. His history books had given place to a Medical Dictionary that he would study in fearful silence, set aside with sudden resolution and timidly return to again and again. When she tried to persuade him to come away to a hotel at the seaside he had fiercely enquired where the money was to come from.

The lengthening days brought a measure of relief to Edith. It ended for a while the dreaded hours of sitting opposite one another over the fire. She could sit for long evenings by her sunlit bedroom window or take her work into the Park, but always the sight of her in a hat would bring the eternal "Where are you going?" and the closing of the front door the maddening, "Where have you been?"

There were times when he was pitifully anxious to please her. One evening he went out alone and returned with a small jade brooch that she had admired while shopping on the previous evening; at other times he would return with a bag of cakes for tea. But these were tiny oases in a desert of petty quarrels—nagging over money—futile arguments that would die away: fester and break out again and drag on for days—rising at times to terrible bursts of temper: "Why don't you read the papers properly and find something sensible to talk about!"

And sometimes her own patience would collapse under the strain and she would feel her voice rising to a shrill cry:

"Go out!—join a Club or something!—get some friends! For heaven's sake *do* something!"

" What the devil can I join ! "

" The Bowling Club in the Park: I see them enjoying themselves every night ! "

" Those idiotic old bores !—I'm not dead yet ! "

And once, in an agony of spirit she cried out : " Go to a Public House and get drunk !—anything !—anything ! "

She had never seen such a wild look come into his eyes. " By God, I will ! " He crushed on a hat—went out into the twilight without his stick or overcoat and slammed the door.

It frightened her, and she was ashamed. An hour passed, and she was terrified : she pictured him lying help-less in the Park with a bottle clenched in his hand : then the gate squeaked and he came in quite normally with a pound of eating apples.

Worst of all were the long silences after a quarrel : some-times a whole day without a word : a half-hour of silent torture at lunch—another at dinner, while Edith wondered whether he or she, or both of them, were going mad. She hated him : despised him, and pitied him. His eyes never met hers except when he was carried away by anger, and then for a horrid moment she would see the eyes of a hostile stranger.

And this was to go on now till the end—until they died. The days began to draw in, and with the gathering dark-ness came the nameless dread of another winter.

There was a golden autumn evening, and Edith was sitting at work by her bedroom window. Through the gap between the houses opposite she had a glimpse of the Park —of two elms that met and intertwined their branches,

G₀

and the dusky sunset behind them brought the memory
of a walk that she and Tom had been very fond of in the
years before the war—a walk particularly suited to an
autumn afternoon. It began unexpectedly in a right of
way through a farmyard into unfrequented fields—three
miles of woods and meadows that rose gently to a crest
that looked down upon the little village of Welden in its
valley of gorse and elms. They would reach the crest in the
dusk, and the twinkling lights below would summon them
forward to an old-fashioned cake shop in the village—to a
glowing wood fire and an alcove, hot muffins and a generous pot of tea. An hour of drowsy rest: a stroll through the
night to the rural station and home in time for dinner: a
walk for the autumn, when the fading light would shade
each stage of their progress with a quality that lingered in
the memory.

It occurred to Edith that she might persuade Tom to
take this walk again. It was a forlorn hope, but to do it
once and enjoy it might lead to a weekly habit that would
draw him out of his desperate stagnation and bring new
scenes and thoughts to stimulate him.

It was time for dinner: she put her work aside, tidied
herself and went downstairs. There was a mustiness in the
dining-room, for Tom insisted upon closed windows now
that the autumn was coming. The room was in twilight
and he was sitting by the window reading the evening
paper in the scanty light. His latest fad was to save the
electricity by sitting in the darkness.

He glanced up as she came in and switched on the light.
" Well ? " he said, " what have you been doing ? "
" Odds and ends," she said.
There was silence until Ada had brought the dinner in.

He was in a quiet, friendly mood, and Edith decided to seize the opportunity before the inevitable squabble began.

"I was thinking just now about those walks we used to go on Saturday afternoons before the war. D'you remember how you used to hurry home for lunch—and how we used to take the bus out to Stanmore—and that tea-shop in Welden ? "

" Those were good days," he said.

" Let's go next Saturday—over the same ground—exactly as we used to——"

He looked at her as though she had said, " Let's drown ourselves," but before he could reply she hurried on with a desperate eagerness : shy wings of memory went fluttering through the tips of the larch woods, over bramble hedges and rutted fields : they descended abruptly and breathlessly to anticipate one of the objections he was certain to make——

" Tea about one and six—fares half a crown—it wouldn't cost much compared with the fun we'd get."

He listened with the sidelong, impatient glance that was his habit nowadays when she talked too much.

" D'you realise that walk's a three mile climb uphill ? "

" Well—what of it ? " she demanded.

" What of it !—you used to get tired out when we did it fifteen years ago."

" I don't mind."

" You mightn't—but what about me ? I suppose you've forgotten I've had lumbago for nearly a month."

" Exercise is good for lumbago."

He snorted, and helped himself to potatoes : she saw her plan tottering to extinction and gave a final, despairing puff to the dying spark.

" You might come for my sake, Tom. I feel I want a good walk. I can't read a map like you can: I'd lose my way if I went alone."

" Why didn't you think of it in the summer instead of waiting for this treacherous east wind ? "

" Because it's an autumn walk,"—and she thrust in a glowing picture of the tea-shop—so eagerly that his supercilious smile began to give place to surprise. But all he said was:

" Getting hot and sitting in a cold train. Are you going to answer for that ? "

" But we shall cool down at tea ! "

" And then go out of a hot tea-shop into the night air."

" For heaven's sake, Tom !—we're not invalids ! "

He looked down at his plate, and she saw him flush. She expected a burst of temper, but he said quite quietly:

" *I* can do it, if you can."

" Of course I can."

The battle was won. When he rose from dinner he went to his bureau, searched in a drawer and produced a tattered Ordnance Map that had served them on many a past adventure into unknown fields. With a good deal of argument they traced the route of the walk that Edith had spoken of: they pored over it—their heads came nearer together than for many a weary day, and when at last they folded the map Mr. Baldwin went upstairs and routed out his old walking boots.

He took them for a trial in the Park next morning and pronounced them in good running order, and when, at two o'clock on the following Saturday afternoon Miss Freeland thought her dull old neighbours were going to the Pictures, she was quite wrong.

CHAPTER X

" September 1914?—as long ago as that ! "

" It must be," said Mrs. Baldwin, " because you joined the Specials in October and naturally we gave up the walks then."

" And never began them again. I wonder why ? "

The bus was beyond Hendon, and the discussion as to when they had last come out this way had arisen from the changed appearance of the country bordering the main road. To the best of their recollection it had opened out into green fields when Hendon had been left behind, but now there was little to be seen but rows of small new houses with an occasional sports ground in the distance.

But there was nothing depressing about the change: the long road was buzzing with the light-hearted business of Saturday afternoon: people were working in almost every garden: little groups of young men hurried by with small bags and dangling football boots: a party of excited girls with hockey sticks travelled with them for a mile: then clattered off and disappeared up a lane towards some distant goal-posts.

" *That* was there ! I remember it," said Mr. Baldwin, pointing to a tall, sad house lying a little back from the road. He looked at it in silence, as if drawing some memory from it, he followed it round with his head as the bus drew away then turned suddenly to Edith and said:

" What have we been doing these last ten years ?—I mean—it seems extraordinary we've never been out here since."

" Four of the years were the war," said Mrs. Baldwin.

" The last six, then ? "

She knew what had happened in the last *one*—but five years had passed between the end of the war and her husband's retirement.

" You used to do a lot of overtime work after the war : that took most evenings."

" Yes, of course—but Saturday afternoons—and Sundays ? "

Edith gave a little laugh. " *I* don't know. You just—get out of doing things."

They had the two front seats of the bus : he lowered his eyes from the road in front of him and looked across at her with an earnest smile.

" You know, Edie, I think we were letting ourselves run to seed. Fancy forgetting the country was only half an hour away ! "

Edith dared not rejoice too soon. Too often, in the past hopeless year she had known brief moments when he had pulled himself together and been as eager and as happy as this. And yet his present mood was more genuine than anything she had seen since the first days of his retirement : it was building up, and she scarcely dared say a word that might destroy it.

He was sitting well forward on his seat, tapping the floor impatiently with his walking stick—pointing out old landmarks—deploring the appearance of new ones, but fretting all the time to be off, and walking. He seemed to have forgotten all about his lumbago.

At least the beginning of their favourite walk had not been disturbed: they saw to their joy the battered old signboard: "FOOTPATH TO WELDEN." It seemed to have shrunk back into the trees to avoid the greedy paws of London. The same old smelly farmyard with a heap of steaming manure—the same big, ramshackle gate that had to be heaved up before it could be opened, the same broad, rutted track beside the stubble field—in ten minutes there was not a soul in sight.

" It looks as if they *knew* this was our walk," said Mr. Baldwin, " and left it for us ! "

" It's lovely," said Edith.

They came to the first wood, and some young rabbits went bouncing away into the undergrowth: they picked some blackberries, and took a rest upon a stile.

" Before the war," mused Mr. Baldwin, " think of all the things that have happened since we got over this stile last time." He fumbled for his tobacco pouch, filled his pipe and lit it. He sat looking into the wood—slowly swinging his stick—puffing little clouds of smoke into the quiet, frosty air.

" You know, Edie—I often wish I'd gone in for Natural History. I don't know what any of these trees are called."

" Those are just thorn trees," began Edith, " and of course those are silver . . . ," but he broke in as though he had not heard.

" If only we'd got a bit of land like this at home—something to clear and really work in—you know—sort of virgin soil—with tough things growing in it. There's nothing in our garden that's got enough spirit to catch hold of your trouser legs and tear them."

There was a nip in the air, and they rose to go on. Far away to the left, behind a group of trees, some tiny red and white specks were eddying to and fro at football, but ahead of them the path wound slowly upwards in solitude. In her eagerness to encourage her husband Edith had not questioned her own ability to cover three rough, uphill miles, but half the distance was behind them before she began to feel fatigue. The walk was turning out a wonderful success and tiring feet were nothing to the exhilaration she was feeling. If they could do this every week ! It would lift the dread clouds of winter: it might bring him new interests. His birthday was in a fortnight's time and she decided to get him a Natural History book and possibly something about country rambles.

They frequently paused to recollect small incidents that had happened in the past: a spot where Mrs. Baldwin's shoe-lace had once broken and the bank they had rested on to make repairs: the wild corner of a meadow where on two succeeding walks they had discovered a hedgehog in exactly the same place, and the evergreen oak that once sheltered them from a sudden shower. In half an hour they found more to say than in the past two months.

It was half-past four as they climbed the last gentle slope towards the crest that concealed the village of Welden in its valley. The sun was beginning to set behind them, there would be a mist, a trail of wood smoke—a few flickering lights beckoning them down the slope to the log fire, toast and tea. The last half mile down-hill was the best part of the whole walk, with its great solitary elms and clumps of gorse—a lovely little valley that marked the twilit, peaceful end of their journey.

" Thank goodness nobody's tried to spoil it," said Mr. Baldwin as he reached the summit a little ahead of his wife.

And then he stopped dead. She saw his jaw drop and heard his exclamation of astonishment.

In a moment she was beside him, and they stood together in speechless dismay. There below them lay the valley : the sun was sinking beneath a dark strip of cloud, and as they looked it sent a long pale stream of light across the land as though to say : " Look what's happened while you've been away ! "

The desolate charm of it—the wild, fragrant peace—had gone for ever : through the soft gorse field stretched broad, hideous gashes of naked yellow clay, and clustering along them, like evil fungus to a fallen tree were hideous new houses—stacks of bricks—pyramids of sewage pipes—piles of white timber—mud-stained lorries and sheets of hunched tarpaulin—a nightmare of perverted progress.

Aloof and unchanged lay their footpath and the hedge that skirted it, for it lay some little distance from the ghastly mess—unchanged, from this distance, lay Welden Village, but a new road had buried itself in its very heart. Untouched, for the moment, were the solitary elms, brooding over the desecration beneath them—silently awaiting their fate.

" We might have known," whispered Mr. Baldwin.

Edith could not reply, for suddenly a leaden weariness had fallen on her. A three mile walk over rough, uphill ground was no light undertaking, but she had faced it stubbornly and joyfully because of the things it had promised them. And now, at the moment of its climax, when it seemed as if nothing could prevent the success of the adventure, the whole thing was shattered by the view before them. She knew that they could never repeat this walk with the knowledge that the destruction of their favourite valley awaited them at its end: Their tea-shop had probably been swept away by now: they would drag themselves to the station—there would be a cold, hungry journey home—the same sordid squabbling would begin again—it would all begin again for another hopeless, pitiless winter.

They walked on in silence, their eyes averted from the houses as from something naked and unclean. All that they wanted now was to pass it by and forget it if they could. Even the path was theirs no longer: it had been churned by the hobnailed boots of workmen—paper bags hung suspended in the gorse bushes—bottles lay in the ditch—a filthy rag of a waistcoat assaulted them.

At one point the footpath led them within a few yards of the new road, and they could not avoid a repugnant glance at the houses beside it. Three appeared to be finished: two more were completed except for their roofs, and another half dozen stood in various stages of stark, skeletoned ugliness.

But new built, empty houses have an attraction for human beings that new haystacks have for cows, and despite their disgust and indignation, Mr. and Mrs. Baldwin could not resist a moment's pause.

In different circumstances they might have admitted them quite pleasant. The first was square built and snug looking—cream walled and green shuttered, with a sturdy green front door. The house beside it was entirely different but not incongruous: it had the irregular, inconsequential charm of a Tudor cottage, with oak beams and gables. And each stood comfortably in its own land.

" They'll be falling to bits in five years," said Mr. Baldwin. " The first big storm'll wash them away. Jerry built—all show and no strength. I pity the people who live in them. Come on."

" May I show you round ? " came a pleasant voice that startled them with its unexpectedness. When he had recovered from his surprise, Mr. Baldwin discovered a young man beside them—a pleasant looking young man in a sports coat and grey flannel trousers. He wore no hat, and a big, unruly tuft of light brown hair lay across his forehead. He looked more like a tall schoolboy than a young man. Where he had sprung from was a mystery, for a moment ago, Mr. Baldwin and his wife seemed the only living souls in the twilit valley.

The young man appeared to understand their surprise, and began to explain.

" We've only just started this Estate and we're going to make it our best. It's a lovely spot, isn't it ? We've just opened a Show House across here. I thought perhaps if you were looking for a nice house. . . ."

" We're *not* looking for a house," said Mr. Baldwin rather curtly.

" Oh, I'm sorry."

The young man took the snub so pleasantly that Mr. Baldwin felt ashamed of his rudeness.

" I mean," he said, " we should only be wasting your time."

The young man brushed the hair off his forehead and laughed.

" You won't do that because I shall waste it in any case.

I'm here to show people round and nobody's turned up this afternoon at all. We've hardly begun advertising it yet, you see. I'm new to the job, too. If you've got five minutes to spare I can practise on you. It would do me good."

Despite his annoyance Mr. Baldwin could not help a smile. There was something attractive and disarming about the boy. Although the afternoon was cold he was not even wearing a waistcoat: his tweed jacket was open and a striped, coloured tie swayed carelessly across his chest. He looked as if he ought to be playing football somewhere instead of standing about in this desolate place on a Saturday afternoon. He was one of the new kind of boys one saw about these days—rather like Musgrave at the office. They looked so much as if they ought to be playing games that people took it for granted that they would be no good at work—and yet they tackled their jobs with an inspiring sort of eagerness to get on and succeed. Mr. Baldwin glanced at the boy, then across at the little cream-painted house that gleamed in the dusk.

" Well," he said, " if you're sure you don't mind . . . would you like to look over it, Edie ? "

" Very much indeed," said Mrs. Baldwin.

They followed the boy across the maze of yellow ruts that would one day be a road : they crossed a deep trench of glistening pipes and through the oak gate of the Show House.

" I must apologise for all this," said their guide, pointing to the rubble-strewn front garden. " It's too late to put down grass this year, but we shall do all that in the spring. It's awfully good, light soil—with lots of gravel underneath." He swung round on Mr. Baldwin with a broad, mischievous smile. " That's the way to begin, isn't it ? Tell people about the soil ! "

" That's the way," said Mr. Baldwin, with an artful smile back.

He was beginning to enter into the fun. It was a good joke to go round a house like this: to be one of the actors in a sort of dress rehearsal. He nearly said: " I knew this valley before you were born, my boy," but checked himself for fear of putting the young man off his stride.

The front door stood invitingly open and their guide switched on the light in the entrance hall. He patted a strange flat metal affair let into the wall.

" Central heating, you see. This radiator keeps the hall nice and warm: there are radiators in all the rooms, of course."

" Is it hot now ? " asked Mrs. Baldwin in surprise.

" Oh, yes. Feel it. The house still wants a bit of drying. It was only finished last week."

Even with the front door open and the frosty air curling in there was a delightful warmth in the house—a clean, fresh warmth flavoured with wood shavings, fresh paint and new furniture.

" The radiators are heated directly from the kitchen boiler. There's no extra expense at all."

" Very convenient," murmured Mrs. Baldwin. Her eyes were roving curiously round the entrance hall. At home there was nothing but a high-ceilinged, narrow passage, crowded with the coat-stand and umbrella-rack, with doors leading stiffly off from it. But this hall was far more spacious: almost a room in itself, with the stairs leading up at an attractive angle and a long, interesting window on the first landing. She noticed that the carpet

covered the whole floor, and there were no ugly borders
of bare, stained boards. It was a warm, generous carpet,
a simple powder blue with no tedious design to grow tired
of.

" There's plenty of room for coats and things in here,"
said the young man, throwing open a spacious cupboard
that completely lacked the stale stuffiness of their cupboards at home. It had the freshness of pine needles in it.

The first big surprise was the downstairs cloak-room,
with wash-basin and lavatory. All their lives Mr. and Mrs.
Baldwin had associated the act of washing with going
upstairs: they did this, on an average, six times a day,
making an annual ascent equivalent to the conquest of
Mount Everest. " Saves lots of time," said Mr. Baldwin,
peering into the compact little closet.

" And here's the dining-room."

A bit plain, thought Mr. Baldwin. A funny-looking
table and set of chairs that did not look quite finished.

" Weathered oak," said their guide, " the latest thing.
Don't you think it's rather attractive ? "

It grew on one, certainly. Clean and healthy looking.
Perhaps it was because this vigorous young man approved
it, but Mr. Baldwin could not imagine feeling bilious
after eating a meal from such a table.

But the whole room was so gloriously clean and airy.
Its very plainness and simplicity captured the imagination
and gave one the feeling of being on a ship bound for some
high spirited adventure. One could never feel depressed
or old in such a room, with such generous windows and
bright cream walls.

" Service hatch to kitchen," said the young man,
opening a little door beside the fireplace.

And the kitchen itself! Nothing in it, of course—but Edith could picture glistening rows of saucepans on its spotless shelves. It was more like a scientist's laboratory than a kitchen. . . .

" You see how the corners of the floor and ceiling are rounded to make sweeping easy. There's nowhere for dust to collect. Electric stove. . . ."

" Very expensive," said Mr. Baldwin, feeling it high time to put in a little criticism.

" On the contrary," said the young man, " far less expensive than the old fashioned range."

' " But you've got to have a coal fire as well to heat those radiators."

The young man's eyes lit up in triumph:

" No, sir !—this boiler scarcely needs any coal at all: it burns up all the kitchen rubbish. You make your rubbish warm your house and give you hot baths ! Now let me show you the lounge."

The kitchen and dining-room had already taken most of Mrs. Baldwin's breath away, and the lounge removed the little that remained. She saw it first in semi-darkness, with a panel of sunset upon one wall and a twilit stretch of the valley through the broad windows that opened boldly upon the garden. Then the young man switched on the light and the room was floating in a soft amber glow. It took in the full breadth of the house, with deep bow windows upon the road, but there was nothing gaunt about it: there seemed to be nooks and crannies— unexpected little alcoves and recesses—an intriguing little oval window like a ship's porthole high up in the wall. The settee drawn up to the fireplace looked almost too comfortable to be real, and the armchairs opened their arms to her when she looked at them. The fireplace itself was of small, mellowed bricks: it looked like the arched gateway to a miniature Tudor mansion and made one think of crackling logs and moorland peat. The colour scheme was impossible to define at a glance: all kinds of colours sang out from the cushions and curtains, and seemed to blend themselves into a bold, light-hearted melody. There were no odds and ends—no knick-knacks or protruding furniture to bruise the thighs. There was a friendliness, a simplicity—a clean freshness—a gaiety about this room. It thrilled Edith and saddened her, for it was no more than a dream. In a few minutes they would be on the road to the village and the magic of this little house would be a memory: a dwindling, dark patch in a darkening valley. Twice, it seemed, she heard the word " bedrooms "—and then a quiet laugh brought her to a consciousness of other things: her husband had gone, but the young man was standing by the door.

" Would you like to see the bedrooms ? "

She followed him, wishing very much that there might have been some means of keeping the bedrooms for another day: her mind was buzzing with a score of little things that were searching for places to settle in her memory: she would have preferred to give them time to sort themselves out before opening the doors to new ones.

Tom was standing motionless in the window recess of the chief bedroom as she entered: he was obviously impressed, for he had removed his hat. He turned his head and said: " Come here."

" Funny to see our old footpath from the window of a house," he said.

It was certainly a queer experience. From this window they could trace the footpath up the side of the valley until it disappeared over the crest. They could see the point from which a few minutes ago they had looked down in such astonishment and disgust, and Edith wondered what her husband was thinking now.

The young man looked surprised at Mr. Baldwin's remark.

" You're not strangers then, sir ? "

" No," said Mr. Baldwin, with an attempt at truculence, " we've come down that footpath many a time: we used to come miles to enjoy the view of Welden Valley and now you've—you've done this to it . . ."

The young man seemed at a loss for a reply. Then he said :

" I'm afraid somebody would have built sooner or later. We shan't spoil it: we're leaving a lot of open spaces: every house'll be in its own ground. Somebody might have packed it with horrible rows of cheap things and ruined it. Besides, nobody can touch your footpath."

" No, but—— It's a pity, you know." Mr. Baldwin felt he had fizzled out rather lamely. He turned and inspected the bedrooms. There were four altogether—two were very small, and although the light distempered walls made up for it, Mr. Baldwin felt it was high time to assert himself in earnest.

" Our bedrooms at home are much bigger than this. It must be rather depressing, sleeping in such small places."

" Of course," said the young man, " they *are* small, but lots of people prefer them small nowadays. You see there are lavatory basins in all of them—hot and cold

Ho

water night and day—and you see the furniture's almost all built in." He opened an unexpectedly big cupboard that was fitted like a wardrobe.

The lavatory basins were a revelation: the Baldwins had heard about them, but had never actually seen them. They had imagined them to be rather disgusting, and insanitary—but Mr. Baldwin could not help picturing himself getting out of the sturdy, weathered oak bed, strolling to the basin, turning a tap and shaving in luxury. He thought of the little can of hot water that Ada brought up—the rickety washhand-stand and ungainly jug and basin—the eternal search for a match to light the geyser.

The young man treated the bathroom with a casualness that must have been artificial. It was impossible to be calm and blasé in the face of that final, glistening wonder. The walls were covered to the height of four feet with shining white tiles and above the tiles lay an azure sea, with sailing ships heeling to the wind: the bath itself was partly sunk into the floor and might have come from the palace of a Roman Emperor: there were glistening taps: recesses in the wall for soap and flannels—a bell you could press while in the bath—and a shower. . . .

" We're much obliged," said Mr. Baldwin at the gate: " very interesting." They had been in the house far longer than they had realised, for stars were shining overhead and a frosty crust was gathering upon the clay ruts of the road.

" Pity we don't want a new house," he added in a weak voice.

" I suppose that's a lot of money," said Mrs. Baldwin.

"More than *I* could afford," replied the young man with a wistful laugh: "but it's extraordinarily cheap considering the way it's built. You see, when you put up a number of houses on the same Estate you naturally cut down costs all round."

"How much is that one?" asked Mr. Baldwin

"Well, the one you've seen is £1,175. We're not building anything to spoil the value of the place. Prices range from £1,950 to £1,050 according to size. Furnishing's cheap because so much is built in: you don't need wash-hand-stands or wardrobes or old fashioned stuff like that. That house was furnished complete for £350."

"Really?" said Mrs. Baldwin. She could scarcely believe it. She would have said a thousand. "£350?"

"That's all." A little white card gleamed in the darkness. "If you know of anyone looking for a house—will you give them my card? It'd do me a lot of good if you *did* happen to put someone my way."

"Certainly," said Mr. Baldwin. "Certainly I will. Good evening—and thank you."

He wondered for a moment if a tip were expected, but the way the young man smiled and turned away was quite sufficient to show that everything was all right.

"I must go and turn those lights off," he said. "Good night."

"Nice young chap," said Mr. Baldwin, as they picked their way back to the footpath. "Ought to do well."

After a silence he said, "I think it was the way he showed us the house that made it seem so attractive."

"Perhaps so," replied Edith after a thoughtful pause.

Lights had been shining from every window when they left the house. When Mrs. Baldwin glanced back she saw

one solitary panel glowing through the darkness. Even
as she looked it disappeared, and the house was swallowed
in the night.

The moon was rising as they reached the village, and
when the bye lane joined the old world High Street they
were delighted to see their cake shop as brilliantly lit—
as resplendent with fancy cakes and doughnuts as of old.
Even the buxom woman—(whom they had always assumed, from the name over the door, to be Mrs. Chambers)
—was still there, as rosy and as buxom as ever.

" Well, this *is* a surprise ! " exclaimed Mrs. Chambers.
" It's just about this time of a Saturday afternoon you used
to arrive in the old days. Toasted scones ?—some nice
assorted cakes ?—will that fire be too hot ?—it's certainly
coming over chilly."

They confirmed that their train left at 6.24 and settled
down comfortably for an hour's rest. Mrs. Baldwin was
ready for it : a three mile walk in untried shoes had tired
her more than she cared to admit, but their interesting
visit to the Show House had compensated in a curious
way for the ruination of their favourite walk. She was
even beginning to wonder whether the houses had ruined
it after all. It might possibly add interest to the walk,
for every time they came over the crest and down the hill
there would be something new to see. Having actually
been inside one of the houses made all the difference.
They would not be strangers : they might even meet their
pleasant young friend again and have a joke with him
about the number of houses he had sold. One by one
they would see the houses springing up and the gardens
coming to life. With all her heart she envied the lucky
people who were to live in Welden Valley, for to them

would come the romance of pioneers, and however old they might be in years they would have youth in spirit, for no one could feel age in such a house as the one they had just seen.

Tom was very silent after tea, but not morosely silent. He sat puffing his pipe—his feet up on the window seat— the wood fire flickering in his face. The walk had brought a healthy colour to his cheeks and had obviously dispersed his lumbago. When he caught her looking at him he pulled out his map and began to study it.

Edith closed her eyes and tried to doze, but all kinds of odds and ends kept passing beneath her closed lids. One thing that kept pushing itself forward was the wonderful built-in dresser in the Show House kitchen, with an ironing board and pastry board that drew out like drawers.

The wind had risen while they were resting in the tea-shop: a few dark rags of cloud were scurrying across the moon and the lane to the station was pregnant with power and danger from the massive, straining trunks of the elms. Some pigs were squealing in a farmyard: a man with a bucket came out of the gate and said, " Good evening."

" Good evening," said Mr. Baldwin, feeling like the village squire. Then he said to Edith: " You know, you might easily be a hundred miles from London here."

They said very little to one another during the journey home. They had a compartment to themselves and Mrs. Baldwin was able to sit with her legs resting along the seat. She had a pain like toothache in her shin bones and the small of her back was so stiff that she resolved upon a hot mustard bath before going to bed. It would be a poor business if the walk cured Tom's lumbago and gave her an attack in exchange.

Mr. Baldwin stretched his legs along the opposite seat, but after a while he grew tired of looking into the carriage: he brought his feet down and sat for a long while in silence with his eyes upon the moonlit, ghostly fields.

A circular in a halfpenny envelope lay on the hall mat when they opened the door. How cold and ill-lit and clammy the passage seemed—how badly the damp-stains showed up on the wallpaper above the coat rack. Edith, on her way home, had begun to scheme and plan. She had wondered whether they could possibly save up a little and gradually transform their house into something like the one they had seen in the valley: they could easily have the depressing wallpaper taken off and a bright cream distemper in its place: central heating—lavatory basins—she had resolved to make secret enquiries in Maida Vale—but the first cold whiff of stagnant air in the passage dispersed her dreams—the whole house would need pulling down and re-shaping, for nothing could brighten this narrow, hopeless passage and the steep cramped stairs. She began to wish they had not accepted the young man's invitation to see the new house—for though the memories might fade she would never be able to quench the sadness and discontent that they would leave behind.

But although the shabbiness of the old house destroyed her plans it did not depress her spirit, for the walk had splendidly justified its purpose. They both felt bigger and stronger: their hands and faces tingled. The long uphill

climb had given both of them a new pride in themselves:
they had both been through a gruelling test and emerged
with flying colours. Despite the new houses in Welden
Valley she was confident that Tom would want to go
again.

She went to her bedroom and changed her stockings:
there was a blister under one toe but otherwise her feet
appeared all right. And because she felt well and happy
she put on the black velvet dress that was reserved for
special occasions. Tom's cheerful whistling in the bathroom drew her thoughts away from the drabness of the
bedroom, and she went happily downstairs.

She picked up the evening paper that Tom had been
reading in the train and stood by the fire with it, waiting
for him to come down to dinner. She could not avoid a
glance at the heavy old fashioned mantelpiece, and the
big, cumbersome mirror above it: she tried to concentrate
upon the news, but she was thinking all the time of a
sturdy, simple fireplace in mellowed brick, and a romantic
little oval window high up in the wall, framing the evening
sky and the swaying tips of an elm.

Her eyes wandered to the Stop Press column of the
paper: there were a few football results and a blank
space below—but in this space were some faint, pencilled
figures. She wondered what they were, and fumbled for
her reading glasses on the mantelpiece. She could see at
once, by their neatness, that the figures were in Tom's
handwriting, and first of all was written—£1,175. Something gripped her weary shin bones: it seemed to gather
and race through her body until it touched her heart
and sent it wildly throbbing. £1,175 !—the figures that
had been buzzing in her brain for the past three hours—

since the boy had casually mentioned them in the valley.
So Tom had been thinking about it, too. She had thought
that he had put the house from his mind in the first steps
away from it towards the tea-shop, for he had avoided
all mention of it on the journey home. There were more
figures underneath—uncertain and difficult to decipher:
it was a small sum—£1,000, £200, £37 10s. 0d.—
added up to £1,237 10s. 0d., and underneath were a few
unmeaning little squares and criss-crossed lines—a kind of
futuristic picture of his thoughts. . . .

She dropped the paper as he came in, briskly rubbing
his hands: there was a glow in his cheeks and he looked
at her with steady smiling eyes.

" How d'you feel, Edie ? Tired ? "

" Legs ache a bit—but not tired."

" Mine ache, too."

" But the lumbago's gone," she said with a mischievous
smile.

He was guarded about that. " I don't know yet. I'll
tell you in the morning. It was a risk."

" You're looking awfully well, though."

" I feel it, Edie. It was a good idea of yours—that
walk."

Ada brought dinner in, and he lifted the lid of the
casserole. " Irish stew, eh ! Just the thing for hungry
tramps like us ! I oughtn't to want any after that big
tea—but I do ! "

They talked mainly of the walk as they had their dinner:
of the woods, and the tea-shop, and the village, and
although Tom grew indignant at the way the bus route
had been disfigured by new factories, he did not mention
the houses in Welden Valley.

When dinner was over, he rose and stood lighting his pipe by the fire.

" I bet you aren't going out for a walk to-night ! " said Edith.

He made no answer for a moment. He was just about to say something as Ada came in to clear away, and he turned abruptly and went to the windows.

By force of habit he looked between the curtains to see if the windows were closed. He usually muttered something about a dangerous draught as he did this, but to-night he said nothing. He gave the curtains an extra pull as if to ensure secrecy and when Ada had made her final departure with the table-cloth, he came and stood by the fire again.

" Edie," he said, " why shouldn't we have one of those houses in Welden Valley ? "

She looked up breathlessly from her needlework. She did not want to interrupt by saying anything. Her own mind had taken her as yet no further than the question he had asked, but she felt that his must have probed the dark, exciting spaces beyond. A pointless remark from her might destroy everything—she wanted to sit in silence, and listen—but all he said was:

" Why *shouldn't* we ? "

" D'you mean it, Tom ? *Could* we ? "

He nodded. " I'd have laughed at the idea a couple of days ago. People like us get timid, you know—fixed down —afraid to move. As we get older we get more and more afraid until at last we think we'd die if anything happened to disturb us." He turned away and stood looking into the fire. " You know, Edie—we've had a rotten year, haven't we ? Nothing wrong with us—enough to eat—

plenty of comfort—but, oh, you know—hopeless: it's all
so old and dingy here. Nothing to—to keep us young.
Think of that—that lovely house . . ."

"That lovely house," whispered Edith.

He swung round eagerly: "You liked it?"

"Liked it?—what a question!"

He was at the table now—he drew up a chair beside
her—a sheet of paper before him and a pencil in his hand.
He looked like a General planning a battle.

"Look here. This house is ours. It's worth £1,000—say
£900 at the lowest. We could sell it quite easily. Then I've
got £200 in the Bank and £37 10*s.* in the Post Office.
I've put that by since I retired. You've often thought
I've been mean and stingy."

"I've never!"

"Oh, yes, you have—or you ought to have anyway—
but—but—*I* don't know—money's got on my nerves and
I've put by when there's really no need. Anyway—it'll
stand in good stead now." He threw his pencil down.
"There you are, Edie! £1,137 10*s.* and the new house
is only £1,175!"

She hated throwing even a thimbleful of cold water.

"But there'd be lots of extras, Tom—fittings—lamp-
shades—and the garden. . . ."

"The garden!" His eyes lit up with a new light—
"perhaps we'd get a piece with one of those big
elms!"

He could sit still no longer: he rose and paced the room:
he stood in odd corners where he had never stood before:
his eyes took in the walls, the floor, the ceiling: they were
measuring the height of the bookcase—the breadth of the
sideboard—the shape of the carpet.

" I'd say all this furniture would go in, wouldn't you ? This ceiling's higher, of course, but there's a good clear foot above the bookcase there. It'd all go in, wouldn't it, Edie ? "

His excitement suddenly seemed to fade into uneasiness and doubt: his last words were more like an appeal for help than a direct question, and she understood what had suddenly come to trouble him.

Her own heart, too, had fallen when she glanced round at the ponderous furniture surrounding them. It was so terribly ugly and depressing in the light of what they had seen that afternoon. She pictured their enormous mahogany sideboard, with its ancient scars and musty, unwholesome drawers, wedged against the delicate cream walls of that fragrant little dining-room: the sullen, carved oak bookcase, almost black with age, squeezing out the sunlight, hopelessly out of place—would be like a resentful, stooping giant in a fairy house. Most of the stuff had come from Tom's family home in Colchester, and the drawing-room furniture from her father's vicarage. The bedstead upstairs, with its loose brass knobs, had been bought secondhand when they had married, together with the yellow pine wardrobe and dressing-table. The rest had come at odd times, from here and there. Nothing really matched, and although it had never pleased her, it had never brought such revulsion as it did now: each room of the Show House was furnished with an entrancing little suite of uniform design.

Their first frantic enthusiasm had been far too wonderful to last: Tom's calculation far too plausible to bear the test of hard reasoning: even as she listened she felt there must be a snag somewhere, and sure enough there was.

She saw her husband's splendid new dream about to crumble away like all his others. They would need every penny to buy the new house and to think of a new set of furniture was out of the question. And yet it would be a mockery to move and be followed by all this faded, depressing furniture: it did not look so bad in a faded house, but in a new house it would look ghastly. It would carry the seeds of the misery they had suffered in the past year, and in a little while it would all spring up again.

Mr. Baldwin still stood by the table, but he was no longer sizing up the furniture with eager, critical eyes: he was looking at it sadly and hopelessly: his hands were twitching, and she saw the little droop return to the corners of his mouth. In a moment he would give way, and she knew what the reaction would mean. She knew instinctively that a chance such as this would never in their lives come again. They would never recapture the reckless spirit of adventure that had swept them for one glorious moment beyond the timid reasoning of middle age. If the devil had appeared in this moment of need she would gladly have given him her soul for the money to buy that new furniture and sweep this hopeless stuff away. And in answer to her thought came an idea that frightened her: that she fearfully repulsed: that gathered and flashed up again.

Upon the death of her mother, Edith had received some legacies that she had treasured as a sacred trust. There were several rings and two small diamond brooches, hallowed by memories and locked away in a small box in her bedroom cupboard. There was also a mysterious gift described by the lawyer as London Chatham & Dover Railway 5 per cent Debentures: she had never seen them and had never quite understood what Debentures were. They sounded like some kind of office furniture. They had always been locked up in the vaults of the Midland Bank and twice a year a remittance of £10 arrived like a fairy gift which never failed. Tom refused to allow her to spend it on the house, so it went upon new clothing and a few small luxuries, including birthday and Christmas presents. She had been given to understand that these Debentures were worth £400, but she no more thought of disturbing them than she would have pawned her mother's jewellery. She guarded them as her mother before her had guarded them—as a perpetual monument to the self-sacrificing determination of her grandfather that the women of his blood should never be quite penniless.

But something had happened this night that had never happened before: to clench her teeth—to abuse her trust and to sell those Debentures might mean the raising of two struggling souls from a living purgatory.

She hardly recognised her voice: it sounded loud and hollow—like someone else's when one is half asleep.

"Tom!—we're not going to take a stick of this old stuff with us!—we're going to sweep it all away and start all over again!—absolutely afresh—with lovely new things from beginning to end! We can do it, Tom!"

He looked at her in astonishment: she was bouncing up and down in her chair as she jerked out the words, and he suddenly felt afraid: Edith had never fainted or had hysterics, but this appeared to be the onset of something very queer. He wondered what he ought to do.

"Why, Edith?—what d'you mean, dear?"

Breathlessly she explained: she was out of her depth when she tried to talk about simple finance, and Debentures were even worse—but one thing she knew: they were worth money: £400: and they weren't going to lie asleep in the Bank for another day—they were coming out to buy glorious new furniture: gleaming pots and pans for the kitchen: powder blue carpets: bright chintz curtains—suites of weathered oak—everything—everything they needed for their new home in Welden Valley!

He listened in silence—then shook his head.

"No, Edie, dear. It's—it's awfully—good of you—but those Debentures are yours. This is my responsibility."

"They're not mine!" she cried, "they're ours!—everything's ours!"

He began to pace the room again. He had never tried pacing the dining-room before and it made him realise for the first time how hopelessly big and cumbersome everything was: the old leather chairs were clutching at his knees, imploring to be spared, but he had no time for sentiment. It was a magnificent idea of Edith's: the fresh, healthy furniture of the Show House danced before his eyes: it beckoned and sang to him. He stopped abruptly, sat down beside Edith and lay a hand upon her arm.

"Listen, dear! Even if we buy everything new we shall never need *all* that money. We'll sell all this: it's good sound stuff and some people like old furniture. We might get enough to buy everything new without touching your money at all!"

"We might," said Edith, looking at the brown stain behind the mirror.

"But it's magnificent to have that money in reserve!

—it makes it all possible "—his hand closed tightly upon her arm—" it's wonderful, Edie, isn't it ? "

He looked up at the clock and then at his watch. He got up and went on apologetically—like a small boy who expects a scolding.

" You know Martins—the furniture shop at the corner of Edgware Road ? There's a light in the window all night. I'll—I'll just pop down and see if I can get an idea of prices—it'll be interesting."

" Why not let's go together in the morning ? "

" To-morrow's Sunday."

" But we could look in the window."

" It won't take half an hour. You go up to bed, dear. I'll come up and tell you directly I get back."

He was gone for more than half an hour. When he came up to the bedroom he explained that he had gone for a walk round to have a good think. He sat on the foot of the bed, fingering one of the loose brass knobs.

" Edie—there's a lovely bedroom suite—the whole thing—bed—dressing-table—everything—guess ? "

She had not the slightest idea without seeing it, but made a most fortunate attempt:

" Twenty pounds ? "

" Eighteen pound fifteen shillings ! " he said triumphantly. " We'll do it, Edie !—we'll do it easily—the whole thing ! "

Edith laughed and hitched herself up a little stiffly in bed.

" Tom—I meant to have a hot bath and get rid of this stiffness—and I forgot all about it ! "

He threw up his head and laughed so loudly that she had to remind him that Ada was asleep upstairs.

"What about Ada?" he said, "shall we take her? I suppose we must." Then he bent forward and said in a low, impressive voice:

"In the new house you are going to have a hot bath every night and no wretched wheezing old geyser to wait for!"

He got up. "I've just got to work out a few more figures downstairs."

"Don't stay up too late. It's been a tiring day."

"No—only half an hour."

She heard him run downstairs. She heard the dining-room door close and a chair being drawn up to the table.

CHAPTER XI

Edith woke to the thud of a fog signal and cold rims to her nostrils. The first white frost of the winter was upon them, and it brought back to her the first days of her husband's retirement a year ago.

He was still heavily asleep beside her. He had come up far later than he had promised, and it must have been past midnight when she half awakened to hear him stealthily undressing in the dark.

He had risen on his first morning of retirement with such brave hopes for his new life and the fine things it promised him: in a little while he would be rising to meet the new hope that had come to take the place of what had so painfully and pitifully died.

She lay watching the faint, slow trail of mist creep through the curtains and she felt the muffled stillness of the fog-bound Sunday morning. Would this new endeavour fade out as the past one had? Would they wake to the first fog signals of next year's winter in this bedroom, a little more worn and shabby, themselves a little more tired? There was a man and his wife whom they had once known and extracted secret amusement from: they were people who always had some wonderful plan in mind, who were always on the verge of doing something remarkable but never quite did it. One really never knew oneself: perhaps she and Tom were like that without

IG

realising it. It had all sounded so easy and magnificent last night, but it was a little too easy and magnificent to believe in the cold light of a frosty, fog-bound morning.

She prepared herself with all her philosophy to meet her husband's awakening. She could picture him turning over and looking at her with dull, shamed eyes—and saying—" Edie, I thought it all over last night—and I don't *think* we can do it. You see, dear . . ."

She did not want him to wake until he had slept his fill. She decided to go down and tell Ada to hold up breakfast for half an hour, but when she moved to get out of bed she let out such a gasp of surprise and pain that Tom turned over and opened his eyes.

He was a slow waker, and for a little while he stared at her. She was sitting bolt upright in bed as if she had seen a ghost.

" What's the matter ? " he asked.

She gave an uneasy laugh.

" What is it, Edie ? "

" I don't know—I can't move. My—my back and legs —they're. . . ."

" Poor old Edie !—it was that walk." He raised himself and cried out : " Ooh !—mine're the same."

It was a huge relief: for a moment she had had visions of crippling rheumatism.

" My legs . . . they're like bits of board."

" Bound to be after a walk like that. You ought to have had that hot bath last night. I tell you what. I'll go and turn on the geyser and tell Ada we'll have breakfast in bed."

Edith protested. " Ada with a tray on those stairs ? "

" Do her good," said Mr. Baldwin lightly. He climbed

gingerly out of bed and put on his slippers and dressing-gown. He paused at the door and said :

" I'm glad we're feeling stiff, Edie. It shows we didn't dream what happened yesterday."

" You're still keen ? "

" Keen ? Don't be silly ! "

She heard the husky pop of the geyser and lay back thoughtfully in bed : she knew that she ought to be relieved and delighted at his buoyant mood—but the very ease and casualness of his confidence disturbed her a little : she would have felt happier if he had awakened with some tough problem to grapple with but he seemed to have swept all problems aside. She wished with all her heart that she could feel as he did—but to her it was still too easy—too magnificent to be free from hidden danger.

He returned with the Sunday paper and climbed back into bed more easily than he got out.

" Healthy stiffness soon wears off," he said. " We'll have an easy morning and get down to things in the afternoon."

" What did Ada say ? "

Mr. Baldwin laughed. " Not much. Too surprised. We've got bigger things to face than Ada now." He began to turn the paper and suddenly sat up in excitement.

" Look here !—a whole page advertising new Estates ! Funny we've never noticed this before."

Edith had vaguely glanced at the Estate page on many a Sunday morning and passed it by without a thought. It was now as fascinating as in the past it had been dull. The broad page was filled with announcements of different shapes and sizes : Estates jostled each other and pushed their attractions eagerly and frantically before the reader's eye. The Meadow Hall Estate was exquisitely

situated in a centuries old garden: the Pitberry Hill
Estate offered a glorious view over three of nature's most
favoured Counties: the Chawley Down Estate invited
one to enjoy a breeze that blew one's cares away: a
lovely reach of the noble Thames was at one's feet for
18s. 7d. weekly : "£10 down and no legal charges": £5
secured possession of a home to be proud of. Houses at
£699 sounded suspiciously more expensive than those at
£700 : there were solitary aristocrats standing amidst
pines at £1,875, but nothing, in the final opinion of Mr.
and Mrs. Baldwin, to rival the Show House in Welden
Valley.

It was good to have before them every kind of alternative and slowly whittle them away until their valley
remained supreme. The banks of the Thames meant
dampness and fog—the Downs would rattle windows
too boisterously and keep one awake: a house in a centuries old garden offered no crisp virgin soil to break
and tame. " It's all right," he said, " all these are nice—
but there's nothing quite so good." He lay the paper
down and gazed at the ceiling with his hands behind his
head.

When Edith returned from her bath the breakfast tray
lay on the bed and Mr. Baldwin was industriously at work
with a writing pad.

" Young Mr. Morrison's going to have a pleasant
surprise in the morning," he said.

" Who's Mr. Morrison ? "

He began to tease her. " Ronald Morrison !—*you* know
Mr. Ronald Morrison ! "

" I've never heard of him," said Edith.

" But you said you liked him ? "

"What are you talking about?" she began, and then she said, "Oh!" and laughed. He was holding up a card which she recognised as the one their young friend in the valley had given them the night before. "Oh—is that his name? Ronald Morrison?" She took the card and read with interest:

MR. RONALD MORRISON

Welden Valley Estate,
　　Welden,
　　　　Middlesex.　　　　Phone: Welden 801.

"How does this sound?" said Mr. Baldwin. He picked up the sheet of paper and began to read:

"DEAR MR. MORRISON,—When we met you yesterday we had no intention whatever of buying a new house. Thanks, however, to the interesting manner in which you explained your Estate, we are persuaded that, subject to the satisfactory arrangement of terms, we should like you to build us a nice house somewhat after the style of the one you showed us.

"We are free on Wednesday afternoon and shall be pleased to meet you upon the Estate at 3 p.m. to discuss the matter further."
　　　　　　"Yours sincerely, etc. . ."

"That's awfully nice," said Edith.

"No harm in giving the boy a lift up. He'll naturally show it to his boss and it ought to do him a lot of good. Some people would write a formal business letter direct to the Estate, but it's the personal touch I like. You'll find that boy'll be useful to us over lots of little things."

" Can't you picture his face when he reads it ! " said Edith, as she carefully sat up and poured out the tea. " His hair'll flop over his face and he'll probably start singing."

" He'll probably get married on the strength of it."

" I hope he does," said Edith. " Mind how you eat that egg ! "

They stayed in bed for an hour after breakfast and calculated how much they would get for the bedroom furniture. They agreed it conservatively at £15, although Mr. Baldwin thought the tallboy in the corner, which came from his father's house in Colchester, was probably an antique and might fetch almost anything. " You never know," he said.

A shroud of steel grey, motionless fog wrapped Brondesbury Terrace when they drew the curtains. Towards midday the sun appeared : a flavourless pink ball that groped for an hour then packed up in despair and moved on to more responsive lands. But the weather mattered little to the Baldwins now. After lunch they went all over the house making an inventory of the furniture and placing estimated values against everything. It reached the satisfactory figure of £400.

" If all goes well," said Mr. Baldwin, " we shall scarcely have to touch those Debentures of yours."

They had both secretly feared that the old house might hold a subtle power to shame their light-hearted plans. Once or twice, as they went from room to room, some little, unexpected thing would stir a memory and arouse a pang, but as the day drew on the old place slowly released its feeble grip and by the evening it scarcely seemed their home any longer. As they drew the curtains and turned on the lamp they felt as if they were settled for a night's lodging in some old Harbour-side hotel: that a ship nearby was waiting for the morning, when it would take them aboard and sail for mystic far-off lands.

Mr. Baldwin made a fair copy of his letter to the young man of Welden Valley and went down to catch the early evening post to ensure its delivery in the morning. He added a short postscript:

"P.S. Perhaps you would see if you can arrange a piece of land for us that includes one of the big elm trees that are such a pleasant feature of Welden Valley."

"To-morrow morning we start in earnest," he said when he got back. "First of all we must go to an Estate Agent about selling this house." He threw himself into an armchair by the fire.

"By Jove ! I'm stiffer than I thought ! "

"We oughtn't to have walked so far," said Edith.

Mr. Baldwin sat up and stared at her across the fire.

"Supposing we hadn't !—supposing we'd turned back before we got to the crest of that hill ?—and had never seen the valley—and those houses ?—I wonder . . ."

"I wonder," murmured Edith.

CHAPTER XII

THE OFFICES of Timbrell & Dove, Auctioneers and
Estate Agents, were situated in Station Approach. Mr.
Baldwin had passed the place thousands of times on his
way to catch his train, but nothing until now had given
him reason to go inside. His first view of the interior was
a little disappointing: he had pictured a spacious office
buzzing with officials managing Estates and people buying and selling houses: he discovered a small dingy room:
half office, half shop, and nobody to be seen.

But voices came from an inner room, and presently a
pale, weedy young man appeared and looked at Mr. and
Mrs. Baldwin in surprise. He had a boil on the back of
his neck which made it look as if he were peering over
the top of a pair of invisible spectacles. It was obvious at
a glance that he was neither Timbrell nor Dove.

" Yes, sir ? "

Mr. Baldwin approached the counter. " We want to
sell a house." he announced.

The flutter he had expected failed to materialise: whatever interest the youth had shown immediately disappeared. He picked up a grubby looking piece of paper,
handed it to Mr. Baldwin, nodded stiffly towards a
rickety little table in a corner and said:

" Fill in this form, please."

Mr. Baldwin was so surprised that he felt it was up to

him to do something unexpected, but as nothing occurred to him he took the form and sat down. It was an insult to his house and an insult to him to have the matter treated as if he were registering for a housemaid. What he had expected he could not, perhaps, explain: vaguely he had hoped to find kindred spirits in this office who would enter into his own enthusiasm about it all: keen business men who would jump at the prospect of selling a sound, well built house so near the station, shops and Park, who would applaud the bold step that he and his wife were taking. Their visit to the Estate Agent was the first move into the open: Sunday had been packed with secret discussions: they had worked until midnight in a fever heat of suppressed excitement, and it was depressing that the first outside person to know about it should be an insipid young man with a boil on his neck.

It occurred to Mr. Baldwin that he should have asked at once to see one of the partners, but that was too late now. He drew the form towards him and picked up the pen he was expected to use. The nib was so bloated with clotted ink that it looked more like a prune than a writing instrument. He drew out his fountain pen and began:

Address of Property:	Grasmere, 14 Brondesbury Terrace.
Freehold or Leasehold:	Freehold.
Sitting Rooms:	2
Bedrooms:	4
Bathroom:	Yes.
Garage:	No.
Telephone:	No.

It was a little disturbing to sit at this drab rickety table and fill in poor old " Grasmere's " death warrant: he had an uncomfortable feeling that he was playing the old house a dirty trick behind its back. It was waiting for them to return, patiently and trustingly, like an old, devoted dog that they were planning to have destroyed.

The form itself was so unattractive that " Grasmere " seemed to shrivel up and decay as he filled up the bare, commonplace particulars. " Sitting rooms: 2 " was a travesty of fact: he wanted to add: " large folding doors between drawing- and dining-room opening upon wrought-iron balcony and steps to spacious garden," but something told him that it would mean nothing to the dreary minds of Timbrell & Dove. He left blank the space after " Price demanded " because it looked like a trap. He rose and pushed the form across to the waiting clerk, who glanced at it, blotted it and disappeared with it into the back room.

Mr. Baldwin winked at Edith to show that he was feeling all right about everything: but inwardly he had never felt less like winking. Until this moment he had not doubted that a ready and eager purchaser would appear. The difficulty had not been connected with the selling: it had been in the mustering of courage to burn their boats and sell. They had done that triumphantly: they had left home upon the wings of adventure, determined not to hesitate or falter, and now something in this drab, cheerless office had made him feel horribly different about it all. Supposing nobody would buy " Grasmere ? "—that would mean . . . he dared not face what it would mean. . . . As he stood waiting, he watched the heads of passers-by. They did not glance at the office: none of them looked as if they would dream of buying " Gras-mere." . . .

" Would you come through, please ? "

The clerk was standing at the inner door. Mr. Baldwin made way for Edith with an encouraging smile, but a heavy, anxious heart.

" Good morning ! " said a fat man with a large tobacco stained moustache. " Sit down, madam. Sit down, sir."

It was a small office, smothered, like the rest of the place with large, flimsy notices. How it would burn, thought Edith.

The fat man sat down at his desk and pushed aside some papers to make room for Mr. Baldwin's form.

" ' Grasmere '—Brondesbury Terrace," he read. (He might, thought Mr. Baldwin, have added: " Of course—I know the house.")

" We are moving into the country," said Mr. Baldwin.

The Estate Agent looked up in sudden interest.

" The country ? Have you decided upon the district ? We represent several very charming new Estates—no doubt we . . ."

" That's all decided," said Mr. Baldwin, somewhat irritated, and he noticed a distinct cooling off in the fat man's interest.

" Quite. I only mentioned it because we have special facilities for purchase, etc. When—er—do you wish to move ? "

" Not until our new house is ready, of course."

" Is it near completion ? "

" It isn't started yet."

" Oh. That means at least six months. It'll give us more chance of doing something with this."

He raised the form containing the particulars of "Grasmere" as though it were contaminated.

"I'm afraid there's not much demand for houses in Brondesbury Terrace."

"No demand!" exclaimed Mr. Baldwin—"there hasn't been a house for sale there all this year!"

The Estate Agent looked at him with a weary smile.

"Quite. But you know, some people object to notices being stuck up."

Mr. Baldwin felt cold, and slightly sick. The egg he had eaten so hastily for breakfast in his hurry to call at this dreary place had formed into a hard lump in his stomach. "Some people object to notices being stuck up,"—that meant presumably that everybody in Brondesbury Terrace was secretly and hopelessly trying to sell their house.

The man had a genius for stirring up annoyance: he sat back, stuck his thumbs into his waistcoat and said: "Basement?"

"*All* the houses round here have got basements," snapped Mr. Baldwin.

"That's the trouble," replied the fat man. "Basements are the curse of our business." He peered at the form and added: "No garage, I see."

"'Grasmere's' near the station—five minutes from the shops and Park—it's . . ."

"Oh, I know—but, you see—it's the wrong *side* of the station: it's not a district people are looking for in these days."

Mr. Baldwin curtly rose and Edith looked up in surprise. His face was pinched and pale, and his hand was quivering as he reached for his hat. He was staring over the Estate Agent's head—through the bleak uncurtained window that faced the Railway. But there was a halting dignity about the way he said:

" You mean you would prefer not to act as our agent ? "

This time the man behind the desk looked surprised. There was a little note of respect when he answered.

" Not at all, sir ! I shall be delighted to act for you. Only you know, sir—I find my clients frequently think it's easier to sell than to—er——"

" Buy ? " enquired Mr. Baldwin.

The man laughed. " You've got it, sir ! "

" Of course I realise there's not a queue of people waiting outside to buy my house."

The Estate Agent laughed again. He pulled out a tarnished case, straightened the cigarettes in it with a fat, stained finger and offered it to Mr. Baldwin.

" I'm sorry if I gave you the wrong impression, sir. I don't often fail to sell when I get busy on a house. I only wanted you not to expect anything too—er— exceptional. Let me come up and see it. Will you be in at "—(he opened an appointment book and quickly covered the blank page with his hand)—" three o'clock ? Very good, sir."

" And, by the way," said Mr. Baldwin at the door— " we intend to sell *all* our present furniture and buy everything completely new for our new house. I shall want to auction it."

" Certainly, sir. Thank you. My partner Mr. Dove attends to valuations : he's away to-day, but I'll ask him to make an inventory. Good morning, sir. Good morning, madam. Three o'clock, then."

"I didn't like him at first," said Mr. Baldwin.

"I don't like him much now," replied Edith. She had not said a word during the interview, but she had seen a good deal. "I think we might do better, Tom. There's a much nicer looking place in the High Street."

"Give him a trial," said Mr. Baldwin. "After all, he's on the spot. He'll give us more personal attention than you'd get from a big place."

They turned into Brondesbury Terrace and walked down towards their house. Both were wondering, as they returned, whether half-burned boats could ever be patched and launched again if the worst came to the worst.

Mr. Timbrell turned up promptly at three o'clock and seemed much more interested in the furniture than the house. He took the house in at a glance—as much as to say—"I know the type"—but he spent a long time in the drawing-room examining the furniture and china in the bureau.

Mr. and Mrs. Baldwin showed him everything: pointing out good features and stressing the fact that a good deal came from old country houses. "Yes," said the Estate Agent—then "Yes," again. He looked thoughtful and interested, and Mr. Baldwin's spirits began to rise. It looked as if the man had spotted something really good. "You're going to sell *everything*?"

"Everything," chorused Mr. and Mrs. Baldwin.

Mr. Timbrell nodded approval. "It's an original idea: an excellent one if you ask me. You ought to see the old junk some people cart about with them."

The last remark detracted a little from the first. There was an unpleasant flavour about " old junk " that Mr. Baldwin did not like.

" Now, sir ! " said Mr. Timbrell, drawing up a chair to the table. It *would* be the one with the split leather, thought Edith, and the man would naturally put his fingers into the grey, dirty-looking stuffing.

" Now, sir. The house. We ought to agree upon a limit price. You can depend upon me to get the highest figure, of course, but we must fix a limit."

Mr. Baldwin's heart began to thump. The time for pleasant speculation was over and they were to face hard facts at last.

" I paid £750 in 1913 and I've made a good many improvements since then, of course." He kept his eyes from the ceiling, where above the electric light bowl lay the brown tinge from the gas-lit days. " I imagine all property has risen in value a good deal since 1913. It's freehold, of course, and not mortgaged in any way."

" Quite," said the Agent. He sat silent for a while, drumming the table with his fingers. A greasy bowler hat lay beside him and his open overcoat hung almost to the floor. Mr. Baldwin watched him steadily, and suddenly remembered another point.

" I'm certain there's never anything empty in this road : people never seem to go."

Mr. Timbrell glanced up quickly. " Quite. I know— but—but you see, they're mostly the kind of people who— who stay—if you know what I mean——"

" Because it's a good neighbourhood," suggested Mr. Baldwin with a smile.

" I didn't mean it like that," put in the Estate Agent.

" Don't think I'm trying to run the house down: it's sound enough—but it's old fashioned: that basement kitchen, you know——"

" Our servant never complains," said Edith—but Mr. Timbrell appeared not to hear.

" It's a wrong impression to believe that house property of this kind has risen in value—the trouble is that such a lot of new houses are going up nowadays and people naturally go for modern places."

Mr. Baldwin felt his irritation rising again. They had been through all this once.

" Well," he said, " what price are we going to fix? "

Mr. Timbrell drummed with his fingers again.

" We shall be very lucky if we get the price you paid."

" The—the price—I paid? . . . £750? "

The man nodded, and there was a grim finality in his nod.

" But, my dear sir, you're—you're not serious? I paid £750 before the war—when a sovereign was made of gold. I consider it worth at least £900 now."

" But, think, Mr. Baldwin—why *should* we get more? You've had years of wear and tear out of the place! You wouldn't expect to sell a suit of clothes for the price you gave for it, would you? "

" That's different."

" Wear and tear's the same with everything, though: there's a going out of fashion. I assure you, Mr. Baldwin, I've been an Estate Agent for twenty-five years. . . ."

Mr. Baldwin glanced up. His eagerness had gone: he looked tired and listless.

" We—we must consider it," he said in a low voice. " We—we didn't realise. . . ."

At the door he remembered something that had been tremendously important a little while ago.

"The furniture?—what would you think we ought to—er . . .?"

"I'd put it round about £90," said the Estate Agent, "but I'll send Mr. Dove to make an inventory. Then you'll let me know, sir? Good day. Good day, madam."

That evening Mr. Baldwin drew up a little statement, and Edith and he sat looking at it in silence for a long time.

DEBIT	£	s.	d.	CREDIT	£	s.	d.
New house	1,175	0	0	Old house	750	0	0
Additional				Sale of furniture	90	0	0
Fittings, say	50	0	0	In Bank	200	0	0
New Furniture	400	0	0	Post Office	18	15	0
Extras unpro-				Edith's Deben-			
vided for, say	25	0	0	tures	400	0	0
	£1,650	0	0		£1,458	15	0

K G

CHAPTER XIII

A HOUSE proudly valued at £1,000 battered by an expert to £750 : its furniture carefully calculated to £400 shrunk to a fantastic £90 : every penny of the reserve Debentures swallowed up and a crushing debt of £200 remaining with no earthly prospect of repayment.

Mr. Baldwin lay in bed, weary and heavy eyed from a sleepless night, wrapped in the misery of his return from a fool's paradise. A move to Welden Valley would carry the torments of financial suicide that none but a lunatic would bring upon himself. He should have known from the beginning that it was too good and easy looking to be true : that the beaten track, with all its dullness, remained the only secure path for the man no longer young. He should have known the ominous reason for the lack of footprints upon tall green grass and glistening, undrying sands. If it were easy to slip out of one's threadbare envelope of existence then every dreary road within call of London would be a desert of empty houses.

A year ago he had thought that he alone of all the thousands who retired had found the secret door to a new life : he had wondered why others had never used it, and as the months passed he had found out why. It needed younger, stronger arms than those of a man of sixty to lift the latch. And now—a year later, when another door had revealed itself and enticed him to its entrance, a single day had proved it too narrow for the lorry load of cares that follow a man in middle age.

The crushing little statement of figures, with a pencil beside it, lay on the bedside table. He had brought it to bed with him in the fruitless hope that some revelation might come in the night. He picked it up and lay staring at it in the curtained dimness of the autumn morning; he added it up again and put it aside. Forty years in a profession that glutted itself upon caution had taught him one thing at least: that figures, to be properly digested, must be taken cold and raw. He was a fool who tried to boil them into different shape and dry them before a radiant imagination. As he had climbed into bed at the end of the dreary Monday of disillusionment, Edith had turned with a wan smile and said: " Whatever happens—nobody can say we haven't tried."

He heard the gate squeak, and the heavy clump of the postman up the steps. It should have set his heart thudding with anticipation but it meant nothing now.

Two letters came up when Ada brought the morning tea: both bore Welden postmarks—one was addressed in typescript, the other on private paper in a round, schoolboyish hand.

WELDEN VALLEY ESTATES LTD.

Directors.	Welden,
W. N. Turnbull.	Middlesex.,
R. Sovretti.	24th October, 1924.
T. S. Sotherby.	

" DEAR SIR,—We beg to acknowledge with thanks receipt of your letter of the 22nd inst., addressed to our Mr. Morrison.

" We are very pleased to learn of your desire to have us build you a house on our new Estate. One or two very delightful positions remain available and our Manager, Mr. Watkinson, will meet you at our Estate Office on Wednesday afternoon at 3 p.m.

" A car will be waiting for you at Welden Station and a convenient train is that arriving at 2.48 p.m."

The other, in the round, boyish hand:

" DEAR MR. BALDWIN,—I don't suppose it's the proper thing to write like this, but I really must tell you how grateful and delighted I was to get your charming letter. You can't think what it means to me. It's my first big success, and. . . ."

Mr. Baldwin lowered the letter to the crumpled counterpane. He could not read the rest, for a hot, smarting mist had filled his eyes. Poor boy—his first big success—his first big disillusionment. Fools that they were to have written and sent those youthful hopes bounding before they had made certain that the move could be made. What could he write in reply?—altered plans?—a weak lie about postponement? Whatever he wrote and whatever he did the boy would remember him as one of the type that fed a cheap vanity upon deference extracted by big talk and false promises.

He picked up the typewritten letter and glanced at it again: " one or two delightful positions are still available." Through the mist he saw the span of meadowland: turf rolled up and set aside: the outline of a house drawn in broad strips of naked soil: walls rising: window-frames settling in place: dark tiles and chimneys and the first

shy wisp of smoke. Welden Valley would spring to life
and soften to maturity and they would not be there.

Edith was sipping her tea. She had seen the letters
but had not asked to read them. But to her at least an
idea had come during the night:

" Tom. What about all the money you've paid into the
Life Insurance ? Couldn't you borrow that ? "

He shook his head. If anything were to happen to him
there would be just enough from the insurance, together
with her widow's pension, to keep her from need.

" No, Edie. We can't touch that."

But even as he spoke an inspiration jerked him up in
bed.

He often wondered afterwards why the idea had not
come to him before: why he should have spent a day of
misery with the way out staring him clearly in the face.
Probably because the word " mortgage " was a funereal
way of saying " loan," because a loan meant financial
failure—moral collapse and every other disturbing thing
that his laborious but honourable creed had stiffly turned
its back upon. When he had left home to come to London
his father had given him a piece of valuable advice:
" Never borrow—and never lend."

It was particularly good advice in Mr. Baldwin's case,
because while he had never had any cause to borrow,
men in the office had frequently invited him to lend.

But he had no false ideas about these things: to live
within one's income without a call upon one's self restraint
was nothing to be proud of. It showed, on the contrary,
an anæmic grip of life. All the really attractive and
vigorous men he had known were chronically in want of
money and usually in debt and he admired them because

their embarrassment came from vigour, imagination and a fierce desire for the things that money could buy.

He admired them because they showed contempt for the things he feared: moneylenders—sleepless nights and the losing of his job. To raise a mortgage upon his house to cover overspending in other directions would have been in his eyes the first step to a midnight seat on the Thames Embankment. But several old shibboleths had gone overboard in this memorable week-end and suddenly the one about mortgagers went over with a smooth slip and scarcely a struggle. It was no longer an ominous word of failure. To raise a mortgage of £200 upon a house worth £400 more than " Grasmere " was a step forward rather than a step back and the word took upon itself a sweet sounding note of honourable rescue: a march from a fallen city with flying flags and undelivered swords. He swallowed a mouthful of tea and said to Edith:

" What would you think if I were to say that whatever we have to do—whatever the risks we have to take—we shall have that house in Welden Valley ? "

Two round eyes looked at him over the tea cup: the sip that Edith was on the point of taking was indefinitely postponed, and in fact never taken. Half an hour later Ada discovered a half cup of cold, forgotten tea upon the dressing-table.

" I'd say," said Edith, " that whatever it means— whatever we have to do—even if I have to go out and do dressmaking—I'm with you, Tom."

He felt quite moved and had to recover himself before he began to explain.

" You see, dear, a mortgage doesn't mean you've really *borrowed* money. It simply means we exchange a small part of the house for what we need to pay for it."

Edith did not quite understand—nor did Mr. Baldwin, exactly—and he tried to make it clearer.

" If you were to borrow money and spend it on a holiday that you can't afford—then that's a different thing altogether, because you've spent the holiday *and* the money. All we do is to sell a house worth £750 and get one worth £1,175—we are £425 better off but £200 worth of the new house still belongs to the Estate. We are £225 to the good, you see. The little piece of the house that belongs to the Estate is always *there*; we haven't spent it and we gradually pay it back until one day the whole house is ours. We pay £10 a year interest, but we save that by growing our own vegetables. We'll easily do it, Edie. We shan't want to spend much on ourselves in the new house because it'll be so fine just to live in and work in. So it's all right, Edie—it's absolutely all right after all ! "

And Edith, in her joy, did an embarrassing thing. She pressed his hand, quickly kissed him, and said: " Bravo ! " She used to do things like that when she was young, and it had always made him feel a bit awkward. It made him wriggle somewhat hastily out of bed, but he was too happy to feel irritated. He understood how Edith was feeling: he could have run all over the house shouting, " Bravo ! " himself, at the top of his voice. The dark clouds of failure that had closed upon them the previous evening had lifted now without possibility of return, and their lifting had set the fires of excitement blazing more fiercely than ever before. They knew the worst and they knew that the worst could not stop them: if " Grasmere " only sold for £600 instead of £750, they could still go on: it would only mean an extra £150 mortgage—£7 10s. od. a year

in extra interest. Edith had inspired him more than she
knew when she had said that about doing dressmaking :
he would do anything : go out gardening—address
envelopes at a thousand a shilling—anything would be
joy with the house in Welden Valley.

Plans they had made for the day and sadly set aside,
sprang to life again : they had arranged to go to London,
to call at the Bank and arrange about Edith's Debentures,
and spend the afternoon at a big furniture store in the
West End. In the course of a hurried shave Mr. Baldwin
decided that while he was in the City he would pay a visit
to the old office. He had not been near the office since
his retirement : he had shrunk from joining the ranks of
the decrepit old dodderers who went in to waste the time
and patience of the active staff. But he could go with
a purpose now, and chuckled at the surprise he would
give them all. . . .

They called at the Estate Office on their way to the
station and told Mr. Timbrell to go ahead as quickly
as possible with the sale of " Grasmere." Mr. Timbrell
looked as if he had not expected to see the Baldwins
again and was both pleased and surprised to receive
such prompt instructions. He promised to get busy at
once and the Baldwins said they had no objection whatever to a " FOR SALE " board being put up in their
front garden.

Mr. Timbrell introduced them to Mr. Dove, his
partner, who was to value their furniture for the auction.
Mr. Dove was inclined to be patronising, and after

reference to his engagement book, informed them that he would call at three o'clock that afternoon.

But Mr. Baldwin shook his head.

" I'm sorry—we're absolutely full up all day—we haven't a moment."

Mr. Dove began suggesting Wednesday.

" I'm afraid Wednesday's no good either. We've got an important engagement in the country."

It was clear that he was building up a good impression, and after a discussion, Saturday morning at ten o'clock was settled.

It was pleasant to walk the old City streets again: to breathe that old familiar smell of wine vaults and stability: to cross at old familiar places with Edith on his arm. The Bank Manager was polite but obviously surprised: he was very pleased to meet a lady whose Debentures he had protected for so many years. They were no longer called " London Chatham and Dover Debentures," owing to the big Railway Merger, but they were just as good—if not better. Yes, certainly: they could be sold at any time. He consulted the *Financial Times* and stated that the Debentures stood slightly over par, at 102⅝. That meant that after deducting brokerage they would receive a clear £400, and as Mr. Baldwin heard this he gave a sigh of relief. The tide had turned at last: at last something was worth what they had estimated. It was arranged that the sale should be effected when the money was needed in the spring: the Manager personally accompanied them to the door and they were able to bask for an extra half minute in the flattering deference paid to Capitalists.

" Now," said Mr. Baldwin, as they stood outside, " we'll look in at the old office."

He stepped out confidently, but an overpowering shyness crept over him as he approached the familiar doors. It was going to be a big ordeal to walk in after such a long, unexplained absence. He had promised to look them up quite frequently and his failure to appear must have caused some speculation amongst his old friends. Had he broken up ?—he was just the kind that would : the eyes of the whole staff would be upon him : upon his face, upon his clothes, upon Edith. It was not like entering a drawing-room and being at once surrounded : the staff, during office hours, would have to remain more or less in their places, and it would mean long distant, embarrassed smiles and nods to most of them across the tops of desks and around brass railings and stone columns. His courage almost failed, and he was on the point of turning aside when Henslip the old Messenger, in his seedy top hat and brass-buttoned tail coat appeared, approaching the door from the other direction. Mr. Baldwin joyfully hurried forward and called out to the Messenger as he was about to go in.

" Hi, there ! Henslip !—how are you ? "

It took the Messenger a moment or two to realise who it was, then a broad smile and a firm handshake broke the ice.

" Why, if it isn't Mr. Baldwin !—You're a nice one, sir ! You promised to come in and see us months ago."

" I know. I've been so terribly busy—haven't had a moment—but here I am, and this is my wife."

" You're looking five years younger than when you left, sir ! "

"And I feel ten years younger," beamed Mr. Baldwin in reply. "I want to see Mr. Wilson. Take me in, Henslip. I'm feeling shy!"

His entrance was impressive, beyond all his expectations: he made his way down the broad marble flagged aisle in earnest conversation with Henslip, glancing up now and then to wave friendly but brief acknowledgment to his old friends. He caught sight of several new, boyish faces as he went along, but in all other respects everything was absurdly the same—except, perhaps, the little glassed-in cubicle where he had spent his last years of active service. That somehow looked remote and strange.

Wilson, the Manager, looked absurdly the same, too. He might easily have just sat down after delivering his speech and handing Mr. Baldwin the clock. Mr. Baldwin half expected to see the shavings from the parcel still lying on the desk.

"Well, this *is* a surprise! We thought we were never going to see you again! How do you do, Mrs. Baldwin. Sit down."

He produced a box of cigarettes, and Mr. Baldwin felt agreeably surprised and happy. He realised what a very wise thing it was to be elusive, and to make rare appearances.

"You're looking extremely well, Baldwin."

"I feel it."

"Enjoying yourself?"

"I'm enjoying every minute of it. There's so much to do, you see. And now we're just going to start building a new house in the country. You can realise what that means: new furniture—new everything."

He had meant to keep this back for a bit, but he could

not resist firing off all his artillery at once. Wilson, a younger man, had passed over his head to the Managership and had never been able to conceal a little touch of tolerance that Mr. Baldwin had resented. It was a pleasant experience to sit back balancing his hat on his umbrella handle, puffing Wilson's cigarette and telling him about his new house. " We're off to Harrod's this afternoon to see about furnishing."

Wilson looked at him incredulously.

" Why—have you—have you had some luck, or something ? "

Mr. Baldwin enjoyed a silent chuckle and shot a furtive wink at Edith. How true to type this fellow was ! He took it for granted that a retired Insurance Clerk should potter out the rest of his days in obscurity, thinking in humble little ways, doing humble little things—clutching his little pension in humble gratitude and warming his toes gratefully beside his humble little fire.

" Luck ? " he said. " No. No special luck. We just happen to be tired of the old house, so we're selling it and buying a new one, that's all. We're tired of our old furniture, so we're selling that, too, and buying new, modern stuff. We're going to rather a delightful spot in Welden Valley, beyond Stanmore. After all, the whole point of retiring is to get out of the rut and start afresh, isn't it ? "

Mr. Wilson gave it up. It beat him. Baldwin of all people. He shifted a little in his chair, for he was feeling vaguely irritated. Baldwin's eyes were upon him with a clear, amused steadiness: Baldwin reached forward and casually flicked his cigarette ash into the wastepaper basket. He was behaving like an important client when he should behave diffidently and gratefully like the retired clerk he was. He ought to be sitting with awkward embarrassment, not knowing what to do with the long grey ash on his cigarette and dreading lest it fell on the Managerial carpet until he, the Manager, lightly pushed forward the ashtray on his desk to the accompaniment of grateful thanks. He felt irritated.

"I just came along to say I'd like to insure the new house in the old office: I'll drop a line and tell you when it's ready. It'll be for £1,175—probably £1,250 with fittings, and £400 on furniture."

"And a Rolls-Royce car?" enquired Mr. Wilson with a hint of malice.

"Not yet," smiled Mr. Baldwin, "I'll try and get the new owner of 'Grasmere' to keep the insurance of it in the old office, too."

"Splendid!" said Mr. Wilson, without much conviction. He turned to Mrs. Baldwin with a gracious smile.

"I expect you're enjoying the excitement, Mrs. Baldwin?"

"Very much, thank you," said Edith.

That was better. She was timid, in any case, she was a retired clerk's wife, even if the husband were a bit above himself. "I wish I could ask you to lunch with me, but I'm lunching with Mr. Addison Cotter, who's just back from America. You remember the Addison Cotter Estate, Baldwin?"

Mr. Baldwin certainly did. An awe-inspiring list of properties that filled six ledger pages. He had a feeling that the Addison Cotter Estate had been fired at him in retaliation.

"Well," said the Manager, "come in and see us again.

I'm glad to see you looking so well. Good-bye, Mrs. Baldwin."

Edith went out and sat on the leather seat beneath the window while Mr. Baldwin strolled round to shake a number of hands in the main office. She heard the words " Welden Valley " several times, and each time she heard it the sound of larks and the sigh of the wind seemed to rise above the dull roar of the City traffic. She heard someone say, " Are you going to keep a cow ? " and she saw Tom join heartily in the laughter. How different he looked—what a miracle had been wrought in the past four days !—only four days ! She had swelled with pride in the Manager's office. Tom looked ten years the younger of the two—bright eyed—healthy cheeked—keen and alert—nicely dressed—a country gentleman. The Manager had looked tired and dusty—there were dark shadows under his eyes and some grey, crumby-looking fallen hairs on his coat collar.

She was thinking of the wonderful change in her husband : she had no mirror to reveal how she, too, had changed. She only knew that never in her life, until this moment, had she felt the happiness and excitement that life was ready to give to those who did not fear its shadows and uncertainties.

It was chance rather than design that carried them home in the very train that Mr. Baldwin used to catch on his homeward journey in his office days, and chance that placed Mr. Baldwin in the same corner that had been his on the night when the clock in its parcel lay above his head. It was a queer, uncanny experience to look round the crowded carriage and see once again the kind of people he had known so well—two girls deep in library books—an office lad with a paper backed thriller—men with pipes and newspapers—a youth with a text-book and a man with nothing to read but a whisky advertisement on the panel opposite him. The same atmosphere: the same rattle: the same electric signs. Mr. Baldwin sat thinking of his last journey; a year ago but as clear as yesterday. He thought with a sad wistful-ness of the fantastic plans that had carried him home on the last evening of his working days—how futile and unsubstantial they had been; how splendidly real were the things that lay ahead this time.

He leant forward, touched Edith on the knee and whispered through the rattle of the train:

" To-morrow we go to Welden Valley and pick our piece of land."

Edith leant back again, nodded several times, and smiled.

CHAPTER XIV

THE TREES were waving excited branches over the lane that led from Welden Village to the station: they tossed up little handfuls of russet leaves and bent over the road to watch them fall. They grew much too near the road, thought the chauffeur of a large saloon car. One day one of those enormous elms would lose its balance and turn a good car into scrap iron and a good chauffeur into pulp. They seemed to grow straight out of the farmyards, a mere yard or two from the low grey walls that girded the lane.

The chauffeur was a sensitive man, and each time a great gust boomed overhead he thought he could hear giant branches cracking, and ducked towards the driving wheel of his car. It sounded like the sea. An eddy of leaves smacked the window, chased each other round to the back of the car and followed like demented little boys.

A lovely day: a clean October sky: a clear cut landscape and a smell of wood smoke and pigs. It was certainly rural, this Welden Valley. For himself he preferred the Hampstead Estate that the Governor had just finished. You could see the whole of London from there and you could be in the heart of it in twenty minutes. Down here in Welden Valley you felt like a beetle in a basin.

There was time for a cigarette before the 2.48 arrived: he pulled up in the station yard and smoked inside the

car, for the wind outside gave him a headache and red
eyelids.

It was quiet enough for anybody down here: a man
breaking coal on a truck in a siding seemed to begin and
complete the whole sum of human endeavour. A solitary
porter appeared and gazed up the line as though somebody had told him a train was coming and he thought he
was having his leg pulled.

Still, the Governor would wake things up a bit. Five
hundred houses he talked about building—each in its
own land and separated from the others, and when the
Governor planned a thing he usually completed it. He
glanced back at the sleepy village and wondered how it
would take the strain. A funny man, the Governor: he
really did seem to try and make his Estates worth living
in: he gave up good bits of land simply to turn into green
verges, and what he called " Closes."

He climbed out of the car, opened the windows to let
the smoke out and stood by the barrier as the train came
in. Doors crept furtively open and pale hands held them
an inch apart until the brakes had squeaked into silence.
Only about half a dozen people got out: a workman—a
schoolgirl—a traveller with a bag of samples: the chauffeur's practised eye quickly singled out his quarry—he
could not mistake them as they climbed out of the middle
of the train. An alert, slightly built man of about fifty—
looked like a solicitor—grey hair—jaunty tweed cap, grey
flannel trousers and immaculate brown shoes. Plenty of
money, decided the chauffeur. He carried a burberry and
a stout walking-stick: obviously a town gentleman out for
a country house: he had all the symptoms, even to the
way he carried his burberry carelessly over one shoulder.

Lᴏ

The lady had lost something: she was fumbling hastily with her bag and umbrella: a plump, pleasant little lady with grey hair and a brown coat and skirt: she was searching the platform rather short-sightedly. The husband darted forward just in time to retrieve a small suede glove that was on the point of beginning a precarious journey to St. Albans on the footboard of the train.

The chauffeur saluted. " Mr. Baldwin, sir ? "

" Yes. That's right."

" I've come to drive you to the Estate, sir."

" This is business efficiency and no mistake ! " said Mr. Baldwin.

" It is indeed," murmured Edith.

She turned in her deep, bouncing leather seat, put her arm through the leather rest and peered up at the trees as they waved their boisterous welcome. " Isn't it lovely ! "

Mr. Baldwin was pretending as hard as possible that he was not entirely a stranger to luxurious Daimlers. He was also thinking, a little uneasily, that the Welden Valley Estates Ltd., must make quite a good profit out of their houses to afford this sort of thing.

" D'you realise," said Edith, " that this is the first time we've seen Welden Valley in broad daylight ? It's always been dark by the time we've had tea and come along here to the station."

" Yes. Funny, isn't it ? " Mr. Baldwin would have preferred the new Estate to have come upon them gradually in a leisurely walk from the station: he would have enjoyed drawing out this period of rare anticipation. He looked through the window at the village that was soon

to be their home—at an old brown church lying back
amongst the trees, at a snug village street to stroll along
in pipe-lit ease on summer nights—meadow-paths and
wild flowers—a square of amber light in the valley
beckoning him home. A little way ahead, hidden for the
moment by the old houses of the main street, lay a green,
unsuspecting square of land—unaware of those who were
swiftly approaching it, who were soon to claim it and
begin to tame its wild virgin heart. Mr. Baldwin lay back
in the car and thought to himself, " This is a moment
that'll never come again—hold it tight, and keep its
memory."

They swung to the left in the centre of the village, up
the lane that used to end in their footpath from Stanmore.
But now, where the lane used to fade into the heathland,
the new road began, and presently they were swaying
slowly and gently along a broad ribbon of billowy clay.

The ride was over. They stopped beside a neat little
Estate Office that might have been built from an expensive
box of toy bricks.

" Here we are, sir," said the chauffeur, jumping down
and opening the door. " Lovely day."

" Beautiful," said Mr. Baldwin, bumping his head on
the roof of the car. " Thank you."

" The wind's dried everything up nicely," added the
man as he took Mrs. Baldwin politely by the arm and
helped her out.

The Baldwins had no precise idea of what the Manager
of a select Building Estate should look like. If a large
weather-beaten man in Scotch tweeds had appeared they
would probably have said afterwards: " Exactly what we
thought ! "

But Mr. Watkinson was a surprise. They would not have come near him in a dozen guesses. He was short and square, with a smooth pink face and little polished red patches on his cheekbones: a bald, pear-shaped head and a little pointed beard—rather like Shakespeare. His dress seemed quite unsuitable to his profession, for he wore a large butterfly collar, a dark suit and pointed black shoes. But after all, thought Mr. Baldwin, he was a business man, and most of his time was probably spent at Board Meetings in luxurious offices that demanded pointed black shoes. He could not change each time he came to the Estate to meet a client.

He greeted them warmly but briskly, and conducted them through the outer room to his private office. Mr. Baldwin noticed interesting maps on the wall as he passed through: a girl at a typewriter, a few small fragments of up-to-date houses piled in a corner—a glazed brick, a door-knocker—an interesting looking bath tap. It all looked very busy and prosperous.

Mr. Watkinson wasted no time in coming to the point; he waved aside Mr. Baldwin's faltering explanation that they had not quite decided upon the exact house they needed.

" There's plenty of time to arrange that: you must have a quiet look at all these plans. What we must do first of all is to fix down a good position: you must have one of the best before they're all gone."

" Are they—going ? " enquired Mr. Baldwin, pleased but a little anxious. He felt certain there would be a rush for the positions that had the big elms upon them.

" *Going !* We sold seven last week: twenty-nine this month : roughly one a day—and the demand's increasing.

I expected it would go quickly but I've never known anything like this ! " He sat back and threw out his hands to show how helpless he had been in stemming the rush, and Mr. Baldwin was very thankful they had not delayed.

Then he noticed that Mr. Watkinson was eyeing them both—keenly and thoughtfully. Mr. Baldwin began to wish he had not dressed so smartly, as it might give a wrong impression. On the other hand, he reflected, it might be all to the good if the man over-estimated them at first : he would give them more attention and show them the best. He probably handed shabby people to assistants who packed them away in the worst positions.

Then Mr. Watkinson suddenly appeared to make up his mind. He looked at Mr. Baldwin firmly and decisively and said : " You must build your house in Welden Close."

" Welden Close ? " enquired Mr. Baldwin—guiltily, as though he ought to have known all about it.

For answer Mr. Watkinson briskly rolled out a plan, secured its corners with an inkpot and paperweight and pointed rather dramatically to a green square towards the top of the paper.

" Here," he said.

" That looks quite nice," said Edith.

" It's the only place that will really satisfy you," answered Mr. Watkinson. " You see, first of all we have Bracklesham Avenue and Cymbeline Road—here. Well, that's very nice indeed for people prepared to live in an ordinary road, facing other houses, but the people I like are those who are *not* prepared to live in ordinary, formal roads, and for those people I have designed Welden

Close. This," he said, pointing to the green square, " will remain open for ever—a village green—a close—and the houses that are built round it will look out for all time upon a stretch of green turf with trees round it— upon gorse bushes—in fact, upon nature undisturbed."

Mr. Baldwin noticed that several of the positions round the Close were coloured in pink.

" Are they—er—gone ? "

Mr. Watkinson nodded. " I'm not showing Welden Close to everybody," he said. Then he looked at them keenly again and added slowly and deliberately: " but if you'll allow me to be very personal—you are the right kind of people."

It was certainly rather personal, and a little embarras- sing, but Mr. Baldwin knew what he meant and appre- ciated the point all the more when Mr. Watkinson explained.

" Why do you join any Club ? Not because of its name—or its age—or its reputation, but because of the kind of people you see going in and coming out. The kind of people—that's the only thing that matters."

" Quite," said Mr. Baldwin.

" And I apply that test to my Estates. It may sound snobbish, but I'm a business man. The right kind of people attract *more* of the right kind of people. I apply that," he went on hastily, " to the *whole* Estate: to Welden Close I apply it in the highest degree—because," he whispered confidently, " because I intend to build a house and live in Welden Close myself ! "

He gave them a slow, artful smile as he rolled up the plan, and the Baldwins laughed. It was beginning to sound a bit too buttery and flattering until he had added that last very human remark. "Now then, come along and look for yourselves!"

They walked with Mr. Watkinson along the churned clay road: it was quite obvious that all these positions had gone, for besides three houses that were finished, and the three nearing completion, there were piles of scaffolding and stacks of bricks on almost every vacant plot and men were busy cutting foundations on one.

There was a brisk tapping: a cheerful whistling: a steady vigorous hammering—men paused with bricks in their hands to look down at them over the edges of scaffolding and an old aproned carpenter peered over his steel-rimmed spectacles. The whole thing looked very vigorous and successful.

"It's wonderful where all the people come from to buy these houses," said Mr. Baldwin.

Mr. Watkinson smiled but did not answer: it seemed as if he had discovered a secret reservoir of homeless people somewhere and was not going to risk the chance of its whereabouts becoming known to his competitors. But Mr. Baldwin was very interested in this house-building mystery and felt that the Manager of an Estate was the man to solve it: he pursued the matter.

"It's not as though the population's increasing at this speed—or as if the older places were being left empty. Where *do* they come from?"

But Mr. Watkinson was not to be drawn. He changed the subject by pointing down a broad road cut at right angles. "We shall develop these roads later on: we've got fifty acres altogether."

The road they were following faded into trampled grass: ahead lay an untouched sweep of heathland, spotted with gorse bushes and clamped down with stout girthed oaks and elms.

Mr. Watkinson paused, blew his nose and blinked round with a dreaminess that contrasted strikingly with his brisk manner of a moment ago. Apparently the view before him conjured visions.

" There's nothing to see for the moment, of course—but you must picture the whole of this centre part as an old world village green—the grass cut and rolled—the bushes trimmed a little—the big trees just as they are. Now follow my finger—you see those white tapes ? They mark a road that will enclose the green. The houses will be fifty feet back from the road—each in its own grounds."

He paused, and permitted himself a moment's rapture. " Perhaps I ought not to say it, but this will be one of the loveliest features ever embodied in a modern Estate: three acres of valuable land sacrificed for the benefit of those who live around it."

Mr. Baldwin was overwhelmed by the grandeur and generosity of the scheme. The summit of his ambition had been just an ordinary house in this valley: a house in an ordinary road, looking across at other houses. But a home overlooking this lovely open space—a view from the back to the crest of the ridge—a long view to the front, between thorn trees and elms to a sunset that would linger behind the dark little embowered houses on the opposite of the Close . . . it . . . there must be a catch in it ! No wonder Mr. Watkinson had looked dreamy. Mr. Baldwin was dreamy now—he saw it all on a summer evening, with the lazy shadows over it: children playing—dogs running for bouncing balls—the little dream houses lying bliss-fully back—each in its snug dominion of evergreen and flowers. He was hardly conscious of Mr. Watkinson as he followed him across the rough grassland towards the further side—the houses down by the Estate Office were nothing now: they were as commonplace and as trivial as those in the dusty neighbourhood of his old home.

He awoke from his daydream with a start: Edith tripped over one of the tapes, tossed her umbrella and bag into the air and fell down. Both men ran to her assistance: she was shaken, but fortunately unhurt. Her bag had flown open and a powder puff and eightpence were recovered from the grass.

" All right, dear ? "

" Quite all right, thanks."

" I'm sorry, Mrs. Baldwin. I ought to have warned you of these tapes," said Mr. Watkinson. " We're starting the road to-morrow. It should have been started last week, but we've been delayed by the gravel."

The accident brought Mr. Watkinson back to earth and business. He unrolled the plan and supported it on his knee, and Mr. Baldwin noticed with some concern the number of positions round the Close that were painted over in pink.

" Those have gone, I assume ? "

The Estate Manager nodded. " And these marked with pencilled crosses are being held for confirmation."

It disturbed Mr. Baldwin: there seemed very few positions available.

" Now how would this suit you ? " suggested Mr. Watkinson.

He led them across to one of the pegged out squares of land and tapped it with his heel to show that it was solid.

Tom and Edith stood upon it—they peered round enquiringly like two staid old ponies on a new grazing ground.

" It's very nice," said Edith; she looked up at her husband for confirmation but his eyes were not upon the ground: he was gazing ahead.

" We should like," he said, " a piece with one of those old trees on it—if that's possible."

" Certainly," said Mr. Watkinson.

A little ahead stood a great silent elm: the wind had fallen, but the old tree was secretly beckoning to them with its delicate, lacy branch tips. It seemed to say: " Come over here—I'll look after you: I'll rustle you to sleep on summer nights and roar the ghosts away in winter —I'll give you shade—I'll never change: I'll give you peace—and something that'll make your cares and troubles feel very small and trivial. . . ."

" What about that one ? " said Mr. Baldwin in as calm a voice as he could muster.

The Manager gave a slow, artful smile.

" You've picked the plum: the finest site of all."

Mr. Baldwin knew that without being told. He stepped over the tapes and stood upon the only piece of land in the world that could make him happy. The wiry grass sent a thrill of understanding up his legs: he felt the iron-rooted muscles of the giant that towered above them.

" This is our place," he said.

The land sloped towards its further end, and their footpath formed its limit: a great wild mass of bramble marked its frontier and a stout little may-tree stood sentinel beside it. " This is our place," repeated Mr. Baldwin.

" It's the finest, as I've said," remarked the Manager, " you face due south—you see where the sun's setting— you're at a corner—away from what little traffic there'll be—you also get a much wider plot because it opens fan-shaped towards the end, to fit the corner, you see ? "

He pointed out the position on the plan—and Mr. Baldwin suddenly felt faint: the plot was painted pink— it had gone—it was sold !—and that was the end. He would never be able to live in Welden Valley and see this lovely—this only spot in someone else's hands. It would drive him mad. He felt sick, and suddenly angry. Why hadn't the blundering fool seen that. . . .

" But," he stammered, " it's—it's gone—it's marked in, in pink ? "

Mr. Watkinson looked momentarily disconcerted, but he quickly pulled himself together.

" Oh, yes. Yes. I'm sorry. What am I thinking about ? " He examined the square closely, as if for some secret mark, and then looked up reassuringly. " But I think it can be arranged. It's not definitely decided and I haven't heard from the people. It's their fault entirely for not con-firming it. Besides," he added with a guilty glance round, " I want you to have it. You *can* have it." And with a gesture of finality he drew out a pencil and made a triumphant tick upon the square—" It's yours ! "

Mr. Baldwin suddenly became conscious of his heart: it was thudding like a sledge hammer. He was not a fool —and although he knew beyond doubt that this was the gem of the whole Estate, he was beginning to feel terribly afraid that things were not going to be plain sailing . . . this man had flattered them so obviously, and lured them on : he prepared himself for the struggle of his life. . . .

" I suppose," he began, " we could build a house like your Show House here ? "

" Certainly ! "

" The cost, I mean—would it be the same ? "

" This land is £7 a foot."

It was as if Mr. Baldwin's hammering heart had missed the anvil and hit him in the throat: the shock passed, leaving a dull pain of weariness. At the summit of ecstasy had come a death-warrant. The land, then, was extra. The boy had never told them that—he had just said: " This house is £1,175," and had cruelly concealed the price of the land. £7 a foot—that would be hundreds of pounds. It was fiendish to have led him here—to have flattered his selection—then crucified him with £7 a foot.

" But surely," he began in a voice that was suddenly loud and hollow, " the Show House *includes* the land ! "

" The Show House ?—oh, yes, certainly."

His heart rose—he felt himself attacking—Mr. Watkinson was on the defence.

" Then for £1,175 we could build a house on this plot exactly like the Show House ? "

Mr. Watkinson began to smile, then stopped. Something in the trembling voice—in the thin, lined face and burning grey eyes stopped him smiling. He was used to hammering out these things with pitifully eager purchasers—sometimes perhaps he had taken advantage of the power he held, for at no time is a man more vulnerable to extravagance and recklessness than when his feet first grip a piece of land that has captured his imagination. He knew how to face bluster and crafty bargaining, but there was something different about the man beside him now—

something a proud fugitive might have in begging
sanctuary. . . .

He pulled out his cigarette-case and held it forward.
He did not look up, but he felt his client's head shaking
and he saw that no hand reached out for a cigarette.
He took one himself and lit it.

" You see, this is a far better position than the Show
House."

" Yes, I know, but . . ."

" The land in the road where the Show House is built
is £3 10s. a foot. There's a fifty-foot frontage, so you see
the house works out at £1,000, and the land, £175. This
frontage is really worth *more* than double—there's at least
an extra twenty foot depth and I'm not charging for the
extra width at the bottom. I tell you it's cheap, Mr.
Baldwin ! "

Mr. Baldwin turned his head. A deep, stormy sunset was
gathering behind the trees across the Close : they could
have a rustic seat to encircle their elm—the morning sun,
and the evening sun would shine upon it and the ridge
behind would throw the pink glow upon the cool
weathered oak in the lounge.

" I know," murmured Mr. Baldwin, " I know it's worth
it." He looked at the Manager puffing hard at his cigarette. " But it means this would cost £175 more. I'm
awfully afraid . . . you see, I've retired."

Mr. Watkinson did not reply for a moment. " Would
you require us to build the house ? "

" Certainly."

The Manager looked up more hopefully. " It makes
a difference, you see. Some people engage their own
builders. I tell you what I'll do, Mr. Baldwin ! I'll knock

£75 off the land !—that means you could have a house
built, including everything, for £1,275 !—It's ridiculous,
Mr. Baldwin ! I'll get called over the coals, but I *want*
you to have this land because—well, I guess you'll never
be happy on any other bit ! "

It was awful how the devil of ambition could get a
cautious man by the ears and turn him into a spendthrift.
Mr. Baldwin understood now what he had never understood before—how clever, sane men could come the most
dreadful crashes over money, simply through ambition—
simply because the devil got them by the ears. The devil
certainly had Mr. Baldwin at this moment. A week ago,
if a plumber had asked for an extra pound to make a
better job than his first estimate allowed for, he would
have considered it and brooded over it for days before
deciding. And now, having faced and won a fight to
place £200 on mortgage, it seemed to matter nothing that
an extra £100 were added.

Never had Mr. Baldwin sunk to bargaining, but it
came now as naturally as if he had done it all his life.
" Make it £1,250 and it's done ! " he cried, and when
the Manager shook his head—" I'll give you my cheque
for the deposit now—this very moment ! "

" We'll lose over it," said Mr. Watkinson. " I could
sell that land any day for £7 a foot."

" Sell it to me *now* !—and begin the house to-morrow ! "

There was a final, pregnant silence. The whole valley
seemed to be waiting for the Manager's reply. He looked
at the man in front of him—the burberry had slipped
through his arm and was dangling partly on the ground—

he looked at the plump little lady, fiercely gripping her bag between her fingers.

"All right," he said. And for some reason that was quite unusual on such occasions, he reached forward and shook Mr. Baldwin's hand. "You've won!"

CHAPTER XV

"I t's these little set-backs that make it so worth doing," said Edith. " I mean, if it was all easy it wouldn't mean nearly so much."

" I know," sighed Mr. Baldwin. " I know."

Edith had said very little in Welden Valley, but she found herself doing most of the talking on the journey home. The strain and excitement had brought a violent reaction upon her husband, and he had almost collapsed in the corner of the carriage. His face was turned to the window—his mind was assaulted with forebodings darker than the fields outside. Now and then an erratic firework would shoot up in the distance and split into a few disappointing sparks : the train rattled over a crossing and some waiting children with fierce moustachios and a shapeless figure in a perambulator reminded them how deeply they had penetrated into the autumn.

" I mean," went on Edith, " if it were easy, everybody would do it, and that would end all the fun and excitement of it."

" That's right," agreed Mr. Baldwin. There was something in everything that Edith said, but nothing, somehow, that got to the root of what was worrying him. The train stopped at a station and went on before he spoke again.

" D'you realise, Edie, what an awful mess we're in ? "

Edith laughed a little uneasily. " How d'you mean, Tom ? "

A touch of his old impatience returned: " Well—think, dear—ask yourself ! We've just agreed to put down £1,250 for a new house : we've got to spend nearly £400 on furniture—there's legal charges—removal expenses—all kinds of things, and we've actually got in cash—£218 ! "

" But we've got the Debentures."

" I know, Edie——"

" And ' Grasmere.' "

He looked up. " ' Grasmere '—I know—but supposing nobody buys it, dear ? After all, how do we know ? "

" Of course somebody'll buy it ! "

He shrugged his shoulders and lapsed into silence. Edith felt it better not to disturb him again, and the rest of the homeward journey was disappointingly solemn.

It should have been a progress of triumph: they had walked into Welden Valley and staked their claim upon the finest position on the Estate : they had been overwhelmed by the prospect of simply securing a square, formal position beside houses in an ordinary road, with other houses looking at them at close range opposite. Reality had been unbelievably finer : they had twenty feet more land than the others : it was not only deeper, but it widened out : there was room for vegetables—room for almost anything. They should have journeyed home in a blaze of triumph.

But Mr. Baldwin began to cheer up after supper. The first thing that greeted them upon their arrival home, was a large notice board in the garden : " THIS CHARMING HOUSE FOR SALE." Timbrell and Dove were obviously

MG

smart people to respond so quickly to instructions and it promised well for the future.

And Edith enlarged considerably upon the idea of growing all their own vegetables. " We'll grow at least ten pounds worth a year," she said. " That'll pay the interest on the mortgage. Then there's room for chickens and we could sell a lot of eggs——"

" That's certainly an idea, Edie. It'll be grand to have our own vegetables out of that good fresh soil."

The chickens and a whisky and soda were the turning point of his depression. His spirits rose steadily as they sat talking it over by the fire after dinner.

" I'm terribly glad we did what we did this afternoon, Edie: we went much further than we ought to—we've taken a big risk, but I don't mind because it's—it's worth it a thousand times ! Supposing we hadn't taken the land in Welden Close—supposing we'd been satisfied with a cheap piece in that road—think how awful it would have been to see the spaces filling up round that open green—to have lived in sight of it all the time—watching the houses being built there—watching a house being built on *our* land ! It would have driven us mad, Edie: we'd have always felt so cheap and mean." A new thought came, and his eyes gleamed across the fire. " D'you realise we're going to be *important* people, living up there in Welden Close ! "

Edith laughed, and rose to go to bed.

" Don't you go getting too proud ! " she said. " You know the saying about pride—and falls."

" I know—well, I'll be up soon, dear. Good night."

" Good night, you reckless old gambler ! "

He lay back in the armchair to finish his pipe alone—

"reckless old gambler": Edith had said it: she had said it in fun, but it was true. Sixty-one next Thursday and suddenly, unbelievably a gambler. For the first time in his life he felt himself tossing rudderless upon a sea of financial obscurity: for the first time in his life he could not—if suddenly called upon—meet the financial obligations he had made, and yet never in his life had he felt so confident in himself—so sure that he could face unexpected troubles and overcome them. He felt taller, stronger—younger at heart than ever he could remember.

He rose and crossed to the window to see that the latch was fastened, and suddenly wondered why he troubled about locking the house up when he went to bed. It was a fussy little habit dating back to his timid, solvent days. If a burglar or two came in now he would look over the banisters and laugh at them, and then go down and give them a drink and good-humouredly kick them out. There was a faint autumn mist round the lamp-post outside: a field mist would be round the trunk of their tree in the valley—the clump of brambles would just have its crown showing above it: a dark lump like a porpoise in a flat grey sea. Brambles!—fancy going down the garden with a paper bag and walking-stick to do an afternoon's blackberrying upon one's own private bushes!

He turned off the light and tiptoed up to bed.

CHAPTER XVI

T HE FORTUNE that is traditionally supposed to favour
the brave, but which usually gets them into such a mess,
came along to give Mr. and Mrs. Baldwin a most encouraging fillip on Saturday morning when Mr. Dove arrived
to make the inventory of their furniture.

Mr. Dove was a seedy, battered little man. He had a
shaving cut on his chin that had bled and dried : his
clothes were creased in curious directions and his thin,
sandy hair was scurfy and dishevelled. He looked as if
he had been run over and hastily cleaned up so as not
to miss his appointment. He had a cold in his head and he
seemed to sniff contemptuously at each piece of furniture
in turn. He explained several times that there was a
terrible slump in second-hand furniture, and that it was
cruel to see lovely old stuff knocked down for a song.
The Baldwins were thoroughly sick of him by the time
he got to the drawing-room.

He was explaining that nobody had drawing-rooms
nowadays and was going into it at such length that Mr.
Baldwin could have kicked him through the windows
into the garden, when he suddenly and unexpectedly
became silent. He had opened the little walnut-wood
cabinet and taken out one of the dainty shell-like pieces
of china that had come to Edith from the Vicarage. He
looked at it closely and intently : he turned it over, pushed

his glasses on to his forehead, and peered at the mark with bulbous, faded eyes.

Then he blinked at Tom and Edith.

" You want to sell these ? "

" Certainly. Everything."

" These are good."

" Oh ? " said Mr. Baldwin, overlooking in his pleasure the inference that everything else in the house was bad.

Mr. Dove took out several other pieces and examined them in turn.

" They came from my home," said Edith.

Mr. Dove did not answer this, but after a moment said :

" You don't want to put these in the auction. You wouldn't have the sort of people to give the proper price."

To ask bluntly what they were worth, seemed to Mr. Baldwin like shattering them on the floor. He had a feeling that they would grow in value if nobody talked about the price for a little while, but his imagination was leaping nimbly upwards—five—ten—fifty pounds ? Supposing it turned out to be one of those fantastic discoveries one read about ?—supposing they were a unique set that experts had been searching for, for years and years ?

" I'm not an antique valuer," said Mr. Dove, " I'll send a friend of mine this afternoon." He turned his attention once more to the furniture, and began to sniff again : the stuff in the bedrooms brought a bead to his nose, but the Baldwins were so pleased with him over the china that they gave him a glass of sherry before he went. It was a drop that had been in the bottle ever since the Tarrants came to Bridge, but he drank it with relish.

" Anyway, he's honest," remarked Mr. Baldwin when he had gone. " Some men wouldn't have said a word

about good stuff like that, and bought it themselves at
the auction for a knock-down price."

The friend came in the afternoon. He also was rather
dilapidated and looked as if he had been in the same
accident that had crumpled Mr. Dove. He was a slow
moving, elderly man with long white hair, a blue veined
nose and a strong smell of tobacco. He did not take so
long to examine the china as Mr. Dove. He offered
fifteen pounds.

The Baldwins had hoped for more, but it might easily
have been less. In any case, it was a lot more than they
had ever expected. But Mr. Baldwin was a business man,
and he felt it was perfectly in order to get a second opinion.

"We'll consider it and let you know to-morrow,"
he said, and the elderly man, with a slow and apparently
fruitless glance round the drawing-room, took his departure.

There was an interesting old antique shop in Edgware
Road, and that night, after dark, they approached it
furtively, with one of the little saucers wrapped in a silk
handkerchief.

An elderly woman peered at the little piece of china,
turned on another light and went to the narrow stairs
and called out, "Joseph!"

"I'll get my husband to look at it," she said.

There was a slow shambling down the stairs, and then,
to the Baldwins' unspeakable horror, came a strong and
unmistakable odour of stale tobacco, followed by the
elderly man with the blue veined nose who had called
that afternoon.

It was the darkest moment in the Baldwins' united
lives: never before had they felt so bewildered and

humiliated. For one wild, groping moment, Mr. Baldwin thought he would pretend he had come to accept the offered price—then he remembered that he had already asked the woman what it was worth.

He was no diplomatist: when forced to think quickly he fell back upon honesty. With a laugh that sounded hollow and unlike his own, he started to explain that they had really come to seek a second opinion and that it was an extraordinary coincidence. . . .

The antique dealer waved aside the explanation and showed no sign of annoyance: he went so far as to tell Mr. Baldwin that it was a perfectly correct precaution: there was another antique shop further down the road—perhaps Mr. Baldwin would like to enquire there.

A humbled Mr. Baldwin said he was perfectly satisfied—he had no desire to enquire further, but the dealer was still anxious to reassure him. " I tell you what. We'll ask the wife—she doesn't know the price I've offered. What would you say to a full set like that, Alice ? Half a dozen of each ? "

" Ten pounds," said the woman.

The man laughed. " I've made it fifteen pounds."

" If you took more notice of what *I* say," said the woman, " we'd have a bigger shop than what we've got."

" Maybe," said her husband, pulling out his pipe—and Mr. Baldwin hastily repeated his desire to accept.

" Very well, sir. Fifteen pounds. It's a good fair price. I'll arrange with the Auctioneer, and he will credit you. Good evening, sir. You've forgotten the saucer. Better keep it all together till the sale."

" Thank you," said Mr. Baldwin with heartfelt meaning. They laughed it off on the way home, but Mr.

Baldwin still felt as if he had just had a piece of plaster ripped off his stomach.

"I think we must tell Ada," said Edith, after dinner.

"I think we must," said Mr. Baldwin. "Pity we didn't tell her before the notice was put up in the garden—and before Mr. Dove came. She *must* know now."

They had meant to tell Ada a week ago: their first thought had been that she would revel in the comforts and conveniences of a modern home. Their second thoughts had been different. Ada was ten years older than either of them: she had been with them seventeen years, and her roots extended a good way beneath the basement. She was really old, and the more Edith thought of it, the less she could picture Ada in Welden Valley: it worried her, and made her feel unhappy, and she knew that it was best to get it over. . . .

Ada was washing up. She stood with her back half turned to Mrs. Baldwin and listened in silence—a silence that was like a piece of thick wet flannel. When it was over she partly turned her head and said: "Well, it's nothing to do with me, is it?"

"It's a lot to do with you, Ada. You're one of us and you know what you mean to us. You're in the house far more than us, too."

"But you never told me nothing about it until now." Then she added: "Mind you, it's your business and there's no reason why you should."

"The work'll be so much easier," began Mrs. Baldwin, "you've no idea how convenient everything is . . ."

Then Ada put down the plate she was drying and began.

She was not insolent: there was more of sorrow than of anger. What was she going to do on her nights out—in a lot of dark fields without any lamp-posts—falling over cows—and no cinema? And all these modern cleaning ideas—she was not too proud to get down on her knees and scrub. All her friends lived in Brondesbury: they weren't going to come with her to this country place and she couldn't start making a new lot at her age. " I know you and the master don't care about friends, but I do ! "

She began to lay the plates along the dresser—gleaming, spotless plates; there were two little patches of colour in her seamed face. Mrs. Baldwin looked at the old black uniform, the clean starched apron, the prim little lace cap that modern servants laughed at—and felt suddenly ashamed.

" I'm sorry, Ada . . ."

" There's no need to be sorry, m'am. You want to make a clean sweep and a clean start in the new house and you can't do that with me around. I'm too old to break in a new set of saucepans now. I got my pension and my sister in Paddington. Don't you worry about me, m'am—I'll be all right. Maybe I'd have gone in any case soon—what with being near seventy and them basement stairs. . . ."

" I don't like saying it," said Mr. Baldwin, " but I think I'm rather glad. She'd never have settled in. Without a basement she would have been so near to us—and —and—that would have been very difficult when she was in one of her bad moods. I think it's best, Edie : and as she says, she would have gone soon in any case. We'll get a young country girl—everything fresh and new."

CHAPTER XVII

On three successive afternoons the Baldwins went to Welden Valley, partly to discuss the form of their new house, partly to make sure that their land was still there, and that nobody was building a house on it by mistake. Their anxiety in this respect was relieved on the third day when a board marked " SOLD " appeared on it.

They went over all the completed houses and climbed precariously amongst the skeletons of those under construction: they studied piles of plans, admired numerous attractive designs and decided in the end that nothing was better than the Show House they had originally seen.

Apart from the charm of its design the Baldwins knew that they would never forget their first visit to it. They owed everything to it, and to possess a house exactly like it would enshrine a memory.

Mr. Watkinson suggested several small but excellent improvements: the deepening of the bay window in the dining-room to catch the sunset: a small additional window in the best bedroom to give a view of the foot-path up to its disappearance over the crest of the hill: a slightly darker tile: a recess to let the front door mat flush with the surface of the carpet—" We're finding things out every day," he said, " and your house will have the benefit of it, right up till the moment it is finished." By having a house exactly the dimensions of the Show House Edith was able to measure up for the curtains and begin making them at once.

They thought at first that they could not better the colour scheme of the Show House, but Mr. Watkinson was very honest about it. "If I were furnishing that house again," he said, "I would not have powder blue carpets. They're very charming but they're not suited to the country. People are in and out so much and every little spot shows." He took them across and illustrated what he meant.

They decided upon fawn as the predominating colour —a heathery shade of fawn for the carpets and a slightly deeper shade for the mats: cream scrumbled walls and blue upholstery and curtains. Mr. Watkinson entered into everything as though he were going to live in the house himself. When they explained their colour scheme he seemed overcome at the very thought of it. If anything he was a bit too interested, and once or twice Mr. Baldwin found himself in heated argument, particularly when Mr. Watkinson made the appalling suggestion that they should have the branches of their elm lopped off, apparently down to its bare trunk. Mr. Baldwin stared at him in amazement.

"It'll sprout again in a couple of years," said Mr. Watkinson.

"You suggest—having—our elm lopped!"

Mr. Watkinson nodded. "It's entirely up to you, Mr. Baldwin. It's your tree, but, you know, it's very big, and elms are treacherous things."

"I wouldn't dream of it!" exclaimed Mr. Baldwin.

The Manager shrugged his shoulders: "We had a

big one blown down on our Cobham Estate: cracked a garage open like an egg."

" I'll risk that."

" It's not only your own property to consider. It may fall the other way upon someone else's house."

" I can insure against that," replied Mr. Baldwin very curtly, and the matter dropped.

For an extra £50 they arranged to have cupboards built in, and wardrobes with long mirrors in their doors.

" We shall begin building," announced the Manager, " in a fortnight's time. I shall have the road up to your plot by then."

" And when," asked Mr. Baldwin, " can we move in ? "

" Don't make it before the end of March," said Mr. Watkinson.

" The end of March—but—but—that's five months ! "

Mr. Watkinson nodded. " I don't want you to be disappointed. I should not be treating you fairly by letting you in before. Let me have the drying March winds on the house before I do the painting. If I paint before the walls have dried you will only have to paint again. Give me time, Mr. Baldwin, time to let the foundations settle, time to give you something we can both be proud of ! "

Despite their disappointment they had to agree. The houses in the road by the Estate Office seemed to be growing before their eyes and they had confidently hoped to be in by Christmas. It was awful to face a lingering winter in " Grasmere," for the sale's board in their garden had broken their last bonds with the old house and they felt like restless, discontented lodgers.

" And yet," said Edith, " the spring will be a wonderful time."

They could have spared their disappointment, for now that things had really started time gathered wings and flew with amazing swiftness. They scarcely noticed the days deepening into winter, and the long dark evenings that Edith had dreaded were not long enough for all they had to do. They began an orgy of mat making. Estimates showed that they would need eight in all: two large ones for the reception rooms and six smaller ones for the doorways. It was no longer a matter of spinning out the work to fill in time. Mr. Baldwin set himself to do a square foot per day and grew feverishly impatient when he had to lay off for a week with cramp in his fingers. From tea until dinner he would read by the fire while Edith sat up at the table for the light to work upon the curtains. His books were *Garden Planning*, *Bird Life in England*, and magazines that told him a hundred and one things about the making of a home. Sometimes he would lay down his book and watch Edith with a wistful smile as she bent over the delicate, filmy curtains. Even with her spectacles on her nose and the pool of light shining upon her whitening hair she seemed like a girl wife working with trembling and caressing eagerness upon the tiny clothes of a baby that would come to her in the spring.

One day Mr. Baldwin steeled his heart and undertook a terrific clean out of old papers and letters and made a bonfire in the garden. It needed a special mood to destroy the hoarded relics of a lifetime and he worked like a demon while the mood was upon him. If old receipts had been attractive to collectors he could have made a fortune at Sotheby's: there was a complete set of Water Board receipts from 1899 in perfect condition, and the stamps upon them covered three reigns. There were stacks of letters that he burned with a blind recklessness, knowing full well that if he opened and read one he would sit down and read the rest and keep them. He emptied every drawer right down to the fluff encompassed pins, and when it was over he dug the little grey heap of smoking flakes into the soil of the shrubbery.

One afternoon there was an unexpected knock at the door, and a young couple arrived with an order from the Estate Agent to view the house. They were the first people to come, and they inspected everything with polite appreciation: they were getting married, the young man said, and his father-in-law had promised them a house. They were interested in " Grasmere " but suddenly got much more interested when the Baldwins explained why they intended to sell. They said they thought it was a splendid idea and would build a house themselves. They left with grateful expressions of thanks and the Baldwins decided to keep their plans to themselves another time.

The Estate Agents were getting very lively, for people arrived, upon an average, twice a week. The Baldwins began to get tired of pointing out the beauties of " Grasmere," particularly as some people obviously came out of curiosity without any idea of buying.

Some were polite, some were indifferent, one or two were quite rude.

" It's scandalous ! " exclaimed Mr. Baldwin, after a visit from a woman with a harsh voice and a sharp nose who had used the words " dark," " damp," " stuffy," and " inconvenient," at least three times each in as many minutes. " I shall tell Timbrell to be more careful about the people he sends in future."

But as it happened, one of the rudest and most thoroughly unattractive visitors sprang the first surprise.

He called himself Ranken-Dudley: he was a very tall, dusty looking man with a mane of.black hair and a big pale, pitted face. He brought with him a disconcerting young woman who was not his wife but whom he called " kiddy." He introduced her as Miss Sarda Northcote and she had vivid carmine lips and green earrings.

He was a teacher of Elocution and explained that he had been in Hollywood for some years, teaching silent film stars how to talk. He had returned with a view to opening a School of Voice Production in London. He looked about him as if he were searching for somebody he disliked and soon decided that " Grasmere " was quite unsuitable.

" I shall require a big room for my classes," he said.

For answer Mr. Baldwin threw open the partition between the dining- and drawing-room.

" We've sat thirty people here at a whist drive—and once had forty to a Tennis Club musical evening."

Mr. Ranken-Dudley was impressed but not convinced.

" If we did that we'd have nowhere to live ourselves."

" There are three large rooms upstairs—and two on the second floor. How many would there be in family ? "

" Just us two," said Mr. Ranken-Dudley a trifle shortly.

" Well," said Mr. Baldwin.

They went away but came back next afternoon. Mr. Ranken-Dudley wanted to look at the big room again to see if alterations could be made. They were the first people to make a second visit, and the Baldwins offered them a cup of tea. Miss Sarda Northcote left a large Turkish cigarette end in her saucer and a bright carmine lip print on her cup.

Next morning came a letter from Timbrell & Dove:

"DEAR MR. BALDWIN,—I am very pleased to inform you that our client Mr. Ranken-Dudley is definitely interested in ' Grasmere.' It is somewhat small for his purpose but he is considering the possibility of certain structural alterations.

"We have informed Mr. Ranken-Dudley that your price is £850, and having in mind the limit of £750 recently fixed with you we are given room for negotiation.

"I trust that we shall have further news in the course of a few days."

Nothing happened for a week, and then Mr. Timbrell himself appeared. He tried to put on a casual manner but he was obviously pleased with himself.

"I've brought you some good news, Mr. Baldwin."

"Oh ?—good."

"Mr. Ranken-Dudley has been to see us this morning. He offers £800."

"Eight hundred pounds? By Jove—that's—that's good ! "

Mr. Timbrell crossed his legs—put his finger tips together and smiled.

"I told him you would not consider it. I stood firm at £825."

Mr. Baldwin curdled inside and stared at the Agent in

disgusted astonishment: it was the sort of fool thing he *would* do—a little man of his type *would* get above himself and let a good thing slip away out of sheer conceit!

" But, surely ! Eight hundred pounds is fifty more than. . . ."

" I stood firm," broke in Mr. Timbrell, " at £825— after a hard fight I got him to agree."

" You mean he'll—he'll pay £825 ? "

Mr. Timbrell nodded and beamed. " I knew you would be pleased."

The sherry had all gone, so they gave Mr. Timbrell a whisky and soda and a biscuit. Although it was only eleven o'clock he appeared quite at ease with it.

" He would like to take possession at Lady Day, so you can practically step straight out of this house into your new one."

Mr. Baldwin promised to get the Deeds from his Solicitor and Mr. Timbrell departed smelling brightly of the hospitality afforded him.

" Well, Edie," said Mr. Baldwin, " what d'you think about that ? Seventy-five pounds more than we expected—£15 for that china ! There's still a chance of keeping out of the Bankruptcy Courts ! What a good thing it was we stuck to the land we wanted. We might have been kicking ourselves now for funking that grand bit in Welden Close and taking a miserable piece down the road ! "

" Thank goodness we didn't," said Edith. " I think you were wonderful that first day with Mr. Watkinson—the way you stuck to what you wanted—and got it ! "

No

And Mr. Baldwin, modest though he was, had to agree.

They sat silent for a while, then Edith voiced what both of them were thinking:

" So poor old ' Grasmere's ' really gone."

CHAPTER XVIII

ONE GLORIOUS MORNING in mid-December Mr. Baldwin conceived the idea of taking their walk from Stanmore once again. He wanted to come out upon the crest of the ridge and look down at his land : he was aching to see whether they had started work, but he wanted to see by himself, without the Estate Manager at his elbow.

"D'you realise, Edie, that we've been there six times and we've never really been *alone*? They won't be working on a Saturday afternoon so we can just stay as long as we like and really *look* at it."

They took sandwiches this time, and lunched on the stile beside the copse where they had seen the hedgehog. He insisted upon Edith taking frequent rests as they began to mount the higher ground, although he was itching to get on to make the most of the short December afternoon. As they drew near the crest of the hill, the elms in the valley gently reared their crowns above the horizon, and they paused to guess which crown was theirs.

And then the valley lay beneath them and they stood for a while like explorers upon the rim of a promised land. It was near the shortest day, and the fading sun had lain soft beams across the meadows, blackening the thorn trees and lighting the grey winter streaks in the wiry grass. It took them some moments to get their bearings, for even in six weeks the valley had changed beyond belief. Two houses that had been but a thicket of scaffolding had grown stout walls, and a ribbon of white road had swept along two sides of Welden Close. They saw the white tapes that marked the unmade road: they followed them past the gorse clumps and close beneath two elms —and suddenly Mr. Baldwin squeezed Edith's arm.

" Look ! "

It was hard to make out exactly what had happened: their tree was all right, and they could see the white pegs that marked their boundaries. Beneath the tree lay something that looked like a ladder, and beside it was a pile of something, either bricks or timber. Then, as their eyes grew accustomed to the light they could see rolled stacks of turf and the faint outlines of foundations.

" They've started ! " said Mr. Baldwin. " Come on ! "

The workmen at one of the half-built houses had left a bonfire smouldering, and some time during the afternoon an eddy of wind had smudged a streak of smoke across the valley and left it there. The valley seemed quite desolate, but remembering the surprising way in which young Mr. Morrison had once appeared from nowhere, the Baldwins descended the slope with stealth and wellnigh tiptoed to their land under cover of the gorse bushes. They wanted no one with them this afternoon.

It was certainly a ladder beneath the tree—an old, paint encrusted ladder that looked as if it had served many a growing house—but the heap that looked from a distance like bricks or timber was actually an old tarpaulin thrown over two wheelbarrows, a pile of sand and some bags of cement.

" Of course," remarked Mr. Baldwin, " cement—

foundations." He looked triumphantly at Edith. " Things
are beginning all right now ! "

Mr. Baldwin produced a tape measure. It was only
five feet long but quite adequate for measuring their
boundaries. He began from one of the front pegs and
instructed Edith to mark each point it reached with the
tip of her umbrella. He also told her to keep an eye open
for Mr. Watkinson, for although he was perfectly within
his rights in measuring up the land, he did not want to
be caught doing it.

He found, on twice measuring the frontage that he was
three inches short.

" That's near enough," said Edith, who was getting a
bit tired of it.

" At £7 a foot, my dear, an inch is worth over 10s. 0d."

One peg was leaning inwards a little which no doubt
accounted for the discrepancy. So he kicked it straight,
and in doing so it went comfortably over towards the
next plot, adding a couple of inches to his territory.
" You often find," he pointed out, " that those tape
measures shrink, and we must allow for it."

It was good to be alone: it was possible to plan something of the garden and he drew a rough sketch showing
the position of the elm, the house, the thorn tree and the
tower of brambles. He wanted to elaborate this at leisure
so that the permanent features could be woven into his
final design.

As the sun dropped below the crest, the valley was
filled with a strange uncertain glow that lingered on
beyond the normal span of sunset: the ground was dark
but the sky remained light grey and faintly sunlit.

The foundations of the house were puzzling at first:

the front door seemed so extremely narrow and they appeared to have forgotten to make an entrance to the dining-room.

" I expect they know," said Edith, as Mr. Baldwin stood scratching his forehead. " It'll straighten itself out as it goes along and I'm sure good people wouldn't forget a doorway."

" It all looks frightfully small, doesn't it ? " said Mr. Baldwin. " I mean—look here—surely the lounge is going to be bigger than this ? "

The little square of grass within the clay borders of the room seemed no larger than a tool-shed, but it was certainly eighteen feet by fifteen feet when they measured it. It was very deceptive, but it was also a unique experience to stand upon soil they would never see again when once the strong white boards had spanned it. " You see the fireplace here, Edie ? This is where your chair will be —and this is where I shall have mine. It's nice to see how clean and fresh it's going to be underneath."

" Funny," said Edith, " to think of my chair being right on top of this rabbit hole ! "

" And mine," put in Mr. Baldwin, " on top of a bunch of thistles ! "

They lingered on their land till a ground mist lapped their knees and lights began to twinkle in Welden Village. Mr. Baldwin strolled up and down within his pegged-out frontiers: he saw where the rustic pergola would go: he planned a gate at its far end to open upon the footpath.

" We ought to have brought our tea with us and had it in the lounge ! "

As they went towards the village, they met two other people gazing at the houses in the road beside the Estate

Office: two pleasant, youngish people who looked interestedly at Tom and Edith as they passed.

" Good evening," said the man.

" Good evening," said Mr. Baldwin, and then, unlike himself, he added, " Coming to live here ? "

" Yes ! " said the man, " this is our house," and he pointed to the one with the Tudor gables.

" Oh, really ?—Mr. Watkinson allowed us to look inside. I think it's charming."

" You do ? " said the young man in an eager voice, " we—we thought so, too. Are you going to live here ? "

" Why, yes. Up there in Welden Close—by that elm, there."

" Splendid—I expect we shall meet again."

And the woman, who was really only a girl, flashed a smile at Mrs. Baldwin and said: " We're starting to furnish next week."

" We're getting ready to," said Edith.

" You must come in soon and see what kind of a mess I've made of it ! "

" I'm certain it won't be a mess," laughed Edith, " but I'd love to see it."

" Fancy talking to strangers in a way like that in Brondesbury Terrace ! " said Mr. Baldwin as they went their way. He took Edith's arm and drew her towards him. " I believe it's going to be splendid here."

" I'm sure of it," she said.

They broke their news to the lady in the tea-shop as they sat in the alcove by the fire. She was delighted. " It's going to be a beautiful Estate," she told them.

" Lots of people have been coming to see it : nice people—
and I know three already who are having houses built.
It's going to be a wonderful thing for the Village."

They asked the woman if she knew of a girl who would
like to come and work for them and the woman promised
to keep an eye open and let them know. They also told
her they would certainly want to have their cakes and
bread off her. " And that means we shall eat too much ! "
called back Mr. Baldwin to the broad figure in the
glowing doorway. " Come on, Edie—we'll have to
hurry ! "

CHAPTER XIX

As the days sped by with gathering swiftness, and
the evenings began to stretch out lingering trailers of twilight, the Baldwins grew increasingly thankful that they
had not attempted to move before the end of March.
Five months, upon first reflection seemed a hideous time
to wait, but when it came to the point, five months contained not a day too many for the countless things to
be done. Half the enjoyment, reflected Mr. Baldwin,
would have been lost in the hopeless disorganisation and
anxiety of a hurried move to a damp, half furnished
house.

The buying of the new furniture alone demanded a
fortnight's concentration. Mr. Baldwin had hit upon the
idea of making the furniture a definite purchase out of
the money from Edith's Debentures, so that, while the
house and land were his, the furniture was Edith's. By
this means he made her feel that her sacrifice had gained
her a definite and visible stake in the new home. They
wandered miles through a labyrinth of sideboards and
bedroom suites : they glutted themselves upon weathered
oak and well-nigh suffocated themselves in mattresses and
quilts, and Mr. Baldwin discovered the remarkable difference between buying and selling. When he had marched
into a small, shabby Estate Office and announced in a
crisp, authoritative voice : " We want to sell a house," he

had felt as though somebody had opened a refrigerator door with one hand and cut the heels off his boots with the other. But when he had walked timidly into a palatial West End store and murmured: " We want to buy some furniture," it seemed as if his heels were replaced with a deep bow and the whole building quivered with deference. It appeared to Mr. Baldwin a little strange, for selling seemed to him as honourable as buying.

But while furnishing preparations were completed by the middle of January, they grew seriously concerned about the progress of the new house. As far as they could see, the builders had spent a few days laying the foundations and making a thorough mess upon their future garden, and then disappeared and completely lost interest in it. Upon three successive visits in three successive weeks, they were disgusted and disturbed to find nothing but a few dreary grey layers of cement and a muddy, trampled patch of grass. It looked terribly as if the builders had got into some awful kind of mess, and did not know how to continue the job. Mr. Baldwin began to wonder if what he had feared was actually true, and that they had completely forgotten the doorway to the lounge and were frightened to admit it.

On the fourth visit, not only was there nothing further done, but some workmen had had the stupidity to throw a heap of scaffold poles across their blackberry clump and beaten the bushes down. Mr. Baldwin strode down to the Estate Office with his blood boiling.

Mr. Watkinson was away in London and the Foreman builder seemed more surprised than apologetic.

" You mean those blackberry bushes, sir ? "

" Yes !—I mean those blackberry bushes ! "

"We never thought for a moment you'd be leaving 'em there, sir—we thought you'd have them out so as to make the garden. But I'll have the stuff moved at once."

"And when," proceeded Mr. Baldwin, " do you intend to begin my house ?—Nothing seems to have been touched for six weeks."

" Well, sir. You can't build on soft cement. You'd have the walls cracking in a few months. You've got to let the foundations settle in a bit."

" Excuses ! " burst out Mr. Baldwin as he stalked away. " It's always the same—give people plenty of time to make a thorough job and they ignore it completely and go ahead on jobs that people worry for : then you make a fuss and there's a mad rush at the last moment ! Here's the end of January and nothing done ! "

They kept clear of Welden Valley for a fortnight, but when they made their next visit there was such a scene of activity that Mr. Baldwin felt a little ashamed of his impatience. It was as if a magician had waved his wand, the scene had altered so incredibly : the walls were at least twelve feet high and a dozen or more men were creeping amongst a mass of scaffolding, hammering, clicking, scraping, whistling. A carpenter was planing window frames—two labourers were digging a trench for drains— the Foreman builder himself, in a bowler hat with a patch of white powder on it was consulting with a keen eyed, plus-foured young man in the roofless lounge.

" It's only because you made a fuss," whispered Edith.

Mr. Baldwin nodded with a grim smile, but even now he did not look entirely satisfied.

" I hope they don't hurry too much," he said.

He would have been happier if the men in the scaffolding had been laying the bricks more deliberately—had whistled less and concentrated more.

The next visit revealed an even more fevered scene: the house was crawling with men and Mr. Watkinson himself came out of the front door as they approached.

" Ah ! Mr. Baldwin !—Good morning, Mrs. Baldwin ! " and he turned with a contented grunt to view the house in perspective. It was difficult for the Baldwins to grow accustomed to the fact that all this turmoil—all this human activity was for them—and them alone: it did not, somehow, look like the house they had ordered—and yet, as they stood looking at it, it gradually seemed to mould itself into what they had expected. It seemed a little squat and crouching—the window frames were at present a bright startling pink and against the pale, unfinished plastered walls they made the house look like a surprised white cow with inflamed eyelids.

" We'll have the roof on in a fortnight," said Mr. Watkinson. " In five weeks from now we'll be finished. That'll give us a good month for decorating and drying. And then," he said proudly, " we start three more houses—there—and there—and there."

" All round us ? " laughed Mr. Baldwin.

" All round you," confirmed the Manager—" but don't worry !—the noisy part will be over before you come in."

The Baldwins took their departure with lighter hearts. The furnishers were to have a fortnight to lay the carpets and set the furniture. " And now," said Mr. Baldwin, " we simply *must* settle on a name."

The finding of a name should have been an amusing little pastime compared with the hard material side of the adventure, but repeated attempts to agree had brought a widening divergence that threatened to develop into serious conflict. Both were thinking along different avenues, and they had reached a stage when they instinctively disagreed with the other's suggestions almost before they were made. Edith's ideas, to Mr. Baldwin's mind were far too sweet and sentimental to last out a winter: " Restnook," " Larksrise," " Lavender Corner," " Peace Haven," while Mr. Baldwin, in Edith's opinion, was asking for trouble with thinly disguised puns and jokes like " Firstcome," " Open House," and " Clean Sweep." He stuck to " Firstcome," with irritating pig-headedness. " After all, we *did* come first, to Welden Close—so why not be proud of it ? "

" I know," said Edith, " but it's ugly."

He suggested " Chetleigh "—the name of the village where Edith was born: but she was against it, and retaliated with " Baronsmead," after the road in which his father's house had stood.

And like so many long drawn, awkward problems it was settled in the end, as Mr. Baldwin put it—" with a sudden click." The roof was on, and the lavatory basins were being carried in by a procession of men who looked like dishbearers at a mediæval banquet. They were standing with the Manager, discussing the final painting of the exterior. " Green," agreed Tom and Edith, " a rich, deep green."

" You're right," said the Manager. " You're never wrong with green : it'll look well against light coffee-cream walls. And the gates ? "

" Green," said Mr. Baldwin, " green gates."

" And that's the name of the house ! " said Edith.
" Green Gates ! "

" No," said Mr. Baldwin, by force of habit. And then, after a pause: " Edith, you're right. ' Green Gates ' is right."

And " Greengates " it became.

Six weeks: a month. Three weeks: a fortnight. The sands were running out at " Grasmere " and the last few days slipped by in a fever of forgotten details. Mysterious forms had to be filled in concerning the surrender of their gas stove: meters had to be checked: there were visits to London concerning the £200 mortgage —the Deeds of " Grasmere "—the sale of the Debentures —the insurance. Mr. Baldwin wrote by hand and posted to all concerned:

" Kindly note that, as from the 26th March, the address of Mr. and Mrs. T. H. Baldwin will be:

> ' Greengates,'
>> Welden Close,
>>> Welden Valley.

Telephone: Welden 327.
Station: Welden."

One afternoon the Notice of Auction appeared in the front garden in place of the " FOR SALE " board and Mr. Dove came to label the furniture. He said that the house must be entirely surrendered to him on the day before the Sale.

" I'll want to strip the beds and do up the blankets and everything," he explained.

But the Baldwins were adamant.

" We don't care what the house is like—we're going to sleep the last night here and move straight away to Welden Valley directly the Sale's over."

But the Auctioneer also dug his heels in. " We've got to do up all the kitchen utensils—tie the curtains up in bundles—the house'll be impossible that night. There's a comfortable little Boarding House opposite our office that'd make you welcome."

But this was not according to Mr. Baldwin's plan: he wanted to avoid an indefinite period between the old home and the new: he wanted to sleep at " Grasmere " on the last night, attend the Sale in the morning, and when the Sale was over he wanted to close the door, surrender the key and allow the new life to open upon the moment that the old one closed.

It was clear that Mr. Dove did not appreciate the drama and sentiment of the scheme: he finally shrugged his shoulders and said: " Well, if you insist. But I warn you that Thursday's not going to be comfortable—and our men'll have to be in here by eight o'clock on Friday morning."

" We'll be up and ready for them," said Mr. Baldwin. " And anything that's disturbed by us that night will be put back as the men leave it."

" Very well," said Mr. Dove, with an ominous look in his eye.

Tom and Edith were early astir on the morning before the Auction, and they caught the 8.15 to Welden Valley.

" Greengates " was ready and the furniture was promised
at ten o'clock. They arrived soon after nine and opened
the glistening front door with a glistening little mortice
key that Mr. Watkinson handed them with ceremony at
the Estate Office. For an hour they roamed the clean,
paint-odoured rooms: " We shall never see it like this
again," said Mr. Baldwin.

Soon after ten, two big motor-vans came swaying
slowly into Welden Close. The first van jolted several
times, lurched dangerously and stopped dead a hundred
yards from the house. The Baldwins went down to investigate and found that its front wheels had sunk deeply
and hopelessly into the sticky yellow clay. It moaned on
low gear once or twice, sank lower, and stopped exhausted. The driver climbed down in disgust, and half
an hour passed before a fussy little tractor belonging to
the Estate came along and pulled the lorry out.

" Better keep off the road and try and get across the
grass," advised the tractor driver. It was not a very encouraging beginning: the furniture men began work in
a bad temper and Edith was terrified lest they banged the
stuff about. But in a few minutes the work was in full
swing: the carpets had been laid the previous day and the
Baldwins went from room to room, directing operations
and occasionally getting a bump that once or twice seemed
intentional.

By lunch-time the lounge and dining-room were ready
and the Baldwins undid a packet of sandwiches and ate
them upon a newspaper spread out on the weathered
oak table while the men retired to refresh themselves in
their vans. By tea-time the work was done: Mr. Baldwin gave the chief man a ten-shilling note, the vans

gingerly departed across the grass, and they were alone in a furnished " Greengates " for the first time.

There was too much to be done to give much time for meditation : a large crate in the kitchen contained all the new pots and pans and china : another crate, brought by carrier from " Grasmere " contained the few things that had survived from the old house : their own clothing— the clock presented to Mr. Baldwin by the staff of the office—and a few wedding presents and personal belongings that could not be destroyed or sold.

Mrs. Chambers of the tea-shop had fulfilled her promise to find them a girl, and produced no less a person than her own niece, Peggy—a girl exactly after the style the Baldwins hoped for. Peggy arrived at four o'clock for an interview : a sturdy, country-looking girl with a round, rosy face, surprised grey eyes and large pink hands. It was arranged that she should come in next day, make the beds, generally clear up, learn how to work the stove and prepare dinner for them at 7.30.

A man arrived to fix the electric lamps and Edith worked like a Trojan on the curtains and bedrooms while Mr. Baldwin packed the new linen in the heated cupboard and boiled out the new saucepans and kettle.

They left soon after tea, for the Auctioneer's men were at " Grasmere," and the Baldwins wanted to keep an eye on them to see that they did not dismantle their bed. As they dragged themselves wearily to the station they were happy to think that everything was ready for them in Welden Valley when the door of " Grasmere " closed next day.

" Phew ! " said Mr. Baldwin, " what a time it's been ! "

Og

And Edith, with a wan smile, said : "It *has* been harder than I thought ! "

They were glad to have found a promising girl like Peggy—but their happiness even now was tinged with a little sadness. For after dinner that evening at " Grasmere "—after their last dinner in the old house—after the dinner things had been washed up and put into their places in the sad old basement kitchen, Ada would take off her stiff starched apron, put on her rusty old coat and green hat with the artificial cherries in it, and come up to say good-bye.

CHAPTER XX

THE OMINOUS PROPHECIES of Mr. Dove were more than fulfilled when they returned home, and the ravages within " Grasmere " were apparent even from the front gate. The window curtains had disappeared and the old house stared at them reproachfully with gaunt, lashless eyes. The front door stood listlessly ajar and their feet echoed across the matless, carpetless hall.

Mr. Baldwin dropped his umbrella into Lot 1 and hung his hat upon Lot 2. The partition between the dining-room and drawing-room had been thrown back and all the chairs in the house had been collected and lined up in rows for the comfort of those who were to attend the Sale next day. A small rostrum had been built in front of the drawing-room window and the dining-room table had been pushed far away into a corner.

Even the old pendulum clock on the mantelpiece had been defaced by a large white ticket marked Lot 29 and Tom and Edith were very thankful that their absence in Welden Valley had spared them from watching the end of the old house. They realised how right Mr. Dove had been in urging them to sleep elsewhere on this last evening. In every room the curtains were down and the carpets rolled and stacked in corners, and every piece of furniture, large and small, had been removed from its old position and placed in readiness for disposal. Their bedroom alone remained a small oasis in a desert of bare floors and walls, although even there the carpet had been rolled up and the furniture labelled.

The men departed at six o'clock, and it was uncanny to see Ada come up the basement stairs in her same old uniform, a cloth under her arm and a handful of cutlery for dinner. Her face was like a mask as she edged her way between the chairs to spread the cloth on the table in the corner. The Baldwins did not attempt either to joke or apologise to her over the appalling muddle, and the old lady appeared to expect nothing to be said. She moved to and fro in her stiff black uniform like the ghost of an old serving lady in the twilit ruins of an ancient home.

Edith went up to wash and Mr. Baldwin tried to cheer up the dull, ash-laden fire.

It was a sad, incongruous little dinner: incongruous because despite its queer position in a corner of the drawing-room, the table was set exactly as if the evening were one of the thousands that were past. Mr. Baldwin's place was laid upon the usual side, facing the dining-room window, Edith's on the side towards the door and nearest to the bell. The salt cellar, the pepper pot and the mustard jar stood huddled in their usual corner like three little fugitives upon a desert island.

It was almost as if Ada had maliciously planned to stir remorse within her master and mistress on this final evening, for Edith, in the hurry of the day, had left the old lady to arrange the last meal at " Grasmere " herself. She brought them a mixed grill, and an apple tart with junket: dishes she had been told were her most successful and most relished by her people.

Tom and Edith could well have managed upon a few

makeshift slices of pressed beef, for the festive little meal gathered memories that tightened the throat. At such moments the bad times slink away and the good ones crowd in with all their wistful sadness. Mr. Baldwin had not expected to feel sad: he had anticipated a keen romance and excitement—and he was disturbed that such unexpected memories came to him. The wide open partition reminded him of the far-off days when he had been Treasurer of the Acacia Tennis Club and the two rooms had been thrown together and used for General Meetings. He could almost hear the babble and merriment of the Musical Evenings that had followed the official business. Good days—but memories: the Members of the old Club had scattered far and wide and he had no reason to feel sad. They were strangers in Brondesbury now and they had no ties to break with old neighbours. . . .

" Pity Ada's not coming," he said, and even his low voice brought an echo from the curtainless window pane. " Did you ask that girl if she could cook ? "

" She's been helping Mrs. Chambers in the bakery," said Edith, " she's bound to be all right."

" Poor old Ada. Pity she's not ten years younger. She would have enjoyed ' Greengates.' I wonder what she's thinking about down there ? "

He had to climb over three rows of chairs to reach the bell and ring for Ada to clear away. There was nowhere to sit comfortably in the dining-room, for their arm-chairs were wedged in a corner and buried under piles of books. They went upstairs and wandered aimlessly from room to room, waiting for the sound of Ada coming up the basement stairs to say good-bye. Even in their bed-room they felt conspicuous against the uncurtained window, so they switched off the light and stood looking down the dark road until they felt that Ada must be ready.

Once or twice Mr. Baldwin went to the head of the stairs and stood listening for the signs of the old lady's departure. He could hear the familiar sounds of running water—cupboards opening—plates being lined on the dresser shelves: he heard her poking the fire from the kitchen range: he heard the kitchen door open and the clang of the dustbin lid. Then there was a long silence, and at last the slow, heavy tread on the basement stairs.

They went down to the hall to meet her. She had a shapeless little attaché-case with a strap round it for safety, and a short, stubby umbrella. The cherries in her hat nodded grimly at them as she put down her bag to shake hands.

" It's not ' Good-bye,' Ada," said Mrs. Baldwin, " because you've got to come and see us often in Welden Valley."

" I'll be pleased to, m'am. You'll find everything's put straight in the kitchen. There's a good sackful of coal in the shed they ought to allow you for, and the man never came for the jam jars. I've put some cold sausages and the cold tart in the cupboard so as you'll have a bite for lunch. Good-bye, sir. Good-bye, m'am. I hope you'll be all right in that new house."

Mr. Baldwin fumbled in his pocket, produced an envelope and pressed it into Ada's hand. " Something from us both, Ada. We wish you were coming with us."

" Thank you, sir." She put the envelope in her purse and picked up her bag. She turned to go down the basement stairs to the kitchen door, and for the first time in

all the years Mr. Baldwin laid his hand upon her arm.
He led her to the front door and opened it for her. They
watched her fumble with the gate, close it carefully, and
go away into the night, and when they turned back into
the house it seemed suddenly to have grown cold and
dead. An icy stillness lay in the black shadows of the
basement stairs; a solitary glowing eye peered at them
from the dining-room fire; Mr. Baldwin looked at his
wife, and their eyes met.

" Let's go to the pictures, Edie. We can't stay here."

They got home at eleven o'clock, glanced round the
dark, deserted house and went straight to bed.

CHAPTER XXI

THE SALE was announced to begin at ten o'clock, and at nine-thirty Mr. Dove arrived with his clerk and two middle-aged, shapeless men who put on green aprons in the hall. Mr. Dove looked round suspiciously and asked Mrs. Baldwin whether she was quite certain that everything they had used had been returned to the exact position of the previous night. " I once knew a Sale ruined because some of the Lots had been moved and couldn't be found. It's got to run slick—without a hitch: you've got to keep people concentrated."

The Baldwins left Mr. Dove checking over the catalogue with his clerk, and went up to sit at their bedroom window. It was nearly ten o'clock and they were very curious to see what kind of people were coming to the Sale.

As the clock struck ten it looked terribly as though the whole thing was going to be a ghastly fiasco. Exactly three people had arrived. A young, shabbily dressed couple and a stout lady who looked as if she had come out of curiosity. The young couple did not even appear to have any original intention of coming at all, for they peered up at the Notice in the garden, discussed the matter at some length, looked at their watches and entered self-consciously as people to a circus side-show.

Mr. Baldwin was in an agony of suspense: he even thought of going down to tell Mr. Dove to call the Sale off to avoid the stout lady buying everything at a shilling a Lot—and then, gradually, things began to happen. People arrived in twos and threes and some even came in cars. Most of them were women and they recognised several people from the neighbourhood. Then came a few men, singly: men of a type, whom the Baldwins took to be Furniture Dealers: they were pleased at the arrival of the old tobacco-odoured man of the Antique Shop, for he had evidently spotted something during his visit and had come to snap it up.

Mr. Dove had told them it was not unusual for people to attend the sale of their own furniture but to avoid being conspicuous they put on their hats and coats to make it appear as if they were ordinary people, and went downstairs.

About a dozen people were wandering about, looking at the Lots and comparing them with their catalogues, and still a few were coming in.

They could see no sign of Mr. Dove and were beginning to wonder what had happened when Edith touched her husband's arm and pointed to the windows leading into the garden. There was Mr. Dove, and he was behaving in a most extraordinary way. He was standing on the iron balcony outside the windows, leaning on the balustrade, gazing into the garden with his back to the room. He was languidly smoking a cigarette and appeared completely oblivious to the things happening within the house. He might have been a thousand miles at sea, lounging on the promenade deck of a liner.

The Baldwins wondered what on earth he was doing— until suddenly a remarkable change took place. He pulled out his watch and seemed to brace himself for a great exertion: he threw the cigarette into the garden, swung round and strode into the room.

He had obviously staged his entrance, for he banged the windows to behind him and the clatter brought immediate attention: he stood motionless before stepping on to his rostrum: the audience seated themselves and he rapped the table with a small mallet:

" Ladies and Gentlemen.

" We have a great deal to do to-day: we have one hundred and twenty-seven valuable Lots to dispose of and I shall be very obliged if you will help me by giving me your attention as closely as possible.

" I need say little in introducing this interesting Sale: I have carefully examined every piece and can guarantee its condition without reserve. The majority of these choice pieces have come from old country houses and the owners are reluctantly disposing of them for one reason alone: they are moving to a new house and wish to furnish afresh. I can only add that pieces of this quality and condition very rarely come into the market and I hope you will give everything the consideration it deserves. All right, Bert ! "

The speech ended surprisingly and abruptly and all eyes were turned towards the door as one of the green-aproned assistants wheezed in with Lot 1—the Umbrella stand. Mr. Baldwin felt a pang as he saw his old friend held up before twenty pairs of curious eyes: he wondered how many thousand times the tin base had rung with the plop of his umbrella. But he soon found himself too interested in the proceedings to think of the personal side.

Mr. Dove obviously realised the need of a little wit to warm up his audience.

" Now, Ladies and Gentlemen !—What above all things do we need in this good old country of ours ?—an umbrella ! Second only to our umbrellas we need a stand to put them in—and here's an opportunity to give your umbrellas a home to be proud of ! Lot 1 : Umbrella stand of seasoned oak : sound lead base : perfect shape to fit any hall—large or small. Now then, Ladies and Gentlemen : who's going to be the lucky possessor of Lot 1 ? Remember that Lot 1 brings luck ! "

" Half a crown," said the stout lady who had been the first arrival. Her effort brought on a fit of coughing, followed by three incredibly quick, staccato sneezes.

There was a suppressed laugh, and the Baldwins looked anxiously at Mr. Dove to see whether he was annoyed. But Mr. Dove turned the incident cleverly to advantage :

" Madam !—you're wise—next time you go out in the rain you must have an umbrella—and a stand to put it in ! "

Everybody laughed except the Dealers, who wanted to get on with the business, but a friendly intimate atmosphere was established :

" Now then—let's begin ! This lady has opened the Sale with a bid of half a crown for a stand that cost £2 10s., and is as good as new ! Now then——"

" Three shillings," came a squeak from a wistful little face at the back.

" Three and six," said the stout lady.

Mr. Baldwin felt his blood coursing with excitement.

" Four shillings," returned the little lady.

" Four shillings," repeated Mr. Dove. " Now we're beginning ! "

He spoke too soon, for this optimistic prediction seemed to freeze the audience into silence.

"Come along now! Who's going to say 'Five shillings'?"

No one seemed inclined to say, "Five shillings"—the umbrella stand looked as if it were shrivelling up in the hands of the green-aproned assistant.

"Four shillings?" It's a sacrifice! Any advance on four shillings? Going, going—Gone!"

Mr. Baldwin listened to the brief formalities with a heavy heart. The first wicket had fallen very cheaply.

Never had he and Edith passed a morning so filled with conflicting emotions and violent reactions: periods of bitter disappointment would give place to a sudden, exultant surprise, which just as suddenly would fade in the face of a heart-rending sacrifice. Mr. Baldwin's twelve-volume *History of England*, together with the *Gems of International Literature* in ten volumes, were knocked down for a shilling. The dining-room curtains fell for half a crown: there were moments when the Baldwins felt as if it were a hideous nightmare. They observed that it was when the Dealers stepped in for the larger stuff that fairly good prices were forthcoming. Three of them put up quite a struggle for the dining-room table, which was of old mahogany and well carved. It reached the highest price of the morning at £7 10s., followed by the large bookcase at £6 and the walnut-wood china-cabinet in the drawing-room at £5 15s.

Despite the disasters the figures steadily mounted up, and as Tom and Edith lunched in the kitchen they jotted up a total of £59 12s. 6d., which covered eighty-nine Lots, or the whole of the ground floor.

The afternoon was devoted to the bedrooms and a miscellany of kitchen utensils and box-room odds and ends. Three Dealers alone returned after lunch and they remained only to bid for the tallboy in the best bedroom. Here was a genuine surprise, for although Mr. Baldwin had always thought a lot of it he was too disillusioned to expect the £10 that it fetched. The Dealers then departed, leaving the beds and bedding to the women.

At five o'clock a weary, bloodshot-eyed Mr. Dove sat at the kitchen table and after much muttering and arguing with his clerk announced to Mr. Baldwin the satisfactory figure of £98 17s. 6d. The £8 17s. 6d., which was over and above the first rough estimate disappeared immediately when Mr. Dove reminded them that commission and cost of catalogue had to be taken into account, but despite everything the result was not so bad.

Mr. Dove sat back and sighed—took out a cigarette and motioned to his clerk to go upstairs and supervise the removal of such furniture that was being taken away that evening. Heavy boots were thudding overhead on the bare boards of the dining-room: the Dealers' vans had arrived before the Sale was over and a great deal of stuff had disappeared.

Edith had taken the precaution to make a thermos flask of tea and Mr. Dove had a cup with the remaining slice of tart.

" Well," he said, " that's that."

" I must say you did it wonderfully," remarked Mr. Baldwin. " It must be a strain to talk for five hours practically without stopping."

" It's not so much the talking," said Mr. Dove, " it's the concentration. You've got to know human nature—

sum 'em all up and lead 'em on—tickle their fancy—you know ? "

" It must be very interesting," said Edith.

Mr. Dove smiled and rose to take his leave. " Well. I hope we'll meet again. Let me know if I can ever do anything. We'll be sending you a cheque in a day or two and the balance on the house ought to be along Thursday. Are you leaving now ? "

" We're catching the 6.24 for Welden Valley : we've got half an hour before we go."

" I better take the keys with me, and you can just slam the front door when you go. Well, good-bye, Mrs. Baldwin —good-bye, sir. Good luck to the new house ! "

They followed him up the basement stairs and down the bare passage to the front door. The last of the Dealers' men was leaving with two of the drawing-room chairs : a woman was stacking a pile of blankets in a perambulator and another was leaning on the door of a small car, laying the three landscape pictures from the drawing-room on the back seat with a care that scarcely justified the three shillings and sixpence she had paid for each.

The clerk closed his greasy register and followed his master. " There won't be anything else called for to-night," he said. " The rest'll be collected in the morning. Good night, sir."

" Good night," said Mr. Baldwin. He closed the door and was alone with Edith in " Grasmere " for the last time. " It's still ours until midnight," he said with a little twisted smile. " What a time it's been ! We ought to sleep soundly to-night—at ' Greengates.' "

" If Peggy cooks us a supper that doesn't keep us awake," said Edith.

They went over to close and lock the French windows and stood for a moment on the iron balcony. A few autumn leaves were still lying on the paths, for Mr. Baldwin had scarcely touched the garden in the past busy months. They reminded him of the trouble with Ada over the broom and he thought how long ago it seemed. Against the lower wall lay the stack of leaves he had made in the autumn of the previous year: a little heap of embalmed sadness: a little monument to a futile groping for a happiness that had sidestepped him and slipped away.

" We'd better go," he said, and as he turned from the garden the evening light caught the pale green shoots that were forming in the grizzled shrubs beneath the wall.

They went up to their bedroom for the small bags that contained their needs for the previous night and as the clock was striking six they closed the door, pulled back the squeaking gate and turned towards the station.

CHAPTER XXII

MOST long-looked-forward-to events are worn-out before they happen. The best times of all sweep down upon
us so unexpectedly that anticipation gets no chance to
water down the pleasure of reality: and they pass so swiftly
that even reality never gets a chance to bore its ugly holes
into the memories that remain.

Mr. Baldwin had no doubt looked forward a little
too long to the thrill of slamming the front door of
" Grasmere " for the last time. He had thought a little
too much about the great moment when he would turn
his back upon a faded, worn-out life and stride away
through the spring evening towards gleaming horizons of
unblistered varnish.

Everything happened perfectly to plan until the moment came for slamming the front door. The chaos of the
auction had risen to his highest expectations: the departure of the bargain hunters and the last wistful half-hour
with Edith in the old house had worked out entirely as
he had pictured—and then, suddenly, everything went
wrong.

Possibly he stared for a moment too long into the forlorn, umbrella-standless passage, for in that fatal moment
of delay a torrent of memories poured from every nook
and cranny of the sad old house and filled him with a
sudden agony of remorse. The mad stupidity of it all rose

up before him, and he realised, too late, what an unspeakable fool he had been. A few days of trivial discontent had blinded him to a thousand solid, well-tested contentments that " Grasmere " stood for, and because his retirement had made his old home temporarily distasteful he had deliberately broken it to pieces and thrown it away ! The hollow echo of that slamming door seemed to carry away with it everything that he could trust and rely upon. He had understood " Grasmere " and " Grasmere " had understood him. Every rattle of its windows had become the inconsequential chattering of an old, well-tried friend : every chair had patiently moulded itself to the whims of his joints : every stick of furniture, every cup and saucer and door knob had proved itself and would have stood by him to the end. And now he had destroyed it beyond hope of repair. He had destroyed it in a fruitless gamble to cheat the years by discarding the trusted companions of a lifetime—by hobbling away to flirt with a new life that would have nothing in common with him ! The house in Welden Valley was young : it would be hard-muscled, unsympathetic and impatient. He thought with a sudden revulsion of the hard, strange armchairs : the hard, bright lights : the restive, untamed bed that would jerk him impatiently away from it and call for youth to lie with it at night. It had been his happy conviction that he would never feel old or out of sorts in a young, vigorous house like " Greengates." How true that was—but how true with a terribly different meaning ! If he were ill— he would never dare let young " Greengates " know about it : it would despise him for it and turn its back upon him. The old house had always understood : it had always soothed him in its pools of undemanding quietness.

Pᴏ

Only the sight of Edith, waiting by the gate, gave him the strength to turn away and face the frightening, uncharted future. He could have rushed to the Estate Agent's office—begged for the key—slept upon the bare boards of " Grasmere " that night and begged Mr. Ranken-Dudley next morning to give him back his home at any cost. He would have called from door to door upon the people who had taken his furniture and begged them to restore it to him. He would have made it his life's work to replace everything in " Grasmere " as he had known it and loved it. . . . But Edith was waiting. Nothing on earth could restore " Grasmere " to him now—no power on earth could replace it with all that it had once possessed for him.

" Come along," said Edith.

He could see that she, too, was suffering, and he pitied her and despised himself for what he had done to her. Loose brass knobs on a bedstead had nothing to do with the comfort of one's bed. She walked in tight-lipped, stricken silence, like some old Flemish peasant woman driven from her home by war. She clutched her bag in a way that told him that she had smuggled some secret relics away. In bitter truth they were refugees in that dark moment: refugees dragging themselves to the shelter of a strange, hard building in a strange, uncertain country. . . .

" Two singles—Welden Valley," he mumbled through the ticket-office window.

Right back in the autumn, when first they had heard that " Greengates " would not be ready until the end of March, Edith had said: " The spring will be a splendid time to move." Her words came back to Mr. Baldwin as he sat waiting disconsolately for the train. A few bright tufts of grass were sprouting from the borders of the gravelled platform and a half-starved, stunted chestnut tree beside the signal-box had gathered its frail resources to push forth a cluster of soft, sticky buds. Even here— in this drab old suburb, the spring found cracks to sprout through: out there in Welden Valley it would stretch its limbs in wild exultancy. He rose to meet the train with a desperate effort to be cheerful.

" Well, Edie," he said, " off at last ! "

" We'll come back one day and have a look round," said Edith, picking up her bag and following him to the bleak, empty train.

" Of course we will. Often. We'll walk down the old road and see what that fellow does to ' Grasmere ' ! "

" And if we're homesick we can go and have some Elocution lessons off him ! "

" Good heavens, yes !—it's not as if we were going across the world. I mean—*supposing*—supposing you didn't like Welden Valley—we could always buy the old house back."

" Of course we could," said Edith.

And suddenly the clouds began to clear. The train surged westward, and no passage of time will quench man's longing to cheat the darkness by roaming in the evening towards the setting sun. And Edith did an unexpected thing that warmed and brightened Mr. Baldwin's heart. She opened her bag and produced a flask of sherry.

" There was a good deal left in the bottle," she explained. " It seemed a pity to waste it."

" I should think so, indeed ! " exclaimed Mr. Baldwin.

She had even brought something to drink it from: a small tooth glass that had saved itself from the auction by hiding in the bathroom cupboard behind a bottle of liniment.

Edith took her share; Mr. Baldwin sipped from the flask, and gradually, in all its glory, the journey that Mr. Baldwin had begun to dread burst into robust blossom. Not for the first time in history did a man feel his destiny reviving from an opportune glass of sherry upon an empty stomach. His forebodings and remorse were so completely swept away that he felt well-nigh ashamed of himself. He sprawled out his legs and lit his pipe as the train gathered speed and rattled through the dusk.

"I *was* a fool just now, Edie. Did you see me standing at the front door after I'd slammed it ?—pretending I was making sure that it was properly shut ? I felt *awful* !— I felt I couldn't bear it. I felt we'd made a horrible, ghastly mistake ! "

Edith nodded and sipped her sherry. "I know," she said.

" You felt it, too ? "

" Of course I did. We shouldn't be human if we didn't. Standing there by the gate I thought of all the times I had gone in and out."

He nodded. " I felt I wanted to scream and hammer at the door—like a little boy shut out in the night. D'you know what I mean ? "

" It'll pass off," said Edith.

" But it *has* passed off ! " he cried. " That's the extraordinary thing ! Coming along to the station just now I felt we'd absolutely ruined our lives: I felt we were—sort of—roaming off into a kind of utter emptiness. Isn't this

sherry good ?—It's so smooth.—I mean, Edie—*supposing*
we suddenly woke up and found we'd dreamt it all—and
were just on our way back to the old house to carry on
exactly the same—would you be glad ? "

" No," said Edith in a firm voice.

The sherry had chased away the last remaining houses
from the carriage window—they were running out
through the open fields, and a light green down upon
them gleamed in the sunset.

" D'you realise," he said, " we aren't suburban people
any longer ?—we're country people ! " He leaned back
in his seat and folded his hand round the bowl of his pipe.
" Supposing we'd funked all this ?—we'd just be sitting
back there. . . ."

The long day was beginning to tell upon them. They
lapsed into silence and turned their faces to the window.
After a while Mr. Baldwin said : " I still can't believe it :
I shan't believe it's real till I wake up to-morrow in
Welden Valley . . ."

He puffed slowly at his pipe. What did it all mean ?—
what was it all leading them to ? The future gleamed
excitingly ahead, but it lay beyond a veil that no thought
could penetrate. New friends ? What kind of friends ?—
new interests ?—new pleasures ?

" I hope Peggy goes in all right to get dinner," remarked
Edith. " I hope she understood it was to-night. . . ."

" I don't care ! " he said with a laugh that rang with
bravado. " We'll cook it ourselves if she doesn't turn up ! "

There were far more lights in Welden Valley than they
had expected : at least a dozen houses were brightly

illuminated and despite the late hour the Estate Office was still in full activity. Lights blazed from every window; they could see girls busily typing letters and men moving to and fro. It was reassuring and heartening, for they had expected a groping walk of half a mile through a darkened valley.

Their fears concerning the arrival of Peggy were quickly set at rest, for as they reached the corner where the road turned into Welden Close they saw a clear-cut square of light gleaming ahead of them.

" She's there," said Edith with a sigh of relief.

There was something symbolic in the picture that framed itself in the light from the kitchen window. As they drew near they could see Peggy at work by the table —standing sturdily against the clean distempered wall. She was wearing a light blue uniform and her sleeves were rolled up nearly to her shoulders. Gleaming pink arms moved over a white-topped table, a row of shining plates behind. There were none of the lurking shadows that haunted old Ada's kitchen in Brondesbury Terrace: it was a picture scowered and thrown up by the sea.

The green gates clicked behind them and the lantern light over the front door clicked on soon after they rang the bell. It seemed as if everything in " Greengates " were going to happen in a series of cheerful clicks.

Peggy threw open the door with surprising quickness. When you rang the bell at the old house there was almost time to go and buy a paper while Ada wheezed up the basement stairs.

" You've got here safely ! " said Peggy—and a cheerful smile made up for the missing " m'am."

" Yes," said Mrs. Baldwin, " quite safely."

They entered the little hall and stood for a moment as if expecting Peggy to tell them to wait while she went to see if the people of the house were at home. "Well!" said Mr. Baldwin, "I suppose we'd better hang up our coats and hats."

He went to the downstairs cloakroom, touched the switch outside the door and plunged the hall into darkness. "You turn on the w.c. light from inside," explained Peggy. Mr. Baldwin fumbled in the dark—touched another switch and the light flicked up on the first-floor landing. "Takes a bit of getting used to," he muttered.

It was certainly a little puzzling, for the lighting at the old house had been on very simple lines. In "Greengates" you were able to perform complicated manœuvres with a little practice. When you wanted to go to bed, a switch in the hall turned on the light upstairs: having ascended you extinguished the downstairs light from a switch beside your bedroom door, and it seemed that almost any of the switches turned on or turned out the lantern light in the porch. By the time Mr. Baldwin had mastered these details he was beginning to feel at home.

It transpired that Mrs. Chambers of the cake shop had come up to "Greengates" herself that afternoon to help her niece prepare the dinner. "Not," hastily added Peggy, "that I can't cook myself—only Auntie thought I might have trouble with the stiff taps and things."

"That was very good of Mrs. Chambers," said Edith. "Was everything all right?"

"Quite all right," said Peggy, "and Auntie took the liberty of making a steak pie instead of frying cutlets. She thought it'd be better in case anything delayed you."

"Excellent," said Mr. Baldwin. Peggy looked so new

that it was hard to believe she had been alive for nineteen years: she looked as if she had been supplied with the house and polished to match it. There were no odds and ends about her: no spots or stains; her bright blue eyes matched the curtains; her bright pink face and arms blended with the fresh, distempered walls. She only appeared to wear three pieces of clothing: a blue cotton dress, a pair of distemper-coloured stockings and brown shoes. Ada always looked as if you could undress her indefinitely without making much change in her appearance. Mrs. Baldwin looked at the girl in wonder and a little sadness: no human being that walked about and touched things could remain in such spotless condition for long.

She felt the same touch of sadness about the house itself, for it was too wonderful at present to be a genuine home. She and her husband were so creased and time-worn in comparison that every movement—every step they took seemed to threaten destruction to their virgin surroundings. Her umbrella and Tom's walking-stick looked awful in that trim little weathered oak stand: they looked like a battered old Punch and Judy from a worn-out side show peeping out of the Queen's doll's house. When Mr. Baldwin hung up his hat in the cloak-room it looked so dusty and greasy that he was ashamed of it and quickly hung his burberry beside it to lessen the comparison.

It was their first view of " Greengates " by artificial light. They would have declared it impossible for the little house to look better by night than it had by day, but it did: it eclipsed their wildest dreams.

The wrought-iron knocker on the front door was

shaped like a miniature sailing ship: it would be a luxury
in itself to lift that knocker: it would be worth going out
for the pleasure of rapping out one's return upon it. The
gleaming letter-box seemed to be crouching back in
readiness to seize hold of letters like a playful puppy and
swallow them into its little wire stomach. When the door
opened you came upon the tough little cocoanut mat let
into the floor and flush with the carpet. All previous
front-door mats that the Baldwins had known were cumbersome, contrary things that turned up their corners,
stopped the door from opening and slid with the feet: this
little mat promised never to push itself forward: it gently
seized one's feet, wiped them and passed them on without
a murmur to smooth stretches of fawn, unpatterned
carpet that flowed up the stairs, lapped against the walls,
streamed into the various rooms and into the furthest
corners without pause or break.

Mr. and Mrs. Baldwin went upstairs. Beginning life
afresh had decided them upon doing away with the old-
fashioned business of sharing a double bed: they were
each to have their own bedroom now: Edith's looked out
towards the sunset across Welden Close, Tom's towards
where the dawn would come, over the crest of the hill
with the time-honoured footpath winding up its side.
The beds were made with the new linen and blankets:
their pyjamas lay folded beside the turned-back sheets,
they flicked on the neat, shell-shaped reading lamps over
the beds, and Mr. Baldwin gave a sudden queer little
sigh—" *I* don't know," he said, " it's all too . . . well,
too good to believe, isn't it ?—I can't help feeling there's
a catch in it. Can you believe it's all ours, Edie ? "

Edith neither nodded nor shook her head.

" We're bound to find something that's . . . that's not quite right," she said.

" I almost hope we do," replied Mr. Baldwin. " It looks too much like an Ideal Home at the Exhibition. I feel somebody's going to come along to-morrow and say the Show's over—and pull it all down."

Even the crackling fire in the dining-room looked almost too good to be warm. Dinner was set out upon a spotless cloth that gleamed as if it had been varnished: the new cutlery shone like silver: the new earthenware dinner-service looked too pure to take the pie that Edith cut and served.

They began the meal with a light-hearted gust of conversation, but gradually the deep quietness of Welden Close compelled their voices to undertones. In Brondesbury Terrace it was never completely still: there were always the footsteps of a passer-by: the rumble of a lorry upon the main road: a neighbour calling in his cat—a window closing—a clock chiming—a train hooting: there was always, even in the depths of the night, some tiny sound to break the quietness. Here, in Welden Valley, Tom and Edith sat and listened, for the first time since their busless, lorryless childhood, to the compelling wonder of deep, unblemished silence. The windows framed a clear-cut fathomless square of indigo night and Mr. Baldwin had the queer feeling of being upon a bright-lit stage—of being an actor in a dinner scene: that the dark night enwrapped a vast, silent audience that watched a man and his wife play out the first scene of a drama.

" We ought to sleep wonderfully here," he said, wiping his mouth on a new serviette that was so stiff and shiny that it passed across a crumb and left it on his lip . . .

" wonderfully," he added, removing the crumb with his fingers.

Steak pie, brussels-sprouts, and mashed potatoes: stewed pears and a piece of Cheddar that looked so new and clean that it might have been a chunk cut bodily from the distempered wall. Mr. Baldwin rose, and stared out of the window. Faintly he could see the great trunk of his elm, and gradually, as his eyes accustomed themselves to the darkness, the green gates outlined themselves. A pang of loneliness came and he tried to shake it off. They seemed so utterly removed out here from the noisy, friendly world of an hour ago. There was not a light to be seen: the intense stillness was broken by a faint rustle in the tree, and in the silence that followed the little house seemed to sink another hundred fathoms into a soundless ocean.

Edith, by force of habit, was piling the dinner plates together—then she remembered there was no basement and no Ada—and pressed the bell.

" I don't see why we shouldn't have the light in the porch," said Mr. Baldwin.

" Certainly not," said Edith. " I thought it *was* on."

" I turned it off trying to turn on the light in the hall," he said.

It was pleasant to meet Peggy in the passage and to feel that there was life in the world besides their own. He switched on the outside light and returned to the dining-room. He felt like the Captain of a ship with broken engines—drifting in the black emptiness of an Atlantic night—turning on every light in the vain hope of companionship.

The porch lantern certainly improved things: it threw

a pale, ghostly gleam across the little front garden, and
he could pick out details here and there: a pile of stone
slabs he had ordered for his crazy paving—a few tufts of
grass that had escaped the builders' feet. He felt restless,
and angry with himself for feeling so. No fire could look
more inviting than the one before him—no chairs more
anxious to make his acquaintance and become his friends.
He ought now to settle down with Edith opposite him—
to spread his legs to the fire, light his pipe, and have a
long talk with her over the absorbing things that had
happened in this eventful day.

But he could think of no more to say at present: everything had been talked out: they had slept fitfully on the
last night in the old house and they had been up before
seven.   Bed seemed the obvious thing—and yet he felt
too restless for bed—too restless to talk. He told himself
that it was natural to be restless on the first night in a
new house—but it did not comfort him. Supposing their
lives were to go on exactly as before?—supposing, after
all, they found no friends and no new interests—that
everything turned out to be too young and out of key for
them in Welden Valley? It was easy to be lonely in the
old house, for most of their neighbours kept themselves
to themselves. There were busy streets, cinemas, endless
shops to look into in Brondesbury . . . and a house that
understood them. Supposing the people in Welden
Valley labelled them as a couple of old bores with no
claim upon the buoyant life of a new city?—what would
happen if Edith and he were thrown back upon each
other?—night after night—month after month, in this
utter, impenetrable stillness? He shivered—gave his head
a little shake to clear it—and turned to the fire.

Edith was stifling a yawn : she saw him looking at her and smiled apologetically. " I'd sleep anywhere to-night," she said. " I shall sleep like a log in that lovely new bedroom."

" You go to bed right away," he said. " I'll just get my hat and stick and go for a stroll." He took her arm and they went upstairs.

Edith's room looked rather cold and bare when the time came to think seriously of bed. The bed itself looked a little too self-centred and proud of itself to welcome a timid newcomer: it seemed to stick up its chest and stomach a little too high.

" What a charming room it is," said Mr. Baldwin. " You've planned it and thought it all out wonderfully."

It occurred to him for the first time what a struggle poor Edith must have had to keep her love of freshness alive at the old house. She had been a mere girl when they had furnished it over thirty years ago: she had thrown her youthful heart and soul into it—and then for over thirty years she had fought a heart-breaking battle against decay. Now and then she had replaced old, worn-out things with tiny, hard won improvements that in his blindness he had scoffed at and fought against. For all those years her love of fresh, modern things had been stifled: one would have thought her desires would have paled and died; that when the time came to furnish " Greengates " her mind would have groped back feebly towards the old fashioned things that she had understood as beautiful in years gone by.

But lo and behold !—when the chance came—when her desires and dreams should in the normal course of things have passed away, her genius had burst out as freshly as ever. How on earth had she kept up to date and understood so perfectly what would look right in a modern house ?

" You've done it all beautifully," he said. " Everything's so exactly right."

She turned from her new dressing-table with its pivoting, frameless side mirrors and low-built surface : she was laying out her toilet set—and her brushes and scent bottle looked a little uneasy in their grand surroundings.

" You were the one that made it possible, Tom."

She smiled at him and he turned abruptly to the windows. He had a strong dislike for Darby and Joan scenes, and Edith, on occasions, was a little too inclined to set the stage for them.

" Don't be silly. Anybody can do this with a little"— he nearly said " courage "—" energy."

" It wants more than . . . just energy . . ."

There she was again !—she was always saying things that his own restraint so carefully avoided !

" Anyway," he said, " I couldn't have done it alone— so that's that ! Sure you won't be lonely if I go out for a stroll ? "

" Of course I won't. Peggy's here. But don't forget where the house is—it'd be silly to sleep out under a hedge on the first night ! "

He kissed her. " You get along into bed. I shan't go far. I'll be back in ten minutes."

It did not seem correct to muffle himself in an overcoat now that he was a countryman. He took his hat and stick, thrust out his chest and strolled off into the night.

CHAPTER XXIII

THE LANTERN LIGHT over the door guided him to
the gate, but he had to grope carefully over the rough
grass verge that lay between his fence and the road. How
extraordinarily dark and quiet it was out there ! When you
went out in Brondesbury Terrace you would always see a
bus or car slip by on the main road : there would always
be someone walking nearby : a row of lived-in, lit-up
houses opposite and a line of moth-infested lamp-posts.
He found himself longing for the very things he had most
longed to be rid of !

Out here there was a cool, sweet country dampness in
the air—a rustle of trees, and a smell of earth and stars—
and yet, when he turned at a little distance to look at his
new home he was filled with a strange melancholy.
Nothing could look more inviting than its clean-cut
outline and its mellowed lights. It lacked nothing : it was
a perfect home—but its very perfection called upon him
to achieve the impossible : to live ravenously in the present
and to blot out past and future.

Darkness to the front of him : darkness to the right of
him—only to the left lay a few glimmering lights, and his
lonely steps rang out on the concrete road that skirted
Welden Close. As he passed the dim white pegs that
marked the empty building sites he began to wonder about
the little pinked-in squares on the Estate Agent's map—

sites that he understood had been sold. He realised now that those coloured squares had been decoys: that he had been duped into building out here in this wilderness away from the other people—that his house was to serve as a piece of ground bait for the convenience of the Estate Management. There were probably some awful, unforeseen drawbacks to Welden Close that everyone but he had realised. He had come to Welden Valley with a hunger for companionship and they had stuck him out here where nobody would ever come. . . .

Oh, well—he was depressed, and that was the end of it. Maybe it would be better in the morning. He decided to walk as far as the village—to go slowly by the new houses in Cymbeline Road and see if he could spot through some of the windows the people who were to be his neighbours, but never, probably, his friends. Then home to bed. . . .

"Good evening!" came a voice through the darkness.

Mr. Baldwin glanced up with a start of surprise. He was passing the gate of the first new house and a rotund little man was standing there. He could not see the man's face—for the bright light over the front door revealed nothing but a stubby little silhouette in plus fours, smoking a cigar.

"Good evening," replied Mr. Baldwin, and he braced himself to walk on. He had always shrunk from people who were too suddenly familiar and his instinct told him to withdraw politely, and have a look at the little man by daylight before taking further steps. But second thoughts warned him that his whole future in Welden Valley might depend upon what he did now. If he were to walk straight by without a word this little man might tell the people of Welden Valley that the newcomers at "Greengates" were too proud of themselves to know their neighbours.

It would mean the very isolation he was dreading. He stopped dead, and said: " Lovely night ! "

" It is indeed," replied the little man. " Are you the chap from ' Greengates ' ? "

Mr. Baldwin felt a twinge of disappointment. For general purposes he divided the human race into three broad categories:

(a) Men who referred to their wives as " my wife."

(b) Men who referred to them as " *the* wife."

(c) Those who called them " my old lady."

He sadly placed his new acquaintance in category (b). He had hoped that no one in Welden Valley would fall below (a). But what did it matter ?—they were brother pioneers. He gave a friendly laugh.

" That's right," he said. " How did you know ? "

" Sherlock Holmes ! " replied the little man, jerking his thumb towards Welden Close. " One house up the road : one man comes down the road ! "

Mr. Baldwin responded in a spirit that surprised him.

" I'll have a shot now—and guess you live there ! " he said, nodding towards the house that lay behind the little man.

The little man chuckled, and turned round to admire his new home in the light of Mr. Baldwin's pointing finger.

" I think it's a delightful house," said Mr. Baldwin. He and Edith had noticed it in particular as they had passed : it was a dignified, Regency sort of house with long windows and green shutters, with two neat little box trees in green tubs to either side of the door.

" D'you like it ? " said the little man. " I'm not sure whether I don't prefer the Tudor ones myself—but the wife voted for a Regency one because of the high ceilings.

Qɢ

You've got a nice place up there. I'd have built in Welden Close myself if I'd known somebody else was going there."

Mr. Baldwin never knew quite how it happened, but suddenly he found himself strolling down the road with his new friend and talking to him about Welden Valley as if he had known him for a lifetime. Such a thing would have been unthinkable in Brondesbury Terrace !— nobody would dream of picking up a total stranger and diving into a heart-to-heart talk about Brondesbury, because Brondesbury was not an absorbing subject to discuss : the building of it had been completed years ago and it was now a place that one merely lived in, in silence.

" Van Doon's my name," said the little man. " Nothing Dutch about me though."

Whatever he was he proved himself a good and sympathetic listener. Mr. Baldwin forgot to look at the houses he was passing : he found himself telling Mr. van Doon the whole story of his adventure : how he and his wife had known the Valley when it was a desolate place : how furious they had been when first they had seen its dawning development—he told Mr. van Doon about their unexpected visit to the Show House and all that it had led to. He even told him of his emotions at leaving his old house that afternoon.

" I know," said the little man. " We all take roots and it hurts to pull 'em up. But you're right in coming here : it's got a future, you know—a big future."

" What made you come ? " asked Mr. Baldwin.

" Well—the Estate Manager's a pal of mine for one thing."

" Mr. Watkinson ? "

" Yes—old Tom Watkinson. I knew him in Singapore."

" You've lived abroad ? " enquired Mr. Baldwin with a new interest.

" Knocked about a good deal out East," said Mr. van Doon.

" Watkinson tells me he's going to build a house for himself in Welden Close."

Mr. van Doon threw back his head and laughed.

" He always tells people that when he's selling 'em a house. Nothing like it for giving confidence ! " He glanced quickly at Mr. Baldwin and added: " I don't mean he's dishonest—I reckon he really *does* believe he's going to build for himself—but when the time comes he always shuts down and clears off to the next place."

Mr. van Doon was interested in rubber. The whole of his youth, it seemed, had been spent upon remote plantations, but the time had come when the old country had called. " There's always a time," he said, " when a man wants to sleep safely without a revolver under his pillow."

" That's true," said Mr. Baldwin. He would never have placed this comfortable, rather smug little man as an Empire Builder. They had reached the main road of the old village and he was able to see a little more of his new friend by the light of the street lamps. His face matched his body : it was clean-shaven, round and chubby. He had a snub nose and little twinkling grey eyes. He bore no trace of his life in the tropics.

It was a splendid, starlit night. Mr. van Doon threw away his cigar stub and the two men paused to fill their pipes at an old hump-backed bridge that spanned a narrow stream. Beside them lay an inviting village inn and

Mr. van Doon nodded towards it over the flame of his match.

" What about a night-cap ? " he said.

The remark pulled Mr. Baldwin back to earth. In the excitement of this new and unexpected companionship he had almost forgotten Edith waiting anxiously in their lonely house for the sound of his returning footsteps.

" To tell you the truth," he stammered with an apologetic laugh, " I only meant to come out for five minutes. It's our first night, and naturally my wife . . ."

Mr. van Doon nodded understandingly, and finished what Mr. Baldwin was groping to say.

" I know," he said, " she's bound to feel lonesome. Mine did to begin with, but she's got a dog now. We'll pop in and have one another night. It's a decent little pub."

They left the bridge, and began to stroll back towards the valley. Mr. Baldwin puffed at his pipe. For the first time a silence fell between the two men, but it was an easy, sympathetic silence. There was something unreal to Mr. Baldwin about this delightful, informal companionship. It had sprung from a darkness that had seemed so utterly empty. No doubt it meant little to Mr. van Doon: he was probably accustomed to picking men out of the night and turning them into companions for a leisure hour —but it meant something to Mr. Baldwin that his new friend, with all his insight, would never have dreamed of. It was his first real heart-to-heart talk to another man for over a year, and he was delighted to find that his powers of conversation had survived the weary months of loneliness. At first he had talked stiffly and jerkily, as a parched man might sip the first drops of water from the pool of an oasis, but now he was talking freely and easily: he was aching to prolong the pleasure of it and suddenly he remembered that amongst the goods ordered from the village to stock their larder were a crate of ale, a bottle of whisky and some port. They had reached the gate of Mr. van Doon's house, and Mr. Baldwin hesitatingly delayed him with a hand upon his arm.

" Why not stroll back to my house and have a spot with me there ? "

" Good enough ! " said Mr. van Doon, promptly re-closing his gate.

It may have been the decisive manner of his new friend's acceptance, but directly Mr. Baldwin had made the suggestion he regretted it. It would be magnificent to settle down by his own fireside for a lazy yarn with a friend, but what on earth would Edith think of it ?—what on earth would she think of him, dragging a total stranger into the house at half past ten at night ?—on their first night, when naturally she would want to enjoy " Green-gates " alone with him ?

They were in sight of the house now : he could see the light gleaming over the porch, and the subdued glow behind the bedroom curtains where Edith lay listening for his return. He wanted to get rid of Mr. van Doon: he wanted to go in by himself—to be alone with his wife —to sit at the foot of her bed and tell her about the first friend he had made in Welden Valley. He floundered for an excuse to put Mr. van Doon off until another night, but in place of the excuse came a sudden exultant joy that made him feel like taking his new friend by the arm and racing away with him up the dark hillside. The futile suburban conventions that had plunged him into loneliness were gone for ever !—the Pioneers of Welden Valley were bound in a common companionship, sharing the same ideals—the same absorbing interests. His house was open to every man and theirs to him ! As he closed the gate he looked up at Edith's window and thought of her lying there alone. He was longing to run upstairs and tell her that their days of lonely wayfaring were over: she knew nothing as yet of Mr. van Doon and the companionship that he symbolised. He threw the gate open with a flourish and stood aside for his friend to enter.

" I expect I can rout up something to christen the new house in," he said.

The green gates clicked behind him. He opened the front door with his glistening new mortice key and flicked on the light in the dining-room. The fire had fallen to a peaceful glow and he was proud to ask a friend in without shame of disorder and shabbiness.

" Make yourself comfortable," he said. " I expect the maid's gone to bed—I'll just go out and see what I can find."

He did not go directly to the kitchen. He hastened upstairs to Edith's room.

She was reading in the luxury of the light above her bed. She lowered her book and looked at him enquiringly.

" Bed comfortable ? " he enquired; " it looks fine."

" Lovely," said Edith. " Who's that downstairs ? "

He looked up at her with a guilty chuckle.

" Why, Edie . . . it's funny . . . I was just strolling down the road, and I came across the chap who lives at the white house with the green shutters: the first house you come to . . . you know . . . at the corner: we had a walk together—and I asked him to drop in and have a drink. He's an awfully nice chap: he's asked us both to go and have tea and meet his wife."

The last remark was not strictly true, but he felt certain an invitation would come, and he was burning to draw Edith into it. She raised herself upon her elbow. " That's splendid !—what's he like ? "

" Well," began Mr. Baldwin, " he's a short, cheery chap —lived abroad a lot . . . awfully interesting . . ."

But Edith pulled him up. " Don't leave him sitting there by himself ! The drinks are in the larder. I expect he'd prefer whisky if he's lived abroad."

Mr. Baldwin got up, went to the head of the bed and kissed her. " You don't mind, Edie ? I'm sure he won't stay long."

" Mind ?—it's splendid to meet somebody so quickly ! "

He left her wondering what she was going to wear when they went to the van Doons to tea. He hastened downstairs, found the whisky and a syphon, and hurried back to the dining-room.

Mr. van Doon was sitting well forward in his armchair : he was filling his pipe and his eyes were reflectively upon the fire.

" Who did your fireplace ? " he enquired.

" Oh—the Estate people. D'you like it ? "

Mr. van Doon nodded. " It's a nice job."

Mr. Baldwin tasted the first fruits of the house-proud : he felt that the fireplace in Mr. van Doon's dining-room was not quite so good—that Mr. van Doon was wishing he had a fireplace like the one in front of him. . . .

" We picked it out from a lot of designs," he said. " Say when."

" When," said Mr. van Doon, after a disturbingly long silence.

" Right up ? " enquired Mr. Baldwin with the syphon.

" Half and half," said his friend. " Well, chin-chin."

" Here's to Welden Valley ! " said Mr. Baldwin.

" That's it !—Welden Valley—and let's hope our walls don't crack ! "

Mr. Baldwin pulled out his pipe and pouch and sat opposite his friend. Here was perfect happiness : a fire— a home—a drink and a companion : and a wife tucked comfortably in bed upstairs : the things he had pictured so often had come true at last.

Mr. van Doon lounged back in his chair : he looked more at home in " Greengates " than its owner did at present.

" It's good to have a new house," he said. " It's all so clean and fresh—it's nice to know that nobody's ever died in any of the bedrooms."

Mr. Baldwin lit his pipe and nodded agreement. " I expect you've seen a lot of queer places," he said.

Mr. van Doon required little encouragement : he sank deeper and deeper in his chair : his pipe sank deeper and deeper into his mouth : he balanced his glass on the arm of his chair, and talked.

He was a good talker : and Mr. Baldwin desired nothing more than to lie back, in his chair, to puff at his pipe and to listen.

It seemed that Mr. van Doon was born at Croydon and had owned one of the first motor-bicycles ever built. Incessant punctures had drawn his attention to the poor quality of the rubber then obtainable, and he had gone to the Malay States, opened up a rubber plantation and done a great deal to remedy things. He told Mr. Baldwin how one reared the trees and tapped their juices: how one stored it and sold it: how one treated the black men to make them respect one: " You've got to hang them now and then," he said; " it's the only way." It amazed Mr. Baldwin to think that here before him, at his own fireside, sat a man who had hanged natives like hams—and yet it seemed in perfect keeping with the free, devil-may-care life of the Pioneers of Welden Valley.

Welden Valley itself threatened to fall a bit flat after such lurid excursions into the backwoods, but Mr. van Doon's eyes lit up with a new fire when the conversation turned to the life that they had come to share together.

" What are our neighbours like? " enquired Mr. Baldwin. " D'you know much about them? "

Mr. van Doon knew all about them. He began with the house next to his own and worked methodically round the entire Estate. They were very much the kind of people Mr. Baldwin had expected. There appeared to be no outstanding personalities: no film actors or racing motorists, but there was something solid and satisfying about them. They were all people of good estate—living in their own houses in apparent ease. There were no families living in basements: no tenements disguised as " maisonettes " as there were in Brondesbury Terrace: a dozen in all: a dozen pioneers: three or four young married couples, three or four men in middle life with families, three or four elderly retired couples and one old lady with a parrot and a girl companion.

" They sound quite interesting," said Mr. Baldwin. He had made up the fire while his friend was talking and

a blue jet of gas was gushing through the black lumps
in the grate: the smoke was surging up the chimney with
a firm decision that promised complete relief from freak
chimney-pots and unsightly cowls. But these were things
that lay only in his subconscious thoughts: it needed all
his will power to keep his mind firmly planted in reality.
Even if he had returned from his walk alone, and sat
quietly for an hour by the dying fire with the silence of
the valley for companionship, he would still have found
it hard to associate himself with the Mr. Baldwin who had
once worked for the Temple Insurance Office and lived
in Brondesbury Terrace. The difficulty was tenfold in
the present circumstances. His second and third whiskies
were very modest compared with those he had given his
friend, but how the room glowed with light !—it seemed
to grow brighter and brighter until the very walls poured
radiance from their glistening distemper. It rushed into
his veins, and pulsed up to his temples, and overwhelmed
him with a sense of unreality. He kept thinking of a Mr.
Baldwin sitting in an old dining-room at Brondesbury
Terrace, watching the fire die out and listening to the
footsteps passing by. He kept wondering who this was
who sat by the fire in this strange new room that shouted
with light, who listened to a tubby little man with a red
face who talked and talked. . . .

"They *might* be interesting," said the little tubby man,
" if they were properly handled."

They ? Who were they ? With a struggle he pulled himself together. Of course, they were talking about their
neighbours. The strange people who lived out there in
the darkness were " they."

" How d'you mean ? " His voice sounded as if it flew

out of a loud speaker, and he cleared his throat gently to adjust things.

The little man in the opposite armchair removed the mouthpiece of his pipe and blew a spray of evil liquid into the fire. " They might be *very* interesting—if somebody took the lead." The clock on the mantelpiece chimed the first quarter past eleven—the blue squirt of gas in the fireplace matured into a soft, leisurely flame. Mr. van Doon relit his pipe, took a sip of whisky and edged his chair nearer to his host.

" If we act quickly—if we do it now—it can be done. If we wait until the place has grown too big, we've lost our chance."

Mr. Baldwin was no good at solving cryptograms. " What's the idea ? " he said.

" It's just this," replied Mr. van Doon. " You were saying just now that nobody really cared about the place you come from—that people just lived in their houses and never did anything *together*. That's because they weren't interested in the place: it was built and finished years before they went there—there were no surprises left—nothing more to be built or developed. See what I mean ? "

" Quite," said Mr. Baldwin, with a shrewd nod.

" Now think of Welden Valley: it's new: just beginning—and it depends upon us firstcomers what happens to it in the end. See what I mean ?—we've got a duty and so far nobody's done anything about it. We're just going the same way as the people in them older places: we just dig our gardens and go shopping—say " How d'you do ? " over each other's gates and when the night comes we just shut ourselves up in our houses like a lot of hermits—

everybody wishing somebody'd *do* something to bring us together and liven us up ! See ? "

" Absolutely true," murmured Mr. Baldwin.

" Now's the time," said Mr. van Doon.

He removed his pipe and waved it confidentially towards the window.

" D'you know that old barn over there ?—a big rambling, tumbledown place that used to belong to Welden Farm ? It would make a wonderful Club House if it was rebuilt, and those flat meadows round it would make wonderful playing fields for tennis and bowls and cricket. It would pay the Estate hands down to take on the job. A big social and sports club would add pounds to the value of this place."

Mr. Baldwin sat up. Clubs had always interested him, but during the past years, in one way and another, he had dropped away from those he had belonged to. " That's a great idea," he said. " Why not suggest it to the Estate ? "

Mr. van Doon sat back in his chair and held up his hand for silence.

" I have," he said. " They'd start to-morrow—only they're afraid of it: afraid it might be a white elephant. They won't do it on their own responsibility, but they'd do it like a shot if they knew for certain that the people in Welden Valley would support it."

" Then why not get them to support it ? "

" They wouldn't want asking twice: they'd jump at it." Mr. van Doon paused and firmly emphasised his final words: " but they must have a leader ! "

Light dawned upon Mr. Baldwin: suddenly he realised what the little man was getting at. He wanted to be the leader himself, but naturally he wanted someone else to suggest it.

" We want," continued Mr. van Doon, " a man to take the lead : a man who can get all these people together and put some pep into them. Once we've got these first-comers bound together the whole thing would grow and grow. Every new arrival would join as a matter of course. We'd start with a dozen foundation members. In a year there'd be a hundred—in two years five hundred !—there wouldn't be a club like it in the whole of England ! "

" You're the man to do it," said Mr. Baldwin.

He was prepared for a smug smile and a little self-deprecation from Mr. van Doon : he prepared himself to persuade his friend and promise to canvass for support from their neighbours. As far as he was concerned he cared little who took the lead as long as a lead was taken. It thrilled him. It was a splendid scheme. As one of the foundation members he might find himself upon the committee, with an engrossing hobby for the winter evenings. It would give both Edith and himself the social life they longed for. He was by no means sure that Mr. van Doon was the right man—but the right man very rarely did take on these jobs. They were nearly always run by the men who were not quite right—who were tolerated because of their energy—" I'm certain you're the man," he said.

And then a surprising thing happened. There was no smug smile or deprecating shake of the head. Mr. van Doon leant forward in his chair, pointed at Mr. Baldwin and said : " No. You're the man."

Mr. Baldwin could not reply : the surprise of it took his breath away.

"It's good of you to say I'm the chap," continued Mr. van Doon, "but I'm not. I don't like fellows who run themselves down. I'm not doing that. I reckon I've got my good points like the rest of us—but my good points aren't the sort for taking on a social job like this. If you want a chap to settle a spot of bother with a bunch of niggers, good enough, but I'm a self-made man: rough diamond if you like—I don't mind saying it. I haven't got the education."

He paused abruptly—almost pugnaciously, and Mr. Baldwin felt embarrassed. Mr. van Doon had summed himself up with surprising insight. Mr. Baldwin admired him for it but it was hardly polite to express his admiration in the circumstances. But uppermost in his mind was the quite bewildering suggestion that he himself was the man to lead the people of Welden Valley. A few hours ago, in the barren loneliness of his arrival he would have ignored the idea as a stupid joke. Who in his right mind would pick upon an elderly, retired insurance clerk, whose very friendliness gave damning evidence against his ability to lead and inspire his fellows? But queer things had happened since his lonely arrival in Welden Valley—queer things that shone out of these new distempered walls and clicking electric points: that radiated from the strange little man in the arm-chair opposite—that flowed out of the amber bottle on the gleaming table. He was a new man whom no one, not even himself, had a right to judge. Leaders sprang from strange, unexpected corners. Little incidents flashed across his mind: incidents that led nowhere in themselves, but hinted at exciting things that might have happened. His year as Treasurer of the Acacia Tennis Club had been a golden one. He had been popular in the office and the younger men especially had shown their respect for him. Many a potentially great leader had passed through life in obscurity—because the man and the hour had never synchronised. Was this the hour ?—was he the man ? It was too bewildering to disentangle at a moment's notice. He could only shake his head with a weak smile and say—" Don't be silly. *I'm* not the man. I'm certain of that."

Mr. van Doon leant further forward in his chair. " D'you mind me being personal ? " he said.

" Not a bit," replied Mr. Baldwin, feeling sure that something nice was going to happen.

" First of all," said Mr. van Doon, " you're the right age. Not too old and not too young. People would respect you, and that's essential. Then again, you've had a business training: you know how many shillings go to the pound. Then—if you don't mind me saying it—you're a man of the world, you've got education and polish. I reckon you could stand up to anybody and give 'em points on polish. You've got enthusiasm—but I've seen enough of you to know you haven't got any silly unpractical ideas. You'd always know what can be done and what can't—and if that isn't enough I'd like to know what is ! "

Mr. Baldwin stirred in his chair: it was pleasant to listen to this remarkable analysis of his character—and yet he felt a little uneasy—at any moment he felt that Mr. van Doon might ask for an urgent loan. The queer little man was looking him straight in the face, with piercing, glistening grey eyes.

" I . . . " he began, not knowing in the slightest what

he would have said if Mr. van Doon had not abruptly stopped him.

" Wait a minute ! I know what you're going to say—you haven't got time: you don't want to push yourself forward. Maybe you're not even sure of yourself—but I tell you that you're the man for the job and I know the right man when I see him ! Think of it as a duty ! "

Mr. Baldwin leant forward and gulped his whisky. One of his ears cracked and began to buzz : it was as if a shaft of inspiration had pierced his brain. He remembered how once, in an emergency, he had captained the office cricket team—how easily and smoothly he had moved his fieldsmen about—how effortless had been his duty in ushering the opposing team into the luncheon tent and seating them between his own men—he remembered two wide eyes in the darkness of the office stairs upon the night he had retired and a boyish voice that had said : " We shall miss you badly, sir ! "

" I'd do anything I could to bring people together and make them happy," he said.

" Splendid ! " said Mr. van Doon, slapping himself on the knee. " You'll always have me behind you—I shall back you up all I know."

" The power behind the throne ! " said Mr. Baldwin, with a knowing little laugh. Mr. van Doon knew his limitations, but he intended to be in the fun all right !

" The power behind the throne ! " laughed Mr. van Doon. " It's going to be grand fun. It'll be a terrific success—a tremendous job, but a terrific success. We'll start to-morrow !—I'll get a notice round asking everybody to a meeting at my house. I've got a nice big room that'll take fifty at a pinch. Even if they all come—if they all bring their wives—it'll only mean twenty-five. Twenty-five Pioneers !—I'll fix up cakes and coffee."

The clock began to chime and Mr. van Doon looked up in sudden dismay.

" Is that clock right ?—it can't be twelve ! "

" It *is* twelve," said Mr. Baldwin, glancing at his watch.

His guest sprang to his feet, pulled his waistcoat down and brushed some ash away. " I shall catch it all right this time ! The wife'll think I've been locked up ! "

" Won't you have a spot before you go ? " asked Mr. Baldwin.

" Not a drop ! " said Mr. van Doon. " You're a nice one to lead me astray like this ! " His face was very red, but despite three whiskies he was perfectly sober as far as Mr. Baldwin could see : he knocked his pipe out, dropped it in his pocket and walked briskly to the door.

" Well, it's been a wonderful evening," he said. " I shouldn't be surprised if we haven't made history to-night ! I'll drop in to-morrow morning with that notice. I'd like you to see it before it goes out."

" Splendid ! " said Mr. Baldwin. He opened the door and watched his new friend go briskly down the rough path. " The gate opens inwards."

" So does mine and every sensible one ! " called back Mr. van Doon. " Chin, chin ! "

" Chin, chin ! " called Mr. Baldwin, feeling a little annoyed at ending the evening with a silly remark. He closed the door. In the sudden silence he became conscious of a queer, high-pitched singing in his ears : he felt about ten feet tall and the veins in the backs of his hands were so big that he could scarcely close his fingers. He stooped to push home the bright little brass bolt and

R G

his head billowed out like a balloon. The pounding of a
waterfall came to his ears. He stood upright and steadied
himself against the wall. The house was ablaze with
lights, and suddenly he realised what a firm hold he would
have to take upon himself to turn them all off in their
correct order.

He knew quite well what was wrong. He had had too
much whisky. On the first night in his new house he was
going to bed intoxicated—a thing that had not happened
for years and years. He tried to think out what it all meant
—but it was far beyond him—he was too bewildered to
think—too bewildered to do anything but concentrate his
whole will-power upon the glaring lights——

He reached out towards the three little switches in front
of him and gave the lowest one a cautious twitch. The
light in the outside porch went out and he found himself
laughing out loud. A fluke !—a bull's eye first time !
Emboldened by his success he pushed up the second
switch : something darkened above him but for the
moment he could not locate it. Then he saw that the light
upstairs had disappeared. That was wrong. He would need
that when he went upstairs. He switched it on again—
tried the upper switch and plunged the hall in darkness.
When he returned to the dining-room he was staggered
by the reek of tobacco : it closed around him and made
him feel a little sick. The fire was blazing brightly and
unconcerned.

He took the tongs and groped amongst the red-hot coals
to remove the largest pieces and push them under the
grate. But the heat pounded upon his face and he lay the
tongs down with elaborate care to avoid a sound that
might disturb Edith. What did the fire matter ?—it was

an absurd, old-maidish idea to rake it out every night before going to bed.

The grate was full of the white ash from their pipes. There were wet rings on the table from their glasses. Good old, hard living Pioneers !—smoking like furnaces and swilling liquor !—what a life !

He flicked out the light in the dining-room, but as he went to the stairs he saw that he had forgotten to turn off the kitchen light when he had gone to get the whisky.

What a gorgeous little kitchen it was !—clean as a new pin : flick !—it was gone—the house was in darkness save for the glimmer on the upstairs landing that would guide him to bed.

He stood in front of his bedroom mirror : he looked surprisingly—disappointingly normal. His hair was ruffled from lying back in his armchair and his face was a little more highly-coloured than usual—but his head was the correct size and his eyes looked clear and steady. It was probably excitement, and not the whisky that had given such a strange flavour of unreality to the evening. He stood by the window : a clean fresh breeze sponged gently over his face and cleared his thoughts. The hill crest was faintly visible in the dark, starlit night. Somewhere up there the footpath spanned the crest—somewhere up there he and Edith had stood six months ago and looked down upon the valley in anger and dismay. From the same place they had looked down and seen the first stack of bricks and scaffolding, the first vestiges of " Greengates " lying under the elm.

The call of a night bird and a rustle of wind came through the darkness. He felt very tired, but his mind was seething with the turmoil of the fantastic evening. Dictator of Welden Valley: leader of the people—leader of the Pioneers: it was too fantastic to believe. Even Mr. van Doon now seemed a ghostly visitor without substance or future. But Mr. van Doon had been real: Mr. van Doon was a shrewd judge of men: he had been genuine and sincere in everything he had said. The intense, husky little voice still rang in his ears:

" *You* are the man !—*You* are the man to lead ! "

He could still see the piercing little eyes. He went to the mirror. There was no doubt about it: in a certain light and at a certain angle strong, masterful lines formed round his jaw. He was seized with an overwhelming desire to go back to the dining-room: to take pen and paper and write a stirring manifesto to the People of Welden Valley. But even as the desire came an aching weariness crept over him. It was an effort even to raise his hands to undo his collar—it was an exertion even to climb into the cool, unfamiliar, springy bed, to grope for the switch and to plunge the room into the fathomless darkness of the valley.

CHAPTER XXIV

Between the small hours of three and four that morning Mr. Baldwin turned wearily upon his back and stared up at the dark ceiling of his bedroom. It was a new bedroom no longer: no room could have remained bright and spotless through such an eternity of darkness. He felt that he had been lying in it for half his lifetime—that if he were to turn on the light he would find that the bright distemper of the walls had peeled and littered the floor with aged, discoloured powder.

It was a cruel disappointment, for above all things he had wanted to awake fresh to his first morning in Welden Valley. At half past twelve he had struggled against sleep to draw the bedclothes around him. Five minutes later he had never been more starkly, staringly awake in his life. A riotous crowd of thoughts began to race each other round and round his brain, missing the curves and bouncing off the inside of his skull. For a little while he tried to control them: to cut down their pace and to sort them into order. He tried to begin his plans for the Welden Valley Club, but every time they began to take shape the tubby little body of Mr. van Doon came somersaulting round to send them flying in all directions. It was Mr. van Doon who was keeping him awake. Mr. van Doon became a menace: he wanted to run Welden Valley with Mr. Baldwin as a spineless figurehead: he wanted Mr. Baldwin to do exactly what he was told.

The whole thing was ridiculous. He turned irritably on to his side and tried to get rid of his lower arm by resting it upon the bedside table. It was ridiculous to begin worrying about a club that had not even started. The grand Welden Valley scheme was probably stone dead: still-born from a bottle of whisky and a pipe of tobacco, for Mr. van Doon would probably wake up in the morning and decide that it was not worth while. Life in Welden Valley would probably turn out as he had expected all along—a quiet, peaceful existence: a few good books, a few pleasant walks—vigorous hours in the garden, and perhaps a few quiet, pleasant friends. But when he tried to persuade himself that a peaceful existence was all he needed there would come the fascinating vision of a clubroom filled with people—of a spacious office wherein he sat behind a huge desk covered with papers—of a green field speckled with flannelled tennis players—of people saying, " See Baldwin about it: Baldwin'll put it right." . . .

It was useless to think any more about it until the morning. He summoned his will power, determined to lie perfectly still, to close his eyes, make his mind a blank, and count slowly to a thousand. He had never been any good at counting imaginary sheep passing through an imaginary gate: he had never been able to conjure up a sufficiently clear picture of the gate or to collect enough imaginary sheep to make the effort worth while. He lay counting grimly, sticking out a finger to mark each hundred, but before the fingers of one hand were stretched, Mr. van Doon swept past and knocked them flying.

He tried an old trick that had sometimes induced sleep on nights of restlessness in the past: he began an imaginary journey from his home in Brondesbury Terrace to his office in the City: he walked to the station, visualising each landmark on the way: he climbed into the train and conjured up each detail of the panorama that flowed by the carriage window. But he lost himself in the maze of chimney-pots round Camden Town: the pillow was closing one of his nostrils and by the time he had rearranged it the imaginary train had arrived at the London terminus without him.

What did one do with one's arms upon a normal night in bed? Wherever he put them they either slipped down or tugged his pyjamas. One arm was a yard too long—the other a yard too short. He tried laying one across his chest, holding it in place with a thumb through the buttonhole of his pyjama coat, but this drew the coat so tightly under his arm that it threatened to burst his veins. The human body seemed shaped to meet every emergency of life with the one exception of sleep. He stretched an arm above his head and groped for something to hold on to. The old bed at " Grasmere " had comforting brass rails to grasp: this new bed had a smooth, heartless wooden back devoid of fingerhold. It proved what he had suspected all along: it was the kind of bed that took no further interest in a man from the moment its winning smile had rescued it from the showroom.

The whisky had parched his mouth and he would have given anything for a cool glass of fruit salts. He felt desperately lonely without Edith beside him. He began to feel that it was the room that was keeping him awake: its shadowy corners were so utterly barren—so strange—and still, and destitute of character: the room felt like a railway station waiting-room closed for the night.

With every restless movement he edged the pillow closer to the side of his bed: with monotonous regularity he raised himself upon his elbow and pulled it back. The quiet was so intense that it seemed to be thinning the very air. He longed for the early sounds that used to keep him company on wakeful nights in the old house—the slow, lumbering luggage train that passed on the main line soon after four—the clock of St. Mary's Church that separated the black slabs of time into digestible slices. Once he felt that sleep was coming at last: he scarcely dared to breathe lest he frightened it away, and then his chin irritated and the rubbing of it brought him wider awake than ever before.

Leader of Welden Valley ! What a farce ! A born leader would never have sprawled for five meaningless hours: he would have risen and spent the night upon his plans. He pictured van Doon, rolled up in his blankets like a fat cocoon . . . van Doon . . . cocoon. . . .

Vaguely he heard someone moving nearby, but he was too tired to open his eyes. Blearily and indistinctly he heard something chink down upon the bedside table, and then a voice cut through the clouds . . .

" Good morning, sir ! "

It was Peggy: Peggy with his tea: Peggy in broad daylight. He jerked himself abruptly on to his elbow.

" Good morning, Peggy. What's the time ? "

" Eight o'clock, sir . . . and two letters."

Peggy at least had survived the night's eternity with

success. If anything she looked younger: her arms and face shone more brightly in the daylight than they had by night.

" Sleep well, Peggy ? "

" Like a top, sir. Was *you* comfortable ? "

" Yes, wonderfully."

And he meant it. As Peggy closed the door he closed his eyes—he forgave the pillow—he forgave the bed—he forgave everything in thanksgiving for the deep, dreamless sleep that had come so stealthily and unexpectedly in the end. The tea completed his recovery and he felt ready for anything.

The letters were only two circulars with halfpenny stamps on them: one from a coal merchant and the other from a dairy: but they pleased him nevertheless. They seemed to announce his election to full membership of Welden Valley.

He jumped out of bed and went to the window. A pale spring sunlight lay upon the hillside—there was a smear of mist upon the grass and a tang in the air that smelt of September but tasted of spring. He threw open the window and performed the breathing exercises that he had promised himself ever since the evening when they had first seen their land. The cool air bubbled in his lungs: the new life had begun. He threw on his dressing-gown and went to Edith's room.

Edith was sitting up in bed opening letters: she had beaten him easily, for the bed was littered with envelopes bearing halfpenny stamps. There were two from laundries, three from dairies, two from butchers and a catalogue of wines.

" I didn't know there were so many tradespeople in the

place." He sat on the foot of her bed. " How did you sleep, Edie ? "

" Quite well," said Edith. But the rumpled bedclothes gave her away. " It's a beautiful bed, but . . ."

" I know," said Mr. Baldwin. " I didn't sleep much. It wants getting used to."

Edith was bursting with questions about Mr. van Doon. " I felt terribly curious. I kept wondering what you were talking about down there. I wanted to come down and listen outside the door."

He looked up in sudden concern. " Could you hear us ? "

" The dining-room's right underneath."

" I'm terribly sorry . . ."

" Don't be silly—it didn't keep me awake. I *wanted* to keep awake. I lay there wondering what I'd wear when we go to tea with them to-day."

Mr. Baldwin felt awful. Drunkard and liar—that was what he had come to. He had kept her awake till midnight—and Mr. van Doon had never asked them to tea at all. . . .

" As a matter of fact," he stammered, " it wasn't definitely arranged—it . . . it was left indefinite."

" In that case we'll ask *them* to tea," said Edith. And Mr. Baldwin, humbled and grateful, went to his room and shaved.

Edith's curiosity about Mr. van Doon was very quickly satisfied. They had scarcely risen from breakfast before the gate clicked, and the little man himself came smartly up the path. Peggy was told to show him into the lounge and Mr. Baldwin's heart fell as he took Edith in to introduce her.

For Mr. van Doon, in the pale morning sunlight, was not nearly so impressive as he had been in the darkness, and in the mellow, forgiving glow of the dining-room on the previous night. His change of clothes had a good deal to do with it. The plus fours and tweed jacket had given him a breezy, open-air appearance, but the tight, natty little blue serge suit he was now wearing made him look like a retired publican, and the light brown, pointed shoes, together with the daffodil in his buttonhole reminded Mr. Baldwin of Whit Monday at Brighton. But his face was the greatest disappointment: it had glowed so rosily under the lamplights of Welden High Street: it had been so chubby and Pickwickian in the light of the dining-room fire, but the rosy flush had now retired, and shut itself up in a multitude of tiny blue-tinted blood vessels around his cheekbones and nose.

But his buoyancy remained. He bounced up from the sofa with an " Ah ! " of delight and took Edith's hand in both of his as if he had been longing to meet her for years.

" I expect you heard about the little binge me and your hubby had last night ! "

Edith laughed. " I heard you come in: I'm sorry I was in bed."

Mr. Baldwin did not like the way his visitor had jerked his head suggestively towards him and winked artfully at his wife: he did not like the word " binge," or " hubby " very much—and he began to realise the horrible mistake he had made. He should have known that the best kind of people are not picked up so casually in the night.

But Edith was charming to Mr. van Doon: whatever

disappointment she felt after her husband's glowing reports was magnificently concealed: she drew him into a conversation about Welden Valley and the little man began to improve at once: he was so vitally interested in everything: he flattered Edith about the taste she had displayed in decorating the lounge, and when he frankly admitted that he liked their fireplaces better than his own, Mr. Baldwin began to like Mr. van Doon better than he did the blue suit and daffodil.

Van Doon got quickly to business. He produced a sheet of bright blue notepaper and handed it to his host.

" I scribbled this out when I got home last night. D'you think it'll do ? "

Mr. Baldwin took the paper and read:

WELDEN VALLEY CLUB

A number of residents have expressed a desire for the establishment of a club to form the centre of the social and athletic life of Welden Valley.

I am writing at their request to invite you to an informal meeting at my house at 9 p.m. on Thursday next, the 6th inst., to discuss the project and consider ways and means. I sincerely hope you will be free that evening to attend.

Very truly yours,

PERCY VAN DOON.

" Brief and to the point, don't you think ? " enquired Mr. van Doon.

" Perfectly," said Mr. Baldwin. There was a restraint about the notice that surprised him. He had feared a long and repellent manifesto. " I didn't know other people had asked for it ? "

" They haven't," replied van Doon with a knowing smile, " but that's the way to get people keen. I'll copy that out and send everybody one to-night." He rose briskly and slipped the notice into his pocket. " Now what about strolling down and having a look at the old barn ? "

Mr. Baldwin was torn between two earnest and conflicting desires : he was longing to get out into his new garden—to get hold of his shining new tools and begin work—but his eagerness for the club had returned : his spirits had risen and he was burning to see the barn that might soon become the centre of his new life.

" I ought to get busy on my garden . . . " he began, but van Doon waved the garden vigorously aside. " Gardens can be done any time—this club business is urgent ! "

Urgent ! Nothing in Mr. Baldwin's life had been urgent for close on two years. It was a splendid thing to be concerned in something urgent. He took his hat—gripped his walking-stick and set off with his new friend across the broad field in front of his house.

It was a morning to lift the heart and make the nostrils quiver. The spring lay crouching in the grass : the rising sap had given a plump sleekness to the elm trunks, and their branches were gathering around them a pale green haze that shone against the sky. Some crows were bustling amongst the trees, and Mr. Baldwin felt the ground beneath him murmur with the tiny yawns of a million little creatures to whom the call had come. Specks of colour glistened in the bank beside the field path, and a cluster of snowdrops, weary little pioneers of spring,

were trying to forget their battles against the last rude
blasts of winter by raising their tired, grimy faces to the
sun.

Mr. Baldwin had yearned many a time in the past two
years for a companion upon his walks, and now that a
companion was beside him he would rather have been
alone. He wanted to stride on and on, up hill, down dale—
to realise that from now on—upon every morning until he
died he would walk out of his house each morning and feel
the crunch of virgin grass beneath his heels.

Van Doon seemed quite unaware of the splendour
surrounding him: he trotted along beside his tall companion, three steps to his two, and prattled incessantly
about the new club—about subscriptions and hot water
pipes and the crockery he would get from a friend in the
wholesale line. He discussed the club tie that they would
have; Mr. Baldwin was fond of club ties, and he wished
he could look forward a little more keenly to wearing the
same colours as Mr. van Doon.

They came to a lane that curled away towards a dell of
trees and presently van Doon stopped beside a ramshackle
old gate and pointed up a cart track, grass-grown, and
apparently disused for many years.

" There you are ! " he said.

Mr. Baldwin's antiquarian instincts leapt within him
as he approached the dark old building at the end of the
lane. It was a magnificent old place—far and away
beyond his expectations. He had pictured a gaunt wooden
shed, devoid of character, but this was built of brick:
narrow, wine-red Tudor brick, with sturdy oak beams
in its sides. The tiles were of the kind that people snapped
up and put on new, expensive houses, for no craftsman

could imitate their mellowness, their fascinating twists and gentle, time-worn undulations.

What a place it was to conjure with! He peered into its dark interior: massive beams spanned its roof—cobwebby, broken machinery littered its floor—but what a clubroom it would make! A great open hearth could be built in its far end—it was as big as an ordinary village hall and could be divided into several rooms. And the meadow beyond cried out for bowls, and tennis and cricket.

"It'll want a lot done to it," said Mr. van Doon. "This barn can be patched up and made into a sort of entrance hall, and the Club House Proper can be built on behind."

The hard little voice cut gratingly across Mr. Baldwin's thoughts: he was thinking of labourers, stacking those twilit corners with sweet hay: labourers in tattered knee-breeches and greasy three-cornered hats—with old leather jerkins they had smuggled home from the wars of Marlborough: very softly the ripples of history must have lapped against these walls.

"We must be careful not to damage this," he said.

Mr. van Doon looked at him with surprised round eyes. "Damage it! You'd want a clever man to damage it any more than what it is!"

"I mean," said Mr. Baldwin, "it's—it's a perfect piece of Tudor work: if we do anything to destroy its appearance we should be vandals."

"But it's only a barn! How can you have a Tudor *barn*!"

Mr. Baldwin made no reply. He stood gazing at the old place in silence.

" Let's go down and see if we can catch old Tom Watkinson at the Estate Office," suggested Mr. van Doon. " We'll have a talk about the whole thing."

The Estate Manager was talking to a self-conscious young couple at the door of his office, and while they stood waiting van Doon nudged Mr. Baldwin and whispered : " Two more members for the club ! "

Mr. Baldwin heard the Manager say : " I assure you, sir—it's the only place to build—in fact, I'm going to build there myself." He saw the young man nervously stroke his little fair moustache and the girl clutching her bag : he knew what they were thinking : he hoped with all his heart that things would work out right for them. He heard the young man murmur : " We'll—we'll drop you a line."

" Not later than Friday," warned Mr. Watkinson.

" Not later than Friday," said the young man.

He watched them walk away and he saw a queer little smile flicker round the corners of the Manager's mouth.

Mr. Watkinson did not appear to know Mr. van Doon quite so intimately as Mr. van Doon seemed to know Mr. Watkinson, for while Mr. Watkinson said : " Good morning, Mr. van Doon," Mr. van Doon said : " Cheerio, Tom."

They were invited into the office, and the Manager listened attentively to all that Mr. van Doon had to say. He was silent for some while after the little man had finished.

" You mean," he said at last, " that you want the Estate to bear the cost of converting that barn and building a large club house on to it—and then to stand the risk ? "

" There won't be no risk," exclaimed van Doon. " We'll rope in everybody to join—we'll have hundreds of members in a year or two."

As Mr. Baldwin sat listening in silence it was borne home to him that van Doon had not been altogether straightforward: he had given him distinctly to understand that the Estate Manager knew all about the scheme and was ready to support it if the residents were ready. It was now quite clear, from Mr. Watkinson's manner, that this was the first he had heard about it.

Mr. Watkinson began to grow impatient: he glanced at his watch: Mr. Baldwin rose to go, but van Doon sat stubbornly on:

" But, Tom, old boy—can't you see what it'll mean to the Estate ! The biggest and grandest club for miles around ! People are going to fall over each other to build nearby to get the use of it ! You'll not only get more for your land, but in a year or two you'll get a profit out of the club as well ! "

" I know," said Mr. Watkinson, " I know."

" If I bring you a definite list of people who'll support it. . . . "

" All right," interrupted the Estate Manager, " you have your meeting and see me again. I can't promise anything—but it's a good scheme and I'll see what I can do."

Mr. Baldwin made an elaborate excuse to get rid of his persistent little friend outside the Estate Office. He referred to numerous duties in the village and a meeting with his wife at the baker's shop. To his relief van Doon decided to go home and write out the notices for the meeting at once, and Mr. Baldwin walked away alone. As

Sɑ

he passed through the sleepy old village he caught a glimpse of the young couple, sitting in the cake shop, drinking coffee. He felt he would like to go in and speak to them, to urge them on: to encourage them to fight their difficulties and reap their reward. But at the moment he wanted to be alone to think. He crossed the little hump-backed bridge and followed the road up its winding course towards the ridge.

He wondered whether he was a bigger snob than he had suspected. The long and short of it was that van Doon was not good enough. Class counted for nothing and character everything: old Henslip, the Messenger at the office, was in conventional terms a common man, but he was a gentleman with whom Mr. Baldwin had many an evening played dominoes in the office basement. He would welcome Henslip as a member of the Welden Valley Club because he was modest and simple and unaffected and had a jolly sense of fun. Mr. van Doon was far cleverer than Henslip: far better off and better educated, but Mr. Baldwin had no desire whatever to meet him socially: he was perky—he was bogus: he was not genuine.

For two pins he would wash his hands of the whole scheme—but something inside him kept urging him to reflect and think: he reached the crest of the hill and followed a path that looked down upon the valley from the opposite side to his own. It was while he stood there in the spring sunlight, with the cluster of new houses beneath him, that he made his resolution. There would be a Welden Valley Club after all, but it would be the club of his own dreams and not the one that van Doon was thinking of. It would not be " the biggest, grandest club for miles around ": it would not have " hundreds of

members in a few years' time ": there would be no
" Club House Proper " built on to the barn. That grand
old barn alone would be the club: it would be restored
with reverent care and its members would be few—just
the best: the people that mattered—regardless of class
or calling—and a small committee would select those
members with jealous care.

Instinctively he knew that everything he desired would
clash with van Doon. It was an unscrupulous thing to
contemplate fighting the very man who had first suggested the scheme, but he was ready and fiercely happy to
be unscrupulous if it led to something fine.

CHAPTER XXV

A few days of residence at " Greengates " revealed to Mr. and Mrs. Baldwin several small but important adjustments that called for the attention of the builder. The plumbing appeared to be a little too delicately balanced, for if the front door was slammed too hard the lavatory flushed. This was not a nice thing to happen each time a visitor arrived and left, but when Mr. Baldwin tried to demonstrate the trouble to the Estate Manager it naturally refused to happen: the slam of the door was followed by a stony silence from the lavatory. Another thing was due to pure carelessness upon the builder's part, for after Mr. Baldwin had run the hot tap in the cloakroom for half an hour in an attempt to get hot water, he found that the hot water came immediately from the tap marked " cold." He was sharply instructing the plumber to see that the pipes were immediately taken up and relaid correctly when the plumber somewhat insolently replied that it would be quicker to change the labels on the taps.

But these were trivial troubles that did little to mar the happiness of those first spring days in Welden Valley, for Tom and Edith Baldwin felt all the joy, and all the freshness, all that superb enhancement of self-respect that comes from association with things that are clean and new.

One felt a different kind of cleanness after a bath at "Greengates": it was almost like bathing in the open air. The bathroom in the old house had always been a musty, soul-destroying place. It faced the gaunt brick wall of the house opposite, and on the brightest day it was plunged in sulky, dark brown shadow. The window, for as long as they could remember, had been jammed irrevocably open to the extent of two inches at the top: the room used to fill with steam, and a dismal rainbow would form around the choking, gasping gas jets beneath the geyser. You undressed furtively in your bedroom, and as you crept into the bath you felt that pneumonia germs sat waiting for you upon the soap-stained, brown painted ledges. You were oppressed with a sense of doom as you pushed open the steam-slimed door and faced the black coldness of the passage.

But the morning sun shone into the "Greengates" bathroom: the glistening white tiles made one's body look pink and aglow with health: the window stood boldly open and you felt the country air brush softly upon your thighs. There was room to throw out the arms and do rhythmic breathing exercises—you could throw a towel around you, poke your head out of the window and see the hills and trees.

Mr. Baldwin felt almost ashamed to dig his spade into the strong, tuzzled turf behind the house: it was like digging a knife into a magnificent birthday cake and destroying its graceful lines. He felt reluctant to soil his beautiful new tools with their shining blades and spotless ashen handles. But once he had set aside these scruples he forgot everything in a mighty struggle against the vigorous, untamed turf that wrestled with him until great beads

of perspiration plopped into the grass. Here at last was
a garden worthy of a strong man's toil ! He taped out
the position of paths and flower beds with mathematical
precision: the great cubes of turf clung to the earth and
came up with a fierce despairing hiss. He piled them together behind the brambles to weather down into top-spit
for his beds and he struggled round the house with slabs of
crazy paving. He mixed cement upon the box the beer
came in and consolidated each foot of hard won land
before adventuring further into the wilderness beyond.
By lunch-time upon the third morning, five yards of
stone-flagged path stretched boldly away from the
windows of the lounge: by lunch-time every day his vest
and shirt were wringing with sweat and he would take
a tepid bath and change his clothes before sitting down
to the meal.

Edith spent adventurous mornings in the village: the
finding of new shops had always amused her, and here
was a paradise on earth—a place in which every shop
was new to her. She discovered a greengrocer who grew
his own vegetables, a dairyman with his own cows, and
a butcher with his own farm. Mr. Baldwin jocularly
enquired whether the grocer tinned his own tongue.
All the tradesmen urged her to open an account and
permit them to call for orders, but Edith was a wise old
hand at shopping. She told them all that she had not
decided which shops to give regular orders to. She kept
them all on tiptoe and extracted remarkably good service
from them as a result.

A pleasant surprise for Edith was the return of her
afternoon nap that she had thought was gone for ever.
It came about through Mr. Baldwin deciding upon a

regular afternoon rest on his bed after such strenuous work in the garden, and so for an hour after lunch Edith was able to draw the blinds, plunge the drawing-room into twilight and recapture the happiest memory of years gone by.

The time between tea and dinner became for Mr. Baldwin the best of all. He had bought a large scale map of the country around Welden Valley: the sun now lingered until well past six, and when tea was over he would take his stick and pipe (but not his hat), and stride away upon a new exploration every evening. Sometimes he would pass through the village and follow the valley until he came to the beech wood with its maze of moss-green paths: at other times he would climb the ridge and take the bridle path to Polegate Hill. On a fallen tree he would sit and watch London slowly appear in the sky as the night clouds gathered up its glow. The set of the sun became the signal for return and the lights were always beginning to pop up around him in Welden Valley as he came in sight of " Greengates." Edith had been granted sole and exclusive rights over the rose beds in the front garden, and often as he returned in the twilight he would see her blue overalled figure moving to and fro amongst her frail young trees. In the few minutes before dinner he would take the Naturalist's Diary that Edith had given him at Christmas and jot down a few notes for comparison next year—" First primrose in Harless Wood "— " Heard cuckoo by bridge on Thurston Road."

But there was a wistful quality in these days as well, for every evening brought them nearer to the night of the meeting at van Doon's to discuss the club, and something told Mr. Baldwin that these were to be the last days he would ever spend as a lonely man. On the coming Thursday he would meet all the people at present hidden from him behind the curtained windows of the houses in Cymbeline Road. Some would emerge as friends—others as enemies: some would support his scheme for the club—others would support van Doon. Most nights on his return through the Valley he would pass a stranger, and nod, and say " Good night." And always he would walk on with the thought—" Will he be with me—or with van Doon ? " When Edith had gone to bed and he sat working at the dining-room table upon his plans, he would sometimes lay down his pen and wonder whether it was all worth while. Life was very pleasant as it was: why throw himself into a struggle that was certain to lead to restless days and sleepless nights ? Defeat would mean embitterment—victory would lead to ceaseless work—disappointments—the clashing of conflicting ambitions —jealousies and enmity. But he always picked up his pen again and went on with his plans. One night van Doon dropped in to say that he had followed up his circular letter with a personal call upon everyone concerned, and he felt confident that there was great interest, and the meeting would be well attended.

Mr. Baldwin took the opportunity of telling van Doon his second thoughts about the club: that a small select club would be far better than a large, public place open to all. Van Doon had looked at him in surprise and said: " Oh, no—the Estate won't help unless everyone in the place can join."

And Mr. Baldwin quietly braced himself to fight.

CHAPTER XXVI

THE DAY OF THE MEETING dawned with a strong
northerly wind that ferreted amongst the hedgerows and
found a few weary, half-skeletoned leaves to play with.
Towards evening there came dark clouds and a gusty,
uncertain rain that threw ominous shadows towards the
critical events that lay so close at hand.

The Baldwins dined lightly upon fish to avoid risk of
discomfort or drowsiness at the meeting, for above all
things Mr. Baldwin desired a clear brain and sharp wits
about him. He said little during the meal, and Edith
made no attempt to force a conversation. Since tea-time
he had been silently at work, and his final notes, neatly
folded, lay ready upon the hall-stand beside his hat. He
was restless and ill at ease, and more than once glanced
up at the windows as the gale spattered them with rain.

" This is certain to keep people away from the meeting," he said at last.

" Not if they're keen," replied Edith. " In any case
nobody's got far to come."

At moments Mr. Baldwin weakly hoped that no one
would be at the meeting at all: that the whole thing
would be a fiasco. At the next moment he prayed for a
room full of people: to have as many there as possible
to witness his fight against van Doon and the second-rate
things that van Doon stood for.

It was less than a minute's walk to the van Doons' house and although the Baldwins ate slowly there was nearly half an hour to spare when the meal was over. They sat by the fire: they tried to talk of other things: of the garden: of the small library they had discovered in a room behind the newsagent's shop, from which they had that morning drawn two tattered but amusing books. But the time lagged interminably, and Mr. Baldwin wondered how many other people were sitting by firesides, waiting for the time to go to the meeting.

"Whatever happens, we're going to meet our neighbours," said Edith; "there's bound to be some nice people amongst them. I like the look of that woman who goes by every morning with that big Airedale dog. I hope she's there." She paused for a moment, then added: "Even if they don't support your plan, we shall still find some nice friends. Some are certain to be on your side."

Mr. Baldwin did not answer at once. He threw a log on the fire and said: "I hope it doesn't end in an awful row: van Doon's the sort of chap who might easily turn nasty: it's the pity the meeting's in his house."

"There's no need for him to be unpleasant," replied Edith. "It's just your scheme against his. They'll discuss it and then vote. There's no reason for it to get personal."

But he shook his head. "It's extraordinary how easily things *can* get personal," he said. "Sometimes I think I'm a fool to trouble about it. It'd be much more pleasant just to go to the meeting and enjoy listening—and just be one of the crowd. But you know how it is, Edie. The world's made up of unpleasant, pushing people and nice,

retiring people. If you mix the two kinds together in a
club the nice ones always go and the nasty ones remain.
A club either keeps its social standing with a terrific
struggle—or it goes down. No club ever goes *up* socially,
ever. I simply want a club for the nice people, that's all.
I want all the rules to protect the nice ones and keep the
nasty ones out. The nasty ones can go and have a club
to themselves. We could have such a grand little club
down in that old barn if we fight for it. Can't you picture
it ? A jolly little club room for the winter ?—a tea garden
for the summer ?—with just the people that matter ?—
simple, interesting people. I want to limit the membership
to thirty men and thirty women; half to be under thirty
years of age so that it'll never turn into an old fogeys'
club. The two things that make people proud of a club
is a waiting list, and a rumour that the committee had
refused to accept somebody."

" I think everybody will vote for that," said Edith, but
Mr. Baldwin shook his head with a smile.

" Not everybody. Not the people who know they
wouldn't be elected to a really exclusive club. Van Doon
wants to lord it over a colossal club with hundreds of
members. He wants quantity: quality doesn't appeal to
him. But it does to me."

He rose from the fire and went upstairs to brush his
hair and prepare for the battle. He was wearing a dark-
grey suit that had seen very little service since his City
days. At ten minutes to nine they slammed the front door
and heard the lavatory flush defiantly behind them.

" I shall insist upon the builder putting that right," he
said. He spoke mechanically, neither in sorrow nor in
anger. It was curious how remote and unimportant little

" Greengates " had suddenly become, when a few days ago it had meant everything in the world.

They pushed open their umbrellas and leant against the gale.

Mr. van Doon had specially invited the Baldwins to arrive early in order that they might say " How d'you do ? " to his wife before the crowd arrived. Lights were shining from every window of the van Doon house as they walked up the path and stood between the smug little bay trees by the front door. Mrs. Baldwin had caught sight of someone peering between the front-room curtains as they had entered the gate, but the head had disappeared as if jerked by a string and there was a somewhat tedious, nerve-wracking wait before the door was opened by a superior-looking maid in brown uniform. The maid took their umbrellas away from them like a nurse removing unclean toys from little children. She was asking them for their names when Mr. van Doon himself emerged from a room and advanced with outstretched hand. He was wearing yet another suit: a double-breasted jacket, striped trousers and a large butterfly collar that made him look like a solicitor in a film. He was carrying a cigar that had obviously just been lit.

" Here we are !—Come along in and meet the wife !— I hope the rain doesn't keep 'em away. I'll get busy on the telephone if it does !—I'll rout 'em out ! "

" We must have a good big meeting ! " replied Mr. Baldwin.

" We shall !—even if I have to fetch 'em in the car ! "

Mrs. van Doon was tall and plump, with startling blue eyes and beads to match. She had bright pink cheeks, full red lips and was in every way the kind of lady men married when they came home from Rubber Plantations.

" Percy's never stopped talking about you both ! " she exclaimed. " It's quite an occasion to meet you in the flesh ! "

This made Mr. Baldwin feel as if he had come without any trousers on, but he gallantly replied that he, too, had looked forward to their meeting with barely concealed impatience. The house was full of bright amber light and a smell of coffee. A startled, resentful cat peered round a corner and shot upstairs.

Mrs. van Doon took Edith by the arm and ushered her away to remove her coat. Mr. van Doon took Mr. Baldwin by the arm and led him into the large front room.

It was a very fine room—much bigger than the lounge at " Greengates." It was painted a cream colour and the Regency mouldings on either side of the fireplace looked very impressive and correct. The designs embodied bundles of flutes done up in ribbon, small cherubs with trumpets and decorative wind instruments in profusion. Everything was in such harmony, and so cream coloured that Mr. Baldwin could not help feeling it a pity that coal could not be secured in cream-coloured knobs. It was an elegant, impressive room, but not the sort that one could do a piece of toast in. The wind boomed in the chimney and a scurry of rain came faintly from the night.

Mr. van Doon had spared no pains to get everything as perfect as possible for the meeting. A table had been placed at one end of the room, with two chairs behind it. Upon the table were pens and ink and a copy of Whitaker's *Almanack* for reference if needed.

The rest of the room had been arranged in a pleasant,

informal circle of chairs with a settee and two large armchairs by the fire.

Mr. Baldwin declared that it looked first rate, but van
Doon held up his hand and said: " Wait a minute !—
have a look in here ! " He led the way across the passage
and threw open the dining-room door.

The sight took Mr. Baldwin's breath away. He had
never seen such a reckless display of refreshments. There
were plates of sandwiches of every type from cress to
lobster: sausage rolls, éclairs, large cream buns—slips of
toast with sardines on them and a large purple jelly. Upon
the sideboard, glowing in the amber light and catching
dancing reflections from the fire, stood a small battalion
of bottles and glasses: from home-made lemonade to a
crusty-looking bottle of port and a large jug of yellow
fluid with fruit floating in it or lying on the bottom,
according to the kind of fruit it was. Mr. Baldwin looked
round in astonishment. It must have cost pounds. And
as he looked, he felt all his fine, carefully-prepared plans
crumbling to pieces. No one who came to the meeting
could do anything but support a man who entertained
them like this. . . .

" There's just a point that's worrying me," said van
Doon. " We must have a Chairman for the meeting."

" You must be in the Chair," said Mr. Baldwin. " I
shall propose you myself."

" I mean," went on the little man, "just because it
happens to be my house I don't want to . . ."

" Nonsense," broke in Mr. Baldwin, " you planned the
meeting: it's your idea."

" All right. If you think so. But you might slip the word
to someone else to propose me. You see, if you propose

me and I propose you as Secretary, it'll look a bit fishy—a put-up show—if you see what I mean."

"Quite," said Mr. Baldwin. "I'll mention it to somebody. And then you'll propose me as Secretary before the meeting starts? We must have proper notes taken from the beginning."

"Certainly I shall. Directly I'm in the Chair," assured van Doon.

Mr. Baldwin felt relieved. He also felt that he had played a slightly dirty trick: he wanted to be safely elected as Secretary before he declared himself against van Doon's plan. If the election were to come afterwards van Doon might have second thoughts . . . he might even contrive to be elected Secretary himself—and that would wreck every remaining hope in Mr. Baldwin's heart.

But he quickly shook off his scruples: he knew that he would have to be unscrupulous to succeed: he was prepared to ride rough-shod over everyone—over van Doon himself if necessary. . . .

He waved his hand towards the table with a laugh:

"You ought to have had some crackers—then we could have finished the meeting blowing whistles in paper hats."

Van Doon did not laugh very much at this joke: Mr. Baldwin felt he had made a tactless remark, that he had belittled van Doon's hospitality. He was just beginning to put himself right when the front-door bell rang and the little man bristled into activity.

"Come along!—we'll meet them in the lounge!"

They were just in time to regain the lounge before the door reopened and the maid announced: "Mr. Forbes Whitehead!"

"Ah!" said van Doon. "The very man we most wanted! I'm glad you got down in time!"

"I *made* time," said Mr. Forbes Whitehead. "Just scrambled into the seven-fifteen."

Mr. Whitehead was a sturdy, thick-set man. He was very bald, but his keen, aquiline face and piercing eyes made up for his lack of hair and stamped him as a young and vigorous personality. He was dressed in the conventional black coat and striped trousers of the City, but while Mr. van Doon had obviously dressed in the same style for this special occasion, Mr. Baldwin knew that Forbes Whitehead was dressed this way through lack of time to change into something easier. Van Doon was bogus: Whitehead was real.

"You two ought to find plenty to talk about!" said van Doon as he introduced them. "Two City men!"

The new-comer turned a pair of such penetrating eyes upon Mr. Baldwin that they would have been disconcerting without the broad, humorous smile beneath them.

"Were you on the seven-fifteen?" enquired Mr. Whitehead.

"No," replied Mr. Baldwin, "I've retired."

"Lucky man!"

Mr. Baldwin discovered that his new friend was a member of the Stock Exchange and he felt a little awed. The aloof, top-hatted men who came and went through Throgmorton Street and disappeared through the mysterious, forbidden door of "The House" were rather a class apart from the lesser, bowler-hatted men of the Banks and Insurance Offices. But the common interests of Welden Valley soon broke down the barriers, and in a few minutes Mr. Baldwin found himself in a deep and surprising conversation about swallows, cuckoos and migratory birds in general. Birds were Mr. Whitehead's hobby, and he was literally bursting with them. In five minutes he told Mr. Baldwin more about them than he had learned in sixty years. He promised to take Mr. Baldwin out one day and show him how to observe nature unobserved: he was just explaining how it was possible to lie in secret within six feet of a thrush's nest when van Doon broke in to introduce a talkative white-haired lady named Mrs. McKinney. Mr. Whitehead escaped, but Mrs. McKinney hemmed Mr. Baldwin into a corner and began in a rapid, high-pitched voice to tell him everything he knew about everything.

Mr. Whitehead had interested him so deeply that he had quite failed to notice how quickly the room was filling with people. There were at least eight or nine already, and as he abstractedly nodded and listened to Mrs. McKinney he keenly watched the door over her shoulder as further people arrived. He was glad to see Edith sitting on the couch in conversation with a pleasant lady in horn-rimmed glasses, and he enviously watched Mr. Whitehead discussing motor-cars with a large fat man as vigorously as he had discussed birds with him. Mr. and Mrs. van Doon bustled to and fro, excited and happy that every-body was finding so much to say. The room was throbbing with conversation: the bell kept ringing: somebody said: " The rain's stopped—the moon's out! " and Mr. Baldwin nervously felt for his notes in his waistcoat pocket. The babble was so intense that he began to feel light-headed: it was a long time since he had been in a room with so many people, and it frightened him to think that in a little while they would all be silent—listening to his

TG

speech. Mrs. McKinney prattled on about how nice new houses were and what a treat it was to live in the country and had Mr. Baldwin noticed that the spring was coming. He glanced furtively at his watch and saw that it was ten past nine: he noticed with relief that the buzz of conversation had begun to die away: that some of the guests were glancing around with a look of expectancy. He caught Mr. van Doon's eye through the crowd and they exchanged a nod of agreement: the little man made his way to the table and tapped upon it with a pencil. There was no response and he tapped more loudly.

" Ladies and gentlemen ! " he called out.

There was instant silence except from an old lady who was apparently deaf, who went on talking in a shrill, solitary voice until her listener gesticulated her into silence.

" Ladies and gentlemen ! " repeated Mr. van Doon. " Shall we begin ? "

There was some pointless but friendly laughter; one or two " hear ! hears ! " and then silence. Everyone was looking towards van Doon: van Doon stood by the table in expectancy, and with a thud of the heart Mr. Baldwin realised that he had forgotten to tell anybody to propose van Doon as Chairman. He was upon the point of doing it himself when Mr. Whitehead called out:

" We must have a Chairman to keep us in order ! May I propose our host ? "

This was carried with acclaim, and Mr. van Doon edged round behind the table with a bashful smile.

" Thank you, ladies and gentlemen. This is rather sudden, but I'll do my best. Now will you all make yourselves comfortable ? I hope there's enough seats. I wouldn't like anybody to come to my house and sit on the floor ! "

There was further laughter at this remark and Mr. Baldwin could not help feeling what a heaven-sent opportunity a meeting of this kind offered to a man who never managed to raise a laugh at anything he ever said at any other time in his life.

There seemed to be far fewer people when everyone was seated. There appeared to have been at least fifty when they were all standing up—but now, from his stiff chair beneath the window Mr. Baldwin was disappointed at counting only seventeen.

But they were pleasant, friendly, well-to-do looking people : much better than the sort one saw passing the old house in Brondesbury. There was one exceedingly aristocratic old gentleman with a grey, military moustache and a nice old aristocratic wife—two young, obviously newly-married couples—two single old ladies—a stout, commonplace man in pince-nez, a shrivelled little man in a high collar and a few people behind whom he could not clearly see. He was pleased to note that Edith had retained her seat on the sofa beside the lady in horn-rimmed glasses : she looked flushed and happy, and threw him an encouraging smile.

Van Doon looked as if he had grown six inches as he stood behind the table puffing with circumstance. " I wonder if anyone will feel a draught if we just open the window a little at the top ?—I'm afraid it'll get a little close."

There were cries of " Yes !—let's ! " and the meeting was entirely upset while all the men got up and looked for the windows behind the numerous curtains. Mr. van

Doon called out: " No !—please !—the maids can do it
—let the maids come in and do it ! " But the resourceful
Mr. Whitehead had already opened a window and was
enquiring of a lady beneath whether she would feel it.
All the men got up again and offered to change seats if she
felt any inconvenience. The maids arrived and were sent
away—and Mr. Baldwin felt certain that the whole
window business had been manœuvred to display the
fact that van Doon's domestic staff was in the plural.

" Now, ladies and gentlemen ! I'm sure we all want a
businesslike meeting and I suggest we begin by appointing a Secretary to keep proper records."

There was a murmur of approval : Mr. Baldwin's heart
began to thump and his tongue grew dry. " I had a word
just now," went on the little man, " with my friend
Mr. Baldwin, and he expressed his willingness to act if
that is your desire."

There was another murmur, followed by a ghostly
silence. Mr. Baldwin's heart was thudding like a sledge-
hammer. The silence continued : he saw people exchange
glances, raise their eyebrows, and shake their heads—
obviously indicating that they didn't know who Mr.
Baldwin was. After an eternity, van Doon remarked
in a drawling voice : " Will anybody propose Mr.
Baldwin ? "

Mr. Baldwin felt suddenly humiliated and angry : he
felt that van Doon had deliberately staged this drawn-out
delay in order to belittle him. Once more the resourceful
Mr. Whitehead jumped up :

" I'd like to propose Mr. Baldwin ! "

" Proposed by Mr. Whitehead," drawled out van Doon.
" Will somebody second that proposal ? "

Again there came the awful silence: were the whole lot dumb !—had only Whitehead got a voice !

" I second Mr. Baldwin," came a thin, nervous voice from the back. It came from one of the young newly-married men: Mr. Baldwin noted him and vowed eternal friendship.

" Mr. Baldwin is proposed by Mr. Whitehead and seconded by Mr. Fitzgerald. Any other nominations ? "

This time the silence was correct and comforting.

" Those in favour ? "

Some hands went up—then several more.

" Carried," remarked van Doon in a voice that sounded full of relief after a ticklish and difficult business. " Will you sit up here, Mr. Baldwin ?—there's plenty of paper and ink."

There was a little applause and some sympathetic laughter as Mr. Baldwin arose and went to his seat beside van Doon. He felt that he had made a sorry and undignified entrance to public life and he knew that van Doon had deliberately made his election seem futile and unsubstantial. He felt like a beaten man: he had no chance against the fates that were fighting upon the side of van Doon to-night: van Doon was in his own house: he was host and Chairman: everyone in the room except Mr. Whitehead seemed dumb: they would follow van Doon like sheep . . . he drew the paper towards him, took out his fountain-pen and prepared with a heavy heart to make notes of what transpired as the little man got up to speak.

Van Doon talked for half an hour and Mr. Baldwin had to admit that he talked well. What he said was no doubt well prepared and his vitality gave a rough eloquence to his words that deeply impressed his listeners.

He began by ridiculing the feeble, squabble-ridden, poverty-stricken little clubs that usually grew up like mushrooms in every new residential area—" They are feeble because they devote themselves to one solitary game or interest which cannot possibly attract sufficient people to make each pay its way. Jealousy prevents them from combining into one strong club embracing every sport. They grow like mushrooms and shrivel up like mushrooms.

" But we people of Welden Valley have got a unique opportunity—and we shall be lunatics if we don't take advantage of it !

" We have a far-sighted, intelligent Estate Management alive to the golden possibilities of one really fine, centralised club as the hub of the social life of the Estate. The Estate themselves will find the money : they will build the club : they will relieve us of all the dull, back-breaking work of founding it. We can be certain of it being a fine, impressive building, because the more attractive they make it, the more people will come and live here—the more people will buy their land—and pay them to build their houses. From their point of view it is a great business proposition because it will double the value of the land they have to sell : from our point of view it is something for nothing ! We have already bought our land and houses—it will only be the newcomers who have to pay more. The subscription will be moderate : the Estate will not attempt to make money out of the club itself : they will probably lose by it—but they will gain ten times their loss in other directions !

" All they need is an assurance from us—the pioneer residents—that we shall give our whole-hearted support and confidence ! Let us send them a message of support to-night and I guarantee they will begin the club to-morrow ! "

There was great applause when he sat down, and enough stamping of feet to set the purple jelly wobbling in the dining-room. During the ovation van Doon leant over towards Mr. Baldwin with glistening eyes and said: " How was that ? "

" Magnificent," replied Mr. Baldwin with all the heartiness that he could muster. " I wish I could speak like that."

" I'm sure you can," replied van Doon with a sympathy in his voice that said: " I know you can't."

When silence returned van Doon half rose with an apologetic modesty at having to rise again. " I hope we shall have a full expression of opinion from the meeting."

The stout man in pince-nez got up without delay. He heartily congratulated Mr. van Doon upon his very excellent speech and proceeded to make one himself that he obviously considered to be still more excellent. It was, in fact, a considerable feat of memory, for he repeated almost everything that Mr. van Doon had said: he then said a good deal of his own and when finally he sat down one gathered that he was in favour.

Mrs. McKinney then got up and strongly advocated the encouragement of archery. At some length she described the attempts made by her late husband and herself to instil an enthusiasm for this royal and ancient game into the residents of Wimbledon Park, and ascribed their failure to numerous reasons, the majority of which were not quite clear to the audience.

She received a sympathetic ovation when she took her seat, and continued to enlarge upon her idea in a whisper to an uncomfortable looking lady next to her who kept nodding and rolling her eyes.

The next speaker was the shrivelled little man in a high collar who arose from the obscurity of a small seat in a corner.

" Dentist," muttered van Doon to Mr. Baldwin.

" May I ask," began the little man in a thin, apologetic voice, " whether the club committee will be composed of residents—whether we, in this room, shall be eligible to serve on it ? "

" Certainly," replied van Doon. " The Estate Management will expect us to elect our own committee."

" What," asked the dentist, " will be our power if the Estate are, in fact, Owners and Managers of the club ? "

Mr. Baldwin felt a sudden glow of pleasure : here was the first opposition : the little dentist was on his side : his friend. For the first time van Doon showed hesitancy as he arose to reply.

" I've already said that the residents will themselves manage the club."

" I know—but what power will they possess if they do not control the one vital element in a club—its finances ? "

" I've always imagined that members are the one vital element," retorted Mr. van Doon. He smiled with a return of his self-assurance when some laughter followed this reply—but Mr. Baldwin noticed that the laughter was by no means general.

"Another point," pursued the dentist. "A committee protects a club by refusing membership to those whom they consider undesirable. If the Estate sells land to a man at a high price because they have provided an excellent club nearby, what will the Estate say if the committee refuses membership to that man—and what will the man say to the Estate when he realises that he has paid a high price under false pretences?"

"I assume," replied van Doon, "that all of us who possess the financial standing and discrimination to live in Welden Valley would be desirable members."

His face was flushed and he was fidgeting angrily with a piece of blotting-paper. There was an attempt at sarcasm in his answer: an attempt to make it seem as if the dentist were casting reflections upon those present in the room. But his efforts missed fire and there was no response from the audience. All eyes were turned towards the fragile little dentist, standing against the wall, fingering his watch-chain. There was a tenseness in the room that comes from an audience hoping to witness an exciting little breeze.

"I see," replied the dentist. "In other words, the residents who form the committee will be forced to accept, even against their will, everyone to whom the Estate sells a house?"

"I've already said," snapped Mr. van Doon, "the Estate are very particular about the people they sell houses to."

"Thank you," said the little man, disappearing from view upon his seat on the Regency coal-scuttle. There was no applause, but a murmur came that was far more eloquent than hand-clapping.

The stout man in pince-nez stood up again. He was

pugnacious and a little unpleasant. He said that it was nothing short of defamation of character and a criminal offence for a smug, self-righteous committee to exclude a man from a club he wished to join. Some men had suffered all their lives from the venom and spite of people who got on to committees and set themselves up as judges of other men's characters. All committees turned into little cliques who took too much to themselves and it would be an excellent thing if there *were* a power above them to let them know they weren't everybody. He enlarged upon this theme to such an extent and with such venom that it became evident to everybody that at some time in his life he had badly wanted to be on a committee and failed to achieve it.

There was no applause at all when the stout man sat down: if he had intended his outburst as support for van Doon's scheme it dismally failed: the little dentist had pointed out possible weaknesses: the stout man had proved conclusively that the dentist's theories were correct.

In the space of ten minutes the atmosphere of the meeting had undergone an astonishing change. Until the little dentist had risen, it had been like a friendly, rather aimless little tea-party. Now the air seemed charged with electricity: at any moment a careless word might cause a violent storm: people were speaking in undertones—nodding and shaking their heads. They seemed to be realising for the first time that they were dealing with a far bigger issue than they had anticipated, that the club was something that might profoundly affect the future of Welden Valley and all who lived in it. The smile had disappeared from van Doon's face: he sat back in his chair, obviously annoyed at the unofficial discussions proceeding in every corner of the room.

Mr. Baldwin realised that his turn had come at last. He had purposely refrained from speaking until he had been able to gauge the feeling of the meeting: so far van Doon alone had spoken constructively—and the little dentist, in a few penetrating questions, had brought van Doon's plan to the brink of destruction. Another attack might end everything, and he saw now that he alone was ready with a constructive alternative that would not only save the club, but save van Doon—for suddenly and unaccountably he felt sorry for van Doon . . . The stout man in pince-nez, in an attempt to support him, had done the little man a hideous disservice that he did not deserve . . .

He stood up, cleared his throat and took a firm grip of his watch chain. Van Doon looked up in surprise, and tapped the table for order.

" Is the poor, downtrodden Secretary allowed to open his mouth ? " began Mr. Baldwin.

There were cries of " Yes ! "—" No ! "—" Sit down ! " —" Go on ! " and a lot of friendly laughter.

Mr. Baldwin was delighted to find that his unrehearsed opening had struck the right note. He had planned to begin with a graceful compliment to the Chairman, but these good-natured interruptions were more helpful than an ocean of polite applause. They eased the tension, broke down the barriers between him and his audience, and all his nervousness had disappeared when silence permitted him to proceed.

" The rottenest thing in the world," he said, " is destructive criticism. To attempt to pull down and destroy the

carefully considered proposals of our Chairman would
be worthy of contempt, and I hope that nothing I say will
bring that charge upon me. When the Welden Valley
club is a hundred years old I hope it will be clearly
remembered that the man whose energy and enthusiasm
inspired it is the man sitting beside me to-night."

He bowed slightly towards Mr. van Doon amidst
appreciative applause, and he was happy to see the smile
return to the little man's face.

" I support his plans with admiration and enthusiasm :
it was a splendid proposal of his that one strong, centralised club should take the place of half a dozen futile ones.
I disagree with him upon one point only. I disagree with
the Estate having any interest or control whatsoever. I
believe that would not only ruin its spirit and destroy its
character ; it would also deprive us of the joy of scheming
it out and fighting for it and creating something with our
own hands that we can be justly proud of.

" I know that the Estate could build a far grander place
than we can hope for by our own efforts—but don't you
think we shall enjoy it more if it is a little less grand and a
little more our own ?

" Let us go to the Estate and say : ' Give us that barn
and meadow upon a yearly rental and leave us to do the
rest.' I want all of you to go down and see that barn and
picture what we can make of it : it is too fine, and old, and
unspoiled to be vandalised into a large modern club. If
we make this club with our own hands we shall fight
each other—clash our characters one against the other—
face disappointment and struggle through to far more
enduring friendships than we shall ever find by walking
like pampered guests into a glorified hotel—built and

managed for us by the Estate. We shall be free to elect only the people we desire: we shall set a standard that newcomers will try and live up to: membership will be a proud honour, jealously guarded, and not merely something thrown in by a builder with a plot of land ! "

Mr. Baldwin sat down. From his unclenched palm there fell a piece of paper—hot and damp and twisted. It contained his notes: planned with meticulous care through half a dozen long evenings of labour and he had not used a word of them. They contained suggestions for altering the barn: plans of the club's activities, carefully modelled to attract both young and old, with a dozen other details. He had planned a businesslike, cool-headed speech, and instead he had ranted like a soap-box orator . . .

But they were applauding him—and the applause seemed to go on for a long time: he turned round to find van Doon's little round face in his, and van Doon, who should by now have been his bitter enemy, was smiling. " Who said you couldn't speak ? " said van Doon.

Mr. Baldwin felt bewildered. Were they laughing at him ?—was the applause ironical ?—was van Doon's remark a crowning insult ?—or could it be a generous compliment ? He cursed himself for losing his head and forgetting all his best and most carefully reasoned arguments—and yet as the applause ended a murmur arose— a keen, excited murmur from half a dozen impromptu meetings around him.

Vaguely Mr. Baldwin realised that somebody was standing up talking. Mrs. McKinney was telling the meeting that when she and her late husband had tried to found the Archery Club at Wimbledon Park it had been their intention to keep it select and have nobody who was likely to fool about, because bows and arrows were delicate things, and expensive and easily broken and she knew by experience what a lot of damage one stupid person could do. She thought the best way to avoid this would be to limit the club as Mr. Baldwin suggested because it did not follow that because a man bought a house in Welden Valley he would understand how to treat the delicate implements of archery.

Mrs. McKinney's speech was opportune because it broke the silence and gave everybody a chance of thinking about what Mr. Baldwin had just said. But it remained for the aristocratic old gentleman in spats to voice what all were thinking and to set the seal upon Mr. Baldwin's triumph.

The old man had said nothing so far. Once he had looked at his wife and gravely nodded: once he had glanced at her and shaken his head with a smile. For the rest he had sat motionless, thoughtfully stroking his moustache. He was slight and very thin: he wore an old fashioned suit and an old world tie. His shoulders drooped a little but there was a quiet dignity that compelled attention.

" Colonel Henderson," whispered van Doon into Mr. Baldwin's ear, and Mr. Baldwin was pleased that appearances had not deceived him. He had hoped all along that the old man might turn out to be a Colonel, but spats can be treacherous things and he had feared they might have turned out to be mere decoys round the ankles of a retired grocer.

Van Doon tapped upon the table and the meeting became silent when it saw the old man standing up.

" May I say a word ? " began the old man in a gentle,

cultured voice. " May I tell Mr. van Doon how grateful my wife and I feel towards him for a very happy and stimulating evening ? When we came to Welden Valley we expected to be rather lonely old people. We did not expect an invitation to a meeting such as this. We both admired and respected our Chairman's speech: at first we were both ready to support a club managed by the Estate—but after sitting here and listening, and—may I say ?—feeling the fine independent spirit of everyone present this evening I am sure we can have splendid fun if we build up the club on our own—just as Mr. Baldwin has so admirably suggested. I say that if necessary we will both support a club built by the Estate because I think it our duty—but if we have our *own* club—if we have that fine old barn all to ourselves, then I shall take my coat off and mow the grass and wash the cups and do everything in the world for it. Perhaps I am a selfish old snob: a diehard Tory if you like—but I do want the spirit in this room to be kept safe and sound so that it may set a standard for those who follow us."

They applauded Colonel Henderson more for himself than for his words: they applauded him because they all wanted to be like him when they were old.

The two young men at the back were inspired to their feet: they spoke briefly but vigorously. " Our own club or nothing ! " was the gist of their remarks, and through a haze of happiness Mr. Baldwin caught sight of Edith, almost bouncing on the sofa—almost slapping the second young man on the back.

Van Doon behaved admirably. If he felt any disappointment he concealed it with a completeness that won Mr. Baldwin's heart. He stood up and said that his own proposal was only put forward as an idea to stimulate the meeting to a full expression of views. All that he desired was a first-rate club and his heart and soul would be with whatever the meeting decided upon.

" As Chairman I will ask you to decide by a show of hands. Those in favour of our own private club ? "

Fourteen hands shot up. The deaf lady and the stout man in pince-nez were the only ones who remained aloof.

" Those in favour of the Estate-managed club ? "

No hands went up at all : the stout man in pince-nez stared at the ceiling and continued to remain aloof, and the deaf lady was asking her companion what the first lot of hands were all about.

" Carried ! " said Mr. van Doon amidst enthusiastic applause.

Mr. Forbes Whitehead got up and made some keen businesslike remarks. " To vote for a club doesn't mean it's built and furnished," he said ; " we've got a long way to go, but I do suggest we try by some means to buy that barn and meadow so that the club will be ours in fact as well as spirit ! "

A small executive committee was then formed consisting of Mr. Baldwin as Secretary, Mr. van Doon, Colonel Henderson, Mr. Whitehead the stockbroker and Mr. Fitzgerald, a young architect who offered his professional services in an honorary capacity. Everyone agreed that it was an admirable committee. It was to start work immediately and report progress in two weeks' time. All present were invited to submit their names for membership without formality and to be elected at the next meeting. All future members were to be proposed and seconded and carefully considered by the committee before election.

A very complimentary vote of thanks to the Chairman was proposed by Mr. Whitehead and passed with acclamation. Mr. van Doon replied that no one in the room was happier than he at the result of the meeting and concluded by inviting the company to adjourn to the dining-room for refreshments.

Mr. Baldwin never forgot the last hour of that evening. He never forgot the gay, bewildering atmosphere of that throbbing, panelled dining-room : the warm amber lights, the smell of coffee and log fire and shrimp paste and new hearth-rug and chocolate sponge : the keen babble of voices and bubbling gusts of laughter : the jogging of elbows and the gushing of coffee into saucers—cries of warning, apologies and more laughter. There seemed to be hundreds of people crowded there, and all of them appeared to have something to confide to Mr. Baldwin, their new Secretary. Five different people came up to register their names as members without delay, and with a rock-bun in one hand and note-book in the other Mr. Baldwin jotted down their names and addresses and promised to communicate with them at the earliest possible moment. Colonel Henderson came up to introduce his wife and ask whether the committee would honour him by meeting in his house for their first meeting on Friday night. " You made a magnificent speech," said the old man with a hand upon Mr. Baldwin's arm. " It was your speech that did it."

" It was yours that did it," said Mr. Baldwin, but Colonel Henderson shook his head and smiled.

Mr. van Doon, with a large, half-eaten cream-bun in his hand and a small piece of cream upon his nose, came

Uσ

up and asked what time to-morrow would suit Mr. Baldwin for an interview with the Estate Manager about the barn and meadow. Mrs. McKinney pushed her way through the crowd and asked Mr. Baldwin what he really felt about archery, and the young architect wanted to know whether Mr. Baldwin would walk down to the barn directly he got home from London to-morrow evening to discuss the alterations. At one time there were half a dozen people standing round Mr. Baldwin, and he had to slip the rock-bun into his pocket to give more freedom to write. Mr. van Doon kept calling out: " Jelly !—who says jelly ! " and Mrs. van Doon kept going round asking everybody whether the room was too hot for them and whether they were quite sure it wasn't, and whether they would promise faithfully to tell her at once if it was. The young architect pushed through the crowd with a large whisky-and-soda and insisted upon Mr. Baldwin drinking it before he exhausted himself any further.

It was past eleven before the first guest said " goodbye " to Mrs. van Doon. It was Mrs. Morrison, the deaf lady, and she asked Mr. Baldwin whether she might make some d'oyleys for putting under the plates at the new club and Mr. Baldwin thanked her and promised to lay her generous offer before the committee.

Gradually the room emptied and the table reappeared in all its battered glory. It looked as if a bomb had exploded upon it: the sandwiches had entirely gone, and only a plate of large sausage rolls had been spared intact as a monument to Prudence. Although the purple jelly now had a large crater in its summit, numerous small pieces of it were visible upon plates pushed furtively on to the window ledge, the sideboard and other secluded places, for it had not been quite sweet enough and had tasted slightly of paraffin.

By mutual accord the committee lingered until the end. They were arranging their first meeting at the Colonel's house when the little dentist popped back from the front door in a large green muffler. He drew Mr. Baldwin aside to tell him that a friend of his was in the wholesale printing line and would no doubt be pleased to prepare all the printed matter of the club at exceptional prices. Mr. Baldwin thanked him and promised to lay the generous offer before the committee.

He caught sight of Edith peeping into the room to see if he were ready, and he gathered up his papers to go.

" To-morrow night, then, at Colonel Henderson's."

" Eleven o'clock at the Estate Office ! " warned van Doon.

" And six o'clock at the barn ! " reminded the young architect.

" You've got your time cut out now ! " called the Colonel.

" I shall work it all in somehow !—Good night ! "

" Good night, Mr. Secretary ! "

The storm had passed, and Tom and Edith Baldwin walked home through a quiet, starlit night. They could still hear van Doon calling out to his departing guests as they opened the green front gates of their home and picked their way through the puddles of the unfinished pathway to the front door. The dining-room was cool and peaceful after the heat and babble of the past hour : the fire glowed faintly beneath a soft grey fur of ash as they sat down beside it for a little while before they went to bed.

"Well," said Mr. Baldwin with a laugh. "What d'you think about it?"

"I think it's wonderful," said Edith.

"Van Doon seems quite happy. He took it well."

"He was happy directly after that compliment you paid him about people remembering him in a hundred years' time. He didn't mind what happened after that."

Mr. Baldwin pulled on his slippers and smiled. "People won't remember: they never do. But van Doon won't be there to know."

He lay back in his chair and although it was nearly midnight he filled and lit his pipe.

"From now on," he murmured, "it's work—and work —and work. We shall have to reorganise everything, Edie. Less time for the garden—less time for sleep—less time for everything."

CHAPTER XXVII

WITH THE MEETING of the Pioneers, and the birth of the Welden Valley Club upon that blusterous, rain-spattered night our story of Tom and Edith Baldwin is really over. It concerned their lonely struggle in the wilderness and was not intended to draw the curtains from the brimming days that followed.

Ten years have passed since that April night, and this final chapter comes more by chance than by design.

I had need this autumn to visit some friends in Buckingham and my way from London led along the Edgware Road. I was held up by the traffic beside one of those many quiet roads that join the main thoroughfare at right angles. I glanced up as I waited for the traffic to move on, and the name-plate " Brondesbury Terrace " revived a memory. I had worked beside Mr. Baldwin for several years in the Temple Insurance Office: I had subscribed my half-crown towards his clock and stood by the wall in the Manager's room when it was presented to him upon the night of his retirement. I had been one of the first visitors to his new house in Welden Valley, but since then, for over ten years, our ways had parted, and except for an annual Christmas Card I had heard no news of him at all.

The impulse came to swing into Brondesbury Terrace, to drive past old " Grasmere " to see what had happened to it, and then to break my journey at " Greengates " for a cup of tea. I wriggled my car around the tail-end of a lorry and drove slowly down the road that Mr. Baldwin had lived in for so many years.

Brondesbury Terrace has let the years slide over it with little sign of wear, and the same old houses turn their brown, placid faces towards you as you pass. I began to look for the large notice-board that advertised Mr. Ranken-Dudley's School of Elocution, but as I drew opposite " Grasmere " I saw that the notice-board had disappeared. Mr. Ranken-Dudley has vanished into the noise from whence he came and " Grasmere " has settled down once more into the dignity of a private residence. The front door and railings have been painted a rather disturbing ginger-brown, but the old laurel hedge that Mr. Baldwin worked so hard upon still lingers there in its dusty, chronic baldness. A boy in a green cap came whistling down the steps on his way to afternoon school and a pleasant-looking young mother closed the door behind him. The curtains were clean and tidy, and I looked forward to telling Mr. Baldwin that the old house had taken on a new and happy lease of life.

As I drove on I saw the walnut tree in the neighbouring garden shake its tousled old head and throw a shower of leaves over the " Grasmere " wall. I wondered if anyone had used the heap that Mr. Baldwin had made and whether anyone would stack this year's supply against the lower wall.

If you have not been to Welden Valley in the past ten years a visit will surprise you. A vast iron-grey by-pass road sweeps round upon its northern side, missing the old village by a hairsbreadth. " To Welden ½-mile " brings you to a railway station, far different from the one that Tom and Edith Baldwin knew in the days when " Greengates " was being built. You can no longer hear a solitary porter yawn through the stillness, for the sleepy little station has been attacked and captured by Metroland: colonised and civilised into producing six train-loads of lively City people a day. The elms no longer creak their joints above the narrow, twisting lane that led to the village: the lane has grown into a broad, curving, concrete avenue upon which Woolworth's, Sainsbury's, Boots' and Lyons' have built their mansions and settled down.

The old village, with its brown turreted church and elm trees, remains almost as it used to be because it lies in a backwater, but the Bell Inn beside the humped-back bridge has swollen into the Bell Hotel and a delicate operation upon the bridge has broadened its back and removed its hump, so that people in dickey seats of cars no longer come down after the car has hurtled on.

As I drove out of the old village and turned into the road that leads to Welden Close I came to a far different corner of the modern world from the screeching, concrete-spattered stretch beside the by-pass. Broad white avenues curve away towards the low hills that rim the valley: quiet, sane avenues with well-spaced, embowered houses that do not stare rudely into each other's bedrooms. Most of them look politely over each other's shoulders towards the southern sky, and everywhere there is a sense of rest and quiet. Welden Valley will always be quiet, for it has been given the golden privilege of leading to nowhere.

The Estate Office has packed up and disappeared. It has sold all its land in Welden Valley and has got its teeth into the naked haunches of a hill three miles away.

Welden Close remains open and inviolate. It has mellowed and softened, and is slowly gathering to itself the tranquil spirit of a village green. But " Greengates " no longer stands there in solitude. Houses surround it on all sides, but they are well spaced and already secluded amongst their fast-growing evergreens. The shrubs that hedge the front of " Greengates " are no longer shivering little striplings, frightened of themselves and suspicious of one another. Their sturdy growth has given them confidence. They have made friends with each other and thrown their arms around each other's shoulders so that the lower windows of the house are hidden from view until you reach the gate.

I could not have called at a better time as far as Mrs. Baldwin was concerned. The season had been kind and her roses were putting up a great show for the lateness of the year. She came to meet me in a business-like blue overall and pulled off a bulky leather glove to shake hands. There was a Committee Meeting at " Greengates " that night, she told me, and her best trees were offering up their choicest blooms to decorate the room.

" Tom's upstairs at work. Come round and see the back garden before we call him down."

" Back garden " is a poor name to describe the little paradise they have made behind the house. The clefts of the stone-flagged path are filled with moss; shy rock flowers specking it here and there with violet and gold.

But the moss is allowed to explore no further than the path, and the lawn, unlike most lawns, is reserved exclusively for grass.

" The lawns are my husband's special interest," said Edith. " He's never laid an inch of new turf or set any seed. It's just the meadow land, brought up to behave itself like a civilised lawn."

A pergola of briar roses spans the garden at the lower end of the lawn, and at either end of the path beneath the rustic archway two small banked-up rockeries have been built. They cleverly conceal the boundaries of the Baldwin territory and give a sense of width and spaciousness.

Upon one side of the lower garden are the vegetables. Upon the other side, beyond a small thicket of currant trees, a corner has been left in its native wildness. In this corner the grass lies tough and wild around the trunk of Mr. Baldwin's elm and the clump of blackberry bushes are as they were upon the first day of the Baldwins' visit.

" We come blackberrying down here with a hooked walking-stick and a jam jar," said Edith. " It's nice to know there's one wild bush in the world that we can go blackberrying around without other people getting there before us and leaving us the green ones."

In this wild corner they have built a rustic summer-house. It is out of view of the house when the trees are in leaf: out of view of all buildings. It might be right away in the wilds, and it looks up towards the hill crest, to where the footpath meets the summit.

" They'll never build up there," said Edith, " because the owner's given it as an open space. Tom brings his work down here quite often."

I gathered that Edith has, by degrees, taken over all the garden except for this wild corner and the lawns. At first the rose trees alone were hers, but she has taken it piece by piece as the work of the Club has steadily increased upon Mr. Baldwin's shoulders.

The Club ? Yes, the Club was doing wonderfully well, but Edith felt very strongly that her husband should have an assistant to relieve him of part of the work. " He's at it day and night. He attends all the sub-Committees and hasn't missed a meeting since the Club was formed. When he had lumbago last spring he insisted upon having a meeting in his bedroom ! He likes to keep everything under his hand and know exactly what's happening everywhere."

She was telling me how Mr. Baldwin had offered to resign after his tenth year as Secretary last April, and how the General Meeting had shouted him back to his seat, when she was interrupted by the French windows flying open and Mr. Baldwin himself came hurrying down the path to meet us.

He will be seventy-one next year. His hair is quite white now, but his face is the colour of polished oak and his eyes are clearer and keener than ever I saw them in his office days.

He took me upstairs to his bedroom, if it can still be called a bedroom, for it looks more like the sleeping quarters of an Adjutant upon Active Service. The bed has been shoved carelessly away into a corner as an irritating necessity that calls for too much valuable time, and beneath the window that looks across the open country to the hill crest there stands a large table piled with books and papers. Open shelves along the walls are lined with

Club Minute Books, files of correspondence, reference volumes and some new books on Gardening and History.

"You must excuse the mess," said Mr. Baldwin. "I do most of my work up here to be out of reach of people who call. I simply have to make it a rule to be 'out' to everybody in the afternoons or I'd never get through any work at all. The Club ?—Yes, most of it's the Club."

I began to congratulate him upon the success he had made of it, but he quickly broke in to stop me.

"It's not me: it's team work. We struck lucky with our original Committee; that's the key to it all. We've got a fellow named Forbes Whitehead. He's a stockbroker— a wonderful chap. He took charge of the finances: he raised a loan and fixed up a plan to buy the barn and meadow. He arranged a sinking fund and in three years we pay back the last penny and the Club's ours ! Everybody does something. Colonel Henderson runs the garden : he lends his own gardener twice a week and works on it himself like a trojan. A young architect gave his services and made a magnificent job of the barn. It's just like an old Tudor Hall inside, with big curtains to divide it into separate rooms when we need them. The Club's full up now : a hundred members and a waiting list of seventeen. We've kept half the membership reserved for young people : we're running a rugger team for the first time this season and of course the cricket and tennis have been going on for several years. Van Doon ? Yes—he's still here. He's useful because he does odd jobs other people don't want. But you have to sit on him now and then. If you're too nice to him he gets uppish and rude, and if you're rude to him he offers you a cigar. You know the sort of man."

I noticed a pile of open books on his table, and several

sheets of closely written notes. It was pleasant to see again that neat round hand that I knew so well from the ledgers in the office. I asked him whether he were writing a book of his own, and he laughed self-consciously.

" Notes for my next lecture ! " he said. " We've had a series each winter for the last five years and they've turned out quite a success. We often get as many as sixty or seventy members to them." He handed me a neat little booklet. " Here's the list for the new season."

Oct. 10th.	" Memories of the North-West Frontier," by Colonel G. S. Henderson, C.M.G.
Nov. 6th.	" Nature at Night," by Forbes Whitehead.
Dec. 5th.	" Adventures of a Rubber Planter," by Percy van Doon.
Jan. 6th.	" Cricket in Trinidad," by Major Allan Keeble.
Feb. 7th.	" Books to read and books to light the fire with," by Rev. Walter Fenn.
March 10th.	" A Civil War Skirmish in Welden Valley," by T. H. Baldwin.

" We encourage members to prepare lectures and submit them to the Lecture sub-Committee. Everybody's had some kind of adventures, or got some kind of interest or hobby worth listening to. I was always rather interested in History. I'm making a study of the history of this little corner of the world and it's twice as interesting if you can stand up and talk about what you've discovered. People ask questions and often come round and discuss them afterwards. I began with ' Welden Valley in the Stone Age,' then ' The Romans in Welden Valley ' ; last year I did 'What William the Conqueror did with Welden Valley,' and next year it's 'Member of Parliament for Welden!' I've discovered that Welden was one of the Rotten Boroughs and until the Reform Act stopped it, a farmer and six labourers had the right to elect a Member! I'm hoping to begin an Archæological Society one day— but it's difficult to find time for everything one wants to do."

Mr. Baldwin was tilting back in his chair with his hands behind his head. He looked like a Company Director enjoying a brief relaxation. The sun was setting. Through the window I could see the trunk of his elm and the foot-path winding up the hillside. Faintly I could hear the roar of traffic from the by-pass. He apologised for talking so much: he asked me for my news, and was glad to hear that old " Grasmere " looked well and happy again.

" Funny how long ago that seems," he said. " As you grow older your memory seems to twist right round and point the furthest end at you. I remember my father's old house in Colchester much clearer now than I remember " Grasmere." The Grammar School's much clearer to me now than the office. Come down and have some tea ! "

As we went downstairs I noticed a number of framed photographs of cricket teams upon the wall, and that Mr. Baldwin appeared in all of them in a long white coat.

" Yes," he said, " we've had our cricket team for six years now—ever since we collected enough money to lay the pitch in the meadow. I'm the official umpire—which probably accounts for us winning eight matches this season ! It reminds me I've got to get those batting and bowling averages worked out for the Club Magazine."

During tea I discovered that Edith's activities were not

entirely confined to the house and garden. She is on the Ladies Committee and she reminded Mr. Baldwin that there would be an insurrection amongst the ladies if they were not given the Club for an extra afternoon a week for their new scheme of House and Garden debates.

Mr. Baldwin threw out his hands in a gesture of helplessness.

" It can't be done, Edie ! You know quite well there are only seven days in a week ! They begin rehearsing the Christmas play on Wednesday: the juniors want their weekly dances again and with twenty-eight entries for the Ping Pong tournament we shall have to play as many games as we can in the afternoons. You've got three afternoons already ! "

" There's Friday," put in Edith.

" Friday's the only day when members who don't want to do anything can sit about in peace. Nice time we shall have if the Committee turns them out for your needlework and cookery lectures ! " He reached forward and took his cup of tea. " Still, I'll sound the Committee to-night. I'll see what I can do, but I can't promise anything."

" Which means," said Edith with a wink at me, " that we can have an extra afternoon without the slightest trouble if you say so."

" Rot ! " said Mr. Baldwin, " I'm only Secretary ! " But Edith only laughed and winked at me again.

The evenings were beginning to draw in, and I wanted to make as much progress as possible along an unfamiliar road before it grew dark. In any case I could not have taken up much more of Mr. and Mrs. Baldwin's time, for

Mr. Baldwin had got to hurry down to the Club to supervise the draw of the Ping Pong tournament and get back for a hasty dinner before the Committee Meeting, and a lady named Mrs. McKinney was coming in to see Mrs. Baldwin to discuss the possibility of having an afternoon a week in the meadow for Archery.

" Try and come over one Saturday and see one of our rugger games," said Mr. Baldwin. "·Young Whitehead's Captain: he's the son of old Forbes Whitehead and was Captain of his school last year. It'll be a great triumph if we can win a few games in our first season. Here's a fixture card—to save you coming on a Saturday when we're playing away. But you must come in the spring to see the Club at its best: come one evening when the garden's worth seeing and when there's tennis going on and some youngsters practising cricket at the nets."

They came to the gate to see me off: Edith still in the blue overall she had forgotten to remove for tea, Mr. Baldwin in his grey flannels and white sweater. They waved good-bye as I turned the corner that led me away from Welden Close. I drove slowly through the old village where the falling sun was giving a ruddy glow to the church tower behind the trees. I drove more quickly along the new road past Woolworth's, Sainsbury's, Boots' and Lyons'. I skirted the station as a crowd of returning City men and girls came hurrying out towards their new homes in Welden Valley. I just had time to wonder how many of them were members of the Club as the roaring by-pass caught me and swept me away towards the North.

THE END

If you have enjoyed this Persephone book why not telephone or write to us for a copy of the Persephone Catalogue and the current Persephone Biannually? All Persephone books ordered from us cost £14 or three for £36 plus £3 postage per book within the UK.

PERSEPHONE BOOKS LTD
8 Edgar Buildings
Bath BA1 2EE

Telephone: 01225 425050
sales@persephonebooks.co.uk
www.persephonebooks.co.uk